A

Merseyside Town

in the

Industrial Revolution

St. Helens

1750-1900

T. C. BARKER
*Lecturer in Economic History at the London School of Economics
and Political Science, University of London*

and

J. R. HARRIS
Lecturer in Economic History at the University of Liverpool

FRANK CASS & COMPANY LTD
LONDON
1959

First published by the
Liverpool University Press
1954

Reprinted with corrections
1959

©

Printed in Monotype Times 10 pt. by C Tinling & Co Ltd
of Liverpool London and Prescot for Frank Cass & Co Ltd London

[Photo: R. K. Robertson]

COLLIERY (ABOUT 1800)

The Walker Art Gallery, Liverpool

CONTENTS

PART ONE

DEVELOPMENT IN THE CANAL AGE

PART TWO

THE AGE OF PETER GREENALL
1830-1845

PART THREE

THE MIDDLE YEARS
1845-1870

PART FOUR

INDUSTRIAL PROGRESS AND THE RISE OF RESPECTABILITY, 1870-1900

LIST OF ILLUSTRATIONS AND MAPS

INTRODUCTION

MODERN St. Helens can justly be described as a product of the Industrial Revolution. The local coal industry received a powerful stimulus from the cutting of the first English canal, and to the coalfield were attracted the furnace industries, glass, copper and chemicals. These industries have received relatively little attention at the hands of economic historians, and no apology is made for devoting much of the book to them. The new industries brought people from far and near, and many pages have also been given to the life and condition of the population during the years when the town was growing rapidly.

We have been particularly fortunate in discovering much documentary evidence which seems to modify to a considerable extent what has been written on town life at this period. At all times we have tried to keep in mind that St. Helens is part of Merseyside, and that the life and trade of Merseyside are part of a national picture. We are emphatic that the history of any industrial town, seeking its raw materials over a wide area and selling its finished products over the whole world, cannot be studied in isolation. We have accordingly related the growth of the town to the economic pattern of Merseyside and to national events. It is our hope therefore, that this book will be of interest not only to the people of St. Helens, and to other inhabitants of Merseyside, but to those interested in economic history generally.

This study has been largely based upon hitherto unpublished documents in local, county and national archives, and upon other materials which we have unearthed for ourselves. Newspapers have also been of great importance, particularly the Liverpool papers from 1757 and the St. Helens press from the middle of the following century. It is from these two types of source that much of the detail is derived, and if that detail serves to show readers that the growth of a modern industrial town was an extremely complex process, brought about by influences both small and great, it will not have been presented in vain.

This book is a work of collaboration ; a task made easier by the fact that both the writers have spent most of their lives in the district which they are describing. Although, generally speaking, the eighteenth century has been the responsibility of Dr. Harris and the nineteenth of Dr. Barker, there has been a constant interchange of ideas and notes during the five years over which this study has extended. Certain chapters have, in fact, been written jointly. These are : I, II, V, IX, and X. Chapters III, IV, VI, VII, VIII, XI and XII have been the work of Dr. Harris, Chapters XIII to XXIX of Dr. Barker.

So many people have helped us in the writing of this book that we cannot thank them all here. From the outset we have received the warmest support from Mr. N. F. Newbury, the Director of Education for St. Helens, without whose personal interest this book would not have been attempted. The University of Manchester provided the generous post-graduate scholarships which enabled the necessary research to be undertaken. Professor Arthur Redford and Dr. W. H. Chaloner gave us the wise advice and careful training in research which we hope has enabled us to produce a book which will be worthy of the tradition of the Manchester History School. St. Helens Corporation not only helped to defray the expenses of research, but also made a most liberal grant towards the cost of publication. We are deeply indebted to Professor F. E. Hyde for the great interest he has shown in our book, and for recommending it to the University Press of Liverpool, whose Secretary, Mr. R. A. Downie has given us much helpful advice.

Among those who have assisted us by putting manuscript material at our disposal we would especially wish to thank Col. H. A. Bromilow, Mr. Griffith of Greenall, Whitley & Co Ltd., Lt.-Col. M. Hughes-Young and his agent, Mr. W. V. Spencer, and Sir Harry Pilkington, Chairman of Pilkington Brothers Ltd. The number of references to documents at the Lancashire Record Office and at the St. Helens Library sufficiently show our indebtedness to Mr. R. Sharpe France, Mr. H. C. Caistor and their staffs. We have received splendid co-operation from the local press from the very outset. Mr. R. P. Brady of Cowley School planned the maps, the cartography of which has been the responsibility of Mr. A. G. Hotchkiss of the Department of Geography in the University of Liverpool. The Historic Society of Lancashire and Cheshire kindly lent the block of the illustration at p. 18. We have not space to thank all the hundreds of people, particularly at St. Helens, whom we have burdened with enquiries or who have brought material to our attention ; we hope they will not be disappointed with the book they have helped to make.

Certain sections of the book have received helpful criticism from Dr. W. H. Chaloner at Manchester, from Mr. G. Clayton, Dr. S. B. Saul and Mr. B. B. Parkinson at Liverpool, from Mr. A. J. Taylor of University College, London, from Dr. E. M. Hampson of the University of Aberdeen, from Dr. R. Dickinson and Dr. D. W. F. Hardie of Imperial Chemical Industries, from Mr. M. N. Leathwood and Dr. W. B. Price of Pilkington Brothers Limited, and from Mr. F. A. Bailey and Mr. N. H. Barker. They are in no way responsible for any of our errors or opinions.

T. C. B.   London School of Economics and Political Science, University of London.

J. R. H.   University of Liverpool.

SOURCES

ORIGINAL MANUSCRIPT
AND UNPUBLISHED MATERIAL

(a) At St. Helens.

At the Town Hall.

Minutes of the St. Helens Improvement Commission, 1845-68.
Minutes of the Sewering and Highways Purposes Committee of the St. Helens Improvement Commission, 1845-68.
Minute Book of the Sutton Local Board, 1864-69.
Miscellaneous Papers of the St. Helens Improvement Commission 1845-68 (package 157).
Statements for Counsel's Opinion (package 209).
Minutes of the Select Committees (Commons and Lords) on the St. Helens Improvement Bill, 1869.
Papers of the Cowley Trustees.
Deeds of the United Alkali Co. Ltd.

At the Reference Library, the Gamble Institute.

Parr Poor Law Papers to 1828.
Parr Poor Rate Books, 1840-49.
Account Book of the Management of Sarah Cowley's Estate.
Orderly Book of the Highways of the Hamlet of Hardshaw, 1839-93.
Minute Books of the St. Helens Public Library, 1853-70, 1877-81.
Minute Book of the St. Helens Mechanics Institute, 1861-73.
Note on the Quarterly Meeting of the St. Helens District, of the Independent Order of Oddfellows (Manchester Unity), 1839.
Time Tables of the St. Helens Railway, 1842, 1853.
Papers of John Ansdell, including the Minutes of the Select Committees (Commons and Lords) on the St. Helens Gas Bill, 1870.
Annual Reports of the Medical Officer of Health, 1873-1900.
Annual Reports of the St. Helens Hospital and the Providence Hospital.

At the Parish Church.
Registers from 1713.
Minutes of Vestry Meetings and Trustees Meetings (in Baptism Register, 1713-77).

At the Congregational Church.
Deeds and Miscellaneous Papers.
Registers from 1778.

At Lowe House.
Registers from 1785.

At the Wesley Church.
St. Helens : A Brief History of Its Religious and Other Institutions . . . Also a Concise Account of its Productions, Trades, Manufactures, Topography and Antiquities, MS written by T. Cook in 1867.

At the Westminster Bank.
Papers of the Trustees of the St. Helens Parish Church.

At Sherdley Estate Office.
Papers of the Hughes Family.
Letters.
Accounts.
Pocket Books.

At Hardshaw Brook Depot.
Rate Books of the St. Helens Improvement Commission 1845-68.

At the Office of Maxwell Wood, Brewis and Co., Solicitors.
Deeds of the St. Helens Waterworks Co.

At Pilkington Brothers Limited.
Papers relating to the St. Helens Crown Glassworks from 1826.
Minutes of the British Plate Glass Company to 1861.
Minutes of the Ravenhead Colliery, 1868-73.
Minutes of the St. Helens Collieries Co. Ltd., 1876-89.
Miscellaneous Deeds.

At Greenall Whitley and Company's Brewery.
Brewery Letter Books, 1786-1817.
Hardshaw Colliery Letter Book, 1805-1816.
Rent Books, 1820-41.
Diary, 1845-59.

At S. and C. Bishop and Company Limited.
Books containing results of experiments (colouring of glass) from 1 January, 1836.
Miscellaneous Deeds.

At Beechams Pills Limited.
Wages Books. Miscellaneous Deeds.

At the St. Helens Industrial Co-operative Society Limited.
Minute Books of the Society, 1883-1900.
Deeds relating to Moorflat School and the Windle Workhouse.

At the Office of the Superintendent Registrar of Births, Marriages and Deaths.
Registers, 1837-50.

(*b*) ELSEWHERE.

At the Public Record Office.

Palatinate of Lancaster—
  Chancery Records :
    Bills P.L.6. Answers P.L.7.
    Papers relating to the St. Helens Graveyard, 25 July, 1816. P.L.14.
    In the Matter Relating to Sarah Cowley's Charity, 1822. C13/2789.
    Kurtz v. Darcy, 1839. C13/2307.
  Home Office Papers :
    Census Returns, 1841, for Eccleston, Parr, Sutton and Windle. H.O. 107/516-7.
    Correspondence relating to Disturbances 1830/1 H.O. 40/26, 53/13.
    Correspondence relating to the Poor Law, 1837-9. H.O. 73/52-6.

At the British Museum.
Add MSS. 36914. Documents concerning the Weaver Navigation, chiefly the correspondence of Sir Thomas Aston.

At the House of Lords Record Office.
Committee Minutes of the British Plate Glass Bill, 1841.
Committee Minutes of the St. Helens Improvement Bills, 1845 and 1855.
Committee Minutes of the St. Helens Canal and Railway Bills, 1845, 1846, 1847, 1853, 1864.
Committee Minutes of the St. Helens and Wigan Junction Railway Bill, 1885.

At the British Transport Commission, Historical Records, 66, Porchester Road, London, W.2.

Minutes of the St. Helens and Runcorn Gap Railway, 1830-64.

At the Library of H.M. Customs and Excise, King's Beam House, London, E.C.3.

Treasury and Excise Papers, **125**, petition of William Pilkington, jr., 23 Dec., 1825, **124**, petition of Bevan and Rigby, 7 Oct., 1826.
Treasury and Excise Papers, 1829/30, T.E.1432. Papers relating to the fraud at the Eccleston Crown Glassworks.

At the Registry of Friendly Societies, North Audley Street, London.

Rules of Friendly Societies in Eccleston, Parr, Sutton and Windle from 1776.

At the National Debt Office (Belsize Park Repository).

Savings Banks Journals, 1820-50.

At Chance Brothers Ltd., Smethwick.

Minutes and correspondence.

At Messrs. Doulton & Co. Ltd., Lambeth.

Memoir on the firm's factory at St. Helens, by A. E. Marshall.

At the Lancashire Record Office, County Hall, Preston.

Papers deposited by Henry Cross and Son, Solicitors, Prescot. (DDCS).
Gerard Papers (DDGe).
Molyneux Papers (DDM).
Pilkington Papers (DDPi).
Wills proved at Chester prior to 1858.
Tithe Awards and Plans, Eccleston (1843), Parr (1843), Sutton (1840) and Windle (1840).
Land Tax Assessments, Eccleston, Parr, Sutton, Windle, 1781-1831.
Lists of Persons Entitled to Vote (1833-40).
Proceedings of the Constabulary Committee from 1840. (QEC).
Accounts of the Constabulary Committee from 1840. (QEC).
Minutes of the Prescot Guardians from 1837. (P.U.P.).
Returns of Places of Worship Not of the Church of England, 1829 (QDV).

At the Cheshire Record Office.

Weaver Tonnage Books.

At the Liverpool Record Office, Picton Reference Library, Liverpool.

Tarleton MSS.
Holt and Gregson MSS.
The Diaries of Sir Willoughby Aston.
The Account Books of Case and Southworth.
Liverpool Town Books.

At the British Electricity Authority Offices, Clarke's Gardens, Liverpool.

Deeds of land at St. Helens.

At Manchester Central Reference Library.

Proceedings of the Committee of the House of Commons on the Liverpool and Manchester Railroad Bill, Session 1825.

At the Headquarters of the Independent Order of Oddfellows (Manchester Unity), Grosvenor Street, Manchester.

Minutes and other Documents of the Grand Committees.

At the Miners' Offices, Bolton.

Minute Books of the Lancashire Miners' Federation : Particulars of Correspondence and Proceedings of Meetings in Connection with the Negotiations for a Sliding Scale in West Lancashire, 1885-86.
Minutes of the Lancashire and Cheshire Miners' Federation from 1894.

At Wigan Public Library.

Dicconson Papers.

At Warrington Public Library.

Papers of the Rev. Edmund Sibson, Vicar of Ashton-in-Makerfield.
Minutes of the Flint Glass Manufacturers' Association, 1829-31, kept by T. K. Glazebrook.

At Walton Old Hall, Stockton Heath, Warrington.

Typescript History of Greenall Whitley and Co. Ltd.
Abstract of Title of Peter Greenall to an Estate called Williamson's in Eccleston.

At Birmingham Public Library.

The Boulton and Watt Collection : papers relating to the erection of engines for the British Cast Plate Glass Co. (1786-90), for the Union Plate Glass Co. in 1838 and the British Plate Glass Co. in 1843.

At the Library of the University College of North Wales. Bangor.

Plasnewydd Collection.
Hughes of Kinmel MSS.
The Mona Mine MSS.
Bangor MSS.

At Brasenose College, Oxford.

Maps, deeds and papers relating to Barton's Bank Estate in Sutton.

At Black Park, Chirk.

Letters, diaries, deeds, etc., belonging to the Bromilow family, in the possession of Col. H. A. Bromilow.

At the National Archives, Washington.

Despatches from Liverpool, vol. 32.
Record of Fees, 1873-92.

(c) THESES.

T. C. Barker :

The Economic and Social History of St. Helens, 1830-1900. (Ph.D. Thesis at the University of Manchester, 1951).

J. R. Harris :

Economic and Social Development in St. Helens in the Latter Half of the Eighteenth Century. (M.A. Thesis at the University of Manchester, 1950.)

Emlyn Rogers :

The History of Trade Unionism in the Coal Mining Industry of North Wales to 1914. (M.A. Thesis at the University College of North Wales, 1928.)

(d) MISCELLANEOUS.

Patten Papers at the Winmarleigh Estate Office, Warrington.

W. H. Chaloner : " Price Regulation and Output Restriction in the Cheshire Salt Trade, 1815-88." (Unpublished paper in the possession of Dr. Chaloner.)

The Flint Glassmakers' Magazine (from 1851) in the possession of Mr. C. D. Stanier, O.B.E., 125, Parkfield Road, Stourbridge.

Memoir written by Sir Frederick Norman (transcript in the possession of Dr. D. W. F. Hardie).

Minute Book of the Cheadle Brass Wire Co. (in the possession of Thomas Bolton and Sons, Ltd., Widnes).

Ledger of a local builder, 1840-41 (in the possession of Mr. Thomas, Mill Lane, St. Helens).

Minutes of the St. Helens Book Club, 1830-1919 (lately in the possession of Mr. J. Hammill, Solicitor, St. Helens).

Wage lists relating to the colliery of John Cross at Thatto Heath, 1875 (in the possession of Mr. Walter Fogg, St. Helens).

Sutton Heath Price List, August, 1917 (in the possession of the Miners' Lodge, Sutton Heath).

Diary of H. R. Lacey, 1843-45, and Diary of Newton Lacey, 1871-92 (in the possession of Mrs. Campbell, " Moness," Abbey Grove, Rhos-on-Sea).

Valuation of land at Prescot, 1808 (King's College, Cambridge ; transcript in the possession of Mr. F. A. Bailey, Prescot).

Minutes of the Joint Committee of the St. Helens Trades Council and the St. Helens Socialist Society to adopt an I.L.P. candidate, 1903 (in the possession of Mrs. Standring, 50 Orange Hill Road, Heaton Park, Prestwich).

The Township Book of Sutton. In the possession of the Prescot Historic Society.

Marriage Settlement of John Mackay. In the possession of Mr. C. I. Fraser, Reelig House, Kirkhill, Inverness-shire.

ABBREVIATIONS USED IN THE FOOTNOTES

B.P.G. Mins.	Minutes of the British Plate Glass Co.
B.M.	British Museum.
Chet. Soc.	Chetham Society.
C.J.	*Journals of the House of Commons.*
C.S.P. Dom.	*Calendar of State Papers Domestic.*
Chem. News	*Chemical News.*
Chem. Trade Jour. ...	*Chemical Trade Journal.*
Ch. Emp. Comm. ...	Children's Employment Commission.
D.N.B.	*Dictionary of National Biography.*
Econ. Jour. (Ec. Hist. Ser.)	*Economic Journal (Economic History Series).*
Econ. Hist. Rev.	*Economic History Review.*
Eng. Hist. Rev.	*English Historical Review.*
Guard Mins.	Minutes of the Prescot Poor Law Guardians.
Gore's Gen. Ad.	*Gore's General Advertiser* (Liverpool).
Inst. C.E.	Institution of Civil Engineers.
Inst. M.E.	Institution of Mechanical Engineers.
Lancs. Par. Reg. Soc. ...	Lancashire Parish Register Society.
L. & C. Antiq. Soc. ...	Lancashire and Cheshire Antiquarian Society.
L. & C. Hist. Soc. ...	Lancashire and Cheshire Historic Society.
L. & C. Rec. Soc.... ...	Lancashire and Cheshire Record Society.
L.R.O.	Lancashire Record Office.
Lpool.	Liverpool.
Lpool Chron.	*Liverpool Chronicle.*
Lpool. Merc.	*Liverpool Mercury.*
Phil. Trans. Royal Soc. ...	*Philosophical Transactions of the Royal Society.*
P.R.O.	Public Record Office.
Ref. Lib.	Reference Library.
R.C.	Royal Commission.
St. H.	St. Helens.
St. H. C. & R.	St. Helens Canal and Railway.
St. H. Cong. Ch. ...	St. Helens Congregational Church.
St. H.I.C.	St. Helens Improvement Commission.
St. H.N.	*St. Helens Newspaper.*
St. H.R.	*St. Helens Reporter.*
St. H. and R. G. Mins. ...	Minutes of the St. Helens and Runcorn Gap Railway (later the St. Helens Canal and Railway).
S.C.	Select Committee.
Soc. Chem. Ind. ...	Society of the Chemical Industry.
Soc. Glass Tech. ...	Society of Glass Technology.
U.C.N.W.	University College of North Wales, Bangor.
V.C.H.	Victoria County History.
Williamson's Lpool. Ad. ...	*Williamson's Liverpool Advertiser.*

Parliamentary Papers are cited in the form in which they appear in the official indexes, with the year of publication first, then the number of the particular paper (in square brackets), and the volume in which it is bound (in Roman numerals). E.g. 1878 [2159] XLIV.

PART ONE

DEVELOPMENT IN THE
CANAL AGE

THE LOWER MERSEY 1750-1950

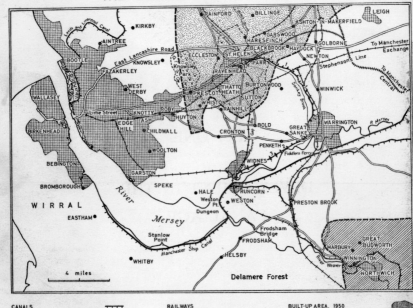

CANALS   ━┼┼┼━

MANCHESTER SHIP CANAL

SANKEY CANAL   First opened
             First extension
             Second extension

RAILWAYS

L.M.S.R. (LNWR)   ━┼━┼━

L.NER (G.CR.)   ┿┿┿┿┿┿

ROADS   ━━━━

BUILT-UP AREA, 1950

BOUNDARY OF ST. HELENS, 1954

COALFIELD

SALTFIELD

CHAPTER I

COAL AND SALT

THE South Lancashire town of St. Helens takes its name from that of a chapel-of-ease which stood on a busy stretch of highway. The chapel was situated at the junction of the boundaries of the four manors and townships of Windle, Sutton, Eccleston and Parr, and near it the roads from Liverpool to Bolton and from Warrington to Ormskirk converged.

About the year 1700 the district around St. Helen's Chapel wore a very different aspect from that which it presents today. A predominantly agricultural population tilled fields already enclosed. A mixed farming prevailed, but the acres of arable and pasture were frequently interrupted by barren stretches, indicated on the modern map by place-names embodying elements like " Heath " and " Moss." Amid the oatfields and the barley, the " scores " for cattle and the fruit gardens, the peat mosses and the wild heaths, the first signs of the industrial age could just be discerned, but these did not as yet seriously affect the essentially country atmosphere. Here and there in each of the four manor-townships a few fields or patches of waste were scarred by tips and coal banks, where, to the creaking of primitive windlasses, the colliers of the district disappeared from the light of day to pursue their grimy and dangerous calling. Close by one of these small collieries, marked out as rather more important than the others by its horse-propelled gear, a new cone-like chimney and a trail of smoke gave evidence that another race of industrial workers, the glassblowers, had just made their appearance.

Many of the industrial activities already carried on were not, however, pursued in mine or works, even on the smallest scale, but in the scattered houses and cottages of the four townships. Linen-weaving was carried on in many homes (though cotton was soon to begin to supplant linen), some farms were combined with nailmakers' forges, and there was at least one combmaker. Even brewing was virtually a domestic industry at this time, being carried on either in the mansions of the gentry and the well-to-do for the benefit of their households, or in the brewhouses which formed an essential adjunct of most inns.

These industrial beginnings, however, must not be over-emphasised. It would be the reverse of the truth to suppose that it was by a gradual growth of existing trades and crafts that the modern town was created. Nor was its good position in relation to road communications—though responsible for the existence of the small hamlet of Hardshaw-within-Windle which already lay close to the chapel—the real reason for the phenomenal growth of the place. Changes of a different nature came to this obscure neighbourhood, changes which had a threefold origin; in certain raw materials, hitherto little exploited, of which the district possessed an abundance; in new and momentous economic events taking place on the Cheshire saltfield and at the rising port of Liverpool; and in the presence of an insignificant stream, the Sankey, formed from the confluence of several local brooks, and running down to the Mersey near Warrington.

The raw materials present were coal, sand, and fireclay. St. Helens was situated near the south-western tip of the South Lancashire coalfield, and in the early eighteenth century its position gave the district two advantages. It was on the side of the coalfield nearest to the mouth of the Weaver, the artery of the saltfield ; equally important, it was only twelve miles from Liverpool. The possibility of water communication with the Mersey and the presence of the essentials for glass and other furnace industries were, to begin with, of secondary importance as compared with the juxtaposition of coal and salt. Indeed the whole economic history of St. Helens is a lengthy commentary on the inter-relationship between these two vital and complementary raw materials as they have been organized and manipulated by the men of Merseyside, and upon the world-wide trades to which they have given rise. To understand why a vigorous coal trade developed in the St. Helens district it is first necessary to realise what was happening on the other side of the Mersey.

Before the middle of the seventeenth century coal replaced wood as the fuel employed in the Cheshire saltfield.[1] This started a train of events which was to determine to a very large degree the industrial character of the Merseyside region. At first the salt-boilers looked to the Staffordshire coalfield as their main source of supply. By the later years of the seventeenth century, however, Lancashire coal was carried by pack-horse to Hale,[2] shipped across the Mersey and transferred to waiting carts or pack-horses at Frodsham Bridge.[3] It was delivered at the most westerly saltworks in the vicinity of Winnington Bridge for 11s. 10d. a ton,

[1] " Some Inquiries Concerning the Salt Springs and Ways of Salt Making at Nantwich in Cheshire," Answered by Wm. Jackson, Dr. of Physick, *Philosophical Trans. of the Royal Society of England* No. 53, 15 Nov., 1669, 1065. For a more detailed account of the Cheshire salt trade see T. C. Barker, " Lancashire Coal, Cheshire Salt and the Rise of Liverpool," *Trans. L. & C. Hist. Soc.* **103** (1951), 83-101.

[2] Lpool Ref. Lib., Holt and Gregson MSS. X, 263.

[3] " Considerations concerning a project to make ye River Weaver in Cheshire Navigable from Frodsham Bridge to Northwich." B.M. Add. MSS. 36914 fo. 94 *et seq.*

a shilling or two cheaper than the Staffordshire coal which had to be brought a longer distance overland.[1] Although this was a slight saving for the saltboilers concerned, carriage continued to be a most expensive item. It still cost more than twice as much to transport the coal from the colliery to the saltworks as it did to raise the coal out of the ground. A reduction in these disproportionately heavy transport charges would greatly reduce the saltboilers' production costs, for they burnt a ton of coal every time they made one and a half tons of salt.[2] In an attempt to effect such an economy some of the Cheshire men started to prospect for coal at the saltfield itself. One of them, William Marbury, conducted a search under his land at Marbury, near Great Budworth, in 1670. The borers failed to strike coal; instead they discovered a deposit of rock salt.[3]

This altogether unexpected find was a severe blow to the Cheshire brinemen. It not only disappointed their hopes of obtaining a cheaper supply of coal but also opened the way to competition in the salt trade which might have proved their ruin had not Parliament intervened in the struggle. The brinemen were burdened by two costly transport charges; for coal carried into Cheshire (either from Lancashire or from Staffordshire) and for white salt transported away from the saltfield. The newly-found rock salt, however, could be carried towards the coalfield for refining and only one transport charge was incurred.

Liverpool, the natural outlet for the produce of the Cheshire wiches, profited the most from Marbury's discovery of 1670, for rock salt was soon being despatched by sea from that port for boiling elsewhere. Moreover, enterprising manufacturers were able to export from Liverpool cargoes of white salt refined on the shores of the Mersey. There supplies of rock salt from Cheshire met the pack-horses carrying fuel from the nearest pits of the Lancashire coalfield. This, in turn, reduced the price at which the producer of salt from brine sold his product to merchants in Liverpool. John Holt, the Liverpool historian, was probably writing with his customary care when he expressed the opinion that

" The Salt Trade is generally acknowledged to have been the Nursing Mother and to have contributed more to the first rise, gradual increase, and present flourishing state of the Town of Liverpool than any other Article of Commerce."[4]

The traffic in rock salt increased rapidly at the close of the

---

[1] B.M. Add. MSS. 36914. Note attached to a letter dated 29 Aug., 1699. Staffordshire coal cost between 9/2 and 10/- per ton at Middlewich and the cost of transport to Winnington Bridge was a further 4/6. (*Ibid*).

[2] T. S. Willan, *The Navigation of the River Weaver in the Eighteenth Century*, Chet. Soc. 3rd Ser. III (1951), 3. For the pithead price of coal, see below, p. 10.

[3] *Phil. Trans. Royal Soc.*, No. 66, 12 Dec., 1670, 2015-7.

[4] Holt and Gregson MSS., X, 253.

seventeenth century to the growing dismay of the brinemen. In 1702 they obtained an Act of Parliament restricting the number of refineries to those already in being and to any erected within ten miles of the rock pits.[1] Petitions from refiners of rock salt at Bristol[2] and Bideford[3] indicate the extent of the trade by 1701. By that date salt was already being refined at Frodsham[4] and Dungeon[5] and the names of Thomas Johnson and John Blackburne, powerful men in the Liverpool rock trade, are encountered for the first time at the end of the seventeenth century.[6]

The Act of 1702 which closed the growing industry of refining rock salt to all newcomers must have been highly acceptable to the existing refiners, even though later legislation permitted the boiling of rock salt at several other places in England and Wales.[7] It is reasonable to suppose that the refineries at Liverpool, Dungeon and Frodsham increased in size during the early decades of the eighteenth century, and the opening of the Weaver Navigation to traffic on January 1, 1732,[8] which eliminated the costly pack-horse journeys between the salt mines and Frodsham Bridge, led to the doubling of rock salt cargoes carried down the Weaver in the next twenty years.[9] The Weaver Navigation also stimulated the brine trade at Northwich by reducing the price of fuel. Coal shipments up the Weaver increased from 2,634 tons in 1732-3 to 9,400 tons in 1752-3.[10]

It is very appropriate, considering the primacy of coal in the economy of the St. Helens district, that mining is the earliest local industry of which we have evidence. How early the existence of

---

[1] 1 Anne cap. XXI, section 10.

[2] C.J. **13**, 599. 6 June, 1701.

[3] *Ibid.* Philip Doubt, John Adams and Robert Wren were the petitioners.

[4] W. R. Scott, *English, Scottish and Irish Joint-Stock Companies to 1720* (Cambridge, 1910), II, 470.

[5] B.M.Add. MSS. 36914 includes a pamphlet (n.p.) printed in 1697 entitled *Reasons for Continuing the Duty of Eight Pence Upon Each One hundred and twenty Pounds Weight of Rock Salt without allowing a Drawback upon the same by comparing the Brine Salt made at Northwitche in Cheshire with the Salt-Rock Refined at the Dungeon near Leverpoole in Lancashire.* Dungeon, near Hale, situated close to the place where coal was shipped for Cheshire, was the most obvious position for such a refinery.

[6] Edward Hughes, *Studies in Administration and Finance 1558-1825* (Manchester, 1934), 225.

[7] *Ibid.*, 396n.   [8] Willan, *op cit.*, 31.

[9] 7,954 tons of rock salt were carried down the Weaver between Michaelmas 1732 and Michaelmas 1733 and 14,359 tons between Michaelmas 1752-3. Willan, *op cit.*, 39-40.

[10] *Ibid.*

coal was either known or suspected, it is impossible to say ; in the contiguous township of Ashton-in-Makerfield mining was taking place as early as 1330,[1] and it is likely that outcrop coal was used as soon as wood became scarce. Such a scarcity may have occurred quite early, for in 1327 Alan, lord of the manor of Eccleston, was altering his tenants' right to gather fuel in the wood of Eccleston " which now begins to decay " to the right of turbary in the heaths and mosses of the manor.[2]

Possibly the very fact that so much of the land was desolate peat moss helped to delay the coming of the coal age. Turves were used in brick-making until the opening of the nineteenth century, " moss reeves " were appointed by the township of Sutton until 1750, if not later,[3] and even Michael Hughes, a man of broad acres and industrial wealth, was not above noting in a pocket book in 1796[4] his right to " turf-rooms " on Sutton Heath.

Nevertheless it was in the midst of this very source of turf, Sutton Heath, that about 1540[5] the first recorded mining took place, the coal being discovered by accident during the digging of a clay pit. The opening of mines about this period was general rather than local. Nef has shown a widespread expansion in Lancashire coal-getting about the middle of the sixteenth century,[6] and very important mines at nearby Prescot were entered into in 1521.[7] The discovery of the Sutton mines meant a severe struggle between those who claimed rights on the now valuable piece of waste, and the Bolds of Bold, the lords of the manor, started to enclose it. Between the 1540s and the 1630s there was a series of lawsuits between the Bolds and the principal freeholders, led by the Eltonhead family, who endeavoured to claim, without much success, that their land was a manor in its own right. It was in 1580, during the taking of depositions for these lawsuits, that an elderly inhabitant stated that mining had begun about forty years before. The evidence makes it clear that the presence of coal in common land was often a reason for enclosure, and helps to explain why this process was so advanced in the district by the

[1] H. T. Crofton, " Lancashire and Cheshire Coal Mining Records," *Trans. L. & C. Antiq. Soc.*, 7 (1889), 35.

[2] A. J. Hawkes, " Some Thirteenth and Fourteenth Century Documents relating to Parbold, Ince, and Sutton." *Trans. L. & C. Antiq. Soc.*, 51 (1936), 72. Right of turbary allows the collection of turf or peat as fuel.

[3] The Township Book of Sutton (1658-1750). In the possession of the Prescot Historic Society.

[4] Hughes Papers, Sherdley Estate Office. Michael Hughes's Pocket Book, 1796, April 30.

[5] P.R.O. Duchy of Lancs. Depositions, 30 Eliz. No. 25, Sept., 1588. Transcript at St. Helens Ref. Lib.

[6] J. U. Nef. *The Rise of the British Coal Industry* (1932), I, 60.

[7] F. A. Bailey. " Early Coalmining in Prescot, Lancashire," *Trans. L. & C. Hist. Soc.*, 99 (1947), 2.

mid-eighteenth century. At the same time the importance of the lord of the manor in colliery development is underlined ; he possessed the coal rights not only under his own estates and demesne, but also under the highways and wastes.

From the middle of the sixteenth century down to the Restoration scattered references to mining occur, involving all the constituent townships of the modern St. Helens. In addition to the activity in Sutton, coal-getting is mentioned in Windle in 1610,[1] in Parr in 1655[2] and in Eccleston in 1660.[3] This part of Lancashire, however, saw no development in the scale or technique of coal mining to equal the contemporary achievements in the North-East. In this period the economics of transport were overwhelmingly in favour of water communication ; the prospects of collieries close to the sea, or to a river either naturally navigable or improved by the making of a "Navigation" were vastly better than those of merely " land-sale " collieries. The distance over which coals could be moved by cart, pack-horse or donkey was limited, ten miles seems to have been the rough economic radius of the land-sale colliery, and on occasion even that short journey may have multiplied the pit-head price of coal five times. Against this physical barrier to sales various forces could operate, the growth and intensity of demand of adjacent markets (Liverpool and the saltfield in the case of the St. Helens collieries), the turnpiking of roads, the making of navigations (like the Weaver Navigation), or, most powerful of all, the cutting of canals. In fact all these remedies were applied one by one to remove the disabilities under which the St. Helens coalfield laboured.

No difficulty appears to have been placed in the way of mining expansion by the local lords of manors. The Bolds in Sutton, the Ecclestons in Eccleston, the Gerards in Windle, the Byroms in Parr were all willing to have their coal exploited. But even if they had been reluctant to see their fields torn up and their land subsiding, the variety of other freehold landowners within the manors would have made the entry of the colliery speculator easy. There was a surprising diversity in the ownership of coal rights. Between the Restoration and the nineteenth century the local colliers hewed away coal their masters had bought or leased from Catherine of Braganza, George III, the Society of Friends, two Colleges (King's and Brasenose), and, at the other end of the scale, innkeepers, cabinet makers and yeomen.

Between the Restoration and the canal era the coalfield saw a number of attempts to make mining a regular and paying business. One difficulty was that the St. Helens district was long a " marginal " mining area as far as the Cheshire saltfield and the

---

[1] L.R.O., Cross Papers DDCs., 53/16.

[2] L.R.O., Gerard Papers, DDGe., 844.

[3] L.R.O., Scarisbrick Papers DDSc., 12/16.

Liverpool market were concerned ; pits at Prescot, Whiston and Huyton were closer to the destinations of the coal, and would certainly have the preference. This factor alone tends to account for the sporadic nature of many of the ventures, the local collieries chiefly being engaged in taking up the slack in the market. There were, however, other factors inherent in the nature and technique of early eighteenth-century mining which served to make it an uneven and irregular process. Many of the local entrepreneurs were acutely short of capital ; a windlass, a few baskets, buckets and picks, a string of horses or donkeys to carry away the coal, a stock of hay and candles—these few simple demands on their resources were as much as they could handle. Sometimes the piece of land they leased was small ; once they had worked out the coal within it neighbouring owners might not be prepared to lease them more on suitable terms, and the colliery might stop. Perhaps the greatest problem was drainage. In the flat Lancashire plain the favourite drainage device of the period, the ' adit,' a tunnel running from the workings to a point on the surface at a lower level, was generally impracticable. Hence coal was often taken only near the outcrop or from very shallow seams, and once water came in fast the pits were left. Mines generally consisted of several small workings dispersed over a number of fields, each perhaps employing only three or four colliers. Sometimes a mine drained by bucket and windlass was abandoned, to be resumed later by means of a whimsey, a sort of capstan turned by a horse, which enabled deeper working, and was then abandoned again only to be revived when the steam pumping engine was introduced, an innovation which reached St. Helens a decade before water transport. In some cases these various degrees of exploitation might be attained by entirely separate successive groups of partners, for each required a greater investment of capital than did its predecessor. This again helps to account for the way these collieries tended to die out and then come to life again on a more ambitious scale.

Space does not permit the examination of all the known colliery ventures prior to 1750, but one example is so typical that it should be given. In 1690 a gentleman of Frodsham in Cheshire leased from the Crown (in the person of the Queen Dowager, Catherine of Braganza) part of the common or waste of Thatto Heath on the borders of Sutton and Eccleston townships. He obtained permission to mine and drain the land, and in the following year extended the area of his operations in association with a London capitalist. Also involved was a Sutton yeoman, John Shaw, who lent the Cheshire man money, supported him when he was arrested for debt, and bought out his widow's share after his death. Shaw then became involved with the Turners, another Cheshire family, of Middlewich and Norley, who invested in the mine in 1715 and sent horses into Lancashire to be employed in draining. By 1718 the mine was a prosperous concern, with ' three hundred works of coal set upon the bank or Brow,' and we are told of 11,400 works raised at 7s. 6d. the work, and 1,200 works at 10s. the work, in all worth £4,000.[1] In the subsequent period mining around Thatto Heath was less active, but in 1770, in the canal and steam engine era, the collieries were revived amid great stir by a remarkable Scots industrialist, John Mackay.[2]

This single example shows the succession of speculators and of techniques which was necessary to develop one corner of the St. Helens coalfield, and how it was often only after long efforts that a short period of great prosperity came, until once again the limits of capital or technique were reached for the time being. It is also noteworthy that, when no further expansion could be achieved on local capital, the collieries of the area were a sufficiently good business proposition to attract outside investors, even so early as 1700. It was not, however, until the middle of the eighteenth century that by means of an infusion of capital into its communications system the coalfield became the centre of a vigorous, even hectic, economic life. That infusion did not come from the metropolis or even from Cheshire, but from the members of a new and vital commercial oligarchy, the merchants who dominated the Common Council of Liverpool.

---

[1] P.R.O., P.L. 6. 61/11. A work was about three tons.

[2] See below, pp. 43-4

Chapter II

THE FIRST ENGLISH CANAL

THE later 1660s and early 1670s saw significant changes at the port of Liverpool. As the Town Books of the day reveal,[1] to the existing coastal and fishing trade there was added a wider overseas connection. This is corroborated by a statement, issued at the end of the century by the Corporation :

"It was formerly a small fishing town, but many people coming from London, in time of the sickness and after the fire, several ingenious men settled in Leverpool, which caused them to trade to the plantations and other places, which occasioned sundry other tradesmen to come and settle there, which hath so enlarged their trade, that from scarce paying the salary of the officers of the customs it is now the third part of the trade of England, and pays upwards of £50,000 per annum to the king ; and by reason of such increase, many new streets are built, and still in building; and many gentlemen's sons of the counties of Lancaster, Yorkshire, Derbyshire, Staffordshire, Cheshire and North Wales, are put out apprentices in the town . . ."[2]

Defoe had the same story to tell. On his second visit to Liverpool, in 1690, the inhabitants claimed that the town was twice as large as it had been in 1670 and he himself testified that it had again doubled in size between 1690 and his third visit in 1705.[3] Liverpool, he thought, was "one of the wonders of Britain."[4] Another traveller, Celia Fiennes, was so impressed by the new streets and buildings that she proclaimed the town "London in miniature."[5] This remarkable expansion continued throughout the first half of the eighteenth century. All the indications seem to point to the fact that the population and trade of the port grew

[1] The Town Books for this period have not yet been published. They are kept at the Lpool. Record Office.

[2] "The case of the Corporation of Liverpool, in relation to a bill for making a new parish and erecting a new church there," c. 1699, printed in The Moore Rental ed. Thomas Heywood, Chet. Soc. 12 O.S. (1847) 77n.

[3] Daniel Defoe, A Tour Through England and Wales ed. Cole (1928) II, 255-6. Defoe does not state the date of his third visit but Mr. Hall wrote to Richard Norris on 28 Sept., 1705 : "Danl. Defoe hath been some days in town which hath been the great subject talked of, and been great matter of speculation to some persons." The Norris Papers ed. Thomas Heywood, Chet. Soc. 9 O.S. (1846), 145.

[4] Defoe, op. cit. II, 255.

[5] The Journeys of Celia Fiennes, ed. C. Morris (1947), 184.

roughly threefold between 1700 and 1750.[1] Each additional hearth increased the pressure on the town's fuel supply.

There was also an industrial demand for fuel which was almost certainly quite as great as, and probably considerably greater than, that of the domestic consumers. Sugar baking, a direct result of the new West Indies trade, began about 1670.[2] Salt boiling, as we have noticed, started in the mid-90s. A thriving pottery industry, which included not only common earthenware mugs, sugar moulds and the like but also the high-class Delft ware, arose in the eighteenth century.[3] Glassmaking can be traced back to 1724.[4]

[1] E.g. the number of christenings at St. Peter's exceeded 200 a year after 1708 and 600 a year after 1747. William Enfield, *An Essay Towards the History of Leverpool* (1773), 25-6. The average amount of shipping which entered and cleared the port of Liverpool in the seven years ending 1716 was 18,371 tons and in the seven years ending 1751 was 32,702. Thomas Baines, *History of the Commerce and Town of Liverpool* (1852), 491. The earlier returns are not given but it would seem probable that the figures for about 1700 were appreciably smaller and the increase over the period 1700-50 nearer threefold than double.

[2] Moore recorded in 1667-8 :

". . . one Mr. Smith, a great sugar baker at London, a man, as report says, worth forty thousand pounds, came from London on purpose to treat with me ; and, according to agreement, he is to build all the front twenty-seven yards, a stately house of good hewn stone, four story high, and then to go through the same building with a large entry ; and there, on the back side, to erect a house for boiling and drying sugar, otherwise called a sugar baker's house." *Rental*, 76-7. William Fergusson Irvine in his edition of the Rental, *Liverpool in King Charles the Second's Time* (L'pool, 1899), 99, points out that the earliest reference to a refinery is in Redcross Street. Therefore, if the refinery was ever built on the site mentioned by Moore, it must have been soon removed. No doubt Smith was one of the " ingenious men " whom the Corporation had in mind when they drafted their statement. An instruction to a Liverpool captain, dated 1700, shows that Liverpool ships were already engaged in the slave trade by that date. Picton Ref. Lib. Norris Papers, 2/199, 2/567. A number of broadsides and pamphlets issued by the Royal African Company between 1708-10 makes it clear that the Company's monopoly started to be infringed by interloping soon after 1688. By 9 and 10 Wm. III., cap. XXVI, merchants who were not members of the Company were permitted from 24 June, 1698, to engage in the Africa trade on a payment of 10% on all cargoes, slaves excepted.

[3] For sugar moulds, see James Touzeau, *The Rise and Progress of Liverpool* (Lpool, 1910) I, 401, and *Williamson's Lpool. Ad.*, 18 June, 1756, quoted in *V.C.H. Lancs.*, II, 404. For Delft Ware see articles by Joseph Mayer in the *Trans. L. & C. Hist. Soc.* 7 O.S. (1854) ; Llewellynn Jewitt, *The Ceramic Art of Great Britain* (New York, 1883), 310-27 ; V. W. Bladen, " The Potteries in the Industrial Revolution". *Econ. Jour.* (*Ec. Hist. Ser.*), Jan., 1926.

[4] The transcribed registers of St. Nicholas's Church, Liverpool, at the L.R.O., contain no references to glassmakers until 6 July, 1724. Thereafter glassmakers are mentioned with regularity. A glasshouse is marked on Chadwick's map of Liverpool, 1725, and George Skene, a visiting Scot, noted in his journal on 17 Sept., 1729, that there were then two glasshouses in operation. *The Miscellany of the Third Spalding Club* (Aberdeen, 1940), II, 132. It would seem, therefore, that Francis Buckley was probably incorrect in stating that the first glassworks were built at Liverpool in 1715. " Old Lancashire Glasshouses," *Trans. Soc. Glass Tech.*, XIII, Sept., 1929.

Beer-brewing was probably an even older occupation. All these industries required large and—perhaps just as important—regular deliveries of coal. To these must be added the cargoes of coal which were shipped from Liverpool up and down the coast, to Ireland or abroad.[1] While it is true that salt boiling in Cheshire and, later, salt refining on the Mersey, were the chief reasons for the more vigorous exploitation of the coal measures in south-west Lancashire, it is also true that Liverpool, with its growing population, its developing industries and its commercial commitments, was geographically the most important single destination for these coals.

Now Liverpool was highly articulate. In its Common Council it had a body of able and resourceful men who knew their own minds and were not afraid to voice their opinions. As the port became wealthier, the Council was able not only to protest against shortage and inefficiency; it was in a position to embark upon (or to give material encouragement to) development schemes which would eradicate them. By the eighteenth century, Liverpool Corporation was a power to be reckoned with.

The need for an abundant supply of cheap fuel gained the attention of the Council more and more as the eighteenth century wore on. So early as February 1698, very soon after the saltworks had been built, they authorised the expenditure of not more than £10 on an experimental bore for coals,[2] and in March 1717 they allowed one of their number, Alderman Gildart, to carry out another search within Corporation lands.[3] But neither of these investigations yielded any satisfactory result and Liverpool continued to rely for its deliveries of coal upon the precarious link with Prescot. This road was " almost unpassable "[4] for traffic, particularly in the wet weather when the heavy rains washed away the surface and transformed it into a succession of deep holes and ruts surrounded by a sea of mud.[5] It was customary, therefore,

[1] In August, 1663, the Common Council took notice of damage to the roads of the town on account of carts laden with " Coales and Muggs etc. to ye waterside . . . to be transported and carried away". (Touzeau, *op. cit.* I, 263). When the Sankey Canal was opened, special delivery prices were always quoted for loading upon vessels in the river.

[2] Touzeau, *op. cit.*, I, 344.

[3] *Ibid.* I, 404. In 1723 Gildart sought permission to find lead and other ore as well as coal.

[4] Liverpool Town Books, Nov., 1725, quoted in Touzeau, *op. cit.*, I, 417. " Several Gentlemen, Merchants, Tradesmen, and other Inhabitants living in and near the road from Liverpoole to Prescott " in a petition to Parliament, claimed that " several Parts of the said Road are so very deep, and other Parts so narrow, that Coaches, Waggons, and other Wheel-carriages, cannot pass through the same". (*C.J.* 20, 568, 12 Feb., 1725/6).

[5] For observations on the pre-turnpike road, see F. A. Bailey, " The Minutes of the Trustees of the Turnpike Roads from Liverpool to Prescot, St. Helens, Warrington and Ashton-in-Makerfield, 1726-89," *Trans. L. & C. Hist. Soc.* 88 (1937), 160-4. This paper, which covers pages 159-200 of this vol. and pages 31-90 of vol. 89, is based on the minutes of the Trust.

for most of the coal to be transported during the drier summer months, the road having been repaired in the spring by statute labour.[1] But the summer of 1725 was very wet and the people of Liverpool are said to " have suffer'd much for want of getting their Coales home Dureing the Summer season, thro' the Great Rains that have happen'd in these parts".[2] This led the Corporation to seek Parliamentary sanction for turnpiking the road. The necessary Bill received the Royal Assent on 26 April, 1726.

This Act authorised the formation of a Turnpike Trust for twenty-one years. By 1746, when this term had almost expired and the Trust was obliged to seek a further Act to prolong its existence, there is a clear indication that the output from the collieries at Prescot and Whiston no longer sufficed to meet the growing demand. Permission was sought to extend the Turnpike from Prescot to St. Helens in order to open " a Way to several Ranks of Coal-Pits, whereby all the Country adjacent, and particularly the Inhabitants of the Town of Liverpoole (now become very numerous) and also the shipping of the said Port, may be commodiously served, both in Winter and Summer, with Coals".[3] A witness told the Committee of the House of Commons that the extension would enable customers to be "more certainly and commodiously supplied with Coals than they now are . . . [and] if any Accident should happen to the Collieries at Prescot, Liverpoole could not be served with Coals, other than from St. Helens".[4] He also spoke of "People often being obliged to wait a considerable time at Prescot, before they could be supplied, there not being, in general, a sufficient Quantity of Coals upon the Bank to answer the Demand". In his opinion the collieries at Prescot would not suffer as a result of opening the road to St. Helens for heavy, wheeled traffic "because Prescot, being Three Miles nearer to Liverpoole than St. Helens, Persons will naturally go to the former Place for Coals, if they can be supplied as well and as cheap there as at the latter".[5] But the very fact that Liverpool was so anxious to obtain easier access to the pits which lay beyond Prescot was a sure sign that coals were not, in fact, being supplied so well or so cheaply as was required.

The improvement of the road to St. Helens, carried out in

[1] *Ibid.*, 162.

[3] Liverpool Town Books, Nov., 1725, quoted in Touzeau, *op. cit.*, I, 417.

[2] *C.J.*, **25**, 43, 28 Jan., 1745/6.   Petition of the Trustees.

[4] This is a clear statement that coal from the Wigan field was not, as yet, making its appearance in any quantity at Liverpool.   Although several inhabitants of the " Borough Town of Wigan " presented a petition against the Bill on 25 March, others from the town and the townships to the south of it were among those who signed a petition in favour which was laid on the table of the House on 8 April, along with seven other favourable petitions.

[5] *C.J.* **25**, 80, 28 Feb., 1745/6.   Evidence of John Eyes.

1749,[1] does not appear to have made the supply of coal as cheap and plentiful as its promoters had hoped. The mounting fuel crisis came to a head in 1753 when the Turnpike Trustees reimposed a toll on back-carriage which they had lifted in 1746,[2] and, almost simultaneously, the proprietors of Prescot Hall Colliery, the most important on the coalfield, advanced their prices by 20% in order to pay for a new pumping engine which they had just installed. These two acts of unwise self-interest transformed what had previously been an irritating hardship into an intolerable imposition. The Corporation decided to explore the possibility of providing a link by water between the coalfield at St. Helens and the river Mersey. Such a waterway, by permitting regular boatloads of coal to be brought all the year round from the coalfield down to the Mersey and from there to Liverpool or the wiches, would eliminate the costly road transport altogether and would make the consumers of coal independent of the pits in Prescot and Whiston.

On 5 June, 1754, the Council ordered that "two able and skilful surveyors" should, at the Council's expense, survey the Sankey Brook to see if it could be made navigable.[3] Their report was apparently favourable, for on 25 October the Council resolved to lend £300 towards securing the necessary Act of Parliament.[4] Four of the five Liverpool merchants whose names appear as the undertakers were prominent members of the Corporation. James Crosbie was Mayor, Charles Goore was Mayor in the following year, Richard Trafford was Mayor's Bailiff in October, 1755, and John Ashton had been Town Bailiff in 1749. The fifth undertaker was John Blackburne, junior, the owner of the Liverpool salt works. He joined the others on the Council in July, 1755. The measure could hardly have had more influential backing. Two enthusiastic petitions were presented by the interested parties: one was from the merchants, proprietors of salt works, sugar bakers, glass makers, distillers, beer brewers, maltsters and other tradesmen in and near the Borough and Port of Liverpool, the second from the proprietors of salt works at and near Northwich and Winsford.[5] William Taylor, one of the surveyors, testified that

---

[1] F. A. Bailey, *Trans. L. & C. Hist. Soc.* **88**, 196-7.

[2] In April, 1753, the Trustees were permitted to extend the Turnpike from St. Helens to Ashton and from Prescot to Warrington. The Warrington Road was improved first. Apart from erecting a toll gate at Ashton Cross in December, 1753, the St. Helens to Ashton road was not touched until after the opening of the Canal. The reimposition of the toll on back-carriage was supposed to meet the additional costs incurred in connection with the 1753 Act. Bailey, *op. cit.*, **89**, 45-9.

[3] *Town Books.* 5 June, 1754.

[4] *Town Books.* 25 October, 1754.

[5] *C.J.* **27**, 55-6, 17 December, 1754.

" large Quantities of Coals are consumed in the Salt Works at Liverpoole, Dungeon, Northwich and Winsford and by the Inhabitants of the aforesaid Towns and Places who have met great Complaints of the advanced Price which Coals have been sold for of late and of the short and uncertain Measure thereof ; and that he apprehends such advanced price is owing as well to the Difficulty of the Carriage as the Scarcity of the Coals."[1]

The Bill received the Royal Assent on 8 April, 1755.[2]

The two men who were chiefly responsible for the successful completion of the Sankey Brook Navigation, John Ashton and Henry Berry, were both of local origin. John Ashton's father, Nicholas, who died in 1728, possessed estates in Ashton, Parr and Eccleston and described himself in his will as " of Parr."[3] We do not know when John Ashton left home to seek his fortune in Liverpool nor have we any information about his activities there until 1749 when, as we have seen, he acted as Town Bailiff. When he came to make his will in November, 1753, he styled himself " Merchant and Cheesemonger "[4] and we know from another source that he was at that time engaged in the Africa trade.[5] He had also entered the salt industry on a large scale, for he owned the important Dungeon Salt Works,[6] having probably

---

[1] *C.J.* 27, 102, 17 Jan., 1755. On 7 February the principal landowners and coalmine proprietors upon the upper parts of the three branches of the Sankey Brook petitioned that the northern limits of the Navigation be extended to reach their collieries. An agreement on this was reached between the undertakers and Sir Thomas Gerard on 4 February, 1755. L.R.O., Gerard Papers DDGe 882.

[2] 28 Geo. II. cap. VIII.

[3] Will of Nicholas Ashton, of Parr, yeoman, proved Chester 9 May, 1729. He married " Margaret, daughter of James Orrell of Ashton," according to the family pedigree, but as his will mentions his brother-in-law " Humphrey Orrell of Parr " it is obviously the Blackbrook (Parr) family of that name. They were large farmers or small squires, possessed coal mines by 1750, and regarded themselves as gentry, and as protectors of the local Catholic community. We are indebted to Mr. N. C. E. Ashton of Kensington for use of the family pedigree compiled by Richmond Herald in 1787 and for access to a collection of material on the family formed by the late J. W. Ashton.

[4] Will proved at Chester 29 July, 1760.

[5] Gomer Williams, *History of Liverpool Privateers* (1897). Appendix VI, 674.

[6] Will of John Ashton.

acquired it at the time of its sale in 1746.[1] If we add to these varied interests the information that he was accused in 1757 of engrossing corn,[2] we have the picture of a man who rose to a position of eminence by shrewdly speculating in the numerous business ventures in which Liverpool was involved. The Sankey Brook Navigation was yet another of his successful speculations. He was its financer-in-chief, advancing close on £9,000 in all and holding 51 of the 120 shares.[3] In the first eighty years the Navigation was to pay an average yearly dividend of $33\frac{1}{8}$%.[4]

Henry Berry, who also hailed from Parr, was born in 1719 or 1720,[5] and came of a dissenting family. His elder brother John was a trustee of the Independent Chapel in the 1720s[6] and Henry Berry himself, described as " of Parr Batchellor," is mentioned in a trust deed of 1742.[7] In the following year he acted as township surveyor for Parr and his name occurs frequently in the Parr township papers during the next four years.[8] In 1747, however, he disappears from these local records and we next encounter the name in the Liverpool Town Books on 7 November, 1750 when, shortly after the death of Thomas Steers, the dock engineer Henry Berry, styled " late clerk to him ", was instructed to " continue to oversee the works till further notice."[9] By the following year, Steer's clerk was himself engineer at the Liverpool Docks.[10]

There can be no doubt that the man who at the age of thirty

---

[1] When these works were advertised for sale in *Adams Weekly Courant*, 9 December, 1746, it was stated that the premises were in the possession of a Mr. Ford. Further particulars were to be had from Jonathan Case at Wills Coffee House opposite Lincoln's Inn Gate, London, or from Richard Eccleston, attorney at law, Liverpool. The advertisement is quoted by the late Mr. A. C. Wardle in his paper, " Some Glimpses of Liverpool During the First Half of the Eighteenth Century," *Trans. L. & C. Hist. Soc.* **97**. (1945), 150. For Jonathan Case's tenure see below p. 25.

[2] *Lpool. Chron.*, 18 Nov., 1757.

[3] Will of John Ashton. £155 was paid up on each share. P.R.O., P.L.6. 84/3.

[4] See below, p. 185.

[5] When he died on 31 July, 1812, he was stated to have been " in the 93rd year of his age." Tombstone at St. Helens Congregational Church, cited in S. A. Harris, " Henry Berry (1720-1812) : Liverpool's Second Dock Engineer," *Trans. L. & C. Hist. Soc.*, **89** (1938), 107.

[6] Trust deeds at St. Helens Congregational Church, 2 Feb., 1726, 22 March, 1728.

[7] Trust deed at St. Helens Congregational Church, 10 Nov., 1742.

[8] He was highway surveyor in 1743, overseer of the poor and constable in 1742. About this time, when not in office, he featured as an intermediary. He was paid for clothing for the poor on several occasions ; it is just possible he kept a shop.

[9] *Town Books.* 7 Nov., 1750, quoted in S. A. Harris, *op. cit.* 93.

[10] *Town Books.* 3 July, 1751, quoted by S. A. Harris in an additional note to the above paper, *Trans. L. & C. Hist. Soc.*, **90** (1939), 197.

was entrusted with the responsibility for the completion of Liverpool's second dock was the same person who, only a few years
before, was repairing the lanes of Parr.[1] When new trustees were
appointed at the Independent Chapel at St. Helens in 1753, Berry
was described as " late of Parr and now of Liverpool, yeoman "[2]
and in 1756 in a deed relating to Parr, he was styled " of Liverpool,
Engineer."[3] Many years later when he died in Liverpool at the
great age of 92, his body was carried, at his own request, to the
Independent Chapel of St. Helens to be buried, " not in the
Chapel, where my parents are buried, but in the Chapel Yard."[4]

Unfortunately we do not know whether the ratepayers of Parr
made such constant use of Berry because he had already served his
apprenticeship as a millwright or in some other trade where he
could acquire engineering skill, or whether they were merely taking
advantage of an able young man who revealed a natural bent for
that kind of work. There can be no dispute, however, that once he
came under the tuition of Thomas Steers at Liverpool, he received
the finest instruction from one of the few experienced dock engineers of the day. The suggestion has been made that Steers had
been George Sorocold's chief assistant in the construction of the
famous Rotherhithe Dock in 1700.[5] Liverpool Corporation was
certainly advised by Sorocold before embarking on its first dock,[6]
and that may explain how Steers was sent up from London in 1708
to undertake the task.[7] By the late 1740s, when Berry came into
contact with him, Steers had a long line of engineering successes
to his credit and a full lifetime of valuable experience. On several
occasions he had turned his attention to inland navigation. He
had been connected with the Mersey-Irwell, Weaver, and Douglas
schemes and, between 1736 and 1741, was Adviser to the Newry
Navigation Commission.[8] Young Henry Berry was, therefore, in
a position to learn at first hand all the theoretical principles and
practical methods of waterway construction.

[1] The Parr Township Papers (Surveyors) St. H. Ref. Lib. include
the following entries written by Berry in 1743 :

July 11	For myself a day laying a plat in the cartway of						
	old Simcock's	...	...	...	...	0 0 5	
12	For myself letting of water	...	...	...	0 0 10	
Aug. 5	Paid John Berry for 2 Load of Stones ...	...	0 2 0	

[2] Trust deed at St. Helens Congregational Church, 11 Dec., 1753.

[3] St. H. Town Hall. Indenture dated 7 October, 1756.

[4] Second codicil to will of Henry Berry dated 4 June, 1808. Will proved
at Chester 5 Aug., 1812.

[5] H. Peet, " Thomas Steers, The Engineer of Liverpool's First Dock,
A Memoir," Trans. L. & C. Hist. Soc., 82 (1930), 170.

[6] Norris Papers, 165.

[7] Peet, op. cit., 170.

[8] Ibid., 183-4.

It was not surprising that Liverpool Common Council, having decided to explore the possibility of making a navigable waterway up to the coalfield, should turn to their able young dock engineer who had just proved his worth by completing the Salthouse Dock. He also had an additional recommendation : an intimate knowledge of the upper reaches of the Sankey Brook, where he had spent his childhood. This resourceful and well-informed servant of the Council was an obvious choice for the preliminary survey[1] and, when Parliamentary permission had been obtained, the Council resolved

> " That liberty be given to Mr. Berry for Two Days a Week to Attend the making Sankey Brooke Navigable—he providing and paying a skilfull person to superintend the works of the docks in his absence—to be approved by the Council."[2]

It was generally believed at the outset that the Council's order and the Act of Parliament would be adhered to and that the project was to be yet another river improvement scheme—dredging and widening the stream, making cuts to eliminate awkward bends and erecting locks to maintain the water level—on the same lines as the Mersey-Irwell, Douglas, and Weaver Navigations in which Liverpool had been interested. The Sankey Brook had already been made navigable from its mouth up to Sankey Bridges where it ran under the Warrington-Prescot road[3] and it was assumed that this improvement of the existing channel would be continued northwards until the coalfield was reached.

But the Sankey was only a brook. It was narrow and in wet weather overflowed its banks.[4] Such a small and unreliable stream was quite unsuitable for vessels and Berry was aware of this. But he also knew that, were he to come out into the open and suggest that the entire waterway be made a " cut "—or a canal, as we should call it—he would risk a complete and overwhelming defeat in Parliament. Only a few months before, in March, 1754, a Bill to make such a navigable channel from Salford to Leigh and Wigan had been thrown out by the Commons.[5] Berry's predicament

[1] He undertook the survey in company with William Taylor during the summer of 1754.

[2] *Town Books*, 7 May, 1755. Berry was paid 16s. 6d. per day for this work. T. S. Willan, *The Navigation of the River Weaver in the Eighteenth Century*, Chet. Soc., 3rd Ser., III (1951), 57. The proprietors presented him with a silver cup on its completion. Will of Henry Berry.

[3] Thomas Pennant, *A Tour from Downing to Alston Moor* (1801), 17. The will of John Woodcock of Warrington, merchant, dated 15 June, 1745, proved at Chester, 25 May, 1751, mentions " my share in the Navigation at Sankey Bridges".

[4] E. A. Pratt, *A History of Inland Transport and Communication in England* (1912), 166.

[5] *C.J.*, **26**, 944, 968-9, 972-3, 977 ; 4, 25, 28 Feb., 5 Mar. 1754.

is ably summarised by the well-informed writer who was later called upon to compose his obituary notice :—

" after an attentive survey he [Berry] found the measure [making the Brook navigable] impracticable and, knowing that the object they had in view could be answered by a canal, he communicated his sentiments to one of the proprietors who, approving the plan, the work was commenced on 5 September, 1755, but the project was carefully concealed from the other proprietors, it being apprehended that so novel an undertaking would have met with their opposition".[1]

The proprietor in question was almost certainly John Ashton, by far the largest single shareholder.

The extremely sketchy information relating to the actual construction of the Canal and the manner in which Berry used the Sankey Brook merely as a source of water supply and a means of overflow for his ten-mile cut, have been outlined elsewhere and need not detain us here.[2] The Canal joined the navigable portion of the Brook by a lock at Sankey Bridges and from this junction the waterway was gradually raised 80 feet by eight further locks to the point in Parr township where it forked into two arms, the northern branch continuing towards Penny Bridge at Blackbrook and the westerly branch towards Gerard's Bridge. A plan of 1763, based upon an earlier survey, shows that the Canal had been completed as far as Gerard's Bridge by the spring of 1759, at which date the northerly arm was half-finished.[3] The new waterway had been open to traffic along two-thirds of its length eighteen months before this : on 4 November, 1757, the *Liverpool Chronicle* carried the advertisement that " Sankey Brook Navigation is now open for the passage of flats to the Haydock and Par collierys." The Sankey Canal, opened almost four years before Brindley's much publicized waterway from Worsley to Manchester, ushered in the Canal Age.[4]

[1] *Lpool Merc.*   7 Aug. 1812.

[2] T. C. Barker, " The Sankey Navigation : The First Lancashire Canal," *Trans. L. & C. Hist. Soc.*, **100**, 139-143.

[3] " A Plan of the Sankey Navigation From the River Mersey into the Townships of Parr and Windle in the County of Lancaster. Survey in April and May 1759 by John Eyes and Thomas Gaskell and Plan by John Eyes in July, 1763," at the Estate Manager's Office, Euston Station, London. The northerly arm does not appear to have been completed until about 1770. Evidence was given to a parliamentary committee in 1829 that " In 1769 an application was made by Mr. Legh of Lyme for a Canal to be cut up towards La Fog [Laffak] Colliery . . . which was executed very shortly afterwards." (Quoted by L. W. Evans in evidence on the St. Helens Railway (Transfer) Bill 1864). The southern spur into Sutton was completed about the same time. See below, p. 44.

[4] For similarities between the Sankey and Bridgewater Canals and the suggestion that Brindley may have been aware of Berry's work twelve miles away, see Barker, *op. cit.*, 152-3.

The opening of the Canal had an illuminating sequel. Throughout the growing fuel crisis, in all its official pronouncements Liverpool had emphasised the sufferings of the townspeople rather than the industrial shortages which had undoubtedly occurred. The shortage of coal in the domestic grate was, no doubt, calculated to win the most widespread public sympathy. At the same time, it must not be forgotten that the inhabitants' claims were being pressed by members of the Council, prominent merchants and industrialists who had their own business reasons for wanting a more plentiful and cheaper supply of coal. John Ashton and John Blackburne, who always featured as the chief promoters of the Canal, were the leading salt refiners on the Mersey, the former at Dungeon, the latter in Liverpool itself. By this time back-cargoes of salt had become an integral part of the commercial life of Merseyside in which almost every merchant was interested in one way or another.

From the point of view of this all-pervasive salt interest, the Sankey Canal was the logical conclusion to the Weaver Navigation, for it secured access to the coal just as the Weaver Navigation had opened a route for the carriage of salt. The two waterways were complementary. It was obviously the intention of the promoters of the Sankey scheme that the same flats should sail[1] up to St. Helens for a cargo of coal which they would then ship across to Northwich, returning to Liverpool laden with salt. As soon as the Canal was ready to be opened in the autumn of 1757, Liverpool Corporation, having received a petition from several merchants of the port " complaining of the ill management of the navigation of the river Weaver," offered to " bear the expenses of any gentleman who shall take the trouble to go and order a survey of the said river and to meet any gentleman concerned in the said navigation, in order to have the inconvenience and mismanagement of the said river redressed."[2] This was the signal for the beginning of protracted negotiations in which the Liverpool men brought extreme pressure to bear on the trustees of the Weaver to improve the river, enlarge the locks (and so make the Navigation a five-foot waterway, as was the Sankey Canal)[3] and accept receipts given on the Sankey as valid statements of cargo.[4] The Liverpool men gained their objectives and the improvements and alterations in the Weaver were effected by the early 1760s.[5] At the outset they

[1] The Canal was navigated by barges fitted with sails. For this reason swivel bridges were used.

[2] J. A. Picton, *City of Liverpool Municipal Archives and Records* (1886), II, 145-6, quoted in Willan, *op. cit.*, 49.

[3] Willan, *op. cit.*, 54.

[4] The negotiations are fully treated in Willan, *op. cit.*, caps. IV & V.

[5] *Ibid.*, 82.

even had Henry Berry (whom a Cheshire gentleman referred to as their agent)[1] in charge of the work. But the assignment was to prove his undoing as a canal engineer. In March, 1759, while he was building a new lock, weir and cut at Pickerings, a " fresh " coming suddenly in the river breached the banks of a temporary channel which he had dug to take off the water while he was constructing the cut.[2] Shortly afterwards the weir was " intirely washed away " and the Commissioners thought it " imprudent to employ him any longer."[3]

It would appear that Berry, outstandingly successful though he was in harnessing the stream of a mere brook, was unable to manage the more variable currents of a river. But it must not be forgotten that he was looked upon as the agent of the pushing Liverpool men in the land of the more leisurely Cheshire gentlemen who showed an intense dislike to the changes being imposed upon them. It is certain that the people of Cheshire would be only too glad to make the most of every imperfection, however small, in order to discredit this symbol of foreign dictation. And it may be significant that, in the midst of these trials, Berry lost his staunchest and most influential supporter. John Ashton died in August, 1759.[4]

There can be little doubt that the events of 1759, whether entirely Berry's fault or not, explain his eclipse as a canal builder. When in 1762 the Sankey Canal was extended from Sankey Bridges to Fidler's Ferry in order to cut out the winding mile and a quarter of original waterway down to the Mersey, Berry was not placed in charge.[5] By that time James Brindley had already caught the public imagination and Berry returned to his important work at the Liverpool docks, the forgotten pioneer.[6]

By the beginning of the 1760s the salt interest had instituted an internal triangular trade between Liverpool, the St. Helens coalfield and the Cheshire saltfield. In one respect in particular—the provision of a valuable back-cargo—this was as crucial to the

---

[1] Sir Peter Warburton to John Stafford, *ibid.*, 186.

[2] *Ibid.*, 58-9. In a letter to Sir Peter Warburton, written on 13 March, immediately after the accident had occurred, Berry protested that " the breach is not as bad as was represented to you. If the weather hold good, I think we can make it good in about three or four days time." *Ibid.*, 166.

[3] *Ibid.*, 81.

[4] *Williamson's Lpool Ad.* and the *Lpool Chron.* noticed his death, in the briefest of obituaries, on 10 Aug., 1759.

[5] Barker, *op. cit.*, 143.

[6] Berry, however, was not so discredited that his opinion as an engineer could not be sought on important projects. He achieved some prominence in the mid-1780s in connection with the first proposal to bridge the Menai Strait and his favourite device of the swivel-bridge was one of the most debated features of this project. U.C.N.W. Bangor. Plasnewydd Colln. Bundle of uncatalogued papers, 1785-6. *Gore's Gen. Ad.*, 14 July, 1785.

port's growing prosperity as was that other, better-known triangular trade to Africa and the West Indies in which Liverpool vessels were engaged. The Weaver Navigation had, in effect, taken the Mersey traffic up to the Cheshire wiches and the Sankey Canal brought it into the St. Helens district. The Canal was an extension of the Mersey and its northern terminus became an extension of Merseyside.

For the next seventy-five years the economic life of the St. Helens district was dominated by this waterway, and in relation to most of the chief developments its significance will scarcely need stressing. One interesting example of its influence is, however, worth noting. Advertisements in the Liverpool papers when land, coal rights, or works sites were to be sold almost invariably mentioned the distance from the canal. " The Sankey Canal flows through the estate " appears to have been the highest commendation possible. Even property at Rainford, a good four miles from the waterway's extremity, seems to have appreciated because of its construction. Colliery expansion was largely governed by proximity to the Canal; every hundred yards of distance from its banks diminished the value of a mine and every mile further north on the canal itself meant that flats would prefer to load coals lower down ; even the increased use of the waggon-way never seems to have offset the disadvantage of distance from the banks. For St. Helens and its industries this was indeed the Canal Age.

CHAPTER III

THE EARLY COAL MAGNATES: THE CASES OF HUYTON AND SARAH CLAYTON OF LIVERPOOL,
1757-1762

IN the early eighteenth century the most important coalowners on the western side of the St. Helens-Prescot coalfield were the Cases of Redhasles. They held the manor of Huyton and, by intermarriage with the Ogles of Whiston, they had come into possession of that manor and its important coal measures.[1] In 1701 a Jonathan Case figured prominently in a petition of rock salt proprietors interested in the Cheshire trade,[2] and in 1714 he was partner in a Huyton colliery supplying the great salt proprietors Sir Thomas Johnson and John Blackburne. Significantly, as will appear, there were also among the colliery's customers a Mr. Clayton and other owners of the ship called the " Clayton Galley ".[3]

As early as 1719 the diarist Nicholas Blundell recorded that the Cases had a remarkable new pumping engine near Prescot :

" I went to Mr. Case his, but he was not at home so I smoaked a Pipe with his Son Henry and then went to ye New Engin as is to draw up water from one of ye Cole-pits, thence I went to ye New Glass-hous, Mr. Case came past whilst I was there so I followed him to his Hous where I stayed awhile and desired him to be one of my Executors."[4]

An abstract of title to the Case property shows that the engine was in fact a " fire engine " or Newcomen steam engine. The permission to erect it together with the expense of erection had cost Jonathan Case's son Thomas at least £1,500.[5] Since the first Newcomen engine was only erected in 1712, the one owned by the

---

[1] L.R.O., Cross Papers, Abstract of Title of Henry Case : Lease from Cuthbert Ogle of Whiston, Esq., to Jonathan Case of Redhasles in Huyton, Esq., 1701. Matthew Gregson. *Portfolio of Fragments*. (Manchester, 1869) 176.

[2] *C.J.* **13.** 6 June, 1701.

[3] P.R.O., P.L. 6. 56/49.

[4] *Diary of Nicholas Blundell of Crosby*. Ed. Rev. T. E. Gibson. (Lpool, 1895) 154.

[5] L.R.O., Cross Papers, Abstract of Title of Henry Case, quoting will of Jonathan Case, 1721. For this and other local Newcomen engines see J. R. Harris, " The Early Steam-Engine on Merseyside." *Trans. L. & C. Hist. Soc.* **106,** 109-16.

Cases must be among the earliest, and may be claimed as the first Lancashire steam engine.[1]

The capital outlay involved in running the collieries became increasingly heavy, and must have come near to ruining the family. In 1731, two years after his father's death, Thomas Case already owed £1,000 to Elizabeth Clayton, the widow of his former customer, and borrowed a further £1,500. Ten years later the debt to Elizabeth Clayton was " £690 and no more," but Case owed her daughter Sarah £940. Lands in Whiston had been mortgaged to a celebrated capitalist, Nicholas Fazackerly of Lincoln's Inn, for £1,500; by the transfer of one of the debts formerly owed to Elizabeth Clayton a lesser lawyer-financier, Thomas Barron of Prescot, was involved. In 1744 the creditors set up a trust for administering the Case property, one of the administrators being Sarah Clayton. These trustees strictly limited the income which Thomas Case and his son Jonathan were to receive from the estates and mines, provided for the discharge of some of the mortgages, and sold off property in Prescot, Whiston, Huyton and Hale, including the " Salt Works in Hale," the well-sited and very important Dungeon Works.[2] As already shown, the acquisition of this works by John Ashton had a bearing on the building of the Sankey Canal.

Sarah Clayton was to be of the greatest importance in the creating of the St. Helens coalfield, and her mining concerns become at this point integral to the narrative. Her father, William Clayton, was descended through the Claytons of Fullwood from the Claytons of Clayton Hall, near Manchester. During the reigns of William and Mary and of Anne he was one of the greatest Liverpool merchants; Mayor of Liverpool in 1689, he represented the port in six Parliaments from 1698 to 1713.[3] A few years before his death he purchased the manor of Parr, formerly owned by the Byroms, who were going rapidly downhill at this period. Several mentions of lunacy in the family are recorded and Samuel Byrom, the last of the line, died in York Castle in 1741.[4] Long before this the Claytons had taken their

---

[1] For the early history of the Newcomen engine and its exploitation by a company of proprietors under the Savery patent see H. W. Dickinson, *A Short History of the Steam Engine* (1938), Chaps. I-IV ; and a document published in " The First Steam Engines on the Durham Coalfield " by Prof. E. Hughes. *Archaeologia Aeliana* (1949) 41-3.

[2] L.R.O., Cross Papers, Abstract Title of Henry Case : Agreement of 15 and 16 March, 1744.

[3] S. A. Harris, " Sarah Clayton's Letter and John Wood of Bath." *Trans. L. & C. Hist. Soc.* 100, 55-8.

[4] James Byrom was mentioned as being mad when owning the manor in 1655.   Roger Lowe the diarist also records : " 14 March, 1665. Henry Houghton came to me and William and had me to go with them to Parr Hall to seale lease to Mr. Byrom.   He seald it, and Mr. Edward Byrom and his two Brothers that were destructed went and brought us to an Ale

place in the manor; the Hall was in their hands in 1713, and the demesne coal mine in the next year.[1] The following year William Clayton died, and the manor passed to his widow, Elizabeth, who long outlived him. On her death in 1745 the manor descended to her daughter Sarah.

Sarah Clayton seems to have lived with considerable ostentation. From 1752 she began to lay out the Liverpool square still bearing her name, now in the centre of the city, but then in a field of the suburbs, and she herself occupied the largest house.[2] In the early 1750s she was one of the four people in Liverpool owning their own coach,[3] and her frequent residence at Bath enabled her to meet John Wood the architect and advocate his employment in the design of Liverpool's new Exchange.[4] Few charitable causes seem to have been advanced in her native town without her support. Both the Clayton ladies were rather particular in their choice of title, for Elizabeth Clayton, at least during her widowhood, was called " Madame Clayton," while Sarah was referred to as " Mistress Clayton," which explains why, though unmarried, she is always " Mrs. Clayton." She appears to have rejected the title of " Miss " which was becoming the rule.

The Claytons were not merely bound to the Cases by financial ties, for Sarah's sister Margaret had married Thomas Case in 1721 ; it was in fact to his mother-in-law and sister-in-law that his chief debts were owed.[5] From this it followed that the change

---

house, where we sat drinking a good while." *The Diary of Roger Lowe of Ashton-in-Makerfield, Lancashire, 1663-74.* Ed. William L. Sachse, (1938), 81. See also Administration of Samuel Byrom, Wills at L.R.O. 22 Oct. 1741. Two creditors were administrators, one of whom was an innkeeper, the bond taken out being for only £80.

[1] St. H. Ref. Lib. Parr Township Papers. Land Tax Returns. Only a few of this period are preserved ; returns for the County are not available before 1781.

[2] S. A. Harris, *op. cit.,* 56.

[3] J. A. Picton, *Memorials of Liverpool, Historical and Topographical.* (Lpool, 1903), **1,** 182.

[4] S. A. Harris, *op. cit.,* 58-62.

[5] L.R.O., Cross Papers, Abstract of Title of Henry Case. Marriage settlement of 5 & 6 March, 1721. While dealing with the Clayton family, it may be remarked that Elizabeth Clayton's tomb in St. Nicholas' Church was one of the sights of Liverpool in the late eighteenth century A photograph of the monument is frontispiece to H. Peet, *Liverpool in the Reign of Queen Anne,* (1908). Her epitaph and that of her daughter Sarah may be of interest :

" Near this Place lieth deposited the Mortal part of Elizabeth, Daughter of George Leigh of Oughtrington in the County of Chester, and Relict of William Clayton of Liverpool, Esqrs. to whom She was Married the 7th of August 1690, and had Issue 2 Sons and 7 Daughters, viz. Eleanor married to Mr Richard Houghton of this Place Merchant ; Anne Married to Banastre Parker of Cuerden in the County of Lancaster Esqre.; Margaret, Married to Thomas Case of Red-Hasles in the same

in the control of the coal supply to the Cheshire saltfield and to Liverpool which was a consequence of the building of the Sankey Canal was not so great as might have been expected. There was of course a strong shift in the balance of the trade from one end of the local coalfield to the other. Huyton, Prescot and Whiston became relatively less important than Sutton, Eccleston, Parr, Garswood and Haydock. As far as the capitalists were concerned, however, the effect was largely to take some of the trade from the Cases and place it in the hands of Sarah Clayton, for Parr was the first mining township to be reached by the canal and for many years remained the most important. Indeed the process can be regarded from Sarah Clayton's point of view simply as an extension of an existing interest in the coal trade, a change from financing other colliery venturers to operating her own mines. The fact that the prices of coal on the new canal did not long remain as low as the citizens of Liverpool desired and considered feasible may well have been due to Sarah Clayton's wish to safeguard her allies and relatives in Huyton, for even after her direct participation in the trade the Cases remained of importance. After the death of Thomas Case his eldest son Jonathan began to extend his interests eastwards towards the St. Helens district, whilst his younger son Thomas, a great Africa and West India trader, many years later became associated with Sarah Clayton's mines. In a way the extension of the Clayton-Case control of the coalfield may be likened to a military pincer-movement, Jonathan Case's attack being on the line of the turnpike, Sarah Clayton's on that of the canal.

As soon as the canal reached the Parr collieries Sarah Clayton and her agents were in evidence.

" The Collieries belonging to Mrs. Clayton in Parr, adjoining to Sankey Brook Navigation, are opened; where there are two Delfs already worked, and a Quantity of each Delf got ready for Sale.

Mrs. Clayton proposes to put the new raised Coal on board the Flats in the Navigation at Four Shillings and Twopence a Ton. The Waggon Road and other conveniencies are fixed in such a manner that Flatts may be loaden in a few hours.

Orders will be received, and punctually obeyed, on these Terms

County, Esq. and Sarah Clayton, by whom this Monument was erected to her Memory : the Rest died Young. She died after a Life well spent in her Duty to God, and the care of her Family in the 78th Year of her Age, A.D. 1745."

The length of Sarah Clayton's epitaph to her mother is in ironic contrast to her own, when the family star had set.

" Mrs. Sarah Clayton exchanged this life for a better May the 1st, 1779, Aged 67, and was interred in the vault with the Remains of her late Father William Clayton, Esqe, many years Representative in Parliament for this Borough".

by Richard Sherrat, at Parr Collieries aforesaid, or Alexander Tarbuck at Mrs. Clayton's in Liverpool.

N.B.—A Quantity of Coals, that was raised last Winter in the first entrance into these works, will be sold something under the above Price."[1]

This advertisement was to appear at frequent intervals for over two years.

In the February of 1759 Sarah Clayton stated her prices for delivery at Liverpool ; coals would be supplied to ships at 7s. for 30 bushels, about a ton in weight, and to householders at 7s. 6d. per ton.[2] Comparing this with the prices at the pit-head or wharf, as quoted previously, it is obvious that even accounting for the 10d. per ton toll on coal on the Navigation there was plenty of room for profit between 7s. or 7s. 6d. and 4s. 2d.

As the 'sixties opened the Clayton interest and the Canal interest were a little on the defensive, and a note of explanation and reassurance crept into their insertions in the Liverpool papers.

" At a General Annual Assembly of the Proprietors of the Sankey Brook Navigation, 30th April, 1761. It being represented in this Assembly, that the toll or duty of 10d. per Ton on Charcoal, Coal and Cinders, is too great a Duty, and more than those commodities will well bear : it is therefore ordered That for the encouragement of Persons to convey these Commodities down the Navigation, the Collector of the Tolls and Duties shall, for the future, . . . take no greater Duty than the Sum of Seven-pence . . . "[3]

The day of graceful gestures was not over. The very next issue of the paper carried this insertion :

" Whereas there has been a kind of Smiths Coals carried down the Sankey Navigation and sold in Liverpool for Winstanly Coals, tho' much inferior in Quality ; these are therefore to acquaint the public, that there is now in carting, down to the Sankey Navigation, a Quantity of the right Winstanley Coals as good in Quality as any that was ever yet there raised and intended for Sale. Who ever wants any of the said coals, may depend upon being well used upon reasonable terms, by applying to John Foster, Blockmaker in King Street, Liverpool ; Alexander Tarbuck at Parr Colliery, or Thomas Farnworth, agent to the said Winstanley Colliery . . ."[4]

---

[1] *Williamson's Lpool. Ad.* 16 Dec., 1757.

[2] *Ibid.* 16 Feb., 1759. The Sankey Canal Act was not only concerned with the construction of the waterway, but with the establishing of a correct and fair measure of the coal which was to be supplied by it. A standard bushel was specified, which would contain a bushel and a quart of water, Winchester measure. Thirty such bushels made about one ton.

[3] *Williamson's Lpool. Ad.*, 1 May, 1761.

[4] *Ibid.*, 8 May, 1761.

The Parr Colliery must be that of Sarah Clayton, for Alexander Tarbuck was her agent. Another six months passed and reform was again in the air.

" Whereas it has been represented to the Proprietors of Sankey Navigation that some of the Sellers of Coal which are brought down the said Navigation and sold at Liverpool, do frequently give short measure, by not filling the Tubs even with the Top or brim to the great Detriment of the Inhabitants of the said Town . . ." [the Proprietors are printing those clauses of the Act of 1755 which legislate against short measure, and the penalty of £50 wherever recovered will be given half to the informer and half to the poor].[1]

This would seem admirable on the part of the Proprietors, did not the notice have very much the air of what contemporaries termed a " puff." Obviously the coalmasters and canal proprietors felt that there was a great need to conciliate public opinion.

Strong light is thrown on their apprehensions by a letter which appeared in the Liverpool press only a month later. After referring to the coal dealers as " Coal Jews " and comparing them to the corn monopolists of the famine year of 1757, the writer went on to give the reasons for shortage and high prices.

" It is not long since we were dependent on Prescot and places adjoining for our Coal, which we looked on as a very great Grievance ; And in Order to remedy the Evil petitioned for an Act of Parliament, to get a navigation opened from Sankey Brook into the River Mersey; which was granted, suffered, and looked upon, by everybody, to be for the Good of the Town, by reducing the Price of Coal ; but instead of reducing the Price or increasing the Quantity, they have lessened[2] the one, and consequently raised the other. The Country Carters, at the opening of the new Navigation, found there would not be the Demand for Coal that there formerly had been ; therefore, as their Livelihood chiefly depended on that of leading Coal, they were obliged to convert their Carts to other Uses, which discouraged the Proprietors from raising the Quantities they had done. The Engrossers of the Navigation Coal, finding that the Town was likely to be distressed (which

---

[1] *Ibid.*, 8 Jan., 1762.

[2] It is difficult to believe that, however monopolistic the canal proprietors and coal-masters may have been, the building of the canal actually resulted in *less* coal arriving in Liverpool than in the previous period when only land-sale coal was available. The position was doubtless that the town was growing so rapidly and industrial use extending so quickly that the newly increased supplies were swiftly absorbed, leaving the householder as badly off as before.

they certainly are at present, especially the Poor, who are not able to buy above a Load, or what is called a Ton at a time) takes all means they possibly can to distress the Inhabitants. They began the sales at Seven Shillings per Ton, and in the space of Four Years . . . has got them to Eight Shillings and Sixpence ; nay I may safely say, any Price they please to demand for there is none to be sold to the Poor ; Therefore how dangerous . . . is the consequences.[1]

I observe . . . a Part of the aforementioned Act, printed in this Paper of the 29th ult., quoted I suppose to skreen the Proprietors, and throw the Culpableness on the Persons employed by them ; or rather to clear them all from, I believe, a just Imputation of retailing out bad measure . . ."[2]

This letter is a perfectly good explanation of the conciliatory attitude recently shown by the Sankey Canal party. It must be borne in mind that we have here a Liverpool newspaper, owned by a mercantile family, the Williamsons, attacking—or allowing others to attack—the most powerful group in commercial Liverpool, a very dangerous set of people to quarrel with. There can be no doubt that for the letter to appear at all the newspaper must have been sure that a strong public opinion was behind it, and the Sankey Canal proprietors and the coal owners seem to have thought the opposition dangerous enough to make some show of giving way.

---

[1] The writer may have had in mind the several food riots about Liverpool and Prescot in 1757.

[2] *Williamson's Lpool. Ad.*, 12 Feb., 1762.

CHAPTER IV

THE GROWTH OF COMPETITION ON THE COALFIELD
1763-1775

BEFORE 1763 Sarah Clayton and her associates did not have things entirely their own way in the coal trade, but the opposition was not nearly so serious as it later became. Down to this time the competitors of the Clayton interest can be divided into two groups. Firstly, there were the proprietors of "land-sale " collieries to the west of St. Helens, and nearer to Liverpool. The importance of this threat was reduced by the fact that the coalfield terminated some six miles from the port, and this fixed a limit to the effectiveness of such competition. The second set of rivals consisted of other coal-masters on or near the Sankey Canal itself ; these would appear to have been the more immediately dangerous as they might have split the alliance between the Canal proprietors and the Clayton-Case coalowners. So long as one group of coal-masters had something of a monopoly, the Canal proprietors would be content to make their profit by charging high tolls on a restricted traffic, but, as soon as the monopoly was seriously impaired, their best prospects would lie in obtaining the maximum traffic on the Canal. This local competition had been in evidence before the price reduction of 1761, but had generally come from small speculators without the resources which the Claytons and Cases derived from their extensive commercial wealth and landed property.

In 1756, just as Sarah Clayton was opening up her Parr collieries, a local yeoman family, the Tarbucks, began in a humbler way. Two brothers, Robert and John Tarbuck, sank mines in Windle at their joint cost, and continued to work them for over a decade. John Tarbuck acted as manager on the spot while his brother Robert resided at Liverpool, possibly so as to superintend the sales. It became necessary for them to rent more land, if the mines were to be kept going, and they leased a small estate from Sir William Gerard and other lands from the Revd. Mr. Moss. Even after their expenses were deducted the mines were very profitable. In 1766 Robert Tarbuck left Liverpool and came to reside near the colliery, and about this time Richard Sherrat, who was the coal agent (which probably means that he was looking after the technical part of the business) was desirous of purchasing a half-share, for which he offered £660. An agreement on these lines was drawn up between the three men, though the " Windey Engine, the Rail Road, the Waggons and the Hovel " were not included in the contract. But on the 25th of December, 1768, the colliery stopped work because Gerard's lease had expired, and the coals of the other owners were worked out. The colliery must have been near the Canal, because coal was being sent by flat to Liverpool and other places.[1] In this case, as in others, we can see from the fact that only horse-gins were being used that the mine was shallow. The reason for closing the colliery—the failure to obtain extensions of leases and coal rights—was a common one with the smaller concerns.

By 1758 another local colliery was selling coal in Liverpool :—

" Notice is hereby given, that there is good COALS mixed with small Kennel, at St. Helen's Coal-Work, that will be laid down at Liverpool at five-pence per Basket, ready Money, so any Persons that has a mind to try them may be supplied, by enquiring of Mr. John Berry, at side of dry Dock."[2]

This colliery was worked by Peter Berry, a Sutton yeoman, who had rented part of it in 1754 from Thomas Golden (or Goulden) of Hardshaw Hall. The lease was for twenty years and involved a monopoly of mining on the Hardshaw estate, Golden's own colliery excepted. The venture was short-lived ; an advertisement appeared for its sale at the Raven Inn, St. Helens, on July 18, 1759, with this description :

" A coal mine, consisting of eleven feet of coal, with an addition of one foot of cannel ; held by Peter Berry for the space of Twenty Years from several Proprietors or Lords, Five of which years are expired ; now in extreme good condition, situate and lying in St. Hellens, on the Turnpike Road to Liverpool, and within seventy roods distance of the Sankey Navigation. There are several new pits sunk, a good Fire Engine lately erected, and all other Utensils to compleat the said work . . . apply to . . . Peter Berry, who will shew . . . an exact scheme and Map of the Whole Work."[3]

Charles Dagnall is the most interesting of the smaller local

---

[1] P.R.O., P.L. 6. 85/35. Sherrat worked the ironstone mine on the Tyrer Estate in Parr (the Tyrer family were related to the Claytons) in 1743, and we have seen that he was acting as Mrs. Clayton's agent at Parr Colliery in 1757. (Above, p. 28). At his death in 1792 he was worth less than £300 in personal estate, L.R.O. Will.

[2] *Williamson's Lpool. Ad.*, 5 May ,1758.

[3] *Ibid.* 29 June, 1759. A renewal of the advertisement on 13 Nov., 1761, shows that the mine was near the line of modern Church Street, the town's main shopping centre, and that land was leased from the Trustees of St. Helen's Chapel, the Gascoyne family, and the Society of Friends, in addition to Golden. The Newcomen engine mentioned is the second met with on the coalfield. Peter Berry, we know from other evidence, also mined in the Ravenhead area, but at what date is uncertain. See below p. 43.

coal-masters of this period. He had begun operations over ten years before the construction of the Canal and the opening of Mrs. Clayton's Parr mines, and persisted into the era of the great coal-masters. This half-literate and rather dishonest man combined the calling of coal-master with his original occupation of ivory-combmaker.[1] In 1746 he began mining in land leased from the squire of Eccleston and from two substantial yeomen of that township, Henry Seddon and George Rice, and very soon he entered lands owned by Mr. Lancaster of Rainhill.[2] The site of his operations can be fixed; he was sinking pits in fields stretching from the modern Croppers Hill and Boundary Road towards Thatto Heath—in other words on the flank of the Ravenhead area, afterwards so celebrated for its Rushy Park coal. Originally Dagnall paid Mr. B. T. Eccleston 1s. 9d. per work for the coal he raised, but at the expiry of the original seven-year lease the squire realised that he could demand more, and increased the rent to 3s. per work. In June, 1755, at the end of the first year's working at the higher rent, Dagnall professed willingness to stand by his agreement, but said he would be ruined if he had to pay the same rate to other owners from whom he " farmed " land for coal mines. While paying in full, he asked Mr. Eccleston to give him a receipt for a much smaller amount, in order to deceive the other coalowners. A little over a year later, however, the mine was worked out. Dagnall delayed paying the outstanding coal rent, and claimed (with his receipt as witness) that he only had to pay at the original rate. Eventually Mr. Eccleston had to take him to the Palatinate Court of Chancery.[3]

Charles Dagnall's venture is remarkable for two things. Firstly, he declared his intention, as early as 1746, of erecting a Newcomen-type engine, and this was certainly at work by 1750/1. Secondly, it provides our first recorded instance of concessionary coal being allowed to St. Helens colliers, and, incidentally, of an allowance being made for the coal consumed by a colliery steam engine.[4]

In the mid-1750s, apart from his mines in Eccleston, Dagnall possessed a colliery at Barton's Bank, on the boundaries of Parr and Sutton. A few years later he opened pits at Ashes Farm

---

[1] For the Dagnalls and the local comb-making industry, see below, p. 170n.

[2] Wigan Ref. Lib., Dicconson Papers, Eccleston Coal Leases A series of accounts of the output from Dagnall's pits in Mr. Eccleston's land, together with several letters, survives in this collection. The amount of coal raised varied greatly from year to year, from about 500 works to about 1,400. Mr. Eccleston had his own manorial colliery at Gillars Green by 1753, and this is marked as still in operation on a coal map of the Eccleston Estates in the possession of Pilkington Brothers, Ltd., which may be dated to within a few years of 1765.

[3] P.R.O., P.L. 6, 82/27.

[4] See below, p. 64.

in Windle, an out-of-the-way site between St. Helens and Rainford.
By 1765 this colliery was up for sale, and it was again advertised
in the following year. It was rather ominous that in 1765 two
separate workshops in Eccleston were for sale with the colliery—
presumably Dagnall's premises as a combmaker—and that his
creditors were to send in their accounts. In 1766 a fire engine
was to be sold as well as the colliery, which was untruthfully
described as being in " an excellent situation for Country Sale."
Dagnall was by this time in the hands of assignees; his fall was
complete in 1770 when he was declared bankrupt.[1]

These activities of the lesser coal-masters, while illustrating
the new spirit of enterprise on the coalfield, were not, as their
relatively short duration testifies, a permanent threat to Sarah
Clayton and the Cases. From the early 1760s, however,
competition quickly intensified as a new industrialist of great
ambition and an almost reckless speculative zeal entered this
developing area. His original introduction to coalmining, as
far as can be ascertained, was an indirect one. On the 19 May,
1762, Basil Thomas Eccleston made an agreement with
Thomas Leigh of Warrington, apothecary, for certain coals in
that part of his estate which lay outside the boundary of Eccleston
Manor and within the Township of Sutton, under two estates
known as " the Tickles " and " Burtonhead." Leigh's tenure
was for 100 years, and he contracted to raise a " Fire Engine "
within three years, to sink an engine pit over sixty yards deep, and
to get at least 2,000 works per annum, to be paid for at 2s. 6d. per
work. This ambitious programme was perhaps too much for
him, for by the next year he sought to introduce a partner with
whom he drew up a draft lease, which was apparently never
executed.[2]

The partner described himself as " John Mackay, Esq. of
Belfield Co. Chester". As the name implied, he was not a Cheshire
man but a Scot. His grandfather had been a notary, his father an
Inverness merchant. By 1757 he was resident in St. Martin-in-the-

[1] *Williamson's Lpool. Ad.*, 28 June, 1765, 3 Oct., 1766. The assignees
included Richard Melling, a celebrated Wigan coal surveyor, and William
Hill of Dentons Green. Dagnall was over £2,000 in debt at the time of
his bankruptcy, and, with his usual lack of scruple, tried to conceal certain
effects from his creditors. P.R.O., P.L. 6, 86/32.

[2] Wigan Ref. Lib., Dicconson Papers, Eccleston Box   Parcel of
" Old Coal Leases " Leases from Basil Thomas Eccleston to Thos. Leigh,
19 May, 1762 ; Eccleston to Leigh and Mackay, 1763 n.d.

Fields, when he married a London woman, Millicent Neate, who brought him a fortune of £3,000.[1] In 1761, then living in Holborn, he formed his first known connection with the St. Helens district when he was associated with a Parr man, Jonathan Greenall, in obtaining a patent.[2] This patent was for an improved method of salt refining, and if we take this in conjunction with Mackay's residence in Cheshire in the following year, it is clear that his activities on the coalfield originated with an interest in salt. On the day after the two men took out the salt patent, Greenall secured another for an improved atmospheric steam-engine or " fire engine".[3] While Mackay is not mentioned this time it is probable he was Greenall's patron, for he supported a later steam-engine project. Nor was this his last connection with salt inventions. In 1772, together with a London partner, he took out a patent for the " making of salt from sea water or brine by steam".[4] That he had saltfield interests as yet unidentified is confirmed by his sending cargoes down the Weaver in the 1760s.[5]

Mackay's interest in salt soon drew him to the district whence the fuel for the Cheshire saltworks was supplied, and his later ventures were in coal and the industries of the coalfield. In 1768 he advertised for twenty colliers who could work " longwall " instead of " pillar and stall " to come to his Parr colliery, one of the earliest mentions of this technique in Lancashire. In this as in later instances, he was careful to make the job seem attractive to the workmen, offering to provide lodgings for those unable to get home at night, and cottages with gardens in six months' time.[6]

Parr, however, was not to be Mackay's chief centre of operations. He spent the late 1760s and early 1770s in developing a series of mines of the greatest importance a mile or so to the west. These were in the district which came to be called " Ravenhead " after a farm of that name purchased by the coal-master. Here,

---

[1] Marriage settlement of 31 May, 1783. This document is in the possession of Mr. C. I. Fraser, a descendant of Millicent, the daughter of John Mackay, who married Col. James Fraser of the army of the Hon. East India Company in 1783, the year of her father's death. We are indebted to Mr. Fraser for providing (from his specialist knowledge of pedigrees as Dingwall Poursuivant) many particulars of the Fraser and Mackay families. Mackay died in the later summer of 1783, at Buxton. (Gore's Lpool. Ad. 7 Aug. 1783).

[2] Specifications of Patents. Chemical Compositions (1629-1824), 1761, No. 760. John Mackay and Jonathan Greenall. Manufacturing Salt.

[3] Ibid. Steam Engine (1736-91), 1761 No. 761. Jonathan Greenall.

[4] Ibid. Chemical Compositions (1629-1824), 1772, No. 1006.

[5] Chester Record Office. Weaver Toll Books, 1762. From Northwich.

[6] Lpool. Chron., 3 Nov. 1768.

before 1780, this great industrialist had built Ravenhead House, a mansion influenced by the new " Gothic " style.[1]

It is the measure of Mackay's energy and insight that he understood the importance of the high-grade Rushy Park seam, and that he succeeded in attracting to his collieries two of the largest concerns of the eighteenth century, the casting department of the British Cast Plate Glass Company and the smelting works of the Parys Mine Co. Strangely enough, the very name of John Mackay has long been forgotten in the district, but the great industrial area which now covers the lands he developed is his sufficient memorial. The modern St. Helens largely owes its existence to this Scottish contemporary of Dr. Johnson who, having taken the road to England, came to see the potentialities of this district. Mackay was ahead of his contemporaries in that, while they only saw the St. Helens coalfield as a centre of supply for the saltfield and for Liverpool, his greater vision foresaw its future as a site for coal-burning furnace industries.

Mackay's development of Ravenhead was not easy or inexpensive ; together with his industrial projects it meant heavy borrowing and a very heavy burden of debts bequeathed to his daughter Millicent and her husband James Fraser.[2] Nor was he without competitors, even at Ravenhead. In the 1760s and 70s much depended upon the rivalry between the Scot and Jonathan Case, the colliery-owner nephew of Sarah Clayton. Before this struggle is outlined, however, it will be necessary to describe a movement of wider importance which had implications for every owner of collieries or coal rights whose profits or " lord's part " depended on Sankey Navigation.

In 1759 Brindley's career as engineer to the Duke of Bridgewater began with the planning of the celebrated Worsley Canal. By 20 August, 1766, a Liverpool-Hull canal project was mooted in Liverpool,[3] and this pointed the way to a series of great cross-country canals. It was the Leeds and Liverpool canal, announced in Liverpool in December, 1768,[4] which was to be the greatest threat to the Sankey. The course of the canal into Liverpool was planned in a great arc ; from Wigan it connected with the Douglas Navigation and then swept round through Burscough before entering Liverpool by its northern suburbs. While the projectors preferred this course as the cheapest and as reducing the need for

---

[1] Manchester Cent. Ref. Lib. (MS. F942, S113), Vol. 13, Lancs. Nos. 1 & 2. C. R. Sherbourne, Watercolour Drawings. These drawings of Ravenhead House show it as left by Mackay, and as altered into the classical style by Col. Fraser. They are dated 1791 and 1810. Sherbourne was the manager of the Ravenhead plate glassworks.

[2] See below, p. 113n.

[3] *Williamson's Lpool. Ad.*, 29 Aug., 1766.

[4] *Ibid.*, 23 Dec., 1768.

locks, the citizens of Liverpool did not take this easy view. It is obvious that they were chiefly concerned to obtain a canal as short and direct as possible to the Wigan coalfield, so as to provide a better competitor to the Sankey Canal than the old Douglas Navigation had been. A newspaper of 13 January, 1769, reported[1] that a proposal was before the Conversation Club that it should discuss the idea of bringing the Leeds and Liverpool canal on a line to the south of Ormskirk, so as to pass through more coal and quarrying districts. In the next issue an account of the debate was given.

" It was thought by several Gentlemen, who knew the country, from the observations which they had made, that the new intended canal might be brought, if not south of Ormskirk, yet so as to join with the present Sankey Navigation ; which would be attended with the most advantageous consequences, as a union might thereby be made with the Staffordshire canal, proposed to cross the River Mersey into this county from Runkhorn in Cheshire ; and the eligibility of the alteration was so evident, that a survey of the country was deemed highly necessary."[2]

This particular plan was obviously engineered by the Sankey proprietors to forestall the blow which the Leeds and Liverpool canal would give them, and to turn that rival enterprise into an ally by joining it with the existing canal. We may be sure that the Conversation Club was not unconnected with the Common Council, for it simultaneously put forward a plan, the setting up of a Chamber of Commerce in Liverpool, which was in fact adopted not long afterwards by the creation of a co-opted committee of the Council.[3]

There were now three parties in the field, the promoters of the Leeds and Liverpool Canal on its originally projected course, the opposition party of the Sankey Canal proprietors, who wished to divert it so as to join with their waterway, and the direct route party. The third group joined the fray in October, 1770, by opening subscriptions for their scheme.[4] The canal contest reached its height a year later when it was announced that subscription books for the Runcorn Gap Canal were to be opened,[5] and towards the

---

[1] *Gore's Gen. Ad.*, 13 Jan., 1769.

[2] *Ibid.*, 20 Jan., 1769.

[3] J. A. Picton, *City of Liverpool Municipal Archives and Records* (1886) 238. The body was sometimes described as a Committee of Trade.

[4] *Gore's Gen. Ad.*, 12, 26 Oct., 1770. This canal seems to have been originally envisaged as reaching Bolton, and as crossing the Mersey to join the Staffordshire canal. For the Liverpool Canal schemes of this period see J. R. Harris, " Liverpool Canal Controversies 1769-1772," *Journal of Transport History*, Vol. II, No. 3, May 1956.

[5] *Ibid.*, 11 Oct., 1771.

end of 1771 a spate of letters on the rival canals flooded the newspapers.

By the early weeks of 1772 the struggle had been carried to the House of Commons, and on the 22 January the project for a direct Liverpool to Wigan Canal was introduced there, leave being sought to bring in a Bill for a canal which was to pass through Everton, Kirkdale, Walton-on-the-Hill, West Derby, Roby, Huyton, Whiston, Tarbuck, Cronton, Widnes, Appleton, Cuerdley, Bold, Burtonwood, Newton, Golbourne, Lowton, Abram and Ince, and terminate at or near Wigan. The obvious intention was to open up the coalfield to the south of that town. It is not at all surprising that the inhabitants of Wigan and Liverpool were among the supporters of the canal, but it is noteworthy that a similar petition was backed by the Mayor, Bailiffs and Burgesses of Liverpool. In other words the Sankey Canal proprietors and their friends had been abandoned by official Liverpool.[1]

This, however, did not cause them to admit defeat. The House heard on the 10 February :

" A Petition . . . [of the] . . . Proprietors or owners of and in Sankey Navigation . . . Setting forth that by two acts the . . . River or Brook . . . hath been made and compleated at great expence and risque, the object of which was, to procure a sufficient supply of coal for the town and port of Liverpool and its shipping, and for the Salt Works upon the River Mersey in the County of Lancaster, and at Northwich and other places in the County of Chester ; and, in consequence thereof, very great quantities of coal have been and are sent down the said navigation . . . and that the River Mersey is naturally navigable . . . by the flowing and reflowing of the tide, several miles higher than its junction with Sankey Navigation, by means whereof there is a complete Navigation from or near the Great Coal Mines adjoining or near the said Navigation to Liverpool for vessells upwards of Forty Tons Burthen ; and the petitioners are informed, a Bill is intended to be brought in . . ." [i.e. the south project, which will necessitate a crossing of their canal] . . . " upon such a height or level, that it will be necessary to carry or convey the same by an Aquaduct, across the said Sankey Navigation, to the great injury of vessells passing and repassing thereon."[2]   They maintained that with the Leeds and Liverpool canal, the newly projected Bridgewater canal, and their own, there would be all the transportation needed.[3]

---

[1] *C.J.*, 33, 22 Jan., 1772. It was in opposition to this scheme that the Leeds and Liverpool proprieters bought out the Douglas Navigation (Holt & Gregson Papers X, 221).

[2] Presumably because the bridge would have been too low to allow barges to pass beneath with sails set.

[3] *C.J.*, 33, 10 Feb., 1772.

This petition nevertheless showed a considerable deterioration in the Sankey proprietors' position ; they no longer opposed the Leeds and Liverpool project openly, or tried to suggest its junction with their own canal, and they seem to have been on the defensive, not without cause as we shall soon see, in trying to prove that their canal was technically efficient. Their sole aim was to prevent the construction of a fourth canal radiating from Liverpool, in other words to attack the weakest of their several opponents. Here they were not in isolation, even though deserted by the Common Council, for both the Leeds and Liverpool proprietors and various landowners attacked the scheme of the direct or southerly Liverpool-Wigan canal. The landowners were headed by the greatest nobleman in Lancashire, the Earl of Derby. They objected to having their land cut through by the new canal and stated that " Liverpool and its neighbourhood are now supplied with great quantities of coal at a moderate price, by land carriage, from certain coal mines in and about Prescot, Whiston, and other places adjacent thereto, . . . by means of a good Turn-pike Road,"[1] a conclusion which the inhabitants of Liverpool would have indignantly rejected.

While Parliament was being approached in an endeavour to gain a verdict, the battle still continued in the Liverpool press. One " Candidus," an opponent of the Sankey proprietors, contributed some useful opinions.

" The attempt to cut a Navigable Canal from Sankey Bridges to the coal mines in Parr, Haddock, and St. Helens and for supplying the towns of Liverpool and Warrington and the salt works at Dungeon, Northwich, etc., with coals, was the first undertaking of the kind in this county, and as such justly invited the admiration and attention of the public at that time, but the principle of making canals being then little understood, and the practice still less known, of course the performance must be liable to many imperfections. The public have long seen and the proprietors have long acknowledged, the improprietory and inconvenience of falling into the tideway, instead of carrying it on a higher level through the country to Liverpool. This needs no better proof, than the several alterations in the work ; an amendment of the Act to empower them to cut from Sankey Bridges to Fiddlers Ferry a little lower down upon the Mersey, and their intention of still further powers to continue their canal to Bower's Pool near Runcorn Gap.

When the last act for the Sankey Canal was to be obtained, we were amused with the hopes of a constant supply of coals at a much lower price than at any time before ; but the coal owners at Prescot, Whiston, etc., well apprised of the many dangers, delays and uncertainties of such conveyance through the tide-

[1] *C.J.* **33**, 10 Feb., 1772.

way, raise the coals 2s. 6d. a work while the bill was soliciting,
which has continued a burden on the public ever since, without
any hopes of being removed by the Sankey Canal. The proprietors of Sankey Brook are so far from wishing the town of
Liverpool may be supplied with greater quantities or better
quality of coals, with more certainty, or at lower prices, that, I
am credibly informed, they intend to oppose the present laudable
scheme of a level canal between Liverpool and Wigan, and are
for offering to the Public 'A Plan for making a Navigable Cut or
Canal from Winick Pond on Sankey Navigation to or near
Wigan and Pemberton.' . . . this will certainly be the most
effectual means of raising the price of coals at Liverpool, and
merits an address of thanks from the coal owners and carters
in the neighbourhood of Whiston, Prescot, Eccleston, etc. . . .
Whereas [the Sankey branch] . . . can only be proposed to
aggrandize the present proprietor [sic] . . . the object of this
design is not local, it is not confined to any particular place or
persons ; it is a scheme of general public utility, no part is
intended to be private property."[1]

To these accusations a correspondent in the first weeks of
1772 added that of bad measure, declaring that the Sankey
proprietors were charging 9s. for a ton of 15 to 17 cwts., varying
with the quality of the coal. The Bridgewater Canal was chiefly
serving Cheshire and had made little difference as yet to the
Liverpool market.[2]

These attacks in the newspapers may be summarized as directed
against (1) monopoly ; (2), the engineering deficiencies of the
Sankey Canal and its projected Wigan branch ; and (3), the in-
difference of the proprietors who allowed the public to be swindled
by their agents.

While accusations against individuals were rare, the various
correspondents all assumed that the Sankey coalowners and
proprietors were in fact in league against the public and acted in
concert, so much so that departures from the practice were noted.
There appears to have been no doubt in the minds of Liverpool
writers that, if they so wished, the coalowners could have sold
cheaper, an opinion for which they seem to have had good
evidence. At the same time the correspondents' obvious inability
to point to any actual machinery of cartel, regular meetings or
contractual agreements, is not evidence of the non-existence of
monopoly. The group involved was small, intimately connected,
and in day-to-day contact on Liverpool's new Exchange, while
the concerns were so localized that there was no need of extensive
administrative machinery. The one reference which it is possible
to pin down is that to " the present proprietor". Actually Nicholas

[1] Gore's Gen. Ad., 1 Nov., 1771.   [2] Ibid., 17 Jan., 1772.

Ashton himself held only 15 out of 120 shares, but the family as a whole was left 51 by John Ashton.

The Wigan branch now planned by the Sankey proprietors was an alternative to their former proposal for a junction with the Leeds and Liverpool canal. It was to run, a statement of theirs declared, " from Winick Pond . . . through the townships of Winick, Newton, Lowton, Abram, and Golbourne . . . to the south side of Brin Moss in the township of Ashton . . . and thence to be continued by one branch southwards to . . . a place called the Black Rock . . . in Ince near Wigan . . . and by another branch along the west side of Brin Moss to . . . Smithy Brook in the township of Pemberton."[1]

Both the Liverpool South Canal and the Sankey Branch schemes were pressed to the point of subscription,[2] probably in the belief that this would help their petitions to Parliament for leave to obtain Bills. The Sankey proprietors, trying to dispel the impression of monopoly, declared that no one was to have more than 10 out of the 240 shares in their new branch. So confident were they that on the 8 November, 1771, they advertised the opening of subscription books on the next day at 1 p.m., to be continued to 2 p.m. if they were not already filled before ! Next week they were able to announce that the whole sum of £24,000 was subscribed on the 9th " in less than a quarter of an hour, and a much larger one might have been raised if necessary." The same issue carried a notice by the Liverpool [South] Canal which said £30,000 had already been raised for their enterprise, anticipated that the necessary £60,000 would be raised in a few weeks, and announced the places where subscription books might be found.

This is almost the last we hear of the matter. After the brief Parliamentary fuss the alternative schemes were quietly forgotten, and the Leeds and Liverpool Canal continued its leisurely progress undisturbed. It seems possible, indeed, that, towards the end, the Sankey proprietors may have been more concerned with blocking the Liverpool South Canal than with obtaining a new Act of their own.

The Sankey proprietors would have been better advised to employ their capital in making good the deficiencies of their original navigation than in projecting new branches. Despite the alteration of route in 1762 the flats or sailing barges were still dependent on a favourable wind and the Mersey tide, and the proprietors appear to have let the canal get seriously out of repair, a practice to which they were prone for over half a century. The reason appears to have been that they were so assured of the steadily-growing Cheshire salt trade, if of nothing else, that they

[1] *Gore's Gen. Ad.*, 8 Nov., 1771.
[2] *Ibid.*, 8 & 15 Nov., 1771.

were indifferent as to the inconveniences they caused their customers. From 1771 to 1775 stoppages were frequent, indicating that repairs were seriously overdue.[1]

Both the Sankey Proprietors and the coal-masters had much to fear from the cutting of canals to new coalfields, but the latter had in addition a more immediate anxiety. Between 1765 and 1778 their mutual competition gradually intensified.

Sir Thomas Gerard was the first to cause a fall in the market. " In the year 1765, and in 1766, the great supply of coals from Garswood reduced the price, and caused an export of more than 8,000 chaldrons, since that time the exports have been very trifling, chiefly owing to the advanced price . . ."[2] stated a writer in 1771. This would imply that once he was established in the market Gerard saw no need to continue undercutting ; by 1769 he had his own coal-office in Liverpool.[3]

During the years 1769-1773, however, the chief interest seems to lie in the contest between John Mackay and Jonathan Case.[4] In 1769 Case extended his hold on the land-sale cart trade to Liverpool by opening a second colliery at Whiston. This, the so-called Carr Colliery, near the boundaries of Prescot and Whiston, was the first in his series of eastward extensions.[5] On 31 July of that year he proceeded to go several miles further afield, and to lease a mine on the boundaries of Sutton and Eccleston,[6] at the extreme limit of the land-sale collieries, and near enough to the Sankey Navigation for him to carry his coals there. The land leased was on the estate rented from B. T. Eccleston by John Barnes, gentleman, as was the site mentioned in the 1762 lease to Thomas Leigh and in the proposed lease to Leigh and Mackay of 1763. Similarities in the field-names show that the colliery sites of the rival coal-masters must have been very close, if indeed some of the fields formerly leased by Leigh were not now taken by Case. Already the industrial importance of the Ravenhead site was foreshadowed.

[1] *Gore's Gen. Ad.*, 26 April, 1771 ; *Williamson's Lpool. Ad.*, 30 April, 1773, 8 April, 1774 ; *Gore's Gen. Ad.*, 24 March, 1775.

[2] *Ibid.*, 1 Nov., 1771.

[3] *Ibid.*, 31 March, 1769. A John Berry is mentioned in connection with the office, perhaps the same man who was formerly selling coal for Peter Berry's St. Helens coalmine ; see above, p. 32.

[4] Tactical objects in the struggle were (a) to get the most advantageous position astride the Ravenhead branch of the canal, extended in 1773 (b) to get the best working position on the valuable Rushy Park seam.

[5] P.R.O. P.L. 6. 87/10.

[6] Wigan Ref. Lib. Dicconson Papers : Lease from B. T. Eccleston to Jonathan Case, 31 July, 1769.

Under his agreement Case was to hand over one third of the profit from such coals as " can be gott dry in the said Basil Thomas Eccleston's land by the present sough or by cutting into the old work or by driving in the [middle ?] to the old sough or levell that was made and carried forward by Peter Berry." He undertook to get all the coals as deep as 70 yards, provided the seam fell to that depth from the outcrop in the land he leased, and to raise at least 2,016 works of coals per annum before the erection of an atmospheric engine and 3,000 works after that had been accomplished.

There were two further clauses of importance. One stated that if the coals did not sell for 12s. 6d. per work (this would be pithead price) either of the parties could " put a stop to the Colliery " on six months notice. The second was very significant. " Also he the said . . . [B. T. Eccleston] . . . doth hereby promise and agree not to lett, sett, sell or dispose of any Coals or mines of Coal to any other persons or persons, without the consent and advice of the said Jonathan Case his Executors or Administrators while they are employed in working or carrying on the colliery herein intended to be granted . . . save only and except Burrows Lane pitt to be allowed to be gotten to the Levell of going down brow below the Eye in the said pitt Provided they are only gotten at the same or any other pitt on the same Levell."[1] In other words Case was trying to prevent competition and secure to himself a monopoly of deep mining in the Eccleston lands.[2]

On Mackay's side the measures to open up the Ravenhead area were even more energetic. In 1765 he leased the common or waste of Thatto Heath from the King and a few years later bought the Ravenhead Farm from the Archbishop of York, also acquiring the little Kitt's Bridge Estate.[3] In 1770 he was ready to begin sinking his shafts :

" January, 1770.
" If any number of good Colliers or sinkers will apply at Hatto Heath Colliery, near Prescot in Lancashire, they will meet with constant employ, and the best encouragement."[4]

[1] For the existence of a pit at Gillars Green (which is very near to Burrows Lane) as early as 1753, see above, p. 33n. As a colliery worked by the lord of the manor this had naturally to be excluded from Case's monopoly.

[2] For a previous grant of an estate mining monopoly in Hardshaw see above, p. 32.

[3] Pilkington Brothers Limited, Deeds. Abstract of Title of John Mackay: Lease from Geo. III to John Mackay, Esq., 31 May, 1765 ; Archbishop of York to John Mackay, Esq , 22 May, 1772. Thatto Heath was part of the Honour of Widnes and of the Duchy of Lancaster. The Archbishop of York became trustee for Ravenhead Farm on behalf of his sister, formerly Lady Hay, after the failure of her husband, Robert Roper. The spelling of " Thatto Heath " was vague at this period, " Hatto " and " Thatway " were common.

[4] Gore's Gen. Ad., 2 Feb., 1770.

The operations were apparently extensive and took time, for it was almost eighteen months after Mackay's sinkers were advertised for before his next advertisement appeared in the Liverpool papers.

" It is with great pleasure we give the inhabitants of Liverpool, and the country, the earliest notice, that the mines of J. Mackay, Esq., are in most extensive opening, will be compleated this year, and that Sankey Navigation is now bringing up to the new ones in his own land. We are told by that gentleman's agent who brought the following for insertion, that no part of the Kingdom will be better supplied for coals than this town and neighbourhood, they now being in such condition as to get immense quantities, that colliers are their only want, and the encouragement given them there is great, that the proximity of the town of St. Hellen, together with the extent and probable durability of the mines, renders it so inviting a situation for Colliers and their families to settle in that he makes no doubt (when once known) they will have great plenty of men ... His master, for the convenience of his people, has now built, and is still in building, a considerable number of comfortable houses, at the higher end of the collieries ... "

23rd May, 1771.

" The Public hereby have notice, that Mr. Mackay has lowered the price of coals at Hatto Heath and the Ravenhead, to Twopence halfpenny per basket. The excellence of the upper mine for house firing, and the lower one for manufacturing uses, are too well remembered in this country, to need saying anything further of them."[1]

This was an immediate slashing of prices down to 4s. 2d. per ton or 12s. 6d. per work, the rate below which Case had indicated it was not worth working his Sutton mine, and this before the new Ravenhead arm of the Sankey Navigation had reached the collieries !

For the time being, notwithstanding, all the advantages did not go to Mackay. One of the first developments after the opening of the mines was that a Liverpool coal dealer, Thomas Lyon, announced that he had " engaged Country Carters to supply him with COALS; from Hatto Heath colliery Which are the best in Quality that come into Liverpool, and will serve his customers at sixpence per basket, with a Ticket from the Pits delivered along with them, by which he hopes to give entire satisfaction to the Public."[2] By 25 September, however, Lyon had changed his pit

[1] *Gore's Gen. Ad.*, 24 May, 1771.
[2] *Ibid.* 17 April, 1772.

to Mr. Case's Carr Colliery ; he was still charging 6d. per basket or 8s. 6d. per ton.[1]

If in this small instance Case came off best, he must have been disgruntled to find a second rival once more becoming dangerous. On 5 June, 1772, Sir Thomas Gerard announced that he was putting coals on board flats on the Sankey at 4s 3d. per ton, allowing threepence per ton discount for ready money.

" The said coals are suitable for salt, copper, or any other works ; and will be warranted full twenty-five-hundred to the ton, of a hundred and twenty to the hundred."

At his office at the New Dock Gerard was selling coal for industry, export and domestic use, it would be put on vessels at 6s. 8d. per ton, and delivered at 7s. 4d. per ton anywhere in Liverpool, rating 20 cwts. to the ton and 120 lbs. to the cwt.[2]

By March, 1773, Mackay's flat-men were moving coals down the Canal and being very arrogant about it.[3] In June of that year James Gildart, a member of one of the Liverpool mercantile families who were interested in salt, opened his own mines at Whiston,[4] and in August Mackay began to ship his high quality smiths' coal down to Liverpool.

" The Shippers of Smiths' Coal, for America, are requested to take notice, that by Application to Mr. Churchill of Edmond Street, they may be supplied with those of an excellent quality, for that Market, from the NEW PITS of John Mackay, Esq., at Ravenhead, at 8s. 4d. the Ton of 120 Pounds to the Hundred Weight, delivered on Board at Liverpool.
N.B.—The Coal [sic] are so much on Demand, that a weeks notice would be required, for any considerable Quantity."[5]

This rivalry and price-cutting by the local coal-masters may have been resorted to as a preparation to meet the competition of Wigan and Worsley coals brought down the new canals, rather than out of a wish to harm each other. Nevertheless this was precisely the effect, and there is good evidence that Jonathan Case and Sarah Clayton were hard hit.

A note appended by Matthew Ellam, Case's agent, to the foot of the 1769 " monopoly " lease he had obtained from Mr. Eccleston, shows that this colliery was abandoned on the 8 October, 1773, the clause allowing Case's withdrawal if prices fell below 12s. 6d. a work having come into operation. It was arranged that if prices rose again Case could take up his lease once more :

---

[1] *Gore's Gen. Ad.*, 2 Oct., 1772.   Case's Colliery was at least two miles nearer Liverpool.

[2] *Ibid.*, 5 June, 1772.   A copper works was erected on Gerard's land in this year. See below, p. 76.

[3] *Williamson's Lpool. Ad.*, 19 March, 1773.

[4] *Ibid.*, 23 July, 1773.

[5] *Ibid.*, 20 Aug., 1773.

" the Price of the Coals being by the Parties consent first offered to Sale at Ten Shillings a work but without disposing of any Quantity to any Purpose to either of the Parties therefore the said Colliery did cease Working or Raising any coals from and after the said eight day of October in the aforesaid year 1773."[1]

These prices, which would represent 3s. 4d. per ton or 2d. per cwt. by modern measure, and even less by any of the local variants, some of which we have already met, are as low as any encountered in the district during the last half of the eighteenth century. To be able to get an entire winter's firing for 6s. 8d. must have been something new even in an age whose prices seem incredibly cheap to us, and the fact that Case had no customers at such rates shows that his competitors must have been selling even lower.

It is in the early 1770s also that we have our first evidence that Sarah Clayton herself was in difficulties. In 1771 she borrowed £10,000 on the security of the Hall, Manor and Mill of Parr and of a number of smaller estates in Parr and Hardshaw, together with their coal rights. In 1773 a further £1,200 was borrowed from a Manchester spinster. These measures were not sufficient, and in 1774 Sarah Clayton took a desperate step. She made over her estates to her nephew, Thomas Case, the brother of Jonathan, and a great Africa merchant, for £17,800. It was subsequently decided in a court of law that this transfer was deliberately made with an intent to deceive her creditors, and in fact Case never paid any money for the estates, merely giving his bond, which it was not intended to honour. From this time until the fraud was revealed, Thomas Case therefore appears as the proprietor of the Parr mines.[2]

During the seventies a factor began to assist Mackay and Gerard which had formerly not been of great significance except to the small land-sale pits. This was the increased consumption of coal on the coalfield itself. The district was of course becoming more populous, but it was the growth of industrial rather than domestic use which caused the greater demand, for three very large works and two industries particularly voracious of fuel arrived during the decade 1770-80. In 1772 Thomas Patten set up a copper-smelting works at Blackbrook, in 1776 the celebrated British Cast Plate Glass Manufactory was founded at Ravenhead and in 1780 the great Ravenhead Copper Works opened. The Patten works was on Gerard's land, and he was always one of its principal suppliers of fuel, while Mackay as one of the proprietors

---

[1] Dicconson Papers, *loc. cit.* above, p. 43.

[2] The loans mentioned are recorded in St. Helens Corporation Deeds, St. Helens Town Hall : (1). United Alkali Co. (Globe) Plots 39-43, I [Parr Mill Estate, Abstract of Title of Devisees of Nicholas Ashton] ; (2). Baxter's Works Bundle, Abstract of Title of Wm. Smart.

is certain to have been supplying the Plate Glass Company, and he early entered into an agreement to supply all the coal required by the Ravenhead Copper Works. Thus Gerard and Mackay now had a guaranteed market for a portion of their coals, and in the copper works they had a munitions industry which, as a rule, would provide a better market in wartime even than in peace. To the Clayton-Case group these significant advantages were denied.

The threat represented by the rival canal projects which has been the background to the story of local rivalry became greater as the schemes neared completion. By the January of 1774, though his canal was not quite finished, the Duke of Bridgewater was able to sell coals in Liverpool at competitive rates, and was creating (probably deliberately) an impression of liberality as compared with the harshness of the Sankey proprietors.

" We cannot do greater honor to his Grace the Duke of Bridgwater, than by telling to the world that, at this time, he is selling at Liverpool, a single pennyworth of coals, to everyone who chooses to purchase at the same rate as by the cartload. For this humane act, the blessings of those who have few friends shall be upon him, and the prayers of the poor shall proclaim him their benefactor... At this severe season he sells twenty-four pounds of coal for one penny, and if it was not for the unfortunate obstruction in Cheshire, which prevents the compleating his canal, he would sell them to the poor even cheaper than that... "[1]

The 21 October in the same year saw the canal competition at its height, when the Leeds and Liverpool canal reached Liverpool, and was suitably celebrated.[2] Just as a previous attack on their position had been met by concessions, so again the Sankey proprietors hastened to put their house in order.

" Many and (it is to be feared) just complaints having been made, by House-keepers and others, of imposition and unjust dealing, by delivery of short measure and other unfair practices, of the common dealers in that most useful article COAL, whereby the coal coming down the Sankey Canal may have fallen into disrepute: To obviate all such complaints, and to secure to all Persons a certainty of having the full quantity and true Quality of all such COAL which they may hereafter pay for, the Proprietors of Sankey Navigation have come to a resolution of Delivering Coal by sworn Agents, in whom the Public may confide.

[1] *Williamson's Lpool. Ad.*, 14 Jan. 1774.

[2] *Ibid.*, 21 Oct., 1774. " On Wednesday last that part of the Leeds Canal between here and Wigan was opened with great festivity and rejoicings . . . The workmen, 215 in number, walked first with their tools on their shoulders and cockades in their hats, and were afterwards plentifully regaled at a dinner provided for them."

E

And for public encouragement, with respect to price, the said Proprietors have studied the means of reducing it, and find that by a saving on the first cost, by paying ready money to the Coal Owners, by reducing the freight and cutting off the unfair profits and advantage hitherto taken by the Dealers or Retailers, Coal [sic] may be and are ready to be delivered, for the use of the Town, at the door of Housekeepers, and for Shipping, at the respective rates and prices undermentioned, and every buyer may rest assured that every Ton of Coal so delivered shall contain *Twenty Hundred weight*, reckoning 120 pounds to the hundred, certified by a ticket from the keeper of the weighing machine with each cart, for Ready money only.

	Delivered to Housekeepers	Delivered to Shipping
Peter Leigh Esq.'s Coal	7s. 2d. per ton	6s. 6d. per ton
John Mackay Esq.'s Coal	7s. 0d. „ „	6s. 4d. „ „
Thos. Case, Esq.'s Coal	6s. 10d. „ „	6s. 2d. „ „
Sir Thomas Gerard's Coal	6s. 6d. „ „	5s. 10d. „ „

Any person taking a Flat load, may have any of the above said Coal, paying the cost at the pits, river dues, freight and cartage ; And to accommodate poor Housekeepers, or such as cannot purchase a Ton at a time, smaller quantities will be delivered at the yard, at fourpence halfpenny per hundred of 120 pounds. Sworn Agents will attend constantly at the Coal Office, adjoining the weighing machine on Nova Scotia, upon Mann's Island, to whom the public may apply.

By order of the Proprietors."[1]

The public of Liverpool, it is to be imagined, would have taken this tender solicitude for their welfare as more genuine had it not followed so closely upon the action of the Duke of Bridgewater, and coincided with the arrival of the competitive Wigan coalowners who announced their prices in the following January.[2] Indeed the Sankey Proprietors were always suspiciously a day after the fair with their gestures of generosity, which gives the impression that their detractors had a deal of justice on their side.

By 1774 mutual rivalry and the competition of other waterways seemed to have done their worst to the local colliery proprietors, but if they thought these the limit of their trials, they were to be undeceived.

---

[1] *Williamson's Lpool. Ad.*, 9 Dec., 1774. While this advertisement has the merit of telling us how the prices of the various colliery owners stood at this time, it must be remembered that coal varies greatly in quality ; for instance, if Mackay was the only one working the highly-prized Rushy Park seam he would be selling a superior article. Leigh's collieries were in Haydock.

[2] *Gore's Gen. Ad.*, 27 Jan., 1775.

CHAPTER V

DEPRESSION, DISASTER AND RECOVERY

1775—1815

IN 1757 the Sankey Canal reached the township of Parr, giving its proprietors a position of semi-monopoly in the Liverpool market and Sarah Clayton a decided advantage over all other coalowners. Between that year and the spring of 1775 competition had so intensified that the collieries of Sarah Clayton and her relatives were in danger of being beaten out of the market, and the Sankey Canal was seriously threatened by the rivalry of other waterways. These difficulties were of a local or regional origin, and would have arisen without the intervention of any more general commercial crisis.

From April, 1775, however, England was at war with her American Colonies, and from 1778 and 1780 with first France and then Holland also. It has been claimed that in the earlier wars of the eighteenth century Liverpool (due to her position at the head of the Irish Channel) was relatively free from the menace of privateers, and less injured in her trade than many other ports. In the American War of Independence this was certainly not the case ; the famous triangular trade to Africa and the West Indies was laid open to attack, and the considerable commerce to the American Colonies in iron goods, salt,[1] textiles and smith's coal was desperately hard hit.

Liverpool merchants were fearful of the consequences of the struggle while it was yet impending, and early in 1775 sought to prevent it by petitioning Parliament concerning the disputes which were preventing harmonious relations between the mother country and the colonies. Their anxieties were completely justified, and by the following September the port was feeling the effects of war severely. A writer in *Gore's Advertiser* stated :

[1] T. Baines, *History of the Commerce and Town of Liverpool* (1852), 450. " On the 26th of June [1775] Captain Crippen, of the Liverpool ship *Albion*, who had attempted to land a cargo of salt at Philadelphia, was compelled to depart, and a resolution was passed in that city, declaring that Mr. Henry Cour and Nicholas Ashton, Esq., of Liverpool, the owners of the salt, had wilfully violated the orders of the American Congress. The inhabitants of Philadelphia were warned not to have any commercial dealings with them." During the war Nicholas Ashton owned privateers, one in partnership with the Marquis of Granby, (Baines *op. cit.*, 456), and fitted out the brig *Woolton* as a privateer. In *Gore's Gen. Ad.*, 4 Jan., 1781 " All brave seamen and landmen who are willing to try their Fortunes," were invited to apply to him at Woolton Hall.

" Our once extensive trade to Africa is at a stand : all commerce with America is at an end. . . . Survey our docks ; count there the gallant ships laid up and useless. When will they be again refitted ? What become of the sailor, the trades-men, the poor labourer, during the approaching winter ? "[1]

Gomer Williams, the historian of the privateering and slave-trading ventures of Liverpool, has written of this period :

" The general effect of the American war of independence on the position of Liverpool, was to put an entire stop to the commercial progress of the port, during seven long and disastrous years. The foreign trade of the port, which had doubled itself between the accession of George the Third, in 1760, and the commencement of hostilities, in 1775, declined in all its branches, from the beginning of the struggle, to its close in 1783. The customs revenue of the port, which amounted to £274,655 at the commencement of the war, had fallen to £188,830 in 1780, the sixth year of the contest. The tonnage declined from 84,792 tons to 79,450 of which a large part consisted of privateers. The population decreased from 35,600 to 34,107 ; and the condition of the inhabitants was deteriorated so greatly in the latter years of the war, that, at its close, not less than 10,000 of the poorer classes, were supported either by the parish, or by charitable donations."[2]

The St. Helens area was so much at this time a subsidiary sphere of operations of the Liverpool merchant that we would naturally expect some repercussions of this disastrous state of affairs on the coalfield. Moreover, it would be expected that those coalowners most deeply involved in the decline of Liverpool trade would be most affected, while those capitalists who were purely industrial would stand a better chance of escaping. Thomas Case, who in 1774 had taken over the nominal ownership and control of Sarah Clayton's Parr collieries, was a partner in the West India firm of Case & Southworth[3] and owned a Jamaica plantation. He was a leading member of the Africa Company in Liverpool, and one of the most prominent owners of slave ships, being associated with William Gregson[4] and John Dobson. He was also interested in insurance as a partner in the

---

[1] G. Williams, *The Liverpool Privateers and the Liverpool Slave Trade* (1897), 181.

[2] *Ibid.*, 301. See also *History of Liverpool from the Earliest Authenticated Period* (Lpool., 1810), 168.

[3] Liverpool Ref. Lib. Account Books of Case & Southworth, 3 vols. The West Indies branch was at Kingston, Jamaica. Sarah Clayton was certainly involved in this concern, but the nature of her interest cannot be readily determined from the accounts.

[4] P.R.O. P.L. 6. 85/26.

firm of Gregson, Case, & Co., presumably an extension of the slave trade interests of the two men.[1] In addition to his association with Gregson and Dobson, Thomas Case was also concerned in a slave trade partnership with his brother, Clayton Case.[2] For him it was very unfortunate that the depression was so general ; not merely were his insurance, West India, and Africa concerns hard hit, but at the same time competition in the coal trade was intense.

It is interesting to notice from the Liverpool newspapers of the time how the Clayton-Case group tried to put a good face on things, and endeavoured to keep away from their anxious creditors on Liverpool Exchange the signs that their concerns were drifting towards insolvency. Perhaps, until near the end, they even convinced themselves that all would blow over.

As early as 1775 Thomas Case sold the house and estate of Crank, near Rainford, a property purchased before 1763 in the hope of exploiting coal and clay measures.[3] Next we hear of his marriage, recorded in the Liverpool press in December, 1776, to " Miss Ashton,"—Anna Ashton, sister of Nicholas Ashton, and daughter of the deceased John Ashton.[4] Did Case hope for assistance from this powerful family ? It is certainly unlikely that Nicholas Ashton would have welcomed the marriage if he had known the position of Case's affairs. His credit was still good, as can be seen from his entering a new firm, the Liverpool Fire Office, at the end of that month, an insurance company founded by a group of distinguished merchants and bankers.[5] On the 18 July, 1777, it was announced that Case was to be one of a committee of Africa merchants who were to hold regular meetings to take evidence and muster support with a view to getting Parliament to do something for the trade, though it is difficult to see, failing peace, what would have given any relief. Included in the committee were such prominent men as William

---

[1] *Gore's Gen. Ad.*, 21 Nov., 1782. See J. Hughes, *Liverpool Banks and Bankers* (Lpool. 1906), 107 *seq.*

[2] For their petition of 1775, seeking to be allowed to export arms for the slave trade, see Journal of Commissioners for Trade and the Plantations, 1768-1775, 436-7

Thomas Case and his brother, John (Jestan) Case are given with the descriptions " merchant " and " Manchester warehouse " in *Gore's Directory* for 1766 ; in 1769 Thomas Case and Thomas & Clayton Case (another brother) are among the firms recorded. In 1772 we find Case, Clayton ; Case, John Jestan ; Case, Thomas ; and Case, Thomas and Clayton ; all firms of merchants with premises in Water Street. Gregson, Case & Co are given as an insurance office in Castle Street, near the Exchange.

[3] P.R.O. P.L. 6. 86/22.

[4] *Gore's Gen' Ad.*, 6 Dec., 1776 ; also Ashton Pedigree by College of Arms, 1787, in possession of Mr. N. C. E. Ashton.

[5] *Gore's Gen. Ad.*, 3 Jan., 1777.

Gregson, Benjamin Heywood, Thomas Staniforth and William Crosbie. During the same year, together with Joseph Daltera, John Chorley, Thomas Staniforth and others of similar standing, Case served on the Chamber of Commerce.[1]

Ever since 1774, however, Case had been liable for more than his own commercial debts. His fictitious purchase and unhonoured bond made him responsible for his aunt's coal mines, now affected by the general depression. It was only when it was too late that Case participated in a scheme which, had it been advanced earlier, might have saved the situation. On the 26 January, 1778, in conjunction with John Mackay, he signed an agreement with the trustees of Sir Thomas Gerard.[2] This remarkable document reveals Mackay and Case guaranteeing to the Gerard trustees the yearly sale of 9,750 tons of coal from their canal wharf at Blackbrook, at 4s. 8d. a ton. If this amount of coal was not sold, Mackay and Case agreed to buy any residue at the stipulated price, if delivered to them on the Navigation. In return, they would peg their prices to within 4d. a ton of Gerard's. The real nature of the agreement grows apparent with the succeeding clauses. The trustees bound themselves not to sell more than 9,750 tons of coal a year, and to deliver to Mackay and Case every month a " true Account of the Quantity of Coals which shall have been sold by or for the said Committees during the month preceding." The present trustees, as long as any two of them lived, would not allow any new pits to be opened or leased for opening except to Case or Mackay, if the coal from such pits was to be for Navigation sale. These regulations could be revised at the end of a five or ten year period, when any of the parties might withdraw providing a year's notice had been given.[3]

Here obviously we have a cartel for the restriction of output, drawn up by the three greatest coal owners on the Sankey. It is probable that this was not the only such agreement, and that similar declarations and guarantees were given by Mackay to the Gerard trustees and Case, and by Case to the trustees and Mackay. The very existence of this agreement is a strong indication of the difficulties experienced by the mining industry and the seriousness of the depression. Had the restriction of output been made a year or two earlier we might have had South Lancashire " Grand Allies;" as it was, the treaty cannot have had force for more than two months ; it was Thomas Case's final bow as an industrialist.

---

[1] *Ibid.*, 27 June, 1777.

[2] L.R.O. DDGe. 1318. Agreement, Committees of Sir T. Gerard to John Mackay and Thomas Case. Gerard was insane.

[3] The Gerard Committees carefully safeguarded their right to sell coal to the industries sited at Stanley in Ashton (Blackbrook), that is to say the Patten copper works and the iron-slitting mill. For these see below, pp. 76 and 126.

He last appeared as a man of means in the newspaper of 13 March, when he and Sarah Clayton undertook, with the usual group of Goores, Heywoods, Staniforths, Blackburnes, Caldwells, Parkes, Gregsons and Crosbies, to give an annual subscription to the Immanuel Hospital for the Blind.[1] A few weeks later all was over.

" The Creditors of Mr. Thomas Case, of Liverpool, merchant, are desired to meet at . . . [The Golden Lion, Dale St.] on Thursday the ninth of April next . . . to examine and take into consideration the State of his Affairs, which will then be laid before them for their Inspection and further direction."[2]

It was the first of a long series of advertisements which were to occupy the columns of local papers for many years ; if in 1778 there were any business acquaintances of the Cases or Claytons who were not acquainted with the Golden Lion in Dale Street, they must have had a melancholy familiarity with the place ten years later.[3]

It was inevitable that Case's brother would be implicated. On 1 May an advertisement was inserted for the settling of Jonathan Case's accounts;[4] by the 15th it was announced that his creditors were to meet. On the 29th it was made clear that just as his agent, Peter Worrall, had preceded Thomas Case in failure, so Barton Tarbuck, a Huyton brewer who had formerly been agent for Jonathan Case, had assigned over his effects to two of his creditors.[5]

Nor was the train of ruined businesses complete. On 19 June the important Liverpool house of Dobson, Daltera & Co. was in trouble. Gregson, Case & Co. was dissolved, and also Gregson, Bridge & Co., another firm of insurance brokers. Other businesses to close about this time were the salt firm of Gildart and Bungay and the flint glasshouse of Heywood, Staniforth & Co.[6]

The most important of the failures was that of Sarah Clayton herself. On 3 July bankruptcy proceedings were announced, and

---

[1] *Gore's Gen. Ad.* 13 March, 1778.

[2] *Gore's Gen Ad.*, 3 April, 1778.

[3] While the first spate of notices concerning the Clayton and Case failures came in this decade, a trickle continued long afterwards. Sarah Clayton's creditors were finally paid in full in 1807 ; newspaper notices in the same year show that Thomas Case's affairs were not settled even then. Lpool. Chron., 10 June, 1807.

[4] *Gore's Gen. Ad.*, 1 May, 1778.

[5] *Ibid.*, 6 Feb., 29 May, 1778.

[6] *Ibid.*, 1 Jan., 1779, 30 April, 1779, 28 Aug., 1778. In the April of 1778 Case's name disappeared from the list of the Fire Office Proprietors, and in the November following the concern was strengthened by bringing in a number of wealthy citizens.

her creditors were asked to meet at the Golden Lion on the 15th of the month, to prove their debts against this famous " dealer in coals."[1] From this advertisement came the first intimation that the selling of the property was not going to be easy, and that the Parr estates and mines were to be claimed by the creditors of both Thomas Case and Sarah Clayton.

Something is known of the final struggles of Jonathan Case before he followed his brother and aunt into bankruptcy. After having to stop his Sutton colliery because of low prices in 1773, he had recovered sufficiently two years later to rent a colliery in Eccleston near to Ravenhead comprising the very fields, " the Rushy Parks," which gave their name to a celebrated coal seam.[2] After only two years' working he had difficulty in paying his rent and claimed that he was being charged too much. In November, 1777, he and the coalowner, Mr. Eccleston, set up arbitration machinery to settle the matter, and the arbitrators decided that Case must pay £370 arrears of rent.[3] In June Case accused two of his mine officials of fraud, bringing lawsuits against John Balmer, his banksman at a Whiston colliery, and Matthew Ellam, who had supervised all his collieries in Whiston, Sutton and Eccleston. Both protested their honesty, implied that he was unjustly putting the blame for failure on them, and demanded that he should be forced to produce the account books which he had taken away. The testimony of Ellam shows that Case had been borrowing extensively, particularly £1,710 from Robert Hesketh, Esq. and £656 from Thomas Case.[4]

Sarah Clayton and the Cases did not long survive their failures. Clayton Case died in the year following the crash,[5] and Jonathan

[1] *Gore's Gen. Ad.*, 3 July, 1778.

[2] Wigan Ref. Lib. Dicconson Papers. Lease, B. T. and T. Eccleston to Jonathan Case, 15 July, 1775.

[3] *Ibid.*, Act of Arbitration by Robt. Moss and Matthew Ellam, 17 Dec., 1777, bond of Jonathan Case, 7 Nov., 1777, general release 19 Jan., 1778.

[4] P.R.O. P.L. 6. 87/10. Sarah Clayton and her nephews were to a great degree indebted to each other, and their financial affairs were almost inextricably tangled. In May, 1774, when Thomas Case gave his bond to his aunt for the Parr Estate " purchase ", she was indebted by " bonds and otherwise both on her own Act. and as surety for the said Thomas Case to various persons in several sums of money to a very large amount." Jonathan Case acted as surety for his aunt in several bonds. On the other hand, Sarah Clayton influenced two great-nieces, Mary and Eleanor Blundell, to lend £900 and £1,200 to Thomas and Clayton Case. (St. Helens Corpn., Deeds, Baxter's Works Bundle, Abstract of Title of Wm. Smart ; Lpool. Pub. Ref. Lib., Tarleton MSS., 11, 11a.).

[5] L.R.O. Wills. Will of 18 Feb., with affidavit that handwriting is that of deceased. The administrators were the assignees of Thomas Case, who had been left sole executor and residuary legatee. The assignees, together with a Liverpool woollen draper, took out a bond for £5,000. Thomas Case, " disabled from contracting business " as a bankrupt, handed over the administration on 12 May, 1779.

Case was dead by 1783.[1] Sarah Clayton, as we know from her own statement, was broken in health by her failure, and no doubt also by the selling up of her houses in Clayton Square and at Parr. In her will of 20 October, 1778 she mentioned a servant, Jane Barrington ; " she hath shown ye greatest attention to me thro my misfortunes and ye ill state of health the [sic] have brought me too [sic]." For a very roof over her head, she had been indebted to a niece, Elizabeth Case ; she recognised in a covering letter to the will " the trouble and expence you have had in purchasing a House for me to live in and your care and Assistance in furnishing the same " and spoke of the " Household goods . . . which my kind friends hath [sic] enabled me to buy."[2] She did not survive 1779, and in this forlorn state died Liverpool's most famous woman merchant, formerly one of the most ostentatiously wealthy of its citizens.[3]

[1] Gore's Gen. Ad., 26 June, 1783. A limited administration of an unimportant part of his property was granted in 1791 ; he died intestate.

[2] Lpool. Pub. Ref. Lib., Tarleton MSS., 11 and 11a.

[3] The sales following the failures of Sarah Clayton and the brothers Case give opportunity for assessing the extent of their property and mines. To Jonathan Case's original Whiston mines another in the same township was added in 1769, his first Sutton mine of 1763 was succeeded by another in 1769 (which we have seen was closed in 1773) and another was opened in Eccleston in 1775. (P.R.O. P.L.6 87/10). For all Case's St. Helens ventures a complete set of leases survives, the chief source being the Dicconson Papers. The expectation of the Sutton mine leased in 1769 was originally assessed at 3,000 works a year, and that in Eccleston at 2,016 works. Jonathan Case also possessed mineral rights in Hardshaw and Windle. The Carrs and his other Whiston colliery had fire-engines as did the Rushy Park (Eccleston) colliery. Other property included an interest in the family mansion of Redhasles, Burtonhead Farm in Sutton and some adjacent closes, a tannery in Windle and the Red Lion Inn in that township.

The local properties of Sarah Clayton and Thomas Case, before the claims of the rival creditors were settled, were unseparated and virtually identical. As first advertised for letting they were described as

" A VERY VALUABLE COAL MINE, situate in Parr . . . upon the banks of Sankey Brook Navigation, and by that means rendered convenient for a speedy and cheap conveyance to Warrington, Northwich and Liverpool, with all the horses, waggons and other carriages, railed roads, ways, windlasses, materials and utensils thereunto belonging, particularly a remarkable good FIRE ENGINE, lately erected and in thorough repair, so as to require little expence during the time the coals may reasonably be expected to take in getting; The quantity about THIRTY THOUSAND WORKS, part of it subject to a small Lord's rent; and either with or without the capital Mansion House, called PARR HALL . . and demesne lands . . . containing . . . ONE HUNDRED and SIXTY ACRES . . . well situated, in the centre of the several market towns of Warrington, Wigan and Prescot." (Gore's Gen. Ad. 19 June, 1778).

In addition the Parr property included the demesne, the estates formerly Greenough's and Tarbuck's (the latter containing coal), that part of Parr Great Delphs (coal seams) which were under waste or highway, and Bate's, Roughley's, Byrom's, Barton's, Arrowsmith's and Hill's estates and the Ship Inn (formerly called the Sloop). In Hardshaw, Sarah Clayton owned a moiety of the coal and iron mines in the estate of James Glover (the King's Head Estate by St. Helen's chapel).

Of those who participated in the carving-up of the Clayton and Case properties John Mackay, as perhaps might be expected, took the best pickings. In the June of 1778 he leased mines from the squire of Eccleston which seem to have been in part those worked earlier by Peter Berry and by Jonathan Case.[1] Land Tax returns, available from 1781, show that by that time he was in occupation of three Sutton estates formerly owned by Jonathan Case. In Parr he occupied Bate's and Ashton's estates, which indicates that he took over the principal mines of Sarah Clayton. He also possessed 22 cottages in Parr, no doubt tenanted by colliers.[2]

Another coal-master to take over some of the mines of the bankrupts was James Orrell of Blackbrook, who came of a family of small squires whom Parr Township Papers show to have been selling coal at least as early as 1750.[3] Without ever being quite in the front rank, they became notable coal owners in the decades after 1780. In 1778, before the actual collapse of the Cases had occurred, Orrell leased from the Eccleston family the " Rushy Park Delft " which Jonathan Case had formerly mined, occupying some of the same fields and agreeing to an estimate of yield based on the same rather odd amount, 2,016 works.[4] He did not occupy all the site of the previous lessee, however, for the administrators of the insolvent Jonathan Case kept the old colliery going till it was worked out. As was to be expected, Orrell's chief acquisitions from the estates and mines suddenly thrown on the market were nearer his own Blackbrook Estate ; by 1781 he had occupied all of Parr Hall Estate and part of that called Britche's, and in 1785 it was stated that there was a colliery on the property.

In contrast to these men, whose importance as industrialists was already established, three new coalowners are to be noted. One was Thomas West, who took over Jonathan Case's Sutton

Thomas Case possessed in his own right an estate in Crank and Rainford and the small Dutton's Estate in Parr. The income from the Parr properties of aunt or nephew is not known, though six years after their opening the mines were expected to produce upwards of £600 profit per year. Sarah Clayton's Liverpool estate included a large number of houses and pew-rents. The assignees of Thomas Case were William Gregson, Thomas Earle and Thomas Parke, and those of Sarah Clayton, John Blackburne and John Williamson. Not until 1780 was any dividend paid, when 4/3 in the £ was returned on Thomas Case's account both in his sole capacity and as partner with his late brother Clayton Case.

[1] Wigan Ref. Lib., Dicconson Papers. B. T. Eccleston to John Mackay, 24 June, 1778.

[2] L.R.O., Land Tax Returns, under townships.

[3] Parr Township Papers. Overseers Accts., 1750/1.

[4] Wigan Ref. Lib., Dicconson Papers. B. T. and T. Eccleston to J. Orrell, 20 Feb., 1778.

The Walker Art Gallery, Liverpool

SARAH CLAYTON (1712-1779)

estate of Burtonhead, and went in for coalmining and glassmaking; another was William Bromilow, who moved into part of Aspinall's Estate in Parr. A third coal-master whose family, like the Wests and the Bromilows, was to be of great importance in the nineteenth century, was Thomas Speakman. Roughley's Estate in Parr was his share of the spoils.[1] When he left a good property for a self-made man by his will of 1793, it included this estate " Under which are fully expected to grow a very Considerable Quantity of coal and Canal [cannel] . . . which I purchased from the assignees of the late Sarah Clayton."[2]

After the great disasters of 1778 an important change came over the coalfield. The age when the important mines were controlled by a handful of powerful individuals was passing, and was being succeeded by an age of many owners, none of them dominant. This tendency was helped by the death of John Mackay in 1783. His trustee, Admiral Philip Affleck, was content to administer the property so as to recoup the heavy borrowings of the dead capitalist from the mines. Attention was concentrated on the profitable Ravenhead colliery, and the restless enterprise of the Scot was not matched by his successors.

The disappearance from the scene of Sarah Clayton, Case and Mackay removed possible obstacles to an even closer relationship between the St. Helens coalfield and the Cheshire saltfield. Again it was the Liverpool merchants who were responsible for forcing the pace. Having produced a most efficient water transport system linking the coalfields, the saltfield and the docks, they were obliged to intervene yet again to maintain adequate supplies, first of salt and then of coal.

Output from the Cheshire saltfield continued to rise in the 1760s and 1770s; white salt shipments down the Weaver increased from 20,000 tons a year in 1760 to 40,000 tons twenty years later.[3] But even this rate of increase did not satisfy the men of Liverpool who by the 1780s were contracting to supply more salt to their customers than the Cheshire boilers were able, or willing, to

[1] *Ibid.*

[2] L.R.O., Wills, Will of 20 April, 1793, proved 1797 and again in 1835. This conception that coal beds " grew " was by no means uncommon at this period.

[3] T. S. Willan, *The Navigation of the River Weaver in the Eighteenth Century*, Chet. Soc., 3rd Ser. III (1951) 208, 220.

make. The position has been well summarised by a Liverpool
pamphleteer, writing in 1804 :

> " In the year 1784 . . . some exporters in Liverpool obtained a
> considerable increase of demand by forming some extensive
> connections abroad. Instead of being encouraged for so doing,
> the then salt proprietors (who, all but two, lived in Cheshire[1])
> considered it as a favour to let these exporters have salt for their
> contracts ; and when the least complaint of quality, or any
> other circumstance, occurred, they were told they need not come
> for any more salt ; they might take it or leave it. The conse-
> quence was, the people so used revolted at the treatment and
> erected salt works themselves, which caused more to follow
> their steps ; and, at this period, the interest in the salt works
> rests, for two-thirds, with the proprietors residing in Liverpool."[2]

The result of Liverpool's intervention in the brine trade was,
indeed, striking. White salt shipments down the Weaver increased
rapidly to 58,000 tons in the year 1792-3 and to 106,000 tons in
the year 1799-1800.[3] Much of this increase was obtained from
Winsford where just under 2,500 tons of salt were made in 1781-2,
more than 18,000 tons ten years later and no less than 38,000 tons
in 1799-1800.[4] Among the shippers of this Winsford salt were
Joseph Leigh and Co., Henry Wilckens and Co., and Leigh
Hewson and Co., all Liverpool firms.[5] By the 1790s Philip
London reported eighty-three flats unloading salt simultaneously
at Liverpool, and the Marquis of Bentivoglio, a visiting Milanese
nobleman, thought that " Salt is Liverpool's chief article of
commerce."[6] Yet, despite this extremely flourishing state of
affairs, the worries of the Liverpool salt interest were not yet over.
Having broken two monopolies by building the Sankey Canal and
by entering the brine trade, they had now to break a third, the
product of their own success.

The coal proprietors on the banks of the Sankey Canal took
full advantage of the rapid expansion of the salt industry at
the end of the eighteenth century. Between 1800 and 1804

---

[1] One of them was John Blackburne. In his will, dated 17 June, 1779,
and proved at Chester, 27 May, 1790, he mentions a brine pit and brine
salt works at Anderton.

[2] Anon. *Remarks on the Salt Trade of the Counties of Chester and
Lancaster*. (Lpool. 1804) 11-12.

[3] Willan, *op. cit.*, 224, 228.

[4] *Ibid*. 219, 224, 228.

[5] Cheshire Record Office. Winsford Tonnage Books.

[6] E. Hughes, *Studies in Administration, and Finance 1558-1825* (Manchester, 1934) 401.

when the Liverpool pamphleteer was writing, the price of coal had been advanced on three separate occasions, the total increase being 43 per cent.

" One should suppose [wrote the pamphleteer] that such customers as the saltboilers deserved attention, that the interests of buyer and seller were so mutually connected, that what hurts one must hurt the other. But it is a lamentable fact that this is not discerned, and that the proprietors at the collieries have as late deemed the saltworks as a kind of appendage to them, whom they by necessity can keep in a state of vassalage ; who cannot get supplied with coals any where else, whose complaints they therefore need not heed, and to whom they can set the price at their own pleasure. . . . The high price of coal causes new speculators to embark in a trade which is so lucrative that even the professionalist in law and physic can perceive and catch at it. The new comers give advanced wages and higher rents to get on ; no opportunity escapes their grasp to partake of the golden fleece at which they are aiming."[1]

Perhaps the writer was unduly hard on the coal proprietor who raised his prices in time of war and uneasy peace as an examination of the Hardshaw Colliery books shows ;[2] but there can be no disputing that the high price of coal and the guaranteed market enjoyed by the St. Helens coalowners tempted the salt boilers to sink pits to ensure their own supplies of fuel.

The reference to " the professionalist . . . in physic " makes it clear that the writer had in mind a combination of salt proprietors and others who entered upon a thirty-year lease of a mine of coal near Gerard's Bridge, St. Helens, in 1801. The partners in the new colliery were : William Leigh of Liverpool, merchant ; John Hewson of Middlewich, doctor in physic ; John Thompson of Northwich, salt proprietor ; George Leigh of Middlewich, salt proprietor ; John Leigh of London, gentleman ; Joseph Leigh of Liverpool, merchant; George Jackson of Liverpool, merchant ; William Carter of Northwich, salt proprietor ; John Whitley of Ashton-in-Makerfield, merchant ;[3] and Thomas Bridge of Davenham, salt proprietor.[4] Joseph Leigh and Co. and Leigh Hewson

---

[1] Anon. *Remarks on the Salt Trade . . .*, 10-11.

[2] Below, pp. 72, 73.

[3] Almost certainly the John Whitley of Clowes and Whitley who had dealings with Peter Stubs. See T. C. Barker, *The Economic and Social History of St. Helens, 1830-1900*, Ph.D. Thesis at Manchester University (1951) 10n.

[4] Lease dated 19 Aug., 1801, among the private papers of Col. H. A. Bromilow, Black Park, Chirk. We are much indebted to Col. Bromilow for permitting us to investigate this deed and other documents in his valuable collection of family papers.

and Co. were, as we have seen, two of the newly-established brine boiling firms at Winsford. Joseph Leigh and Co. were shippers to the Baltic and Joseph Leigh himself was a partner in Leigh and Sherlocks, trading with America.[1] A note, written in Whitley's hand and pinned to a draft of the lease,[2] confirms that this partnership in what was to be known as the Rushy Park Colliery was an association of salt companies formed to meet an emergency rather than a combination of speculators bent on holding the salt boilers to ransom, as suggested by our anonymous pamphleteer :

" Mr. Whitley conceives that it is not necessary that anything should be said in the articles of the managing partner, as Mr. W. would not wish to be such any longer than it is agreeable to himself or to the other partners. With respect to the partners being supplied with coal, of course it must be in turn as the Flatts come up the Canal, other sale the partners can settle how they shall be served at anytime.

The preference to partners in the disposal of any share, Mr. W. thinks, should first be to their own sett of salt proprietors, then, if refused, to the whole concern . . ."

The Rushy Park Colliery was no isolated example of the Liverpool-dominated saltmakers' becoming coal proprietors. John Ashton's son, Nicholas, leased mines in Parr before 1790 and extended the scope of his operations to tne immediate vicinity of St. Helens in 1800.[3] He was followed to the coalfield by John Bourne, the brother of Thomas Bourne, who was (in his own opinion) the greatest man in the rock trade,[4] by Thomas Claughton who, if he did not aspire to such heights in the rock trade, was certainly a salt merchant on a large scale owning extensive estates,[5] and by Thomas Chantler.[6] A strong and unified connection was being established between the Lancashire coalfield and the Cheshire saltfield. Before long the coal proprietors were themselves starting to acquire saltworks, not a difficult task in an industry where over-production brought swift retribution and drove the small man into bankruptcy.

---

[1] *Report from the Select Committee on the Laws Relating to the Salt Duties* 1818 [393] V. Evidence of Joseph Leigh, 155.

[2] L.R.O. Cross Papers, draft of lease dated 3 Aug., 1801.

[3] *Ibid.*, Conveyance, Nicholas Ashton to Ravenhead Colliery, 20 Sept., 1823 ; L.R.O., Land Tax Returns.

[4] *Report from the Select Committee on the Use of Rock Salt in Fisheries* (1817) [247] III, 24 ; L.R.O., Cross Papers, draft lease from Anna Maria Bold ; St. H. Corpn. Deeds, United Alkali Co. Ltd., deeds of Kurtz Works.

[5] Claughton went bankrupt in March, 1824. For the extent of his estates and his coal interests in the St. Helens district, see sale notices in the *Lpool. Merc.* 22 April, 1825, 18 Aug., 1826.

[6] L.R.O. Cross Papers, West v. Chantler, bill filed 13 May, 1809 ; draft indenture relating to Cowley Hill Colliery, 1833, fo. 22-3.

By the early 1830s the bond between Lancashire coal and Cheshire salt was complete. Every coal proprietor in and about St. Helens owned saltworks in Cheshire. The process which started during the seventeenth century had reached completion. Liverpool men had brought new life to the Cheshire salt industry by intervening in the rock salt trade. Then they had stimulated production by cutting out the land carriage between the wiches and Frodsham Bridge and, when this was so successful that it caused an acute shortage of coal, they had created a waterway up to the coalfield to connect with the Weaver Navigation. When the salt boilers of Cheshire set limits to their production, they went into the salt industry and when the coal proprietors attempted to restrict output, they became coal proprietors as well. Thus, over a period of a century and a half, relentless pressure from the men of Liverpool had brought the coal and salt trade to a high degree of economic organisation with Liverpool as its focal point.

Chapter VI

COLLIERY PROBLEMS AND PRACTICE

WHILE much attention has been given to the capitalist in this account of local eighteenth-century coalmining, little has been said about the working of the mines, the conditions required before the coal-master was allowed to break the soil, the colliery officials, the working collier, or day-to-day administration.

The letting of a colliery was a matter requiring great care and judgment, as well as technical knowledge. Though the main problems which had to be borne in mind were early understood, the means of solving them were only slowly perfected. As early as 1655, in a lease from the Byrom family of Parr to Sir William Gerard, there were clauses on the price of coal, wayleave, rights of sinking and of draining away water, the standard of measure, the prices paid to the lord for different grades of coal, the depth of the mine, the compensation of tenants for damage, and the filling-up of disused pits.[1]

As geological knowledge increased, and as the skill of the local lawyers in drafting such leases grew, methods of valuing and pricing coal seams improved. In the instance of 1655, just quoted, the lessee paid the owner 4d. for every 13 baskets of coal and 8d. for every 12 baskets of cannel " every basket of coal and cannel . . . [to] . . . Contayne so much in measure as are now used at the Coal Mines and works of the said Sir William Gerard in Ashton."

Matters were more exactly regulated a century later. The lease from Mr. Eccleston to Thomas Leigh in 1762 stipulated a rent of 2s. 6d. per work, and a system was adopted by which an annual output was estimated ; if this was not realised in one year, the deficiency could be made good in the next. At the time this lease was signed the selling price of coal was 2½d. the basket ; for each ½d. rise or fall in price Leigh's payment per work (three tons) was adjusted by 6d.[2] The lease of an adjacent colliery seven years later made a distinction between coal which could be got without pumping, and that which had to be pumped for ; on the former one-third of the selling price was paid to the owner, on the latter one-fifth. In this lease the measure was laid down carefully. Sixty

---

[1] L.R.O., DDGe. 844. The local evidence in the early part of this chapter may be usefully compared with the more general findings of T. S. Ashton and J. Sykes in *The Coal Industry of the Eighteenth Century* (1929), especially Chapters II to IV and XI.

[2] Wigan Ref. Lib., Dicconson Papers, lease of 19 May, 1762.

baskets of coal were to make an evenly-filled gauge work, 3 yards long, 2 yards broad, and 6 inches high.[1] Another lease of the same year adopted the device, which later became common, of fixing a definite money-rent for the expected yield of the colliery. This land-sale pit was to pay £112 a year for an output of 1,000 works. If more coal was raised the lessees were to pay the owner one-third of the price, providing it was not greater than 2d. a basket at the pit head ; above 2d. the basket half the price was to be handed over.[2] A lease of the Rushy Park mine in 1775 had an estimate of 2,016 works of 66 baskets at a rent of £252 a year, with a similar sliding-scale,[3] while three agreements for coal in the late 'sixties and 'seventies relating to Ravenhead all fixed a rent of 12s. 6d. per work.[4] An improvement on these earlier methods was made about 1780, by which the sliding-scale of rent and coal prices was regulated by reference to the coal price current on Sankey Navigation. The end of the century saw the general adoption of the method of charging a price based on the surveyed quantity of the coal ; if need be this could be qualified by a guiding figure of rent per annum, a reference to Navigation prices, or concessions based on the depth and cost of working and the quality of the seam.

An unscrupulous lessee could leave a colliery in an unworkable state at the end of his term, and regulations as to the manner of working were often specified. As early as our example of 1655 there were stipulations about the filling up of disused pits and the complete draining of the coal. Colliers were sometimes forbidden to trespass on the surrounding land after ploughing or when it was bearing crops. If a colliery was obtaining coal from the lands of several owners it sometimes was necessary to get permission to bring coals leased from one owner up a shaft leased from another, and to stack them on the " brows." Subsidence was even then a problem. It was alleviated by clauses to prevent the miners from digging within a certain distance of any buildings, or by instructions to leave sufficient pillars to support the roof. In a lease of 1778 John Mackay was allowed a one-fifth rebate of rent for the pillars he would leave, which may indicate the amount of coal lost by this method of mining.[5] When Leigh in 1762 was enjoined to do his mining skilfully and without intermission, it was " to be esteemed a Public Work to all intents and purposes."[6]

---

[1] *Ibid.* Lease of 31 July, 1769.

[2] L.R.O. DDGe. 849.

[3] Dicconson Papers, Lease of 15 July, 1775.

[4] *Ibid.* Leases. J. Case, 31 July, 1769. J. Orrell, 20 Feb., 1778. J. Mackay, 24 June, 1778.

[5] Dicconson Papers, Lease of 24 June, 1778.

[6] *Ibid.* Lease of 19 May, 1762.

F

Often allowances of free coal were made by the parties to a lease. Two very full sets of allowances have survived for Dagnall's collieries ; one fixed in 1746 with Henry Seddon, a yeoman of Eccleston, provided that coals could be taken without payment to the owner to defray

" . . . way candles when there is occasion to use them every getter of Coals to send three Baskets a week a piece one for sharpening of picks one Basket for the letting down of the Coal miners and Drawers one Basket to make the Brow good and every Coal miner or Getter of Coals to have forty Basketts a Year every whole Drawer to have twenty Basketts and every half drawer ten baskets a year and Ginn fire allowed."[1]

Here we have in the one document the earliest record of colliers' concessionary coal at St. Helens and the earliest mention of a fire-engine, or the intention to erect one. A Newcomen engine was not particular as to its diet, and often inferior fuel was allotted for this purpose : " sleck," " culm," and " chitter coal."

Rail-ways or waggon-ways seem to have been used at Prescot as early as 1594,[2] and the distance being so small they were presumably known of at St. Helens almost immediately. Waggon-ways only became prominent, however, after the building of the canal and turnpike, as connecting links between these and the collieries. In the case of the colliery owned by the Tarbuck family there are two references to rails;[3] the Gerards had a railway from Garswood to Blackbrook on the Sankey Canal, and a lease of 1792 mentions the possibility of building a rail-way where the loaded trucks running downhill would drag empty ones up an incline.[4]

Compared with the local evidence on other aspects of mining, little has come to light respecting the working-life of the eighteenth century collier. We know that in mid-century there must have only been a few men in each pit, for a colliery with an annual output in the neighbourhood of 3,000 tons might have half a dozen separate pits.[5] The frequent references to " ranks " of coal pits indicate these successive sinkings along the line of a seam. Evidence from the Prescot district shows that the hewer went to work very early in the morning ; times given are between one and two o'clock and between four and five o'clock. After getting his

---

[1] *Ibid.* Dagnall Bundle, 29 Oct., 1746. " Whole " drawers were presumably adults, " half " drawers children.

[2] F. A. Bailey, " Early Coalmining in Prescot, Lancashire," *Trans. L. & C. Hist. Soc.* **99** (1947) 14.

[3] P.R.O. P.L. 6. 85/35. *Gore's Gen. Ad.*, 14 July, 1769.

[4] Dicconson Papers, Lease from Thomas Eccleston to Gov. & Co. of Plate Glass Mfrs., 11 Oct., 1792.

[5] *Ibid.*, Dagnall Bundle. Numerous statements of output per pit.

stint of coals, presumably based upon the " work'" he came up, probably before noon—eleven o'clock is recorded in one instance. The drawers, mainly boys and girls in their 'teens, went down at about six or seven in the morning, and continued till the coal was cleared. Boys of ten and eleven and a girl of twelve are recorded as working below ground in Prescot ; such child workers would often be assisting their fathers or elder brothers.[1]

The atmospheric steam engine invented by Newcomen and modified by later hands was the means of creating deeper collieries and, necessarily, larger ones. Its arrival on any coalfield was essentially dependent on the market value of the coal and on the degree of capital available for investment, a factor of importance since in the early part of the century such engines frequently cost over £1,000 to erect. At Prescot, the main centre on the local coalfield prior to the building of the Sankey Canal, the erection of an engine seems to have been under discussion as early as 1716.[2] This engine was in course of erection in 1719 and was bequeathed as a going concern in a will of 1729.[3] There is no record of the atmospheric engine being immediately adopted in the St. Helens district, which had at that time poorer communications with the market, and was consequently a less attractive prospect to the mining investor. It is first mentioned about St. Helens in 1746, when Charles Dagnall asked owners from whom he was leasing a colliery to allow him free coal for an engine he was to erect. A statement of 1751 that coal was being consumed for this purpose shows that this engine was then at work.[4] It is interesting that the two local men who first employed " fire-engines "—Charles Dagnall the combmaker and Peter Berry the yeoman—both had to abandon their mining, and do not appear to have derived great profit from their engines. Within a few years Dagnall tried to sell his to a coalowner as a way of settling debts;[5] after leasing mines in 1754 Berry was endeavouring to sell both mines and engine in 1759. Atmospheric engines were more effectively used by the great colliery proprietors of the period after the opening of the canal ; Jonathan Case possessed at least three, while John

<hr>

[1] F. A. Bailey, " Coroners' Inquests held in the Manor of Prescot, 1746-89." *Trans. L. & C. Hist. Soc.* 86 (1934) 25 *seq.*.

[2] When Staniere Parrot, known to be associated with the fire-engine proprietors, leased mines from Lord Molyneux at Tarbock near Whiston. R. Sharpe France " Lancashire Papists' Estates," Vol. I. *Trans. L. & C. Rec. Soc.* (1945) 195. It would be a surprising coincidence if his visit did not connect with the subsequent erection of an engine so very near these mines.

[3] See above, p. 24.

[4] Dicconson Papers, Dagnall Bundle, Account of Dagnall's " get ". 1751-2.

[5] *Ibid.* Dagnall to Thomas Eccleston, 11 March, 1757.

[6] Above, p. 32, 32n.

Mackay not only employed them, but was interested in their technical improvement. By mid-century depths of about 150 feet were being worked on the coalfield with the aid of these engines ; though these were greatly increased thereafter, the levels reached did not compare with contemporary sinkings in Cumberland or on Tyne and Wear. Obviously on the low-lying and well-watered Lancashire plain drainage was the great difficulty. In 1754 Charles Dagnall wrote of land on the Eccleston estates near Boundary Road : " them fields Lets watter like a Sife . . ."[1]

While colliery records of this district provide disappointingly little material on the life of the working collier, they are unusually rich in references to the men who ran the collieries, the banksmen and the agents. The banksman was really the king-pin of the small colliery. He was surface-manager, book-keeper, and the official in charge of weighing machines and the loading of carts and flats, and for this he was apparently not exceptionally well paid. In 1714 Samuel Bure of Sutton, describing himself as a " husbandman," was employed by Jonathan Case of Red-hasles and his partners at a Huyton colliery. He defined his position as " Steward or Banksman in keeping an account what Coals and Slack was got in the said Coalwork and how much thereof was sold and to whom and likewise of the wages that were or should be due . . ." He was also responsible for despatching coals for " leading " to Liverpool. His name was involved in bonds for raising money to carry on the colliery, and he was in dispute with one of the partners over this.[2] Colliery officials seem to have been almost perpetually at variance with the owners.

Banksmen were appointed by the coal-master who ran the colliery and, where he did not own the coal rights, by the owner of the coal as well. For instance, Mr. Eccleston provided in his lease of 1762 to Thomas Leigh that he should be able to appoint his own banksman, who was to be paid reasonable wages by the coal-master, and whom the squire might change at will.[3] The duties of a coalowner's banksman were to see that the lessee did not cheat the owner—a practice only too common—which entailed ensuring that uncounted baskets of coal were not put on the brow, that pillars were not robbed, nor other deceits practised. His life at the colliery, as a sort of licensed spy, cannot have been comfortable. By the terms of a lease of 1759 from Sir Thomas Gerard to Charles Dagnall the coalowner could appoint one " Workman at each working pit as

---

[1] Dicconson Papers, Dagnall's " get " statement, 1755-6. Here, as on many other occasions he made charges of deliberate sabotage—in this case against a farmer, Henry Seddon, for deliberately flooding out his colliery. He also accused one John Wilcock of dropping stones on the heads of his sinkers as they worked. Dagnall to Taylor, 20 Aug. 1754.

[2] P.R.O. P.L. 6. 56/49.

[3] Dicconson Papers, B. T. Eccleston to Thos. Leigh, 19 May, 1762.

drawer, Winder, or Banker," to be paid the same wages by Dagnall as the rest of the men, " And he shall not be put to greater hardships than other Workmen in the Like Stations are."[1] This sort of post tended to die out ; the banksman became redundant once the coal extracted was measured not by counting the number of baskets raised but by surveying the coal at stipulated times after the mine was opened. It seems to have been in the banksman appointed by the lessee that the agent proper, or as we would now call him, colliery manager, had his origin.

The banksman or agent was invariably the first to be accused if things were not going well, as the case of Alexander Tarbuck testifies.[2] Tarbuck, a Parr yeoman, was Sarah Clayton's surface-manager and book-keeper, assuming the post in 1760, when he succeeded Hugh Gomery or Montgomery. In 1763 he was party to a contract with his mistress which gave him one-tenth of the annual profits or not less than £60, with an extra £7 a year for acting as estate manager at Parr and Rainford. He was by his own description book-keeper, cashier and surface manager. By the end of 1768 he had been elevated to the status of business manager, being only required to inspect the colliery once a quarter at most, while one Edward Hall (formerly his assistant) now had the business of managing the colliery. His sins were, typically, discovered at a period of depression in the trade ; in 1772 he was discharged for keeping the books " in a very irregular manner " and in 1774 he was prosecuted for fraud in the buying of timber for Sarah Clayton.[3] The case is interesting if only for indicating the growing difference between the agent and the other officials of a merely foreman status.

Tarbuck did his brother-in-law Matthew Ellam a good turn by recommending him for the post of agent at Jonathan Case's Whiston colliery. Ellam was to look after the colliery, supervise the underlookers, keep an eye on the engines, and also collect estate rents. At that time and for two years afterwards another man did the book-keeping. For his duties Ellam got £65 a year, a house and garden rent-free and the keep of a cow on the payment of £3 a year. At the end of a year his wages were increased to £70 ; presently he took over the sales side of the business and claimed to have increased the market considerably, without receiving any further remuneration. Case tried to make Ellam do the book-keeping also, and, though he refused for some time, a new book-keeper proved unsatisfactory and eventually he was forced to do the work. Subsequently another colliery (Carr

[1] L.R.O. DDGe. 1257. Sir T. Gerard to Charles Dagnall.
[2] P.R.O. P.L. 6. 86/22.
[3] P.R.O. P.L. 6. 86/42.

Colliery) was opened in Whiston, one in Sutton was worked for a
few years (1769-1773), and another was begun in Eccleston in
1775, all of which Ellam had to supervise without increase in pay.
In March, 1774, he remonstrated on the multiplicity of his duties
in a letter to Case, declaring that their extent was harmful to his
health. His ungrateful employer, however, claimed that Ellam
had never settled with him for various debts in the books and
went to law with him.[1] Simultaneously Case prosecuted John
Balmer, the banksman at one of his Whiston collieries, whom he
had employed at the " small wages " of 8s. per week for 16 years.
For this the banksman had to keep an account of the coals raised
at each pit " eye," note the coals sold for ready money and those
sold for credit, pay the colliers, and settle with the main agents of
Case who were successively William Moss, Edward Astley,
Barton Tarbuck, William Ashton, and Matthew Ellam. Balmer
was accused by Case of being in debt to him and of falsifying the
books, despite the fact that they had been settled quite recently.
Case also caused piles of poor coal lying in the fields about the
colliery to be measured and set against the banksman, which
Balmer claimed was wrong as they were " unsaleable and he
ought not to be charged with such Trash because your orator
alleges they ought not to be called Coals." Some had been on the
brow for six or seven years and was only fit for stoking the fire-
engine.[2]

These cases further illustrate the differences creeping into the
work and status of colliery officials. Ellam was agent for several
collieries, chiefly pushing sales and looking after the business
aspect, and (like his brother-in-law Alexander Tarbuck) leaving
the working of the colliery to various under-managers or surface-
managers of whom Balmer was one. Many of the agents seem to
have been substantial men and described themselves till quite late
in the century as " yeomen." Before the Clayton-Case failures,
however, they had not got to the importance of the managers of
the last quarter of the century, such as William Bromilow, Thomas
Speakman and John Haddock, who eventually went into mining
on their own account, founding the St. Helens mine-owning
families of the nineteenth century.[3]

Apart from some fragmentary records we have no evidence of
day-to-day management and business policy in any local mines
until we come to the Hardshaw Colliery in the early years of the
nineteenth century. When the Letter Book opens in 1805 the
important local brewer, Thomas Greenall,[4] had just died leaving

[1] P.R.O. P.L. 6. 87/10.

[2] P.R.O. P.L. 6. 87/9.

[3] See below, pp. 197, 200.

[4] For his brewing and other interests see below, p. 90 et seq.

his share in the colliery to three sons ; the other partner was Joseph Churton, a local doctor who was also interested in a Liverpool glass works. This firm was typical of a number of coal concerns of the second rank, which flourished mainly on the lucrative trade to the saltfields. Their heyday was between the disappearance of the great eighteenth-century proprietors and the emergence, in the early decades of the nineteenth century, of a group of powerful local coal-masters who invaded the salt trade.

It is immediately obvious from the Letter Book that there was supposed to be an agreed price at which coal-masters loaded " flats " on the Navigation. The combination to maintain prices was, however, constantly undermined by secret competition. This can be instanced by one of the very first entries in the Letter Book. Writing to a firm of Liverpool sugar merchants, Churton said :

" I have consulted with my partners (Mr. Greenalls) respecting your being served with Coals at 7/6d. per Ton. We are of Opinion the Price is too low considering the goodness of our Coals. Nevertheless as we expect your consumption will be considerable we will serve you upon those Terms for this Present Year out—You will please to observe that in the Notes or Bills sent by the Flatt Masters the Coals will be charged at 8/4d. and the 10d. shall be deducted at the time of payment. I entirely depend upon your honour and secrecy in this Business as we serve no other person whatever upon the same Terms.
Jos. Churton."[1]

In a further letter to the same customer on the 22nd, Churton admitted others were selling even lower. James Orrell had reduced his price to 6s. 8d. per ton " in consequence we are informed of some ungenteel treatment from some of his neighbours but we apprehend he will not continue selling at that Price long." If there was a general fall of prices at the other collieries Greenalls and Churton would follow, but for the time being the Ashton's Green, Haydock, Ashton, Rushy Park, " Gerrotts " (Gerard's) Bridge, St. Helens and Croppers Hill collieries were all selling at 8s. 4d. Churton agreed " that Ravenhead Colliery and a few that Mrs. Hill has to get are now selling at 7/6d.," but these coals Churton considered not so good as those of the Hardshaw colliery. Three days later a letter was written in reply to Mr. Midgley, a Cheshire salt manufacturer, allowing him a rebate of 8d. per ton.[2]

[1] Greenall, Whitley & Co. Ltd., Hardshaw Colliery Letter Book. Colliery to Bancroft, 19 July, 1805.

[2] Hardshaw Colliery Letter Book. Colliery to Bancroft, 22 and 25 July, 1805.

The next month saw the Colliery writing to the celebrated salt firm of Dudley at Winsford suggesting secret terms.

" As we have now a pretty large Stock of Coals upon hand, the quality of which we have little doubt you will approve of we are inclined to do business with you on terms that we flatter ourselves will be honorable and advantagus [sic] to you.
If you think this worthy of your attention please to give us an answer and we will pay proper attention to it and also explain our meaning in more general terms. In the mean time we trust you will have the goodness and honor not to make known of this to any person whatever."[1]

The price fixed was 7s. 8d. per ton. This policy of price reductions continued to be practised ; on the 21 March, 1807, Midgleys and Co. had their original discount of 8d. per ton increased by 2d. since the colliery owners were " ever desirous to oblige a Steady Customer." By the December of the same year Midgleys had found a colliery which would serve them at the heavily reduced rate of 7s. per ton, and asked Hardshaw Colliery to cut their prices to the same rate. Mr. Bate, the colliery agent, wrote them :

" In answer to this proposal I am desired to assure you that my Employers feel much regret at seeing a probability of being compelled (most reluctantly) to part with a Connection in Trade which they have long served with pleasure to themselves, and are happy to find (by your letter) with satisfaction to you ; but knowing the Coals now getting at this Colly. are as good as any, and much better than some upon the Sankey Canal, they entertain hopes that it will be in their power to dispose of them at the usual Price and consequently are not inclined to sell them for less than 7/6d. p. Ton at present."[2]

Certain details of the working of the colliery appear in the Letter Book. Towards the end of 1805 and during the first half of 1806 the Colliery was endeavouring to get payment from debtors being " much in want of money," " in extreme want of money " and " in the Act of making extensive alterations."[3] The firm purchased a second-hand steam engine which cost them

[1] Hardshaw Colliery Letter Book. Colliery to Dudley & Co., 19 Aug., 1805.

[2] Hardshaw Colliery Letter Book. Colliery to Clay & Midgley, 22 Dec., 1807. In the previous month Litton & Wagstaffe were allowed slack at 2/6d. per ton instead of the usual 3/-, as Clares, the coal merchants of Sankey Bridges, were selling at that rate. " Under the present circumstances it is necessary to keep the Price out of the Note Sent by the Flatmen, as we are now charging 3/- to other People, this it is hoped will not be mentioned by you."

[3] Hardshaw Colliery Letter Book, Letters of 28 Nov., 1805, 11 April and 26 May, 1806.

£220,[1] and they immediately afterwards ordered a " Teagle Fall or Block Rope . . . 55 or 60 yards in length," showing that an engine pit was being opened or re-equipped of about 150 feet deep.[2] Further expansion appears to have taken place in 1807 when they wrote to the celebrated John Curr for

" one of your Patent Round Ropes. . . . The Rope in question must be of equal strength to a Common Round Rope of Nine Inches Circumference the length one Hundred and Eleven Yards. As your own Interest is so deeply concerned with the Reputation which your Ropes may acquire from those who make trial of them, I consider it almost unnecessary to remind you that this Rope ought to be made of the best materials . . ."[3]

An actual contract drawn up with the sinkers of a pit in 1811 is recorded by the agent.

" This Day made a verbal agreement (in the presence of William Appleton Senr. and George Vose) with John Bradshaw, John Johnson, Daniel Wynne, and William Appleton Junr. by which the four last mentioned undertake to Sink the New Engine Pit as this Colliery, down to the four foot Delf at £3 3 0 per yard ; and cut the Horse Tree Holes and put in the Horse Trees at 5/- per Sett ; each man is also to receive 6d. per Hour for every Hour which he may lose by the water being in the way, or any other cause, not being brought on by the said Workmen, or through their neglect ; the said Workmen also agree to forfeit and pay the Proprietors of this Colliery 2/6d. for each and every turn of Eight Hours which any of them may lose through his own Neglect or Illness."

Each of the said Workmen Accepted and Received 5/- as Earnest of the above Agreement.

N.B.—Agreed to give each of the above mentioned four men 8 yards of Blue Cloth for a Sett of Jackets."[4]

It is difficult to estimate the number of people employed at the Hardshaw Colliery, as only those who were paid out are

[1] Hardshaw Colliery Letter Book. Colliery to McConnell & Kennedy, 17 March, 1806.

[2] Hardshaw Colliery Letter Book. Colliery to Mr. Jackson, 8 April, 1806.

[3] Hardshaw Colliery Letter Book. Colliery to Mr. John Curr, 12 Feb., 1807. See T. S. Ashton and J. Sykes, *The Coal Industry of the Eighteenth Century*, (Manchester, 1929), 61. John Curr's patent flat rope had been invented in 1798. It consisted of " several small ropes of circular section stitched together : at the beginning of the operation of winding, the rope to which the loaded corves were attached wound on a small diameter ; but as the corves were raised, and the rope coiled on itself, the diameter increased, while that from which the descending empty corves unwound correspondingly diminished." Curr claimed the speed of winding was increased five-fold.

[4] Hardshaw Colliery Letter Book. 14 Aug., 1811.

recorded in the Account Books, These would be the " getters " or hewers, the boys, women and girls employed as " drawers " and " thrutchers " not being mentioned. Lists for 1803 mention 18 men ; for 1804, 19 ; for 1807, 11 and 17. It might not be too wild a guess to say that the colliery, reckoning two assistants to each collier and allowing for those loading and banking coals on the surface, probably employed at these various periods between thirty-five and seventy people ; but estimates are liable to be affected by such factors as the distance between workings and the shaft. As this colliery was surrounded by others, and had at one time as many as five shafts, the likelihood is that galleries were short, and the number employed in underground transport of coal smaller than usual.[1]

Many references in the books of the Hardshaw Colliery bring out the importance of the salt trade. There is the specific statement of the agent and proprietors on several occasions that the coal supplied by the colliery was particularly suitable for salt boiling : " . . . We are credibly informed they are the best for Manufacturing salt,"[2] ". . . it is a fact established now beyond all doubt that our Coals are superior to most of the other Collieries for the purpose of Manufacturing Salt, tho' this circumstance may have escaped your notice . . ."[3]

By going through the colliery account books it is possible to estimate the influence of the salt trade. It soon becomes apparent that little else counted ; the brewery took considerable amounts of coal and various local works (including the glassworks in which Churton had an interest) purchased the odd flat-load, but these demands were completely overshadowed by those of the salt-boilers. Though, as we have seen, the annual output of the colliery varied between two and four thousand works, or six to twelve thousand tons, on several occasions single salt-boilers took over 1,000 tons in a year. Among the customers in the salt business were the firms of Kent & Naylor, Midgleys, Johnsons, John Blackburne, John Roylance, Nicholas Ashton, the brothers Bourne, Henry Wilckens and the Okells, as well as many others less prominent.

The books of Hardshaw Colliery also enable us to discover how far the pamphleteer of 1804 was justified in his attacks on the coal proprietors for raising their prices.[4] There can be no doubt that prices of coal had risen. This was only to be expected at a time when the Napoleonic Wars had forced England to become an arsenal for herself and her allies, and when the metal

[1] For the practice of having many shafts to one colliery see Ashton & Sykes, *op. cit.*, 7.

[2] Hardshaw Colliery Letter Book. Colliery to Midgleys, 25 July, 1805.

[3] Hardshaw Colliery Letter Book. Colliery to Kent & Naylor, 25 July, 1805.

[4] See above, p. 59.

industries were flourishing, and demanding increasing supplies of fuel. In addition to the tendency for prices to rise because of demand, there was also an increase in overheads. The contemporary Copper Trade Enquiry of 1799 revealed that the increased price of materials used in mining, particularly wood, was having an effect on costs of production. The first of the Hardshaw Colliery account books, running from 1802 to 1811, shows that an increase in coal prices was taking place. Some prices of supply to the brewery, which must represent the pit-head rate, show that coals were 4½d. the basket in 1802, dropping in January, 1803, to 4d., but reaching 6d. by July, and rising to 7d. per basket in the following year. They only achieved stability at 30s. the work, or 6d. the basket, early in 1805. By the time the Letter Book opened in the same year the price was down to 5d. the basket. It would then seem that the pamphleteer of 1804 noted the rises in price, but not the reductions. Moreover, we have seen that the official prices were being secretly and heavily cut, and that favoured customers were being supplied as low as 7s. 6d. per ton.

The Hardshaw Colliery was several times in difficulties because of the actions of an undisciplined group of workers. Possibly the collier was more noted for his independence than any other eighteenth-century workman, but bargees have always been reputed to have wills of their own. The " Flatmen," and particularly the " Captains " of flats on the Sankey, emerged on more than one occasion as a force to be reckoned with. In 1792 there was an important strike of the men working the barges between Liverpool and Northwich, during which it was asserted that flat-masters could earn up to £90 a year, and were known to have refused 50 guineas.[1]

The Sankey flat-masters gave their employers at least as much trouble. On the 19 March, 1773, John Phillips, the Liverpool dockmaster, published a letter to John Mackay concerning one of his " Insolent and drunken " flat-men, a certain Gloster, who had obstructed the passage between the bridges of the North Dock with his vessel during an evening tide.[2] Mackay at once replied regretting the occurrence : " In consequence of your representation . . . I have given directions for his immediate discharge from my employ—I wish the attention of my people but equalled my desire for the service of the public. . . ." It would appear that the flat-masters carried on an interesting sort of blackmail. Apparently salt-boilers, while having a preference for the coal of certain collieries, would be put off with that of others, and the flatmen took advantage of this. Instead of sailing up the Sankey to the designated colliery, possibly right at the extremity of the canal, they would fill with coal at one lower down, thus saving them-

---

[1] *Williamson's Lpool. Ad.*, 7 May, 1792 ; *Gore's Gen. Ad.*, 3, 24 May, 1792.

[2] *Ibid.* 19 March, 1773.

selves time and trouble and getting a quicker trip. The only way to avoid this was to pay them a secret bonus. Just after the turn of the century the Hardshaw Colliery, which was one of the less fortunately placed, was experiencing considerable trouble from this cause. Writing to John Dudley of Winsford in 1805 they announced the price of their coal, but pointed out that it included a bounty paid to the flatmen, " Which must be done otherwise they will report that we give nothing, and by these means we shall be injured in our sales."

Ten years later, in 1815, we get further references to the bounty:

" Your letter by Capt. Musket is received, and the flat Heron is loading . . . as to placing 5/- or thereabouts to the Credit of your account, instead of giving the Captain a small matter to make up the difference of expense which he incurs by coming to one of the higher, instead of loading at one of the lower. Collieries : It is a request so entirely new that I do not feel myself competent to give an answer until I have consulted my employers . . . "[1]

The colliery agent was involved in a similar discussion with another firm, that of Henry Harrison & Co., early in the following year : " . . . You say the Captains are paid from 15/- to 42/- for loading at the Colliery—the former sum was given at this colliery previous to the 17th Nov. last but the latter sum 42/- has never been given here, and your Letter contains the first information I ever had of such a sum being given at any Colliery—since the 17th Nov. the Captains are paid the additional money only which it costs them to get their flats brought from the lower to the higher Collieries as stated in my last. As to the circumstances mentioned in Yours of a Captain returning with his Notes to the Clerk of some Colliery and requesting him to put in four tons more than he had on board in consequence of the liberal fees he had received, I can only say that such a transaction never occurred at this Colliery—and if any Captain had made such a proposal to me I would have acquainted his employer with his conduct. I am also desired to assure you that the practice of giving money to the Captains has always been extremely disagreeable to my Employers and that they never submitted to it but when compelled by the example of others . . . I am aware that unless you enforce the most rigid obedience to your orders on the part of the flatmen, they will find excuses to avoid this colliery altogether, if we attend to your orders and do not [compensate them]."[2]

In the early nineteenth century the coal industry was on the eve of an era of phenomenal expansion, but, particularly among the smaller firms, it is clear that there were plenty of trials and problems to be faced, and not always great profits as compensation.

[1] Hardshaw Colliery Letter Book, 28 Oct., 1815.
[2] Colliery Letter Book, April, 1816.

CHAPTER VII

THE COPPER INDUSTRY : ANGLESEY AND
LANCASHIRE 1770-1815.

THE chief consequence of the development of the local coalfields in the eighteenth century was an indirect one. The
mines had been opened in order to satisfy the demands of
Cheshire saltboilers and Liverpool householders, but they soon
began to deal extensively with the proprietors of important furnace
industries which the coalmasters had succeeded in attracting to the
district. Between 1771 and 1815 St. Helens was deeply involved in
the affairs of the copper industry at the most interesting period of
its history.[1]

Copper mining in Britain declined after the departure of the
Romans, and there was no important revival before the reign of
the first Elizabeth. Two companies were then formed, the Mines
Royal and the Mineral and Battery Company. Both were
administered by German technicians, and partly financed by
German capital; between them they enjoyed a monopoly of copper
mining and smelting. The Civil War suspended their activities
and destroyed the important mining organization which had been
built up in the Lake District. The factors which led to a great
revival of mining and smelting after 1690 are not as yet completely
elucidated, but important reasons were the abandonment of the
royal mining monopoly, the change from smelting with charcoal
to smelting with coal, and a demand for copper not only for
coinage and domestic articles but for export, first to Africa and
subsequently to the East Indies. As the newly-developed copper
mines of Cornwall increased their production, and the smelting
works (principally concentrated in the Bristol and Swansea
districts) multiplied and expanded, the copper and brass imports
from Sweden, Barbary and Holland dwindled, and Britain quickly
became an exporter rather than an importer of those metals.

The Patten family of Warrington first brought the copper
industry to Lancashire. About 1717 they established the Bank
Quay Copper Works, in which they had the celebrated William
Wood as their partner for a few years.[2] From Warrington the

---

[1] For a more complete account and more detailed references, see J. R.
Harris, *The Copper Industry in Lancashire and North Wales, 1760-1815.*
Ph.D. Thesis (Manchester University, 1952).

[2] Harris, *op. cit.*, 31 *seq.* See also Winmarleigh Estate Office, Warrington:
Patten Papers, Parcel 2, Agreement 11 Sept., 1735, citing earlier document
of Aug., 1721. Also *ibid*, agreement of 11 Oct., 1725.

Patten interest soon extended into Staffordshire, and in the early
1730s the family became involved in the Cheadle Company. This
became one of the principal copper and brass concerns of the
eighteenth century, and had branches or works at Alton, Oaka-
moor, and Cheadle in Staffordshire and in South Wales. A
separate firm was founded in 1755 with many of the same
partners, and was styled the Warrington Company; like the
Cheadle Company it dealt extensively in articles for the Africa
trade. Here again the Patten interest was dominant, and the
original partners were all Warrington men; Thomas Watkins,
and William Dumbell being associated with Thomas and Robert
Patten. The Warrington Company had its principal manufacturing works at Holywell in Flintshire, but the making of " Manillas "
—and possibly the smelting—was done at Warrington. In 1767
the firm was partly reorganized, some of the Warrington plant
was sold, and two Cheadle men, Robert Hurst and Joseph Ingleby,
joined Thomas Patten, William Dumbell and John Watkins as
partners.[1]

Shortly after these changes the Warrington Company found
itself with a rival in the Liverpool market. This was the firm of
Charles Roe & Co. of Macclesfield, who set up a Liverpool
smelting works in 1767 in order to deal with the large cargoes of
ore they were shipping from the newly-discovered copper mines
at Parys Mountain in Anglesey, which they had leased a few years
previously. Roe & Co., like the Warrington Co., were supplying
copper and brass goods to merchants in the African slave trade.[2]
It may have been this rivalry which induced the Warrington Co.
to establish a smelting works nearer the source of fuel than either
Liverpool or Warrington. By 1771 they were in negotiation with
the trustees of Sir Thomas Gerard for a works site at Stanley in
Blackbrook, on the borders of Parr and Ashton townships.

A year later the Warrington Co. was able to secure a firm
tenure of the property it desired, close to a branch of the Canal and
just at the point where the Gerard coals from Ashton and Garswood were brought down to the Sankey Canal wharf. The copper
firm agreed to take all its coal from Sir Thomas's representatives,
not only for its furnaces but for the use of its ' Servants, Agents,
and Workmen.' While coal prices were under 4/- a ton the
firm was to pay the ordinary price current on the Canal, but if
the cost rose it received an appreciable discount, amounting to
as much as 5d on a ton costing six shillings. The trustees agreed
to lay down " a planked and railed Road from the said Sankey

[1] Thos. Bolton & Sons, Widnes. Deeds of the Cheadle and Warrington
Companies. Agreements and leases of 1734, 1759, 1780 and Minute Book
of the Cheadle Co. Manillas were brass bangles.

[2] The firm of Roe & Co. is being dealt with by Dr. W. H. Chaloner
in two articles in Trans. L. & C. Antiq. Soc. 62 (for 1950-51) and 63
(for 1952).

Navigation to the said Lessees intended works",—while on its part the Warrington Company promised to compensate the land-owner's tenants for any crops or buildings " in any way annoyed, hurt, smoked, singed, destroyed or damaged by reason of calcining, smelting, roasting or refining of any copper or other ore."[1]

Little is known of these works over the next few years. The Warrington Company was still in occupation in 1775, when the leasing of additional land was contemplated ; this would imply that the works were then a profitable concern.[2] The factory seems to have been still at work in 1778, when the Gerard Committee exempted the coal they supplied to the copper works from a cartel agreement.[3] Prior to 1785, however, the furnaces had been allowed to go out, for when Thomas Williams purchased the works on behalf of the Stanley Smelting Company there was a delay for repairs before production could be resumed.

From 1779 onwards the great organization controlled by Thomas Williams dominated the Lancashire copper industry. Williams, a successful lawyer of Llanidan in Anglesey, became involved in the early 1770s in a lawsuit over the ownership of some remarkable new mines. These were situated on Parys Mountain near Amlwch, and were partly in land owned outright by Sir Nicholas Bayly of Plasnewydd, partly in land owned jointly by the Baronet and by the Rev. Edward Hughes of Llysdulas in right of his wife Mary, born Lewis. These disputes were of a for-midable complexity. It must be sufficient to say that eventually the mines in Sir Nicholas Bayly's lands continued to be operated under lease to Charles Roe & Co., while those in which the Rev. Edward Hughes had a share were formed into the Parys Mine Company, officially founded in 1778.[4]

The Parys Mine Company was a partnership of Edward Hughes, Thomas Williams, and John Dawes, a London banker; from the outset Williams seems to have been the effective manager. He quickly saw that the full advantage of the cheap, easily mined, low-grade Anglesey ores could not be obtained unless the Company controlled its own smelting works. For decades the smelters had been in an efficient combination against the miners of the chief

[1] L.R.O. DDGe. 864, 818, 819, 100-102.

[2] *Ibid.* 459.

[3] See above, p. 52.

[4] The early association of Williams and the Anglesey Mines is dealt with extensively in a collection of records recently discovered. Their owner, Mrs. B. Fetherstonhaugh of Kinmel Manor, Abergele, has placed these papers on permanent loan to the University College of North Wales, Bangor. The construction and activities of the Mona and Parys Mine Companies are set forth in Mona Mine MSS. at the Library of U.C.N.W., Bangor. Useful summaries of the changes in organization at the mines are to be found in M.M. MSS. 3544 and 1267. The writer is now engaged upon an industrial biography of Thomas Williams, *The Copper Kingdom*.

copper-mining region, that of Cornwall, and had paid what they saw fit for the ores. Williams would have none of this, and, before the formation of the Parys Co., endeavoured to have the duty on the coastwise shipment of coal repealed, so as to establish smelting works in Anglesey. Not being immediately successful, he decided to set up works on the Lancashire coalfield, and a year after the formation of the Company he was in negotiation with the most enterprising of the coalmasters of the St. Helens district.

The gravity of the depression years of 1778 and 1779, which had seen the ruin of the powerful Clayton-Case group of coal-owners, and an abortive attempt at a cartel by the chief coal-masters, must have made any furnace industry a welcome immigrant to the coalfield at this time. How Mackay secured the Parys Company's works for his Ravenhead Estate we do not certainly know, though we can make some plausible guesses ; there can be no doubt that he gained a great prize. This was his second coup of this nature, for in 1773 he had brought the great factory of the British Cast Plate Glass Company to Ravenhead.[1]

In September, 1779, Mackay leased land adjoining the Raven-head branch of the Sankey Canal to the Parys Mine Company partners ; there they were to erect plant for smelting ores and houses for their agents and workmen. In addition Mackay allowed the partners free use of his stone quarry and lime kilns, and all the brick clay they required.[2] As well as the main Raven-head site the Company took over part of the " Kitsbridge " estate, where Mackay leased them the Navigation Tavern, a graving dock for barges, and other land. The Company also extended its premises over the next few years by leases from other landowners in the vicinity. The Parys Mine Co. was allowed to renew its leases from Mackay by a fixed fine whenever they fell in.

Together with this there was a coal agreement. Mackay con-sented to supply the Company with all the coal it needed at 5/- the ton of 30 cwt., to be delivered according to the directions of the smelters. This price, as well as that of the fireclay which it agreed to take from him, could if necessary be regulated according to the current price of coal on the Canal. On its part the Parys Company bound itself to take all their coal from Mackay's collieries.

Mackay had done well in that he had secured a steady cus-tomer for a large part of his coal. Nevertheless, the bargain was at least equally advantageous to the Parys Co. By means of the Canal flats could sail from within two miles of the mine almost to the door of the smelting house, while refined copper could have

[1] See below, p. 112.

[2] L.R.O. Cross Papers. " Copy of P.M.Co' s contract with Mr. Mackay for their supply of coals from his colliery." L.R.O. DDGe. 830. Draft Lease, John Mackay to P.M. Co., 29 Sept., 1779. See also Harris, *op. cit.* Chapter IV., " The Parys Company in Lancashire."

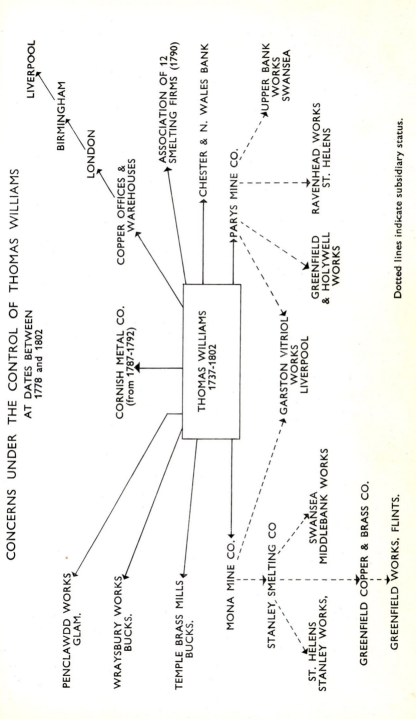

CONCERNS UNDER THE CONTROL OF THOMAS WILLIAMS
AT DATES BETWEEN
1778 and 1802

LIVERPOOL

BIRMINGHAM

LONDON

ASSOCIATION OF 12
SMELTING FIRMS (1790)

CHESTER & N. WALES BANK

UPPER BANK
WORKS
SWANSEA

COPPER OFFICES &
WAREHOUSES

PARYS MINE CO.

RAVENHEAD WORKS
ST. HELENS

CORNISH METAL CO.
(from 1787-1792)

THOMAS WILLIAMS
1737-1802

GREENFIELD
& HOLYWELL
WORKS

PENCLAWDD WORKS
GLAM.

GARSTON VITRIOL
WORKS
LIVERPOOL

WRAYSBURY WORKS
BUCKS.

TEMPLE BRASS MILLS
BUCKS.

MONA MINE CO.

SWANSEA
MIDDLEBANK WORKS

STANLEY SMELTING CO

GREENFIELD COPPER & BRASS CO.

ST. HELENS
STANLEY WORKS,

GREENFIELD WORKS, FLINTS.

Dotted lines indicate subsidiary status.

By permission of Lt.-Col. Hughes-Young

MICHAEL HUGHES OF SHERDLEY (1752-1825)

water carriage from the factory to Liverpool, or, from the Mersey, through a widely-developing canal system. The Rushy Park coal at Ravenhead was already famous for its quality, and by having their works directly on the coalfield the Company were in a better position than their rivals at Warrington and Liverpool. Even as compared with the Stanley Works of the Warrington Co. they had the advantage of cheap working, for they were smelting their own ores.

To manage the large new works which they proceeded to build the Parys partners sent out Michael Hughes, the twenty-eight-year-old youngest brother of the Rev. Edward Hughes. This appointment was not a sinecure for the new manager remained in charge to the end, considerably increased his duties as time went on, and, outside his work for the Anglesey Mines and their subsidiaries, was a successful business man, landowner and magistrate.

Williams soon carried his schemes further. Finding that he would have difficulty in disposing of his refined cake copper because of the activities of the opposing cartel, he followed the setting-up of the Ravenhead refinery by the establishment of copper rolling and manufacturing plant at mills on the Holywell stream in Flintshire.

During the 1780s Williams's power in the copper trade increased by leaps and bounds.[1] He fought a successful price war with the smelting cartel, largely waged at the expense of the Cornish mine adventurers, who were reduced to desperation. He endeavoured to obtain the valuable East India contract for copper in the teeth of his rivals' opposition, and, in 1785, succeeded in obtaining the lion's share. Furthermore, he supported experiments which resulted in the perfecting of copper fastenings suitable for securing sheathing sheets to ships. The practice of copper sheathing, enabling ships to sail faster and to spend much less time in refitting, had first been adopted in the 1760s, but had spread only slowly, and had been nearly abandoned by the British Admiralty because of the way in which ships were endangered by the galvanic action between the copper and the iron with which it was secured. Once the new process was in operation the navies and shipowners of Europe were clamouring for Williams's bolts and nails, very often taking his sheathing as well.

The year 1785 was a remarkable one for the Anglesey Mines. Williams took over the management of the mines of Bayly and his successors, and their lease to Roe & Co. was not renewed. To

---

[1] See H. Hamilton, *The English Brass and Copper Industries to 1800* (1926) esp. Chapters VI and VII ; Harris, *op. cit.* esp. Chapter V., " The Growth of the Anglesey Power " ; and A. H. Dodd, *The Industrial Revolution in North Wales* (2nd ed., Cardiff, 1951), 152 *seq.* ; G. C. Allen, " An Eighteenth Century Combination in the Copper Mining Industry " *Econ. Jour.*, **33** (1923).

exploit these ores he formed a new Company, the Mona Mine Co.
As in the instance of the Parys Co. smelting was undertaken, but in
this case a subsidiary company, the Stanley Smelting Company,
was set up for the purpose.   Works at Middle Bank, in South
Wales, were taken over, but the main plant was the Stanley Works
near St. Helens, which were purchased from the Warrington Company.   Williams also bought the Flintshire works of the Warrington Company, founding the Greenfield Copper and Brass Company, subsidiary to the Mona and Stanley concerns.   This firm
manufactured the refined metal from the smelting houses, principally into naval supplies.

In the same year the Cornish adventurers revolted against the
tyranny of the South Wales and Bristol smelters and set up their
own ore-marketing cartel, which was drawn up under cover of a
general agreement with Williams for the sharing of the national
market.   The Cornish Metal Company agreed to allow Williams
the monoply of the Liverpool market, and to share with him those
of London and Birmingham, reserving only that of Bristol to
themselves.   The two mining companies of Parys Mountain were
allowed to raise one-third of the agreed output of the two mining
centres, a proportion which was later increased to one-half.

Even so, the Cornish Metal Company found it difficult to
remain solvent ; while having agreed to take all ores offered to it,
it was unable to regulate the rate of Cornish ore production to
the level of its sales of fine copper.   By 1787 it had huge unsold
stocks, and was facing bankruptcy.   After much debate and
negotiation it was decided to hand over the marketing and the
large unsold stocks to Williams, who from this time was in control of almost the whole British copper output.

Five years later, however, circumstances had ceased to favour
Williams, and he was forced to relinquish the control of Cornish
ores.   Chief among the new factors which had forced his hand
were a decline in the Anglesey output and an increased demand
for copper.   Prices rose, and the fear of over-production in Cornwall diminished.   Though Williams never again recovered his
supreme power, the Anglesey Mines continued prosperous for
some years.   In 1802, the year of his death, Williams was engaged
upon a considerable reorganization of his works and companies,
a change which reflected the greater decline of the Parys Mine
of the Rev. Edward Hughes as compared with the Mona Mine of
Bayly's successor, the Earl of Uxbridge.   The high wartime price
of copper, founded largely on the naval demand, kept the concerns
going for some years, but from 1809 the old Williams organization
was gradually wound up, or regrouped.   The Vivians of Swansea
contracted for the Mona Mine ores, while the new firm of Williams
and Grenfell took over certain Welsh works and the Liverpool
warehouse, the Lancashire works being sold up.

For the times the size and capital of the Williams organization were altogether exceptional. As late as 1799 the copper concerns in which Williams was involved had a total capital of £800,000, about half the national capital invested in the trade, while he controlled one-fifth of British smelting, consuming 750 chaldrons of coal a day in his works. In addition to the companies mentioned, Williams also owned copper works at Wraysbury and Marlow in Buckinghamshire which were outside the Anglesey Mines organisation, and was with Edward Hughes the founder of the Chester and North Wales Bank. For about seven years the Angelsey Mines also operated a large sulphuric acid works near Liverpool. The recital of the firms under his control is alone sufficient to indicate that Williams was one of the major figures of the industrial revolution.

How did the St. Helens works fit into this remarkable industrial pattern ? The function of the Ravenhead works in relation to the Parys Company was almost identical with that of the Stanley works in relation to the Mona Company. Both existed to smelt the ores of their respective mines, and then despatch the refined copper in cake, shot, rose, or any other required form, either direct to the Liverpool warehouse for sale or to the manufacturing mills which each company owned on the Holywell stream in Flintshire. Minor differences apart—a little nailmaking and brass manufacture at Ravenhead and some japanning at Stanley—the two St. Helens works fulfilled similar purposes.

Descriptions of the factories are few, but a report on Ravenhead drawn up in 1784 was made by a party of men well qualified to assess its importance. In that year a party of French experts on armaments came over to make an inspection of British munitions industries, with a view to submitting a report to their Government. The visit followed close upon Williams's success in making copper sheathing for ships both practicable and safe, and his smelting and manufacturing organization was a principal object of their tour. Ravenhead they described as a " fameuse fonderie de cuivre," and gave a detailed account of the way in which smelting was carried on. At that time the works were receiving 12,000 tons of ore a year, producing on an average 11 per cent. of copper. Though the measure was smaller than that of the ton now used, it is clear that the Ravenhead works had an annual output of over 1,000 modern tons of fine copper, which was probably at least a sixth of the total national production. The Frenchmen thought that the profit of the works, before deducting labour costs and the interest on capital, would be 700,000 livres a year, or over £29,000.[1] Apart from the French account of 1784, only two other descriptions of the works are known. In 1795 Aikin recorded that the Ravenhead and Stanley

[1] Archives Nationales, Paris, T 591/4 et 5. De Givry Papers. We are indebted to Dr. W. H. Chaloner for permission to use his transcript of these documents.

works together smelted 20,000 tons of ore yearly, and that the Ravenhead works made 30 tons of small copper bars every week, which were exported to China, presumably as part of the Anglesey Mines' contract with the East India Company. Another writer about the same time reported that the Ravenhead works consumed 700 tons of coal per week, and went on to state that despite the very harmful effect of the smoke of the works on the surrounding country, the health of the workers was remarkably good.[1] Little as these accounts tell us, they do show that a decade after the visit of the De Givry party the works were still very flourishing, and that the output of copper and the consumption of coal had increased.

From scattered items in the accounts of Michael Hughes, the chief Lancashire agent, and from other local sources, it is possible to add some details about the works and the workers. Ravenhead possessed several subsidiary departments, manufactured brass, and included a brass foundry and a nailmaking department. This works is known to have provided with its material an independent brass foundry which had a short life in the neighbourhood. Some at least of the copper nailmaking was subcontracted, for Michael Hughes mentioned a local woman nailmaker as obtaining an undue profit.[2] No doubt it was the existence of a local iron nailmaking industry which induced the Parys Co. to separate the nail manufacture from the rest of their naval copper manufacture, which was carried on at Holywell.

Both the Parys and Stanley Companies built cottages for their workers, for St. Helens as a town was only coming into existence at this period, and the Parys and Stanley Companies were faced with the problem of housing their men. At Ravenhead 16 cottages were built which, either because of the origin of the Company or that of many of its employees, came to be called Welsh Row. Earlier industrialists like Sarah Clayton and John Mackay had similarly had to provide for their workers, and just as Mackay's Parr property included the Havannah inn, so the Parys Co. took over the Navigation Tavern. This was, as its name implied, on the Sankey Canal, and it seems to have been a social gathering-place for the copper workers ; the company provided newspapers and a sick club was organized under the patronage of Michael Hughes. He was not too proud to accept, as a paying member, their allowances for burying his first wife, though at another time he paid off a small deficit for them. The policy of

[1] J. Aikin, *Description of the Country . . . round Manchester* (1795) 313 ; J. Holt, *General View of the Agriculture of the County of Lancaster* (1795) 208n.

[2] Hughes Papers, Accounts, Sherdley Hall Estate Office. For nail-making, see Pocket Book, 30 April, 1796. See also J. R. Harris, " Michael Hughes of Sutton, The Influence of Welsh Copper on Lancashire Business, 1780-1815 " *Trans. L. & C. Hist. Soc.* **101** (1949) 154-6.

the free provision of medical attention which the Mines adopted in Anglesey was extended to the Ravenhead workers (and presumably those at Stanley).

Next door to the Navigation Tavern lived the Ravenhead works manager. Not a great deal is known of either of the men who occupied this position during the years from 1779 to 1815. The first, Joseph Harris, came from Kingswood, probably from the works of the Bristol Company there ; the second, William Jones, from North Wales. Joseph Harris was probably dead before 1789 and he is remembered to-day for his religious rather than his business qualities. He introduced Methodism to the district, and not only Methodism but its founder, who wrote

"I preached at St. Helens, a small but populous town ten or twelve miles from Liverpool, in Joseph Harris's house, who is removed hither to take care of the copper works. Surely God has brought him hither for good. The people seem to be quite ripe for the Gospel."[1]

By 1790, if not before, Harris was succeeded by William Jones, though his sons continued in responsible posts. Jones was in charge until the end in 1814, and spent his remaining years in the district. The numerous entries in the Hughes Papers concerning him are of a routine nature, and it is only worth recording that he is known to have conducted, in partnership with Hughes, a lime-burning business. The importance of the post of " agent " or manager at either of the St. Helens copper works was decreased by the fact that Michael Hughes, the general superintendent of all the Anglesey Mines' smelting and manufacturing concerns, lived in the district. He had the chief responsibility for the works, corresponded with the senior partners, kept a check on all bills drawn on the London Copper Office, and paid out cash to the local works' managers for their running expenses.

The reasons for establishing copper smelting works in the St. Helens district were the presence of coal, and the accessibility of that coal by means of the Sankey Canal. In the 1770s, when the agreements for the coal used in the Stanley and Ravenhead works were originally made, the proprietors of the local mines passed through several years of great depression, some were ruined, and John Mackay, the owner of Ravenhead, was still heavily burdened with debt at the time of his death in 1783. It was perhaps natural, that, as the prosperity of the industry was restored, the coal proprietors should try to avoid the full force of contracts entered into in a difficult period.

In 1787, only four years after the death of John Mackay, the Parys Mine Co. was in dispute with his trustee, Philip Affleck. In a statement prepared by its solicitor for counsel's opinion, it pointed out that £15,000 had been spent in developing the

[1] John Wesley, *Journal*. Standard ed. of N. Curnock (1915), Re-issue (1938) VI, 348 ; 13 April, 1782.

works on the lands of the late John Mackay. " Their sole inducement to fix upon this spot was Mr. Mackay's coal as shewn and
represented to them before the Agreement being in quantity and
quality quite to their purpose and the price stipulated such as
would justify their preference." However, a poor coal seam had
subsequently been worked in Mackay's mines : " that shewn to
the Lessees called the Main Delph . . . was a good Coal," but
there was an inferior grade, " not properly a coal," containing
sulphur and other metallic substances, " vulgarly called St.
Sebastian." This, after being worked at one period before 1779,
had been abandoned previous to the coming of the Parys Co. but
was now being mined again. After Mackay's death his representatives, to gain greater profit, had started to send the inferior coal
to the copper works. This was a great nuisance to the smelters:
" it retards the Process of Smelting the Copper and injures
both the Metal and the Furnaces, greater quantities of that than
the other are also necessary for any sort of work." It was not that
Mackay's trustees had not got enough good coal to supply the
Company, but that they preferred sending the better article
elsewhere so as " to keep the Country and Sea Custom which
bring in a good deal of ready Money and they supply those
Customers with the good Coal because they will not take the
bad. . . ." The Agent of the Company (presumably Michael
Hughes) had made repeated representations, but over the last
three years 16,297 tons of coal from the poorer seam had been
delivered to the works. " The Lessees have frequently suffered
Losses by being obliged to put out several of the Furnaces for a
time for want of Coals of any Sort and such wants happened thro'
preference given to other Customers."[1]

The dispute was amicably settled by an agreement of 29
August, 1787, by which Michael Hughes (on behalf of the Parys
Company) and Philip Affleck (on behalf of the heirs of John
Mackay) adjusted the various matters at issue. To expedite the
delivery of the coals the Parys Co. was to build a wooden bridge
over the Sankey Canal and Affleck was to advance £40 towards
its cost. Until the bridge was finished three-quarters of the coal
was to be from the better seam, one-quarter from the poorer ;
afterwards five-sixths of the coal was to be Main Delph coals.
Any of the poorer seam supplied must always be screened of the
" Bass and Kennel intermixed therewith." The ability of the
mine to supply a proportion of five-sixths of the better coal was
only guaranteed for six years; after that a larger amount of the
inferior coal could be taken if the other was not available.[2]

The coal question was again raised towards the end of 1804.

[1] L.R.O. DDGe. 834. " 7 July, 1787, Ravenhead Copper Works
Case Respecting the Coal, &c., for Mr. Leycester's Opinion."

[2] L.R.O. Cross Papers. Memorandum 29 Aug., 1787. In handwriting
of Michael Hughes.

At this time Col. James Fraser, Mackay's son-in-law and successor at Ravenhead, tried to reduce the demands of the smelting works on the colliery by ceasing to supply their employees, the nail foundry and the firebrick kilns at the concessionary rate of the coal contract. The contract actually specified the supplying of coal to the partners, " their Agents Servants and Workmen for the use and purposes of the said Smelting and refining works and Business aforesaid," so that Fraser had some justification for his view. Again there was a resort to counsel's opinion, but the outcome is not known, though Fraser certainly continued to supply coals to the Parys Co.[1]

Since the Stanley works were provided with a dam and water-wheel before they were taken over by the Stanley Co., the problem of power there was solved. A water-mill was not feasible at Ravenhead, and Williams was thus interested in obtaining a steam engine very soon after rotative motion became an established fact. He wrote to Boulton in an undated letter, probably of 1783-4, " The Bearer is one of our Agents in Lancashire where we must have a small Engine for a Hammer Mill, etc. . . . Be so good as to let this man see the Modell of Your new Invention and help to him a little on ye Subject."[2] In July, 1785, Williams was still pursuing the topic. " Mr. Willms wants an 18 Inch single Engine at Ravenhead where Coals are of very little Value. I told him such an Eng^n would come to £30 a Year but as he wanted it only for jobs and in order to encourage a beginning he should only pay £20 he said they should not work it half the day and therefore would give us £10 a year or £100. I reply'd that I had not the least objection to making him a present of our Claim, but as a bargain I could not go lower. He is not a man to be trifled with and I know the best way of managing him."[3]

When at Ravenhead, in the previous May, Williams had written to John Wilkinson on the subject. The engine was wanted for grinding clay and brickbats to make firebricks and a 27-in. cylinder was suggested. " I have also mentioned it to Messrs. Watt and Boulton, without any other satisfaction than a good deal of civil conversation on the subject. I am now resolved to wait no longer, but to have one set up in the best and most expeditious manner possible. I should prefer the patent sort and to pay for it in every way as others do. If I cannot have that without delay, I will have the next best that can be made." Boulton and Watt told Wilkinson, who informed them of the letter, that they knew Williams had two years ago made such an enquiry, addressed through Wilkinson, " but as you very incivilly insisted

[1] Hughes Papers. Michael Hughes to Geo. Elleston (?) Solr. 3 Dec., 1804.
[2] Birmingham Ref. Lib. Boulton and Watt Colln. Letter noted as " Mr. Williams-Birmingham." In Thomas Williams's hand, unsigned, n.d.
[3] Ibid. Boulton to Watt, 26 July, 1785.

that it should be executed in a month or some shorter time than it was possible to execute our part, ... chose [to] defer the order ... If Mr. Williams chuses to have such an engine and will give his order in writing to us ... we shall serve him with pleasure. ...."[1]

There is no record of Boulton and Watt ever having supplied an engine to the copper works, though they furnished the Plate Glass Manufactory, on the same estate of Ravenhead, with engines for polishing glass by steam power. What in fact happened was that Williams ordered and erected one of Wilkinson's illegal " pirate " copies of the Boulton and Watt engine. On discovering the Wilkinson frauds the partners drew up on 1 Jan. 1796, an " Account of Premiums due to Boulton and Watt from engines erected by Mr. W. for the use of other persons." This included an engine set up for " Michael Hughes colliery at Ravenhead copper work between Prescot and Wigan," which was described as winding coals. As the Parys Co. did not possess a colliery, the purpose of the engine would seem mistaken. Some calculations made by Michael Hughes in his pocket book for 1796 prove to be an estimate of Wilkinson's debts to Boulton and Watt for engine premiums, and add a further indication that the copper works were involved in his dishonest engine sales.[2]

Only one statement of the numbers employed has survived for Ravenhead works, and one statement as to wages. In the middle 1790s Holt records that between two and three hundred people worked there,[3] while a solitary agreement between a copper refiner, John Evans, and the Parys Co. shows that he received fifteen shillings a week, a house to live in, and a shilling a week in lieu of coals.[4] He, of course, would be a skilled workman.

Turning to Stanley, a very similar picture emerges. It was a smaller works and was not visited by the De Givry party (it may have been idle at the time of their visit) or Holt, and Aikin gives it only vague mention. An early record notes that " Refiners, Chargemen, Cinder pickers, Masons, Smiths, Labourers" were employed and that at the time when Williams took it over the Stanley Co. was engaged in " Repairing the Works and Erecting Buildings, ... making boxes and casks for packing copper .... making a Pool and removing the Rail Road " and purchasing " a Sloop called the Green Linnet." A nearby alehouse was also

---

[1] *Ibid.* Wilkinson to Boulton and Watt, 14 May, 1785, enclosing Williams (Ravenhead) to Wilkinson of 9 May, 1785.

[2] Hughes Papers. Pocket Book (1796). 28 Feb. (?).

Charges estd & awd. agst J. W.	...		15,120
Omiss[s] allwd and estab.	...	...	6,808
			£8,312
J.W. to pay costs of Investn.		...	600
J.W. to pay in all ...	...	...	£8,912

[3] J Holt, *General View, loc. cit.*

[4] Hughes Papers. Memdm. of Agreement, 23 Oct., 1780.

bought. The Ship inn no doubt performed the same function for Copperhouse Row at Blackbrook as did the Navigation to Welsh Row at Ravenhead. An early mention of expenses includes " Allowance of Ale to Workmen £57 15s. 4d."[1]

Stanley, like Ravenhead, added some working-up of materials to its main task of smelting, and in the first years " making Japan and Japan copper " is recorded. Early in 1788 the factory had 22 tons of Japan copper, 14 tons of shot copper, and 23 tons of swages, plates and bolts on hand, as well as " Manillas " weighing over 17 tons and worth about £1,000. As the Greenfield manufacturing side expanded, these items no doubt fell off ; Michael Hughes's accounts and letters mention only smelting. By 1787 Greenfield was taking Stanley's copper in loads of 30-40 tons, the capacity of the average canal "flat." Over the period August, 1786-March, 1788, £41,846 of copper from Stanley and its South Wales subsidiary, Middle Bank, was sold through Pascoe Grenfell of the firm's London department at Williams's Copper Office. The separate profits for March, 1788-November, 1789 survive : they were £5,320 for Middle Bank, £6,985 for Stanley. We know from the records of Middle Bank works that the Stanley Co. was very methodical in its accounts of salaries, sales and output, these being returned fortnightly on specially printed forms, a refinement by no means common in industrial undertakings at this period.[2]

The managers of the Stanley works were successively Alexander Chorley (at one time relieved by his relation, Fothergill Chorley) and William Morgan. Alexander Chorley is to be identified with the man of that name who was partner in the Ashton nail and hinge firm of Chorley and Leech and was also involved in an unsuccessful iron slitting mill, the Stanley Mill Co., which stood adjacent to the works of the Stanley Smelting Co. This works had been for sale about the time of the arrival of the Anglesey firm, and its partners successively went bankrupt.[3] A descendant of the first Stanley manager wrote of him " my grandfather, Alexander Chorley, who was an ironmaster at Stanley-Bank, near Ashton-in-Maker-field, in Lancashire—had not the gift of keeping or of making money. They (the Chorleys) were people of great mother-wit, racy humour, and generous dispositions, but sanguine and self-willed."[4] The Chorleys, like so many other iron-masters, were Quakers.

Chorley's ill-luck with money seems to have followed him into a colliery venture which he undertook with Michael Hughes : this was one of the latter's few unsuccessful schemes, and closed with a small loss. Relations between the Chorleys and the Stanley Co. did not end on the best of terms. In 1803 Owen

---

[1] U.C.N.W. Bangor. Mona Mine MSS., 2500.

[2] Mona Mine MSS. 3043, 3045, 2504, 3056.

[3] See below, p. 126.

[4] H. F. Chorley, *Memoirs*, ed. Hewlett (1873) I, 5-7.

Williams wrote to Michael Hughes that " I have had a very long letter of complaint from young Chorley on the subject of the house etc. at Stanley, as well as the smallness of salary allowed for his brother's services—I have answered that you had already granted his family such indulgences as were not perhaps strictly accordant with the interests of the proprietors who of course looked to you for an exact administration of their concerns, and altho' yourself a partner you were not the less responsible for the property you had undertaken to manage—I for those reasons declined any interference whatever, being likewise full satisfied that you could not entertain a wish beyond doing what is fair and just in the matter."[1] This complaint by the Chorley family seems to coincide with the death or incapacity of Alexander Chorley and the termination of their connection with Stanley.

Early in 1804 Hughes made enquiries for a new manager for this works, and it was a reflection of the technical predominance which the Swansea district was gaining in the smelting industry that John Hughes and Richard Jenkins there were approached for suitable names. One suggested candidate found little favour with Hughes, not only was he too young, but there was another objection :

" . . . if he is a fine Gentleman and foppish in the bargain, he is out of the question . . . for I never will give my consent to have a *Gentleman* Agent at any Copper Works in which I am concerned. . . . If a man can write a legible hand it is sufficient for his business is not to be in the Office but in the Works. . . ."[2]

His choice eventually fell on William Morgan of the English Copper Co.'s Margam works, recommended as a " very sober active little man. . . . He does not pretend to be a thorough book keeper but he understand[s] arithmetic very well."[3] Morgan was taken on at a salary of £100 a year, with a house, coal, candles, and the keep of a cow. He continued to give satisfaction until the Stanley works was wound up, and he was then sent to smelt for the Revd. Edward Hughes at Amlwch.

In 1805, when the peak of the Stanley Works' prosperity would have long passed, there were at least 32 men employed there. Two calciners earned 1s. 6d. a day, as did the six smelters and the three roasters. The three refinery men received 2s. a day, the charge men 2s., the labourers and the farm hands on the land attached to the works the same. Two furnace builders got 3s. and 1s. 4d.—perhaps they were a master and apprentice—the smith 2s. 4d. and the carpenter 2s. One " Mill Man " was paid 2s. 4d., the other 2s. Of the names given, only three, Owen Price, David Vaughan and Robert Jones, indicate a Welsh origin, the others—

---

[1] *Ibid.* Owen Williams to Michael Hughes, 30 Aug., 1803.

[2] Hughes Papers, Michael Hughes to Rd. Jenkins, 9 April, 1804.

[3] *Ibid.* Rd. Jenkins to Michael Hughes, 3 April, 1804.

Atherton, Edelston, Whittle, Travis, Naylor, etc.—are in the main strongly local.[1]

In charge of both Ravenhead and Stanley and of much greater importance and superior social standing than the works managers was Michael Hughes. For his superintendence of the local works he received a salary of £300 ; £200 from the Parys Co. and £100 from Stanley Co. For some years Hughes lived at Sutton Lodge, a house rented for him by the Parys Co., but he later removed to a new mansion, Sherdley House, which he built at the other side of Sutton township.

Hughes's business abilities meant that he was little troubled by inspections from the senior partners, it was one of Thomas Williams's acknowledged qualities that he was able to pick good subordinates, and, having chosen them, that he allowed them to work without needless interference. Nevertheless Williams visited St. Helens on at least three occasions, in 1785, 1788 and 1800. It is also safe to assume that he came to Ravenhead during the negotiations with Mackay in 1779 and during those for the purchase of the Stanley Works from the Warrington Co., probably in 1785.

Michael Hughes's superintendence of the smelting and manufacturing work of the Anglesey Mines was not confined to the St. Helens district, but embraced in a vague way all the works, including the Swansea and Holywell branches. Distance of course precluded him from exercising any very regular supervision, and middle age added a disinclination to travel. Nevertheless, especially at times of change or the winding-up of concerns, he was called upon to visit South or North Wales works and to report on them. As the only member of the Hughes family possessing both the technical knowledge and the business ability for the purpose, he also acted as a specialist adviser to his eldest brother in negotiations with other partners.

In 1815, because of the declining output of Anglesey ores, differences of opinion among the mine partners, and South Wales competition, the Lancashire smelting works closed, and, until the 1830s, the copper industry was not represented in St. Helens. From 1809 to 1814 Michael Hughes conducted a long rearguard action, endeavouring to persuade his business associates to keep at least the Stanley works in operation, but in the end he was forced to give in.

The connection of the coalfield with the great business organization set up by Thomas Williams was severed. The district, however, was long to be influenced by the events of the Anglesey Mines years ; not only was the growing population strengthened by a flow of immigrants, mainly of Welsh origin, but further proof had been given of the merits of St. Helens as a home of furnace industries, and those merits were not long neglected.

[1] St. H. Ref. Lib., Blackbrook Copper Works Wages List.

CHAPTER VIII

THE GREENALLS AND THE BREWING INDUSTRY,

1762-1812

FOR nearly two centuries now the firm of Greenall has been prominent in the St. Helens brewing trade, and today theirs is the town's only remaining brewery. Though they eventually surpassed all their rivals and achieved a much more than local trade, in their early days they had many competitors in the immediate neighbourhood.

In the eighteenth century any district with a sizeable population was bound to contain several brewers. Indeed most large households brewed for themselves, and down to the end of the century it was customary for sales of gentlemen's houses and effects to include brewing utensils and a room or outbuilding set aside as a brewhouse. Most inns of any size or importance also had the necessary equipment, and brewed their own beer on occasion, if not regularly. But, by 1815, most of the upper and middle classes of the district had ceased to brew at home and had begun to rely on the services of the local brewers. There were economic reasons for this which will be discussed later, but minor ones of taste and convenience must not be disregarded. For home brewing to be satisfactory there had to be an adept at the art in each household. At times when there was no one suitable among the servants, or when the master, unlike Parson Woodforde, was not interested enough to take a hand himself, or the mistress decided it was beneath her dignity, there must have been a temptation to order from the nearest wholesale brewer and be rid of the responsibility. Then there was the business of purchasing malt and hops in the right quantity and condition, and the difficulty that the local water supply may not have been the best for the purpose. Indeed the saving by brewing at home may not always have been great, nor the quality of the product markedly superior. It would seem, too, that the upper classes were beginning to drink mainly wine and tea, and to leave ale to the servants.

Most people under the middle class—below, that is to say, the rank of the prosperous shopkeeper or yeoman—were not able to afford the utensils or the large purchases of materials which were necessary if they were to do their own brewing. Consequently the "lower orders" had resort to the alehouse. Often, also, ale was brought to men as they worked, and not merely to labourers in the fields, but to such workers as coal miners and glass blowers who received part of their wages in this form. In December, 1795,

Midland mine owners advertised for colliers in a Liverpool paper :
" Wages from Two Shillings and Six-pence to Three Shillings and
Six-pence per day, with Two quarts of Ale."

Weighty considerations comparable to those influencing the
wealthy householder induced the innkeeper also to turn to the
wholesale brewer. If he could make sufficient by selling beer, why
have the trouble—and the risk—of brewing it ? If the quality
caused unfavourable comment from his customers, he could then
always shift the blame, or order a barrel from another brewer and
invite his "regulars" to sample it; a new brewer would very likely
send the first barrel cheap or even free.

In addition to the Greenalls, the Fosters, the Crosses, the
Greenoughs, the Glovers and the Hills were engaged in local
beer-brewing in the last half of the eighteenth century and
we are fortunate enough to know a little about all of them.
While the details we possess are fragmentary, chiefly consisting of
wills and a few newspaper advertisements, they reveal some
interesting common factors. All these brewers seem to have been
men in a fairly prosperous way of business, and several, for the
times, were almost wealthy. None of them gave any signs of
wishing to abandon the business, and three of them, Joseph
Greenough, William Hill and James Cross, were very insistent
that their successors should carry on the trade after their deaths,
and took what legal steps they could to ensure that they did
so. With the exception of the Crosses, all those mentioned, in
addition to brewing, either kept an inn themselves, or owned inns.
There is, too, an indication that brewers tended to dabble in more
than one business. In all these things we may see parallels in the
firm of Greenall, the trout among the minnows.[1]

Thomas Greenall, the founder of the firm, was the son of
Richard Greenhalgh of Parr, the family having moved from
Ashton to Parr before 1684. He was born in 1733, and it was
through his marriage to a certain Mary Turton that he became
acquainted with the industry which was to bring him success.
His father-in-law owned a brewery in Parr, and on his death
the widow gave Greenall the management of the business. At
the age of 29, in 1762, he transferred operations to a site
between St. Helens Chapel and Hardshaw Hall, founding the
Hall Street Brewery which still flourishes.[2] It is not until 1786

---

[1] For detailed references and quotations from several of the wills see
J. R. Harris, *The Economic and Social History of St. Helens in the Latter
Half of the Eighteenth Century*, M.A. Thesis, Manchester University
(1950), Chapter III.

[2] Greenall took over the management of Mrs. Turton's brewery in 1754
when he was twenty-one. This brewery was purchased subsequently to
1780 by Joseph Greenough of Parr, another son-in-law of Mrs. Turton,
who had been described as a brewer as early as 1775. From him it passed
jointly to his son, Isaac, and his son-in-law, James Eckersley.

that we are able to obtain any very clear account of the affairs of
the brewery, but from that date letter-books are extant which
carry the story down to 1817.

The most important feature of these records is the connection
between brewing and the grain market ; there naturally appears
to have been a close correspondence between the periods of crisis
and high prices for the brewery and the years which, according to
local or national evidence, were remarkable for the high price of
corn. An odd entry which has survived for 1782 points to an
acute shortage in the November of that year.

> " Markets are unsettled here and very high. Wheat is selling
> for 9s 8d, Barley 5/6 to 6/- p. mea. [measure]. I don't know
> how the poor people will live we have purchased about 1400
> mea. Barley mostly at 5/- so that we have done well . . .
> > For Father
> > > Your mo. hble. Servt.
> > > > Edwd. Greenall."[1]

The spring of 1786, when the letter-books open, shows the
opposite state of affairs. Writing to a barley factor on the 20th of
March, Thomas Greenall said " The Liverpool markets still
keep lower, which makes me of opinion the Warrington People
will not buy much from you."[2] The brewer had two possible
sources for his barley. Sometimes he bought from the home
grower or factor, sometimes from the importer (generally the
Baltic importer) at Liverpool. At the end of the same year, and
writing to the same dealer, Greenall advised him :

> " As your Prices of Barley at present is too high for us
> thought it best to write to you Immediately not to buy any
> more as high as 2s. 6d.—if you can pick up a few loads of the
> very best (*Superfine it must be*) and not to exceed 3s 4d p. Mea.
> could wish you to do so ; if any higher it will not suit us, as we
> can buy from Liverpool at 3s 7d p. for the very best of Barley,
> w'ch is cheaper than yours . . ."[3]

By the middle of December not merely the Liverpool market,
but the local ones of the Lancashire countryside were lower than
the factor was able to quote.[4]

---

[1] Greenall Whitley & Co. Ltd., St. Helens. Letter-books. For purposes
of comparison see references to poor harvests and high-prices in T. S.
Ashton and J. Sykes, *The Coal Industry of the Eighteenth Century*
(Manchester, 1929), Chapter VIII, " Corn Riots," and in D. G. Barnes,
History of the English Corn Laws, 1660-1846 (1930) *passim*.

[2] Letter-books. Thomas Greenall to E. Sutton, 20 March, 1786.

[3] *Ibid*. Greenall to Sutton, 18 Nov., 1786. The economic connection
between Liverpool's salt trade to the Baltic and its imports of Baltic grain
is to be noted.

[4] *Ibid*. Greenall to Sutton, 14 Dec., 1786

Writing to him again about a year later Greenall envisaged a rise, but not a disastrous one, in corn prices. In the eighteenth century the business letter had not yet become entirely impersonal, and it was only after thanking Mr. Sutton for the present of a hare, and remarking on his own late ill-health that Greenall declared his willingness to buy again when the price dropped to 3s. or 3s. 3d. the measure of barley :

"The Ports at L'pool are Shutt against Irish and Foreign Barley which I believe will cause our Marketts to rise : Barley at least 6d. There was some few cargoes of Irish Barley arrived at L'pool before the Ports was shut and sold from 2/8 to 3/-, therefore our Marketts are rather Unsettled, but we expect the best Barley will not sell higher than 3/9. This County or our Neighbouring Farmers sells at 3/8 at present."[1]

At the same season of the next year Lancashire prices were 3s. 4d. and 3s. 6d., and the dealer was not to buy except the best and choicest at 3s. 1d. or 3s. 2d. : at that price he might ship an odd boat load by canal.[2] The early winter thus appears to have been the time when Greenalls were in negotiation with their factors at a distance, as can be understood if we realise that the first step after the harvest, providing the local crop of barley was good, would be to secure what could be obtained from nearby farmers and the adjacent markets before buying from the more distant barley-growing areas and paying the extra cost of carriage.

At the end of 1793 Thomas Greenall was much in need of barley and prepared to pay for 2,000 bushels at the rate of 7s. 1d. for 34½ qts. and scorage ;[3] about this time he sent several remittances to the Liverpool grain dealers Corrie, Gladstone & Co., and Booth & Co.

The year 1795, as we may learn from many sources, was a bad one for grain prices. In May Greenall provided the Windle Overseers of the Poor with an introduction to a grain dealer :

"The Bearer of this is our Officer for the Township of Windle and at present superintends a Subscription for the relief of the poor inhabitants of the said township by selling them Flour etc. at a reduced price. He is now in want of a little Barley for that purpose, as such I recommend him to you. . . . If you have none I will thank you to inform him where he can meet with some as he is a Stranger to the Business."[4]

In the December of that year Greenall wrote to Phillips and Yarranton of Worcester urging them to buy barley and malt on

[1] *Ibid.* Greenall to Sutton, 5 Nov., 1787.
[2] *Ibid.* Greenall to Sutton, 20 Nov., 1788.
[3] *Ibid.* Greenall to John Thomas, 11 Dec., 1793.
[4] *Ibid.* Greenall to Wright and Davies, 26 May, 1795.

his behalf,[1] and in the following month a customer was pressed for prompt payment because of the heavy money outlay required to purchase grain : " we have lately made some large contracts for corn, which is to be paid for immediately on its arrival at Liverpool therefore will be much obliged to you for a remittance."[2]

This period of acute scarcity strengthened the tendency to purchase barley in increasingly large shipments, and over the period 1794-6 there are about a dozen payments of over £100 for single orders of barley or malt. From 1796, however, the market does not seem to have been very high for about two years, and in the December of 1798 Greenall was hoping that the not excessive prices would fall further in the spring.[3]

The harvest of 1799, however, was disastrous, and prices were extremely high early in the following year. In the February of 1800 Greenall told a customer that malt was then selling at Liverpool at 14s. 6d. and 15s. per Liverpool measure of 36 quarts " and scarcely any to be bought even at any price : Barley at 7/- per measure and one half of it will not make *any Malt* . . ."[4]

That year Thomas Greenall sent an order for malt to Hornby Comber & Co. of Liverpool, but only three days later his son Peter, who was by this time assisting him in the office, wrote to them asking for time in which to pay.

" We have been expending very heavy sums of money in Malt etc. and are working without any profit at all it makes us very poor, therefore I must beg it as a favour that you will give us the usual credit with the purchase and we will endeavour to make you amends in the next . . ."[5]

The dire need of cash caused Greenall to be as stern to his debtors as he was suppliant to his creditors. To one he requested : " you will make us a handsome payment, as the conducting of our business requires so large a Capital at present that we cannot possibly lie out of so much Money in one Hand."[6] The harvest of 1800 did not improve the situation, and even as the autumn advanced Hornby Comber & Co. were asked to give Greenalls the preference if more shipments of foreign barley arrived.[7] They apparently obliged : in the November 2,000 bushels were taken from them, while in the January of 1801 Thomas Booth & Co. of

[1] *Ibid*. Greenall to Yarranton, 28 Dec., 1795.
[2] *Ibid*. Greenall to Wardle and Tillards, 1 Jan., 1796.
[3] *Ibid*. Greenall to Thomas Coward, 12 Dec., 1798.
[4] *Ibid*. Greenall to Thomas Makin, Bolton, 2 Feb., 1800.
[5] *Ibid*. Peter Greenall to Hornby, Comber & Co., 4 Oct., 1800.
[6] *Ibid*. Thomas Greenall to Mrs. Mary Lea, 17 July, 1800.
[7] *Ibid*. Greenall to Hornby, Comber & Co., 4 Oct., 1800.

Liverpool forwarded 6,000 bushels. Two separate payments of over £1,000 were made for grain during this critical period. By the end of 1801 Greenalls were going so far as to commission entire shiploads of Scottish barley on their own behalf.[1]

Early in 1802, however, their stocks were improving, and these unusual measures were dropped. The harvest of that year seems to have been fairly good, and in its last months Greenalls were becoming adamant as to price and difficult to please as to quality. From this time until 1812 the letter-books of the brewery give little of interest on the grain situation, and it is to be presumed that it was not particularly difficult. The spring of 1812 was described as being a time of a " stagnated state of trade,"[2] and in April of that year prices were considered cheap. After the harvest increases in price—at least that was the cause on which they laid the blame—made Greenalls raise further the already high cost of their beer.

The last mention of grain prices in the letter books is after the harvest of 1816, when the prospect indicated a difficult year, and a lean one for the poor.

" When I had last the pleasure of writing to you [I] informed you of my intentions of taking a journey to London thro' Suffolk etc. to purchase Old Malts, I returned from the journey a few days ago, on the whole the purchases I made will do well . . . there is a gloomy appearance of Trade and what the poor are to do for Bread God only knows, the higher powers are taking pains to be ready to stop riotting etc., but surely they will soon think of some plan to fill their empty Bellies . . ."[3]

Just as it was essential for the brewer to be well-informed in his purchases of barley and malt, it was similarly important for him to watch the prices and the state of the harvest in the case of hops. The Worcester market was the principal one for Greenalls, though Kent hops were often purchased direct from the gardens or through dealers. In the eighties, in particular, the firm had a strong connection with the house of Phillips and Yarranton at Worcester.

Hop dealers were by this time well organized in their marketing arrangements, and perhaps had some sort of price agreement. In August, 1779, they had announced their intention of establishing a weekly conference at Stourport (upon the Staffordshire and Worcestershire Canal) since " a very numerous and most respectable body of hop planters, residing within the counties of Worcester and Hereford " had decided it was the most suitable

---

[1] *Ibid.* Greenall to Samuel Smith, 27 Nov., 1801.

[2] *Ibid.* E., W. & P. Greenall to John Taylor, 14 March, 1812.

[3] *Ibid.* E. Greenall (?) to J. Pagden, 7 Nov., 1816.

H

place. At such meetings, it was declared, " proper encouragement will be given by the planters to the dealers in and buyers of
hops."[1]

The first mention of prices is in the August of 1790, when
Greenall bought hops at 70s. the pocket.[2] If Phillips and
Yarranton found good yearling hops cheap, they were invited to
buy ten or fifteen pockets for Greenalls and forward them by
wagon from London.[3] The carriage from London would indicate
Kent rather than Worcester hops, and indeed a letter in September
ordered both.[4]

At the end of 1790 the Hardshaw brewery was very short of
hops, and Greenall sent out hurried orders to two dealers.[5] He
was always suspicious when the market opened higher than he
expected, and in the case of the harvest of 1791 his son declared
the firm was " Surprised to observe your Market opens with such
high prices, my Father wishes you therefore to defer buying any
(or not more than 10 Pkts. before Chester Fair) . . ."[6]

The summer of 1793 found both the principals of the firm of
Phillips and Yarranton firm in the belief that hop prices were
going to be high, as crops were unfavourable. " . . . if it is
your real opinion that Hops are likely to be higher I wish you
to send me 20 Pkts. of *clean stout* middling sort of Hops such as
will keep. I am not in present want of them but if you think
there is no probability of their being lower the sooner you send 'em
the better."[7]

Enquiries as to the state of the market next year again produced
a discouraging reply " . . . I am sorry to understand that Hops
have took some little advance in your Market but I still trust that
after the Spirit of Speculation is abated there will still be a
sufficiency of Hops to supply the Country with and we shall have
them at a reasonable price. . . ."[8] This " Spirit " must have
worked very effectively, however, for below a list of hop duties
paid throughout the kingdom, Thomas Greenall noted : " The
above is more duty than ever was known to be paid before in the
memory of any Man."[9]

[1] *Gore's Gen. Ad.*, 20 Aug., 1779.

[2] Through Mr. Lyon of the Wilderspool, Warrington, Brewery (Orrett,
Lyon & Greenall), in which Greenalls were interested. Edward Greenall
had a half interest with Thomas Lyon in a small Liverpool brewery.

[3] Thomas Greenall to Phillips and Yarranton, 20 Aug., 1790.

[4] *Ibid.* Greenall to Phillips and Yarranton (?), 11 Sept., 1790.

[5] Greenall to Phillips and Yarranton, 20 Dec., 1790 ; Greenall to
Hooper, Duncan & Co., 13 Jan., 1791.

[6] *Ibid.* Edward Greenall to Phillips and Yarranton, 21 Sept., 1791.

[7] *Ibid.*, P. Greenall to Phillips and Yarranton, 25 July, 1793.

[8] *Ibid.*, Thomas Greenall to Yarranton, 8 Nov., 1794.

[9] *Ibid.*, Undated entry of March or April, 1795.

Chester Fair appears to have been a great meeting place for dealers in grains and hops ; after hearing a favourable report from Yarranton on the prospects of the 1795 hop harvest the Greenalls invited him to extend his journey to St. Helens when he came to the Fair. But the pleasant predictions were not borne out by the event. By September Greenall's son was distressed to hear of the poor state of Phillips and Yarranton's own plantation, " and at the same time to observe Mr. Phillips supineness in not buying sooner, he certainly must not have had his eyes open or he cou'd not have been guilty of so gross an omission."[1]   Thomas Greenall, according to his son, had passed over favourable offers of hops in order not to let down an old friend, whose discretion and judgment he relied on, and the quality eventually supplied by the firm received unflattering comment.[2] The harvest of 1796 was also poor.

On the 20 January, 1797, Greenalls were sorry to hear of a new advance in prices, but by the 17 April they told Phillips and Yarranton : " we are now pretty well stocked with Hops, and trade very dull, " so that it would be two months before they required more. Again in 1798 Phillips and Yarranton's own harvest was poor, but Greenalls had bought good hops cheap in Liverpool.[3] It was well they did, for, as the year drew to a close, prices increased. To a firm which sent short weight later in 1798 Greenall pointed out that " the price of Hops is now very considerable." [4] By the 3 November the brewer had decided that his stocks were sufficient, but swiftly changed his mind four days later when he asked Weston & Co. to buy both for the St. Helens and Wilderspool concerns as hops seemed likelier to rise than fall.[5]

Hops did not figure largely in the letter-books between 1798 and 1802, when there were complaints to various firms about the disappearance of pockets of hops in transit. The autumn of 1802 saw a sharp rise in price, but in ordering from John Brockholding Greenall's son, Peter, expressed the opinion that it was not the harvest which was at fault. " I feel much surprised at the rapid advance that has taken place but am well persuaded that it is more owing to the *Speculations in the Trade* than any great Demand."[6] The ending of the Peace of Amiens, thought Peter Greenall, in writing to Brockholding a few months later, would diminish demand,

---

[1] *Ibid.*, P. Greenall to Phillips and Yarranton, 17 Sept., 1795.

[2] *Ibid.*, Greenall to Yarranton, 28 Sept., 1795.

[3] *Ibid.*, Greenall to Phillips and Yarranton, 1 Aug., 1798.

[4] *Ibid.*, Greenall to Stephenson, Scholey & Co., 12 Sept., 1798.

[5] *Ibid.*, Greenall to Phillips and Yarranton, 3 Nov., 1798 ; to Weston & Son, 7 Nov., 1798.

[6] *Ibid.*, P. Greenall to John Brockholding, 27 April, 1802.

presumably for both hops and beer. Of an existing order to purchase, it was decided : " perhaps it may be as well not to be in a hurry in doing of it as in case we go to War again (which I am sorry to say at present we have every appearance of) it will most certainly reduce the consumption and in my opinion they will still be lower."[1]

Next year Thomas Greenall was looking forward with pleasure to the likely effects of good weather on those who would like to raise prices, " I think this fine weather will begin to alarm the Speculators and induce them to sell—on any alteration shall be glad to be advised."[2]

One of the most interesting features of the brewery letter-books between 1786 and 1817 is that they give an excellent idea of the sort of difficulty the business man of the late eighteenth century had to contend with if he was to make headway. The entrepreneur of the period had to impose a new degree of reliability and punctuality on others if he was to increase the efficiency or scale of operations of his own firm. For instance, standards of weight and measure, in grain as in coal, were very varied, and even without deliberate deceit were liable to cause trouble between buyer and seller. This provided excuse for bad packing and poor weight. The carriage of goods was precarious, and sacks or barrels were always liable to be lost in transit. Quality, like quantity, was not sufficiently regarded ; here again it was necessary to create one's own standards and impose them on those with whom one dealt. The letters of the Greenall brewery tended to be complaining and querulous but the process was a necessary one—it might almost be said that the Greenalls nagged their way to success.

In 1786 Thomas Greenall wrote to a grain dealer saying that on reweighing the barley received " agreeable to our usual Custom ", he had found it to be " much deficient in Quantity— Pray Sir, was all the sacks full when you shipp'd them—when we received them there was one (in particular) only a part full perhaps about 2½ of your Measures in it and several other sacks that was not full by ¾ of a Measure or More According to what we in general received from you last Year."[3]

One of the most strongly worded of Greenall's letters on bad measure was written in the January of 1796 :

" . . . We wrote to you on the 20th Inst. acknowledging the receipt of 60 Meas. of Malt but had not then measd. any of it not knowing the quantity charg'd but understand by your letter to Wpool [Wilderspool] it is called 300 Measures which is

[1] *Ibid.*, P. Greenall to John Brockholding, 10 March, 1803.
[2] *Ibid.*, Greenall to Robert Felton, 5 May, 1804.
[3] *Ibid.*, Thomas Greenall to E. Sutton, 6 May, 1786.

shameful indeed as it only measured 280 by a standard Winct. [Winchester] Measure, making just 20 Measures short at the lawful standard of England and 'tis short of 30 Qts to the measure, it is very painful to me to make complaint but my experience in trade has taught me better than to pay for one fifteenth more than I really receive, surely the World is not turn'd upside down, if prices are high I ought to have justice done me, I mean the measure should be what it is called, I make no doubt the Man sold it for Wincr. measure and such I mean to have if either Law or equity will relieve me, there is no one more willing to pay for what I call for than I am, honestly dealt with, but this is such treatment I never met with. . . . "[1]

Some further excerpts from correspondence on measure and quality are perhaps worth quoting.

" . . . the Malt you have sent is, has [sic] my Son justly observed shamefully bad, and I was very certain had a great deal of Old Malt mixed with it which I am very much surprised you could think of sending as it is of that [?] pernicious quality that whenever it is Brew'd we cannot tell where the bad effects may end, I would much rather have paid you for it, and you not to have sent it at all than have had such vile stuff mixed in it as it is by no means safe to Brew except in the very depth of Winter, and as the Spring is now advancing, the Weather may be very hot before it can be used.

" With regard to the Measure, I do not say but you may have put it up by a fair Winchester Bushel . . . [but the measure was 24¾ Bushels short] . . . therefore I cannot think of paying for any more than I have received. It was measured by two of our men who chalked down every Bushel and our own Clerk stood by all the time and kept Tally with them, they are all men that I can rely upon, and if required will make Oath that it measured *no more*—Respecting the price of the Malt, if you had sent me a fair honest Article, and such as myself or any other Judge cou'd have approved, tho' the Market should have been 5/- per Bushel lower in price you would never have had a complaint as that is a Stigma I was never before Charg'd with, and I defy the man that can say, I was ever guilty of finding fault with any Article without having a sufficient cause . . . it is extremely unpleasant to me to have any fault to find when I wish allways [sic] to pay my money with cheerfulness."[2]

To a firm who had imposed on them in the price of hops the Brewery wrote, " we have no more to add, but request Mr.

<hr />

[1] *Ibid.*, Greenall to Thomas Booth & Co., 27 April, 1790.
[2] *Ibid.*, Greenall to Mr. Wagstaffe, 22 March, 1802.

Atkinson will not give himself the Trouble of calling either at the house of Orrett Lyon and Greenall or at this place in future . . ."[1]

Having examined the difficulties and trials which beset Greenalls in trying to buy good barley and hops at reasonable prices we must now turn to the problems they faced in disposing of their beer.

In 1786 Greenalls were brewing three sorts of ale, all in barrels of 36 gallons, one at 32s. per barrel, another at 44s. and a strong beer at 48s. Large households where there would be many servants were early customers ; for instance those of Mrs. Williams at Roby Hall, and of John Blackburne at Hale. Already in 1786, Thomas Greenall's customers ranged from Liverpool to Bolton ; it appears to have been his aim to get all the inns on the road between those towns to sell his beer. Many Anglesey public houses are Greenall's customers today ; this connection dates back to the old copper trade days. As early as 1786 the recommendation of Michael Hughes, manager of the Ravenhead Copper Works, had found Greenalls an influential customer in one of his Anglesey relatives. A hogshead of strong beer was sent to Sir Hugh Williams, Bart., of " Ffryars near Beaumaris Anglesea Wales " ; the shipper being asked to forward it " by the first Sloop bound for the Port of Beaumaris."[2]

The practice of both brewer and publican could at times be a little sharp, as can be seen from the following letter :

" We have took the liberty of sending you 2 half Barrels of a second sort of Beer (it is sold at Bolton at 6d pr. Qt.) we have charg'd it you only 44/- per Barrel and wish you to make trial of it, it is good Beer but *rathere* [sic] slenderer than our Strong Beer, however if it will not sell by itself, it will mix very well with the strong Beer ; and make your profit more advantageous —Shou'd it [the second sort of beer] meet your approbation we should be glad to send you a Load, as it would in some measure save your strong Beer ; and we are rathere scarce of that *Article*, at this *Season* of the year than any other."[3]

We have seen that the French wars accentuated the tendency towards rising grain prices. In 1796 Greenalls said that they could not fill some of Mr. John Blackburne's large casks with " slender " ale as it would not keep in them, while they could not

[1] *Ibid.*, Greenall to Scholey & Co., 21 May, 1802. Another example of plain language occurs in a letter to the firm of Ward & Holland, expressing surprise at receiving bad malt " little thinking that the respectability of W. & Holland [could] be tempted to do a dirty action . . . it would have been much better to have put it in the Coal Pit . . . it is impossible to make ale that is fit to be seen from such vile stuff."

[2] *Ibid.*, Thomas Greenall to Sir Hugh William[s], 13 Dec., 1786.

[3] *Ibid.*, Greenall to John Hill, n.d. 1787.

on the other hand brew it any stronger because of the high price of malt.[1] The quality of the beer declined, and Greenalls on several occasions had the candour to admit this to their customers. Thomas Greenall in one letter cautioned an innkeeper against making an unscrupulous profit from this wartime ale :

" . . . the time will very shortly be on that neither me nor any other Person can serve you with Ale at these prices ; we have always done our best to serve you with a good article, and to keep your house in good credit but for you to go and sell such poor cold starv'd stuff (as we are necessitated to brew our Common Ale) at 6d. p. Quart I think neither you nor me will gain any Credit and therefore if you think you can be better served by any other Person you are quite Welcome to change . . . "[2]

In 1800 Thomas Greenall explained to Nicholas Ashton of Woolton Hall that beer " . . . is now brewed so small it will not keep long . . . in consequence of the extreme high price of Malt and Hops we cannot afford to sell this kind of Beer at less than 52/- [a] Barrel."[3] Shortly afterwards he told a Bolton customer ;

" Sir, Malt is now selling in L'pool at 14/6 and 15/- p. measre of 36 Qts. and scarcely any to be bought even at any price ; Barley at 7/- pr. Measre and one half of it will not make *any Malt* under these circumstances and Hops selling at the enormous price of 3/- pr. lb. we are now necessitated to give up Brewg any Comⁿ Ale for the present, and we hope all our customers will be convinced how perfectly impossible it is for us to Brew our Ale *Honestly* and sell at so low a price.

N.B.—The above letter was sent to all our Customers at Bolton."[4]

The Bolton innkeepers appear to have made some reply, to which Greenalls sent the following rejoinder :

" Gentn. In answer to your message by Thomas Sutton—I am sorry it is Not possible for me without being a very great loser, to send you Ale at 42/- p. Barrel as every Barrel I brew for my Bolton Customers cost [sic] me that sum before it is mov'd out of the Brewhouse, and if I charge it at 45/- per Barrel it does no more than merely pay me for the Carting and does not leave me any profit at all ; I shall be glad to do anything in reason to serve you, but I hope there is not any one of you that wishes me to Cart my Ale 20 miles and sell it at a less price than the materials absolutely cost at home.—In a general calamity

[1] *Ibid.*, Greenall to John Blackburne, 7 June, 1796.
[2] *Ibid.*, Greenall to Wm. Jones, 14 Jan., 1800.
[3] *Ibid.*, Greenall to Nichs. Ashton, 29 Jan., 1800.
[4] *Ibid.*, Greenall to John Makin, 3 Feb., 1800.

like this we should all bear a little with each other but really I cannot think of sending it to lose *all* when I know it leaves you so good a profit even at this price ; and here [*sic*] is not one Customer in this Country but what pays me 48/- for Beer very little better than what we charge you at 45/-. If I could afford it at less I should be very willing to do it, but I am very certain that it is neither in my Power or any other Person to serve you with good wholesome Beer at a less price . . . "[1]

Trade had even to be turned away ; " as Malt and Hops are so very high we do not mean to take any Fresh Customers during these hard Times."[2]

At the end of 1800 Greenalls had to inform their friends in Bolton that continued rises in Malt and Barley brought about " the necessity of raising our best Beer to 66/- p. Barrel, and other sorts of Beer we must either Brew weaker or have a better price for it as it is not possible for us to send it at the present prices without being considerable loosers [*sic*]."[3] In 1803 beer again rose in price, this time due to excise increases. An additional duty of 2s. per bushel was laid on malt, including that already in the malthouses. The Bolton customers were asked to lay their heads together and decide what quality of beer they desired in future, and Peter Greenall would call on them in Bolton to receive their answer.[4] Though the poorer beers had deteriorated in quality, Greenalls were, however, still able to preserve a pride in their better brew. Sending a Bolton man a barrel of strong beer as a sample in 1804, Peter Greenall gave a detailed set of instructions as to when and how it should be tapped. " I trust it will be such a Glass of Beer as Bolton cannot produce : the price we sell it at is 66/- but I will leave it to yourself to give me what you think *it is worth*."[5]

A final rise in the price of beer, again following malt prices, occurred in 1812, and a publican was told that he could not be supplied under £3 the barrel, which he would have to sell at 8d. the Quart.[6] On more than one occasion the Greenalls were obliged to turn off old customers who could not pay the prices and to refuse new ones so as not to disappoint the old.

The letter-books contain only one suggestion that beer prices were controlled other than by supply and demand. But brief

[1] *Ibid.*, Greenall to John Hamer for Bolton Customers, 5 Feb., 1800.

[2] *Ibid.*, Greenall to John Powell & Son., 28 Feb., 1800.

[3] *Ibid.* Greenall to John Makin, 19 Dec., 1800.

[4] *Ibid.* P. Greenall to John Hamer, 12 July, 1803.

[5] *Ibid.*, Peter Greenall to John Hamer, 28 Feb., 1804.

[6] *Ibid.*, E. & P. Greenall to Henry Cooke, 23 April, 1812.

though this is, it seems to indicate the existence of some kind of association among local brewers.

" Oct. 6. 1802.
        Messrs. Sharp and Eules,
                Gentn.

                Your favor of the 4th inst. was only received this morning, in reply am sorry that a previous engagement will prevent me the pleasure of attending the meeting of the Brewers Tomorrow but whatever is the general determination I shall most willingly coincide with.

I trust my partner Mr. Lyon will be with you on behalf of the Wilderspool Concern and am.

                Gentn. Your mo. obt. servt.

                                Thos. Greenall."

The curious thing is that despite all the difficulties and embarrassments which the trade passed through, Greenalls emerged after 1815 as a much more influential concern than they had been before the war period, and this has to be explained. Partly of course we have to discount the viewpoint of the letter-books. There Greenalls were trying to place their demands for better service or higher prices before others, whom they sought to impress with the necessity for those changes by saying that they would otherwise be ruined. One factor which must have worked in favour of this and other large breweries, was that it must have been next to impossible for the household or the tavern to do their own brewing during the grain shortages in years like 1795-6 and 1800-1. In the first place prices were high, but even more important was the fact that those able to buy £1,000 worth of barley, or a whole shipload, were able to get a better share of what was available, and at a lower cost. We have seen that Greenalls had to cut down the number of qualities or varieties of beer available in order to keep going ; the smaller producer must have found these difficulties even more acute. War shortages and high prices therefore helped those tendencies, which we noticed at the beginning of this chapter, towards the extension of wholesale brewing.

But while we give some of the credit, paradoxically, to the hard times, we must not forget that without acumen and perseverance no sound concern can be built. These qualities were certainly not lacking either in Thomas Greenall or in the sons, Edward and Peter, who succeeded him, or in the grandson Peter Greenall who, as we shall see in later chapters, dominated the early administrative life of the town of St. Helens.[1] The efforts to obtain supplies of malt and hops to their liking have illustrated the family pertinacity in one aspect of the undertaking, but in other branches of the business this quality was

[1] Below, pp. 290 et seq.

equally desirable. Many of the innkeepers with whom Greenalls had dealings were in a very small way of business, with little or no capital of their own, and to give them long credit was to find the debtor bankrupt and the brewers in receipt only of a fraction in the pound. To be too lenient could be fatal, a lesson which Thomas Greenall learnt early. Indeed he might almost be accused of being mean, were it not apparent that a minute attention to detail, which today might seem almost ludicrous, was the only way to ensure regular payments and to obviate fraudulent practices in an age when the details of business administration were vague and commercial morality very imperfectly established. Not merely was there difficulty in getting payment, there was difficulty in obtaining that payment in good money ; innkeepers were always liable to be imposed on and to take bills of exchange which could not be honoured when presented. Many innkeepers indeed could only be forced to pay by the brewer going to the person who leased them their inn so that pressure might be applied.

Thomas Greenall's epistolary style in addressing bad debtors is quite remarkable, each letter seen separately seems quite individual, but in fact was repeated with some slight difference of phrase in demands to other clients. The valedictory formula generally employed was : " Your ill-used friend, Thomas Greenall." Here is an early and typical example of his dunning letter.

" Mr. Buckley,
        I am much surprised at the small payment you made if you had any thought how you are going on Certainly you would not Use me as you do, you Cannot Expect that I find my goods by the highway or I shall steal them, I have payments to make this Xmas and must pay them, therefore I hope you will on receipt of this raise me some money it is not possible for me to follow my Business as you pay me—If you will look over your Act. you will find that the way you go on in will neither do me nor you any service. I understand you wish to Brew your own and I ashure [sic] you I have no objections if you can do any better for yourself I will not be your hindrance. You shall not have my Ale to lay the fault on, but according to the manage-ment of your house I am clear if I was to give you my Ale, it wou'd all be the same—you are in a fair way to ruin both me and yourself, however if you will not pay some more moneys, *Immediately* you will force me to take such means for recovery thereof as will be very disagreeable to your Ill Used Friend.
                                        Tho. Greenall."[1]

[1] Letter-books, Thomas Greenall to Mr. Buckley, 28 Dec., 1786. In a letter of 13 May, 1788 the last dozen words are almost identical, a letter of 7 Aug., 1789 is a very close parallel. The letter quoted gives the only example of an innkeeper threatening to brew independently. It is obvious that Greenall did not rate his chances of success highly.

Greenalls were very careful not to extend their sales if it meant giving credit to a man whose solvency was doubtful. Writing to a Wigan innkeeper in 1792, Peter Greenall said they would serve him with stocks of Ale if they received " a line from your Father or your Brother James signifying we shall be no losers by the business we do with you . . . no one shall serve you better than we can."[1]

One of the several publicans who defaulted in spite of Greenalls' reluctance to see anyone's account grow long was a man named Whalley, an innholder in the Wigan area. Through the owner of the public house the brewers managed to collect £5 of the £13 owed. " I am sorry Whalley has turn'd out such a Raschal [sic] upon your hands but am glad to observe you have been so fortunate as to procure the above sum, I hope you will have it in your power to receive the remainder."[2] Another innkeeper, John Oliphant, after repeated warnings from Greenalls, fell into the hands of his creditors and an assignee was congratulated on obtaining some cash and a watch from him for their benefit.[3]

A letter to a would-be customer who protested at Greenalls' serving a new client in 1799 after they had turned away others (including himself) reveals an interesting detail. The new customer was apparently a carrier or stage-coach driver ; Peter Greenall points out that he was admitted as a customer by his father while he was away, that he had been an old servant of the brewery and also " that he is now a great Friend to all our houses betwixt L'pool and Bolton as I believe he does not stop at any other upon the road."[4]

If Greenalls were to be able to pay for grain in bulk, particularly about 1800 when the need for immediate cash was pronounced, the bills they received had to be easily negotiable. To one publican Thomas Greenall wrote: " I told you it appeared very suspicious and I was very surprised you would take it with such an endorsement you now see my words are verified, I hope you will never think of paying me any more Bills as I am determined I will never take another Bill from you as long as we do any business together ".[5] In the same month two other men from whom payments were due were told that " nothing but Cash or Bank Notes will do ".[6]

The smaller fry among local brewers endeavoured, as we have

[1] *Ibid.*, P. Greenall to Richard Hartley, 30 Jan., 1792.
[2] *Ibid.*, Thomas Greenall to Jas. Leyland, 6 Feb., 1796.
[3] *Ibid.*, P. Greenall to Mr. Threlfall, 10 May, 1798.
[4] *Ibid.*, P. Greenall to Henry Livesley, 23 Nov., 1799.
[5] *Ibid.*, P. Greenall to Thos Oldfield, 9 April, 1800.
[6] *Ibid.*, P. Greenall to Henry Cooke, 21 April, 1800 ; to George Grime, same date.

seen, to buy an inn or two, and we would naturally expect that Greenalls would carry on the same process on a more extensive scale. Some early mentions of Thomas Greenall's dealings in public houses however, show him offering inns for sale rather than acquiring them. In April, 1778, as one of the assignees of Peter Worrall of Parr, he was selling off the Bowling Green Inn in that township, while in 1782 he offered for sale on his own account a new three-storey inn in St. Helens on the Liverpool to Wigan turnpike " situated in a very populous part of the country."[1]

In 1799 Peter Greenall informed Mr. Turner, the Warrington solicitor, that his father intended to purchase the Havannah Inn in Parr and an estate there from James Fraser, " the money is ready at any time when the Deeds are prepar'd ".[2] The lease of the Black Bull Inn in Church Street was renewed for three lives in 1803 after Thomas Greenall had proferred to buy it out if the owners, the Society of Friends, were willing to sell. It was accordingly rented at £22 4s. per year. Two of the three " fresh young lives " are of interest ; they were those of Joseph Churton junior, aged 6, the son of Greenalls' colliery partner, and Richard Pilkington, son of their friend Dr. William Pilkington. Richard was to become prominent in the glass industry.[3] The Greenall rent book, which opens in 1800, shows rents being received from the " Elephant " in Sutton, the " Bull's Head ", in Prescot, the " Fleece ", " Tontine Coffee House ", " Eagle and Child ", " Turk's Head ", " Angell ", " Navigation Tavern ", " Bull ", " White Hall ", and " White Hart ", all in St. Helens, the " Horns " in Widnes, the " Havannah Inn " in Parr and the " Black Horse " in Moss Bank. It may well be that there was a similar rent-book for the Bolton area, where Greenalls certainly owned taverns. The number of public-houses directly owned or leased by Greenalls will not however present the full number of the " tied " houses. This process sometimes took place by more subtle methods. Landlords sent for a load of beer when setting up in business, without having the ready money to pay for it, and began and continued in debt to the brewer. Several times bonds and security are mentioned ; when the publican became heavily indebted it must have been easy to force him to confine his purchases to one brewer's product.

From the brewer's point of view the owning of public houses had obvious merits. Not merely did he secure a steady market for his beer, but he received the rents of the public houses as well, and he could—and did—raise them as a district became more

[1] Gore's Gen. Ad., 24 April, 1778, 14 Nov., 1782.

[2] Letter-books, P. Greenall to Mr. Turner, 27 Sept., 1799.

[3] Ibid., Thomas Greenall to Mr. Atkinson, Agent to the Quaker Society, Manchester, 24 Feb., 1803 ; Greenall Brothers to Atkinson, 30 Dec., 1805.

populous and prosperous, and the value of the trade done increased. The rent of the " Havannah ", £10 in 1799, was £30 in 1814-16 ; the rent of the " Eagle and Child ", £8 10s. in 1800, was £40 in 1818. Moreover, he could replace the idle landlord who ran a slovenly inn, or who failed to sell enough beer, by a more energetic tenant.

Already by 1800 the brewing industry in this district was moving towards its typical modern pattern ; the household brewer and innkeeper-brewer were disappearing and their place was being taken by the large wholesale brewer ; indeed by 1800 his position was the dominant one. The large brewer was extending his influence firstly by holding shares in more than one brewery, and secondly by buying up inns or becoming the creditor of the public house tenant, so that only his own product was sold. But this change in the industry was only accomplished by establishing the pattern of nineteenth-century organization and efficiency where in the mid-eighteenth century there had been something like an easy-going chaos. This process was not one of mere economics: it was a moral triumph of perseverance and business integrity achieved over an opposition of bad measure, inferior quality, debts, and high prices. Given these conditions, it is not to be wondered at if the qualities necessary for success seemed at times a little harsh.

CHAPTER IX

THE GLASS INDUSTRY IN THE EIGHTEENTH CENTURY

1696-1826

THE town of St. Helens is most widely known nowadays as the home of the glass industry. This was not always the case, however ; the origins of large-scale glassmaking in south-west Lancashire are comparatively recent. It is true that the Romans made glass at Warrington[1] and foreign glass-makers were at work in the Bickerstaffe area at the beginning of the seventeenth century.[2] But it was not till Liverpool began to be a considerable transatlantic port almost a hundred years later that the industry became of any consequence in the Merseyside region.

The first mention of glasshouses on Merseyside is in 1696, when there were two, one at Warrington and one " near Lever-pool ".[3] Where the second was situated is not more accurately specified, but the Sutton district of St. Helens is the probable site. It is known for certain that a Warrington family of glassmakers, the Leafs, moved into Sutton township about this time. John Leaf is first mentioned in the Sutton Township Book[4] in 1696, and he served a township office for the first time in 1701, while a John Leaf senior, described as a glassmaker of Sutton, died there in 1713.[5] It seems very likely that there was a glasshouse in Sutton as well as at Warrington in 1695, and that about that year the Leaf family was in process of transferring the manufacture from one site to the other. At all events there is a subsequent silence on the

---

[1] T. May, " On the Altar and other Relics Found during Recent Excava-tions (1895-6) on the site of the Roman Station at Wilderspool". *Trans. L. & C. Hist. Soc.*, **48** (1897) 16-17.

[2] Ormskirk Parish Register, 10 December 1600. " A stranger slayne by one of the glassemen being a Frenchman then working at Bycarstaff." *Lancs. Par. Reg. Soc.* (1902).

[3] *A Collection of Letters for the Improvement of Husbandry and Trade.* (ed. Houghton) No. 198, 15 May, 1696. The list given was almost cert-ainly identical with that compiled by the Commissioners of Excise in con-nection with the recently-introduced duty on glass.

[4] In the possession of the Prescot Historic Society.

[5] L.R.O., Will proved at Chester, 7 May, 1713. According to Liverpool Town Books, a John Leaf, glassman, son of John Leaf, the Warrington glassmaker, became a freeman on 5 Sept., 1694, and John Leaf junior, described as a glassmaker of Sutton, is mentioned in a marriage bond of 21 July, 1705. See " Marriage Bonds of the Ancient Archdeaconry of Chester," Part I, ed. W. A. Tonge, *Trans. L. & C. Rec. Soc.* **82** (1933), 177. The name appears as Lease, but this is an obvious misreading.

subject of Warrington glassmaking, only broken on the formation of the firm of Peter Seaman & Co. as bottle and flint glass
manufacturers in 1758. The John Leaf who died in 1713 was
succeeded by a namesake who certainly continued glassmaking
into the 1730s, and perhaps longer. He was fairly prosperous in
business ; not only did he lend £280 at interest in the 1730s, but
a bond of administration to the amount of £2,000 was taken out
at his death in 1751.[1]

Apart from the little we know of the Leafs, our knowledge of
mid-eighteenth century St. Helens glassmaking is confined to a
few disconnected scraps of evidence. The Leaf glasshouse was in
the Thatto Heath-Ravenhead district of Sutton,[2] but we are also
told that about 1721 John Hensey, a working partner in a
Prescot glasshouse owned by Thomas Cobham, had removed and
built the " Thattow Heath Glasshouse ".[3] It is uncertain to
which of the glasshouses on the heath it was that Nicholas Blundell of Crosby recorded sending for glass bottles in 1721.[4] Leaf's
glasshouse was put up for sale in 1747, and one of the notices
mentioned the existence of a neighbouring " Wilcock's " glasshouse.[5] Subsequent evidence, however, relates only to a solitary
bottle glasshouse, apparently carried on by a partnership of
working glassmakers. In 1767 this partnership was strengthened
by the inclusion of new members, the firm being thereafter
known as Orrell, Fosters & Co. ; the additional partners were
almost certainly James Orrell, the Parr coal-owner, and the
Thatto Heath brewing family of Foster. The inference is that the
working glassmakers were short of capital, and had to turn to
other industrialists to provide it :

" Notice is hereby given That the Glass-Bottle Manufactory, at Hatto Heath Glass House, near Prescot in the County
of Lancaster, is now carried on by Orrell Fosters & Co.
Where all sorts of the best Wine, Beer, Cardavine and other
Bottles, are made, and sold upon the most reasonable Terms ;
and as all the late Workmen and Partners, at the said house,
are engaged, they humbly hope for the Continuance of their
former Favours and Interest . . . "[6]

[1] Hughes Papers : Leaf Bundle. Indentures of 16 March, 1730, 29 Sept.,
1739, 9 Nov. 1742. L.R.O., Will proved at Chester, 28 Sept., 1751.

[2] Pilkington Brothers Ltd. Ravenhead Deeds, package 7. Abstract of
Title to Woods's Tenement.

[3] King's College, Cambridge, MS. PC 2/132. Quoted by Mrs. R. H.
Hughes in paper on " Early Glassmaking in Prescot," in possession of
the Prescot Historic Society.

[4] *Diary of Nicholas Blundell* ed. T. E. Gibson (Lpool, 1895), 177.

[5] F. Buckley, " Old Lancashire Glasshouses " *Trans. Soc. of Glass
Tech.*, **13** (Sept., 1929) 239, quoting *Manchester Magazine*, 31 March and
18 June, 1747.

[6] *Williamson's Lpool. Ad.*, 21 Aug., 1767.

The names of two more of the partners, Highton and Tarbuck, can be obtained from other sources. In 1775 the will of John Highton of Eccleston,[1] " glass bottle founder", bequeathed all his " share in the Hattow or Thattow-heath Glass-house unto my beloved wife Rachel Highton ", who was to receive his portion of the profits so long as the concern continued. James Tarbuck, who had been one of the witnesses to this will, described himself as " one of the late partners " when offering the glasshouse for sale in the spring of 1782, he having left it for the service of the new plate glass manufactory at Ravenhead.[2] The depression had taken its toll and it was three years before Thomas West and Co. announced that they had taken over " Thatto Heath Bottle Work " and put it into production again.[3] West is first heard of in 1777, when he leased land in Eccleston including a " coalpit hey ",[4] and mining continued to be one of his interests, as well as glassmaking.

Up to this time glassmaking had only been undertaken on a small scale in the St. Helens area. Liverpool was certainly a larger centre of production, and, during the second half of the century, more glass was probably made at Warrington than at Thatto Heath. It was only when the first cast plate glass factory in the country was established at Ravenhead in the mid-'seventies that the district began to be of any significance as a centre of glassmaking.

Plate glass, which seems to take its name from the " looking-glass plates " into which it was generally at first manufactured, was a superior and special variety of glass, made thicker than ordinary window-panes so that it could take grinding and polishing, by which an even, lustrous finish could be obtained. A secondary use of plate glass was for coach windows, where strength, as well as good light-admitting properties, was desired, and for panes of large size. The making of looking-glass plates was introduced into England by the famous glass monopolist Mansell shortly before 1621 ; under him the manufacture was said to employ 500 persons.[5] Grinding and polishing were initially hand operations, but patents for grinding and polishing machinery were taken out in 1678 by John Roberts and in 1696 by Thomas Savery, of steam engine fame.[6] By 1706 there were at

[1] L.R.O.. Will proved at Chester, 14 July, 1775.

[2] *Gore's Gen. Ad.*, 25 April, 1782.

[3] *Ibid.*, 24 Feb., 1785.

[4] L.R.O., DDGe 824.

[5] Notestein, Relf & Simpson. *Commons Debates, 1621* (New Haven, 1935) II, 366.   S.P.Dom. Jas I., Vol. 162, No. 63 in A. Hartshorne *Old English Glasses* (1897), 428.

[6] British Patents Specifications 203, 1678 and 347, 1696.

least two plate glassworks in London, and competition appears to have been keen.[1]

Only the purest materials were used for this glass, the finest soda and lime and thoroughly-washed white sand, the whole batch being very carefully fritted before being placed in the melting-pots. Since the finished glass was thick, discolouration was the more noticeable, while any spots on the glass itself or unevenness of the surface meant that it could only be used for inferior mirrors or for coach glass. Until the end of the seventeenth century plate glass was made by blowing. The glassmaker blew the glass into a cylinder which was then slit along its length and flattened out into a pane. This method had the great disadvantage that size was limited ; if the cylinder was blown more than about 50 inches long the glass became too thin to stand grinding.

The introduction of casting effected a revolutionary change in this manufacture. Instead of blowing a cylinder, the glass was simply ladled from the furnace on to a table and allowed to cool. The resulting dull and hardly transparent sheet was then brought up to a finished state by grinding and polishing. The limitation as to size was not so strict, being no longer governed by the amount of molten glass a blower could gather and blow. Casting was first introduced into France in 1688, when a company was granted Letters Patent giving it a monopoly of the French home market. After many vicissitudes the manufacture eventually found a home at St. Gobain in Picardy, where wood fuel was plentiful. Output is said to have reached 700 tons by 1725, 850 tons by 1750, and, after 1760, to have exceeded 1,150 tons a year.[2]

The chief drawback to the casting process was financial rather than technical. The ordinary small glasshouse could be set up fairly cheaply, but for the new method much more was required : a big melting furnace, a casting-table as large as ten feet by six feet (itself a major problem in metal-casting at that period), cuvettes, or cisterns, in which to transfer metal from the furnace to the casting-table, and the cranes needed to move them. Other necessities were grinding and polishing materials and machinery, accommodation for the unusually large number of officials and workmen and extensive warehousing facilities, due to the large and fragile nature of the product. In a sense glass-making has always been a ' factory ' industry, but the cast plate method demanded unprecedented organization and greatly increased capital.

The French were not long unimitated. In 1691 an attempt was

[1] Guildhall Library, London. Broadsides 13/49, 50.

[2] Articles by Warren C. Scoville on " Technology and the French Glass Industry, 1640-1710," *Journal of Economic History*, I (1941) and " Large Scale Production in the French Plate Glass Industry, 1665-1798," *Journal of Political Economy*, I (1942).

made to float an English cast plate glass concern,[1] and in 1692 and
1701[2] plate glass of unusual size and quality was announced as
for sale, suggesting the practical application of the process.

The method was nevertheless soon abandoned in this country,
and when it eventually came to be revived one of the new proprietors, a descendant of two of the promoters of 1691, admitted
to having long since destroyed the casting apparatus in his own
possession.[3] English manufacturers contented themselves with
making the small sizes by the blown plate process, and glass
merchants had to import the large sizes from St. Gobain. The
demand for these sizeable plates was rapidly increasing, one reason
being the desire of the wealthy for plate glass windows in their
houses. To supply this market, £60,000 to £100,000 worth of
these glasses were being annually imported from France about
1770.

In 1773 a British company was formed to exploit this
neglected field. Since at least £50,000 was required to establish
the process, the intending proprietors sought incorporation by
Act of Parliament in order to secure limited liability. The
technical expert of the company was a Frenchman, Philip
Besnard, who had been working at St. Gobain for 15 years.
According to him, the scheme would succeed because the needful
materials (apart from the alkali barilla) could be obtained in this
country, while coal fuel was cheaper than the wood employed
by the French.

Of the greatest interest, however, is the fact that two of the
proprietors were named Mackay, one of them being the coal-
owner John Mackay, who was certainly responsible for bringing
the factory to Ravenhead. At the time of Besnard's arrival in
England, late in 1771, Mackay had just opened his Thatto Heath
mines, and was, no doubt, anxious to have a large furnace industry
as a customer.

The share of John Mackay in founding this great undertaking
cannot precisely be discovered, but it is noteworthy that his
brother-in-law, Admiral Philip Affleck, was among the distinguished group of proprietors, and that a descendant of the
Admiral later declared that " the concern itself originated with
my family ".[4] Locally, at any rate, Mackay was regarded as the
principal proprietor, and the Land Tax returns on one occasion

[1] *Cal. S. P. Dom.* May 1690—Oct. 1691, 537, 540.

[2] F. Buckley, *The Glass Trade in England in the Seventeenth Century*
(1914), 46, 59.

[3] *C. J.* 34, 150, 24 Feb., 1773. This and the following paragraph are
based upon this source.

[4] Pilkington Brothers Ltd. Minutes of British Plate Glass Co., 20 May,
1829.

entered the glassworks as " John Mackay & Co." He maintained close contact with London business circles, even though he lived in the north after 1762, and it was from Londoners—among whom was David Garrick, the actor—that the capital to finance his colliery and glass investments was borrowed. Nor was his interest in the glass trade simply that of a coal-owner investing in order to secure a fuel contract ; in the early 1780s, just prior to his death, he unsuccessfully tried to establish the manufacture of stained and enamelled glass in Liverpool, using a new process.[1]

The original supporters gathered for the venture included a powerful group of East India investors, two West India merchants, and a number of men of some social standing. Scots were well represented.[2]

By an Act of 1773 an illustrious group of proprietors, somewhat changed from the supporters of the petition for the Bill of incorporation, and by now headed by no less a person than Lord Bute, obtained corporate rights for twenty-one years. Permission was granted to raise a joint-stock of £40,000 in £500 shares, and to raise a further £20,000 if three-fourths of their number were agreeable.[3] The foundations of the great casting-hall at Ravenhead, the largest industrial building of the period, 113 yards long

---

[1] For Mackay's various mortgages see Pilkington Brothers, Ltd., Ravenhead Deeds, Abstract of Title of Ravenhead Estate. He borrowed £2,500 and £2,000 from London men when opening his mines, and £12,000 from the actor David Garrick in 1776, a loan subsequently transferred to Garrick's close friend, the banker Henry Hoare. An account of Mackay's short-lived Liverpool stained glass venture can be gained from P.R.O. P.L. 6. 88/42 and the dissolution of that partnership concern is mentioned in *Gore's Gen. Ad.* 5 Dec., 1782.

[2] The petitioners of 25 Jan., 1773 were :- Charles Fitzroy, the Hon. Robert Digby, Peregrine Cust, Thomas Dundas, John Mackay, Philip Affleck, Henry Dagge, James Bourdieu, Angus Mackay, Henry Hastings, Ranald Macdonald and Samuel Chollet. Bourdieu and Chollet were absent from the list of proprietors actually incorporated, but this was considerably strengthened by new members. These included Lord Bute, Maj. Gen. Lord Fitzroy (first Baron Southampton), (Sir) Herbert Mackworth, a member of a South Wales industrial family, particularly interested in copper smelting, Thomas Patten, the Warrington copper manufacturer, Thomas (later Lord) Dundas, and (Sir) Robert Polk, former governor of Madras. The East India interest was strongly represented, four of the proprietors being members of a Committee for East India Affairs set up at the end of 1772, while Scots were also prominent. When 't was again reformed in 1798 the Company's East India connection still remained very strong ; the Affleck family continued their support, but the Mackays and the industrialists Mackworth and Patten had ceased to be members, as had several others. The chief new supporters gained at this reconstruction were the principals of the financial houses of Boyd, Benfield & Co. and Pybus, Call & Co., the former, in particular, having strong East India connections. 38 Geo. III, cap. XVII, at House of Lords Record Office.

[3] 13 Geo. III cap. 38.

and 50 yards wide, were laid in the same year,[1] and glass was first
cast there in 1776.[2]

The first fifty years of the Company's existence fall into two
sharply contrasted phases ; miserable failure was followed by
brilliant success, the turning point being the appointment of
Robert Sherbourne as manager in 1792.

Nothing further is heard of Philip Besnard, and the introduction of the manufacture at Ravenhead was put into the hands of
Jean Baptist François Graux de la Bruyère, who had been born at
St. Gobain in 1739. He continued in charge of the plant for over
ten years, till his death in 1787. According to his epitaph he was
" the first who brought to perfection in Britain ... the cast plate
glass manufacture ".[3] This claim is scarcely justifiable : indeed
under his direction the Company was on the edge of ruin, mainly
due to the high proportion of waste to saleable glass. One trouble
was that French glassmakers were not used to coal fuel ; it was
not until Sherbourne introduced " caped " or covered pots that
the metal was freed from the black drops which fell into it from
the roof of the furnace.

The plate glass industry in England, unlike that of France, was
burdened with an excise duty. The proprietors of the Company
had originally strengthened their petitions by pointing out the
increased revenue to the Crown which their industry would
provide. They soon changed their tune. Only a year after the
factory at Ravenhead went into production the excise rate was
doubled as a war measure, and this must have greatly upset the
estimated selling price. Since the tax was levied on the weight of
raw materials placed in the melting pot, not on the amount of
glass produced, the large wastage in casting led to serious trouble ;
it greatly exceeded the waste allowance made by the Excise, which
was estimated on the lower wastage of the blown plate glass
manufacturer.[4] The appeals of the proprietors to the Commissioners of Excise were met by retorts that the inexperience and
inefficiency of the workmen was at fault, which was largely the
truth. Repeated protests about this taxation of waste were disregarded and the Company continued to operate at a loss. Over
the period 1780-83, at a time of trade depression, income was only

[1] Date stone at Ravenhead.

[2] Library of H.M. Customs & Excise. Treasury and Excise Papers, **26,**
240. Letter from John Grant, 3 May, 1793.

[3] His grave is in the old Catholic burial ground at Windleshaw, now part
of the St. H. Borough Cemetery. See also L.R.O., Bruyère's will, proved
Chester 17 April, 1788. Two of the executors were Thomas West and
George Mackay.

[4] For the seriousness of the wastage problem see the evidence given by
George Mackay, *C.J.*, **40** ; 806-7 ; for the difference between the French
and British industries in the matter of duty, *ibid.*, **40**, 223. By 17 Geo.
III, cap. 38, the duty on plate glass was raised from 9s. 4d., to 18s. 8d.
per cwt.

£40,000 and expenditure £44,000, of which a quarter went in payment of duty. Only £1,000 worth of glass was sold in a polished state, and the Company by selling it unfinished was neglecting its main source of profit. Such losses could not continue, and in 1784 casting was stopped to avoid further debts; the great works lay idle, apart from blowing of small plates, and casting had still not been resumed a year later.[1]

Further desperate appeals were made to the Commissioners of Excise, and the manufacturers now urged that the duty should be levied on the squared plates, instead of on the weight of raw material melted. This was eventually granted in 1787.[2] Casting was begun once more, and efforts to improve efficiency were made, successful in that between 1787 and 1792 wastage was reduced from 200% to 100%. An attempt was made to increase the production of polished glass, and a Boulton and Watt steam engine was installed to drive the polishing machinery according to a method devised by James Watt himself.[3] Output was much improved, but even so only reached about 80 tons a year,[4] paltry when compared with the 1,000 tons and more of St. Gobain.

It was the appointment of Robert Sherbourne as manager in 1792 which ended a situation where performance always lagged behind expectation. His task was difficult indeed ; the minute books were already full of the " failure of expensive experiments " and the " misconduct of managers."[5] The original capital had long ago been swallowed up, as well as a further £60,000 raised in loans, and within two years of Sherbourne's taking over control of Ravenhead Works the charter of incorporation expired, limited liability ended, and the creditors demanded their money. A new petition for incorporation was granted by the Commons, but did not reach the Statute Book, and the shareholders decided to sell up. At the last moment a London man, Thomas Oakes, arranged with the proprietors to buy the whole concern for £105,000[6] and he and the proprietors continued to run it as an unincorporated company until 1798, when a second attempt at

[1] Treasury and Excise Papers, **19**, 455-6, 482 (12 Feb., 26 April, 1779) ; C.J., **40**, 225-232, 806.

[2] 27 Geo. III, cap. 28. This Act was related to the Eden treaty of the previous year.

[3] Birmingham Pub. Ref. Lib. Boulton & Watt Colln. Particularly Watt to Mackworth, 23 April, 4 May, 1786 ; A Black to B. & W., 23 July, Memorandum of James Watt, 7 Aug., Watt to Mackworth (n.d. Sept.), Watt to Mackay, 14 Sept., Watt to Mackworth, 21 Sept., 1788 ; Watt to Mackay, 13 June, 1789 ; Watt to Mackay, 12 Feb., 1790.

[4] Treasury and Excise Papers, **26**, 240.

[5] Pilkington Brothers, Ltd., Minutes of the British Plate Glass Co. (hereafter given as B.P.G. Mins.), 19 April, 1809.

[6] C.J., **49**, 349, 413, 467, 570, 18 Mar., 3, 15 April, 9 May, 1794 ; Pilkington Brothers Ltd., Deeds, Indenture of 30 Sept., 1794.

re-incorporation met with success.[1]   The concern was thereafter
known as the British Plate Glass Company.

The survival of some of the minute books of the Company for
the early nineteenth century greatly enlarges our knowledge of
the conduct of the business during Sherbourne's period of management ; indeed the amount of material is such as to preclude
its full treatment here, though an outline may be given.

Sherbourne's reforms under the old and new Companies
included the saving of £8,000 worth of broken waste glass (cullet)
which had been left lying about by the previous management, the
perfecting of " caped " or covered melting pots which prevented
the spotting of the glass by furnace soot, the use of cheaper local
sand, the saving of £1,000 a year in the grinding department by
an emery preparation process, the introduction of a convex and
concave mirror manufacture, a further elimination of glass
wastage in 1802—which led to the firm receiving a greater wastage
allowance than they required—and efficient personnel management.   Grateful directors declared :   " the moral order and
regularity of the small community belonging to the works must be
seen to enable the Committee to form a just estimate of the
Superintendent's merits."[2] Sherbourne's salary rose as the profits
increased, from £500 a year to £700 and eventually to £1,000.

In 1793 the superintendent's aim had been limited to raising
an output of £20,000 worth of glass to one of £40,000, but by
1801 the Company was making 7,279 plates in a year, worth
about £90,000, and was holding a stock of glasses valued at
nearly £40,000.   Deficit and borrowing were things of the past ;
by 1806 quarterly 5% dividends were being paid, and an income
tax return for 1808 shows that over the past three years £57,540
had been paid out in dividends, £19,180 per annum.   The increase
continued until in 1815 when the Company was paying 30%
on its nominal capital.   Money was plentiful, and such wartime
charities as funds for the " Suffering Portuguese " and the
Russian victims of the campaign of 1812 received substantial
donations.[3]

The war removed all threat of competition from the only
existing rival, St. Gobain, and until the firm of Cookson and
Cuthbert commenced manufacture at the end of hostilities[4] the
Company had the market to themselves, and did not hesitate to
raise prices.   On the other hand quality was greatly improved,
poor glass made in the early days was written off the stock, and
an imperfect mirror was even removed from the Committee

[1] 38 Geo. III, cap. XVII.

[2] B.P.G. Mins., 12 April, 1815.

[3] Minutes and Account Books of the B.P.G. Co.

[4] 13th Report of the Commissioners of Excise (Glass) 1835 [15] XXXI, 103

Room in London.[1] When output was halved in 1812, because of a new increase of the excise, the firm simply increased prices so as to ensure an at least equal income.[2]

No doubt, however, it was this drop in home sales which made the proprietors eager for exports (on which there was a drawback of duty) as soon as the end of the Napoleonic War was in sight. The only previous direct exports of any importance had been a disastrous speculative consignment to Brussels under the old company in 1782-3, and one considerable order from the United States in 1810 ; but from 1814 the proprietors began a series of " adventures " to various overseas countries, particularly India. A large quantity was sent to Calcutta in 1814, and in the same year glass was despatched to Halifax, Nova Scotia, to be diverted to the American market on the conclusion of a peace with Great Britain. Bombay and Madras, too, were soon supplied with British plate glass, though the reaction of the Company's Madras agents was not enthusiastic : " It would be deceiving the Company were we to hold out hopes of a profitable Sale of the elegant Articles they have been pleased to assign to us. The European Inhabitants of this Presidency are not inclined to decorate their houses with such costly furniture and but few of the Native Inhabitants . . . are in circumstances to gratify their taste in that respect."[3] As a last resort, however, agents would try the " Courts of the Native Princes."

The war years brought their own problems, though none of them developed into a serious threat to the Company's prosperity. The supply of pearl ashes (the main alkali), hitherto obtained from the United States, was derived from Canada during the war of 1812-14, though the Canadian supply was affected by the difficulties of the convoy system and the seasonal freezing of the St. Lawrence. The shortage of barilla, formerly derived from the Mediterranean countries, was a more serious handicap, but the problem was energetically tackled. Lord Dundas, closely associated with early chemical development, was one of the proprietors, and some sort of success was obtained with the manufacture of artificial alkali at Ravenhead, the process apparently owing something to the researches of Lord Dundonald. Other inventors approached the Company with alkali-manufacturing schemes, but with little result.[4]

---

[1] B.P.G. Mins., especially 22 June, 1808.

[2] B.P.G. Mins., 29 July, 1812. No doubt it was this increase in prices and continued high rate of profit which caused Vansittart summarily to reject the Company's appeal in 1815 for a reduction of excise duty. *Ibid.* 9 March, 1815.

[3] B.P.G. Mins., Jan., 1816.

[4] *Ibid.*, 11 Feb., 17 Aug., 1808 ; 29 May, 1811 ; 27 May, 1812 ; 16 March, 1814.

Leaving the Plate Glass Company on the pinnacle of prosperity which it had reached by 1815, we must, to complete our survey of the eighteenth century glass industry in the district, revert to the events of 1792.

George Mackay, brother to Angus Mackay, one of the proprietors, and presumably a relation also of John Mackay, was book-keeper at Ravenhead in 1785. He remained there at least till 1790, when correspondence shows he was still in authority if not actually in charge of the works, for he conducted the Ravenhead end of the arrangements for the installation of the Watt engine and polishing machinery. The coming of Sherbourne seems to have coincided with the ending of the Mackay influence, and it was in 1792 that George Mackay, having quitted the plate glassworks, helped to found the crown glass firm of Mackay, West & Co. in Eccleston.[1] The original partners were George Mackay, his brothers Angus Mackay and Major-General Alexander Mackay, together with James Campbell and Thomas and William West. Thomas West was the leading proprietor of the Thatto Heath bottlehouse, which, as we have seen, he took over in 1785. The new Mackay, West works were situated in what is now Eccleston Street, at the junction of that street with Boundary Road, then Gin Lane, and within half a mile of the plate glassworks at Ravenhead.

The firm took advantage of a changed fashion in window glazing. Broad glass, previously widely used for common window glasses, was blown in a cylinder, roughly sheared down the centre, and then spread out on a stone or other more or less flat surface. The contact with this surface often caused loss of lustre and unevenness, which was not the case with crown glass, where the principle of manufacture was very different. In crown glassmaking a quantity of metal (molten glass) was formed into the shape of a pear by blowing, heating, and rolling on a polished surface. The end of the mass furthest from the blowpipe was flattened, and an iron rod or " punty " was sealed to the centre of the flattened surface. The blowpipe was then broken off, the glass was re-heated at a " flashing furnace ", and as the piece began to soften, it was twirled on the punty. Centrifugal force gradually opened-up or " flashed " the glass into a flat circle, which could be up to 60 ins. in diameter, known as a " table " of crown glass. Because it never came into contact with any surface when soft, crown glass was more highly polished and lustrous in appearance than broad glass, but on the other hand it yielded only small panes and the central bull's-eye and the selvage round the edge were wasted. Its superior quality gradually displaced broad glass. Though manufactured in England in the sixteenth century, crown or " Normandy " glass had been temporarily abandoned and the

[1] *Gore's Gen. Ad.*, 19 April, 1792.

skill lost, but it was reintroduced in 1679, gained a firm hold in the London glasshouses before the end of the seventeenth century[1], and gradually spread to the provincial glasshouses over the next hundred years.

Mackay, West & Co. soon advertised their product in the Liverpool press, but stated that they only wished to sell wholesale, either to export merchants or to glaziers and glass dealers. They quickly found Liverpool agents in Thomas Holt & Co., glass warehousemen.[2]

By the end of the eighteenth century, therefore, bottle and plate glassmaking had been joined in the St. Helens district by the manufacture of crown glass ; of the principal branches of the glass industry only flint glass was as yet unrepresented. It was not until 1822, when John William Bell adapted a disused iron foundry close to the Ravenhead terminal of the Canal for use as a flint glassworks, that wine glasses, shades, and articles of tableware came to be made in the district. Bell, whose origins are obscure, soon added new buildings to his Ravenhead Flint Glassworks where a Thomas Bell, of unknown relationship, was his partner.[3] John William Bell was soon to play a key rôle in a second company in the district, formed to make window glass ; but this important event must await consideration in a later chapter.[4]

All four branches of the glass industry, plate, window, flint and bottle, were now represented in the vicinity of St. Helens, where the chief raw materials, and particularly coal, were readily available. As yet, however, the reputation of the district as a glassmaking centre rested solely upon the giant plate glass factory and not upon the other glasshouses, which were trifling in comparison. It was the name of Ravenhead, until the end of the French Wars the only source of cast plate glass in the kingdom, that was so often on the lips of glass dealers all over the country and it was to this one factory that sightseers came from far and wide to marvel from without the walls. Apart from the manufacture of plate glass, the story of the rise of the industry at St. Helens was still in its early chapters.

[1] *Cal. S.P.D.*, 1694-5, 5 Jan. 1694-5 ; *Collection of Letters from the Improvement of Husbandry and Trade* (ed. Houghton), No. 198, 15 May, 1696.

[2] *Gore's Gen. Ad.* 17 May, 1792.

[3] Pilkington Brothers Ltd., Deeds, package 14.   Lease dated 4 and 5 Oct., 1822.

[4] Below, chapter XVI.

CHAPTER X

OTHER INDUSTRIES

ST. HELENS owes its economic growth to the industries that
have already been considered : to coal ; to the furnace
industries, glass, copper and—in the future—alkali ; and to
brewing. Unlike many other towns in Lancashire, cotton was of
little importance. Although the Poor Law records of Parr in the
middle of the eighteenth century mention some spinning and
weaving of cotton by hand both in the workhouse and at home,
linen weaving was much more in evidence ; sailcloth, in particular, was at that time a most important product of south-west
Lancashire.[1] Attempts were eventually made to weave sailcloth
and spin cotton on a factory scale at St. Helens but neither of
these manufactures took root. They were not a natural growth in
the Merseyside region.

Very little is known about the origin of the sailcloth factory.
It was situated in Tontine Street and was in the possession of
Thomas and William Kidd by 1820.[2] The Kidd family had been
sailcloth makers in the Farnworth area since the early eighteenth
century and had a factory there by the time they went into business at St. Helens.[3] The St. Helens factory appears to have been
of secondary importance, for when the depression of the 1840s
necessitated retrenchment, the Kidds stopped making sailcloth at
St. Helens and concentrated their resources at Farnworth.[4]

Cotton spinning on a factory scale at St. Helens also failed to
survive the great slump of 1841-3 and came to an end under
similar circumstances. The first factory to be built in the district
had the longest life. The partners were Thomas Greenall, the
brewer, his brother Richard, who seems to have had the management of the concern, and Thomas Eccleston of Scarisbrick, a

[1] Linen weaving is a subject about which it is very difficult to discover
any precise information from records in the St. Helens neighbourhood
and it seems probable that sources at Liverpool or in Warrington may
prove more rewarding. For a hint of the importance of linen weaving
in south-west Lancashire, see the petitions to the House of Commons,
C.J., **14**, 504, 515, 31 Jan., 5 Feb., 1704/5 ; **36**, 939, 953-4, 29 April,
5 May, 1778.

[2] L.R.O., Land Tax Assessments, Windle, 1820 ; Pigot's *Directory of
Lancashire* (Manchester, 1834).

[3] Pedigree drawn up by Dr. R. Dickinson and now in the possession of
Mrs. Yesson (née Kidd), 134, Mersey Road, Widnes.

[4] William Kidd and Co., who had supplied the St. Helens Railway with
castings in 1833 (St. H. and R. G. Mins., 26 July, 1833), continued to use
the factory at St. Helens as a foundry until about 1850 (St. H. I. C. Rate
Books).

landed gentleman and heir to the Eccleston estates. The partners erected a water-frame spinning factory in Eccleston township, turning the machinery by a water-mill. This necessitated an expensive operation, the cutting of a channel (known to generations of St. Helens people as the ' cotton cut ') which ran from dams on the demesne near Eccleston Hall and supplied a head of water to the mill. Even so the power was found to be insufficient, and an atmospheric steam engine had to be installed for pumping back water so as to supply the wheel in dry periods.

Early in 1784, at a time of improving trade, Richard Greenall was in correspondence with Thomas Eccleston and suggested that an immediate start be made with the factory. The building was to have four floors. It was estimated that it would cost nearly £500, and that the expense of cutting the watercourse would be about £1,000. The expenditure on machinery was to be considerable: 24 spinning frames would cost £25 each, 5 carding frames, 2 combing frames, 3 roving frames and two drawing frames £20 each, making a total of £940.[1]

There is little information on the running of the concern, but from stray evidence in ledgers which Thomas Greenall later used up for brewery purposes we discover that many of the sales were in small quantities of a few bundles at a time, obviously to small-scale putters-out on the domestic pattern. The abandonment of the works in 1793 might give rise to the impression that the financial crisis of that year affected it, but in fact as early as February, 1792 evidence shows that the firm was in a precarious position. While the concern was owed over £5,000 for cotton twist, it owed its creditors over £13,000. Much of this sum was due to the proprietors themselves, who had obviously been dipping their hands deep in their pockets. One very large debt was that of nearly £1,500 to Phillips & Co. for cotton. In the April of 1793 Thomas Greenall bought the mill, a farm and other properties from the firm for £4,200, and, while the accounts are incomplete, it would seem that the debts were by this time reduced to £6,600. Greenall also had to take over the remaining stock of unsold cotton twist, amounting to more than £650.

Apparently the Eccleston Mill was the victim of the yarn depressions of 1788-9 and 1792, slumps which Mantoux has suggested as possibly " the earliest instances of overproduction due to machine industry ". The precise nature of the crisis has, however, not been determined, owing to the way in which it merged into the more general commercial collapse of 1793.[2]

Cotton was not so important in this part of Lancashire as it was nearer the Pennines, and it is the more remarkable that

[1] L.R.O., Scarisbrick Papers, DDSc., 136-139.

[2] P. Mantoux, *The Industrial Revolution in the Eighteenth Century* (2nd Edn., 1928), 258-262.

between 1793 and 1795 three other mills in Prescot and St. Helens were offered for sale ; indeed their disposal is our only record of them. The other St. Helens factory consisted of three storeys, employed a steam engine with a 20 in. cylinder, and contained 15 spinning jennies, two carding engines, two roving billies, and two twisting and two warping mills. Its ownership is unknown.[1]

The Eccleston Cotton Mill subsequently revived. In 1800 Robert Kirkman of Liverpool, a cotton manufacturer, occupied it, having entered into a bond for £1,000 with Thomas Eccleston to keep the building and machinery in good repair and not to employ any workmen who might become a burden on the township.[2] Nothing further is known of the Mill until 1817 when Richard Wigan, a later proprietor, was declared bankrupt.[3] In 1820 or 1821[4] it was leased from the Greenalls by Hadfield and Frost, a Manchester firm.[5] About the same time, Hadfield and Frost took the lease of another cotton factory from the Greenalls, at Latchford near Warrington,[6] and it seems probable that they were encouraged to embark upon spinning at St. Helens as a result of this Warrington connection. They appear to have made a better success of the Eccleston Cotton Mill than did any of their predecessors, but when the depression of the early 1840s arrived, they, like the Kidds, chose to consolidate production at their other factory away from St. Helens.

Attention has already been drawn to the concentration of the cotton industry in Lancashire in the early 1840s.[7] The departure of Hadfield and Frost shows that this localization also took place within the county itself. The manufacture of glass and

[1] *Gore's Gen. Ad.* 30 Oct., 1794. In 1799 a paper mill, described as " newly-erected," was put up for sale as part of the Eccleston estate. *Billinge's Lpool Ad.* 29 July, 1799. The mill was still in being more than a quarter of a century later but the proprietors, James and John Mercer, who then leased it from Samuel Taylor, went bankrupt in the depression of 1826. *Lpool. Merc.* 31 March, 1826 ; 30 March, 1827. P.R.O., P.L. 6/118, P.L. 7/234.

[2] Wigan Ref. Lib. Dicconson Papers, Box. 1. Bond dated 24 July, 1800.

[3] *Gore's Gen. Ad.* 9 Jan., 1817. The sale was announced in the issue of 24 Feb.

[4] The firm is mentioned in Land Tax Returns for 1821 but not for 1820.

[5] According to a *Commercial Directory* (Manchester, 1816), Thomas Hadfield, dealer in twist and weft, had premises at 18, Back Square, Manchester. These were occupied by Hadfield and Frost in 1825.

[6] Information kindly supplied by Mr. George A. Carter, Chief Librarian of Warrington. A cotton factory at Latchford was advertised for sale in the *Lpool. Merc.* 23 March, 1821.

[7] A. Redford, *Labour Migration in England, 1800-1850* (Manchester, 1926), 111 ; A. J. Taylor, " Concentration and Specialization in the Lancashire Cotton Industry, 1825-1850 ", *Econ. Hist. Rev.*, 1 (2nd Ser.) (1948-9), 114-122.

alkali fitted naturally into the existing coal-salt pattern at St. Helens but the cotton trade did not, and, no doubt, the acidic smoke from the chimneys of the chemical works made the town even more unsuitable for cotton spinning.[1] The famous John Rylands had to remove from the district before he could make a fortune in textiles. Born in Parr in 1801, the son of a local draper and weaver, he began a small weaving concern at St. Helens in association with his father and brothers. When he wanted to start production on a factory scale, however, he moved to Wigan where the cotton manufacture was a natural growth.[2]

While feeble and ultimately unsuccessful attempts were being made at St. Helens to keep pace with the transition from domestic to factory production in the sailcloth and cotton industries, many other local inhabitants who struck nails in their own little forges or made metal goods such as tools, files, hinges, locks, chisels, pliers or watch parts in small workshops, continued to earn a tolerable livelihood, for the machine did not invade these branches of manufacture until the middle of the nineteenth century. The most widely distributed of all these trades was the least skilled, nailmaking. Though there can have been few townships in South Lancashire without a nailmaker, or without a blacksmith who would occasionally strike out a pound or two of nails, there was, even here, some degree of concentration. There were district colonies of these workers at Upholland, Billinge, Winstanley, Ashton, Leigh, Chowbent, and, nearer St. Helens, at Moss Bank and at Parr.

The nailmaker was already, by the mid-eighteenth century, the victim of an over-competitive industry. The nailmaker's degradation was long, beginning in the earliest days of the Industrial Revolution, and ending only with the disappearance of the hand-made nail. The trade was heir to all the many ills of a " domestic " industry. Its unskilled nature meant that it could be entered by anyone, and that apprenticeship was meaningless ; boys, women and girls entered the trade without restriction. The separation of the little colonies from one another often meant that the master could impose low rates of pay without difficulty, and that workers undercut each other to get work at all. The conditions under which work was carried on were filthy, stifling and cramped beyond belief. One surviving nailmaker's workshop at Moss Bank could easily be mistaken for a low and inconvenient wash-house.

Records of nailmaking are very hard to come by ; it is our good fortune that the outline of a short-lived venture into this

[1] James Brockbank, *History of St. Helens* (St. Helens, 1896), 26.

[2] For Rylands, see *D.N.B.*; *In Memoriam* (privately circulated 1889) ; art. in *Manchester Evening News* reprinted in *St. H. N.* 24 May, 1865.

industry, undertaken by the brewer, Thomas Greenall, has come down to us. As in the case of his cotton mill, Greenall subsequently used up some of the books in which he had kept his nailer's records for the purposes of his brewery, thus accidentally preserving them. The business was founded by Thomas Greenall entering into partnership with an established nailmaker, John Rigby of Billinge, the manager at St. Helens being Edward Greenall, the brewer's eldest son. Unfortunately there is nothing in the brief records to show where the nails were made, though the writing of letters from both Billinge and St. Helens, and the employment of St. Helens men in the carriage of nails to Liverpool, may indicate that work was carried on at both places.

A letter sent from Billinge on 14 June, 1777, by Rigby to a firm of Liverpool merchants, tells of the foundation of the partnership.

" Messrs. John & Thomas Hodgson,
        Gentn.
                Having lately join'd Mr. Thos Greenall of St. Helens in the Nail Trade under the firm of Thos. Greenall & Co. shall if you ever want nails as suppose you must be much obliged to you for your orders etc. as I know you have great interest will thank you for it with a few of your Friends. You may depend upon the Nails being well manufactored [*sic*] and of a Good Quality the Price as others, your compliance will oblige.
                        Gentn.
                                Your mo. humble Servt.
                                        John Rigby."

At the very beginning of operations we are thus acquainted with the importance of the Liverpool merchant. Apart from the export of nails, particularly to America where log cabins created an enormous demand, Liverpool was itself an important market because of its shipbuilders ; some of the varieties of nail made by Greenall & Rigby were specifically for ships.

The indebtedness of workers to their masters, a usual feature of the nail and tool trades, has an instance in the firm's records. One Thomas Winstanley applied to Greenall & Rigby for employment, and Edward Greenall took him on but wrote to his former master, John Tarbuck of Ormskirk, to suggest that a debt of £13 should be paid off by stopping three shillings a week out of the nailer's pay.[1] Early in the following year, however, a certain T. Winstanley was in active competition with the firm, though he may not have been the same man. In 1778 Edward Greenall wrote to Robert Sherbourne of the Plate Glass Works at Ravenhead :

[1] St. H. Brewery, Letter of 21 Aug., 1777.

" Sir,

Pursuant to order here sent per Thos. Bromilow as above which hope will please—I think there must be some mistake in your prices of 6d & 20d nails they certainly must be sh[or]t count. Shou'd be much obliged to you if Mr. Foster might be permited to lett me see a Bill parcel of T. Winstanley as I have seen in various places of his charged 6d and 20d. the same prices as you have a list off . . . "[1]

The difficulty of knowing what other firms were charging was not easy to overcome ; at the very outset of their venture Greenall carefully collected as full a range as possible of the prices charged by the chief local nailmakers over the preceding few years.

Much of the remaining interest of this short-lived concern centres on its relations with Liverpool merchants. The credit they were given is surprising. At the end of 1778 William Gregson, Africa merchant and banker, was informed, " Our credit is 6 Mos. or 5 p. cent Ready Money,"[2] showing that this highly competitive industry gave its customers three times as long to pay as did, for instance, copper or brewing. Nor is this the longest credit recorded ; Rigby wrote to another celebrated Liverpool merchant, Thomas Earle,

" . . . I recd. your favour but not in time to get the Paterns [sic] on Saturday have now sent them fast on pasteboard—a reference of the prices weights and counts, which I hope will be in such a manner as to be plainly understood, the prices in the reference are at twelvemonths' credit. We allow seven and a half p. cent discount on being paid in a month."[3]

From 1779 to 1783 the Liverpool exporters Thomas and William Moss were very regular customers and on more than one occasion they were wished " a prosperous voyage and good markets." The cheapness of the commodity must have told against single orders of a high value; £30 or £40 worth seems to have been a large delivery, and the greatest in the books are two of £81 and £85 to this firm.[4]

In 1781 and 1782 Greenalls and Rigby found difficulty in keeping down prices. In April of 1781 Earles were told: " . . . have Charg'd the 6d. Nails 1d per more than we have ever charg'd before, owing to the advance of Iron and Workmens Wages cannot afford them lower your future favours will further oblige . . . "[5] Prices were raised to T. & W. Moss in February

[1] Letter of 11 Jan., 1778.
[2] Letter of 11 Dec., 1778.
[3] Letter of 27 Aug., 1780.
[4] In April and Aug., 1781.
[5] Letter of 28 April, 1781 to Messrs. Earles & Molyneux.

of 1782 : " As within have sent pr. order ... (upon examining
the Bill with the last youl [*sic*] find that there is a difference in the
prices) the present prices are charg'd as low as any person in the
County can afford. . . . "[1]

The closing-down of the nailmaking partnership between
Thomas Greenall and John Rigby was almost certainly due to
difficulties in which Rigby had become involved because of his
participation in a more ambitious scheme. This was an iron
slitting mill at Stanley, Blackbrook, adjacent to the copper
refinery established by Thomas Patten. In this Rigby was
associated with other South Lancashire nailmakers, with the firm
of Chorley and Leech of Ashton and with the Postlethwaite
family, who were in the Liverpool iron trade. These works were
offered for sale early in 1784, and later in the year were briefly
taken over by John Rigby, who bought out his other partners
and continued to manufacture hoop and rod iron. Alexander
Chorley was bankrupt by the end of 1785, Rigby died insolvent
about the same time, and John Postlethwaite became bankrupt
in 1787.[2]

The other metal-working trades were, like nailmaking,
scattered over a wide area, though certain districts had a reputation
for particular lines—Ashton-in-Makerfield for locks and hinges,
for instance. A petition from " Ironmongers, Hinge-makers,
Nail-makers, Lock-makers, Hoe-makers, Smiths and others, in
Ashton, Chowbent, West Leigh and ... Warrington ... on behalf
of themselves and many thousands more employed in the different
branches of the Iron manufactory "[3] reveals the extent of these
metal trades by the middle of the eighteenth century. They were
carried on, in general, on the coalfield to the north and east of
St. Helens, though some of these domestic manufacturers worked
within the St. Helens district itself. To the west and south, away
from the coalfield, were to be found the makers of metal tools :
chisels, pliers, vices, gauges, small lathes and, particularly, files.[4]
Such precision skills and the availability of good tools and
" engines " for cutting wheels were essential for the manufacture
of watches and watch parts. Watchmakers, springmakers and
watch case makers are mentioned in the Liverpool Parish Registers

[1] Letter of 15 Feb., 1782.

[2] *Gore's Gen. Ad.* 5 Feb., 11 Nov., 1784 ; 29 Dec., 1785 ; 12 Jan., 9 Feb.,
1786, 8 Nov., 1787.

[3] *C.J.*, **25**, 1098, 29 March, 1750 ; T. S. Ashton, " The Domestic System
in the Early Lancashire Tool Trade," *Econ. Jour. (Ec. Hist. Ser.)* Jan.
1926, 132.

[4] For the late eighteenth century organisation of this indusry, see T. S
Ashton, *An Eighteenth Century Industrialist, Peter Stubs of Warrington
1756-1806* (Manchester, 1939).

of the 1670s[1] and, as occupations only start to be given at that period, it seems very likely that the craft was being followed in the Liverpool neighbourhood even earlier. By the middle of the eighteenth century, the manufacture of watch parts was already being " put out " among the small farms and cottages which lay scattered across the south-west Lancashire plain, with Prescot as the centre for the distribution of the metal and the collection of the finished parts. A number of these domestic watchmakers, each of whom concentrated on the manufacture of one or two particular parts, lived in the vicinity of St. Helens.

Such a division of labour resulted in lessening the cost of production, since the wages bill was by far the most expensive item in watch manufacture. The raw materials, other than the gold and silver cases, cost a trivial sum.[2] Indeed, the Lancashire putting-out system produced the rough movements at such low prices that by the end of the eighteenth century, if not before, the Lancashire manufacturers were supplying most of the great watch firms in London, Coventry and Liverpool with movements and with the tools necessary to finish them. Aikin's claim, made in 1795, that " all Europe " was " more or less supplied " with watch tools and movements from south-west Lancashire,[3] is as indefinite as it is extravagant. But there can be no disputing the clear statement, made by representatives of the Clockmakers' Company of London in 1817, that it was " at Prescot in Lancashire . . . and its vicinity [that] the greater part of the watch movements used in this country and of the watchmakers' tools, were made ".[4] The man who performed the final operations of finishing and assembling the watch placed his name and town on its dial. This concealed the fact that all the earlier precision work inside the watch had been undertaken by a number of domestic craftsmen in and about Prescot. The contribution of south-west Lancashire to national punctuality, in an age of industrialisation of which the essence was accurate timekeeping, deserves more widespread recognition than it has been so far accorded.

The presence of a considerable force of skilled craftsmen, trained to work in metal to a high pitch of accuracy, was undoubtedly a great help to machine-making and engine-building in Lancashire, particularly after 1800 when the expiry of Watt's

---

[1] *Lanc. Par. Reg. Soc.*, **35** (1909).

[2] Memorial of 8 Feb., 1832 in *Statement of the Various Proceedings . . . between . . . the Clockmakers' Company . . . and His Majesty's Government in Relation to the Importation of Foreign Clocks and Watches . . .* (1832), 63-4.

[3] Aikin, 311.

[4] Petition from the Cttee of the Clockmakers' Company, 21 April, 1817, in Mins. of Ev. on the Petition of the Watchmakers of Coventry, 1817 [504] VI. See also F. A. Bailey, "An Old Watchmakers' Workshop," *Trans. Ancient Monuments Society*, **1** (new ser.) (1953), 107 *seq.*

steam engine patent gave rise to an increasing number of engineering firms. " The national advantages derived from the perfection to which the Art of Clock and Watchmaking has been carried in this Country ", wrote the Clockmakers' Company in 1814, " are not limited to the value of its produce, but extend to every branch of manufacture in which machinery is used."[1]

The link between watchmaking and engineering does not seem to have provided St. Helens with a pool of reliable engineers, at least in the early nineteenth century ; the local colliery proprietors and manufacturers had to depend on firms outside the town, such as the Haigh Ironworks near Wigan, the Bridgewater Foundry at Patricroft or Boulton and Watt at Soho.[2] The St. Helens Foundry, it is true, did try to undertake all kinds of engineering tasks,[3] but, from the number of complaints,[4] it would appear that repair and foundry work was its *forte* at that time. Indeed, one of the earliest products was said to have been large iron pots for the Africa trade.[5] The Foundry had been established in 1798 by Birkett and Postlethwaite, who were succeeded by a man called Fletcher and then by the Watson family.[6] John Watson, proprietor of an iron foundry at Sir Thomas's Buildings, Liverpool, had died about 1800, leaving his wife in charge of the business until their sons, Lee and John, came of age.[7] The Liverpool premises were advertised to be let in 1813[8] : this probably marked the beginning of the Watson interest in the St. Helens Foundry. Six years later, Mrs. Watson, then living at Sutton Cottage near St. Helens, and in partnership with her two sons in the St. Helens Foundry, announced that she was " declining [business] in favour

---

[1] Quoted in *Statement of . . . the Clockmakers' Company* (1832), 11. See also G. H. Tupling, " The Early Metal Trades and the Beginnings of Engineering in Lancashire," *Trans. L. & C. Antiq. Soc.*, (1949), **61**, 22. Cf. the Ev. of Peter Ewart to the S.C. on Artisans and Machinery, 1824, [51] V, 251.

[2] Bromilow Papers. Letter from Benjamin Fletcher, Haigh Ironworks, to William Bromilow, 23 Dec., 1828 ; B.P.G. Mins., 25 July, 1838 ; B. & W. Coll., F. Fincham to Boulton and Watt, 4 Sept., 24 Nov., 1843.

[3] See *A List of Bevel, Spur and Mitre Wheel Patterns Belonging to Lee Watson and Company, St. Helens' Foundry, Lancashire* (printed by C. Hollis, Lpool., 1840).

[4] St. H. and R. G. Mins., 3 April, 1833 ; *Wigan Gazette*, 12 April, 1839.

[5] T. Cook, *St. Helens: A Brief History of Its Religious and Other Institutions . . . Also a Concise Account of Its Productions, Trades, Manufactures, Topography and Antiquities* (MS. at St. H. Wesley Church), 100.

[6] *Ibid.* This may have been the Postlethwaite referred to above,

[7] Letters of Admin. issued at Chester 4 July, 1801 ; *Billinge's Lpool. Ad.* 7 Sept., 1801.

[8] *Lpool. Merc.* 6 Aug., 1813. This foundry was still in the Watsons' hands in 1818 (*Gore's Gen. Ad.*, 3 Sept., 1818).

of any person of respectability " who would " take into partnership either of her sons . . . "[1] Such a person did come forward
and in 1820 the St. Helens Foundry was being conducted by Lee
Watson and Co.[2]

The St. Helens Foundry was not the only works in the district
engaged in manufacture for the Africa trade. Large earthenware
vessels were also sent to Liverpool for shipment to Africa. In
1808, for instance, the potters' clay was said to have been " of
considerable demand during the African and West Indian
Trade, but since the Stoppage of those, and a suspension of
Intercourse with America, there appears a great Want of Sale for
Articles (principally Stone Ware Bottles) manufactured there-
from".[3] This traffic, particularly to Africa and Ireland, was soon
resumed, however, and continued to be of importance throughout
the century.

The local clays in and around St. Helens had been worked for
hundreds of years. They were turned on the potter's wheel into
such articles as coarse earthenware mugs, sugar moulds and
drips, and stoneware bottles.[4] There is no indication that the finer
grades of pottery were ever made near St. Helens, as was the case
in Liverpool which was a centre for Delft ware in the eighteenth
century. The local potteries, some five in number,[5] used to be
called mug works, an apt description.

One of them, situated by the Canal at Greenbank, was said in
1833 to have been established " many years." It had been owned
for some time by Thomas Harley, a man with Staffordshire connections. He apparently sent his wares over to Ireland in some
quantity, for he owned a shop at Thomas Street, Dublin, where

[1] *Gore's Gen. Ad.* 3 Sept., 1818.

[2] L.R.O. Land Tax Returns, Windle, 1820. See below, p. 367.

[3] Valuation of land at Prescot preserved among the archives of King's
College, Cambridge. We are grateful to Mr. F. A. Bailey for this transcript.
Between 28,000 and 47,000 packages of earthenware were exported from
Liverpool and between 4,000 and 7,000 sent coastwise in each year between
1803 and 1811. Parliamentary Return 1812 [324] X.

[4] Mr. T. Davies, of Sutton Heath Pottery, possesses stoneware bottles
which were made there late in the nineteenth century for African markets.

[5] These were : (1) Lightfoot's at Gerard's Bridge, held under leases of
1804 and 1816. (*St. H. Standard* 3 July, 1875 ; L.R.O., Cross Papers,
Assignment of Richard Lightfoot's estate, 1816 ; will of Mary Lightfoot,
proved at Chester, 29 Dec., 1832) ; (2) Bromilow Haddock's adjoining
their Ravenhead Colliery (Land Tax Assessments, Sutton, 1830) ; (3)
Thomas Grace's at Marshall's Cross (*ibid* and below, p.369) ; (4) Swaine's
at Sutton Heath (*ibid.*, 1820 ; Bold sale catalogue 1848, Cross Papers,
DDCS 7/25) ; (5) Harley's at Greenbank mentioned in the next paragraph.

they were sold.[1]   Under different ownership, this pottery was destined to play an important rôle in the draining of some of the large towns of the north.[2]

Metal-working, ironfounding, and pottery-making, though by no means vital to the rise of modern St. Helens, provided employment for several hundred of the local inhabitants scattered throughout the area. The domestic metal-workers were ultimately doomed to extinction ; but at the beginning of the nineteenth century the machinery that was to deprive them of their accustomed livelihood had not yet been invented. As the demand continued to grow, they were to pass through a golden age before the end came.

[1] *Lpool. Merc.* 25 Oct., 1833 ; will of Thomas Harley proved at Chester 4 Feb., 1833. Messrs. Mort and Simpson of the Herculaneum Pottery, Lpool., later took a lease of this pottery and began to work it in 1836. Their manager was James Bayley, a native of Burslem (*Wigan Gazette,* 12 April, 1839 ; *St. H. N.* 6 June, 1874).

[2] Below, p. 319.

CHAPTER XI

SOCIAL LIFE : THE POOR OF PARR

1730-1815

A MONG the best sources of information on how the poor lived in the eighteenth century are collections of parish or township papers dealing with the Old Poor Law. This body of legislation, codified under the first Elizabeth, had a wide application. It covered the care of the aged and infirm poor, the binding of poor children apprentice, the punishment of vagrants and beggars, the employment of those without work, the levying of a poor rate and the appointment of local officials, the overseers of the poor, to control these activities in every parish. The Poor Law of Elizabeth I, with numerous modifications, governed the care of the poor in this country down to 1834. Shortly after the Restoration an alteration was made whereby the law could be administered on a township rather than a parochial basis in the North of England, where parishes were often so large as to make administration difficult.

The township records of Eccleston and Windle have been totally lost, and little survives for Sutton,[1] but for Parr a great bulk of material exists, mostly relating to the mid-eighteenth century.[2] The Parr records are very typical, the accounts being kept sometimes well, sometimes badly, according to the ability or public spirit of the part-time and unpaid townsmen who held the office of overseer in the particular year to which they apply. The chaotic state of the records invalidates any kind of statistical approach, except in those few years when well-kept accounts survive, or in those cases where Parliamentary returns of Poor Law expenditure were made. Nevertheless, though lacking in statistical information, the Township Papers of Parr are a rich source of knowledge on how the poor lived ; their perpetual nearness to want and even to starvation, had not the rough mercy of the Poor Law intervened ; their simple luxuries and

[1] Prescot Historic Society. Sutton Township Book. Vestiges of the old manorial court clung to Sutton township administration, shown in the appointment of " the four men," burleymen and mossreeves. The resolutions of several township meetings are recorded. The whereabouts of the remainder of the township records is unknown.

[2] St. H. Ref. Lib. Parr Township Papers. Apart from the papers of overseers of the poor, there are the records of other township officials, the constables and the surveyors of the highway. The earliest poor law records go back to 1688, so that presumably Parr did not adopt the Settlement and Townships Act of 1662 until about that year.

merry-makings ; their clothes ; their subjection to authority ; their dread of being haled before a Justice, or thrown into the workhouse, or moved into the next township, or forced to serve in the militia.

It is in one respect fortunate that it is the records of Parr, alone out of our four townships, which have survived. The first district reached by the Sankey Canal, Parr was the township the collieries of which first received the benefits of water communication, it was the first township to feel the effect of rising land values due to its coal mines, the first, we may assume, to be as much an industrial as an agricultural community.[1] Moreover Parr was a manor as well as a township, and it was the first of the local manors to fall into the hands of a commercial family, the Claytons of Liverpool. Though Elizabeth and Sarah Clayton, owing to their sex, were unable to exercise the office of Justice to which their influence would otherwise have entitled them, it generally happened that the J.P.s to whom the Parr officials went for warrants, orders and the like, were a similar combination of merchant (or industrialist) and landowner—the Thomas Pattens, father and son, Thomas and Jonathan Case, John Blackburne, Richard Norris, Richard Gildart, William Gregson, Nicholas Ashton, Michael Hughes and James Fraser are typical examples. Church influence on township administration was small, and there was here no dual rule of parson and squire ; Parr was only one of fifteen townships in Prescot parish, and by no means one of the largest. Apart from church leys and occasional demands at times of rebuilding, the parish church troubled the township little. In Parr, therefore, we have an example of the Old Poor Law functioning in a district where the preponderant influences were increasingly industrial.

The longest thread which can be traced in the Poor Law history of Parr is the story of the township's attempt to arrive at a workhouse policy. This has the added interest that Parr persistently endeavoured to implement whatever of the Elizabethan intention survived into eighteenth-century Poor Law administration by " setting the poor on work." The place of parish workhouses became a matter for much public controversy in the late seventeenth and early eighteenth centuries, and the times were full of

---

[1] A Militia Return for Parr covering 1768-9 gives a list of able-bodied men between 18 and 44 years of age, with their occupations. It contains in all the names of 75 men, who must have formed a considerable fraction of the male working population. Agricultural and non-agricultural occupations are nearly balanced; while there were 36 husbandmen, there were 19 colliers, 5 nailers, 2 weavers, 2 shoemakers, 2 tailors, 2 blacksmiths, 2 bricksetters, a watchmaker, a brewer, a carpenter, a saddler and a pavior. There are, in addition, several men on the list whose occupations are not given, but whose callings are known from other sources ; for instance James Orrell, junior, Alexander Tarbuck, his assistant Hill and Thomas Speakman have already been mentioned in connection with the coal trade.

projects for the useful employment of the out-of-work poor, young and old, and even for making a profit from their labours. This tendency culminated in the important Act of 1722, which formed the basis for a widespread experimentation in workhouse policy.[1] The churchwardens and overseers with the consent of the inhabitants of any parish or township were empowered to purchase or hire houses, and to contract for the lodging, employment and maintenance of the poor ; a pauper refusing to be so maintained could be struck off the township books and denied relief. Furthermore, where townships or parishes were small, and unable to support a workhouse on their own, two or more, with the approval of a Justice, might unite in purchasing, hiring or building houses to serve as workhouses. Alternatively, the majority of inhabitants being in agreement, the churchwardens and overseers could contract with the officers of another township or parish for the lodging and maintenance of their poor.   Over a short period this Act often had the effect of the later Act of 1834, in that it imposed a species of workhouse test, and thereby reduced the number of applicants for relief.

How the rumour of the successful application of the Act reached Parr, we do not know, but, after a delay of nearly ten years, the township, in conjunction with the adjacent township of Windle, adopted the Act.   On 1 May, 1732 the township officers of Parr and Windle agreed to lease from William Cooper of Token House Yard in London, gentleman, his house, barn and garden at Pike's Brow in the Moss Bank district of Windle. The lease granted was for eleven years at 30/- per annum, and the townships promised to lay out £35 in making alterations and new apartments and in building new premises, and undertook to keep the place in proper repair.[2]

The opening of the workhouse is indirectly noted in the township records by the ending of outdoor relief, and by the township's temporary abandonment of the practice of assisting paupers by paying their rents.   For instance, there is this receipt for the year 1733 :

" Recd. 2 Aprill 1733 from Edw. Greenough (7/- & 6d.) being for Rent for the house where Jeannet Bruch now dwells for the year past by order of the Towne to the time the poor went to the workhouse

I say Recd.
Esther Tyrer.

[1] 9 Geo. I. cap. VII.   See Sir F. M. Eden, *The State of the Poor* (1797), I, page v.   *Ibid.*, I, 267-9 contains a full discussion of the Act, and 283-5 the initial success of early workhouses set up under it.   Eden considered that a factor in their eventual failure was the lack of a permanent official to undertake the administration of the poor law in each parish.   See also Sir George Nicholls, *A History of the English Poor Law* (1854) II, 14-18.

[2] St. H. Ref. Lib., Parr Township Papers.   Indenture of 1 May, 1732.

A workhouse bill survives for the same year, mentioning the payment of 9d for a " coton whele " to be mended and the purchase of brimstone and quicksilver (presumably for medicinal purposes) together with " half a Quarter of Tobacko ". The supply of sheets, chaff-beds, bed-cord and hand towels to the workhouse shows that elementary comforts were provided.

The workhouse did not long achieve the purposes for which it was founded, for by 1740 the old system of paying paupers' rents instead of sending them to the workhouse had crept back once more. As late as 1743, however, some of the poor of Parr and Windle were still in the joint workhouse. The probability is that the lease was not renewed after the original term of eleven years was out, and the townships then turned to other plans for maintaining their poor.

Parr for a time embarked on a small workhouse venture of its own. In the early 'fifties a house was rented from Sarah Clayton. This can have been no elegant building, for two entries over 1750-1 read : " by leading clay treading daub for the workhouse 3/6 " and " Henry Adamson for . . . beating floor at workhouse 2/-". Nevertheless some attention was paid to the education of child paupers, one and sixpence being disbursed as " firemoney for 3 loads at Schole ". The use of this workhouse does not appear to have caused any great reduction in the paying of paupers' rents, in outdoor relief or in weekly pay. Indeed these occupied a much more important place in the accounts than did the workhouse, which was perhaps only intended as some sort of shelter for those of the poor whom it was difficult to billet on others or to maintain in their own homes. In 1751 a purchase of barley and meal for the poor in the workhouse is recorded, while the cost of brick and lime, a lock and nails points to the carrying out of repairs.

This workhouse was persisted with till 1756 at least, but in 1759 Parr again united with another township in a common establishment. On 1 January of that year articles of agreement were drawn up between the inhabitants of Pemberton, near Wigan, and the inhabitants of Parr " concerning the Inhabitants of Pemberton taking the poor belonging to the Township of Parr aforesaid into their workhouse for the term of one whole year . . ." Other townships not specified were also involved in the agreement. Parr was to pay its proportionate part of the wages of the Governor and Governess of the house, and its share of the rent and of the fuel bill. The document continues with a clause which confirms what is known of the staple diet of the working classes in Lancashire at this period :

" The Inhabitants of Parr are to pay to the Governor of the said Workhouse for every single poor person they put in the workhouse whilst oat meal is under 16/- a load, 12d. per week, but if oatmeal extend to 16/- a load 14d a week, if 20/- a load, then it is referred to the Inhabitants of Pemberton what they are to pay more."

Parr was to provide bed stocks and bedding, and " all Sorts of Apparrell & likewise all sorts of worklooms according to their calling " for every single person or family they sent to the workhouse. No lunatics were to be admitted, nor any child incapable of " tenting [caring for] itself unless they bring some person to look after it." The Governor was to allow the overseers of Parr the money earned by their poor, and they were to meet him on the first Monday in every month to settle accounts " and to see how the poor are provided for, or for every neglect to forfeit the sum of one shilling."[1] In practice the Parr overseers almost invariably " neglected." The educational facilities formerly provided at Parr were not forgotten at Pemberton ; the overseers paid " Entrance for 4 Children to School Master at Pemberton 2-6d " and a further 1/3d for a quarter's schooling.

The contract with Pemberton opened auspiciously, for the monthly bill for May, 1759 reveals that the poor there, four in number, were making by their work half of their monthly maintenance, reckoned at 4/- a head. In the next month the inmates were earning more than half their keep by spinning, but curiously enough the cotton used was carded elsewhere and charged against the paupers' account. In the beginning of 1760 this was rectified by " a pair of cards " being bought at 1/- and paid for by Parr. It is difficult to make out what classes of paupers were directed to the workhouse, and the matter is complicated by workhouse governors entering up the paupers simply as so many " head." Where names survive, they are often those of women who had children with them ; perhaps they were often illegitimate, for the term " brats " was several times used to describe them, and this can scarcely have been a polite term, even two centuries ago.

Able-bodied men rarely entered the workhouse, and many of the adult paupers seem to have died within a few weeks of admission. This may not be due to cruelty in the administration of the workhouse, but to the fact that it was used for people who had nowhere else to go, being a cheaper means of sheltering those who were incapable of work and at death's door than boarding them out, even if anyone could be found to take them. Such persons were not entirely denied creature comforts. Tobacco was a regular purchase, nursing was provided when they were ill, and some attempt was made to sustain the elderly and sick. " Paid for sugar and drink for the old woman 2½d " reads one entry. In the case of this old lady the treatment was not long effective, for two months later an account runs :

[1] Parr Township Papers, Articles of Agreement, 1 Jan., 1759.

pd. for one pound of Candels	0	0	7
pd. for half a pound of sugar			3
pd. for wine			3
pd. for laying her out		1	0
pd. for drink			6
pd. for asking to the buryal			6
pd. for hors hire			8
pd. for going to holand[1] and geting the Cofin maid			4
pd. for tobackow			4

Throughout the 1770s bills were infrequent, and little work was recorded as being done within the walls, until in 1781 a Michael and Alice Taylor entered. Michael was a little boy of about ten, Alice appears to have been older, and was perhaps his mother or sister. In the November, Michael was put under contract with the master of the workhouse who was to teach him to weave for £1 down and £1 later, presumably to be paid when Michael was proficient. By the August of 1782 this diligent child was actually earning more than his monthly keep, and thus justifying the often-dashed hopes of the poor law planners of the age. This no doubt involved long hours of work, for in the December, when light would be poorest, sixpence was put on the bill for candles for his use. The same bill shows the governor providing the exemplary little pauper with a new hat, shoes, and stockings. This remarkable incident in Parr's experiments with a workhouse policy was short-lived. In the December of 1783, at the age of twelve, Michael Taylor was apprenticed to Joseph Winstanley of Wigan, fustian weaver, to learn that trade during the space of eight years. No doubt he proved a good apprentice, but the training would seem from his point of view to have been a waste of time.[2]

In 1799 the workhouse alliance was again changed, Parr joining with the neighbouring township of Newton-le-Willows in a Union in which there were at first seven members.[3] In February, 1800, the paupers were being maintained at 4½d per head per day, though this was increased to 5½d by the August. The inmates were set on work, as in the previous workhouses, and tilled some sort of garden or smallholding, for potato sets and cabbage plants featured in the bill for this year, and garden seeds, beesoms, pots and a wheelbarrow in that for 1801. In the latter year three more

[1] Upholland (?)

[2] Parr Township Papers, Apprentices' Indentures.

[3] Though subsequent to the celebrated Gilbert's Act, this Union does not appear to have been administered under its provisions; there is no mention of Guardians, and while the equipment of the workhouse and the materials used for the paupers' work were paid for in equal shares in all the member townships, there was a varying scale of contributions from each township for the upkeep of the inmates, dependent on the number placed in the workhouse. Eden, *op. cit.* I, 366.

townships must have joined the Union, for Parr's share of articles purchased for the workhouse was down to one-tenth. In this year, too, a certain amount of weaving was done in the institution by the paupers of Parr, though the cost of equipping the weavers with looms and other requisites of their trade largely offset their earnings. An account for part of 1803 records the payment of three shillings to a midwife, and the purchase of tea, sugar, and beer. During the succeeding years down to 1808 the Newton workhouse was never used by more than a couple of Parr paupers at a time, and often the township had no paupers there for a considerable period. The series of bills comes to an end in the November of 1808.[1]

Parr's workhouse experiments were at last abandoned. What success had they met with over the previous seventy years? Only in the first workhouse, shared with Windle, was the workhouse test strictly applied, and then only for a few years. In the subsequent cases, despite the existence of the workhouse, much the same volume of outdoor relief and of paupers' rents continued to be paid. The fact may have been that many people were so near to the relief level, and so easily thrust into pauperism by any rise in prices, or a severe winter, or a depression in their trade, that any rigid policy would have been very difficult to enforce. Despite the generally improving standard of living, the workhouse test may, paradoxically, have become even more difficult to enforce in the second half of the century, when the movements of grain prices tended to become too severe for the purses of the poor to cope with in bad years. But even though a stern application of the workhouse test was abandoned, the usefulness of such an establishment might still be considerable. It could always be used as a threat to particularly idle paupers, as a last refuge for those who were so old or ill that no one would willingly look after them, as a place to which any willing to earn their own bread, but without the necessary equipment, might be directed. In other words a workhouse could be a valuable auxiliary to the more usual outdoor relief.

Before finally leaving the subject of the provision of work for the poor, two other points may be worth making. Firstly, giving the paupers work to do in their own houses was not unknown ; in the 1730s and again as late as the 1780s there were instances

---

[1] It is interesting to note that in 1791 the township of Windle obtained the consent of William Cotham (as lord of the manor of Hardshaw) to the building of a workhouse on the waste near the Moorflat. This building, on the site now occupied by the Baldwin Street premises of the St. Helens Co-operative Society, was in fact erected at the joint cost of the townships of Windle and Eccleston. They made an agreement in 1793 containing rules for the administration of the paupers, and for the sharing of the cost of their upkeep and of any profits from their work, but it is not known how long the arrangement was continued. St. Helens Ind. Co-op. Socy. Ltd., Deeds.

of this. In the receipts for 1785, for example, it is recorded that a pound of cotton at two shillings was purchased for Ellen James, while " Smedhurst's wife " had her cotton wheel mended for a shilling.   Secondly, though this part of Lancashire has been thought of as a linen-weaving area until late in the eighteenth century,[1] and though many local inhabitants described themselves as following that calling down to the 1770s, cotton was the only textile mentioned for either spinning or weaving in the overseers' receipts from 1730 to 1800.

An important duty of the overseers was the provision of relief to paupers outside the workhouse, " outdoor relief " as it is generally termed. This could be administered in several ways. The overseers could pay the rent of the pauper, thus lifting a considerable burden from him, while leaving him to get his living as he could. If a pauper had no house of his own they could pay for his board in the house of any neighbour who was willing to take a lodger ; such a payment was often described as a pauper's " weekly table." Young orphans, as well as homeless adults, were often relieved in this way until they were old enough to be put out apprentice. Occasionally, if the distress was only a temporary matter, food or coals would be given, while there was a very extensive distribution of clothing to paupers and near-paupers, though whether this was out of the poor rates or out of the funds of local charities is at times difficult to determine. Lastly there was the most usual method of outdoor relief, a money dole. This consisted of the weekly payment termed " pay " or " wage ", or, alternatively, " occasional relief," payment at odd times to carry the pauper over periods of unemployment, sickness, or destitution.

Weekly pay and occasional relief cannot now be disentangled, for the carelessness with which the accounts and receipts were drawn up generally makes it impossible to know which was which. For certain years, however, when a person with a superior sense of responsibility or a greater familiarity with book-keeping handled the accounts, it is possible to form an idea of the number of people who, over all or part of a year, needed relief. In 1753, for instance, there were twenty-one. The overseer for 1759 noted those to whom only occasional disbursements were made ; they were fifteen in all, and in ten of the cases it is specifically stated that the money was disbursed at a time when the individual concerned (or one of the family) was sick, so that in this year at least public money was not being distributed heedlessly. The confusion of the accounts is often made worse by looseness of phrasing ; if a pauper was paid the sum of 2s. in two successive weeks, that may be recorded as " weekly pay,"

[1] See A. P. Wadsworth and J. de L. Mann, *The Cotton Trade and Industrial Lancashire, 1600-1780* (Manchester, 1931), 277-8.

whereas another, who received 2s. on half a dozen occasions over two months, may well have had his money entered in the accounts as separate instances of occasional relief, though in fact he was more frequently a charge upon the rates than his fellow-pauper. Some conception of what proportion of the population was dependent on relief can be gained from Parliamentary returns made in 1786. These show that 167 persons in Parr were in need of constant relief in December, 1782, while as many as 72 were relieved in August and September, 1783. When we realise that in 1801 the population of Parr was only 1,183, it is at once clear how near to the brink of pauperism was a large percentage of the working class.[1]

Relief in kind was rare, and was probably a matter of emergency, or of convenience to the overseers. On the 12 June, 1757 we have an entry in the receipts :—" to a Loff of Bread p. Overseers Ord. p. Hannah Brimelow 0 0 6d." Again in the February of 1783 James Orrell & Co. were paid 6s. 6d. for 26 baskets of coal supplied to Ellen James at the cost of the township. This was no very dear rate even at the pit-head prices of the time, and obviously a case where the overseers had decided to relieve a poor woman by giving her winter fuel. The accounts for the early 'fifties contain a number of references to food and clothes bought, though in no large quantities ; these are possibly for the workhouse then open in Parr, for they subsequently tend to die out.

Clothing was given away throughout the period, and it is the most suspect of the activities of the overseers. Very often it was not some local shopkeeper but the overseer who was paid for the clothing distributed, and this was obviously open to abuse. Henry Berry, afterwards the engineer of the Sankey Canal and of Liverpool's docks, was an overseer the township paid in this way. Sometimes it happened that drapers or linen-weavers or cotton manufacturers were the overseers. It is not of course necessary to assume that this state of affairs led to any serious abuse ; the very number of inhabitants in some way connected with textiles may have meant that any sharp practice would have been at once detected.

The clothing, especially in the early decades of the century, was frequently supplied in the cloth, thread and tapes being provided to help in its making-up. Serge, frieze, linen, linsey-woolsey, plain and check were the cloths most frequently supplied, and if a complete garment was given, it had usually been made up by the local tailor. The tailors of that period were dressmakers as well, and made gowns and waistcoats, petticoats

[1] Parr Township Papers. "Answers to the Questions relating to the Poor agreeable to Mr. Gilbert's Bill given in 5th Sept., 1786." (Draft). It should be observed, however, that 1782-3 was a period of particularly high grain prices, as was 1801.

and breeches with equal readiness. The wide variety of the cloths distributed can be seen from a single bill of 1751, which mentions half-thick silk, Welsh linen, blue frieze, serge, handkerchiefs, beggar's inckel (probably some sort of tape), binding, worsted and linsey-woolsey. On one occasion in the early 1780s Michael Taylor, the young weaver previously mentioned, received for his use blue frieze, flannel, linen, buttons, thread, stockings, a hat and buckles, having in all 10s. 7¾d. spent upon him. The list of materials supplied can be greatly extended—milled flannel striped cotton and holland, pocket fustian, corduroy and cotton facing are all mentioned. Women paupers were throughout the period able to demand stays from the overseers, and stay tape was a regular item in the clothing bills.

It is interesting to notice that there were two classes of landlord who received payment from the overseers for the rents of those paupers who were relieved by being allowed free house-room. These were the ordinary townsman who owned a cottage or two in addition to his own dwelling, and the industrialist. It would seem that Sarah Clayton had been building or buying cottages for her colliers; after the Clayton and Case failures the assignees let as many as five cottages at once to the township. Within a year or two John Mackay had largely replaced her as a cottage owner. In other words the coal-owners were becoming considerable owners of house property, their obvious purpose being to house their own colliers, and to be in a position to attract labour by offering accommodation, as we have seen Mackay doing at Parr and at Thatto Heath.[1] The Parr Rate Books which survive for the 1840s show that by then most of Parr's housing was owned by industrialists, principally coal-owners. The coal-owners drew rents whether they employed their colliers or turned them off ; unemployed or aged colliers would plead poverty to the overseers and have their rents paid. The Stanley Smelting Company also on occasion leased cottages to the township ; and for some years after 1814, when it closed its works, the Company drew rents from the overseers, probably for the houses of unemployed copper-workers.

An auxiliary method of relief was to supply the services of a doctor in time of sickness, and in the case of Parr a large number of doctors' accounts are preserved. These bills are not merely informative from the point of view of the Poor Law : they also give amusing glimpses of eighteenth century medical practice. The profession even in those days dearly loved a long word. Items included in the pharmacopoeia were balsamic blysters, carminative powders, balsmic electuaries, cordial febrifuge, deobstruent drops, and sudorific anodyne mixture, as well as more

---

[1] See above, pp. 35 and 44.

prosaic remedies. Sometimes the work of the doctor was unpleasant, and he demanded special fees. A Dr. Thomas Tetlow who had in 1759 been visiting Esther Bromilow included in the bill : " to attendance and dressing the mortifyed parts sixteen weeks, six of which took up nearly two hours every day and was very tedious work . . . £3 3 0." It is interesting that the standard of professional skill seems to have fallen off to some extent in the latter half of the century, and in the 1790s bills for doctoring were received from a bonesetter and a draper and from a certain Henry Boardman. He was perhaps one of the last of the race who combined barbering and surgery, and he described some of his services by the simple and general phrase " working fisick." In 1796, for instance, he charged for " a tending on John Woods dressing his sore legs plastering his broken ribs bleeding working fisick and other measures for a whole year 0 13 4."

We have no evidence whether this decline in the standard of medical practice was due to economy on the part of the township, or to the fact that the population was outrunning the supply of practitioners. However, towards the end of the 'nineties, professional respectability reasserted itself as men like William Pilkington,[1] Joseph Churton and John Casey moved into the district and were employed from time to time by Parr. The system was not regularised till 1823 when the services of a doctor were retained for the township at £12 a year.

The forced marriages which formed such a shocking feature of eighteenth- and early nineteenth-century Poor Law administration[2] do not appear to have been common in Parr, and only two or three such events can be identified with any certainty over a period of seventy years. In 1759 one cost the township as much as £3 17s. 0d. How far payments towards weddings or setting up house necessarily implied a forced marriage is difficult to say ; it may only have been a way of encouraging marriages which would enable the woman to be supported without the aid of the poor rate. Though pauper marriages were a rarity, pauper funerals were very common, but the eighteenth century seems to have catered for them rather more liberally than the nineteenth. Parr funerals were supplied with plenty of beer, mourners were summoned, even from some distance, a seemingly expensive coffin was provided, the church bell was tolled, and indeed, apart from the sermon, the pauper was seen out of this world with as much ceremony as some of his wealthier fellows. A bill of 20 January, 1795, reads :

[1] Below, p. 203 *et seq.*

[2] For examples of this practice in other parts of the country see J. Beresford (ed.) *The Diary of a Country Parson, the Reverend James Woodforde* I (1924) 82 and II (1926) 210, 297.

"to Frances Baldwin sickness and Beariell.

to Bord wage wakeing and atendance and noresment

toe weeks	14	0
to leaing aught and winding	1	0
to cofin	14	0
to drink and expences	7	0
to pall	1	0
to Berieng grouend and Bell	5	2
to duty to King		3
£2	2	5

In addition to the numerous varieties of relief they administered, the township officials had two other important duties under
the Old Poor Law. These were the apprenticing of young paupers[1]
and the supervision of settlements. The apprenticeship records
of Parr are not, on the whole, very remarkable, but they do serve
to confirm the usual picture, and here and there to throw up a
striking illustration. Of sixty-one boys apprenticed between 1713
and 1814 seventeen were apprenticed to linen weavers, five to
fustian weavers, one to a muslin weaver, one to a weaver who was
also a bleacher, and three to weavers whose trade is not more
clearly specified. A solitary boy was apprenticed to cotton
spinning, making a total of 28 boys out of 61 who went to the
textile trades. Five boys went to various branches of the metal
industry, seven were apprenticed to husbandry or farming, seven
to shoemakers or cordwainers, and five to tailors, while there are
single instances of boys apprenticed to a mason, a bricksetter, an
innkeeper, a peruke-maker, a chairmaker and a bodice-maker.
Two were apprenticed to coal miners.

Of twenty-eight girls apprenticed during the same period,
twenty-one went to be domestic servants—an apprenticeship to
" housewifery " as it was euphemistically called—one to linen-
weaving, four to cotton spinning (the spinning jenny being specified
in two of these cases), and two to fustian weaving.

It is apparent that parish apprenticeship was less common in
the case of girls than of boys, the intention often being to take the
burden of their maintenance from the rates by sending them to
anyone who would board them as servants. A certain change in
the trades to which the children were apprenticed must also be
noted. No girl, for instance, was apprenticed to anything but
housewifery till 1787 ; seven out of eleven subsequently went to
the textile trades. Women of course had long been part-time

[1] Parish apprenticeship had been in existence since 1601, but the 8 &
W. & M. cap. XXX forced masters to receive apprentices sent to them b
the parish officers under penalty of £10 " and parish apprenticeshi
henceforth became the most popular method of relieving the paris
of its burden of poor children." J. D. Chambers, *Nottinghamshire in th
Eighteenth Century* (1932) 226.

spinners of cotton in their homes, but this seems to indicate the time when it first became usual for women in this district to become full-time textile workers. For boys linen weaving was the most popular trade down to 1780 ; indeed between 1759 and the end of that year every boy apprenticed (but one) went to a linen weaver. After 1780 the proportion going to linen weaving fell off rapidly, fustian weaving largely replacing it in the next decade, when five boys were apprenticed to that branch.

Taking boys and girls together, sixty-three children were apprenticed outside the township and twenty-six inside it during the century over which the apprenticeship records run. This of course was in agreement with the policy of contemporary overseers all over the country. They always tried to get their pauper children placed outside their district because apprenticeship conferred a settlement : once a child was taken to a distant master in another township the overseers did not have to worry further, they had " saved harmless the Inhabitants of Parr." To a great degree this policy must have been nugatory ; as each township unloaded its young paupers on to others, their efforts would cancel out. To some extent, however, there would be a shift of population, some townships would have a general labour shortage, others a particular opening for juvenile labour. Most of the apprentices Parr sent to the textile industries went to the area round Wigan—Pemberton, Billinge, Orrell, Winstanley, and the townships between Wigan and Bolton.[1] The trades to which pauper children were apprenticed were not necessarily the most prosperous or the most populous, but were in the main those which could be picked up within a few months to an extent to which a child's help would be appreciable. Hence the predominance of weaving.

That parish apprenticeship was unlikely to be very valuable to the boy or girl, and was in fact a way of supplying the master with labour in return for maintenance, can be told from the insignificant premiums paid to the employer, or even the absence of any payment. When in 1718, for instance, Nicholas Ashton of Parr, husbandman, the father of John Ashton, the great Liverpool merchant, took Isobell Houghton as apprentice, he undertook to teach her housewifery but was not paid any fee. When a fee was paid it was customarily about £1 till about 1730, but from that date it became usual to demand £1 down and £1 at the end of the first year, " if the child should live so long." Whether this reflects the death rate among parish apprentices as a class, or merely the general child mortality of the period, the phrase or its equivalent has an ugly sound.

---

[1] This tendency has been noticed in the case of a township only a few miles away. " A large number of the boys placed out by Skelmersdale were apprenticed to linen, fustian, and cotton weavers in or near Wigan." D. Marshall, *The English Poor in the Eighteenth Century* (1926) 196.

There was a gradual tendency for the fees to rise, sums between a guinea and three guineas being common in the eighties and nineties, though even as late as 1810 a girl could be put to weaving without any fee. There were exceptions, however, to these small premiums. A blacksmith was paid £5 as early as 1713, a fustian weaver 6 gns. in 1784, a shoemaker 5 gns. in 1795 and a tailor £10 in 1805. In a solitary instance of 1811 a shoemaker undertook to pay his apprentice the wages of a guinea a year. The township provided the apprentice with two sets of wearing apparel " two sutes of Clothes (one sute for workdays and the other for holy days) " as one indenture describes them, though sometimes money was given as an equivalent. The apprentice was supposed to leave his master at the end of this term equally well clothed. The earlier surviving indentures followed the old formula, and in picturesque language forbade cards, drinking, fornication and marriage, but as early as the 1720s a less comprehensive printed certificate began to come into use, though its adoption was slow.

The period of apprenticeship by no means strictly adhered to what is generally thought of as the customary term of seven years ; nor did it always terminate at twenty-one. While sometimes the apprentice was allowed to leave his master at 18 or 20, a boy was often bound till 24.[1] Eight, nine, ten, eleven, and even twelve-year apprenticeships were served, though eight and nine years were the most common. On the other hand, there were a few instances of five- and six-year apprenticeships. But when we consider how paltry were the skills to be acquired from the master, and how long the apprentice was compelled to serve, there can be little doubt that the system generally was one of licensed slavery. When the ages of the children put out apprentice are given, they are customarily as low as nine or ten, or even " about eight." Nor did the age of the children increase much in our period ; twelve and thirteen perhaps occurred more often towards the end of it, but a girl of seven years and seven months was apprenticed to a cotton spinner near Manchester in 1800, a boy of eight to a Wigan spinner in 1812.

The parish officers had among their duties under the Old Poor Law the superintendence of the Laws of Settlement, dating from the Restoration, framed to make it difficult for poor persons to move about the country if they were not likely to be able to maintain themselves, or liable to be a burden to any parish where they settled. Machinery was devised through " settlement certificates " by which a township or parish might accept the poor of another district as long as they

---

[1] Under the Old Poor Law boys were originally bound till the age of 24 girls till 21 or marriage. The age limit was reduced to 21 for boys also by an Act of 1778, 18 Geo. III cap. 47. However, this did not prevent the children being apprenticed young, and a long term being secured by this means ; as late as 1814 a Parr child was apprenticed for 11 years.

were no charge to it, but was able to return them to their place of origin if they became dependent on the rates. There are over 130 settlement certificates or removal orders surviving in the Parr archives between 1700 and 1827. It might be expected that from these something definite could be discovered about the movement of population into an eighteenth-century industrial area. Indeed, as far as they go, the records do bear out the accepted view that the heaviest migration was of a short-distance nature. If we separate the migrants into three classes—1. those who moved in from townships which lay adjacent, or whose boundaries were only an insignificant distance away ; 2. those who moved from townships within the South-West Lancashire area ; 3. those from more distant parts of Lancashire and from other parts of the country—we find that almost fifty per cent. of those whose movements are recorded belonged to the first group, over thirty per cent. to the second, and only about twenty per cent. to the third. Even in the last group, almost half of the movements are still within the county itself, and Durham and Shropshire represent the extremes of movement recorded.[1]

Unfortunately we cannot record the relative degree of movement into and out of the district, because so few of Parr's copies of certificates given to their own poor survive that it is plain that the officers were far more keen on preserving the certificates of other townships than on keeping copies of those they gave.

While the evidence of the certificates would seem to support the view that the great proportion of population movement took place within a small radius, it is unlikely that they tell the whole story. The small army of men who must have been required to dig the Sankey Canal passed through the district unmentioned and unremarked. Did none of them think of settling in this " boom " township ? Some colliers are noted as entering the district, but in nothing like the numbers that must have been required in the expansion of mining in the years after 1757. It is unlikely that the existing inhabitants of Parr were able to supply all the labour for the new collieries.[2] The Patten copper works at Blackbrook must have brought, among its refiners and skilled workers, men whose settlement was at a distance, but there is no mention of them. The revival of these works by Thomas Williams certainly brought in workmen from Wales and elsewhere, but again there is no record. The only possible explanation is that the overseers took little notice of men who moved into the township when work was

---

[1] Some other and longer migrations are noted in the township records but they relate to persons of an essentially wandering nature (sailors, for instance) who were traversing and not settling in or removing from the township.

[2] See for instance John Mackay's advertisement for colliers, *Lpool. Chron.* 3 Nov., 1768.

awaiting, particularly if they were without families. It would no doubt have been unwise in the township officers to have opposed Sarah Clayton, the lady of the manor, when she desired workers for her mines, or to have displeased Jonathan Case, John Mackay, or Thomas Patten, all industrialists and the very Justices of the Peace who supervised them in the execution of their office. If the overseers had persisted in wishing to move the new entrants, to whom could they have turned ? Would such merchants as John Blackburne, William Gregson, Richard Gildart or John Tarleton have backed them against their fellow-entrepreneurs ? Yet these are among the commonest Justices' names on Parr documents between 1750 and 1785. Later in the century, would Nicholas Ashton, Michael Hughes or James Fraser be likely to oppose anything conducive to a plentiful supply of cheap, mobile labour ?[1] They would be inclined, as good men of business, to balance a low cost of labour against the possibility of a higher poor rate. Nor would they be slow to point out that it was their industries, and particularly their coalmines, which had of late so increased the volume of the rates in Parr and its neighbouring townships. He would be a very daring yeoman or linen-weaver or shopkeeper who, in his short year of office, would risk incurring the wrath of men who were not only Justices but industrial magnates and landowners.[2]

What was the general tendency of poor relief during the period ? Did it increase or diminish ? We can answer with some certainty that it increased, and considerably, but the ending of the annual accounts of the overseers in 1773 and the absence of any supplementary information in the county records breaks off the source of our information just at the moment of maximum

[1] These facts on Merseyside magistrates are in strange contrast to the recent statement: " In Lancashire it was an avowed rule not to tolerate any manufacturer as a colleague on the Bench." J. H. Plumb, *England in the Eighteenth Century* (1950) 85. The view advanced that Turnpike Trusts were " almost " the only county bodies on which industrial capitalists gained a place during the period also seems too strong.

[2] Sir F. M. Eden (unlike Adam Smith, *Wealth of Nations*, ed. McCulloch, 1839, 62-5) did not believe that the Law of Settlement had had a serious effect upon labour migration, in that he did not believe that it had been strictly enforced. He quoted the following view with approval : " Does the tradesman or manufacturer, while his trade or manufacture flourishes, refuse to take an apprentice, or employ a journeyman, because he was born or settled in a different parish, or in a distant part of the kingdom ? On the contrary does he not eagerly look out for him ; and gladly receive him from whatsoever quarter he may come ? Were it otherwise, how has it happened, that Sheffield, Birmingham, and Manchester, have increased from almost mere villages, to populous towns . . . ? See Eden, *op. cit.* I, 297-8, and Marshall, *op. cit.* 180. Further discussion of this question is to be found in G. T. Griffith, *Population Problems of the Age of Malthus* (Cambridge, 1926) 131 *seq.*, and in A. Redford, *Labour Migration in England 1800-1850* (Manchester, 1926) 72-81.

interest. The evidence would seem to indicate that the great period of increase was the middle 'fifties, which would correspond very neatly with the cutting of the Canal and the expansion of the coalfield. While there is difficulty in the interpretation of the accounts, the general indication is that the cost of the administration of the Poor Laws in Parr was fairly steady at £70 to £80 in the early 'fifties. In 1758-9, however, the accounts rose to over £170 per annum, and subsequently tended to remain about that figure. Accounts returned to Parliament for 1776 and 1783-5 give annual assessments of £127 and £194, £193, £188 for these years, and a stray entry shows that in 1781 the Poor Rate topped the £200 mark.[1]

The rise occurred at a time when the township had just taken a step which was usually regarded as making for both improved efficiency and reduced cost. This was the employment of a regular paid overseer. As early as 1758-9 Oswald Greenough, a linen-draper, was filling the posts of overseer and constable " being an hired officer." The township was of course too small for his work to be full-time, but for his part-time services he received £4 a year, while his son, Joseph Greenough the brewer, kept the accounts for a further £1 a year. Oswald Greenough remained in office till 1766. He was then succeeded by a couple of officers who served only the customary year, one of them being Leigh Leaf, nephew of the glassmaker John Leaf, whose beautiful handwriting is a welcome change after the vile hands of his Parr contemporaries. Then James Naylor took over as a paid official, and his tenure lasted well into the 'nineties. Sometimes unpaid assistants were also appointed, but the principle of a senior " hired officer " was now firmly established.

The fact that this gain in the efficiency with which the township was served did not manage to reduce costs seems to argue that the tendency of costs to rise in the late 'fifties was indeed strong. On the one hand the population to be looked after was growing rapidly, but on the other hand the resources of the township were increasing too. The arrival of the Sankey Navigation and the opening of extensive collieries increased the poor rate revenue both from mines and newly-built property, and with a rising yield from the rates the inhabitants of Parr were enabled to spend more on their poor without feeling any increased burden. In other words there was a tendency, under the old system by which each township or parish looked after its own poor, for the care of the

[1] House of Commons Reports IX, 380. Reports on the Laws which concern the Relief and Settlement of the Poor (1777) ; Abstracts of the Returns made by the overseers of the poor in pursuance of an Act (of 26th Geo. III). Also *ibid.*, 615, Further Appendix to the Report on Overseers Returns (1787).

poor to be much bound up with the prosperity of the local community.[1]

If on the one hand we must feel the brutality and coarseness which marked the eighteenth century attitude to the poor occasionally showing through in these Parr records, on the other hand the moral disapproval, the stinginess, the mechanical regulation of the later New Poor Law are absent. The eighteenth-century overseers were not particularly wasteful, as far as we can tell, but they did not grudge the paupers such comforts as their ale and tobacco. If they regulated their diet by the price of oatmeal, that was only because it was the staple diet of the Lancashire labourer of the time. No doubt the machinery was haphazard and chaotic, particularly before the appointment of a paid overseer, but to receive relief the pauper did not, over most of the period, have to enter a workhouse, and he might receive that relief in a variety of forms, as suitable to his need. The boundary, moreover, between pauperism and independence was less strict, and the stigma less cruel ; it was possible for a labouring man's wife, during hard times, to have a new gown from the overseer without any serious diminution of self-respect. This easy-going tolerance was lost when the New Poor Law came in 1834, and its loss was unfortunate. While the eighteenth century saw the constable's stocks and whip grow idle, the old township administration had still its lighter side, the refurbishing of the maypole in spring, the expenditure of a few shillings on a November bonfire, and junkettings at coronations and national victories.

There is an immense change in social attitude towards the poor between the reigns of George III and of Victoria ; while the machinery for the relief of the poor was no doubt more efficient in the Victorian era, comparisons of humanity between the two periods must sometimes favour the earlier age.

[1] That the poor rate in Parr was not considered heavy can be told from an advertisement of property in 1789, which declared : " the roads within Parr and the neighbourhood are very good, and the public taxes within that township very easy." *Gore's Lpool. Ad.* 21 May, 1789.

CHAPTER XII

SOCIAL LIFE : AN INDUSTRIALIST AND MAGISTRATE
1779-1825

WHEN Michael Hughes arrived in St. Helens in 1779, sent
by the Parys Mine Company to be the manager of their
new Ravenhead smelting concern, he could fairly be
described as one of the new rich, for his family had only been
enjoying the profits of their sudden mineral wealth for a few years.[1]
The district was only just beginning to know his social type, soon
to be much more familiar. Significantly, the men who became
Hughes's closest friends were of the new industrialist class :
George Mackay, glass manufacturer,[2] Joseph Churton, surgeon
and partner in a colliery and a glassworks,[3] Robert Sherbourne,
manager of the plate glassworks at Ravenhead.[4] Where we can
trace their origins it is rare to find that the new leaders of industry
had begun right at the bottom of the ladder, but even if speech,
habits or tastes did not betray them, their climb to a prominent
position in society had its difficulties.

Despite the alterations in the origins and nature of national
wealth, it was still commonly felt at this time that the returns from
industry and commerce were no foundation for social position.
Land was as yet the only accepted basis, and the great families of
Stanley, Bold, and Gerard maintained their pre-eminence in this
part of Lancashire without effort. Knowsley, Garswood or
Leoni's immense Bold New Hall had a prestige which quite overshadowed the Ravenhead House, West Park or Sherdley House
built by the St. Helens industrialists, or the more ancient seats of
Eccleston Hall or Hardshaw Hall inhabited by others of their
number.[5] Nevertheless some of the newcomers attempted to

[1] Michael Hughes (1752-1825) was the youngest son of Hugh Hughes, an
Anglesey man who was secretary to the Chancellor of Hereford diocese.
Hugh Hughes was the owner of several estates at his death, including that
of Botenial, but was generally described as of Lleiniog. A memorial to
his wife and himself is in the church at Penmon. Michael Hughes's eldest
brother, the Rev. Edward Hughes, became by marriage a proprietor of
part of the fabulous Parys Mine (see above, p. 77). Edward Hughes's annual
income in the early years of the nineteenth century was estimated at
£14,000 ; Hughes Letters: 12 March, 1808, M. Hughes to John Hughes.

[2] See above, p. 118.   [3] See above, p. 69.   [4] See above, p. 115.

[5] Ravenhead House was the home of John Mackay and later of his son-
in-law, Col. James Fraser ; West Park of Thomas West, glass manufacturer;
For Eccleston and Hardshaw Halls see below, pp. 181n, 182n.

increase their stature in county society by becoming landed gentlemen. To appreciate this ambition it must be remembered that in 1800 England was still largely an agricultural country, and even Lancashire was only slowly changing from a county of rustics to one of industrial workers. The very industrialists were would-be country gentlemen, and their conception of greatness was still to be a squire, to live in a fine house in its own park, with several hundred acres about it, and to be a J.P., Colonel of Militia, Deputy Lieutenant of the County, or possibly, as a crowning glory, High Sheriff. Paradoxically, while Hughes and his contemporaries in industry were creating forces destined to destroy the old society, they were trying to carve out for themselves a place in its hierarchy.

Michael Hughes was therefore not content with being an industrialist and an investor, but began to buy estates. As manager of the copper works at Ravenhead the Parys Company provided him with a house which stood close by, and was rented from the Eccleston family. Its rather homely name " The Tickles " suited neither the dignity nor the £2,000 a year of its new proprietor, and it found itself elevated to " Sutton Lodge." Around this house Hughes centred his early land-buying, though it was the late 'nineties before his chief attention shifted from industrial to land investment.[1] In 1795 he purchased a Sutton estate from John Foster of Thatto Heath for £1,340.[2] In 1796 he paid £1,463 for the estate of the late Henry Ellam in Sutton,[3] in 1797 £1,373 for Whitlow's Estate,[4] in 1798 £3,150 for Sherdley Hall Estate,[5] and in 1800 £2,700 for the Leach Hall Estate.[6] In 1801 came the largest purchase of this group, that of the Manor of Penketh from Lord Lilford for £4,535.[7]

A rude shock, however, awaited Hughes. In 1800, Nicholas Ashton of Woolton Hall, a great salt proprietor, started a colliery on land near Sutton Lodge leased from Mr. Eccleston.[8] This necessitated the aid of an atmospheric or Newcomen-type engine,

[1] A small estate was, however, purchased for £693 in 1789.

[2] Estate List. Feb and March, 1795. Documents cited in this chapter, unless otherwise described, are from the Hughes Collection at Sherdley.

[3] Accounts : 9 Dec. 1796.

[4] Accounts : 9 Oct. 1797. Included a pew in St. Helens Chapel.

[5] Accounts : 21 Feb. 1798. From Executors of Joshua Frodsham, Esq.

[6] Accounts : 11 Nov. 1800. From Edward Falkener Esq., who bought a copyhold West Derby Estate from Hughes for £900.

[7] Accounts : 2 Nov., 1801.

[8] Wigan Ref. Library. Dicconson Papers, lease to Messrs. Clare and Haddock, 28 Oct., 1819.

and its smoke threatened to make Sutton Lodge uninhabitable. Hughes's brother Edward wrote in February, 1801 :

"I am told Mr. Ashton is without loss of time to erect a fumigator close to your door ; and that the ground is already marked to open trenches and batteries against your house and castle. It will be too late to retreat in the last stages of suffocation; and however grating it may be to lament and reflect upon the expence and trouble you have been at to bring your situation to its present state of comfort, yet it will not be unbecoming in a good General to secure a place of safety before the garrison is stormed."[1]

This sound advice was taken, and Michael Hughes began looking about for a new mansion and estate. He had thoughts of moving back to North Wales, in which he was encouraged by his relatives, while Edward Hughes, the proprietor of Kinmel and Llysdulas, fancying himself as a judge of property, bombarded his brother for a year or so with the news of North Wales estates on the market. The ideal of a house of suitable size and amenities surrounded by an estate of 600 acres in a ring-fence was not too easily realized, and by August 1802 Michael Hughes had decided to move his situation to the other end of his Sutton Estates, and to build there.

Once this was settled, Hughes was able to continue his purchases of estates in the Sutton area, to consolidate and to improve. In 1802 £1,267 was laid out for Little Burtonhead Estate, purchased from the glass manufacturer and coal-owner Thomas West, who in turn had purchased it from the great mid-eighteenth century coal-owner Jonathan Case after his bankruptcy of 1778.[2] An estate of similar value was bought in the same year from another bankrupt, William Greenall,[3] and Costeth House Estate near Sherdley Hall rounded off the year's purchases at £2,555.[4] Lea Green Estate was acquired for £6,580 in 1807,[5] and two estates in Eccleston for £5,450 and £2,100 respectively in 1810.[6] The greatest purchase comes near the end of the series, when the Sankey and Penketh Estates of Thomas Claughton, the solicitor, land and coal speculator and

---

[1] Rev. Edward Hughes to Michael Hughes, 1 Feb., 1801.

[2] Accounts : 28 Jan., 12 March, 1803.

[3] Accounts : 2 Nov., 1803 ; 7 Feb., 1804. For £1,225.

[4] Accounts : 19 and 26 July, 1802 ; 29 Sept., 11 Nov., 9 Dec., 1803.

[5] Accounts : 30 July, 1807. The estate was of a little over 76 statute acres and contained a large house with outbuildings. It produced a rent of £130 *per annum*.

[6] Accounts : 6 March ; 9 April ; 7 June, 1810. Bought when the Eccleston estates were in the market. The main block went to Samuel Taylor.

M.P., were bought in 1814 for £15,000.[1] Virtually all Hughes's buying was done at the highly inflated prices of the French Revolutionary and Napoleonic Wars.

The decision to build a new house was accompanied by the engagement of John Harrison as architect,[2] and in 1802 Hughes was burning bricks on a large scale.[3] In 1804 he took down Old Costeth House, but spared Sherdley Old Hall, which has now outlived, as a handsome farm house, its showy supplanter.[4] These preliminaries over, in 1805 and 1806 the main work of building was carried out.[5] In the January of 1806 the building must have been well advanced as the master mason was discharged, and in the June the architect was paid in full, the house being insured at the end of the year for £2,000 and the furniture for £500.[6] Like many who venture on building, Michael Hughes was showered with good advice, of which the most amusing came from a relative by marriage, Sir Robert Williams.

" London, 1 February, 1805."

" I have never altered my opinion on the point that you have acted wisely in building when you can, for a thousand reasons—and now my good Sir allow me to give you my poor advice, of all things make your new house snug and comfortable, instead of attending to great uniformity in the building, a good water closet contiguous to your Bed Chambers—and one out of your house, your rooms high, but small as you please—Carpets to take up in your bedrooms and dressing rooms ; and good fire-places—these are luxuries that all the World like—[take care that] . . . you don't show this to your Brother of Kinmel."

The final caution is due to the fact that Kinmel Park was

[1] Accounts : 10 Nov., 1814. A pew and a threshing machine were included. Perhaps the most spectacular of the land purchases of Thomas Claughton of Haydock Lodge was his contract to buy the reversion of Thomas Johnes's Hafod Estate. (See E. Inglis Jones, *Peacocks in Paradise* (1950), 230 and 240.) Claughton was not over-honest. Hughes had to go to Chancery to obtain possession of the land he had contracted to sell, and in the case of Hafod Claughton seems to have avoided his contract to purchase. See correspondence between Hughes and Claughton, L.R.O., Cross Papers, DDCSs 34, and above, pp. 60, 60n.

[2] Letters : H. R. Hughes to Michael Hughes, 28 Aug., 1802.

[3] Accounts : 26 Feb., 5 June, 1803.

[4] Accounts : 23 Feb., 1804.

[5] Accounts : 16 March, 1805. " By John Harrison on acct. of his Salary for planning and superintending the building of my intended N(ew) House . . . £20.0.0."

[6] Accounts : 30 Jan., 11 June, 6 Dec., 1806. A nineteenth century painting of the house is reproduced in *Trans. L. & C. Hist. Soc.* 103, 116. The main building was demolished in very recent years.

equally celebrated in the family for its magnificence and its discomfort.

The furniture was ordered through W. L. Hughes,[1] the eldest son of the Rev. Edward Hughes, who resided mainly in London. The furniture appears only to have been ordered long after the house was complete, and probably replaced furniture brought over from Sutton Lodge until something more splendid could be procured.

"Hinde St., 25th July 1807.

" My Dear Uncle

"I returned from Worthing last night and went early to Gillars [sic] about your furniture. I have not ceased to stimulate him to exertion ever since the first order and have given him frequent calls to warn him of your impatience. He assures me that everything that can be made at Lancaster is in a great state of forwardness and that what will remain to be sent from this town will be ready in ten days the packages will go by the Canal and be directed to the care of Taylor at Liverpool when you must send your waggon for them. I do flatter myself that your two rooms will be the neatest and most tasteful in your neighbourhood. I have ordered a neat Lantern for the dining room which will light the room sufficiently without the nuisance of candles on the table to obscure the view of your opposite neighbour. One of Gillars men is going into your neighbour-hood and will be ready to put up everything in proper order. It occurs to me that you have never mentioned how your bells pull—inform me of this and tell me also whether you want grate and fenders and fire irons for the two rooms.

" As you get the glass from the Manufactory it will be handsome if it goes to the top of the room and if you will send the dimensions a neat frame may be made in this town."[2]

At the end of the year W. L. Hughes was glad to hear of the success of his buying.

"Kinmel Park, 1 Dec. 1807.

" My dr. Uncle,

" I derive great pleasure from knowing that your furniture meets with your and your friends approbation, and tho' I allow the cost will be considerable, yet I hope you will find it com-pensated in the comfort you will derive from it, & that on the

[1] He is several times mentioned by Creevey, occasionally as " Taffy." See J. Gore (Ed.) *Creevey's Life and Times* (1934) xiv and 132, 293, 404. W. L. Hughes was created Lord Dinorben on the coronation of William IV. He had been in the House since 1802 when he was returned for Wallingford, Berkshire. A number of his letters survive in the Hughes collection.

[2] The present firm of Waring and Gillow states that the business originated in Lancaster in 1695. The " Manufactory " was the British Plate Glass Company's works at Ravenhead.

whole as little has been incurred unnecessarily as possible, in the dining room I think none, the drawing room will of course include some articles of unnecessary adornment to a man, but as I know you will like your female visitants to enjoy every comfort and luxury you can afford them, you will not I conclude deem them misapplied, & as my orders were most particular that every article should be more firm and strong than they are usually made for town, I trust if they are now handsome they will be permanently so."

The final touch to the outward splendour of Hughes's new establishment was to be a new coach to replace his old one, a magnificent town-built equipage which should be the envy of his fellow provincials. This however, though ordered through Owen Williams,[1] the son of his former business colleague Thomas Williams, was a great disappointment. The coach was undoubtedly not as well made as it should have been, but part of Hughes's annoyance may have been due to his failure to appreciate the changed London fashion in carriage fittings.

" Sherdley House 5 August, 1809

" . . . I do not exactly know the Orders wch my friend Mr. Williams gave you respecting it, but the Trimmings in the inside do not conform to my ideas of Prop^y [propriety] . . . And they are upon the whole much plainer and less showy than I could have wished—My Livery is a light Drab Colour, pretty near the Color of the Lining with Crimson and Silver. The Inside of the Carriage should have corresponded, & instead of Lace and Trimmings of the same colour, it should have been a *rich Crimson* which certainly would have given a much handsomer inside appearance.

" The Carriage in its appearance exhibits the Plainess of a Quaker, & is in my opinion not at all handsome. It may be of good workmanship and materials, I trust it is, but its general appearance is much inferior to my old carriage & to those made in Lpool."[2]

After a few miles on the local turnpikes, of which he was a trustee and which were excellently paved with the slag from his own copper works, the springs gave, and Hughes's anger against the unfortunate vehicle and its makers boiled over :

" . . . the [Carriage] you sent me is the most mean paltry thing that ever was sent out of London, & so is deem'd by every Gentleman who has seen it. Whether you look at the Outside or Inside it is equally plain, mean and paltry and this much

---

[1] From 1796 Owen Williams had shared his father's pocket borough of Great Marlow ; after Thomas Williams died in 1802 one of its two seats was filled by Pascoe Grenfell, a colleague in the copper trade.

[2] Hughes to Messrs. Chamberlayne & Co., 5 Aug., 1809.

inferior to any Gentleman's Carriage. From the pompous description of it displayed on your Bill, I should have expected that the *Materials* at least of which it is made had been of very extraordinary quality. To my great Mortification & Cost they are not so, for the Springs, altho' the Carriage since I had it has not run more than 30 Miles in the whole with no other weight than my Wife and Myself, the springs have already given way and must be replaced . . . "[1]

While here he encountered disappointment, in 1810 he ministered to his vanity by having his portrait painted by J. Patrick,[2] a contemporary exhibitor at the Royal Academy. In the following year he enquired the charges of a London sculptor, though it is not known whether anything came of this.[3]

As he was building up an establishment fitting to a man of wealth, dignities conferred upon him were raising Hughes's social prestige.

" Mar. 4 (1800) Paid James Tithington for three Bottles of Claret, being what was drank at the first sessions at Prescot after my induction to the Magistracy of the County...£1. 1s. 0."

In 1801 Hughes was president of the Liverpool Public Infirmary,[4] and by the following year he was a Commissioner under the Property Act for the Prescot division of Lancashire. The year afterwards, together with James Fraser, he played a very active part in raising the St. Helens Volunteers and received as his reward a commission as Lieut.-Colonel[5] and the rank of second-in-command of that force. Hughes, who did not lay claim to any military capacity, was much bothered by Fraser's frequent visits to Edinburgh and to his Scottish estates, when the entire responsibility for the corps fell on his own shoulders. By 1806 Hughes was taking an active interest in the work of the local Turnpike Trust,[6] and in the same year he was a subscriber to the Agricultural Meeting of West Derby Hundred,[7] one of the organizations for the encouragement of good farming through the holding of agricultural shows, which were very popular at this time. In a way this was the proudest year of Hughes's life, for in 1806 he achieved his final distinction, being made a Deputy Lieutenant of the county.

[1] Letters : Hughes to Messrs Chamberlayne & Co., 23 Oct., 1809.

[2] Accounts : 22 Jan., 1810.

[3] Accounts : 24 Sept., 1811.

[4] Accounts : 7 July, 1801.

[5] The commission, dated 28 Aug., 1804, is preserved among Hughes Letters.

[6] Accounts : 21 Jan., 1806.

[7] Accounts : 22 July, 1806.

Hughes's first wife, the daughter of a wealthy Prescot clergyman, died in May 1798,[1] and ten years later he married Ellen Pemberton,[2] the daughter of a neighbouring Sutton landowner. He was over fifty at the time of his second marriage, and his wife long survived him. By this second marriage Hughes had six children. His son and heir, Michael, was born in 1810 ; the christening being a grand affair attended by Owen Williams the M.P., H. R. Hughes the banker, and Mrs. Edward Hughes from Kinmel.[3] Thus late in life Hughes became aware of the anxieties of a family man.

" Paid Mr. Parkes of Lpl. Surgeon, for his attendance on my son Michl. at Bootle, when he was ill of the Hooping Cough, & also for coming here from St. Helens this day, to examine my daughter Ellen who was suspected by her mother to be growing crooked, but in Mr. Parkes opinion without cause...£3. 0. 0."[4]

The education of his children involved not only school fees, but such things as music and dancing lessons, and keeping Mrs. Hughes's pianoforte in tune. Occasionally the happier sides of their upbringing make pleasant reading in the father's account books, as :—

" 21 Jan. 1819. Paid to Mrs. Hughes to go to Lpl. where she took the children to the Circus etc............................£10."[5]

The school reports Hughes received about his son Michael and about a nephew, also named Michael Hughes, whom he educated, are sometimes amusing. They are generally from clergymen, the headmasters of various small private schools, and they are full of the masters' anxiety to persuade the parent or guardian that the boy has some talents, while almost invariably regretting his reluctance to use them to the best advantage. Replying to one of these reports, Hughes had to confess his failure to make his nephew complete his vacation task.

" 7 Feby 1810

" Dear Sir

" Your report of my Nephews Progress is highly gratifying to me—& you claim and have my best thanks for your attention to him.

" Altho' I have endeavoured to enforce the Necessity of his application during the Recess—yet in this I fear I have no

[1] Accounts : 16 June, 1798 ; and Hughes collection " Pedigree of th Hughes Family."

[2] Accounts : 9 Feb., 1808.

[3] Accounts : 12 July ; 7 Nov., 1810.

[4] Accounts : 18 Aug., 1818.

[5] The New Olympic Circus visited Liverpool as early as 1805. S Lpool. Chron., 29 May, 1805.

succeeded, for he has not done so to the extent I wish'd him to do. Indeed without the Controul of a Master, it is difficult to get Boys to study during their Vacation, for they generally consider it an Interval almost exclusively devoted to Amusement and Pleasure—Of his Improvement and Acquirements, especially in his Greek, during the short period which he has been under your care, I can not but speak in the most flattering terms of Praise . . . "[1]

The most important work of Michael Hughes, apart from his business activities, was his service as magistrate, a task which he undertook with fitting seriousness and responsibility. His letters and orders are not only to be found among his own papers but also among most collections relating to the St. Helens district in this period. There are two sides to the story which emerges, displaying not so much differing aspects of Hughes's own character and attitude, as two diverse and even conflicting tasks of the magistrate of the time. On the one hand his duties in preserving the peace involved the welfare of the poor, and interference on their behalf in questions of Poor Law administration, wages and so on. On the other hand the magistrate represented the repressive and punitive side of the law, and was responsible for keeping order at a time when there was virtually no police force. Once a situation went beyond the control of a handful of part-time and sometimes unpaid constables, the only solution was to call in the nearest troops. It is therefore advisable, before judging Hughes as a magistrate, to remember the wide scope of the duties laid upon these men, their lack of legal training, apart from that which they picked up for themselves,[2] and the fact that they were doing singlehanded, without salary, and often without thanks, what modern society deputes to many. Hughes's difficulties, we must bear in mind, were greatly increased by the work presented by the growing boom-town of St. Helens.

[1] Hughes to Rev. Wm. Bordman, Warrington, 7 Feb., 1810.

[2] Six months before he began his magisterial duties Hughes wrote to Joseph Butterworth, Law Bookseller of London, for

" Pickering's *Statutes at Large*, 41 Volumes			£21	0	0
Hutcheson's *Excise Survd.*	...	...	...		4	0
Burns' *Justice*, 4 Volumes	...	...	...	1	16	0
Addington's *Penal Statutes*	...	...	...	1	18	0
Digest of Term Reports	...	...	...		14	0
Jacobs' *Law Dicty.*, 2 Volumes	...	...	3	10	0
Box for above ...	...	...	...	...		4	0
				£29	6	0

It might be thought that Hughes as an employer of labour would have adopted towards the poor the increasingly fashionable attitude of *laissez-faire*. He was not, however, among those who thought that the poor should be left to face unaided the operation of economic laws. To one overseer of the poor he wrote at a time of scarcity and high prices : " these are not times for trifling with the Distresses of the Poor." The township of Parr which had been giving an old man 7s. a week to work on the highways was ordered to pay 9s. a week, the former wage being described as " considerably less than his work deserves." Parr overseers were on more than one occasion ordered to appear before Hughes at Sherdley House about breakfast-time for not giving sufficient relief.[1] Writing to the overseers of Overton, Cheshire, concerning the non-resident relief of one of their certificated poor long settled in Sutton, he declared :—

" as a Magistrate in the Neighbourhood, he required me to represent his Case to you, and in complying with his desire, I feel that I am performing one of the most important and essential Duties of my Office—I therefore hope and trust that I am appealing to the feelings of Men of Humanity and Consideration and that I shall not appeal in vain. . . . I need not tell you that the Times are beyond all Example, hard and distressing on the poorer Class of the Community, and in the strongest manner call for Liberality from all Overseers in relieving their Poor ; Humanity and good Policy require it ; I hope that you are of that Opinion."[2]

On more than one occasion, too, Hughes was called in to prevent men being enlisted in the army against their will.

" 20 March 1813 . . . Thos. Jump of Prescot says that on Wedy Night the 7th May he was hastily enlisted at Prescot, by a recruiting party belonging to the 84th Regt. of foot. The said Thomas Jump came to me on Saturday the 20th and declared his dissent to such Enlistment, and said that all the said recruiting party had left Prescot, so that he could not procure any officer to attend him. . . . He therefore paid into my hand the sum of One Pound, to be paid to them when called upon agreeably to 74th Section of 50 Geo. 3 . . . April 10th returned the said Thomas Jump the said sum of one pd he never having heard anything further."

Only a month later Hughes recorded that the wife of George Fildes of Windle, collier, came to him and said that " on Sunday Morning last the 28th Inst the said George Fildes was enlisted at St. Helens when he was drunk, and this day declared his dissent

---

[1] St. Helens Ref. Library : Parr Township Papers : Hughes to Parr Overseers : 1, 20, 23 April, 5 May, 1801.

[2] Letters : Hughes to Overton Overseers : 20 Feb., 1801.

to such enlistment." Fildes paid up his pound and his king's shilling, but in this case forfeited it, for on 30 June Hughes records that he " paid the above mentioned 21s to Wm Taylor, private in the 172nd Company of Royal Marines, by order of Thos Bason, Lieut, & agit^t [sic], Royal Marines."[1]

In 1807 Hughes was involved in correspondence with Thomas Chantler of Northwich, a salt manufacturer who possessed a colliery near St. Helens. He was able to secure Chantler's support in forcing his colliery agent to pay full wages to a collier from whose earnings it had suddenly been decided to deduct house-rent, and to obtain the payment of a week's wages (14s.) to an engine boy who had been dismissed without notice.[2]

The first important occasion on which the grimmer side of the magistrate's task emerged was in 1812, when in common with the other Deputy Lieutenants Hughes was summoned to a meeting to consider the measures needed to suppress the Luddite riots of the period.[3] In 1819, however, Hughes had a riot all to himself. In that year the St. Helens colliers went on strike, the first time they are known to have taken such a step. This dispute was very well reported in the Liverpool press, and one of the letters written by Hughes to the Earl of Derby on the subject has found its way into Home Office papers, to be unearthed recently by Professor Aspinall. The accounts of the strike given by the letter and the newspapers are to some extent parallel and even over-lapping, but as each contains information not contained in the other, it will be well to give both. On 17 February, 1819, Michael Hughes and George Williams, in a letter written from the Raven Inn at St. Helens to Lord Derby, said :

" . . . It is now some weeks (six or seven) since the colliers of this district indicated disturbance ; that of 13 collieries within this district, the majority of the workmen from seven have withdrawn themselves to the amount of about 250, whose

---

[1] Accounts : 22 and 30 June, 1813.

[2] Letters : Hughes to Thomas Chantler, Northwich, 1 Aug., 1807.

[3] *Lpool. Merc.*, 22 May, 1812. Hughes is given as one of the Deputy Lieutenants of the county present at a meeting at Wigan on 15 May, which called for energetic measures against the rioters, and thanked the military for their assistance. " We view with horror and extreme sorrow the riots, tumults, and breaches of the peace, that have occurred in the county, which disgrace civilized society, and are most dangerous to the common-wealth or public polity of the kingdom.
" [We declare] . . . that it is the bounden duty of every man to protect the community, and each individual therein, from every degree of injury and violence ; and that by law, any of his Majesty's subjects, military as well as civil, without the presence of a peace-officer of any description, may arm themselves, and of course may use the ordinary means of force to suppress riots and disturbances." For the Luddite Riots in Lancashire see J. L. and B. Hammond, *The Skilled Labourer* (1919), X, 271-300.

proceeding has thrown out of work between 300 and 400 others connected with the coal getters.

The discontent arises from a reduction of wages having taken place about three years ago, and to which no opposition was then made, the return to which rate of wages is what they now demand of the proprietors, who on their side state that they have been employing one fourth more of coal getters during a depression of trade for those three years more than prudence would justify actually to keep their men at work ; the coal getters obtaining as wages at that time (at the reduced rate) upon a general average of collieries and weeks about a guinea each man per week.

The discontent is stated however to be insufficiency of wages, and all calculations and reasonings upon the subject we have found utterly unavailing to induce them to return quietly to their employment.

On the 12th instant, being here for this purpose of taking examinations, and of pacifying them, we were obliged to commit one of the conspirators for administering an unlawful oath, which threw them into such a state of exasperation that *our* safety was put to hazard, and on the 13th we thought it advisable to obtain a military force from Warrington of 80 rank-and-file. A company was also marched hither from Liverpool composed of 40 rank-and-file. On the 13th, as some outrages had taken place and more were threatened, we thought it advisable to send to Manchester for a detachment of the 7th Hussars, which arrived this forenoon, consisting of 34 horses, officers and men, commanded by the Earl of Uxbridge."[1]

The dangerous situation which had arisen at the Raven Inn on the 12 February is described in an article in the *Liverpool Mercury* on the 19th.

" The colliers at St. Helen's and the neighbourhood have for some time past been forming themselves into societies, for the purpose of obtaining an advance in wages. The object of this organization, we are informed, was, for the workmen of one colliery to make the demand, and if they succeeded, then it was to be made by the others in succession ; but if it was rejected, then those who made the demand were *to strike*, and were to be supported in their designs by those who remained in employment. The proprietors of the collieries, however, having become acquainted with their intentions, and with the view of frustrating them in their object, came to the resolution of immediately discharging those who were engaged in the combination ; and the whole of them left their work. Up to Friday everything remained quiet ; on that day John Johnson *alias* Cooke, who acted as secretary to the body, was apprehended under warran-

[1] Aspinall, A., *The Early English Trade Unions* (1949), 315-6.

for administering unlawful oaths. Soon after Johnson arrived
in custody at the Raven Inn, in St. Helen's, some hundreds of
colliers assembled, and great apprehension was entertained
that they would endeavour to rescue him ; but very fortunately
Colonel Williams and Michael Hughes, Esq., two magistrates,
were there at the moment, and while the former was addressing
the multitude on the impropriety of their motives, Pollitt, the
constable of Warrington, succeeded in conveying his prisoner
away in chaise from the back of the Inn. As soon, however,
as they were acquainted with the circumstances, the mob
became very clamorous, and followed the chaise, but without
being able to accomplish their object.   The men then dispersed ; but we understand that in the evening they visited the
pits in large bodies, with fire-arms, and put out the fires and
discharged the engineers at the different works. Alarmed at
these proceedings, the constituted authorities thought it
necessary to call in the aid of the military ; and on Saturday
evening, a company of the 52nd regiment and the Liverpool
Light Horse received orders to march for St. Helen's. A party
of infantry also marched from Warrington for the same
purpose. We are happy, however, to state, that up to yesterday
afternoon everything remained perfectly tranquil. It is said
that a meeting of the colliers is to be convened this day at
St. Helen's."[1]

The strikes, it was stated, had not spread to Prescot or Whiston,
but were confined to the St. Helens section of the coalfield, and
Johnson was safely lodged in Liverpool jail.

On the 26th the newspaper had to report that the strikes were
not yet over, though some of the men showed signs of returning
to work.

" The principal objects of attack by the dissatisfied workmen
have been the men who have signified their willingness to
resume their employment at the old rate of wages.   The
magistrates (Michael Hughes and George Williams Esqrs.)
have, therefore, issued a notice of their determination to protect
all such persons[2] . . . and of proceeding against the offenders

---

[1] *Lpool. Merc.*, 19 Feb., 1819.

[2] This read :- " Whereas unpleasant differences have and do exist between
the WORKING COLLIERS in this neighbourhood and their Employers
respecting the RATE OF WAGES : and several of the said Colliers
have in open Violation of the Law proceeded to various Acts of Violence
and Outrage, particularly by threatening those Colliers and others who are
willing to return to their Employers with personal injury if they do so
return.

" The Magistrates desirous of preventing and deterring all Persons
from such disgraceful and illegal Proceedings,

" DO HEREBY GIVE NOTICE :
" That they are determined to proceed with the utmost Rigour of the
Law against all Persons who shall by Threats, Intimidation, Persuasion

'with the utmost rigour of the law.' And on Saturday last the following placard was also published by the same worthy magistrates :—

> 'Whereas it appears that some of the peaceable colliers in this neighbourhood, who are formed into societies for benevolent purposes, have been so far deceived by the combined colliers of Windle, Sutton, and Parr, that those societies have been induced to contribute to the present and pressing wants of the discontented colliers under an idea that they are assisting men who have been unjustly, and without any fault of their own, thrown out of employ ; be it now known to such members of societies, that the majority of coal-getters of Sutton, Windle, and Parr have thrown themselves out of employment, and are now illegally standing out for an increase in wages, have also, most unfeelingly, thrown out and brought to distress a great number of innocent persons, such as drawers, waggoners, &c., &c., and that therefore, however humane the motive may have been in such societies to have aided those coal getters in the first instance, to continue such aid now is only to prolong the refractory spirit existing in the body, as well as the hardships and privations of those dependent persons, and is, besides, to be accessory to their guilt. Such societies are therefore apprized that if contributions are afforded after this notice of illegality, they must expect to be proceeded against with all the severity the law will justify and the magistrates [c]an exercise '."[1]

The soldiers, the paper stated, were still at St. Helens. A guard was placed nightly at the different works to prevent wrecking, and several of the most active agitators had been arrested during the past week.

There were two postscripts to the strike. On 2 March, Hughes informed Lord Derby, " The most complete tranquility has been restored to this neighbourhood, the colliers having very generally

---

or otherwise hinder or prevent any Person or Persons from returning to work for their respective Employers.

" And all such Persons who are inclined and willing to return to their Work as usual, are hereby informed that the Magistrates will most Rigidly put the Law in Force for protecting them from any Violence that may be offered to them or to their Property by any evil disposed Person or Persons, in Consequence of their so returning to their Work.

" And the Magistrates wish to Caution the Coal Miners against Designs of deluded Men, who are persuading them to persevere in their unlawful Proceedings, and they wish also to convince them that AN UNLAWFUL OATH CANNOT BIND THEM TO ANYTHING IN ITSELF UNLAWFUL.

" Given under our Hands at St. Helen's, the 17th Day of February, 1819.

" MICH. HUGHES,
" GEO. WILLIAMS."

[1] *Lpool Merc.*, 26 Feb., 1819.

returned to their work as usual, without the smallest injury having been done to the person or property of any individual."[1]   Three days later the *Liverpool Mercury* announced: "We are happy to state, that the disputes between the coal proprietors and their workmen at St. Helens are at an end.   The masters have selected such of the men as they thought proper, but without any concessions on the part of the former."

Although this was the first known strike of any importance on the St. Helens coalfield, either by colliers or others, the degree of organization was remarkable.   The Combination Acts were still in force in 1819, but a widespread organization with a recognized leader brought out about six hundred men at the one time. Moreover, after three years of trade depression and short-time working, the men appear to have been out on strike for about nine weeks without capitulating.   The device by which workers in different concerns struck successively while being maintained by the others who remained in employment is also proof that this was something more than an instinctive revolt of dissatisfied men ; it anticipated by eleven years the famous tactics of John Doherty in the cotton spinners' strike of 1830, which are often thought to have initiated this technique.[2]   It will be noted too, that this strike was made by men who were well paid, the aristocrats of the working class, for, when in anything like full work, colliers received almost double the wages of unskilled labourers.   The strike was an attempt to win back the high wages gained during the French Wars,[3] and it occurred during a brief trade revival which followed the first rigours of the post-war slump.   It only adds to the general impression that the trade union movement originated not among the most depressed workers, such as those employed on the domestic system in the weaving and light metal industries, but in those occupations where well-paid workers were thrown together in large numbers, as in the mines and the cotton factories. Such men were able to combine more easily than the scattered

[1] Aspinall, *op. cit.* 318.

[2] S. and B. Webb, *The History of Trade Unionism*, 117-119.

[3] A Liverpool pamphlet of 1804, in which an anonymous writer connected with the salt industry attacked the Sankey coal owners, had this to say of the local colliers at a time of rising prices, royalties and wages in the coal trade.

" Thus the labouring collier finding his services sought after, and instead of soliciting employment, that employment courting him, becomes fancy. His earnings permit him to idle half the week in the ale-house, which is to him enjoyment ; and by this debauched state of the working colliers, double the number of hands are required to what used to be, for the same quantum of work, and have not been obtained . . . Any person who has attended to the coal trade with an observing eye for a few years past will allow that the foregoing statement is not overcharged."   *Remarks on the Salt Trade . . . in reference to the Weaver Navigation the Coal Trade and the Revenue Laws* (Lpool. 1804) 23-24.

domestic workers, and their higher wages made it possible for them to have some savings and even strike-funds. The use of money placed in friendly societies for strike purposes, which occurred here, arouses speculation as to whether these societies were in fact a cloak for illegal trade union activities, as was often alleged at this period.[1]

On the side of the magistrates, too, there are points to be noted. Attempts at conciliation seem to have taken place over several weeks before any drastic action was taken. Even after it had been determined to put down the strike the action of the magistrates, despite their use of the military, was not unskilful. First a deliberate attempt was made to drive a wedge between those who were willing to return to work and those who were not, the former being assured of all the support and protection in the power of the authorities. Then in the longer placard an attempt was made to absolve the drawers and waggoners and blame the colliers, and to throw the responsibility for the unemployment of the auxiliary and less well-paid workers on to the better-paid ones. The magistrates were also at pains to assert that the dispute was not a lock-out but a strike. It is unlikely that all the friendly societies concerned had exclusively colliers or their wives as contributors, and the latent threat to seize the " boxes " must have alarmed workers in other trades whose savings were involved. Finally, it must be remembered that all this took place while the country was in a most dangerous state, and the greatest apprehension of internal revolution was entertained by the authorities. Peterloo took place in the following August; the Six Acts were enforced in the autumn. The Cato Street Conspiracy of 1820, miserable failure though it was, excited quite disproportionate fears.

Although an incident of this sort was reported in the newspapers and received the attention of the Home Office, it was not typical of the ordinary work of the magistrate, nor does the suppression of strikes and riots, which was enjoined upon him by the statutes which he was appointed to maintain, mean that the magistrate normally showed a cruel and vindictive attitude to the poor in general. The social history of this period, too largely derived from Home Office records, may perhaps be rewritten in a different light from other sources. Michael Hughes was certainly not regarded as a harsh magistrate by the people of St. Helens. On 19 September, 1833, eight years after his death, the inhabitants of the town, in a document signed by every person of importance in the place, and by the priests and ministers of all the religious

[1] See the Webbs, *op. cit.* 78, 80, 82. During the trial of fifteen Manchester cotton spinners for conspiracy in 1819 it was stated that, " All societies whether benefit societies or otherwise, were only cloaks for the people of England to conspire against the State."

communities, Anglican, Wesleyan, Independent, and Catholic, called upon his son, Michael, to assume the office of J.P.

" The population around us is rapidly increasing, and calls for the presence of Magistrates interested in its welfare. Your father was coeval with the rise of this place to considerable importance ; and inheriting as you do, his station in society, we wish to see you seated in the judicial chair so long, and so ably, filled by him. And we hope, Sir, this expression of our wishes, will induce you to accept a Commission as Magistrate of this County : to obtain which, we feel assured, an intimation in the proper quarter, of your willingness to accept it, is only wanting."[1]

It is scarcely likely that without a sense of respect and affection for the father the people of the neighbourhood would be so eager to secure the services of a young man who had not long become of age.

On the charity of the wealthy man, and particularly of the magistrate, heavy demands were made. In 1801, the year of his Presidency of that institution, Michael Hughes gave £100 to Liverpool Infirmary,[2] and paid for the preaching of the Anniversary sermon. In 1797, when a voluntary contribution to the Government was called for, Hughes was in charge of the donations of St. Helens and district, and himself gave £100 out of a total of £681 0s. 8d.[3] During the grain shortage of 1800 he paid £5 for himself and £10 for the Parys Company on two separate occasions for the relief of the Sutton poor, and in the same year advanced money to the overseer to distribute until such time as a special rate could be raised to defray the heavy expenditure needed during those hard times.[4] Hughes' account books show dozens of examples of small acts of charity involving a few pounds or shillings, to all sorts of people. A typical entry runs, " Gave Mr. Byron a distress'd Player £1."[5]

To outline all the social material in the Hughes account books and papers would be impossible here on the mere score of length. Perhaps from this short account, however, will have emerged something of the personality of the man, generous, irascible, very conscious of his place in society, but no less conscious of his duties and responsibilities to his fellow-men, both rich and poor. The letters and even the account books are full of little details that betray the man. On one occasion he entered a serious prayer—

---

[1] Hughes Letters : Petition of 19 Sept., 1833.
[2] Accounts : 24 March, 7 July, 1801.
[3] Pocket Books : 2 and 17 April, 1798.
[4] Accounts :   3 Feb., 5 March, 9 Dec., 1801.
[5] Accounts : 25 Nov., 1806.

" Slept for the first time in my New House. May God grant me good luck and his Grace to enjoy my New Habitation. Amen ! Amen ! Amen ! ",[1]—on another when he had purchased a lottery ticket, a humorous one—" May God send the good luck— Amen ! " The new age of speed, just making its tentative way, never failed to intrigue him, and he liked to remark the times in which journeys could be made. In 1799 he carefully noted that he set out one Saturday for Swansea with his Stanley Works manager and his servants, and returned home, his business completed, the following Friday at 7 o'clock.[2] Despite his status as a landowner Hughes affected neither the habits nor the tastes of the fine gentleman, nor even the vices. His losses at the card table were in shillings, and, although he liked his wine, his greatest purchases were made with that most altruistic of motives, the laying down of a cellar for future generations. Pleasures, however, do find mention ; the annual visit to Newton Races, or in his younger days the coursing of a hare or two at Rainford or Crosby. Hughes never lost his interest in the countryside, and there are several notes on nature or the seasons :

" Wednesday 6 Jany 1796. Spent in coursing hares at Rainford, Mossborough etc. 7/- N.B. In returning home at abt. 4 o'clock in the afternoon, heard a Thrush singing very loud on the right hand side of the Road leading from Denton's Green to St. Helens—an extraordinary Instance of the mildness of the season."

Or, 16 April, 1819 :

" Memdm. Heard the Cuckoo for the first time this year, which is sooner than I have heard that Bird before for many years."

From a doctrinaire viewpoint Michael Hughes, apparently the very image of the rising industrialist and investor, is a disappointment. A *parvenu*, he arrived at St. Helens without any other influence than that of recently-acquired wealth, yet he became in twenty years the most respected man in the neighbourhood. He eagerly accepted authority and office (though we have no evidence that he toadied for them) but he brought to all his duties and positions a proper seriousness and responsibility, and, if he was not without a trace of self-importance, he had no officiousness. He bought land at the inflated prices of the French Wars, but the nucleus of the estates he collected is only now breaking up, having lasted a century and a half. Himself an industrialist, his successors were landowners and Army officers. As a magistrate he appeared both as a protector of the poor, and as a suppressor of strikes.

[1] Accounts : 14 Oct., 1806.

[2] Accounts : 5 July, 1799. The trip cost just over £40.

He accounted for every penny he spent, sometimes entering his expenses in three separate records, yet his gifts to charities were frequent, and sometimes on a considerable scale.

Michael Hughes, however typical of his times he may have been in some respects, cannot be readily summed-up and labelled for our benefit. His character was too individual, his activities were too varied, for that. Indeed, in virtue of his wealth, influence and public spirit he was as much the leading figure of the St. Helens district in the opening decades of the nineteenth century as was Peter Greenall in its second quarter. The creation of a great industrial town is a matter of personal as well as economic factors ; it is as fitting to speak of the successive ages of Sarah Clayton, John Mackay, Michael Hughes, and Peter Greenall as to talk of the Canal and Railway eras.

CHAPTER XIII

THE BEGINNINGS OF THE TOWN

THE situation of the chapel of St. Helen, from which the modern town takes its name, has already been described.[1] This little chapel-of-ease, a pre-Reformation foundation,[2] easily reached from all four townships by the chief roads traversing them, was at the natural focal point of the district. It stood at the extreme south of Windle township, the southern portion of which was formed into a separate manor, or presumed manor, known as Hardshaw, or Hardshaw-within-Windle.

During the eighteenth century the place was sometimes called St. Helens and sometimes Hardshaw. The name St. Helens (often spelt with an apostrophe) was originally applied to the chapel itself, completely re-built in the middle of the century,[3] to the school attached to it, and to the inn nearby. In the chapel registers, for instance, the incumbent—who also acted as school-master—and the innkeeper were described as " of St. Helens "[4] but those who lived farther afield were said to live either in Hardshaw or in one of the townships. In 1763 " the whole village of Hardshaw or St. Helens," according to an early nineteenth century source, consisted of fewer than thirty houses.[5] Although the two alternative place names continued to vie with each other as the population grew during the next fifty years, by 1800 there was little doubt that St. Helens was coming to be the more widely

[1] Above, p. 3.

[2] The first definite reference to St. Helen's Chapel is contained in an inventory of goods in the churches and chapels of Lancashire made in 1552 (transcript, *Chet. Soc.* 113, 80 ; copy of original P.R.O. doct. in St. H. Ref. Lib.). It was falling down sixty years later and may be presumed, therefore, to have been of some age at the time of the 1552 inventory. In stating that St. Helen's Chapel " was founded by Sir Thomas Gerard of Ince about the year 1540," the Rev. F. G. Paterson (*History of Prescot*, private circulation, n.d., 48) seems to be confusing St. Helen's Chapel with Windleshaw Chantry, founded by Sir Thomas Gerard about 1435 (*q.v.* the Rev. Austin Powell, " Windleshaw Chantry and Cemetery," *Trans. L. & C. Hist. Soc.*, 3 (1887), 11-34 and frontispiece).

[3] A deed of 25 May, 1781 recited that since 1751 the old chapel had been pulled down and a new one erected in its place. Charity Commissioners' Report, 1905 [313]C, 26.

[4] E.g. 7 March, 1725, 30 June, 1734, 16 Nov., 1765.

[5] Sherdley Estate Office. Report of the Proceedings in Ex Parte Hughes and Ors., re Cowley's Charity, 24 Jan., 1823.

accepted and in 1808 a writer even went so far as to assert that the name of Hardshaw was " nearly forgotten."[1] The reason for this is clear : it was the area in the immediate vicinity of the chapel that was the scene of the earliest building activity and not the land to the north, nearer to Hardshaw Hall.   The first houses and cottages flanked the half-mile stretch of road on which the chapel stood.   A series of drawings made in 1805 shows that by that date a long row of buildings occupied both sides of the road for most of the way between the Canal and the Independent Chapel.[2]   Some eight years previously the first completely new street had been laid out ; the St. Helens Tontine,[3] wishing to make a remunerative investment, built a row of cottages and the street thus formed was known as Tontine Street.   Market Street later linked Tontine Street with the highway soon to be generally known as Church Street.   This knot of houses was to form the heart of the new town.

We must beware, however, of calling St. Helens a town too soon.   It is true that those who sought to promote a market and fair in 1780, having laid stress upon the " prodigious increase of inhabitants," were equally lavish in calling the place a town,[4] while Lady Kenyon, who passed through St. Helens in 1797, wrote of it—with apt qualification—as a " pretty country town."[5] Twenty years later a correspondent of a Liverpool newspaper, describing the festivities at St. Helens to celebrate George IV's accession, called the place both a village and a town in the course of the same message.[6] He may be excused for not being able to make up his mind : although there was a vast throng of people present to take part in the celebrations, very few of them were resident in St. Helens itself.   The majority lived at or near the collieries or factories where they worked and these were scattered over the surrounding coalfield.   In the early days the employers had to provide suitable accommodation in order to attract workpeople from outside the district.   When, for example, John Mackay wanted " Twenty Colliers, Industrious Sober Men," to work at his colliery in Parr, he advertised that :

[1] Joseph Aston, *Lancashire Gazeteer* (Manchester, 1808) *sub* St. Hellens. The place was more often than not spelt with the double " l " at that time and often called St. Hellen.

[2] These drawings by John Knowles are to be seen in the St. H. Ref. Lib. Two of them are reproduced in this volume.

[3] A tontine was a form of life insurance popular in the seventeenth and eighteenth centuries.

[4] *Gore's Gen. Ad.* 10 Mar., 1780.

[5] H.M.C., 14th Report, Appendix, Pt. IV., 548.   Lady Kenyon to Lord Kenyon, 3 Aug., 1797.

[6] *Lpool. Merc.* 3 March, 1820.

" Good Lodgings will be immediately provided for those who
cannot return to their Home at Night ; and those who chuse
to occupy Houses will be provided for in a decent Manner,
with Gardens and other Advantages at May next. Drawers
also will find the like Encouragement."[1]

Similarly with the glassmakers : when the Ravenhead works
were in course of construction, there were also being built " sundry
small brick . . . dwelling houses for the occupation of labourers
and persons belonging to the said Glass Manufactory."[2] West's
Row and West's New Row housed the families of those who
worked at the Eccleston Crown Glassworks.[3] All these scattered
islands of population came within the orbit of St. Helens.

As a result of this satellite development, although the number
of people living in the four townships of Windle, Parr, Sutton and
Eccleston increased from 7,573 in 1801 to 10,603 in 1821, the
population of St. Helens itself was very much smaller ; in 1821
it can hardly have exceeded 4,000, for the whole of Windle township, of which St. Helens occupied the southern part, numbered
only 4,820.[4] By that time, however, the demand for accommodation was such that house building had become a most profitable
form of investment. In 1824 the first St. Helens Building Society
was formed " for the purpose of Raising by monthly subscriptions
or payment a sufficient fund to enable each to build or purchase
one or more . . . Dwellinghouses."[5] The members concentrated
their main activities upon the erection of cottages on land belonging to Thomas Milne and the Greenalls[6] at Greenbank in
Eccleston, a little below Combshop Brow.[7] In consequence, there

---

[1] *Lpool. Chron.* 3 Nov., 1768. Mackay also built cottages for his men
at Thatto Heath (above, p. 44).

[2] Pilkington Brothers Ltd., Ravenhead Deeds, package 7. Lease dated
17 Aug., 1774.

[3] See, e.g., sale notice in *Gore's Gen. Ad.* 7 Jan., 1830.

[4] Abstract of Answers and Returns 1801-2 [9], VI ; 1822 [502] XV.

[5] Pilkington Brothers Ltd., package 289. Recital in deed dated 31 May,
1830.

[6] Pilkington Brothers Ltd., package 289. Abstract of Title of Thomas
Milne. See also Abstract of Title of Peter Greenall to an estate called
Williamson's among the Greenall papers at Walton Old Hall, Stockton
Heath, Warrington.

[7]The manufacture of ivory combs was linked with the Africa trade, and the
Dagnalls, a family who made combs in St. Helens and sold them at Liverpool,
were signatories to petitions from Liverpool opposing the abolition of the slave
trade. They are first encountered as comb makers in Windle as soon as Liverpool became interested in the Africa trade. Richard Dagnall, a horn comb
maker of Windle, became a freeman of Liverpool in 1701 (Lpool. Town
Books, 6 Nov., 1700 and 5 March, 1701) and Henry Dagnall of Windle,
comb maker, signed a deed on 27 Jan., of that year (P.R.O. C13/2789).
Charles Dagnall of Eccleston, comb maker, was signatory to a trust deed
of 2 Feb., 1726 (St. H. Cong., Ch., package 1). When a comb manufactory,

was a marked increase of population in that township from 1,931 to 3,259 between 1821 and 1831 ; this was a much quicker rate than that in the other three townships, which only grew from 8,672 to 10,940 in this period,[1] and represented an extension of St. Helens to the west. Taking into account developments in Windle, it seems probable that the town's population reached 6,000 by 1830.

Although St. Helens was growing into a small town, it still displayed many of the characteristics of a country village. Its forms of government were rural. The highways were still the responsibility of a township surveyor and the poor continued to come under the jurisdiction of overseers. About 1800 a sewer had been laid down the main street, " capacious for a man to go through it to cleanse when necessary "[2] but, apart from this precaution against flooding, and such measures as householders had seen fit to take privately on their own behalf, the town remained undrained. It was also unlit : on dark winter nights the only illumination came from lamps placed in shop windows or from lights shining from private houses or local inns. Societies meeting after dark selected the night nearest the full moon.[3]

All meetings had to be held in rooms attached to a church or an inn, for there was no town hall of any kind. Nor was there any particular site for the weekly market, held on Saturdays since March, 1780.[4] When Market Street was laid out about 1800, a

belonging to Barrow and Dagnall, in Great Charlotte Street, Liverpool, was put up for auction in 1843, it was claimed to be two hundred years old. There was still a local connection even at that date, for sale catalogues could be obtained from Thomas Barrow of Barrow Street, St. Helens (*Lpool. Merc.* 10 Nov., 1843). Other families were also interested in the trade at St. Helens. Peter Stubs sold horn and ivory combs for Butler and Bate and for Banner and Doke (Ashton, *Peter Stubs*, 64) and in 1825 James Butler and John Barrow and Son were comb makers in the town. (E. Baines, *Directory*.) According to Cook's MS. Hist. of St. Helens, p. 14, " the manufacture of combs was carried on pretty extensively in St. Helens until the business was removed, chiefly to Liverpool. The name ' Comb Shop Brow ' remains as a memorial to this branch of trade." Since Cook's day the name has reverted to Croppers Hill.

[1] Comparative Account of the Population of Great Britain, 1801-31, 1831 [348] XVIII. It should be borne in mind that Eccleston township extended into Prescot. When it was divided at the census of 1851, 3,022 people lived in Eccleston in Prescot and 5,487 in Eccleston in St. Helens.

[2] St. H. Ref. Lib., Ansdell Papers. Placard issued by William Eckersley, July, 1845.

[3] See e.g., rules of the St. Helens Book Club.

[4] *Gore's Gen. Ad.* of 10 March, 1780, having announced the beginning of a biannual fair at St. Helens (see below, p. 315) went on : " The Public are further to take Notice that a Weekly Market will be held in the said Town of St. Hellen ; to begin the first Saturday after Easter Week, at Two o'clock in the Afternoon of the same Day, for Corn, Flour, Cheese, Butcher's Meat, Butter, Bacon, Eggs, Potatoes and other Necessaries of Life."

space was left at the point where it joined Church Street to give the market people room to sell their wares ; but this soon became inadequate and the vendors' carts and stalls were soon holding up vehicles in Church Street itself.[1]

Among the vehicles using the road were coaches travelling from Liverpool along the turnpike through Prescot to St. Helens and on to Wigan or Bolton and thence into Yorkshire. These picked up passengers at St. Helens in each direction several times a day.[2] But travellers from the south were not so well served. They had to alight from the Liverpool-bound coach at Prescot and make their own way to St. Helens from there. When Adam Bromilow wrote from Lincoln's Inn during July, 1829, asking his father to send a gig to meet him in Prescot, he explained with legal precision exactly how he proposed to travel :

" I think of taking my journey comfortably and pleasantly and therefore purpose starting early on Friday morning and stopping all night at Birmingham and reach Prescot the following day (*Saturday*) at about 3 *o'clock* in the *afternoon*. I know of two coaches which stop all night at Birmingham. The one by which I am thinking of going down is called the *Independent Tallyho*. The other one (called the *Eclipse*) reaches Prescot an hour later. If I am not in the one I shall doubtless be in the other. But if anything should prevent me starting in the *morning* of Friday, I shall come down by the *Rocket* which arrives at Prescot, I believe, about 6 o'clock . . . "[3]

Prescot was also the post town and the mail arrived in St. Helens " by a foot post " at 8 in the morning and was collected at 6.15 at night.[4] The Liverpool mail, however, arrived in the late afternoon and was despatched in the early morning.[5] Richard Greenhalgh, a wine and spirit merchant, dealt with the post of the town as a sideline at his shop in Market Street.[6] His sister, Helen Greenhalgh, later took charge of this branch of their business and eventually opened a separate office in the main street.[7] She

[1] St. H. Town Hall, package 209. Statement for Counsel's Opinion 30 Dec., 1848.

[2] *Pigot's New Commercial Directory for the Counties of Cheshire, Derbyshire and Lancashire*, 1828, *sub* St. Helens.

[3] Bromilow Papers. Letter from Adam Bromilow to William Bromilow 25 July, 1829.

[4] *Directory* 1828. The mails were later brought by cart. *Wigan Gazette* 31 March, 1837.

[5] *Directory* 1828. In 1821 there had been complaints that the Leeds mail carried the Liverpool post on to Wigan from where it was forwarded to St. Helens at a total cost of 7d. *Lpool. Merc.* 15 June, 1821.

[6] James Brockbank, *History of St. Helens* (St. Helens, 1896), 40.

[7] *Ibid.* According to this source Miss Greenhalgh first moved to a house next to the chapel and, in 1826, to premises on the other side of the road.

was raised to the status of deputy postmistress in 1830[1] and remained in charge of the town's postal services until 1866.[2]

On the whole, there is little indication of a readiness to demand improvements in local institutions and services to meet the needs of the growing population. In this respect the churches, which showed themselves more alive to the forces of change, were exceptional. They were quick to enlarge their buildings to accommodate more numerous congregations. A vestry meeting was held in January, 1816, soon after the Rev. Thomas Pigot had become incumbent of St. Helen's Chapel,[3] " for the purpose of considering the Propriety of enlarging the Church and the Church Yard."[4] A plot of land nearby was purchased from Bamber Gascoyne and was consecrated as a churchyard by July, 1816. In April, the building committee accepted the tender of two local builders, James Callon and James Latham, to enlarge the chapel and double its size at a cost of £2,094 and the necessary alterations were made during the summer. It seems strange that the Anglicans chose this opportunity to change the name of the Church, after the town had come to be called after it, but this was in fact what happened. The chapel was re-consecrated not as St. Helen's but as St. Mary's and continued to be known by that name until it was burnt down during the First World War. The present building was consecrated as St. Helens Parish Church.

The Independents also required a larger meeting place. They had worshipped since 1710 in a small stone chapel a short distance from St. Helen's along the road to Ormskirk. The building had been severely shaken by coal-getting at the close of the eighteenth century[5] and was only made safe by means of several stout wooden buttresses. This old chapel was taken down in 1826 at the beginning of the ministry of William Vint[6] and in its place

[1] Returns of Deputy Postmasters and Postmistresses of Great Britain and Ireland, 1835 [264] XLVIII.

[2] *St. H. Standard* 11 March, 1866.

[3] Thomas Pigot was b. at Peplow, Shropshire in 1778 and ed. Newport G. S. and Christ Church. He was appointed curate of All Saints, Wigan in 1808, came from there to St. Helens in March, 1815 and was the incumbent until 1836 when he went to the living of Blymhill, Staffordshire. He died there a few years later (*Wigan Gazette* 7 Feb., 1840). His fifth son, James Creswell Pigot, married Elizabeth, d. of Peter Greenall, on 16 May, 1848.

[4] Mins. of Vestry meetings in the Baptism Register 1713-77 at St. H. Par. Ch.

[5] For details, see packages 12 and 13 at St. H. Cong. Ch.

[6] He was the son of the Rev. William Vint, President of Airedale College. He came to St. H. direct from Idle Academy, near Bradford, and was minister from 1824 until 1840. He died 19 January 1842, aged 40 (*St. H. Intelligencer* 5 April, 1856).

was raised on the same site a larger, brick building which accommodated the growing number of worshippers, some 300 strong by 1829.[1]

St. Helens was situated in the midst of a traditionally Catholic stronghold. At the beginning of the nineteenth century the lords of the manor in three of the four townships—the Ecclestons of Eccleston, the Gerards and Cothams of Windle,[2] and the Orrells of Parr—were Roman Catholics. Mrs. Winefred Eccleston, daughter of Dr. Anthony Lowe " of Milnhouse in the County of Chester "[3] and widow of John Gorsuch Eccleston, presented five acres of land near Crab Lane in Windle to the Society of Jesus. Immediately after her death in June, 1793, a Catholic chapel, called St. Mary's, Lowe House, was built there, possibly, as suggested by Foley,[4] to make good the loss of the Eccleston mission when the family removed from the neighbourhood, or possibly to replace the chapel at Mrs. Eccleston's home in Cowley Hill. In support of the latter contention is the fact that the registers at Lowe House run continuously from 1785 and relate, during the first eight years, to the chapel at Mrs. Eccleston's home. In the year of Catholic emancipation, 1829, about 800 worshippers attended Lowe House.[5]

The Methodists had built a church of their own in Tontine Street in 1815 after having met for thirty-five years in various improvised premises.[6] They also had a small mission in Parr[7] and a church at Nutgrove to serve the Thatto Heath district,[8] built in 1811 by Jonas Nuttall. It was largely through the generosity of Jonas Nuttall, too, that Adam Clarke, the eminent Methodist biblical scholar, with whom Nuttall had come into contact through his business as a printer, was able to retire to Millbrook House, Eccleston in 1815. During Dr. Clarke's

---

[1] L.R.O., QDV 9/410. Returns of places of worship not of the Church of England, 1829.

[2] For the Cotham family, see below, p. 182n.

[3] Wigan Ref. Lib. Dicconson Papers, box 1, package 5. Lease dated 21 Dec., 1742.

[4] H. Foley, *Records of the English Province of the Society of Jesus* (1879) V, 397 ; Reginald J. Riley, S.J., *History of Lowe House, St. Helens* (St Helens, 1940).

[5] L.R.O., QDV 9/410.

[6] St. H. Wesley Church, Cook, MS. Hist. of St. Helens, 13, 16, 36 The Methodists met in a room above a joiner's shop and later, in 1801 or 1802, moved to Market Street, then recently laid out.

[7] *Ibid.*, 34.

[8] *Ibid.*, 78.

residence there, which lasted until 1824, the house became a place of worship for the Methodists of the neighbourhood.[1]

The churches were responsible, either directly or indirectly, for the two main day schools in the town. Adam Martindale, the puritan divine and diarist, received his first education at St. Helen's Chapel so early as the 1630s, though he later thought that the " hindrances were many, as First, many teachers (five in fewer years). Secondly, These none of the best . . . "[2] Forty years later John Lyon built a small school house close to the chapel which came to be known as the Old Grammar School.[3] Early in the eighteenth century Sarah Cowley, a Nonconformist, entrusted part of the income from her newly-acquired, fourteen-acre estate in Hardshaw to the Rev. Joseph Gillibourn, minister of the Independent Chapel, " for the bringing up of poore persons children to the schools at St. Elins "[4] and the income from her estate was, accordingly, paid to the schoolmaster at the Old Grammar School. In 1778 or 1779, however, Gilli-bourn's successors as administrators of Cowley's Charity (all Independents) chose—in the words of the indignant Anglicans— " to sett up an Old Man and Woman (Presbyterians) to teach a few children and pay them out of the rents of this Estate and send no children to the Old School."[5]

In 1793 the Anglicans retorted by building a new school on the Moorflat, close by the workhouse opened in the same year, and the Old Grammar School was pulled down.[6] This improvement in the standards of accommodation caused the trustees of Cowley's Charity not only to put up their own school building but also to offer a superior form of education for those whose parents could pay fees. The first Cowley School was built in 1797 on land belonging to Samuel Cross, one of the trustees, at the end of College Lane, only a stone's throw from the new Anglican foundation.[7] Five years later, the income from the Cowley estate having been considerably augmented by leasing

[1] *Ibid.*, 59. For Jonas Nuttall, see below, p. 356.

[2] *Life of Adam Martindale* (ed. Parkinson) Chet. Soc., IV (O.S.) (1845) 11.

[3] A stone from the old school (still preserved) reads :
   " John Lyon built this schoole house upon his owne cost and charges and gave XXX[s.] a year for ever. June, 1670."

[4] Will of Sarah Cowley proved at Chester 20 June, 1716.

[5] Case for the opinion of Mr. Maddocks, 12 Dec., 1785, among the papers of the St. Helens Par. Ch. Trustees ; letter from Robert Hodgkinson to Cowley Trustees, 3 Dec., 1784, in package 14 at St. H. Cong. Ch.

[6] Report of the Charity Commissioners, 1836, II, 255.

[7] This paragraph is based on information contained in the Chancery case, P.R.O. C13/2789.

N

the subjacent coal measures, the trustees were able to put up a
second school building and in the next year Francis Morley,
" a gentleman competent to give instruction in the higher branches
of education", became the master.[1]

The Anglicans continued to protest that the growing income
from the Cowley estate was being misapplied since the moneys
were intended by the testator " for the bringing up of poore
persons children to the schools at St. Elins." But they were
unable to secure a decision satisfactory to themselves until they
were in a position to add the charge of gross mismanagement.
This led to a bill being filed in Chancery in 1822. Like most
Chancery cases, it was long drawn out, and five years elapsed
before the Anglicans were given the right of nominating four
of the nine trustees. They were thereafter responsible for administering the Charity for the benefit of all poor children in the
district, whether Anglicans or Dissenters.[2]

In 1820, 40 children were being educated at the Anglican
School at Moorflat and 30 at Cowley's School.[3] By 1833, the
numbers had risen to 82 and 80 respectively. At the latter date,
50 pupils also attended a Roman Catholic school and, in addition,
no fewer than 444 boys and girls in Windle township (which included St. Helens) were obtaining their education at 15 private
schools, most of them recent creations. The other townships
appear to have been similarly well served with day schools : the
attendance in Eccleston was 279, in Parr 239, and in Sutton 237.
Most of these children were paid for by their parents at the rate of
a few pence per week, although some scholarships were available.[4]

In common with other Lancashire towns at that time, more
boys and girls received their education on Sundays than on
weekdays. Although the first Sunday School, that of the Independents, was not opened at St. Helens until 1806,[5] the movement
thereafter spread rapidly. The Anglicans joined it in 1808, the
Methodists in 1810, and the Roman Catholics about the same

[1] Previous masters were William Grundy and a Mr. Hope (said to have
been the author of the grammar used at the school). Morley had previously
assisted Hope at Annan, near Gretna Green (Cook, *op. cit.* 95). For
Morley, see below, p. 177-8.

[2] St. H. Town Hall, Cowley Papers. Appointment of new trustees, 30
and 31 Dec., 1827.

[3] E. Baines, *History, Directory and Gazeteer of the County Palatine of
Lancaster* (Lpool, 1825), II, 258.

[4] Abstract of Answers and Returns Relative to the State of Education
in England and Wales, 1833. 1835 [62] XLI. For some words of caution
concerning these returns, see T. S. Ashton, *Economic and Social Investigations in Manchester, 1833-1933* (1934), 27-8.

[5] *Lpool Merc.* 7 March, 1856.

[Photo. : R. K. Robertson]

Two Views of St. Helens in 1805

Raven Street from the Canal Bridge (above)
Church Street from the *Black Bull* (below)

Drawings by John Knowles at St. Helens Reference Library.

[Photo : R. K. Robertson]

PETER GREENALL (1796—1845)

Portrait by Spindler at the St. Helens Town Hall.

PART TWO

THE AGE OF
PETER GREENALL

1830—1845.

Chapter XIV

THE COMING OF THE RAILWAY

THE greatest need of the new industrial towns was for men of public spirit able and willing to play their part in local government. Wise counsels were particularly necessary when urban growth was in its early stages, but it was precisely during these formative years that such leadership was so often lacking. The landed gentlemen often looked askance at the despoilers of the countryside, while the new industrialists were usually too preoccupied with establishing themselves and staving off bankruptcy to divert any of their attention to the local affairs of the communities which they were responsible for creating.

In the case of St. Helens, this was as true of the landowner descendants of the industrialists as of those who had owned landed property for generations. Michael Hughes I, the copper smelter, was actively engaged in local affairs; but his son, Michael Hughes II, for many years an army officer, lacked his father's interest in the neighbourhood. Similarly, when Samuel Taylor, whose father had purchased Eccleston Hall and its estate in 1812,[1] went to live there in the middle of the 1820s,[2] he, too, displayed little concern about the growth of the town or the economic prosperity of the district. Nor did Sir John Gerard of Garswood

---

[1] E. Baines, *History of the County Palatine and Duchy of Lancaster* (1836), II, 109.

[2] Col. Samuel Taylor, who bought Eccleston Hall in 1812, was a native of Moston, near Manchester, where the family had been engaged in the textile industry for many years. In 1723 a Samuel Taylor of Moston had patented a method of stamping and dressing thread and Samuel Taylor and Co. were described in a directory of 1781 as check manufacturers at Moston. Another directory of the same year gives the names of Samuel and Thomas Taylor as manufacturers of check and African goods at Hanging Ditch in Manchester. The Samuel Taylor in question, probably father of the Colonel, said in 1788 that he had been engaged in the slave trade since 1761, three-quarters of his goods being sent to Africa and the rest to the West Indies. Col. Samuel Taylor who bought Eccleston Hall was born in 1771 and is perhaps to be identified with the man of that name who was head of the Anglesey Companies' Liverpool Warehouse and Copper Office. The purchase appears to have been mainly an investment, for Col. Taylor continued to make Moston Hall his home, Eccleston Hall, an old and dilapidated building, being leased for use as a school. He died in 1820 and his son, born 1802, re-built Eccleston Hall in 1825, the year of his marriage, and went to live there. St. H. Ref. Lib., Papers relating to the Taylor family ; Wadsworth and Mann, *The Cotton Trade and Industrial Lancashire* (Manchester, 1931), 303 ; ev. of Samuel Taylor to the Cttee of Council on the Slave Trade, 1788.

New Hall, who became the twelfth baronet in 1826, Charles Orrell, who inherited Blackbrook House in 1824, or William Penketh Cotham, for long the owner of Hardshaw Hall.[1] These men all fulfilled their duties as Justices of the Peace but did not intervene in the day-to-day life of the town, preferring to look on from a distance rather than use their prestige to support any schemes for its planning and improvement.

There was, however, one other prominent local family of standing. Though still in business as brewers, the Greenalls had already become the leading owners of property in the town and also possessed much land on the outskirts: more than 300 acres in Eccleston township, extending from Greenbank as far as Millbrook;[2] another 50 acres adjoining it in Windle and a further small but important piece of property, also in Windle, farther to the eastward.[3] The tenants of their houses were so numerous that rent day involved a large proportion of the population and the event was celebrated by a dinner at their Fleece Inn. The annual income from these rents exceeded £2,500 by 1830.[4] Ownership of property on this scale in a town so small qualified the family to take a lead in local affairs.

By this time the Greenalls had made their home in Warrington, though one member of the family still lived at St. Helens to manage the brewery and take charge of all their business in and about the town. On the death of Thomas Greenall in 1805, his sons, Edward, William and Peter, had assumed control of the two breweries, but Peter died in 1815 and William died in

---

[1] The Cotham family hailed from Claughton near Lancaster. Mary Golden bequeathed Hardshaw Hall and estate to her nephew, William Penketh Cotham, by her will of 3 Oct., 1757. He died 11 May, 1797 at the age of 97. The property appears to have passed to William Penketh Cotham II, possibly his son, who was certainly in possession of it when the Tithe Award for Windle was drawn up in 1840. By that date, however, Cotham had removed to Springfield, Eccleston. At the time of his death, in Jan., 1846, he was described as "late of Springfield near Prescot but now of Macclesfield." His property in St. Helens, together with the family estates at Claughton and in Goosnargh parish, passed to his wife and, on her death, to his sisters, Anna Maria Walmesley, Frances Elizabeth Cotham and Mary Clare Cotham. Hardshaw Hall later became the Providence Hospital (below, p. 465) and Springfield became a Carmelite Convent. L.R.O., Cross Papers, Abstract of Mr. Cotham's Title to Hardshaw Hall; Inscription upon the family grave in Windleshaw Cemetery, quoted in Cook, MS. Hist. of St. Helens., 113; will of William Penketh Cotham proved at Chester, 13 March, 1846.

[2] This land was acquired from the Eccleston family whose estates had been heavily mortgaged throughout the eighteenth century. In 1790 a receiver was appointed, £30,000 being then owed to William Marsh and Henry Creed of London. In 1799 the first of a number of auctions took place. Wigan Ref. Lib., Dicconson Papers, Box 1, package 8 ; St. H. Ref. Lib., auction catalogue among Taylor Papers.

[3] L.R.O., Tithe Awards for Windle, 1840, and for Eccleston, 1843.

[4] St. H. Brewery, rent books.

1817. The following year Edward Greenall, the surviving brother, sent one of his younger sons to St. Helens to take charge of the family's affairs. This son, Peter Greenall, just 21, had outstanding ability and a keen sense of duty. Before long he was using his influential position to exercise a benevolent despotism over the town's development. He emerges as the hero of the piece in the vital years between 1830 and 1845.

" We are all possessed of a Railway Mania," wrote General Gascoyne to William Bromilow at St. Helens on 11 February, 1825. His excited state of mind was caused by the campaign for a railway between Liverpool and Manchester, then at its fiercest in Liverpool, of which Borough the General was a representative in Parliament. He was soon complaining of the " Continual *daily* necessity of taking the Chair at 12 o'clock at L. and M. Railway Com^{ee} ",[1] a duty he was obliged to undertake on thirty-eight occasions before the promoters withdrew their Bill in the face of very strong opposition.[2] Had this original application been sanctioned by Parliament, the line would have taken a more northerly route than the one eventually adopted and would have passed within a mile of St. Helens, close by the Cowley Hill, Gerard's Bridge, Rushy Park and Blackbrook collieries.[3] The promoters made much of this coal traffic, claiming that:

" In addition to the transport of goods between Liverpool and Manchester, an important branch of revenue may be expected to result to the proprietors of the projected road, from the conveyance of coals from the rich mines in the vicinity of St. Helens; an advantage which the water companies do not possess, and which, from its importance and extent, may probably enable the proprietors to reduce the rates of carriage still lower than now contemplated. These coals at present pass along the Sankey Canal, and down the Mersey to Liverpool, a distance of about thirty miles. By the railway the distance will be shortened one-half, and the charge for transit very materially reduced."[4]

Although several coal proprietors near whose pits the projected railway was to pass, signed a petition in favour of the Bill,[5]

[1] Bromilow Papers. Gascoyne to Bromilow, 28 May, 1825.

[2] T. Baines, *History of the Town and Commerce of Liverpool* (1852), 609.

[3] For the route, see James Sherriff's *Map of the Environs of Liverpool*. A more detailed map of the route as it passed through Parr is to be found in the *Proc. of the Cttee. of the House of Commons on the Liverpool and Manchester Railroad Bill*, opp. p. 505.

[4] Baines, *op. cit.*, 602.

[5] *Proc. on the Liverpool and Manchester Railroad Bill.*.

Charles Orrell and Sir William Gerard fought hard against it. Orrell was concerned to prevent the line from passing on a raised embankment only 250 yards from the front of his Blackbrook House. The promoters of the Bill, however, were quick to seize upon the fact that Orrell was himself a coal proprietor and, as such, stood to benefit from the proposed railway. His agent, James Glover, disagreed. Liverpool, he pointed out, was not then an important market for coals from Blackbrook:

> " The chief part of Mr. Orrell's coals are sent by the Sankey Canal to Northwich; and to Mr. Ashton's Dungeon Salt-works, not far from Hale Hill . . . He sends . . . some few to Liverpool but not many—very few except a person comes to buy a load of coals and pays ready money for them."[1]

Although Orrell was undoubtedly more immediately concerned about the view from his own front windows than about the prosperity of his colliery, there is no doubt that his agent was voicing the case of all the coal proprietors in the St. Helens district when he emphasised that the coals were sent to the south rather than to the west. If there was to be a railway, the coal proprietors wanted a line running direct to the Mersey whence the flats could ship the coal straight to the saltworks.

Enthusiasm for railways was encouraged by the successful construction of the Liverpool-Manchester line between 1826 and 1830 along an amended route which passed about two miles to the south of St. Helens. As the "Mania" spread from the chief centre of excitement in Liverpool to the surrounding towns, another cry was heard. Several of the coal and salt proprietors, no longer content with a line running in the wrong direction, started to demand a separate railway of their own down to the Mersey at Runcorn Gap.

A prominent feature of this " Railway Mania " was the attack on the canals. According to a later statement by the treasurer of the St. Helens and Runcorn Gap Railway, it was

> " first projected as a work of competition with the Sankey Canal. The Coal Proprietors were dissatisfied with their treatment under the Canal Monopoly and it was held forth to the public that a Railway from St. Helens to a dock at Runcorn Gap for the transit of coal, whilst it would benefit the Coal Proprietors, would afford a fair prospect of lucrative investment."[2]

Prior to 1829, the Canal had certainly paid its shareholders handsomely. In the closing years of the war, annual dividends of

[1] *Ibid.*, 495, 501.

[2] British Transport Commission, Historical Records, 66, Porchester Road, London. W.2.   Minutes of the St. Helens and Runcorn Gap Railway, 21 Jan., 1839.   This source is referred to hereafter as St. H. and R. G. Mins.

between £50 and £60 were usual on each £155 share.[1] According to one of the directors, Thomas Case, giving evidence in 1829, an average dividend of $33\frac{1}{3}\%$ had been distributed annually since the Canal's opening,[2] a return on capital which would earn a fairly high place in Clapham's list of successful canal companies.[3] Such a state of affairs was tolerated while the leading shareholders were also interested in the salt trade and while there was no other satisfactory mode of transport, but by the 1820s many of the shares had changed hands.[4] The possibility of reducing the profits of the Canal by opening an alternative means of communication now proved a great temptation to all who were engaged in the coal trade.

It is not known when the coal proprietors first entertained the idea of building a railway to Runcorn Gap, though the expenditure of £8,653 on a new lock and half tide basin on the Canal in 1826-7 and a further £1,000 on Carr Mill Dam in the following year,[5] may have been in response to the first murmurings of opposition. It was not until 1829, however, that Charles Blacker Vignoles, who had previously served for a time as engineer of the Liverpool-Manchester Railway when Stephenson was under a cloud following the failure of his original Bill,[6] carried out a survey of the intended line. The original plan appears to have been for it to run from the Cowley Hill Colliery *via* Greenbank, Sutton Hall and Lea Green to a dock on the Mersey west of the site eventually chosen.[7] This was later altered and a more easterly route proposed, crossing over the Liverpool-Manchester Railway by a bridge with an inclined plane on both sides. Branches were

---

[1] The figures were : 1809, £51 5s. ; 1810, £59 7s. ; 1811, £63 7s. ; 1812, £46 17s. ; 1813, £54 12s. ; 1814, £60 2s. ; 1815, £59 5s. ; Picton Ref. Lib., Holt and Gregson MSS, X, 131.

[2] Evidence of Thomas Case to the S.C. of the House of Commons on the Sankey Navigation Bill, 1830, quoted by L. W. Evans to a similar committee hearing evidence on the St. H. Rly (Transfer) Bill 1864.

[3] J. H. Clapham, *An Economic History of Modern Britain*, (Cambridge, 1926), I, 81.

[4] Michael Hughes, for instance, possessed shares in the Canal ; he attempted to sell them at £1,300 each to Thomas Case in 1814. Sherdley Estate Office, letter from Michael Hughes to Thomas Case, 13 Dec., 1814. Although John Ashton held 51 out of the 120 shares in the Canal at the time of his death in 1759, his son Nicholas mentions only 5 in his will dated 23 Jan., 1830 and proved at Chester, 19 Dec., 1834.

[5] Case quoted by Evans to the S.C., 1864. The lease of Stanley Mill and Carr Mill is to be found among the Gerard Papers, DDGe 656, at the L.R.O.

[6] Olinthus J. Vignoles, *The Life of Charles Blacker Vignoles* (1889), 110.

[7] This earlier route was shown on the plan deposited with the Act of Parliament and now in the House of Lords Record Office. It has been crossed out and the later route substituted.

to be laid to connect with most of the local collieries.[1] A subscription list for 1,200 shares, each of £100, was opened at the Fleece Inn at St. Helens in January, 1830.[2] The necessary Bill was introduced into the House of Commons on 16 February and received the Royal Assent on 29 May.[3]

About a third or possibly more of the capital appears to have been raised from among the coal proprietors and saltmakers or from those Liverpool merchants who had an interest in the salt trade. From an early subscription list, dated June 1830, it is possible to identify the owners of 1,030 of the 1,130 shares allocated by that date.[4] Of these 1,030 shares, the coal proprietors and saltmakers held 275.[5] Various Liverpool investors owned no fewer than 505 shares and of these, 160 were in the hands of men calling themselves merchants; some of them may reasonably be supposed to have been concerned in one way or another with the salt trade. Other Liverpool investors, who styled themselves book-keepers and gentlemen, may also have been interested in exporting salt. There is a significant absence of the names of those who were prominent Liverpool railway speculators: the Croppers, Rathbones, Horsfalls, Booths and Sandars. It would seem as if the St. Helens and Runcorn Gap Railway was viewed by many of the investors as a means of gaining greater profits from the coal and salt trades rather than merely as a fruitful source of investment. Even at St. Helens, several of the shareholders outside the coal trade, who collectively held 170 shares, were vitally interested in improved communication with the Mersey: James Muspratt, for instance, who bought shares, William Pilkington and Sons who held 25 and Lee Watson who subscribed for 20. The same may be said of Hazlehursts, the Runcorn soap boilers, who held 5 shares, and Thomas Lyon and Thomas Parr, the Warrington bankers who already had money out on loan in the St. Helens district and possessed 20 shares. There were others among the local population, it is true, for whom the Railway cannot have appeared as anything more

[1] St. H. Ref. Lib., *Plan and Sections of an Intended Line of Railway from St. Helens to West Bank at Runcorn Gap from Surveys made under the Direction of C. B. Vignoles, Esq., 28 Nov., 1829.*

[2] Vignoles, *op. cit.*, 140

[3] 11 Geo. IV. cap. LXI. For petitions presented for and against the Bill, see *C.J.*, 85, 12, 193, 207, 230, 8 Feb., 18, 22, 26 March, 1830.

[4] St. H. Ref. Lib. Subscription List, 5 June, 1830.

[5] Robert Robinson 5, Christopher Robinson 5, Thomas Caldwell 20, William Bromilow 10, James Bromilow 10, William Bromilow, Jr. 5, Charles Orrell 5, John Clare, Jr. 5, John Johnson 10, Thomas Birch Speakman 10, James Underhill West 5, Thomas Haddock 10, Joseph Leigh 10, Peter Bourne 15, John Bourne 10, James Bourne 20, Thomas Firth 20, Thomas Marshall 10, R. P. Hadfield 5, William Worthington 20, Thomas Barker 10, John Dudley 10, John Cheshire 5, Thomas Urmson 15, Richard Crosbie Dawson 20, William Ambrose Dawson 5.

than an investment : for Ellen Hughes, for instance, the widow of Michael Hughes I, who held 15 shares, or William Eckersley, the brewer, who held 5, or the Rev. Thomas Pigot, incumbent of St. Mary's, who had 2. But, on the whole, the parties who were to derive the chief commercial and industrial advantage from the line were very much to the fore. It was 1755 all over again with one important difference: whereas the Sankey Navigation was financed almost entirely from Liverpool, by 1829-30 those concerned in the highly-developed organisation of the salt trade lived not only in Liverpool but also on the coalfield and in Cheshire.

The largest family holdings were those of the Bournes and the Greenalls, each possessing 45 shares. Of the Greenalls, Edward held 20 and his five sons, Thomas, John, Gilbert, Richard and Peter, had 5 each. Although Peter Greenall only possessed the minimum number for eligibility to a directorship, it seems most probable that he was the moving spirit behind the company. When Thomas Caldwell, the coal proprietor, wrote to his partner, William Bromilow, who was away in London attending the committee stage of the Railway Bill, he asked:

" Does it not appear that the *Alderman* [possibly a reference to Peter Bourne, an alderman in Liverpool] has acted towards our Committee with some duplicity—certainly our friend Greenall did not expect or anticipate such opposition."[1]

That " friend Greenall " applied to Peter Greenall is made reasonably certain by two later events: his election to the chair of the new company and the presentation to him of a silver dinner service within a few weeks of the line's opening. Each piece was inscribed:

" Presented to Peter Greenall, Esquire, by the inhabitants of St. Helens and its neighbourhood, as a token of their esteem for his private worth, and of gratitude for his public service, 1833."[2]

Unfortunately nothing is known of the problems he faced in organising the scattered protests of the local Canal users and enlisting their support for the Railway. We are well informed, however, of the troubles confronting him as chairman of the new company, for the minutes of the St. Helens and Runcorn Gap Railway have been carefully preserved.

It was soon evident that the Railway, and particularly the dock on the Mersey, were to cost much more than was originally

[1] Bromilow Papers. Thomas Caldwell to William Bromilow, 1 April 1830.

[2] *Lpool. Merc.* 16 Aug., 1833.

estimated. On 15 August, 1831, the secretary of the Company, John Whitley (Greenall's brother-in-law),[1] took down a resolution:

> " That Mr. Vignoles be requested to revise the whole of the Works of the Railway and Dock and to report to the Directors whether in any and what portions of it any alterations may be safely made so as to effect any saving of expense . . ."[2]

The engineer was obliged to economise by laying a single instead of a double track along part of the line and by reducing the number of branches to the collieries. Despite these economies, by July, 1833 the £120,000 raised in shares and a further £30,000, permitted to be raised by loan, had already been spent and an additional sum of money—at least £10,000—was required.[3] The necessary legislation was obtained in the following year permitting the company to raise £40,000 more on mortgage.[4] The Directors might well report to the Annual Meeting a few months later that

> " The difficulties and disappointment they . . . had to contend with have been greater than they felt reason to expect."[5]

The shareholders would have taken a very gloomy view of the position indeed had they known that, on account of the large debt—equivalent to about half the original share capital—they were not to receive any dividend payments for another ten years. As one of them grumbled in 1844:

> " The railway was constructed in the first instance, not from a conviction that it would ever pay even the smallest dividend but with a view to the convenience and benefit of a few coalowners."[6]

Certainly there was much truth in the latter part of his observation.

The first train of coal waggons passed over the line from Broad Oak Colliery to the Mersey at the end of November, 1832, the result of a wager between a coal proprietor and the engineer of the Canal that a coal train would be able to pass along the line before 1 December.[7] The official opening three months later was rather a fiasco. On 21 February, 1833,

> " The Directors met on the Line and proceeded with

---

[1] Isabella Greenall married John Whitley on 27 April, 1824.

[2] St. H. and R.G. Mins., 15 Aug., 1831.

[3] St. H. and R.G. Mins., 26 July, 1833.

[4] 4 & 5 William IV cap. III.

[5] St. H. and R.G. Mins., 26 July, 1833.

[6] *Railway Times*, 6 July, 1844.

[7] *Lpool. Merc.* 30 Nov., 1832.

several waggons of Coal from the Broad Oak Colliery belonging to Messrs Bournes and Comp[y] to the Dock, where a vessel was in readiness for her cargo but Messrs Lee Watson and Co. having failed in their agreement to complete the Tipping Machines at the dock wall, the Coal could not be shipped. The Stationary Engine was also incomplete though the whole were undertaken by Messrs Lee Watson to be ready by this day . . . and the Coals were obliged to be drawn up the Incline Plane [at Sutton to enable the Railway to be carried over the Liverpool-Manchester line] by Locomotive Engine and also by Men and Horses."[1]

It was not until the middle of the year 1833 that coal was shipped regularly from the dock at Widnes at the rate of 200 tons a day.[2] The dock admitted vessels of up to 300 tons and each coal proprietor possessed his own tipping machine and siding so that coal could be despatched without delay. At the time of the Bill's passage, the coal masters had contended that the new dock would enable flats to be loaded in three or four hours throughout the year, an operation which on the Canal occupied 24 hours " and under adverse circumstances several days and frequently a week ", on account of the neap tides at Fidler's Ferry where the Canal entered the Mersey.[3] In August, 1833, 70 tons of coal were tipped into a flat in 40 minutes.[4]

Perhaps the Railway helped the coal trade most of all by obliging the Canal Company to improve its services and reduce its charges. Even while the Railway Company's Bill was passing through Parliament, the proprietors of the Canal were seeking powers to extend their navigation from Fidler's Ferry to Widnes and form a new company with capital of £96,000 for the purpose. The measure received the Royal Assent on the same day as the Railway Bill,[5] and the Canal directors pressed on with the extension to Widnes. This was opened in July, 1833, about the same time as the Railway was really open to traffic.[6] The dock for the Sankey flats was constructed at Widnes side by side with that of the Railway so that both companies were affected in the same way by the neap tides in the Mersey. The new point of entry, more than three miles down river from Fidler's Ferry, did much

---

[1] St. H. and R.G. Mins., 21 Feb., 1833.

[2] *Ibid.*, 26 July, 1833.

[3] Quoted *ibid.*, 21 Jan., 1839.

[4] *Lpool. Merc.* 30 Aug., 1833.

[5] 11 Geo. IV. cap. L. The new company issued 480 shares of £280 each, share in the old company being equivalent to 4 in the new one. Leave had been granted in 1819 to several of the proprietors to introduce a Bill to extend the Canal to Ditton (*C. J.*, **75**, 36, 56, 8, **13** Dec., 1819) but they took no further action on this occasion.

[6] *Lpool. Merc.* 26 July, 1833.

to prevent the tedious delays of which the coal proprietors had complained, and the Canal Company knew that any further complaints would apply equally to the rival Railway Company's dock as to their own.

The opening of the Railway also led to a reduction in the tolls levied on the Canal. At first the Railway charged 1s. 8d. per " long " ton of 30 cwts.[1] from St. Helens to the dock, " the colliers to find coal for the Locomotive and Stationary Engines ".[2] The toll on the Canal for coal and other merchandise was thereupon reduced by charging the same amount for 45 tons as had previously been levied for 40 tons. This increased the " long " ton by one-eighth in a way which enabled the captains of flats to derive some benefit, since the certificates of cargo granted on the Sankey were also valid on the Weaver. The Railway Company retaliated by reducing their rate from 1s. 8d. to 1s. 6d. per ton of 30 cwts. and by informing the Weaver Trustees of the Canal proprietors' ruse.[3]

Improved and cheaper communication between the coalfield and the Mersey led to a great expansion in coal-getting in the St. Helens district during the 1830s, and both the Railway and Canal shared in this additional traffic. In 1836 coal was passing down the Canal at the rate of about 170,000 tons a year[4] and about 130,000 tons of coal were carried on the railway.[5] Nine years later, in 1845, no less than 440,784 tons were shipped to the Mersey by flat and 252,877 tons carried by railway truck.[6]

The Railway failed to capture the greater part of the coal trade, despite the fact that it was a coal-owners' creation, partly because of the large bond debt which dogged it from the outset and partly for technical reasons. Vignoles's original plan of 1829 assumed branches to eleven collieries. In fact, although the Treasurer of the Company stated in 1833 that four coal-owners had spent £10,000 " in making preparations to carry upon the Railway " and had promised to send more than 160,000 tons of coal per year by it,[7] in 1839 only five proprietors, Bournes and Robinson (Peasley Cross and Broad Oak), Speakman Caldwell and Co. (Gerard's Bridge and Cowley Hill), Johnson Worthington and Co. (Sankey Brook), John Shaw Leigh (Ashton's Green) and

---

[1] For the " long " ton, see below, p. 338.

[2] St. H. and R.G. Mins., 4 Feb., 1833.

[3] *Ibid.*, 25 July, 1834.

[4] Bromilow Papers. Account of the quantity of coal and slack shipped in the months of Feb., June, July, Oct. and Nov., 1836.

[5] St. H. and R.G. Mins., 21 Jan., 1839.

[6] Ev. of Arthur Sinclair to the S.C. on the St. H. Canal and Rly. Bill, 1846.

[7] St. H. and R.G. Mins., 9 Jan., 1833.

Joseph Greenough (Parr Stocks) were using the line.[1] Because of the economies ordered in 1831, branches had not been laid to the other collieries ; their owners, therefore, continued to use the Canal, taking advantage of those reductions in tolls which the building of the Railway had brought about. In the meantime, new and extensive pits had been opened in the Blackbrook district to the north-east of the town and these, lying beyond the limits of the Railway, used the Canal.

By the late 1830s the line was in a grave predicament. In the last five months of 1839 the interest on the bond debt consumed all the profits and a loss of £500 was sustained.[2] The track by this time had deteriorated seriously because money could not be spared for its upkeep. In December, 1840, no fewer than sixty broken rails were reported, " the majority of them ' cobbled up ' in a very dangerous manner."[3] Six months later, Robert Daglish, jr. who had undertaken to supply locomotive power, refused to accept responsibility for any damage that might be caused because

" there are not less than 1000 Rails over which it is really dangerous to pass even with a coal waggon containing 3½ tons of Coals, therefore you will readily conceive the danger incurr'd by the Weight of the Engines varying as they do from 10 to 12 tons each."[4]

Clearly, the St. Helens Railway, though it had achieved the end for which it had been built, was in desperate straits. In January, 1842, when trade was bad and the bondholders were starting to press for the repayment of their loans, the bank even refused to pay interest on them, there being only £286 standing to the Railway's account.[5] " The remedy," wrote the Treasurer,[6]

" is alone with the Coal Proprietors. The Railway is in their power : it was made for them ; they have constantly pledged themselves to support it. The sanguine anticipations from time to time expressed were under the sanction of Coal Proprietors in their capacity of Directors as well as in their commercial character. . . . It is quite clear that the Railway cannot go on as at present."

The ramshackle Railway survived the depression of the early 1840s, no doubt with the aid of the coal-owners and possibly with the knowledge that, despite their own misfortunes, their competition was proving most harmful to the Canal. At a meeting held in Warrington in January, 1838, Thomas Parr, Joseph Crosfield, Thomas Case and Trafford Trafford had discussed the possibility of amalgamation, being " decidedly of opinion that it would be to

[1] St. H. and R.G. Mins., 19 Dec., 1839.   [2] Ibid.

[3] Ibid., 11 Dec., 1840.

[4] Ibid., 16 Aug., 1841. For Daglish, see below, p. 367.

[5] Ibid., 10 Jan., 1842.   [6] Ibid., 21 Jan., 1839.

O

the benefit of the proprietors of both concerns to unite them so
as to have one common Interest," but nothing came of these
negotiations.[1] A second approach was made in January, 1844
(on whose initiative is not known) and, after a little business
manoeuvring on the Railway's part, it was agreed that the Canal
Company should sell out to the Railway at £300 for every £200
share. The capital was to be raised by the issue of 1,440 5%
preference shares each of £100, 480 of which were to be offered
to the Canal shareholders and the remaining 960 to shareholders
in the Railway.[2] The necessary legislation was obtained in the
following year.[3] Peter Greenall, who had remained chairman of
the Railway throughout all its vicissitudes, became chairman of
the new St. Helens Canal and Railway Company.

At first glance, the readiness of the Canal Company to merge
with its new rival may appear surprising, for the Canal seemed to
be holding its own and the Railway was in such grave distress.
But the evidence of John Ashton Case before the Parliamentary
Committee on the Amalgamation Bill makes it clear that the
proprietors of the Canal were also feeling the pinch. The dividends
in the previous four years were just over $5\frac{1}{2}\%$, a great drop from
the $33\frac{1}{3}\%$ which had been customary, and the company had not
been able to spend as much on repairs since the Railway had
opened. The Canal also had a bond debt of £30,000.[4] Bearing
in mind the widespread and justifiable belief that the future
of transport lay with railways rather than canals, it is perhaps
not quite so surprising that the shareholders in the Sankey Brook
Navigation were, according to Case, " nearly unanimous "
for amalgamation. Certainly the two companies, when merged,
inspired more confidence than did the Railway alone : the 5%
preference shares were soon standing at $7\frac{1}{4}\%$ premium.[5]

Although the St. Helens and Runcorn Gap Railway paid no
dividends during its early years and, with its inclined planes and
second-hand engines,[6] was far from being one of the best examples
of British workmanship, it nevertheless bestowed many advantages upon St. Helens and, in particular, upon the coal trade.
It is this, the chief source of the district's wealth, that we must
consider next.

[1] St. H. and R.G. Mins., 22 Jan., 30 July, 1838 ; *Wigan Gazette*, 2, 16
March, 1838.

[2] St. H. and R.G. Mins., 11, 20, 23, 31 Jan., 24 Feb., 1844 ; *Lpool. Merc.*
16 Feb., 1844 ; *Railway Times* 24 Feb., 1844.

[3] 8 and 9 Vict. cap. CXVII. A Bill introduced the previous session was
not permitted to proceed because the necessary notice had not been given.

[4] St. H. and R.G. Mins., 23 Jan., 1844.

[5] Letter from a Proprietor, *Railway Times*, 6 April, 1844.

[6] Letter from B. Baxter, *The Locomotive*, 15 Dec., 1945.

CHAPTER XV

THE MERSEYSIDE COAL TRADE

1830-1845

IN 1830 almost all the coal leaving St. Helens went to the Cheshire wiches ; John Whitley, secretary of the Railway Company, wrote in that year that the Railway was " intended to facilitate the transmission of Coals to the Cheshire Salt Works."[1] By the mid-1840s, however, the saltfield had ceased to be the only large market outside the St. Helens area for local coal. In 1845, as has been seen,[2] almost 700,000 tons were carried down to the Mersey by Canal and Railway ; but considerably less than 200,000 tons of this went on to the saltworks.[3] Extensive new markets had obviously been acquired during the fifteen years between 1830 and 1845. They were a direct result of the introduction to Merseyside of the steamboat.

A very primitive steam vessel, propelled by oars and travelling at a rate of two miles per hour, had sailed on the Sankey Canal so early as 1797[4] and the *Liverpool Courier* reported in its issue of 5 July, 1815, " the first Steam Boat ever seen on our River."[5] By the 1820s, however, " steam at sea was yet little better than a toy."[6] These tiny steam vessels were particularly suited for short journeys and were soon being employed on the regular coastal and Irish services of which Liverpool was the chief English terminus. Specially-built steam packets started to carry mails on the Liverpool-Dublin route in 1826[7] and several small paddle steamers were soon providing rapid transport across the Irish sea for cattle and provisions, required in ever greater quantity

[1] Brasenose College, Oxford, package 876. Letter from John Whitley to the Senior Bursar, 29 Jan., 1830.

[2] Above, p. 190.

[3] Below, p. 195. The Weaver Tonnage Books show that coal was being carried at the rate of 150,000 tons a year in 1830, 163,000 tons in 1840 and 200,000 tons in 1860.

[4] The boat, designed and built by John Smith of St. Helens, carried William Bromilow among its passengers on its original journey from St. Helens to the Newton Races (*Billinge's Lpool. Ad.* 26 June, 1797 ; *Lpool. Merc.* 20 July, 1832 ; 18, 25 Aug., 5, 8, 22, 26 Sept., 6 Oct., 1854).

[5] Quoted by A. C. Wardle, " Early Steamships on the Mersey, 1815-20," *Trans. L. & C. Hist. Soc.*, **92**, (1940), 86.

[6] Clapham, *Econ. Hist. of Mod. Britain*, I, 213.

[7] Communication from the Postmaster General, 1828 [501] XIX.

by the growing population of industrial England. By 1837 steam-boats had invaded the Irish and coastal trades of Liverpool to such an extent that the Clarence and Trafalgar Docks were reserved exclusively for them ;[1] in 1844 more than 600,000 tons of steam shipping cleared the port. In that year more of the coastal and Irish traffic was carried from Liverpool in steam-boats than in sailing ships, and about one-third of all the steam tonnage of England and Wales entered the Mersey.[2] Liverpool had become for a time the largest centre of steam shipping in Britain, if not in the world.

The coal proprietors of St. Helens were not slow to take advantage of this important new market which had been created within the limits of the coal-salt triangle. The rich Rushy Park seam of the St. Helens coalfield was a most suitable fuel for steam-boats on account of its very high calorific value. In July, 1829, the City of Dublin Steam Packet Company was already seeking tenders for the carriage from the St. Helens collieries of 13,000 tons of this steam coal to their vessels at Liverpool and a further 3,000 tons to their stores at Northwall, Dublin, during the following twelve months.[3] One of the first St. Helens firms to enter this new trade was that of Bromilow & Sothern, who worked the Rushy Park colliery to the north of the town. By 1837 this company alone was sending more than 23,000 tons of coal a year to Liverpool for sale to steam vessels.[4] In that year, H.M.S. *Etna*, *Thetis*, *Comet* and *Dolphin* each consumed three or four hundred tons of coal per month and other steamboats took smaller stocks of fuel, ranging from the *Isabella Napier*, for which 303 tons were sold in May, to the *Union* and the *Fairy Queen* which purchased only nine tons each. This coal did not always give satisfaction, however. Lt.-Cmdr. John S. Philipps, R.N., H.M. Packet *Lucifer*, complained in February, 1838, that " the Coal . . . is so very bad that the Engineers find it impossible to keep the steam up with it " and his commanding officer in a covering note added that he had received " so many Complaints lately from the Packet Commander as to the bad quality of the Coals supplied " that, if a better quality was not forthcoming at once, the monthly bills would not be paid.[5] The necessary improvement was, apparently, made, for Bromilow & Sothern supplied the Navy during 1840-3 with some 16,000 tons of coal a year, the largest single consignment to naval establishments

---

[1] T. Baines, *Hist. of Lpool*, 640.

[2] Parliamentary return of steam shipping 1845 [206] XLVII.

[3] *Lpool. Merc.* 10 July, 1829.

[4] Bromilow Papers, Monthly returns, 1837.

[5] Bromilow Papers, Letter from Capt. Chappell to Bromilow and Sothern, 6 Feb., 1838.

at home or abroad.[1]   Larger supplies went to other, privately-owned steam vessels. In 1844 a total of 110,000 tons of St. Helens steam coal was purchased.[2]

While the number of steamships was increasing, there appeared the first hint of openings for St. Helens coal in the Irish market. Before this the export trade from Liverpool was the preserve of the Wigan field whence the coals came down the Leeds and Liverpool Canal. According to Nicholas Ashton, the St. Helens coals were " nearly all used at the Salt or Copper Works ; but few come down to Liverpool, except to some Brewerys."[3] In August, 1832, however, the directors of the Railway in their Report, drew attention to

" the rapid increase of the Coasting trade at Runcorn which has nearly doubled within the last three years and proposals have already been made to load Coal at the Dock as back freight for the Irish Market."[4]

These proposals apparently came to early fruition, for on 25 September, 1834, a complaint was read from J. C. Shaw of the City of Dublin Steam Packet Company, complaining of the inconvenience in procuring coal at the dock.[5] It was evidently the new steamboats, seeking to avoid the high port charges at Liverpool,[6] that were the cause of the increased coasting traffic at Runcorn. These small craft brought over cattle and pro-visions and returned laden with coal. In this way the export of St. Helens coal to Ireland grew almost as fast as the sales of Rushy Park coal to the steamboats. By the summer of 1835 these new developments were already being remarked upon[7] and ten years later the St. Helens collieries had an agent in Dublin and were sending 50,000 tons of coal there a year, one-twelfth of that city's total coal imports.[8]

In 1846 the Secretary of the Canal and Railway calculated that, of 693,000 tons of coal taken from the St. Helens field, 183,000 tons were shipped to the Cheshire salt refineries, and

[1] Returns of Contractors of Coal to H.M. Naval Establishments at Home and Abroad, 1840-4, 1845 [600] XXX.

[2] Report of the Commissioners Appointed to Inquire into the Several Matters Relating to Coal in the United Kingdom, 1871 [435] XVIII, ii, 53.

[3] Holt and Gregson MSS., XIX, 39.

[4] St. H. and R. G. Mins., 8 Aug., 1832.

[5] Ibid., 25 Sept., 1834.

[6] Evidence of James Bennett to the S.C. on the St. H. Canal and Rly. Bill, 1847.

[7] Sir George Head, A Home Tour Through the Manufacturing Districts of England in the Summer of 1835, (1836), 85.

[8] Evidence of Daniel Pallin to the S.C. on the St. H. Canal and Rly. Bill, 1846.

440,000 tons went " down the River,"[1] to be consumed by steam vessels, or to be sent coastwise or exported.[2] St. Helens coal never displaced the Orrell coals of the Wigan coalfield as the mainstay of Liverpool's export trade,[3] but it would be interesting to know how much of the 440,000 tons of St. Helens coal found its way abroad among the 120,000 tons or more exported from Liverpool in 1845.[4]

In order to meet these new commitments and the greater industrial demand for coal locally, a large increase in output from the St. Helens coalfield was called for. By 1845 the new customers were taking more than twice as much coal as the salt-boilers, and between 1830 and 1845 the total output of coal from pits in the St. Helens neighbourhood had certainly been doubled and may possibly have been trebled. The total " get " in 1830 can hardly have exceeded 400,000 tons, for in 1836, when steam coal and Irish shipments were already on the increase, no more than 300,000 tons left the district by Canal and Railway.[5] By 1846, however, between 800,000 and 1,000,000 tons were being raised annually.[6] This remarkable expansion was obtained by greatly extending the existing underground workings and by sinking new pits.

The newly-found markets, unlike the Cheshire saltworks, demanded coal of high quality. For boiling salt, small coal or " burgey " was quite good enough, and in later years H. E. Falk was able to boast that the saltboilers could manage with the " cheapest and worst coal [which] . . . would be wasted if we did not use it."[7] The steamship companies, however, were more particular. They would tolerate nothing but Rushy Park or Little Delf coals from the richest measures in the coalfield.

The Rushy Park seam, about 4 ft. 6 ins. thick, and the Little Delf seam, about 3 ft. thick—also known as the Yard Mine—occurred near the surface to the north and west of St. Helens. Both had been worked in Eccleston township since the

[1] *Ibid.*, Evidence of Arthur Sinclair.

[2] Evidence of John Haddock to the S.C. on the St. H. Canal and Rly. Bill, 1846.

[3] D. Lardner, *The History and Description of Fossil Fuel* (2nd. ed. 1841), 430.

[4] Parliamentary Return, 1847 [477] LIX.

[5] Above, p. 190.

[6] Evidence of John Mercer to the S.C. on the St. H. Canal and Rly. Bill, 1846.

[7] Evidence to the R.C. on Noxious Vapours, 1878 [2159] XLIV, q. 7660.

eighteenth century[1] and were still being exploited after 1830 by the Bromilows at their Royal Colliery near the toll bar on Prescot Road.[2] They also mined Little Delf coals, under the name of the Windle Coal Co., on the western side of Bleak Hill Lane[3] and, as has been noticed,[4] dug both seams at their Rushy Park Colliery, north of Glade Hill. Charles Speakman and Co. had also started to get these coals from the Cowley Hill Colliery, opened in 1821,[5] and, as this colliery was situated to the west of the Rushy Park workings, Bromilow & Sothern[6] were obliged to drive eastwards, leasing mines in Ashton township by 1841.[7] In September 1849 they extended their activities still farther by acquiring the Stanley Colliery (New Concern) at Blackbrook from John and William Stock, who were then on the verge of bankruptcy.[8]   Samuel Stock, another member of the same family, owned a colliery at Blackleyhurst and carried his coals down by his own private railway to the Canal at Blackbrook, two and a half miles to the south. By the mid-1840s he claimed to be raising 70,000 tons of coal a year and exporting nearly 16,000 tons of this to Ireland.[9] Between the Blackleyhurst Colliery and Black-brook, John and Thomas Johnson, whom we shall meet presently in their main rôle as soap boilers and alkali makers at Runcorn, had also branched out into the Rushy Park coal business at Laffack, and in 1843-4 they secured the coal contract for the Navy at Liverpool which had previously been held by Bromilow and Sothern.[10]

Because the coalfield dipped steeply to the south-east, the important Rushy Park and Little Delf mines lay too deep to be

[1] Above, ch. IV.

[2] L.R.O., Cross Papers, Leases. For additional information about this and other collieries, see T. C. Barker, *The Economic and Social History of St. Helens, 1830-1900* (typescript at St. H. Ref. Lib.).

[3] L.R.O., Gerard Papers, DDGe 913.

[4] Above, p. 194.

[5] L.R.O., Cross Papers. Recited in draft indenture, 1833.

[6] John Sothern, of Liverpool, whose sister married David Bromilow, appears to have joined the partnership in this colliery about the time of John Whitley's retirement in 1831.   We do not know to what extent Sothern, a Liverpool merchant, was responsible for coal sales at the port.

[7] L.R.O., Gerard Papers, DDGe 917 ; Bromilow Papers, lease from Thomas Legh, 5 Dec., 1841.

[8] *Lpool. Merc.* 18 Jan., 1850. The colliery was adjacent to the works of the former Stanley Smelting Co.

[9] Evidence of Samuel Stock to the S.C. on the St. H. Canal and Rly. Bill, 1847.

[10] Return of Contractors of Coal to H.M. Naval Establishments at Home and Abroad, 1840-4, 1845 [600] XXX ; L.R.O., Gerard Papers, DDGe 919.

won from the existing collieries at St. Helens at this time. At Sutton Colliery, for instance, the Rushy Park seam was found at 586 yards down. In the 1830s a colliery of such a depth was unknown. General Gascoyne in 1839 expressed to David Bromilow his astonishment at the news that a shaft had been sunk in the north-east of England to a depth of nearly 400 yards and added:

> " I had no conception that coal raised from that *extreme depth* say near 200 fathoms or 1,200 feet could be beneficially raised and sold . . . now in Lancashire if we bore for Coal and do not find it at the depth of 200 or 300 yards, we abandon the search."[1]

A few years later a local mining surveyor confirmed the General's statement: in 1846 no pit at St. Helens had been sunk below 290 yards.[2]

But the mid-1840s saw the first attempts at sinking deeper pits to reach the Rushy Park and Little Delf mines in Parr, a little to the south of Bromilow & Sothern's workings. At the Broad Oak and Sankey Brook Collieries, deep shafts were sunk to these seams. By January, 1845, sinkers at the former had reached a depth of 780 ft.[3] Two and a half years later, in June 1847, Bromilow & Sothern, Johnson, Worthington & Co. (Sankey Brook Colliery) and Bournes & Robinson (Broad Oak Colliery) signed an agreement which set boundaries to their respective shares in this part of the Rushy Park mine.[4]

The opening of this mine at the Broad Oak and Sankey Brook Collieries is a good example of the change that was coming over the coalfield. Both these concerns were owned by the coal and salt interest. The Bournes were leading men in the salt trade and Robert Robinson was their managing partner at St. Helens; similarly, William Worthington, Thomas Firth and R. P. Hadfield all came from Northwich and John Johnson was their partner in charge of the coalmining side of their business at St. Helens. Yet both these collieries, solidly bound to the saltfield by tradition and ownership, were extended at considerable cost to cater for the new market in steam coal. A few years later when some shares in the Sankey Brook Colliery were up for sale, potential purchasers were informed that :

> " The colliery has been established nearly thirty years and enjoys an old and valuable connexion, not only in the im-

[1] Bromilow Papers. Letter dated 14 June, 1839.

[2] Evidence of John Mercer to the S.C. on the St. H. Canal and Rly. Bill, 1846.

[3] *Manchester Courier*, 11 Jan., 1845 ; St. H. Town Hall, United Alkali Co. Ltd., deeds, Baxter's Works, lease to Johnson Worthington and Co., 1 Jan., 1844.

[4] Bromilow Papers, Deed of Covenants, 23 June, 1847.

mediate vicinity but also in Liverpool and in the salt districts
of Cheshire, besides an extensive steam and export trade at
the port of Liverpool."[1]

While the demand for steam coal was causing an intensive
exploitation of the coalfield to the north and north-east of St.
Helens, the older-established collieries in and about the town
itself continued to do a brisk trade and took their share of the
expanding market. Local industry developed rapidly in the
1830s ; as we shall see presently, there was a striking advance
in glass production, the alkali trade became firmly established
and the copper smelters returned. Each new furnace demanded
more coal. By the 1840s the larger works were consuming
20,000 tons apiece[2] and in 1846 a mining surveyor estimated that
the total consumption in the St. Helens district was between
200,000 and 400,000 tons,[3] an estimate which, despite its wide
limits, makes it clear that the factories of St. Helens, many of
which had been built within the shadow of a colliery in order
to obtain supplies of coal at pit-head prices, were already consuming more than the salt-pans of Cheshire. It is probable that
the colliery proprietors of St. Helens itself also shared in the
new-found trade from the Mersey; the better grades of coal,
such as that from the Ravenhead Higher Delf Mine, though
not so suitable as Rushy Park coals for steam raising, were most
suitable for industrial and domestic purposes. Even the poor and
sulphurous variety from the St. Sebastian Mine was supplied
to the crown glass factories not only in St. Helens but also in
Liverpool.[4] Some of the coal from St. Helens found its way
by railway *via* the Liverpool-Manchester line and Newton
Junction (now called Earlestown) to Warrington. By the mid-'40s
some 20,000 tons of St. Helens coal were passing along this line
every year, about 2s. 0d. per ton being paid for carriage.[5] It

[1] *Lpool. Merc.* 31 May, 1850. This colliery had been opened in 1822-3
by Richard Johnson, then managing partner of the Union Colliery at St.
Helens. St. H. Town Hall, United Alkali Co. Ltd., deeds, Baxter's Works ;
P.R.O., C13/2789.

[2] The Ravenhead Works consumed 20,076 tons of coal in the year
1846/7 and between June, 1848 and May, 1850 consumption at the St.
Helens Crown Glassworks rose from 350 tons per week to more than 600
tons (papers at Pilkington Brothers Ltd.). The copper industry used more
coal than the alkali works (evidence to S.C. on Coal, 1873 [313] X, q. 6426).

[3] Evidence of John Mercer to the S.C. on the St. H. Canal and Rly.
Bill, 1846.

[4] Bromilow Papers, Balance sheet of Thatto Heath Colliery for the last
quarter of 1838.

[5] Evidence of Arthur Sinclair to the S.C. on the St. H. Canal and Rly.
Bill, 1846 ; St. H. and R.G. Mins, 15 and 28 Dec., 1831.

is not known how much of this total went on down the Grand Junction Railway in the direction of Crewe. Turner and Evans of the Haydock Collieries, who laid their own mineral line to Newton Junction,[1] seem to have taken the lead in this particular traffic, the St. Helens coal-owners preferring to keep their sales within the Merseyside area.

The main collieries in the immediate vicinity of St. Helens itself in 1845 were the Gerard's Bridge (worked by the West family since the close of the eighteenth century),[2] the Ravenhead (taken over by Bromilow, Haddock and Co. in 1818)[3] and the Sutton (opened by Bournes and Robinson in 1812)[4]. In Eccleston township, in addition to those already mentioned, were the Thatto Heath and Cropper's Hill collieries, the former owned by the Bromilow family[5] and the latter by Bromilow, Brown and Jones.[6] In Parr were Joseph Greenough's Parr Stocks Colliery[7] and the Ashtons Green Colliery, still in the hands of the Leigh family.[8] The depression of the early '40s caused several pits to close. Clare and Co's Union, St. Helens and Burtonhead Collieries were all three put up for auction in 1844,[9] the Barton's Bank Colliery appears to have closed in 1839[10] and Nicholas Ashton's Parr Dam Colliery, operated by Charles Orrell from his nearby Parr Mill Colliery after 1830, came to an end when the Parr Mill Colliery ceased to function about 1840.[11]

The underground workings of each of the larger collieries covered many square miles. An accident at Gerard's Bridge Colliery in 1847, for instance, occurred half a mile from the shaft[12] and there is reason to believe that in 1853 coal was being

[1] This private railway is mentioned in *Lpool. Merc.* 13 April, 1833.

[2] L.R.O., Cross Papers, Draft Instructions to Mr. Cotham in West v. Cotham ; lease, 17 Feb., 1824, DDCS 53/49.

[3] L.R.O., Cross Papers, DDCS 43/7.

[4] St. H. Town Hall, United Alkali Co. Ltd., deeds, Kurtz works.

[5] Bromilow Papers.

[6] St. H.I.C. Rate Books, 1845.

[7] St. H. and R.G. Mins. 14 March, 1832. For the sale of this colliery, *St. H. Intelligencer*, 1 May, 1858.

[8] St. H. Ref. Lib., Parr Poor Rate Books.

[9] *Lpool. Merc.* 11 Oct., 1844.

[10] *Wigan Gazette*, 30 Aug., 1839.

[11] Cross Papers, DDCS 30.

[12] *Lpool. Merc.* 4 June, 1847.　The same company, working the Rushy Park seam from their Cowley Hill Colliery, were getting coal beyond Duke Street shortly after 1846. L.R.O.. DDCS 53/29, lease dated 10 March, 1846.

dug over a mile and a half from the shaft of the Ravenhead
Colliery.[1]   Already many hundreds of thousands of tons had
been raised out of the ground from under St. Helens and its
immediate neighbourhood, and the gigantic task of winning coal
was proceeding by the middle of the 1840s at the rate of about a
million tons per year. Between a quarter and a fifth of this output
was being burnt in the town itself, a large proportion of it by
those great furnace industries, glass, alkali and copper, which
owed their whole existence to an abundant supply of cheap fuel.

[1] Evidence of David Swallow to the S.C. on Accidents in Mines, 1852-3
[740] XX.

CHAPTER XVI

THE GLASS INDUSTRY

1830-1845

ALTHOUGH most of the glass in the Merseyside area was, by 1830, being made at factories in and about St. Helens, the town's reputation as a glassmaking centre still rested upon the one giant plate glassworks at Ravenhead. It is true that in 1832 the various St. Helens glasshouses paid in excise duty £54,000 out of a total of £82,000 raised from the nine firms comprising the Liverpool Collection ; yet the Excise Commissioners' total income from all the factories in the kingdom amounted to £680,000. Almost £300,000 of this came from the Tyne, for more than two centuries the home of the English window glass manufacture, and the Midlands contributed about £150,000. Even Warrington, not thought of as a glassmaking town nowadays, then paid £40,000 in duty.[1] The powerful position of the factories of the north-east seemed well-nigh impregnable for, as one of their proprietors boasted, they made more window glass than all the other works in the country put together.[2] Long before the century was out, however, pre-eminence in this branch of the industry was to pass to St. Helens, as it had already done in the manufacture of plate glass. But in the 1830s the balance of power was only just starting to change ; Newcastle's aim, as William Pilkington of St. Helens wrote to his brother, was " to prevent us upstarts from growing greater."[3]

St. Helens, with its natural advantages, continued to attract glass manufacturers and the new Railway was an additional inducement for them to settle. The line was only just open when Samuel Bishop wrote to the directors informing them that he was about to build a flint glassworks adjoining their track and enquiring whether they would lease him a plot of land for use as a coal dump.[4] Bishop was a Londoner[5] and may possibly have been a descendant of Hawly Bishop, whom the Glass Sellers Company had employed in 1687 to make " christalline or flint

---

[1] 13th Report of the Commissioners of Inquiry into the Excise Establishment (Glass) 1835 [15] XXXI, 74-5.

[2] *Ibid.*, 92.

[3] Pilkington Brothers Ltd., William Pilkington to Richard Pilkington, 18 Dec., 1838.

[4] St. H. and R.G. Mins., 20 July, 1833.

[5] This is stated on his grave in the old churchyard, St. Helens.

glass " for them at the Savoy Glasshouse.[1] Perhaps a reduction
in the duty on flint glass, the result of an Act passed in 1832,[2]
may have been partly responsible for the timing of Bishop's arrival
at St. Helens. He was already 59 years of age, so it may be
assumed that much of the active management of the works was
left to his sons, Samuel and Charles, who assumed complete
control on their father's death in October, 1842.[3]

Meanwhile the Bells were conducting their Ravenhead Flint
Glassworks with some success ; they paid duty on 180 tons of
glass made there in 1832. A few years before this they had been
among the founder-members of a partnership that was destined
to become the leading glass firm in the country.

This was the St. Helens Crown Glass Company, formed in
1826 to build a second window glass factory in the district. Of
the eleven shares in the partnership, John William Bell held two
and Thomas Bell one. The remaining eight were divided equally
among four of the leading local inhabitants. John Barnes was
the town's first successful solicitor[4] and James Bromilow was the
second son of William Bromilow, the coal proprietor. The other
two partners interest us most of all. They were Peter Greenall
and William Pilkington. Greenall by now needs no introduction;
but a few words must be said about the Pilkington family.

William Pilkington was the great-grandson of Richard
Pilkington of Horwich, near Bolton, who in 1759 had successfully laid claim to the manor of Allerton, south of Liverpool.[5]
The successful claimant was an elderly man and it was, therefore,
his son's task to journey twice a year from Horwich, where the
family continued to live, to collect the rents at Allerton.[6] The
route lay through the St. Helens district at the very time when
new industry was starting to settle there. It was obviously a place
with a future. Perhaps these early stirrings and the prospect of
further expansion were responsible for Richard Pilkington junior's
apprenticing his son to William Fildes, a St. Helens doctor, about

---

[1] F. Buckley, *History of Old English Glass* (1925), 26.

[2] 2 & 3 Wm. IV, cap., 102. The duty was reduced from £12/10/0 per
1,000 lbs. to 20/- per 100 lbs. and there was an additional allowance granted
for waste.

[3] Grave in the old churchyard, St. Helens. Samuel Bishop II was the
first chairman of the St. H.I.C. and presided over its affairs until 1851.
He was a very strong Anglican and Tory. Obit. *St. H. N.* 28 Dec., 1878.

[4] Barnes's name is to be seen on many of the early legal documents
relating to the town. His clerk, John Ansdell, became his partner and
continued the business after his death on 30 Dec., 1844. His will was
proved at Chester on 30 April, 1845 at under £5,000.

[5] For this claim, see Ronald Stewart-Brown, *A History of the Manor
and Township of Allerton* (Lpool, 1911).

[6] Much information concerning the Pilkington family at Horwich is
to be found among the Pilkington Papers at the L.R.O.

1781.[1] Four years later, Dr. Fildes' apprentice went to London
to walk the hospitals, the usual medical training at that time,
and in April 1786 he received a certificate from St. George's
Hospital—signed among others by the famous John Hunter—to
show that he had " diligently attended the Practice of Surgery "
for the previous six months.[2] His training over, the young doctor
returned to Lancashire. Within two years he was back at St.
Helens and, in the following year, in partnership with John
Walker, he took over the practice left vacant by the death of
William Fildes.[3]

Dr. Pilkington, a staunch Independent as his family had been
for generations, soon became one of the leading figures in the
growing community. His sister, Elizabeth, who came to keep
house for him, married Joseph Rylands of Parr in 1793. Their
third son, John, was to become one of the most famous textile
manufacturers in the kingdom. In the following year William
Pilkington himself married, his bride being Ann Hatton. She
bore him thirteen children. Of these, Richard (b. 20 August, 1795)
and William (b. 14 May, 1800) grew up to be the Pilkington
Brothers whose name was later perpetuated in the title of the
great glass company.

Like most surgeons elsewhere at that time, Dr. Pilkington
was also an apothecary.[4] He kept a shop and sold, among other
things, wines and spirits. The shop prospered ; so much so, in
fact, that when Dr. Pilkington decided to retire from the medical
partnership with John Walker in 1813, he did not give up the
profitable wine and spirit business attached to it. His sons,
Richard and William, were apprenticed to business firms in
Liverpool, the former to William Ewart and William Taylor,
merchants and brokers, and the latter to Robert Preston the
younger, the proprietor of a distillery.[5] Richard joined the wine
and spirit firm in 1817 and his younger brother followed him
three years later. Thereafter the business was conducted as
William Pilkington and Sons.[6]

---

[1] St. H. Ref. Lib. Parr Poor Law Papers. Doctor's Account Book, 3
Aug. 1781 : " Received the above Contents in ful by Wm. Pilkington
by the Use of Mr. Fildes".

[2] The certificate is kept at Pilkington Brothers Ltd. and is printed in
Now Thus, Now Thus, 19.

[3] L.R.O., Land Tax Returns, Windle, 1788, 1789.

[4] Cecil Wall, The History of the Surgeon's Company 1745-1800 (1937), 90.
Five doctors at Prescot are described as surgeons and apothecaries in
Bailey's Northern Directory of 1781.

[5] Pilkington Brothers Ltd. Indentures of apprenticeship dated 28 April,
1810 ; 13 Sept., 1815.

[6] Library of H.M. Customs and Excise Treasury and Excise Papers,
125, 540-4. Petition of William Pilkington, jr., 23 Dec., 1825. The following
paragraph is based upon this source.

Their affairs prospered to such an extent that they started to rectify and compound spirits themselves. Plant for this purpose was installed at first in buildings near the junction of Bridge Street and Church Street in 1823. The halving of the spirit duties in January, 1826, and the prospect of a vast increase in sales caused them to transfer their plant to the back of their premises in Church Street and to extend it. By that time Dr. Pilkington was already a man of substance ; his share of the Allerton property sold at the end of the eighteenth century,[1] the profits from the wine and spirit business and his professional income all brought in considerable sums of money. In 1826 he was able to retire to Windle Hall, which he rented from Sir John Gerard for £300 a year. When he died a few years later, he left a fortune of £20,000.[2]

In 1821 the Pilkingtons became closely related to the most influential industrialist in the town. On 6 March of that year Dr. Pilkington's second daughter, Eleanor, married Peter Greenall, her father providing her with a dowry of £1,000.[3]

The new family tie had important business repercussions. Peter Greenall and his brother-in-law, William Pilkington, held four of the eleven shares in the St. Helens Crown Glass Company, though it is highly unlikely that either of them at that time regarded the venture as anything more than a financial speculation. Peter Greenall was kept busy at the St. Helens Brewery and William Pilkington was actively engaged in the wine and spirit firm, then yielding a handsome profit of about £5,000 a year.[4] Neither could afford to spare much time to bother themselves with the day-to-day working of the new glass factory. This was to be the task of John William Bell, the glassmaker, James Bromilow being in charge of the counting house.[5]

The time was ripe for such a venture. The early 1820s had witnessed a great building boom ; between 1821 and 1825 brick production in the country increased from 900 millions to 1,950 millions per year[6] and crown glass output rose from 86,000 to 140,000 cwts.[7] There was obviously money to be made in this branch of industry. Moreover, the recession of the mid-1820s,

[1] Stewart-Brown, *op. cit.*, 65.

[2] L.R.O., DDCS 37/20, Lease dated 26 Dec., 1826 ; will proved at Chester, 4 April, 1832.

[3] Will of Dr. Pilkington.

[4] Pilkington Brothers Ltd., Account Book of William Pilkington and Sons.

[5] Pilkington Brothers Ltd., Draft Articles of Co-partnership dated 18 May, 1826. Careful search has failed to reveal any final Articles.

[6] H. A. Shannon, " Bricks : A Trade Index, 1785-1849," *Economica*, Aug., 1934, 316-7.

[7] Return of glass production 1839 419] XLVI.

particularly severe at St. Helens in 1826,[1] meant that labour and materials to build the factory could be obtained on the most advantageous terms.

Acting on behalf of the partnership, Bell bought $2\frac{1}{2}$ statute acres of land, close to his Ravenhead Flint Glassworks, in March, 1826[2] and the first glasshouse was built there later in that year, coming into operation in February, 1827.[3] The building is said to have been modelled on one of the cones at Dumbarton[4] and several of the original glassmakers are believed to have come from Scotland.[5] The company was no sooner in a position to embark upon full-scale production, however, than it ran into serious difficulties. These arose from the impossible burden placed upon the shoulders of Bell, the manager. He was responsible for

" attending to the Workmen, the manufacturing of the Crown Glass and all things incident thereto. And also in the travelling department to effect Sales of Crown Glass when manufactured and purchasing Articles used in the Manufacturing of Crown Glass on the best possible terms . . . "[6]

Moreover, he was not supposed to devote his whole time to the new factory but was " allowed to devote a reasonable part of his time to superintend his Flint Glass Works." While acting as works manager and chief salesman and at the same time keeping an eye on his other concern, he was also to teach the other partners, including Thomas Bell, " the different operations respecting the mixing of metal, manufacturing of crown glass and all other things incident thereto."

On top of all these numerous tasks, in April, 1827, only two months after the new factory had opened, Bell found himself engaged in a long drawn-out tussle with the Commissioners of Excise over the payment of duty on coloured glass at his flint glassworks.[7] The matter was quite trivial but Bell contested the payment because he believed that an important principle was at

---

[1] In March, 1826, for instance, the proprietors of the British Plate Glass Co. granted 100 guineas for relief " their works at Ravenhead being in the distressed district." (B.P.G. Mins., 10 May, 1826).

[2] Pilkington Brothers Ltd., Deeds Package 1. Abstract of Title of the St. H. Crown Glassworks.

[3] Interview with William (Roby) Pilkington, *St. H. Lantern*, 7 June, 1888.

[4] This was stated by Abraham Hartley, who had been in the employment of the St. Helens Crown Glass Co., since 1836, in an interview published in the *St. H. Lantern* 3 Jan., 1889.

[5] *St. H. N.* 21 Sept., 1872.

[6] Draft Articles of Co-partnership.

[7] P.R.O., E.159/733/Mich. 8 Geo. IV m. 299. The following account is based upon this source and Excise Trials at H. M. Customs and Excise, 16 Feb., 25 April, 14, 21 June, 29 Nov., 1828 ; 7 May, 1830 ; *Lpool. Merc.*, 16 Jan., 1829.

[Photo : R. K. Robertson]

WILLIAM PILKINGTON (1800—1872)

An early portrait at Pilkington Brothers Limited

THE UNION PLATE GLASSWORKS, POCKET NOOK, IN 1843

stake. The case was first heard in the Court of Exchequer in February, 1828, and ended in a verdict for the defendant. The Commissioners insisted on a re-trial. This came on in the following November. Again Bell secured a favourable verdict and again the Commissioners refused to let the matter drop. Discussion concerning a third trial was still taking place in May, 1830. Just when it was vital for Bell to devote his attention to the new factory, therefore, his time and energy were diverted to pleading his case in London. Moreover, these trials were expensive and the Bells, unable to meet the further calls on their shares,[1] decided to sell them. At the end of 1827 when the first trial was pending, J. W. Bell parted with one of his shares to Greenall, Bromilow and Pilkington, who divided it equally among them.[2] Five months later, the first trial over and the second pending, he was obliged to sell his remaining share and Thomas Bell also sold his. Greenall and Pilkington each acquired a third of these two-elevenths, and Bromilow and Barnes both took up a sixth. The Bells withdrew altogether from the partnership on 15 April, 1828.[3]

The loss of the pilot just when the new company was particularly in need of expert direction, created an extremely dangerous position. In an attempt to save the situation, William Pilkington was prevailed upon to succeed Bell as manager, leaving the wine and spirit concern in the care of his brother, Richard, assisted by a younger brother, Thomas. William Pilkington was a very shrewd and extraordinarily capable business man and had, presumably, been let into the secrets of glassmaking by Bell as the co-partnership agreement stipulated. He would not tolerate slackness of any kind and soon crossed swords with James Bromilow, the partner in charge of the books, of whom he wrote later :

" There were several amounts came into the acc^ts for 1829, say £500, which Mr. Bromilow ought to have included in 1828, as well as supposed discounts which he made no allowance for, say, £1,200 at the very least."[4]

What Adam Bromilow, with the restraint becoming to one training for the law, was to call " differences " arose between his brother and the glass firm.[5] The estrangement resulted in Bromilow's withdrawal from the concern in January, 1829, and, possibly fearing that the end was not far removed, Barnes also sold his

---

[1] The total capital of the firm rose from £11,000 in Dec., 1827 to £13,500 in May, 1828 (Deeds at Pilkington Brothers Ltd.).

[2] Pilkington Brothers Ltd., Abstract of Title.

[3] *London Gazette* 22 April, 1828.

[4] Pilkington Brothers Ltd. Statement of Production, 1827-40.

[5] Bromilow Papers. Adam Bromilow to James Bromilow, 27 June, 1829.

P

interest.[1] Both men were bought out by the Pilkington family who, between January, 1829 and January, 1830, paid £8,200 for their shares. In all, William Pilkington, acting on behalf of himself and his elder brother, Richard, had paid into the concern more than £13,000 in the space of three years.[2] After this the St. Helens Crown Glass Company came to be known also as Greenall and Pilkingtons, Greenall holding three of the eleven shares and the Pilkingtons the remaining eight. It has remained a family business ever since.

If Bell's departure was a severe setback, the elimination of Greenall and Pilkingtons' nearest competitor was an equally great advantage. In October, 1828, only six months after the Bells' withdrawal, an Examiner of Excise discovered that extensive frauds had been perpetrated for some years at Mackay West and Company's Eccleston Crown Glassworks.[3] The managing partner, William Anthony Augustine West, was personally responsible for these frauds and the news of their detection caused consternation among the other proprietors, James Underhill West, George Mackay and Thomas Holt.[4] Although they eventually compounded with the Excise Commissioners for £5,000, the lack of confidence between William West and the other three completely disrupted the partnership. In January, 1830, the works were advertised for sale by private treaty[5] but did not find a buyer. Shortly afterwards they were leased by Mackay West and Company to William West and James Bromilow, fresh from two years' book-keeping with the rival St. Helens Crown Glass

---

[1] Pilkington Brothers Ltd. Abstract of Title.

[2] *Ibid.*, account book of William Pilkington and Sons. When Richard Pilkington was formally admitted into the partnership in 1835, it was stated that half of William Pilkington's interest was held in trust for his elder brother. The correspondence between the two makes it clear that Richard Pilkington was already actively engaged in the works.

[3] The details of these frauds are to be found in Treasury and Excise Papers, T.E. 1432, at the Library of H.M. Customs and Excise and in the Cross Papers, DDCS 14, at the L.R.O., We are indebted to Mr. R. C. Jarvis, Librarian of H.M. Customs and Excise, for transcripts of T.E. 1432.

[4] Of the original partners, William West, senr., died in 1814, Major-General Alexander Mackay died in 1809, Angus Mackay died in 1819 and Major James Campbell's share was sold in 1820. This left Thomas West and George Mackay as the sole survivors of the original partnership. William Anthony Augustine West received his uncle William's share in 1819 and later purchased that of Alexander Mackay, disposing of half of the latter share to his brother, James Underhill West. James Mackay, son of George, received Angus Mackay's share and James Campbell's went in 1820 to Thomas Holt of Liverpool (L.R.O., Cross Papers, DDCS 14/84 ; Pilkington Brothers Ltd., package 31, extract of wills; will of Thomas West proved at Chester, 23 July, 1828; will of James Mackay proved at Chester, 1 Oct., 1844 ; grave of George and James Mackay in the old Churchyard, St. Helens).

[5] *Gore's Gen. Ad.* 14 Jan., 1830.

Company. Although up to this time Mackay West and Company appear to have had some success in hushing up their misdeeds, William West and the other proprietors were unable to straighten out their differences and in 1831 James West sent a circular to the customers of Mackay West and Company which, though concerned chiefly with the debts owing to them, presented their new tenants, West and Bromilow, in a bad light. Although no copy of this circular has survived, a letter sent by William West to James West makes it quite clear that it was directly responsible for causing many customers to switch their orders to Greenall and Pilkingtons :

" Whatever hostility you have shewn towards me I have said little of it, but when I contemplate the hasty steps you took in sending off the Circulars, I must . . . charitably suppose that you could not be aware of the consequences to the Firm of West and Bromilow ; indeed, I little calculated on the issue, nor can I now tell myself where the mischief will end ; to give you some idea, however, I will just tell you what occurred to me in Manchester. I went round as usual. The first I called on was Mr. Occleshaw. He had given an order for fifty crates and several thousand feet of glass were cutting here for him. The whole was countermanded and transferred to [the] St. Helens [Crown Glass Company]. Next Jos. Elleray who not only countermanded his order for 20 crates but returned four crates and insisted on a receipt in full of all demands. Thence I went to Mr. Winder, on whom Elleray had waited to know whether he has a letter similar to the one he held in his hand. Mr. Winder replied No, but the consequence was that when I asked Mr. Winder for the confirmation of the order for 50 crates, he said he had given it to another house for that under the circumstances he knew not how to act . . . I thence crossed over into Salford where our best customer, William Harrison, recalled his order and gave it to the St. Helen's house ; his next door neighbour did the same, Mr. Livingstone the same . . . In a word here is a sample of what we may expect throughout the country. An alarm is given which will take months to quiet and such is the distress caused by it, what with glass being returned and orders countermanded, I am almost distracted . . ."[1]

For the Eccleston works, the situation went from bad to worse and West must have become even more distracted as the months passed. He tried to recoup his losses by again defrauding the excise, but was again detected.[2] The differences between Mackay

---

[1] L.R.O., DDCS 14/30.

[2] Bromilow Papers. Letters from General Gascoyne to James Bromilow, 14 Oct., 1832, 1 March, 1833 and letter from Bromilow to Gascoyne 29 Oct., 1832 ; 13th Rep. of Excise Comm., 133. Evidence of Robert Lucas Chance.

West and Company and West and Bromilow ripened into open dispute and the whole matter was sent for arbitration in June, 1833.[1] The house of West and Bromilow was tottering. In 1834 it fell. The works were put up for auction on 24 June, 1834, on which day West signed a promise to vacate the premises by 24 December.[2] There were no satisfactory bids, however, and West appears to have contrived to remain in possession for another two years : it was not until October, 1836, that he finally left. At a dinner held on that occasion his workmen presented him with a silver cup " to mark their respect and gratitude towards him for the uniform kindness evinced and practised by him towards them."[3] In January, 1837, he sold his share in Mackay West and Company[4] and built a small flint and crown glassworks nearby. But he soon became insolvent and had to surrender these premises to his assignees.[5]

The decline and fall of the Eccleston Crown Glassworks removed Greenall and Pilkingtons' nearest competitor just at the time when William Pilkington was making his greatest effort to secure new outlets for his firm's glass. It is not unreasonable to suppose that West was fully justified in thinking that the St. Helens company's gain of orders in Manchester and Salford was an augury of what was to happen elsewhere. Certainly William Pilkington, shrewd business man that he was, could be counted upon to exploit the situation to the full. As his order book grew fuller, he could face his competitors with greater confidence.

Since prices were rigidly fixed by the manufacturers' association,[6] competition was chiefly confined to the quality of each company's product. William Pilkington's letters home, as he travelled the country in search of orders, constantly harped on this theme. The following extract from a letter, written in 1831 when he was trying, with some success, to break into the London market, illustrates this point ; it also illuminates the character of the writer himself. Having bewailed the fact that the glass which they had previously sent to London was " very indifferent," he went on :

" the flashing of it[7] is downright bad, and tell both Charles and

[1] L.R.O., Cross Papers.

[2] *Ibid.*, 14/68.

[3] *Wigan Gazette* 18 Oct., 1836.

[4] L.R.O., Cross Papers. Draft deed for settling disputes, 23 Jan., 1837.

[5] The fiat of bankruptcy was dated 28 Sept., 1837. See also letter from Wagstaff and Co. to Henry Rowson, 13 March, 1840 (Cross Papers) and, for the new factory, *Manchester Guardian* 15 Sept., 1838.

[6] Below, p. 252.

[7] The meaning of flashing has changed during the past century. In this context it means the operation of opening out the circular table of glass on the end of the punty by centrifugal force.

Spanton that if we cannot have our work flashed as well as other houses, I will discharge both, if you have not done it by one already, and if James Wood does not give us less bent out of the kiln, I will serve him the same. I am surprised, too, that Roger should say such glass was good. If he does not inform us when the work is bad and be more decided I shall be very angry with him. In consequence of the flashing being so bad and the tables so bent, there is not a crate but what has four, five, or six tables broken. Tell Robert Morgan to make his crates wider at the bottom so that they be not pinched and broken."[1]

Constant vigilance and good salesmanship yielded most satisfactory results. Production at the works rose from just under 1,000 tables a week in 1831 to nearly 1,500 in 1833. Business grew so brisk that the partners decided in 1834 to erect a second glasshouse; this came into use in October of that year. With the aid of this new furnace, output during the whole year averaged 2,000 tables a week and in 1835, when both houses were in operation throughout the twelve months, it exceeded 3,000. In order to meet the ever growing demand, a third house was built during 1836 at a cost of almost £5,500.[2] When the annual turnover continued to grow and the expensive third house was in prospect, the Pilkington brothers decided that the time had arrived to part with the family wine and spirit business and to devote their whole attention to the manufacture of glass.

This decision was dictated by events connected with wine and spirit sales as well as by the success of the glassworks. In 1830 the beer duty had been repealed and this reduced the demand for wines and spirits. In 1826 the scales had been tipped in favour of the distiller and rectifier ; now they were redressed in favour of the brewer. After 1830 the margin between expenditure and receipts in the account book of William Pilkington and Sons grew ever closer. In 1830 the difference was £7,107. In 1831 it had dropped to £5,160, in 1832 to £4,872, in 1833 to £3,496, in 1834 to £3,131 and in 1835 to £2,210. In 1836 Thomas Pilkington, a younger brother and partner in William Pilkington and Sons, decided to retire.[3] This finally decided Richard and William Pilkington to dispose of what had once been a most profitable concern, a course they would not have dreamed of when the glassworks was first established. As they explained at the time of the sale :

" If we could have given up the Glass Works we should, but

[1] Pilkington Brothers Ltd., Letter from William Pilkington to Richard Pilkington, 23 April, 1831.

[2] Pilkington Brothers Ltd., List of production figures drawn up by William Pilkington *c.* 1840 ; list of expenditure drawn up by William Pilkington *c.* 1836.

[3] *London Gazette*, 8 July, 1836.

from the great outlay of Capital, in Building etc. we should find
it next to impossible. You are also aware that this was a step we
at one time never contemplated but from the circumstances of
our brother Thomas giving up active business and the glass
trade growing too heavy for one person to manage to advantage,
we thought it better to give up one than verify the old adage
of having too many irons in the fire and letting some burn."[1]

The capital outlay was growing with every extension. By 1834 the
partners had advanced £24,300 and there was an overdraft at
Parr's Bank in Warrington of just under £10,000.[2] The latter
continued to grow ; after the erection of the third house in 1836
it stood at £17,292 and by 1842, in the midst of the depression,
it had risen to £20,000. In that year the entire partnership capital
was just over £25,600.[3] The willingness of Parr's to permit such a
large overdraft when trade was so bad, suggests strongly that the
St. Helens Crown Glass Company was being specially favoured
on account of Greenall's influence at the bank. His brother, John,
was certainly a partner and he himself may have been intimately
connected with its affairs.[4]

This considerable advance from the bank enabled the company
not only to weather the depression years but also to introduce a
new and important method of making window glass which was
soon to drive crown glass off the market. This was the cylinder
method whereby the molten glass, or metal as it was called,
instead of being blown out into a pear shape and rotated until
the pear-shaped mass opened out into a flat circle, as in crown
glass, was blown into a cylinder, about four feet long, slit down the
centre and opened out into a flat rectangle. The cylinder method
had been considerably improved on the continent where it was in
general use ; more attention was paid to the quality of the raw
materials and more care given to the slitting and flattening. In
Britain, however, the crown method persisted and only the cruder

---

[1] Pilkington Brothers Ltd., Letter from William Pilkington, 8 March,
1836. The rectifying plant was sold and the premises leased to Edward
Webster and Sons from the beginning of 1837. For a note on Edward
Webster, his son Edward and his grandson William, see obit. William
Webster, *St. H. N.*, 23 May, 1891. William Pilkington and his family went
to live at Millbrook House until 1850 when they removed to Eccleston
Hall. Richard Pilkington had succeeded his father at Windle Hall.

[2] Pilkington Brothers Ltd., List of expenditure drawn up by William
Pilkington *c.* 1836.

[3] Pilkington Brothers Ltd., agreement dated 1 Feb., 1842 ; L.R.O.,
DDCS 43/22.

[4] T. E. Gregory, *The Westminster Bank Through a Century* (1936), I, 25.
The obituary notice of Peter Greenall in the *Annual Register*, 1845, 296-7,
stated that he was a partner in Parr and Co., " in which he had acquired
a large fortune." We have not been able to discover any confirmation of
this statement in any other source and it may well be that the *Annual
Register* confused the two brothers. The Westminster Bank has no
information on the subject.

form of cylinder glass, known as broad glass,[1] was manufactured, fit for the commonest glazing. Cylinder glass, however, had obvious advantages over crown, particularly in a country where the excise duty had to be taken into account. Much larger panes could be made out of a rectangle than from a circle ; the whole rectangle could be cut into saleable glass and there was no " bulls-eye " to count as wastage. These were important considerations, for the same rate of duty was charged upon cylinder glass as upon crown. Moreover, since 1813 an additional drawback (or rebate of duty) of one-third had been granted upon squares of window glass exported. This concession, originally intended to compensate manufacturers for waste in cutting crown glass, enabled anyone who exported cylinder glass to claim compensation for a non-existent wastage.

In 1832 the Smethwick firm of Chance and Hartley brought glassmakers from the continent to blow cylinder glass. This in its improved form was known as sheet, or German sheet, glass. For a few years they sold most of their production abroad,[2] there being very little demand at home for the new product because its finish, despite improvements, was very inferior to that of the lustrous product of the crown process. In the later 1830s, however, James Timmins Chance patented a means of smoothing and polishing the thin sheets of glass and, sold as patent plate glass, these polished sheets offered severe competition to crown glass in the home market. In January, 1841, Chance proudly recorded : " our sheet plate [sic] is carrying all before it."[3]

William Pilkington, quick to see the possibilities of the new process, lost no time in establishing a sheet glass department at the St. Helens works. An old employee of Pilkingtons, Abraham Hartley, later recalled how the first foreign glassmakers were recruited :

" The simple facts are these. One day, a Belgian, whom I had known at Chance's named Legget—nay, I don't know how the name is spelt—called on me and asked what sort of masters I had. I told him and he came to terms, I suppose, with them, for he started blowing sheets soon after. The others came along and they worked away amongst us. Certainly they tried to keep their operations as secret as they could but they each had to have a ' gatherer ' and the ' gatherers ' saw how the thing was done. It was all a question of knack ; there was no patent about the business. Gradually our men picked it up and they and the Belgians began to work side by side at the blowing."[4]

[1] For broad glass, see above, p. 118.

[2] 34,975 cwts. were sent abroad and 7,395 cwts. retained for home consumption. Parliamentary Return, 1839 [419] XLVI.

[3] Chance Brothers Ltd., J. T. Chance to William Chance, 28 Jan., 1841.

[4] Interview published in the St. H. Lantern 3 Jan., 1889.

This account is confirmed to some extent by the local census returns of 1841, which include the name of a glassmaker called Jean Baptiste Leguay. He, and another glassmaker named Louis Dartes, were both of foreign birth, but of their six children, only the eldest (aged 12) had been born outside the country, the rest being born in England but not in Lancashire.[1] This makes it certain that they came from Smethwick, for Chances were the only company making sheet glass in Britain before this time.

In saying that there was no patent for the manufacture of sheet glass, Abraham Hartley was strictly correct. But J. T. Chance had patented his process of smoothing and polishing such glass and this finishing machinery could only be used under licence. When, however, Pilkingtons took a lease of the old cotton mill, recently vacated by Hadfield and Frost, and installed smoothing and polishing plant,[2] they paid no royalties. In September, 1842, the owner of the patent complained that he was " quite in the dark " as to how they were finishing their glass and in March of the following year the Board at Chances resolved :

" That J. T. Chance write to Mr. Pilkington to inform him that we are satisfied that he is invading our patent in his mode of grinding and polishing glass."[3]

Chances' conclusion was, however, quite without justification ; they never brought any charge against Pilkingtons as they would surely have done had Pilkingtons been infringing their patent rights. In fact, the St. Helens firm, commendably unwilling to increase its own production costs while at the same time subsidizing those of its keenest rival, sought to adapt the existing machinery for polishing cast plate glass, for which there was no patent. Not being engineers themselves, the Pilkingtons gave this task to a very capable young man called Henry Deacon, who had just served his time at Nasmyth and Gaskell's Bridgewater Foundry, Patricroft. The first evidence of his being in St. Helens is, significantly enough, contained in a statutory declaration that he had " invented Improvements in Apparatus for Grinding and Smoothing Plate Glass, Crown Glass and Sheet Glass." This declaration is dated 17 December, 1844[4] and it is not clear what

[1] P.R.O., H.O., 107/516.

[2] Pilkington Brothers Ltd., Package 27., agreement dated 4 March, 1842. The mill was leased from Peter Greenall for £131/10/0 a year, the first payment to be made six months after the firm " shall commence polishing German Sheet Glass."

[3] Chance Brothers Ltd., J. T. Chance to Wren and Bennett, 14 Sept., 1842 ; Board Mins., 8 March, 1843.

[4] The declaration is preserved at Pilkington Brothers Ltd. In the final patent, 10,686 of 1845, he is described as of Eccleston, engineer. For the general background of Deacon's life, see J. Fenwick Allen's memoir in the *Chem. Trade Jour.* 18 Sept., 1889, later printed in his *Some Founders of the Chemical Industry* (Manchester, 1906).

events had occurred in the previous two or three years. Pilkingtons were making sheet glass from 1841 onwards[1] but they could not have smoothed and polished it at first, for they only leased the Old Cotton Mill in March, 1842, and some time probably elapsed before the necessary machinery was installed. Deacon's meteoric rise at Pilkingtons, though still a man in his early twenties, is proof of the value the firm placed upon his services. By 1847 he had the title of Chemist and Engineer to the company[2] and two years later was earning £5 18s. 6d. per week, by far the highest wage paid by the firm.[3]

The new process was introduced to Pilkingtons during the depression years of the early '40s. When trade picked up again after 1843, they were one of the few firms ready to share in the rapidly-growing market for sheet glass. The demand became particularly heavy in 1845-6 and this led some later writers to attribute the flood of orders to the repeal of the glass excise duty in April, 1845. The glass manufacturers, however, never believed that this duty was an impediment to their business ; the chief target for their attack was rather the window tax which prevented nine out of every ten houses in the country from having more than seven windows.[4] The duty on glass was not such a handicap to them as to those who made flint glass ; since the end of the French wars the duty on window glass had been levied on the finished product[5] and the excise officers did not, therefore, interfere in the actual glassmaking operations. The window tax, on the other hand, by restricting the amount of glass required for glazing each house, set an upper limit to the total demand. When Robert Lucas Chance was asked whether he thought the tax on windows more injurious to consumption than the duty on window glass, he had no hesitation in replying :

" Most assuredly. I think that it is obvious from the style of the building here and on the Continent. If you go to Hamburg and the Northern, or to France and the Southern parts of Europe, the windows are double to what they are here."[6]

The manufacturers, therefore, did not expect that the repeal of the duty would be accompanied by any considerable increase in demand. In fact, however, the repeal happened to coincide

---

[1] Pilkington Brothers Ltd., List of production figures, 1844.

[2] Royal Society of Arts, *Abstract of Proceedings*, 14, 21 April, 9 June, 1847.

[3] Pilkington Brothers Ltd. Wages lists for the weeks ending 12 and 19 May, 1849.

[4] 13th Report of the Excise Commissioners (Glass) 1835 [15] XXXI, 59.

[5] *Ibid.*, Evidence of L. Chance.

[6] *Ibid.*, 138.

with a great building boom ; brick production reached 1,820 millions in 1845, the highest total for twenty years.[1] The industry was taken completely by surprise. " None in our branch," wrote one manufacturer at the beginning of 1846, " had any notion that the demand would have been so extraordinary as it proved . . . The extra make, since the repeal, could not be less than fifty per cent."[2] Sales of sheet glass were particularly heavy and Robert Lucas Chance wrote of " a famine of sheet and sheet plate in London."[3] The sudden clamour for the new product found Pilkingtons in a position to supply their customers, whereas the old giants of the north-east, who continued to pin their faith on crown glass, were unable to do so. A new phase had opened for the St. Helens firm.[4]

Peter Greenall, who had supported the company in its adversity, was no longer a partner when it entered this prosperous period. On 1 February, 1842, he agreed to sell his three-elevenths share to his brothers-in-law for £7,000. The partnership did not cease at once, however ; it was arranged that the £7,000 should be paid in 28 quarterly instalments of £250.[5] It was not until the beginning of 1849, therefore, that Greenall and Pilkingtons ceased to exist and Pilkington Brothers took its place.[6]

It is possible that Greenall's decision to withdraw from the St. Helens Crown Glass Company may have been connected with his venture into plate glass manufacture.

At the beginning of 1836 his brother, Gilbert, leased to the Union Plate Glass Company part of an estate at Pocket Nook, which he had recently acquired on the death of his father.[7] This was a concern with a share capital of £180,000 whose headquarters were in Manchester. It is not known to what extent the Greenalls were interested in its formation but Peter Greenall was certainly one of the five directors, the other four being

Shannon, op. cit., 317.

[2] Communication of an unnamed crown and sheet glass manufacturer, 31 Jan., 1846 in Parliamentary Return, 1846 [109] XLIV.

[3] Chance Brother Ltd., R. L. Chance to J. T. Chance, 8 July, 1845.

[4] Below, p. 358.

[5] Pilkington Brothers Ltd. Agreement dated 1 Feb., 1842.

[6] The partnership terminated in 1849 as from the date of Greenall's death in 1845.

[7] Will of Edward Greenall proved at Chester, 11 Dec., 1835.

Manchester men.[1] The Greenalls stood to gain a twofold advantage from this new undertaking ; they not only secured a valuable tenant but also stimulated coal-getting under their estate. The right of the company to purchase these coals was actually written into the original agreement.

The Union Plate Glassworks were built during 1836-7 and the first glass was cast there in March, 1837.[2] The factory was a large one, with a capacity of 5,000 feet per week. Its casting hall, nearly 90 yards long and more than 30 yards broad, housed two founding and two fining furnaces, four pot arches and twenty annealing kilns.[3] Power for the grinding and polishing machinery was supplied by a 100 horse-power engine built by Boulton & Watt.[4] The manager, rather surprisingly, was William West, the bankrupt. He did not hold the position for long, however. In 1845 he was writing to William Pilkington from the Birmingham Plate and Crown Glassworks at Smethwick, which he then managed, protesting that he was quite innocent of trying to entice Pilkingtons' men away from St. Helens in defiance of their contracts.[5]

While the buildings of the Union Plate Glassworks were being erected at Pocket Nook, yet another plate glass factory was in course of construction farther down the railway at Sutton Oak, the proprietors calling themselves the Manchester and Liverpool Plate Glass Company. Little is known of this venture on account of its short life and the loss of all the company's papers. There may possibly be some truth in the suggestion, made many years later, that only one factory was at first contemplated but a rival company was formed because the proprietors disagreed on the choice of site.[6] The Manchester and Liverpool company was first mentioned in the minutes of the St. Helens and Runcorn Gap Railway in April, 1836, when they applied for a strip of land at

---

[1] *The Deed of Settlement Of the Union Plate Glass Company, Established 1836* (Manchester, 1838). The Manchester directors were David Bellhouse, jun., builder ; Henry Charles Lacy, mail contractor ; Richard Lane, architect ; and Samuel Nichols, merchant.

[2] St. H. and R.G. Mins., 20 April, 1836 ; notes at Pilkington Brothers Ltd.

[3] *The Mirror*, 11, 25 March, 1843.

[4] Birmingham Public Library. Boulton and Watt Collection. Letters from W. Bennett, 24 Sept., 1836 to 18 May, 1837.

[5] *Deed of Settlement* ; L.R.O., Cross Papers. Copy of letter from West to Pilkington, 13 Oct., 1845. When West signed a statutory declaration on 25 May, 1853 (Pilkington Brothers Ltd., package 53), he was described as " of Longsight near Manchester, Gentleman." His wife, Anne née Boothman, came from Higher Ardwick (will of Thomas West proved at Chester, 23 July, 1828).

[6] *St. H. N.* 18 April, 1896.

Sutton Oak.[1] A date stone at the factory bears the year 1837,[2] but the first definite evidence of glass actually being cast there is contained in the *Wigan Gazette* of 16 February, 1838 ; according to this report, several shareholders had just visited the works which were described as " now in a state of completion." Four plates of glass were successfully cast under the direction of Mr. Howard, the manager, " and the colour and quality were considered very perfect." The Sutton Oak factory was not originally so large as the one at Pocket Nook, the casting hall being only half the width ; it contained but three furnaces and fourteen annealing kilns capable of making in all 3,000 feet of glass per week.[3]

The proprietors of the British Plate Glassworks at Ravenhead must have received the news of the arrival of these two competing companies with some apprehension, for all three shared the same local advantages as well as the common disadvantage of being equally remote from London, the chief market for their product. About the same time another concern, calling itself the Thames Plate Glass Company, was about to go into production close to the London market, and yet another competitor, the Birmingham Plate Glass Company, hoped to gain advantages both in location and relative proximity to London, as well as to gain the plate glass market in the Midlands. The sudden appearance of four new companies in a branch of the glass industry previously confined to Ravenhead and Cookson's works on the Tyne,[4] threatened to transform the whole pattern of trade so far as the Ravenhead factory was concerned.

The British Plate Glass Company, however, maintained a close grip on events and the Governor and Directors in London were fortunate in having as their agent at Ravenhead Frederick Fincham, a man of the same calibre as Robert Sherbourne. Fincham had previously dabbled in industrial chemistry and had also made glass bottles and soap. In November, 1835, when he was appointed manager at Ravenhead, he was proprietor of a small glass concern in Manchester.[5] His instructions were to cut down expenditure and increase output ; he was soon able to report success in both these directions. Within two years of his appointment economies at the works had paid for six new cottages and the re-roofing of five buildings, including the casting hall, as well as extensions to the polishing room and many other

---

[1] St. H. and R.G. Mins., 13 April, 1836.

[2] British Sidac Ltd. now use this factory.

[3] *Lpool. Merc.* 5 Aug., 1842 ; 15 March, 1843.

[4] Above, p. 116.

[5] 13th Report of the Excise Commissioners (Glass) 1835 [15] XXXI, 74, 114. Edmund Knowles Muspratt described Fincham as " a very intelligent man familiar with political economy " (*My Life and Work*, 1917, 35).

minor repairs. " I have already reduced my number of Hands," his report went on, " and shall seize every opportunity of weeding out those who are the least effective."[1] By 1839, production costs had been cut by 20 per cent. and output stepped up by an even greater proportion.[2] With the aid of a new founding furnace and additional grinding and polishing machinery, installed in 1838, the capacity of Ravenhead was increased to 5,000 feet per week.[3] The Governor and Directors showed appreciation of their resourceful and energetic manager by advancing his salary from £550 to £700 in 1838 and to £1,000 in 1840.[4]

This attacking policy kept their competitors at bay. The Thames Plate Glass Company proved the most dangerous because many of their London customers had an interest in it,[5] but the competition of the other three factories turned out to be very mild. In June, 1838, Fincham was able to send the comforting news to London :

" I have ascertained that neither of the two Companies here can be in the Market with any effect before next Spring and the Birmingham, which is the most forward, not before Christmas."[6]

In fact, it was not until the beginning of 1840 that competition from the newcomers became sufficiently severe to merit a long communication on the subject from Fincham and even then, in his opinion, three quarters of the trade in the north was still being supplied from Ravenhead.[7] According to him, the glass from the new works was of very low standard. It was most important, therefore, that Ravenhead's product should continue to maintain its reputation for high quality, since customers often insisted upon it for that very reason. Thanks to

" the backing of many private friends in Manchester and Liverpool, the New Companies make very slow progress even at Discounts of 20 to 25 p.Cent. below us . . . I have heard very little of the Birmingham Company in these parts . . . Now we know that Cookson's are more intent upon large sales without caring so much about quality, the Thames Plate Glass Co. are something in the same way and others have not much good glass to offer—it appears to me that the

[1] B.P.G. Mins., 15 Nov., 1837.

[2] *Ibid.*, 8 March, 1837 ; 1 Jan., 1840.

[3] *Ibid.*, 27 June, 11, 25 July, 1838.

[4] *Ibid.*, 7 Feb., 1838 ; 1 Jan., 1840.

[5] *Ibid.*, 7 March, 1838.

[6] *Ibid.*, 27 June, 1838.

[7] *Ibid.*, 1 Jan., 1840.

Battle is to be fought on the Glass for Glazing. Attack them upon this point and they will or cannot interfere with you in plates for silvering."[1]

The battle was hardly joined, however, before the depression of the early 'forties made the contest unequal. By the end of 1840 the Birmingham company found itself in deep water[2] and in December 1841 one of the proprietors came to enquire if the British Plate Glass Company would be interested in buying them out.[3] By September 1841 the Manchester and Liverpool company at Sutton Oak was also in difficulties and in July of the following year the proprietors were trying to persuade Fincham to buy some of their surplus stock; but he refused their offer because there was " a Probability of the quality being very bad." The company soon went into liquidation ; the Sutton Oak factory was put up for auction in September, 1842 but there were no bidders even at £10,000 and the property was withdrawn.[4] A second attempt to sell the works was made two years later but it, too, was unsuccessful.[5]

Although the larger Pocket Nook Works of the Union Plate Glass Company did not suffer a similar fate, the concern was in a very unsteady condition. In May 1842 Fincham forwarded to London a report of its directors showing it to be entirely without funds and £12,000 in debt.[6] But bankruptcy was narrowly averted and, when trade picked up again, a delegation from the company waited upon the proprietors of Ravenhead to enquire if the latter would be willing to discuss with them the fixing of prices. This was refused.[7]

By 1845, therefore, the proprietors of Ravenhead, powerfully aided by the trade cycle, were more than holding their own. The newcomers had either been driven out of business or were seriously weakened. Production was higher than it had ever been and Fincham was looking forward to an output of 7,000 feet per week. But the company had not retained its enviable position as the leading producer of plate glass in the kingdom without many sacrifices and changes. Gone were the days when the shareholders could look forward with confidence to large

[1] *Ibid.*, 8 Jan., 1840.

[2] *Ibid.*, 4 Nov., 1840.

[3] *Ibid.*, 15 Dec., 1841.

[4] *Ibid.*, 1, 22 Sept., 1841 ; 6 July, 10 Aug., 21, 28 Sept., 1842. *Lpool. Merc.* 5 Aug., 1842.

[5] B.P.G. Mins., 17 April, 1 May, 18 June, 1844 ; *Lpool. Merc.* 15 March, 1844. The factory was later advertised to be sold by private treaty in the same paper on 4 Oct., 1844.

[6] B.P.G. Mins., 25 May, 1842.

[7] *Ibid.*, 23 Oct., 1844. See also below, p. 253.

returns on their capital. From 1838 they had to be satisfied with 10 per cent. The prosperous days of unchallenged monopoly, or shared monopoly, were gone.

The failure to renew their Act of Incorporation, which granted them limited liability, was a further indication of these changed circumstances. The Act was due to expire in 1841 and when the proprietors sought its extension in January of that year, great hostility was shown by the other companies, particularly the Union Plate Glass Company which had been refused limited liability only a few years before.[1] The Manchester Chamber of Commerce, no doubt at the instigation of the Union Plate and the Manchester and Liverpool concerns, sent in a petition of protest as did the Thames, Birmingham and Tyne companies.[2] In the face of this strong opposition, the parliamentary committee was only willing to permit the renewal of the charter for ten years instead of the thirty-one that had been sought. The committee's chairman was careful to explain that they felt " great objection on principle to the privilege of limited responsibility " but did not wish the privilege to terminate suddenly because half of the stock was held in trust.[3] This was a moderate success for the opposition : a triumph was soon to follow. When the Bill came up on the Report Stage on 10 May, 1841, Mr. Hodgson, the Member for Berwick, without giving any previous notice as was usual in such cases, introduced the shelving resolution, " That the Report be taken into further consideration upon this day six months." This being pressed to a snap division, was carried by 75 votes to 45 and the original measure was thus completely lost.[4] The proprietors of Ravenhead later applied to the Committee of the Privy Council for Trade for their charter's renewal. This was granted but only for one year in order that the difficulties arising from the loss of limited liability could be given attention.[5] After the year's respite, the company worked on exactly the same footing as its rivals.

The years 1830-45, therefore, despite the excise duty and the window tax, saw a great advance at St. Helens in the manufacture of flat glass : the district retained its position as the chief plate

[1] C. A. Cooke, *Corporation, Trust and Company* (Manchester, 1950), 131.

[2] *C. J.*, **96**, 7, 79, 105, 180, 184, 243, 256, 27 Jan., 25 Feb., 8, 30, 31 March, 29 April, 3 May, 1841.

[3] House of Lords Record Office. Mins. of the Cttee on the British Plate Glass Bill, 5 May, 1841.

[4] B.P.G. Mins., 12 May, 1841.

[5] *Ibid.*, 2 June, 8 Sept., 1841; 27 July, 3 Aug., 1842.

glass centre in the country and in addition the early success of Greenall and Pilkingtons set it well on the way to becoming also the leading source of window glass. In the other branches, however, progress was very slow. In bottle-making, indeed, there does not appear to have been any advance at all : the small glasshouse at Thatto Heath continued to be the only factory producing bottles in the neighbourhood. In the manufacture of flint glass, the firm of Bishops soon became of some consequence but their arrival was later offset by the failure of the Bell's Ravenhead works. John William Bell was killed in 1838 when his horse bolted and threw him out of his gig,[1] and after his death the company lacked a competent manager. There was a serious labour dispute in 1843 and in August 1845 all the property, even including the eight-day office clock, was put up for auction.[2] Here, at all events, was one concern which certainly derived no benefit from the repeal of the exise duty.

[1] *Wigan Gazette,* 19 Jan., 1838.
[2] *Lpool. Merc.,* 20 Sept., 1843 ; *Manchester Courier,* 30 Sept., 1843. St. H. Ref. Lib., Ansdell Papers, Sale notice.

CHAPTER XVII

EARLY YEARS OF THE ALKALI TRADE AND THE REVIVAL OF COPPER SMELTING

THE alkali trade was called into existence chiefly to supply the manufacturers of soap, and its origins in and around Liverpool were closely related to the phenomenal growth of soapmaking on Merseyside. London had long been by far the most important soap-boiling centre in the country; but the great expansion of the textile industry—requiring soft soap for its finishing processes—together with the increase of population in north-western England and the development of Liverpool's export trade—requiring hard soap—all combined to create a small but thriving soap industry on Merseyside towards the close of the eighteenth century. In the early 1790s it was described as " an Encreasing Trade not of many years' standing."[1] Progress was rapid. By 1820 the manufacturers on Merseyside were making twice as much soft soap and two-thirds as much hard soap as the capital.[2]

The two varieties were made with different kinds of alkali, caustic potash being used for soft soap, and caustic soda, with which we are here concerned, for hard. The London boilers imported their soda in the form of barilla, the best kinds of which consisted of ashes from plants of the goosefoot family, *salsola sativa*, grown extensively in Spain, Sicily and Teneriffe.[3] The rising industry of Merseyside, however, drew its soda supplies from kelp, the ash of seaweed. This was brought coastwise from the highlands and islands of Scotland[4] or from northern Ireland. It was not so rich in soda as barilla, yielding about 10 per cent. instead of about 20 per cent., but, unlike the imported product, there was no customs duty to pay. The duty on barilla was fixed sufficiently high to allow kelp to be sold at a competitive price, despite their differing soda content. The London boilers preferred the richer barilla because they had to pay more for their fuel ; the Liverpool soapmakers used kelp, which could be shipped cheaply down the coast or across the Irish Sea. A London

---

[1] Picton Ref. Lib., Holt and Gregson MSS., XXII, 22.

[2] Excise Return, 1821 [73] XVII.

[3] C. T. Kingzett, *The History, Products and Processes of the Alkali Trade* (1877), 70.

[4] Malcolm Gray, " The Kelp Industry in the Highlands and Islands," *Econ. Hist. Rev.*, 2nd ser. IV, No. 2 (1951), 198.

Q

soap manufacturer estimated in 1818 that the industry consumed nine-tenths of the barilla and five-sevenths of the kelp used in the country.[1]

By 1820 the Merseyside boilers were already making 3,000,000 lbs. of soft soap every year, more than any other place in Britain. But quantitively this branch of the industry was not so important as that which manufactured hard soap, of which Merseyside made some 16,000,000 lbs. per year.[2] It was in the development of hard soap manufacture that the men of Merseyside could show most progress, and in this branch the relative price of kelp and barilla was clearly of the utmost importance to them. In August 1822, however, the delicate balance was completely upset by the reduction of the duty on barilla from £11 to £5 5s. 0d.[3] This caused the Merseyside soap interest to send a strongly-worded memorial to the Treasury protesting that the measure would " have the effect of wholly superseding the use of kelp in soap boiling to their very great injury " and would be to the profit " only of the London soap manufacturers and of foreigners."[4] To this the Liverpool agents of the kelp proprietors added that kelp would be " utterly superseded throughout the kingdom " for soap boiling. The reduction of the barilla duty, they claimed, " would have a much more injurious effect on the kelp trade than if salt were to be totally freed from taxation."[5]

This last observation referred to the Chancellor of the Exchequer's promise, made only a month before, that the excise duty on salt would be removed in two years.[6] This promise opened the way to the widespread adoption of a method of making soda by decomposing salt,[7] invented by Nicholas Leblanc on the

---

[1] Evidence of Benjamin Hawes to the S.C. on the Salt Duties, 1818 [393] V, 168.

[2] Excise Returns, 1821 [73, 74] XVII. For duties and national totals, see Excise Returns, 1821 [345, 357] XVII.

[3] C.J., 77, 457, 479, 24 July, 5 Aug., 1822.

[4] Library of H.M. Customs and Excise. Treasury and Excise Papers, 101, 323-4.

[5] Ibid., 101, 326.

[6] Gore's Gen. Ad., 11 July, 1822.

[7] The chemical equations for the Leblanc process are :

Stage 1. $NaCl + H_2SO_4 = NaHSO_4 + HCl$
common salt, sulphuric acid

$NaCl + NaHSO_4 = Na_2SO_4 + HCl$
sodium sulphate, hydrochloric acid gas

Stage 2. $Na_2SO_4 + CaCO_3 + 4C = Na_2CO_3 + CaS + 4CO$
sodium sulphate, limestone, powdered coal, sodium carbonate, calcium sulphide

eve of the French Revolution and developed commercially in France when the wartime blockade drove up the price of barilla in that country. In Britain, however, although prices rose sharply,[1] supplies of barilla and kelp had always been sufficient to make unnecessary the introduction of the Leblanc process, despite the fact that it enabled a much stronger form of soda to be produced. After the war the new process was operated on a small scale by Tennants in Glasgow and by Losh & Co. on the Tyne,[2] but the British soap manufacturers gave no great inducement to industrialists to develop it. The importation from Ireland and France of several thousand hundredweights of ashes other than potash, kelp or barilla, makes it reasonable to suppose that some Leblanc soda was already entering the country.[3] But it was not until the reduction of the barilla duty in 1822 that the Liverpool soapboilers really turned to the new product with any seriousness, and then it was chiefly as a means of maintaining their advantage over their London rivals. The promise that the salt duties would shortly be abolished made the prospects for the Leblanc process all the more inviting. And there could hardly be a better district in which to decompose common salt than Merseyside, with its abundance of salt and coal.

The first arrival was James Muspratt, who removed from Dublin where he had almost certainly been operating the process on a small scale.[4] If our supposition that some artificial soda was already being sent to Britain from Ireland is correct, he may well have had contacts among the Liverpool soapboilers before he settled among them in Vauxhall Road in 1822.[5] Here, as the size of his sulphuric acid chamber attests,[6] the new process was

---

[1] See graph of prices in Archibald and Nan L. Clow, *The Chemica Revolution* (1952), 72.

[2] J. Mactear, *Report of the Alkali and Bleaching Powder Manufacture of the Glasgow District* (1876), 25 ; R. C. Clapham, " An Account of the Commencement of the Soda Manufacture on the Tyne," *Trans. Newcastle-on-Tyne Chem. Soc.*, **1**, (1871), 38.

[3] P.R.O., Customs 5/6-10. Imports 1817-22.

[4] This was explicitly stated in Muspratt's obituary notice in the *Lpool. Daily Post*, 5 May, 1886. Kurtz, who went to Dublin in 1818 to conduct experiments, referred in his notebook to purchasing " soude de Muspratt." J. Fenwick Allen, who printed this reference in *Some Founders of the Chemical Industry* (Manchester, 1906) 122-3, did not consider that it could have referred to the Dublin period but it may well have done so. According to the Dublin directories, Muspratt continued in business there until 1830 in partnership with a man named Abbott.

[5] *Lpool. Daily Post*, 5 May, 1886. *Gore's Lpool. Directory* listed the firm for the first time in 1823 as Muspratt and Abbott. In 1825 it appeared as Muspratt alone.

[6] Its base measured 112 ft. x 24 ft. and is to be compared with Tennants' of 12 ft. x 10ft. We are indebted to Dr. D. W. F. Hardie for these particulars.

worked on a relatively large scale. Leblanc soda gradually replaced kelp as the Liverpool soaperies' mainstay and, by enabling the industry to use palm oil in place of more expensive fats, soon secured for Liverpool almost the whole British export trade in soap as well as a large portion of the sales at home. In 1835 a London soapboiler confessed: " Liverpool is the great market now for the export of soap and there is the great consumption of palm oil and almost all the soap for exportation (certainly nineteen-twentieths) is made from palm oil exclusively."[1] Merseyside had at that date far outstripped London, producing in all 47,750,000 lbs. of hard soap annually to the Londoners' 32,650,000.[2]

The transition from kelp to Leblanc soda and the soap-boilers' increased demands for alkali brought considerable success to Muspratt and to others who became soda makers on Merseyside. But Muspratt's very success eventually caused him to concentrate his main efforts outside Liverpool.

In the first stage of the Leblanc process, hydrochloric acid gas was evolved and in the early days this was allowed to escape into the air. As more and more salt came to be decomposed, those who lived near the works began to protest about these noxious vapours. On 5 October, 1827, the *Liverpool Mercury* carried a letter complaining that Muspratt's works

" pour forth such volumes of sulphureous smoke as to darken the whole atmosphere in that neighbourhood ; so much so that the Church of St. Martin-in-the-Fields now erecting cannot be seen from the houses at about one hundred yards distance, the stones of which are already turned a dark colour from the same cause. The scent is almost insufferable, as well as injurious to the health of persons residing in that neighbourhood."

This letter brought a further contribution :

" For my part I don't mind if they [the walls of St. Martin's] are as black as Warren's blacking, provided the church is white inside. But I am more concerned for my lungs, and likewise for the minister and congregation ; if there should be a north-wester when they meet, I am sure they will feel more for their lungs than they will for the colour of the church walls, because Mr. Muspratt's smoke will enter the sacred pile as well as my humble cottage. I only wish that the replier lived in Limekiln Lane or at the top of Scotland Road, he would then feel the effects of it."[3]

[1] 17th Report of the Excise Commissioners (Soap) 1836 [20] XXVI, 104.

[2] *Ibid.*, 71.

[3] *Lpool. Merc.*, 7 Dec., 1827. Letter from J.H.

If these protests were voiced openly in the public press, no doubt many other complaints and, perhaps, threats, reached Muspratt's ears in private. He knew that, as his business expanded, even more hydrochloric acid gas would be poured out from the chimneys of his works to pollute the atmosphere over a part of north Liverpool that was rapidly gaining favour as a residential district. His factory was developing into a public nuisance and he probably knew that Liverpool Corporation had already removed the copper industry from the town for a similar offence.[1]

It was when Muspratt's success was showing the first signs of leading him to trouble with the authorities that another manufacturing chemist, Josias Christopher Gamble, reached Liverpool from Dublin. Gamble had been trained for the Presbyterian ministry but had forsaken his calling for the world of industry, taking advantage of knowledge gained at a course of medical lectures which he attended as part of his theological training at Glasgow University. He started by making bleaching powder, first in County Monaghan adjoining his native Fermanagh, and then in Dublin, where he produced alum and Glauber's salt and was able to make his own sulphuric acid, instead of importing it from St. Rollox.[2] According to the later evidence of his son, Gamble broke up his business in Dublin in order " to find a situation more economically suitable whence to supply the Lancashire manufacturers."[3] Though seventeen years older than Muspratt, he joined the younger man as his junior partner in a new Leblanc concern, known as Muspratt and Gamble[4] or Muspratt & Co.[5] Land was rented from the Greenalls at £25 per Cheshire acre in the summer of 1828,[6] within the coal-salt triangle but well away from Liverpool and in a district where the chemical industry was as yet represented

---

[1] The copper works of Charles Roe and Co. had been indicted as a public nuisance in 1770.

[2] Article on J. C. Gamble in the *Chem. Trade Jour.*, 1 March, 1890, written by John Fenwick Allen, a copper smelter who came to St. Helens in 1858 and was for many years manager of the Sutton Copper Works. This article was one of a series, based upon information supplied by the descendants of the persons portrayed, later re-printed in *Some Founders of the Chemical Industry* (Manchester, first ed. 1906, 2nd ed. 1907). J. C. Gamble graduated at Glasgow in 1797. W. Innes Addison, *The Matriculation Albums of the University of Glasgow* (Glasgow 1913), 174. Jos. C. Gamble and Co. are described as vitriol manufacturers in Dublin directories between 1814 and 1821.

[3] *St. H. N.*, 6 June, 1885.

[4] Greenall Rent Books.

[5] L.R.O., Land Tax Assessment, Windle, 1830.

[6] Greenall Rent Books.

only by a solitary copperas bed.[1] By choosing a site close to the
New Double Locks on the Sankey Canal near Gerard's Bridge,
Muspratt and Gamble were to enjoy the advantages both of an
abundant supply of cheap coal from the nearby collieries, and of
water either from the Canal or the Windle Brook. Salt could be
brought direct from Cheshire by flat, and limestone, needed for
the second stage of the Leblanc process, could be carried up the
Canal without paying toll on account of a clause in the original
Act of 1755, inserted at that time for the benefit of the farming
community.   And, of no less significance, the town of St. Helens
was then an ideal size for a chemical manufacturer : sufficiently
large to house his workpeople yet sufficiently small not to possess
any organised form of local government which might restrict
the growth of his factory by bringing legal actions against him.

By opening a factory at St. Helens, however, Muspratt and
Gamble were moving away from their chief customers, for St.
Helens was never to become a soapboiling centre. Two aspiring
soapmakers, John Bevan and John Rigby, had opened a small
soapery in 1822 at Greenbank, near to the Ravenhead terminus
of the Canal. But when trade became slack, in 1826, the works
had to be mortgaged for £2,000 to Bevan's brother, Reece Bevan,
a Wigan cotton spinner.[2] In October 1826 Bevan and Rigby
petitioned the Excise Commissioners to be allowed to pay duty
on their soap in arrears, for " owing to the pressure of the Times,"
they were unable to collect the debts owed them.[3] Shortly afterwards the firm went bankrupt and on 21 May, 1828, the soapery
was put up for auction.[4] It was not until 1852 that anyone else

---

[1] This copperas bed appears to have been originally laid out by John
Bethune of Manchester in 1811-2. Its original capacity was 200 tons of
copperas per year, made from raw materials available locally. The bed
was extended in 1817 and its capacity increased to 300 tons per year.
Bethune died in the later 1820s but the works were continued under other
ownership until the depression of the later 1870's. By 1859, 700 tons of
copperas were being produced annually; there was a good demand for it at
the local glassworks where, when manufactured into rouge, it was used for
polishing. L.R.O., Cross Papers, correspondence concerning a conveyance
between Mrs. Beckman and John Bethune ; Pilkington Brothers Ltd.,
package 289, Abstract of Title of Thomas Milne ; Gore's Gen. Ad., 15 Sept.,
1814 ; 6 Feb., 1817 ; Lpool. Merc., 2 June, 1826 ; 27 June, 1828 ; St. H.
Intelligencer, 21 May, 1859 ; ev. of John Crossley to the R.C. on Noxious
Vapours, 1878 [2159] XLIV q. 11,008.
    For the manufacture of copperas (ferrous sulphate), see B. Faujas de
Saint Fond, A Journey Through England and Scotland to the Hebrides in
1784 (ed. Geikie) (Glasgow, 1907), I, 143-5, and Samuel Gray, The Operative
Chemist (1828), 694-5.

[2] Pilkington Brothers Ltd., Deeds, package 289.

[3] Library of H. M. Customs and Excise, Treasury and Excise Papers,
124, sub. 7 Oct., 1826.

[4] Lpool Merc. 9 May, 1828.

tried to enter the soap industry at St. Helens. This later venture, made by F. W. Tinker who had been with Hazlehursts at Runcorn, managed to survive but never grew to any size.[1]

The glassworks of St. Helens, however, offered a steady market for the products of the alkali works and the St. Helens district was to become the largest glassmaking centre in the country. But the glass industry never became such a good customer for soda as a prophet in 1830 might have been tempted to forecast. The makers of window glass substituted saltcake (sodium sulphate, the product of the first stage of the Leblanc process) for the more costly soda during the 1830s.[2] The St. Helens Crown Glass Co. was using saltcake as part of their glassmaking mixture in 1837[3] and it had completely replaced soda by the later 1840s.[4] At the plate glassworks, where purity of raw materials was of greater importance, the substitution came later, soda not being completely abandoned at Ravenhead until about 1868.[5] Even there, however, saltcake seems to have been used to some extent in the early 1830s on a scale that justified the British Plate Glass Company's erecting a special plant for its manufacture.[6] Other glass firms also started to make their own saltcake when their requirements were large enough to justify it. The Eccleston Crown Glassworks made saltcake in the 1830s.[7] An account of the Union Plate Glassworks in 1843 mentions " a salthouse for preparing the alkali " and an accompanying illustration reveals a very tall chimney of the kind used by chemical manufacturers to disperse their " noxious vapours " over a wide area.[8] Pilkingtons, it is true, remained customers of the chemical firms for many years, though even they tried to venture into industrial chemistry in the early 1850s and finally established works of their own more than ten years later.[9] On the whole, therefore, it would seem that, although the glass firms of St. Helens certainly provided a considerable and growing market, close at hand,

[1] *St. H. N.*, 6 Oct., 1888.

[2] Henry Chance, " On the Manufacture of Crown and Sheet Glass," in H. J. Powell, *The Principles of Glass-Making* (1883), 104.

[3] Bills at Pilkington Brothers Ltd.

[4] Evidence of William Windle Pilkington to the R.C. on Noxious Vapours, 1878 [2159] XLIV, q. 11,080.

[5] *Ibid.*, evidence of John Crossley, q. 11,004. The French had devised a means of making plate glass using saltcake and had started to use it during the Napoleonic War. *Journal des Mines*, **12** (1802), 243 ; **30** (1811), 447.

[6] B.P.G. Mins., 9 Oct., 1833 ; 29 July, 1835.

[7] Evidence of William Mercer to the S.C. on Noxious Vapours, 1862 [486] XIV, q. 273.

[8] *The Mirror*, 11 March, 1843.

[9] Below, p. 359.

for the chemical manufacturers, this market was very much secondary to that of the soaperies on the Mersey.

The centre of gravity of these soaperies, as of the soda manufacture, was moving away from Liverpool, though in the case of the soap firms, they kept to the river and did not take root on the coalfield. In 1832 the second largest concern on the Mersey was that of John and Thomas Johnson of Runcorn, which in that year paid more than £38,600 in duty.[1] The principals, one aged 32 and the other 29, had many years before them in which to extend their business still further.[2] Hazlehursts of Runcorn,[3] though little more than half the size of Johnsons judged from the duty they paid, were also to grow enormously and so were Crosfields of Warrington, a firm founded in 1815 and paying in 1832 almost £19,000 in duty.

The partnership between Muspratt and Gamble was short-lived. In 1830 Muspratt withdrew from St. Helens and in 1831[4] built a new factory of his own farther down the Canal. This was situated in Newton township, close to the railways from Liverpool to Manchester and from Newton to Warrington—soon to be connected with the Grand Junction line to the south. In the year this factory was built, the inhabitants of Everton got as far as bringing an action against Muspratt for the nuisance caused by his Vauxhall Road works, but the defence managed to have all the prosecution witnesses excluded on the ground that the case was being heard in Liverpool and they lived outside the borough boundary. Only witnesses friendly to Muspratt were allowed to testify : soapboilers, scientific " experts " and doctors, who even went so far as to claim that hydrochloric acid gas was beneficial to people because it destroyed disease. This surprising claim caused a wag to announce in the *Liverpool Mercury* the formation of " A MURIATIC ACID GAS JOINT STOCK

[1] 17th Report of the Excise Commissioners (Soap) 1836 [20] XXVI, 61-5. The largest firm, Matthew Steele and Co. of Liverpool, paid £40,300.

[2] Memorial inscription, Runcorn Churchyard. We are indebted to Dr. R. Dickinson for this reference. John Johnson, their father, died in 1816 at the age of 37 and was described in his will as a soapboiler of Runcorn. The Johnsons' works previously belonged to Hayes, Ollier and Co. Charles Nickson, *History of Runcorn* (1887), 164.

[3] This concern was in being in 1821 (Nickson, *op. cit.*, 163). A firm in Runcorn called Wright and Hazlehurst had been dealing in writing slates in 1805. T. S. Ashton, *An Eighteenth Century Industrialist, Peter Stubs of Warrington* (Manchester, 1939), 65.

[4] Evidence of William Mercer to the S.C. on Noxious Vapours, 1862, qq. 276-7.

COMPANY to supply the town by means of pipes, with this most valuable article." It also helped to secure a verdict against the suffering public of Everton.[1] In April 1838, however, Liverpool Corporation itself charged Muspratt with " creating . . . a nuisance within the Borough."[2] This time the manufacturer lost the case and, although he did not close his Liverpool works, he was obliged to confine his main soda-making activities to the Newton factory, which were greatly enlarged for that purpose.[3]

While Gamble conducted the Gerard's Bridge works on his own, other would-be manufacturing chemists came to the district to try their luck in a trade which, from Muspratt's success at Liverpool, seemed to show much promise. But whatever Muspratt's formula for success may have been—able management, the scale of his operations, the advantage of an open market or merely good fortune—few of the later alkali makers were able to discover his secret ; most of them came as eager optimists and left as downhearted failures. William Neale Clay for instance, is known to have been a manufacturing chemist at St. Helens only because he is described as such in the fiat of bankruptcy issued against him in 1832 ;[4] he later went down to the Midlands to take charge of Chances' saltcake plant.[5] Others, like Edward Rawlinson, enjoyed slightly longer lives as alkali makers. Rawlinson was a Lancaster attorney who, in October 1829, joined Joseph Williams, believed to have been his brother-in-law,[6] in a small factory on the south bank of the Canal at its Gerard's Bridge terminus. Their original intention appears to have been the manufacture of alum ; Williams is described in a deed of 1830 as an alum maker.[7] Rawlinson, to whom Williams assigned his half share in October 1830, later extended the scope of his operations to include soda manufacture.[8] He soon discovered, however, that he lacked the

[1] Gore's Gen. Ad., 12 May, 1831 ; Lpool. Merc., 13 May., 1831.

[2] Report on the Queen v. Muspratt at Liverpool Spring Assizes (Lpool 1838) ; D. W. F. Hardie, A History of the Chemical Industry in Widnes (I.C.I. Ltd., General Chemical Division, 1950), 19-20.

[3] L.R.O., Cross Papers. Gerard v. Muspratt, draft bill marked 1850, fo. 6.

[4] Lpool. Merc., 24 Feb., 4 May, 29 June, 1832.

[5] James Frederick Chance. A History of the Firm of Chance Brothers and Co. (privately printed, 1919), 18.

[6] Art. on Gamble, Chem. Trade Jour., 1 March, 1890. The register of voters at Lancaster includes Edward Rawlinson of Fenton Street from 1818 to 1867. We are grateful to Mr. G. M. Bland, the City Librarian of Lancaster, for this information.

[7] St. H. Town Hall, United Alkali Co. Ltd., Deeds, Gerard's Bridge Works.

[8] Lpool. Merc., 18 Dec., 1835.

necessary capital and on 1 January, 1831, he had to raise £1,500 on mortgage from Richard Tarrant Bury of Liverpool and John Close of Manchester. In June 1832 he was indebted to West and Co. of the nearby Gerard's Bridge Colliery and was obliged to mortgage the works to them as security for the delivery of up to £1,000 worth of coals. He managed to stagger on for another year but the inevitable could not be long postponed : a fiat of bankruptcy was issued against him on 3 August, 1833.[1]

Two other partnerships which started to make soda early in the 1830s survived until 1841. About 1835 Samuel and William Thompson Clough, who hailed from Seacombe in the Wirral peninsula, occupied the works which had previously been Bevan and Rigby's soapery and may well have been the scene of Clay's ill-fated venture in the interim. The Cloughs conducted their business on some scale but, like Rawlinson and Williams, lacked capital[2] and, when the depression arrived, could survive no longer. Their end was sudden. In September 1841 they were obviously planning to extend their plant, for they were arranging an additional supply of water ; four months later they had failed.[3]

Darcy and Dierden, another firm, were burdened by debt from the start. Young John Darcy, who had been one of Muspratt's men, and his father-in-law, Richard Dierden, a provision merchant of Newton, borrowed £500 from Richard Orford of Marple, Cheshire, and on 9 October, 1832, purchased a small plot of land close to the Canal and Railway and next to the newly-established gas works.[4] In 1837 their plant was extended ; as a neighbouring farmer put it : " they were only in a small way then but they kept enlarging."[5] In 1839 Darcy and Dierden, by that time making twelve tons of soda per week, increased the capacity to eighteen tons per week and attempted to reach an agreement with Andrew Kurtz of Liverpool to raise the total still further.[6] But this led to costly litigation just when the depression was setting in. This firm, too, ran short of money and in June 1841 was obliged to mortgage its property to Parr, Lyon and Greenall, the Warrington bankers—a not uncommon

---

[1] United Alkali Co. Ltd., Deeds, Gerard's Bridge Works.

[2] L.R.O., Cross Papers, Gerard v. Crosfield, 1846, fo. 7 ; DDCS 14/101, William Pilkington to Rowson and Cross, 2 May, 1845.

[3] B.P.G. Mins., 29 Sept., 1841. For the auction notice, Lpool. Merc., 30 Sept., 1842, and for the refusal to certify Samuel Clough as a bankrupt on account of his concealed assets, Lpool. Merc., 17 Feb., 1843.

[4] Art on Andrew Kurtz in the Chem. Trade Jour., 9 Nov., 1889 ; United Alkali Co. Ltd., Deeds, Kurtz Works.

[5] Ibid., Deeds, 23 Sept., 1837 ; evidence of Richard Baxter to the S.C. on Noxious Vapours, 1862, q. 342.

[6] P.R.O., C13/2307.

death-rattle.[1] They failed soon afterwards. J. and T. Frankland
attempted to keep the factory open for a month or two but were
obliged to abandon the attempt. The inevitable auction was
announced for June 1842[2] but there was no sale. The plant was
dismantled and dispersed, the land being eventually sold in
September 1845 to Andrew Kurtz.[3]

Kurtz was the most romantic figure among the select band
of unusual men who founded the alkali trade in Britain. He
learnt chemistry in Paris whither he is believed to have fled from
his native Reutlingen in Wurtemburg during the Revolutionary
War.[4] After the downfall of Napoleon, he crossed the Atlantic
and became an American citizen in order to exploit a gunpowder
invention in that country, and later came to England where he
leased a chemical works on the Thames. In 1818 he was carrying
out experiments in Dublin and in 1820 he removed to Manchester
and specialised in the manufacture of chromate of potash.
Pigments were still his chief concern when he later moved to
Liverpool ; he was then described as " a manufacturing chemist
and colour manufacturer."[5]

In May 1839 he entered into a secret agreement with John Darcy,
promising to provide additional plant at Darcy and Dierden's
works for the production of sulphuric acid, Darcy in return
contracting to supply him with soda cheaper than the trade price.
Kurtz constructed five large chambers for making the acid at a cost
of over £1,200. These were his own property built on land which
he had purchased himself and there was no partnership agreement
between Kurtz, on the one hand, and Darcy and Dierden on the
other, even though Kurtz in fact owned part of the works. As
Darcy's business affairs became more embarrassed, however, he
alleged that Kurtz had become his partner and even went so far
as to advertise the fact in the Liverpool Press and have DARCY
AND KURTZ painted in bold lettering on the gates of his factory.
This led to a case in Chancery, which may have been a major
cause of Darcy and Dierden's failure.[6] Kurtz, left with part of a
factory on his hands, decided to embark on the full Leblanc
process rather than withdraw from the St. Helens district.

[1] United Alkali Co. Ltd., Deeds, Kurtz Works, 3 June, 1841. This
includes an inventory of the property.

[2] *Lpool. Merc.*, 27 May, 1842.

[3] The plant had been " taken down, removed and disposed of " according
to an indenture dated 6 Sept., 1845, by which Parr Lyon and Greenall
sold the land to Kurtz for £995.

[4] For Kurtz see the *Chem. Trade Jour.*, 9 Nov., 1889 and Hardie, *op. cit.*,
23-4.

[5] Gore's *Directory of Liverpool*, 1835.

[6] Kurtz's Bill, dated 3 Dec., 1839 and amended 16 Nov., 1840, and Darcy's
and Dierden's answers, dated 27 April, 1840, are to be found among the
Chancery Records at the P.R.O., C13/2307.

In 1846 he was involved in another lawsuit, on this occasion
with Gamble, over his patenting a saltcake furnace resembling one
patented by Gamble in 1839.[1] The worry of the case appears to
have been fatal to Kurtz, then aged 64. He died on 31 March,
1846, before the verdict in his favour was made known. The
works passed to his son, Andrew George, a young man of 21
who had completed his education in Paris where he had met John
Hutchinson, a fellow student. Hutchinson became Kurtz's
manager for a brief time before moving down to Widnes Dock
in 1847 to start alkali making on his own account.[2] Although
Andrew Kurtz's will was proved at £16,000,[3] its provisions, and
particularly the grant of £7,000 in cash to his widow, led the firm
into difficulties. The works were mortgaged as security for
£1,200 lent in July, 1846, by James and John Woolfall Mullineux,
Liverpool spirit merchants, and in the following year £1,000
worth of furniture at Kurtz's home in Kensington, Liverpool,
had to be sold.[4] For the Kurtz family, the main crisis appears to
have come, not because of the depression of the early 1840s, but
on account of the interference of domestic affairs in business in
and after 1846.

In the light of the failure of Darcy, an experienced chemist, the
success of Morley and Speakman, who entered the alkali trade
without the benefit of serving under a Muspratt, is the more
remarkable. Francis Morley was headmaster of the Cowley Hill
Academy and Thomas Birch Speakman was managing partner
at the Gerard's Bridge Colliery, with interests in its associated
saltworks, and in the Denton's Green Brewery. It would, perhaps,
be illuminating to discover how this strange combination of
school teacher and business man came into being in the year
1834[5] and on what basis they conducted their Parr Alkali Works.
These works were sited along the Broad Oak branch of the Railway
on land adjoining the stream which formed the northern boundary
of the Barton's Bank Estate. Speakman's death in January, 1841,
removed one of the partners at the onset of the slump but Morley
proved a capable manager ; he was worth £10,000 when he died
in 1851.[6] The original partners were also succeeded by local men.

---

[1] British Patent 11,052/1846. For Gamble's patent, see below, p. 237.

[2] Hardie, *op. cit.*, 24. Two letters, dated 6 and 13 July, 1846, written by
Hutchinson from the Sutton Alkali Works, are to be found among the
Cross Papers.

[3] Will proved at Chester 13 May, 1846.

[4] United Alkali Co. Ltd., Deeds, Kurtz Works, 1 July, 1846 and 10 April,
1847, the former containing an inventory.

[5] According to a bank book at Pilkington Brothers Ltd., the St. Helens
Crown Glass Co. made a payment to the firm in December, 1834. The
first entry in the voters' list was in 1835 (L.R.O., E.L.1/4).

L.R.O., Letters of Administration (Chester), 29 May, 1851.

John Marsh, son of the leading draper in St. Helens, purchased Speakman's share and when Morley retired shortly before his death, Marsh's brother-in-law, William Hibbert, a local chemist and druggist, and William Grundy, son of the late headmaster of Parr Hall Academy, became the proprietors.[1]

While these soda firms were springing up, some flourishing and some succumbing, three of the larger soap manufacturers considered it worth their while to build their own alkali factories. The two soap companies at Runcorn were engaged in making soda by the middle of the 1830s; a tall revealing chimney 306 feet high, made its appearance at Hazlehursts at the end of 1836[2] and another, 200 feet high, was built at Johnsons a year or two later.[3] The Runcorn inhabitant who wrote to the *Liverpool Mercury* in April, 1838 warning the soapmakers not to spoil their " healthy little village,"[4] was a little behindhand with his correspondence. A short time before this, Crosfields of Warrington had also decided to become soda makers. They, however, chose to take an interest in an alkali factory already in being rather than build a completely new one. On 7 January, 1836, when Rawlinson's works at Gerard's Bridge were put under the hammer, Joseph Crosfield bid £2,050 for the property on behalf of himself, his brother James, and Josias Christopher Gamble[5] and on 18 March the three men also signed a new lease with Gilbert Greenall for the land on which Muspratt and Gamble's original works had been built.[6] The extension of this latter factory soon brought Gamble and Crosfields into conflict with a powerful landowner, whose estates lay immediately to the north.

Although the alkali makers had chosen in St. Helens a district where they were not likely for some time to be bothered by irate neighbours—apart from nearby farmers who could be kept quiet by small doles of money—they had reckoned without Sir John Gerard, lord of the manor of Windle, whose estates stretched northwards from St. Helens to the family seat at New Hall, Garswood, and beyond. New Hall stood in a park of 260 acres and was surrounded by gardens which had been laid out in 1796 by the landscape gardener, Repton, who, it was later claimed,

---

[1] *St. H. N.*, 11 July, 1890.

[2] *Chester Courant*, 13 Dec., 1836, quoted in Nickson, *op. cit.*, 165.

[3] Nickson, *op. cit.*, 165.

[4] *Lpool. Merc.*, 20 April, 1838.

[5] United Alkali Co. Ltd., Deeds, Gerard's Bridge Works, 24 March, 1836.

[5] United Alkali Co. Ltd., Deeds, Globe Works, 18 March, 1836.

" gave a glowing description of the natural Beauty of the Situation."[1] The alkali works, however, were responsible for inflicting some ugly blemishes upon this natural beauty. As Sir John took a turn around his carefully laid out gardens, which he himself had vastly improved and extended at a cost of £30,000,[2] or followed the hounds in the direction of St. Helens, he started to notice the lethal effects of the acidic smoke as it drifted ominously northwards, bringing sure but slow destruction to his trees and hedgerows. The damage became particularly noticeable about 1837 when Gamble and Crosfields' works started to billow forth hydrochloric acid gas in denser and more frequent clouds.[3] In the following year, probably influenced by the branding of Muspratt's Liverpool factory as a public nuisance, Gerard decided to take his grievances to court and to make a case not only against Gamble and Crosfields, the main offenders, but also against the other local alkali works as well. Accordingly, in the Michaelmas Term, 1838, he preferred Bills of Indictment against Gamble and Crosfields, Cloughs, Darcy and Dierden, and Morley and Speakman. A Grand Jury at Kirkdale Quarter Sessions returned True Bills in every case, but a settlement was reached before the matter reached Queen's Bench. The defendants agreed that four referees should grant certificates to each concern on the following 31 May, if their works were no longer a public nuisance. In this event, no further action would be taken, though the referees were empowered to cancel these certificates at any time before Trinity Term, 1841.[4]

The alkali makers had to choose between condensing their hydrochloric acid gas by means of Gossage towers or facing unending litigation in the courts. It was at this juncture that Gamble and Joseph Crosfield quarrelled. In Fenwick Allen's words :

" Joseph Crosfield, dismayed by the demands made upon their firm for damage to trees, hedges and crops, insisted on the immediate adoption of Gossage's patents ; to this Gamble was strongly opposed as he believed some plans he had himself conceived, would supersede Gossage's patents. Crosfield, however, was so impressed with the urgency of the situation and the value of Gossage's work, that on his own responsibility and in defiance of his partner's wishes, he concluded an agreement with Gossage to erect the necessary plant for them and put his process into operation. Gamble was very indignant

[1] L.R.O., Cross Papers, Gerard v. Crosfield, 1846. Brief for Plaintiff. For Repton, see *D.N.B.*

[2] L.R.O., Cross Papers, Gerard v. Muspratt. Draft Bill, 1850, fo. 4.

[3] *Ibid.*, fo. 10.

[4] *Wigan Gazette*, 9 Nov., 1838 ;   L.R.O., Cross Papers, Gerard v. Crosfield, 1846. Brief for Plaintiff.

at his wishes being disregarded and at a contract being made without his consent ; a quarrel ensued between the partners which was so serious that Joseph Crosfield never put his feet inside the works again."[1]

Although Crosfield saw the critical situation more clearly than his managing partner, we can sympathise with the point of view of Gamble, then busily developing a new and successful type of saltcake furnace, using iron retorts, which he patented in 1839.[2]

Gossage sent a Scot, James Shanks, to St. Helens to super-intend the erection of his towers at Gamble and Crosfields, Cloughs, and Morley and Speakmans.[3] Like Gamble, Shanks had been introduced to chemistry through lectures in medicine at Glasgow University, though as a medical, not a theology, student. This common tie with Glasgow and his visit to St. Helens to erect condensing apparatus may have led to Shanks's appointment as manager at Gamble and Crosfields at the close of 1840.[4] He became Gamble's right-hand man and must have taken most of the burdens of management from the shoulders of the older chemist, then over sixty and not in the best of health. It was in the knowledge that Gamble and Crosfields no longer required his undivided attention that Gamble, while still remaining partner in the original works,[5] once again branched out on his own account. On this last occasion he was concerned to see his son David safely embarked in the alkali business.

David Gamble was one of those favoured industrialists who had received the benefits of a prolonged academic education, first at a school near St. Helens (possibly the Cowley Hill Academy) then at University College, London, and, finally, at the Andersonian College, Glasgow. Like Peter Greenall and William Pilkington, he was a man who dominated his surround-ings. He became the outstanding manufacturing chemist in St. Helens and was recognised by his fellows as

" one of the leading pioneers of the second generation of chemical manufacturers, when apparatus on an extended

[1] Art. on Gamble, *Chem. Trade Jour.*, 1 March, 1890.

[2] British Patent 8,000/1839.

[3] *First Report of the Alkali Inspector* (for 1864), 8. Darcy and Dierden never installed Gossage's towers and went bankrupt before the necessary restraining order could be obtained against them (Gerard *v.* Crosfield. Brief for Plaintiff, fo. 15).

[4] *Ibid.*, Note scribbled on the back of the main document states that Shanks became manager on 5 December, 1840. For Shanks, see biograph-ical art. in *Chem. Trade Jour.*, 22 March, 1890. His name is not included in Addison's list of Glasgow graduates (*op. cit.*).

[5] The partnership was dissolved in 1845. *Chem. Trade Jour.*, 1 March, 1890.

laboratory scale began to be replaced by the machinery and plant of the modern chemical factory. He may be defined as one of the originators of modern chemical engineering."[1]

He was to play a great part in the life of the town in which he was bred though not born, the town he watched grow up and did not desert despite the ugliness, smoke and smell which were largely the product of the alkali trade. His valuable services were recognised in 1868 when he was chosen as the first mayor of the newly-incorporated borough, in 1897, when he was created a baronet, and in 1904, when he became a K.C.B.

David Gamble reached his majority in 1844 and it was in this year, when trade was reviving after the depression, that he joined his father in the " very small "[2] works at Gerard's Bridge where Rawlinson had ventured and failed ten years before.[3] At the Gerard's Bridge works, Gamble condensed his smoke from the start, but he did not allow all the hydrochloric acid to be poured to waste in the brook. Instead, he copied Muspratt's recent practice and commenced the manufacture of bleaching powder, the first man to make this by-product at St. Helens.[4] Muspratt and Gamble learned early the alkali maker's formula for success: to turn to profit those chemicals which other manufacturers were unwise enough to throw away. As the century wore on, the alkali maker could no longer exist by the manufacture of soda alone.

Gossage's towers did not put an end to the escape of hydrochloric acid gas, partly because they were not always worked efficiently (one at Gamble and Crosfields was even permitted to fall down[5]) and partly because the men, paid according to output, were not averse to raising the dampers and driving the gas, uncondensed, directly up the chimney, thereby creating a greater draught and making more saltcake.[6] Nearby farmers continued to receive compensation for damage[7] and Sir John Gerard was always on the look-out for the destructive yet incriminating smoke. In 1840 he and Samuel Taylor of Eccleston Hall obtained

---

[1] Obituary notice in *Jour. Soc. Chem. Ind.*, 30 March, 1907.

[2] Evidence of David Gamble to the S.C. on Noxious Vapours, 1862, q. 1799.

[3] L.R.O., Cross Papers. Gerard *v.* Gamble, 1846. Abel Woodward gave evidence that the Gerard's Bridge works had been operating about two years. It is not clear what happened to this site between March, 1836, when Gamble and Crosfields acquired the property, and 1844 when Gamble started to make soda there.

[4] Evidence of David Gamble to the R.C. on Noxious Vapours, 1878, q. 4753.

[5] L.R.O., Cross Papers. Gerard *v.* Crosfield. 1846. Evidence of Robert Smith.

[6] *Ibid.*, Evidence of Thomas Heyes.

[7] L.R.O., Cross Papers, DDCS 30/34. Arbitration for Thomas Green and Jonathan Binns.

£1,000 and £250 respectively from Gamble and Crosfields and Cloughs.[1] Six years later, in 1846, after having received regular reports from paid smoke-spotters, Sir John brought actions for £20,000 damages against Muspratt at Newton and the Crosfields and the Gambles at St. Helens ; he was awarded £1,000 against Muspratt, £400 against Crosfields and £300 against Gambles.[2] Although the Brief for the Plaintiff included a note that " . . . the late Mr. Kurtz having died very recently, the damages were not thought of sufficient importance to justify an action at the present Assizes and Messrs. Morley and Co's works . . . are too far distant, being at present on a small scale,"[3] £300 was later paid by Kurtz as well.[4] There can be no doubt that enormous damage was by this time being done to the Gerard estate and the payment of £2,000, though an arresting warning to the alkali makers, was no adequate compensation to Sir John, particularly as his law costs amounted to £900.[5] After 1846 he concentrated his attention upon the activities of Muspratt at Newton, for the St. Helens works were more carefully conducted than had previously been the case.[6] As the works grew in size, the noxious vapours became a greater problem despite more careful working ; but by that time the growing mounds of alkali waste and the disposal of the condensed acid were becoming equally deserving of attention. These new difficulties associated with the fully-grown alkali trade must, however, await consideration later.

We shall now turn to consider the copper industry, very akin to alkali manufacture in that it, too, was a source of harmful acidic vapours ; sulphur dioxide was quite as noxious as hydrochloric acid gas. The bonds between the two industries were to become much closer after the revival of copper smelting in St. Helens. The copper smelters had left the town in 1815 because the mines of North Wales could no longer provide ore in quantity: they returned about the end of 1830 when supplies from abroad started to reach Liverpool in appreciable amounts.

[1] Gerard v. Crosfield. The cases were settled out of court. The plaintiffs were to have engaged Sir J. F. Pollock, the eminent lawyer, on a special retainer. (Lpool. Merc., 10 May, 1840).

[2] Lpool. Merc., 4 Sept., 1846 ; evidence of Gerard's agent, Adolphus Moubert, to the S.C. on Noxious Vapours, 1862, q. 60.

[3] Gerard v. Crosfield.

[4] Evidence of Moubert to the S.C. on Noxious Vapours, 1862, q. 60.

[5] Ibid.

[6] Gerard v. Muspratt, 1850.

R

In 1825 the duty on imported copper ore was reduced from 21s. to 12s. per cwt.[1] This concession stimulated the mining in Chile, Cuba, and elsewhere of copper ores sufficiently rich in metal to be able to compete with the low-grade British ores in spite of the duty. The Chilean ore contained from 20 to 60 per cent. copper and the Cuban yielded 12 to 25 per cent. compared with the 5 to 10 per cent. copper content of the ores found in Anglesey, Cornwall or other parts of Britain.[2] After a few years cargoes of foreign copper started to reach this country, first a trickle (282 tons in 1828 and 1,055 tons in 1829) but soon a growing flood (5,000 tons in 1833 ; 13,000 tons in 1835 ; 30,000 tons in 1839 and 55,000 tons in 1843[3]). By 1847 those who were engaged in the copper trade claimed that the foreign ore " has been the means of securing to this country the manufacture and supply of full three-fourths of all the copper consumed in the world."[4]

At first, most of the vessels carrying copper ore from overseas docked at Liverpool: 2,185 tons arrived there in 1832, for instance, compared with 1,292 reaching the great smelting port of Swansea.[5] The coalfield at St. Helens, easily accessible from Liverpool by the Canal, was well situated for smelting this ore. In the autumn of 1829 the available sites were surveyed by William Keates, an astute young man who, though not yet thirty, could look back upon eight years as manager of copper works in Staffordshire and in South Wales.[6] He finally decided upon a place at the Ravenhead

[1] Rates of Customs Duty Payable on Copper, 1808-46, 1847 [637] LIX.

[2] Copies of All Memorials and Petitions Respecting the Duty on Copper Ore. 1847 [184] LIX.

[3] Return of imports and exports of copper ore, 1824-46, 1847 [637] LIX.

[4] Copies of All Memorials, 1847 [184] LIX.

[5] Parliamentary return, 1833 [361] XXXIII. Swansea's imports soon caught up upon, and soon far exceeded, those of Liverpool.

[6] Evidence of William Keates to the R.C. on Noxious Vapours, 1878, q. 3210. The outline of Keates's early life is to be found in several resolutions in the Minute Book of the Cheadle Brass Wire Co. (now in the possession of Thomas Bolton and Sons Ltd.) : 10 Oct. 1815 : " That John Keates's Son be taken into the Brass Works to assist his Father in the Warehouse . . . "

15 September, 1818 : " The Company understanding that William Keates has devoted his leisure Hours to Chymistry with a view to the benefit of the Concern, do hereby vote him a present of 10 Guineas as a reward for his application and industry."

27 September, 1819 : " That from the exertions of Mr. William Keates to benefit the Concern he appears deserving of every encouragement, the Gentlemen present authorize Mr. Ingleby to send him to London for a few months for the purpose of studying Chymistry at the Expence of the Company."

In London he is believed to have received some tuition from Faraday and his analysis of brass (Annals of Philosophy, new ser., III, 325 and

terminus of the Canal, not far from where the Parys company's works had been. In the summer of 1830 while searching for low grade ore, necessary as a flux, he visited Anglesey with a Mr. Lyon,[1] who may reasonably be identified as partner in Newton, Lyon and Co., copper and lead merchants of Liverpool, who already owned works at Greenfield and were almost certainly interested in the new smeltery at St. Helens.[2] At the beginning of December 1830, he wrote to Lord Anglesey's agent to enquire if some Anglesey ore could be sent to the works at Ravenhead :

> " Having recommended my friends (The St. Helens Smelting and Copper Co.) to purchase some parcels of British Copper Ore for the purpose of smelting with those we obtain from South America, they have commissioned me to do so, and bearing in mind your declaration that you would sell Mona Ores whenever you could do so with more advantage than by smelting them, I am induced to make the first application to you in hopes that we may transact some business on mutually satisfactory terms."[3]

This application was refused[4] but on 20 September, 1832, Keates wrote again, on this occasion as smelting agent to the Bolivar Mining Association " who now carry on this concern."[5] Why the St. Helens Smelting and Copper Co. had such a short life, we do not know, but it seems likely that the change came about through the decision of Newton, Lyon and Co., who may have been but one of a number of firms with an interest in the Raven-head concern, to erect works of their own on the newly-opened railway at Sutton Oak, trading under the name of the British

---

Annales de Chimie et de Physique, **20**, 240, may have been carried out at this time. His brief stay in the capital over, he was sent to wind up the Cheadle Company's Neath Abbey Works and on 6 November, 1821, the Company recorded : " That William Keates be presented with £30 for his good con-duct in winding up the Neath Copper Concern. But as the Company in the present state of things are compelled to practise every Economy and . . . have lately *lowered all* the Salaries and Wages, they cannot with any propriety advance his Salary." This refusal appears to have caused him to break with the Cheadle Company, for in 1822 he became manager of the Whiston Copper Works near Cheadle and two years later went as manager to the Spitty Copper Works near Lougher (Minute Book ; obit. *St. H. N.*, 26 May, 1888 ; J. F. Allen, *Some Founders*, 2nd ed. app. 1 ; C. Grant Francis, *The Smelting of Copper in the Swansea District*, 1881, 124, 136).

[1] Univ. Coll. of North Wales : Mona Mines Letters, MML 1643.

[2] Newton, Lyon and Co. are mentioned in Gore's *Lpool. Directory* as early as 1818 and their Greenfield works in *Pigot's National and Commercial Directory*, 1828-9, *sub* Holywell.

[3] U.C.N.W., MML 2654. Keates to Sanderson, 1 Dec., 1830.

[4] U.C.N.W., MML 2654. Sanderson to Keates, 8 Jan., 1831.

[5] U.C.N.W., MML 1653.

and Foreign Copper Co.[1] Keates began to smelt at these new
works in 1833, yet remained as agent for the Bolivar Mining
Association until 1835.[2] He lived at Ravenhead House, St. Helens
for a few years but, when the two copper smelteries were both
working satisfactorily and no longer required his personal supervision, he went to live in Liverpool, where the offices of the British
and Foreign Copper Co. were situated.[3]   Keates was soon
controlling not only the works at St. Helens but also the buying
and selling of ore at Liverpool and the firm's interests at Greenfield.   Eight years after his unsuccessful negotiation for ore in
Anglesey, he was in a position to offer the smelters there " our
services for the purchase of Foreign Copper Ores at this Port
and their transhipment to Amlwch" at $1\frac{1}{4}$ per cent. commission.[4]
Ten years later, after the reduction of the import duty on copper
to a nominal 1s. per ton,[5] Keates, by this time a leading partner
in the business, now Newton, Keates and Co.[6], proposed to rent
the smelting works in Anglesey[7] and four years after that
approached Lord Anglesey with suggestions of a partnership.[8]
He was able to build up a trade in copper, based on Liverpool,
St. Helens and North Wales, approximating to the pattern of the
industry in the eighteenth century and capable of holding its own
against Swansea and Llanelly where more than 90 per cent. of the
copper smelting in the United Kingdom took place.[9]

The growing trade in foreign copper caused satisfaction among
the shipowners of Liverpool, for they were able to make from
£2 10s. to £6 profit on every ton they carried ; and the trade was
" enjoyed exclusively by British ships with two exceptions only."[10]
By 1846 cargoes to and from Cuba were carried in specially-
constructed craft

" and copper ore from Chili and Peru is imported in British

[1] Evidence of William Keates to the R.C. on Noxious Vapours, 1878,
q. 3184.

[2] Evidence of William Keates to the S.C. on Noxious Vapours, 1862
q. 2209.

[3] Ravenhead House was advertised to be let in the *Lpool. Merc..*, 23 Jan.
1835 and *Gore's Lpool. Directory*, 1835, gives Keates, " copper merchant
Newton Lyon and Co." as living at 8 Huskisson Street.

[4] U.C.N.W., MML 1721.   Keates to Beer, 26 Dec., 1828.

[5] The Bill received the Royal Assent on 5 Sept., 1848.

[6] U.C.N.W., MML 3309.   A letter was sent from Newton, Lyon and Co
on 4 Nov., 1845 and from Newton, Keates and Co., on 3 Sept., 1846.

[7] U.C.N.W., MML 3309.   Minute by Beer, 16 July, 1849.

[8] U.C.N.W., MML 3311.   Minutes of a conversation with Keates and
Newton at Liverpool, 1 April, 1852.

[9] A. H. John, *The Industrial Development of South Wales* (Cardiff, 1950)
108n, 111-3.

[10] Memorials and Petitions Respecting the Duty on Copper Ore, 1847
10-12.

sulphuric acid from copper pyrites[1] and Darcy was also hoping to use cheap pyrites from the Isle of Sheppey.[2] The proximity of the copper works certainly hurried on this transition, even though the price of natural sulphur was later reduced. When Keates decided to erect his smelting plant at St. Helens, neither he nor the alkali makers could have foreseen that within ten years the two industries would be sharing the same raw material. This was an unexpected advantage bestowed upon the St. Helens district by events far away.

The transition from sulphur to pyrites, no doubt, was also the cause of William Longmaid's carrying out experiments to discover a more direct method of producing saltcake by calcining together salt and iron pyrites, thereby avoiding the use of sulphuric acid and cutting out a stage of manufacture. On 1 June, 1844, Thomas Spencer, an earthenware manufacturer whose pottery was situated in Prescot, and Josiah Churchill, who described himself as a commission agent of St. Helens, leased a plot of land in Greenbank, previously part of Clough's factory,[3] and there started to build plant to work Longmaid's process. But all did not go well. On 21 January, 1845, the commission agent, who had contributed nothing, transferred his interest to Spencer, who had contributed £1,300,[4] and a few months later a renewed effort was made to launch the project on the same site. A glowing description of the practical results of Longmaid's process at the Greenbank works, written by Balmain and Parnell, Liverpool chemists, was widely circulated in the hope of winning some financial support for the venture. This was eventually forthcoming from a group of businessmen who formed the Patent Alkali Co. to operate the process.[5] In May, 1847, Thomas Finnimore Evans of Fenchurch Street, merchant, Richard Harmer of Stepney Grove, silk merchant and James Jennings of Mile End Road, salesman, leased the works at Greenbank.[6] The firm's headquarters were in London.[7]

This is a convenient point at which to interrupt this account of the alkali and copper industries at St. Helens, for by the middle of the 1840s the pioneering period was already over and the pioneers were ceasing to control the works which they had created. Speakman died in 1841, Kurtz in 1846, Gamble in 1848

[1] British Patent 7793/1838.

[2] P.R.O., C13/2307. Kurtz v. Darcy.

[3] Pilkington Brothers Ltd., Deeds, package 289.

[4] Ibid., L.R.O., Cross Papers, DDCS, 14/100.

[5] L.R.O., Cross Papers.

[6] Pilkington Brothers Ltd., Deeds, package 289.

[7] Lpool. Merc., 1 Feb., 1848.

vessels, sometimes as ballast under coffee, wood, hides and other goods but more frequently in whole cargoes, thus affording a valuable return to vessels trading to the Pacific, Australia, and New Zealand ; and as the West Coast of South America supplies few articles and these generally in small quantities (which has been and is seriously felt by other nations) securing to the British shipowner great advantages over the Danes and Hamburghers trading from countries belonging to the Zollverein."[1]

Among the Liverpool shipping houses which were benefiting from carrying copper ore in ballast was that of John Bibby and Co.[2] They had for some years been gaining an additional profit by smelting at Seacombe the copper they had carried half way round the world. As commercial agents to the Bolivar Mining Association, they became interested in the Ravenhead Copper Works and they acquired them as their own property about the year 1838.[3]

The chemical and copper industries had not long been established at St. Helens when, in 1838, they were driven closer together by an advance from £5 to £14 per ton in the price of Sicilian sulphur.[4] As no alternative supply of natural sulphur could be found, the manufacturing chemists were obliged to fall back on pyrites, a source of sulphur used in the manufacture of sulphuric acid for more than fifty years.[5] According to E. K. Muspratt, his father extracted the sulphur from " large quantities " of pyrites and

" as some of the pyrites contained copper, the residue, after burning, was delivered to the Sutton Copper Company [The British and Foreign Copper Co.] at St. Helens, so the utilisation of the copper . . . was attempted at its first introduction."[6]

The local alkali makers followed suit. In 1838 W. T. Clough thought it was worth his while to patent a method of making

---

[1] *Ibid.*

[2] Aleyn Lyell Reade, *The Millards and their Descendants Including the Bibbys of Liverpool* (privately printed, 1915), 25 *et seq.*

[3] J. F. Allen, 2nd ed., app. p. ii. According to E. Cuthbert Woods and P. Culverwell Brown (*The Rise and Progress of Wallasey*, Liverpool, 1929, 13), the Seacombe Copper Works were founded in 1812. Bibbys were certainly selling copper bolts and nails two years later (*Gore's Gen. Ad.*, 1 Sept., 1814). They opened a rolling mill at Garston some years after they started to smelt at St. Helens.

[4] W. Gossage, " History of Alkali Manufacture," *Proceedings of the British Association at Manchester* (1861), 102.

[5] B. Faujas de Saint-Fond, *Tour in England and Scotland in* 1784 (Glasgow, 1907), I, 142.

[6] Presidential address to the Society of the Chem. Ind., published in its *Journal*, 29 July, 1886.

recently taken over the Thatto Heath Bottle Works from the Wests,[1] met together to fix the price of quart bottles at 21s. per gross, and pint and soda water bottles at 19s., with 5 per cent. discount for payment within a month.[2]

The most highly-developed and smoothly-running of the glass manufacturers' associations, however, was that of the window branch of the industry. This was certainly in existence in 1825 and a series of minutes record its highly successful progress during the following twenty years.[3] Like the flint glass association, it covered all the firms in England and Scotland and there were, in addition, occasional meetings of Lancashire firms on a regional basis. Prices were regularly fixed for the whole country and five separate lists were drawn up : for sales in London ; for Newcastle glass sold " to country dealers " ; for the rest of England ; for Scotland ; and for Ireland. One of the members of the association, acting as its secretary, was empowered to summon a full meeting on receipt of complaints of undercutting. The organisation worked extremely well—so well, in fact, that in 1838, when trade became depressed, the association found it possible to restrict the total output of British glass; each firm's quota was then fixed at 10 per cent. less than its production over the previous four years. When sheet glass came to be produced on a considerable scale after 1841, it, too, was made on a quota basis. The records of Pilkingtons show that these quotas were rigidly adhered to by the St. Helens Crown Glass Co. and the absence of complaints in the manufacturers' minutes indicates that this was generally the case.

The manufacture of plate glass was the only branch of the industry without an association of any kind prior to 1845. In this case price fixing by agreement was not necessary, for the British Plate Glass Co. itself controlled the market. The only competitor until the late 1830s was the Newcastle firm of Cookson and Cuthbert and the two companies appear to have been content to share the trade together, apparently without any formal agreement existing between them. When the effects of the new plate glass companies began to make themselves felt in 1840, Fincham, the manager at Ravenhead, reported :

" I keep on good terms with Cookson's Agent at Liverpool who professes that his principals are quite disposed to go hand in hand with you in any measures that may be agreed upon to meet the competition."[4]

[1] Below, p. 356.

[2] Agreement dated 18 March, 1845, among miscellaneous papers in Glazebrook Minute Book.

[3] Copies of the minutes are to be found among the archives at Pilkington Brothers Ltd., St. Helens and Chance Brothers Ltd., Smethwick.

[4] B.P.G. Mins., 8 Jan., 1840.

it ; the consequence of which is that they apparently agree to the proceedings of the meeting who go away dissatisfied and undetermined. The non-attendance is to be attributed to an opinion of the inefficiency of meetings, generally, to the inconvenience and often, the impossibility of attending at a distance ; whilst the hostility of some parties arises from the immediate breach of faith, which has followed the agreement to a list of Prices. . . ."[1]

The delegates met at Lichfield from 12 to 14 December, 1831—a month later than was originally planned—and a circular issued on the 15th confidently expected that the minimum price would meet with universal approbation. But this was certainly not the case in the Warrington District, of which Bell and Co. of the Raven-head Flint Glassworks were members. At a meeting held at the George Inn, Warrington, later in December, Glazebrook noted :

" There can be no fear of any deviation below the Nett Minimum Price recommended by the Deputies at Lichfield inasmuch as it is not only not a remunerating price but in most instances so much below the prices now obtained in this District, that the Circulation of the Lichfield Nett Minimum List will be extremely injurious to all the Manufacturers, not being equal, in a great many articles, to the materials, workmanship and Duty and therefore that this meeting now request an early re-consideration of the whole List."

The members of the Warrington District then resolved :

" That this District now form its own List of Prices, each Manufacturer pledging himself not to sell below or lower than the Lichfield Net Minimum List.
This Meeting cannot help expressing its surprise at the ruinous prices generally fixed, particularly of vials, and recommend an advance on them at the next District Meeting at Birmingham."

Unfortunately the Minutes end at the close of 1831 but we know from another source that the association of English and Scottish flint glass manufacturers was still in being more than a year later. At a meeting held at the Angel Inn at Ferrybridge near Pontefract on 2 January, 1833, two Warrington representatives were present and J. W. Bell sent a letter of apology for absence.[2]

Price fixing is also encountered in the bottle branch of the glass industry, though at a later date. Just before the repeal of the duty in 1845, representatives of the Bank Quay Glass Co. of Warrington, William Foster of Liverpool, Woolfall and Percival of Manchester and Francis Dixon and Co., who had

[1] *Ibid.*, 26 Oct., 1831.

[2] *The Glass Works, Rotherham, 1751-1951* (privately printed by Beatson Clark and Co., Ltd.), 15.

of Orford Lane Glassworks, Warrington, provide a helpful picture of the degree of organisation which had been reached among the flint glass manufacturers of England and Scotland at that time. Although the minutes are chiefly concerned with the excise talks, the question of price regulation cropped up with regularity. This was apparently no new topic, for the Birmingham district was said to be " desirous of again uniting to establish an uniform list of prices if other Districts will co-operate with them."[1] The suggestion apparently found general favour and, in October, 1831, having failed to secure the repeal of the duty upon their branch of the industry, the delegates sent out the following note to the trade before they left London :

> " The Undersigned Deputies of the Flint Glass Trade of England and Scotland cannot separate without expressing their conviction that great good would ensue, were there to be a General Meeting of the Trade called, to be held at the George Inn, Lichfield, on Wednesday the ninth of November next ensuing, at twelve o'clock, to take into consideration the distressed state of Trade, and the ruinous prices at which the Manufacturers are generally selling.

> Hence they strongly recommend the proposed measure, in order to regulate prices and to arrange a List, which being the result of a General Meeting, would be more likely to be permanent. In order to promote and secure the object in view, it is suggested that there be separate District Meetings held, *prior* to the General Meeting and that the result of such Meetings as to their opinions upon the basis on which to calculate a List, be signed and brought to the General Meeting by the several Deputies . . . "[2]

A few days later, a memorandum was circulated summarising the reasons why previous efforts to regulate prices had been ineffectual :

> " Among many others, the chief evils are : a concurrence merely nominal on the part of some members in the proceedings of the Meetings ; non-attendance of many ; the hostility of others ; . . . no plan by which a charge can be made against any party, which occasions many rumours to be believed, which would otherwise be confuted and thereby destroys confidence in others. . . .

> The cause of the first evil arises in great measure from the number of persons of which a General Meeting is composed ; being more than will admit of a full discussion of the subject before them, especially in the short time which is allowed for

[1] *Ibid.*, 18 Oct., 1830.
[2] *Ibid.*, 20 Oct., 1831.

later to remark with some misgiving, it was very difficult to discover the trade price :[1]

"In a large colliery there must be contracts made which are generally private contracts and those who make them do not like to divulge the prices at which they are made. Therefore it is very difficult . . . to ascertain the exact price of the whole coal produced at any colliery . . . the retail price . . . often misleads . . . as to the average price obtainable."[2]

Price-fixing appears to have established the ceiling figure from which discounts were privately given.

Associations which regulated output were much more effective because they called for regular returns of production. This was the case in the salt industry where printed forms were circulated containing the production of every firm and the amounts by which each had exceeded or failed to reach its quota. It is just possible that the collieries at St. Helens had a similar quota system in operation in the 1830s, for a printed list headed *An Account of the quantity of COAL and SLACK shipped at the under-mentioned COLLIERIES on the SANKEY NAVIGATION* was sent monthly to the local coal masters.[3] Although the lists do not mention the amounts over and short, thereby pre-supposing a quota, the very existence of such lists opens up the possibility of some form of output regulation among the coal-owners who used the Canal. The evidence at present available is too insubstantial to allow any firm conclusion to be reached ; nevertheless, it may be pertinent to recall that so early as 1778 several coal proprietors had agreed to just such a quota system based upon monthly returns of Canal shipments.[4]

The local glass firms, like the collieries, were also members of manufacturers' associations. Perhaps collaboration in this case arose out of the need to form delegations now and again to negotiate with the Treasury on matters relating to the excise duty. In the flint glass branch, for instance, representations were made to the Government in 1812 and again in 1825.[5] In 1830 and 1831 delegates of the flint glass manufacturers were in constant consultation with firms throughout the country and with the Treasury in the hope of securing a repeal of the duty on their branch of the trade ; the minutes of the delegation, kept by T. K. Glazebrook

[1] Evidence of William Pickard to the Commissioners Appointed to Inquire into the Organisation and Rules of Trade Unions and other Associations, 1868 [3980] XXXIX, q. 15,801.

[2] *Ibid.*, q. 15,811. Reply of Mr. Briggs in the course of Pickard's evidence.

[3] Bromilow Papers. Returns for Feb., June, July, Oct., and Nov., 1836, sent to the Ravenhead Colliery.

[4] Above, p. 52.

[5] Warrington Ref. Lib., Minutes kept by T. K. Glazebrook, 8 Sept., 1830.

A few months later Cuthbert and Cookson junior waited upon
the committee of the British Plate Glass Co. in London to suggest
that both companies should reduce their prices. This suggestion
was rejected, however, and the delegates on their return to the
Tyne resolved to make no changes on their own.[1] A few years
later, representatives of the recently-formed Union Plate Glass
Co. of St. Helens waited upon the owners of the Ravenhead Works.
The minutes taken on that occasion leave no doubt about the
dominant position of the latter. The members of the deputation

> " stated their conviction of the Desirableness of some agree
> ment between all the Companies as to Terms of Credit, Charges
> for Packing and Guaranteeing Risk and Breakage and
> Glazing and Putting in the Glass and also as to a Minimum
> price being fixed, below which no Glass should be supplied to
> any order. The Governor and Directors having stated that
> they considered any such agreement impracticable, the
> Deputation withdrew."[2]

The lead of the Ravenhead Works over all its rivals had to be
considerably reduced before there was the remotest possibility
of price agreements being reached in the plate glass trade.

The high bankruptcy rate among makers of alkali is proof
that open and unrestrained competition prevailed at least among
the smaller manufacturers. The Alkali Association is usually
taken to date either from 1860, when Holbrook Gaskell and
E. K. Muspratt represented the trade in Paris at the time of the
Cobden Treaty, or from 1862 when a paid secretary was appointed
to keep a watchful eye upon all parliamentary business concerning
the industry.[3] But there may well have been agreements within
the trade before this time. A statistical report of output had been
drawn up in 1852, based upon full returns from sixteen manufacturers " representing 46 per cent. of the whole make " and
partial returns from eleven, representing a further 35 per cent.[4]
An estimate such as this could only have resulted from a frank
pooling of information. The returns are divided into districts,
which may mean that by then there existed local agreements, rather
like those in the coal and glass industries, and the words " the
whole make " have a distinctly familiar ring. Moreover, it is
known that an association was formed in December 1838 consisting of the Tyneside soda makers, the Tennant concerns at Glasgow,
Liverpool and London, Chances, and the British Alkali Co. of

---

[1] *Ibid.*, 14 Oct., 1840.

[2] *Ibid.*, 23 Oct., 1844.

[3] E. K. Muspratt, *My Life and Work* (1917), 104, 106, 132.

[4] Evidence of Christian Allhusen to the S.C. on Noxious Vapours, 1862,
137.

Bromsgrove.[1] This association was "for the purpose of endeavouring to avoid the evils likely to result from injurious competition in the sales of the articles of their manufacture." It was to "fix the prices of soda and alkali both for the home and foreign trade with places of delivery, allowances and other necessary regulations . . ." The penalty for underselling was rather unusual. The culprit had to "forfeit a dinner to the other members . . . and those connected with the trade who usually attend the meetings ; the dinner to be held at one of the principal inns in Newcastle, to be ordered by . . . three members not including the offending party and paid by the latter within one month from the time of its taking place." Unfortunately we do not know how effectively this league of some of the greatest men in the trade was able to control the market, nor if any of the St. Helens firms joined it. Perhaps, being primarily concerned with the Merseyside soap trade and with the export trade from Liverpool, the St. Helens manufacturers remained outside. But such a curbing of competition among the great cannot have failed to influence the smaller firms and it is just possible that by the 1840s even the local alkali trade, outwardly highly competitive and a dangerous financial speculation for those who lacked the necessary capital, was not without its "understandings" ; the case of Kurtz v. Darcy showed that there was a trade price for soda in Liverpool in 1839.[2]

Before the mid-1840s, therefore, the St. Helens coal proprietors, glass manufacturers and, possibly, some of the alkali makers and copper smelters as well, were regularly discussing matters of common interest. In addition to these organisations formed by members of the same trade, there was a considerable local liaison between employers in the different industries. In a small town, the rising industrialist naturally found himself regularly in the company of other men in the same walk of life. At the quarterly meetings of the St. Helens Book Club, for instance, Peter Greenall, Thomas Caldwell, Robert Robinson, Thomas Haddock, William Bromilow and his son William, John Johnson and T. B. Speakman, all coal proprietors, met Lee Watson, the ironfounder, William and Richard Pilkington, partners in the glass firm, and Francis Morley, the manufacturing chemist. This connection between the various local employers was by no means restricted to such social occasions. By the 1830s many of them were related by marriage.

---

[1] Rules and Regulations of the Soda Makers' Association, Newcastle-upon-Tyne, December, 1838, at the back of the book containing the minutes of the window glass manufacturers' association at Chance Brothers Ltd.

[2] Above, p. 233. A similar, tentative conclusion had been reached elsewhere with regard to the copper industry at this time. A. H. John, *The Industrial Development of South Wales* (Cardiff, 1950), 131-2.

We have already noticed that the families of Greenall and Pilkington had been united by the marriage of Peter Greenall with Eleanor, the sister of Richard and William Pilkington. Marriages of various members of the Speakman family had important industrial consequences, too. Of the daughters of Charles Speakman, the coal proprietor and brewer, Mary married Thomas Caldwell, another coal proprietor,[1] Alice married Lee Watson, the iron founder,[2] and Harriet married Robert Daglish, junior, Lee Watson's successor at the St. Helens Foundry.[3] These marriages brought two of the husbands into the Speakman coal and brewing businesses. Thomas Caldwell was appointed an executor of his father-in-law's will and thus became one of three persons entrusted with managing the important Speakman business concerns for fourteen years after Charles Speakman's death.[4] Between 1824 and 1838, therefore, he had an interest, as trustee, in the Gerard's Bridge and Cowley Hill Collieries and their associated saltworks and in the Denton's Green Brewery, in addition to his own coal and salt undertakings. In 1830 one of Charles Speakman's sons, Richard, married Betsy Ann, the daughter of Thomas Ferguson, another of the partners in the Denton's Green Brewery,[5] and Ferguson appointed Lee Watson, together with Thomas Birch Speakman, to act on his behalf after his death.[6] This they did from 1834 until 1838 when Ferguson's share in the Denton's Green Brewery was sold to Thomas Caldwell. Caldwell also became a partner in the coal companies about that time and, on the death of T. B. Speakman in 1841, the company became known as Speakman, Caldwell and Co. Whether Lee Watson ever had an interest in the collieries, we do not know, but there would seem to be a connection between his relationship by marriage with Thomas Caldwell and his partnership in the Bridge Foundry at Warrington, with which the Caldwell family had for long been closely associated.[7] So far as we know, only Robert Daglish failed to extend his business

---

[1] Date of marriage not known, but prior to 1824.

[2] Marriage at St. Mary's Church, 28 April, 1824.

[3] Marriage at St. Mary's Church, 2 July, 1834.

[4] Will of Charles Speakman proved at Chester, 27 Aug., 1824 and re-proved 21 May, 1849.

[5] Marriage at St. Mary's Church, 20 July, 1830. Charles Speakman and Thomas Ferguson bought the Denton's Green Brewery in 1821 from the assignees of William Hill. *Lpool. Merc.*, 15 Sept., 3 Nov., 1820, 19 Jan., 1821 ; L.R.O., Cross Papers, deed of co-partnership 24 Oct., 1821.

[6] Will of Thomas Ferguson proved at Chester, 18 Dec., 1834 ; Cross Papers, DDCS 14/143, copy of reconveyance of the Angel Public House.

[7] The proprietors of the Bridge Foundry early in the nineteenth century were Caldwell and Whitley (Ashton, *Peter Stubs*, 50n), the former being Thomas Caldwell's father. Lee Watson's interest in the Bridge Foundry is mentioned in his will, proved at Chester, 16 Jan., 1844.

S

interests through marrying into the Speakman family. The reason is not far to seek. His wife died less than two years after their marriage.

The unusual provision in Charles Speakman's will, that fourteen years were to elapse before his shares passed to his sons, and the succession of deaths in the family during the 1830s (seven out of the eleven children died between 1830 and 1841) serve to emphasise how important, industrially, marriages could be in the growing town. One is led to suspect that the founders of the new fortunes in trade were just as keen on a good match as were the landed classes to whom an heiress meant so much. Repeatedly the leading industrial families extended or confirmed their influence and interests by marriage. David Bromilow, for instance, married into the Sothern family who were Liverpool merchants, and Bromilow and Sothern of the Rushy Park Colliery were partners in a thriving coal trade to the steamers at that port. David Gamble married Elizabeth Haddock, sister of the managing partner in the Ravenhead Colliery, of which he later became a partner. The list could be extended to cover every stratum of business enterprise.

Associations among industrialists and the intermarriage of members of the various local industrial families tended to exert a settling influence. Perhaps this explains to some extent why the leading figures in industry at St. Helens were by the 1840s remarkable for being men of good background. They may no longer be described, as their predecessors have been, as " ill-educated, coarse and rough, with an extremely limited range of ideas."[1]   Of the manufacturing chemists in the district, Sir John Gerard, a hostile critic, was obliged to admit in 1846 :

> " It must be remembered that the conductors of these Works are not mere Mechanics or people in a small way of business . . . They . . . are persons of much private respectability. They have become in a measure fixed in the goodwill of the trading population and none but persons of a very high or a very humble station in society can venture to say much against them."[2]

J. C. Gamble, educated at Glasgow University, had, for a time, been a Presbyterian minister. His son, David, went to college at London and Glasgow. Andrew Kurtz was, from all accounts, a most cultured man with a passionate love of music shared by his son, Andrew George, who completed his education in Paris. James Shanks was also a Glasgow graduate and had practised as a doctor. Francis Morley had been headmaster of a school where John Marsh, who later became his partner in the Parr

[1] A. Redford, *The Economic History of England* (1931), 45.

[2] L.R.O., Cross Papers.   Gerard *v.* Crosfield.   Brief for Plaintiff.

Alkali Works, had been educated. None of these men were jumped-up foremen ; to each of them the all-important late Victorian adjective " respectable " could be applied.

The same is true of the coal proprietors. Although William Bromilow's spelling was not entirely faultless, he saw to it that his children were well-educated at the best local schools,[1] and his youngest daughter went to a private school in London.[2] John Bromilow went up to St. John's College, Cambridge, where he took his degree in 1824.[3] He entered the Church and was curate at Wigan and, later, incumbent of Billinge.[4] His younger brother, Adam, went in for the Law, received his training in London and afterwards practised at Lincoln's Inn.[5] The indications are that what has been said of the Bromilows, who lived in some style at Merton Bank and, later, at Haresfinch House[6] may also be applied, though in somewhat lesser degree, to the other coal-owners in the neighbourhood.

The same is true, too, of the proprietors of the glassworks. Richard and William Pilkington, as has been seen,[7] were the sons of an extremely well-to-do doctor. The Wests were in the same walk of life prior to their troubles with the Excise Commissioners. At the end of the eighteenth century Thomas West was able to send his sons to Stonyhurst College and one of them, Francis, became a Jesuit and a church architect of some prominence.[8]

Indeed, the more one probes into the family histories of these industrialists, the more it becomes evident that they conform very little to the widely-held conception of the captains of industry at that time : men who struggled out of their humble surroundings by being good at organisation and sharp, sometimes to the point of dishonesty ; men who succeeded by con-

---

[1] Fees were paid to Francis Morley and William Grundy. Diary of William Bromilow, 14 Aug., 1820.

[2] Bromilow Papers, Catherine May Bromilow to David Bromilow, 20 June, 1837.

[3] Bromilow Papers.

[4] *Lpool. Merc.*, 22 May, 1829 ; Bromilow Papers, letter from the Rev. John Bromilow to David Bromilow, 7 Dec., 1836.

[5] Bromilow Papers. He married a close relative of Admiral Sir Ross Donnelly, K.C.B.

[6] The exact date at which David Bromilow went to live at Haresfinch House, is not known. According to a printed agreement of 8 Nov., 1839 among the family papers, he was then in residence. Two years before this Adam Bromilow addressed a letter to him at Merton Bank.

[7] Above, p. 205.

[8] When paying fees on one occasion, Thomas West included a box of glass and a diamond, valued at £7/8/6 (information kindly supplied by the Librarian of Stonyhurst College).

centrating on coining money to the exclusion of all else, often insisting that what was good enough for them in their early days was good enough for their children. There is little doubt that by the 1840s the foremost business men at St. Helens were still kept fully occupied at their offices and had not yet reached the stage when they could sit back and delegate some responsibility to others. But, for the most part, they had not themselves risen from the rank and file nor were they devoid of culture or refinement.

While the masters had their own trading arrangements and social and family ties, their employees joined together in clubs, or, as they are more often called, friendly societies. These clubs fulfilled two functions. They provided opportunities to meet regularly, at fortnightly or monthly intervals, to chat and drink ; and they also provided a most valuable system of insurance. The members agreed to contribute to a common fund upon which each of them had a claim in case of need, through illness, death or misfortune of any kind. Friendly societies were an instrument of self-help providing a means of insurance for millions in the new towns, particularly after the Friendly Society Act of 1793 (Rose's Act) had put them on a sound footing. Sir Frederick Morton Eden estimated at the beginning of the nineteenth century that nearly a quarter of the population obtained relief from these clubs.[1] By the 'thirties and 'forties their influence in the St. Helens district was even more pronounced.

Prior to the appointment of a Registrar whose duty it was to scrutinise the rules of all new friendly societies, these rules had been kept by the Clerk of the Peace in each county. When the Registrar set up office in 1846, the rules of some of the existing societies were forwarded to him and many of them are still preserved at the Registry of Friendly Societies in London. Unfortunately we have good reason to suppose that many clubs—" obscure and shy societies " as the late Sir John Clapham called them[2]—never sent their rules to the Clerk of the Peace in the first place and we know that the lodges of the larger bodies, the Unitys such as the Oddfellows, Druids and Rechabites, were not enrolled until after 1850.[3] Nevertheless, it is possible, by piecing together the surviving enrolments at the Registry and local evidence, to gain a general impression of the very considerable extent of the friendly society movement at St. Helens.

[1] *Observations on Friendly Societies* (1801) quoted in Clapham, *Economic History of Modern Britain* (Cambridge, 1926), I, 296.

[2] Clapham, *op. cit.*, I, 297.

[3] R. W. Moffrey, *A Century of Oddfellowship* (Manchester, 1910), 63.

Six local societies deposited their rules with the Clerk of the Peace between 1794 and 1799, twelve between 1800 and 1809, ten between 1810 and 1819 and fourteen between 1820 and 1844.[1] The apparent falling-off in enrolments after 1820 was almost certainly caused by the coming of the larger Unity friendly societies, organised from outside the district. By the end of the 1850s, eleven lodges of the Grand United Order of Oddfellows had been registered from the St. Helens neighbourhood, five of the Ancient Order of Druids, two of the Grand Order of Modern Druids, two of the Ancient Order of Foresters, seven of the Loyal Order of Ancient Shepherds, and four of the United Order of Free Gardeners. That some of these lodges had been opened long before they were registered, is evident from a glance at the history of the Independent Order of Oddfellows (Manchester Unity), of which the first nine lodges at St. Helens were not enrolled until the years 1852-6.

The Duke of Lancaster Lodge at St. Helens was opened in 1825 by the Duke of Norfolk Lodge, Wigan.[2] It withstood a costly lawsuit brought against it by another friendly society,[3] and in 1830 was strong enough to stage a demonstration in the town " aided by a respectable attendance of brothers from Warrington and Runcorn," which increased its numbers to 150.[4] A report in the *Oddfellows' Magazine* added :

" Since our procession, we have the pleasure to say, our Order has experienced a revival in St. Helens, and several respectable characters have been initiated into our honourable Order ; among whom is Peter Greenall, Esq., who I doubt not, will be an ornament to our Lodge and to the Order in general."[5]

From this humble beginning the Order spread rapidly in the district. By 1835 there were twelve lodges and 642 members[6] and by 1839 nineteen lodges and 1,058 members.[7] Their procession in 1841 was very different from the feeble demonstration of eleven years before. Members appeared in full regalia, the total cost of which was estimated to exceed £2,000, and marched through the streets of St. Helens to the music of four bands.

---

[1] Enrolments at the Registry of Friendly Societies. For the names of these societies, see T. C. Barker *The Economic and Social History of St. Helens, 1830-1900* (MS. at St. Helens Ref. Lib.) I, 150-1.

[2] Minutes of the Manchester Quarterly Committee, 12 Sept., 1825 at the headquarters of the Order, Grosvenor Street, Manchester.

[3] *Ibid.*, 10 Dec., 1827 ; 9 March, 1829.

[4] *Oddfellows Magazine*, Sept., 1830.

[5] *Ibid.*

[6] Year Book at the headquarters of the Manchester Unity.

[7] *Quarterly Meeting of the St. Helens District* (Manchester, 1839). Copy at St. H. Ref. Lib.

" The business of the town was almost suspended and bore
more of the appearance of a general holiday . . . but such rapid
strides has the institution made of late in St. Helen's and its
neighbourhood that a great proportion of that place have
entered within its pale . . . The increase of the order here has
certainly been overwhelming."[1]

That 1,000 men out of a population in the four townships of
less than 20,000 should have been members of one friendly society
alone, gives some indication of the appeal of the movement as a
whole. Of course, the Manchester Unity was abnormally large—
hence the newspaper publicity—but it would be surprising if the
six other big organisations enrolled in the 1850s had not possessed
at least several hundred members in their St. Helens lodges ten
years before. The Foresters and both the Ancient and Loyal
Orders of Druids were, all three, strong enough to be separately
represented in a procession held to mark the proclamation of
Queen Victoria in 1837.[2] The local Foresters held their third
anniversary ball in January, 1839[3] and organised an archery
contest at Cowley Hill in the following summer.[4] Added to the
large membership of these Unity societies was the very considerable strength of the older independent societies, enrolled
before 1846 and still thriving. They, too, probably had several
hundred members. Although it is quite impossible to calculate
the grand total with any exact precision, it seems likely, assuming
five to a family, that the majority of the population of St. Helens
and district in the 1840s derived friendly society benefits. And the
St. Helens Savings Bank, founded in 1818, a kindred organisation
with 367 depositors in 1830 and 556 in 1844,[5] ought to be mentioned in passing, for it was another means of making provision
for sudden emergencies and hard times.

The rules of the smaller independent clubs do not show any
great variation in amounts of contribution or rates of benefit.
An entrance fee was levied which rose from about 5s. at 18 years
of age to £1 at 36 or 40. Members usually met once a fortnight
when they paid 1s. as a contribution and 2d. or 3d. for liquor.
In return they received about 7s. a week in the first year of sickness and 3s. 6d. thereafter. £7 7s. 0d. was paid on a member's
death and £5 on the death of his wife. The Oddfellows (Manchester Unity) appear to have paid a rather higher rate of benefit:

[1] *Wigan Gazette*, 20 Aug., 1841.

[2] *Ibid.*, 14 July, 1837.

[3] *Ibid.*, 11 Jan., 1839.

[4] *Ibid.*, 5 and 19 July, 1839.

[5] John Tidd Pratt, *The History of Savings Banks* (1830), 101 ; 2nd ed.,
1846.

10s. a week for a year and 5s. a week thereafter with £10 on the death of a member and £10 also on his wife's death. Members were often expected to attend funerals and one set of rules includes the injunction :

> " Every member residing within the prescribed limits shall on the death of a member attend his funeral in a deacent [*sic*] clean orderly manner or pay a fine of one shilling."[1]

It is difficult to discover to what extent these clubs assisted members in times of unemployment and distress. The Oddfellows, like the early trade unions,[2] certainly made provision for those who left their homes in search of work. In each town there was an examining officer to whom the unemployed man on the tramp could present his card. Before 1853 lodges accepted responsibility for these men without charge but in that year

> " instead of lodges having to take any member who pleased to deposit his travelling card, or came furnished with a form of clearance, without fee or question, an entrance fee rising from 1s. 6d. to £1 was imposed."[3]

As the actuaries came to be able to show what risks might legitimately be taken by friendly societies, the benefits provided were reduced from a basis of mere chance to one of mathematical calculation. But in the 1840s risks were still being taken and higher benefits continued to be paid. The Oddfellows were able to make provision for unemployment as well as sickness and death, and it seems probable that the smaller and older societies would also make similar provision, possibly by special levies, though they had not, of course, the advantage of branches in other towns.

When membership of a friendly society was restricted to workmen of one craft or industry, the society became a trade club, a form of trade union which ostensibly concerned itself with providing for its members in time of need. These trade clubs appear to have been fairly numerous in the town. The rules of the Chemists' Friendly, Burrieal, Sick and Accidental Society of St. Helens [*sic*], for instance, laid down that " its members shall consist of the trade alone."[4] The glass bottle makers had a friendly society which dated back certainly to 1825;[5]

---

[1] Rules of the Provident Friendly Society of St. Helens, enrolled 1841.

[2] For trade union support of members in search of work, see E. J. Hobsbawm, " The Tramping Artisan," *Econ. Hist. Rev.*, 2nd ser. III (1951), 299-320.

[3] Moffrey, *op. cit.*, 66.

[4] Registry of Friendly Societies.   Enrolled 1839.

[5] *The Lancashire Glass Bottle Trade.   Brief Summary of the Trade* (St. Helens, 1905).   Thomas Chadwick, who joined the society in 1835, was in some measure responsible for the Lancashire Society of 1853 and the national society after the strike of 1857 (*St. H. Intelligencer*, 25 Dec., 1858).

it may well have been in existence, unregistered, before that time, not daring to come out into the open on account of the Combination Laws. The rules of the British Crown Glass Makers' Society were drawn up in 1846[1] but a more local organisation may have preceded this comprehensive association which included both Midland and Lancashire houses. The same may be true of the Flint Glass Makers' Society, started in 1849, for in the second number of its magazine, published in 1850, a writer stated that " in our recollection there have been five different systems ; each system of society has shown the necessity of union, and yet four of the movements have been failures."[2] The shoemakers,[3] carpenters and joiners[4] also had their local clubs and the No. 10 branch of the Steam Engine Makers' Society was formed in 1836.[5] The St. Helens iron founders were certainly members before 1838 ; it is significant to note that during the trade union activity of 1831 the Tontine Coffee House, across the road from the St. Helens Foundry, was for a time re-named the Moulders' Arms.[6]

These early trade clubs were not confined entirely to skilled craftsmen. The Chemists' Society, just mentioned, was made up of workers in the alkali industry. The coalminers, too, the largest group in the local community, were powerful supporters of friendly societies. When a speaker at the Miners' Association meeting in Manchester in January 1844 urged the extension of friendly society facilities to union members, objections were raised on the grounds that " as probably the majority of colliers already belonged to benefit societies ... it would be hard to require them to subscribe to one in connection with the union."[7] The miners' enthusiasm for friendly societies was of comparatively long standing. The earliest club in the St. Helens district of which we have any record is the Fire Engine Society of Parr, the rules

---

[1] Rules at Pilkington Brothers Ltd.

[2] The file of the *Flint Glassmakers' Magazine* mentioned by the Webbs in their *History of Trade Unionism* (1935, 197n) as being in the possession of the Birmingham Trades Council, is now kept by C.D. Stanier, Esq., M.B.E., General Secretary of the National Union of Flint Glassworkers.

[3] *Lpool. Merc.*, 30 Oct., 1846.

[4] The Operative House Carpenters and Joiners of St. Helens held their 34th anniversary in 1864. *St. H. N.*, 10 Sept., 1864.

[5] 29th anniversary reported in the *St. H. Standard*, 1 Sept., 1865.

[6] Annual Report of the Friendly Society of Iron Founders, 1894 ; P.R.O., H.O. 52/13, deposition of James Chisnall.

[7] *Manchester Guardian*, 6 Jan., 1844.

of which are dated 6 July, 1776.[1] At this time, Parr, where the Canal first entered the coalfield, was the chief centre of mining activity and it seems certain that membership of the Fire Engine Society, as its name implies, was made up mostly, if not entirely, of miners. The parchment on which the rules have been written is in such a decayed condition that its survival is nothing less than a stroke of good fortune. Indeed, one wonders how many other such societies there may have been whose records have been lost on account of the toll taken by age and damp.

The historian may perhaps be permitted to cite human nature as his authority in claiming that men from the same industry do not meet together regularly without discussing their work and their pay, and it becomes very difficult to distinguish between the friendly society confined to workers in one industry and the trade union, particularly in these early days when friendly societies were blessed as instruments of thrift and trade unions were damned as hotbeds of radicalism. The glassmakers' societies certainly negotiated hours of work and rates of pay with their masters as well as providing friendly society facilities. It seems likely that the other craft societies did the same. For the coal-miner, however, such action was not so easy, partly because he was more often than not illterate—in 1884 a delegate claimed that three-quarters of the union's 32,000 members could not read[2]; partly because there was a greater gulf fixed between the collier and his master than between the trained craftsman and his employer; and partly because the miners were scattered in relatively small groups throughout each mining district. The colliers belonged to a number of different friendly societies while the proprietors were members of one association. It is hardly surprising that when, in 1819,[3] we learn of the local miners' first efforts to take strike action, there is more than a suggestion that the attempted union was based upon an amalgamation of the several friendly societies in which the miners were interested.

This first strike collapsed and it was not until the wave of trade union activity in 1830-1 that another general stoppage occurred at the St. Helens coalfield. On this second occasion the men were no longer making an isolated demonstration for the benefit of their own particular masters but were taking part in

[1] Registry of Friendly Societies. No. 547 Lancs. Members contributed 8d. per month and an additional 6d., per month if the funds amounted to less than £1 per head. The only benefit that can still be read is a super-annuation payment of 3/- per week for infirm members. " Every member reduced by misfortunes (who cannot come under the denomination of superannuated) is recommended to the Society as worthy of their pity and regard. And that they do receive such an allowance as a majority of a full club shall judge proper."

[2] *Manchester Guardian*, 10 Jan., 1844.

[3] Above, pp. 159-64.

a much wider movement which deserves to be given greater
attention than it has so far received. From headquarters at
Bolton, the union directed the activities of lodges throughout
the Lancashire, Shropshire and North and South Wales coalfields.[1] The original hope was to stage a general strike but this
could not be done ; the union, therefore, fell back upon demanding increases in pay district by district.[2] At the beginning
of October 1830, it was reported that the colliers at Worsley,
Hulton, Radcliffe, Hindley, Ringley, Darwen, Pendleton, West-
leigh, Tyldesley, Shackerley, Bedford " and other places "
returned to work for a 25 per cent. increase in pay.[3] The next
month the miners of Oldham, Ashton and Stalybridge obtained
a 33⅓ per cent. advance,[4] and in January 1831 the North Wales
men secured an addition to their slender earnings.[5] It was now
the turn of St. Helens to stand out for higher wages ; early in
February, 1831, every collier in the neighbourhood was reported
to be on strike and the inhabitants were expecting to have to buy
their coal from other parts of the county.[6]

At the beginning of March, Charles Orrell reported to Lord
Derby that

> " there have been several processions of colliers in large bodies
> with waggons attended by music parading the country begging
> coals, money or liquor, the continuance of which has been
> properly put an end to by the interference of the police at
> Liverpool and other distant places to which they had pro-
> ceeded . . ."[7]

The union members had secured some arms and at night used to
fire at the windows of cottages inhabited by knobsticks, as the
non-union men were called.[8] These processions and acts of
violence struck fear into the hearts of the rest of the population
many of whom remembered 1819 only too well. When a number
of miners were brought to St. Helens from other coalfields in an

[1] Emlyn Rogers, *The History of Trade Unionism in the Coal Mining
Industry of North Wales to 1914* (M.A. thesis, U.C.N.W., 1928), 80 ;
A. H. John, *op. cit.*, 91.

[2] P.R.O., H.O. 40/26. Communication from William Hulton, 22 Oct.,
1830.

[3] *Manchester Courier*, 2 Oct., 1830.

[4] Rogers, *op. cit.*, 33.

[5] *Chester Chronicle*, 14 Jan., 1831, quoted in Rogers, *op. cit.*, 52.

[6] *Lpool. Merc.*, 11 Feb., 1831. See also correspondence in this paper
on 14, 28 Jan., 25 Feb., 11, 18, 25 March and 1 April, 1831.

[7] P.R.O., H.O., 52/13.

[8] *Ibid.*, deposition of Richard Fletcher, collier, of Peasley Cross, 2 March,
1831.

attempt to break the strike, the local property owners, fearing greater acts of lawlessness, petitioned for a troop of horse to be sent to prevent further disorder. Cavalry was particularly requested because experience during the previous strike had shown that Special Constables were " not of the slightest utility and even Infantry Soldiers were at that time of little service." A regiment of the 10th Hussars, *en route* to Ireland, was diverted to St. Helens in response to this appeal for protection.[1]

At the end of March Charles Orrell wrote again to Lord Derby reporting that the differences between masters and men had been " adjusted . . . partially " at collieries on the estates of Sir John Gerard and Mr. Legh in Ashton and Haydock townships, but that

" in the works nearer to St. Helens the diabolical spirit, if I may be allowed the expression, appears to have increased. A meeting of the masters and a deputation from the men took place at Prescot on Monday 14th at the suggestion and particular request of Col. Williams who wished to act as umpire with some other Gentlemen. The result of the meeting was such as might well be anticipated, the deputation could not stand the charge but abruptly left the town hall to the great chagrin and disappointment of the Col : the effect of the discomfiture upon the colliers has been such as to increase the spirit of disaffection and disorder and had drawn forth repeated and most dreadful threats. Very late on Tuesday evening last I received intimation that some dreadful outrages were meditated that night and the following, upon which I immediately wrote to Captain Wallington the officer in command of the division of the 10th Hussars stationed at St. Helens with a request that a party of the troops might be in immediate readiness if wanted, which was most promptly complied with ; I also sent instructions to the various collieries for an increase of the number of their private or workingmen's guard. These precautions undoubtedly prevented greater outrages than really did take place. Between 12 and one o'clock in the morning an attack was made upon the persons stationed at a small colliery a short distance from my house by a party armed with guns loaded with bullets and notwithstanding the repeated firing, most providentially no one was hurt. . . . Such occurrences as the above and many more which we are unfortunately obliged to witness call most urgently upon Goverment [*sic*] for its interference and exertions to destroy the union which exists to an alarming degree in this country."[2]

In the end " adjustments " were made at St. Helens as they had

---

[1] *Ibid.*, Orrell to Melbourne, 13 April, 1831.

[2] *Ibid.*, letter dated 28 March, 1831.

been made elsewhere.[1] But the union was not strong enough to last. Having gained its immediate object, the men withdrew their support and the branches fell away.

The sworn testimony of ex-members of the union, enclosed by Orrell with his reports, reveal in its procedure and organisation much that was based upon friendly society practice. One man, for example, described taking the oath of allegiance to the union as follows :

> " The Members met in a Room up Stairs, at the bottom of the Stairs stood a Man who asked me to walk up, when I got up stairs another Man whose name I do not know put a Handkerchief round my Eyes and took me into a small Room adjoining the one where the Members were assembled—some person here gave me a Book which I believe was a Bible. I was then desired to go down upon my knees. I did so and the person administered an oath to me. I cannot recollect the precise words of the oath . . . after I had taken the Oath, the bandage was taken off my Eyes and I was pushed into the Room where the members were assembled."[2]

This form of swearing-in was very reminiscent of the mummery then the fashion when new members were admitted to friendly societies. On the occasion just cited the ceremony took place at the Seven Stars in Eccleston, where the union had a branch lodge. The local headquarters were at the Tontine Coffee House in St. Helens.[3] This was the same kind of district organisation as the rapidly-spreading Oddfellows were using. The parallels are too close to escape notice.

Twelve years passed before the St. Helens miners again combined in an attempt to secure an increase in their earnings. On this occasion they were part of the Miners' Association of Great Britain and Ireland, formed at Wakefield late in 1842.[4] At a meeting held on the Moorflat at St. Helens in October, 1843, between 1,500 and 2,000 colliers heard a union spokesman refer with contempt to the previous " little strikes and little unions [which] had done ill instead of good." Another proclaimed that

---

[1] A union leader named Berry told a meeting of colliers at St. Helens in 1843 that, in 1831, " they apparently gained their object ; they induced the masters to consent to an advance ; an advance of 1/- a ton was gained and the masters pocketed 9½d. or 10d. and gave the men only 2d. or 2½d." *Lpool. Merc.*, 13 Oct., 1843.

[2] P.R.O., H.O. 52/13. Deposition of Thomas Hartleigh.

[3] *Ibid.*, Orrell to Melbourne, 13 April, 1831. The Tontine Coffee House did not specialise in the sale of coffee.

[4] Information from Mr. A. J. Taylor, University College, London.

" In the strike of 1831 they had taught the masters their alphabet, and now they would teach them the reading-made-easy."[1]

This provides an interesting sidelight upon the growth of education in the mining districts, but it proved to be an empty boast so far as the strength of the union was concerned.

The union's weaknesses were clearly revealed at a national delegate meeting held in Manchester in January, 1844. Its official policy had already been outlined to a gathering of miners at St. Helens only a fortnight before :

" Work short time ; bare the banks ; and if they do not do you justice . . . strike from Land's End to John o' Groats. After that let there be no parading through the streets—no mobbing. Go home and play with the children. Sit by the fireside and if you have fire to burn, play at marbles with the cinders. Stop there for a week ; and will they come to ? Yes. And why ? Because they dare do no other. If such a thing as a strike took place, Sir Robert Peel would not feel comfortable in his seat ; because if they stood out, they would put a stop to all the machinery and manufactures and there would be a revolution, which all well-meaning men would wish to drive from the country. The consequence would be that they would have the sympathy of the public, and the masters would be compelled to give them their wages."[2]

At Manchester, however, there was a sharp division of opinion as to the efficacy of a strike at that time and when a delegate moved that the strike question be held over until the next conference, " a tumultuous discussion " is said to have taken place.[3] The great coalfield of the north-east was in favour of strike action, but only in April when their yearly bond expired. Some speakers counselled moderation and others stressed that many of their members were straining at the leash and expecting the conference to order an immediate stoppage. Lancashire, in particular, " was expecting nothing but a general strike " and, indeed, even while the delegates were still involved in their heated argument, news arrived that some colliers had stopped work that very day at St. Helens and Bolton. The conference finally decided not to call a strike until the next meeting. Until then no partial strikes were to be recognized and delegates were to be sent to explain the position to the strikers in an effort to get them back to work until such time as a general strike could be called. In the meantime the miners' leaders were to try to negotiate an increase in pay with the masters' representatives.

[1] *Lpool. Merc.*, 13 Oct., 1843.

[2] *Lpool. Merc.* 15 Dec., 1843.

[3] *Manchester Guardian*, 6 Jan., 1844. See also issues of 3 and 10 Jan.

But at St. Helens the irresponsible and emotional oratory of the agitators had proved most effective. The men turned down an offer of an increase in pay of 9d. per work[1] and numbers of them went on strike, to be followed soon afterwards by the rest, even though, as it was reported at the time, " the men are conscious that they have made no preparation for such a move and know that their masters are fully aware of the fact."[2]   A week came and went but there were no signs that the masters would come to terms as the union agitator had forecast. Three weeks later acute distress was being experienced, for the strikers received no aid from elsewhere since their action had not been officially endorsed.   Some sought other work ; others scoured the countryside for food or were forced to beg in the town.[3] A week later, after the strike had lasted a month, the men offered to return to work at the advance which they had turned down,[4] but the stoppage was prolonged by the masters' demand that they should bind themselves for a year—a practice customary in the north-east but not in Lancashire—and renounce the union. These demands were refused and the coal proprietors thereupon sought labour from Staffordshire and Shropshire.   The arrival of these knobsticks provoked a serious riot, in the course of which the miners stoned the newly-introduced police force as well as the strike breakers.[5]   Ten of the ringleaders were sent to Kirkdale Gaol to await trial and a detachment of Foot was brought over from Manchester to preserve order.[6] A settlement was eventually reached. The owners agreed not to debar union men from their employment nor to introduce the yearly bond.

The men returned to work early in March[7] ; a month later the colliers of the north-east came out on strike as they had promised to do.[8] The union's lack of co-ordination discredited it in the eyes of many local miners and, though an association of some kind was usual among them after 1844, it was many years before any union gained such a large and enthusiastic membership as there had been at the close of 1843 before the ill-timed and disastrous strike took place.

[1] *Manchester Guardian*, 10 Jan., 1844.

[2] *Ibid.*, 24 Jan., 1844.

[3] *Ibid.*, 14 Feb., 1844.

[4] *Lpool. Merc.*, 23 Feb., 1844.

[5] *Lpool. Merc.*, 1 March, 1844 ; L.R.O., QJD 1/194, depositions of Supt. Storey and others.

[6] *Lpool. Merc.*, 1 March, 1844.

[7] *Ibid.*, 15 March, 1844.

[8] *The Times*, 15 Sept., 1845 ; E. Welbourne, *The Miner's Unions of Northumberland and Durham* (Cambridge, 1923), 66 *et seq.*

By the 1840s, then, the principle of association was well known at St. Helens both among masters and men and the unit of association, though usually quite small, was tending to grow. The window glass manufacturers had progressed beyond the regional group. The coalminers were already feeling their way towards a national body. The skilled craftsmen had already achieved some measure of success in this direction. The large Unity friendly societies were gradually ousting the older, independent clubs.

At first glance, these modest organisations may appear of little moment when set alongside their later counterparts, much larger and all-embracing. The benefit club may seem a very poor substitute for the lodge of a powerful trade union, for instance. That such a high proportion of the local community could afford to contribute to these organisations is, however, significant.

CHAPTER XIX

COLLIERS, IRISH, GLASSMAKERS AND OTHERS

IN 1830 St. Helens was still little more than a coalmining district. As the glass and chemical industries grew up and became more important, coal gradually ceased to predominate and, by the end of the century, more people were employed at the glassworks than in the coalmines. But in the 1840s this transition was only in its early stages and the grimy face of the collier returning from his day's work was still the most familiar sight in the neighbourhood.[1]

To some extent the miner lived a life of isolation ; his place of work, near to which he was obliged to live, was often some distance from any town. The population of Parr, for instance, was made up very largely of a number of scattered mining communities, and the families of colliers had little occasion to mix with anyone else. They were separate and distinct from the rest of the population who, in turn, tended to look down upon them for peculiarities and habits which were bred by isolation and the rough nature of their work. Samuel Bishop, the flint glass manufacturer, remarked in the middle of the century :

" Colliers have a bad name ; they used to live as it were isolated from every one, and were rough and ignorant ; to some extent they are so still but towns have grown up round coal pits of late years . . . the colliers have now been forced to mix more with their fellows and have improved accordingly."[2]

The outstanding trait of the collier was, without doubt, his independent spirit and this arose from his terms of employment. He acted, as a visitor to Parr remarked, " more in the character of a contractor with the proprietor for the delivery of coal than as a regular labourer."[3] He was paid according to the amount of coal he hewed and, in turn, out of his fortnightly reckoning, he paid his assistants, known as drawers or waggoners, to transport the coal he had cut to the foot of the pit shaft. At St. Helens the collier's hours of work were not set out in any bond or fixed contract dictating the terms of employment. He worked only until he had earned enough to maintain himself and his family ; in practice, during the 1840s he usually went down the pit for

---

[1] In 1851, of the 14, 675 men over 20 years of age in the Prescot registration district, 1,422 described themselves as coalminers and 615 as glassmakers. For the figures at the end of the century, see below, p. 451.

[2] Ch. Emp. Comm., 4th Report, 1865 [8357] XX, 271.

[3] *An Illustrated Itinerary of the County of Lancaster* (1842) 100.

eight hours a day on five days a week.[1] His assistants took longer to remove the coal to the foot of the shaft than the collier had taken to cut it. In consequence, the drawers worked a longer day of eleven or twelve hours.[2]

A miner, if possible, employed his own family, and it was usually to assist husbands and fathers that many women and children descended the pit. The visitor to Parr reported in 1842 :

> " A proprietor engages a collier, who himself excavates the coal alone, and he employs either his own family (if he have any), or pays assistants, generally women and children, to convey the coal which he has cut out, to the foot of the shaft. . . . A collier would pay twelve or thirteen shillings a week to these assistants ; but if they are of his own family he saves money, as generally his wife and all his children are employed in the pits . . ."[3]

It would seem, therefore, that the underground employment of women and children was the logical outcome of the miner's direct contract with his master. Under the domestic system it was customary for the wife and children to assist the head of the family and this method of work appears to have been applied to coalmining. Instead of the raw materials being " put out," a seam of coal, leased by the coal proprietor from the landowner, was made accessible for the collier to hew, and the rest of the family assisted by carrying it away. To present-day thinking, the employment of women and young children in the darkness underground is abhorrent. Yet, it is possible that in the earliest stages of coal-getting when the coal pit was often little more than a shallow working of the outcrop, the employment of a few families to cut the surface seam was not necessarily open to grave abuse. It was when the pits became deeper and the workings more extensive, causing the accident rate to increase and the labour of the drawers to be heavier, that the family system became quite outdated and totally unsuited to the changed conditions. In time, women and children came to be employed indiscriminately

---

[1] *Ibid.*, J. L. Kennedy, in a report on the South Lancashire coalfield to the Ch. Emp. Comm. (1842 [382] XVII, 176), stated that regular colliers worked about eight hours a day on not more than ten days to the fortnight " excepting under peculiar circumstances when they may probably reach eleven." This was confirmed by a trade union leader, speaking at St. Helens in 1843 : " Five shillings a day for eight hours of work was only 25/- a week ; for anybody who knew anything of the working of a colliery knew that Monday and Saturday never made more than one day between them". (*Lpool. Merc.* 15 Dec., 1843).

[2] Ch. Emp. Comm. Kennedy, *op. cit.*, 176.

[3] *Illustrated Itinerary*, 100. The Civil Death Registers show that in a local colliery accident in 1847, of 8 people killed, 5 belonged to one family, 2 of them being colliers aged 45 and 22, and 3 drawers, aged 17, 15 and 10. The son of another victim had been with his father just before the accident. *Lpool. Merc.* 8 June, 1847).

T

as hired servants, though in the St. Helens Civil Death Registers
women and children killed in mining accidents were still usually
described in the 1840s not generically as drawers, but as the
wives or daughters of particular colliers.   By the 1830s the
industry was growing at such a rate that their presence in the
mines had become a disgrace.[1]

Of the dangers of the collier's occupation, there can be no
doubt. In the years immediately before a code of mining regulations was formulated and backed by legislation, gruesome
accidents occurred. There was a particularly dangerous interval
between the more intensive exploitation of the coalfields and the
beginning of effective supervision underground. During this
period accidents in the pits were a frequent occurrence.

Some of them were caused by overwinding, the engineman
not stopping the ascending tub until both it and its occupants
had been carried over the headgear.[2] Other mishaps occurred
when the men were tipped out of tubs descending or about to
descend. We learn, for instance, that Joseph Whittle, an engine
tenter at Blackbrook,

" stepping into the bucket at the top . . . somehow over-reached
himself, and, falling out of the tub, was dashed to pieces. A
fellow-workman who was at the bottom, hearing a noise of
something coming down, hastily stepped out of the way, when
two legs and a thigh and arm fell where he had been standing ;
also a hat and lamp, and immediately after the head, body and
remaining arm and thigh, all of which he gathered up, put in a
sheet and conveyed to the top, while a shell, hastily made up
by the carpenter, was used to convey the remains to his
dwelling—Verdict, accidental death."[3]

Before the days of adequate guides and cages,[4] the ascending tub

[1] Although the banishment of women and children from underground
work in the coalmines is usually considered from the moral point of view,
there were also strong material considerations to be taken into account
Women and children cannot have been at all suited to the additional exertions which the larger underground workings demanded.   In the north-east
at the end of the eighteenth century, when extensive pits came into being,
women ceased to be employed there underground.   T. S. Ashton and J
Sykes, *The Coal Industry of the Eighteenth Century* (Manchester, 1929), 21.

[2] E.g. *Wigan Gazette* 13 July, 1838.   Twenty years later, Knowles's
Patent Disconnecting Apparatus was introduced to the district.

[3] *Lpool. Merc.* 7 Feb., 1845.

[4] An accident at a St. Helens coalpit in 1829 was attributed to " want
of conductors " (*Lpool. Merc.* 6 Feb., 1829).   In 1842, however, Kennedy
(*op. cit.*, 153) stated that at the deep mines at St. Helens, wooden side
girders were usual.   Cages were used in the north-east so early as 1834
(Robert L. Galloway, *A History of Coal Mining in Great Britain*, 1882, 216)
but the first indication of their introduction into the St. Helens coalfield
is a note in the Civil Death Register on 17 Aug., 1849 that a cage had killed
a blacksmith working in a coalmine.

sometimes caught against the other tub on its way down and the men were tipped out, if they were unable to hold on to the bucket or the rope.[1] Pieces of stone or earth, protruding from the sides of the shaft, also led to accidents of this kind.

In the workings themselves deaths were caused regularly from falls of roof. Explosions were very occasional but became more frequent in the later 1840s. These explosions, however, usually affected only a small number who happened to be at work in that part of the pit and there is no evidence at St. Helens of colliery disasters on the scale of those already occurring in other coalfields.[2]

From July, 1837, it is possible to calculate the total number of colliery deaths from the Civil Death Registers. About a dozen or fourteen people lost their lives in local coalmines every year up to 1849, excluding those killed in explosions. Such greater calamities increased the total to 20 in 1838 and to 27 in 1847. These were the deaths. We do not know how many more poor unfortunates were partially or totally maimed, crippled or burnt in pits which were becoming more dangerous every year.

Such were the conditions which the women and children endured for longer hours than the colliers, because it was impossible to clear the coal as quickly as it was cut. As the miners extended their labyrinth of galleries farther from the foot of the shaft, the drawers' labour became more arduous. In some collieries, moreover, all the coal had been dug on the rise and down-brows had to be cut, the drawers having to drag, pull or carry their loads up a slope to the main levels instead of having the force of gravity in their favour.[3] To what extent their task had been made easier by the introduction of ponies and underground tramways, is not clear. On the one hand, the Rushy Park Colliery was equipped not only with tramways but with an underground gin to haul the trucks.[4] On the other, St. Helens

---

[1] E.g. *Lpool. Merc.* 6 Feb., 1829 ; *Wigan Gazette* 29 Oct., 1841.

[2] For the chief explosions, see *Lpool. Merc.* 13 Feb., 1835 ; *Wigan Gazette* 8 June, 1838 ; *Lpool. Merc.* 29 Jan., 4 June, 1847 ; 22 Feb., 1848 ; 5 March, 26 June and 12 July, 1849. The purchase of safety lamps is first encountered in the Bromilow Diary, 22 April, 1829, and most of the explosions in the 1830s and 1840s appear to have been caused by miners removing the tops of their lamps to obtain a brighter light so that they could cut more coal. In some pits, thought to be free of explosive gas, candles continued to be used (q.v. *Lpool. Merc.*, 8 June, 1847).

[3] Ch. Emp. Comm., Kennedy, *op. cit.*, 152.

[4] *Ibid.*, 152, 160. Steam engines are said to have been introduced to the Lancashire coalfield in 1822 for hauling from the dip (*Historical Review of Coal Mining*, 1924, 95). According to his Diary, Bromilow was installing trams and railways underground in 1829 at one of his collieries. The visitor to Parr in 1842 (*Illustrated Itinerary*, 100) stated that coal was taken to the pit bottom " in baskets on a kind of railway laid along the different levels." In 1847 ponies were being used underground at Gerard's Bridge (*Lpool. Merc.* 4 June, 1847).

was singled out as one of those districts where the tubs
of coal were still placed on a wooden sledge and dragged along
the floor by the drawer, possibly assisted by a thrutcher who
pushed the sledge from behind.[1]

State intervention to end the dangerous drudgery of these
women and young children and to establish a system of careful
inspection was long overdue in 1842 when the first Mines
Regulation Act was passed.[2]   By its provisions, women and
children under ten were forbidden to work underground from
1 March, 1843, and a mining commissioner was appointed. The
measure had no immediate effect at St. Helens, however, for the
miners themselves were not anxious to dispense with the services
of women and children, who continued to be employed underground in the St. Helens district until the autumn of 1846.[3]
Moreover Mr. Tremenheere, the Commissioner, was not empowered to inspect the workings underground but conducted his
investigations by correspondence.[4] This farcical state of affairs
was ended in 1850 when a small force of inspectors started to go
down the pits to " inspect, report and suggest."[5] This was only
the beginning of effective control ; the earliest surviving copies of
safety regulations at local collieries date from the early 1850s.[6]

The wage which the collier received for his hard and dangerous
daily stint is not easy to assess, for there are so many variables
to be taken into account. To a large degree, the miner himself
decided the amount of his fortnightly reckoning. If he worked
hard, he would obviously be earning considerably more than if he
played half the week. To some extent local conditions in the mine
were an important factor, too. If he worked a fiery seam, he
received proportionately higher pay, a form of danger money,
but, on the other hand, if he was clearing rubbish or dirt or
cutting brows he received proportionately less. Some seams were
easier to get than others and consequently miners in one part of a
colliery could earn more than miners in another, though it was
usual for the rate to depend on the difficulty of the seam. Then
there were the payments which the collier had to make to his
drawers ; and other payments to the proprietor for candles and
for the repair and sharpening of his tools. There are also to be
taken into account the more general wage fluctuations according

[1] Ch. Emp. Comm., Kennedy, *op. cit.*, 154.

[2] 5 & 6 Vict., cap. 99.

[3] *Lpool. Merc.* 7 Nov., 1845 ; 25 Sept., 1846.   Reports of the Mining
Commissioner, 1845-7.

[4] Evidence of Tremenheere to the S.C. (House of Lords) on Accidents
in Coal Mines, 1849 [613] VII, qq. 196, 261.

[5] Evidence of David Swallow to the S.C. on Accidents in Coal Mines,
1853 [691] XX, 29.

[6] Bromilow Papers.

to the state of trade, for the miner's pay always depended on the selling price of coal.

It is possible, however, bearing in mind these variations, to reach a rough idea of a collier's earnings from the various claims made by the masters and the unions during the strikes in 1818, 1831 and 1844.

In 1819 the coal trade was slack. Wages had been reduced three years previously and the demand was so small that only three-quarters of the total available labour force could be kept fully employed. But instead of laying off a quarter of the men, the proprietors had chosen to reduce the hours of work of everyone by a quarter. It was, therefore, a period when earnings were abnormally low. Yet some of the colliers' wages, published by the J.P.'s early in 1819 in an effort to allay discontent, showed that, after deducting pay for candles and drawers, it was still possible, despite the slump, for a miner to take home between 17s. and 24s. 2d. per week, as well as 3 cwts. of free coal if he was a householder. From these figures, argued the Justices, a conscientious workman, despite the depression, could still earn a guinea a week himself, in addition to whatever the rest of his family could make.[1]

Unfortunately we do not possess the miners' counter claims, so we cannot tell what the minimum reckonings were. In 1831, however, the position was reversed, for the union leaders were busily writing to the press, while the coal proprietors held their peace. John Finch—possibly the temperance reformer who later became governor of Robert Owen's Queenwood Community—asserted that some colliers were only receiving 13s. a week after making the necessary deductions.[2] Another propagandist, who claimed to have inspected the books, found that some workmen received only 11s. and, although he admitted that others received 15s., it was, he submitted, " very rare " for a collier to reach this figure.[3] That these claims were almost certainly set too low, is clear from a letter sent by James Bromilow to his father at the time of the strike. James Bromilow happened to be visiting Wrexham just after the miners there had secured their increase and he wrote :

" Our Colliers have little reason to complain in comparison with those about Wrexham. As Mr. Briscoe says, at the advanced price it would be barely possible for a man to get 3/- p. day . . . they have been getting as little as 9/- or 10/- a week."[4]

Presumably, therefore, at St. Helens it was customary at this time

[1] Above, pp. 159-63.   Bromilow Papers, poster dated 19 Feb., 1819.
[2] Lpool. Merc. 14 Jan., 1831.
[3] Lpool. Merc. 1 April, 1831.   Letter from " A Friend of the Union."
[4] Bromilow Papers.   James Bromilow to William Bromilow, 9 Feb., 1831.

for the collier to earn more than 3s. a day for five days a week and this seems to be confirmed by the demand of the union for 5s. a day of eight hours and 6s. " if it was wet work."[1]

More information about rates of pay has survived from the struggle of 1844. At the close of 1843 the miners sent their employers a series of notes in which was stated the price they were receiving per work of six tons at various collieries : 5s. for the Rushy Park seam and 9s. for the thinner and more difficult Little Delf seam at the Rushy Park Colliery, for instance ; 5s. and 5s. 9d. at the Bird i' th' Hand (or Royal) and Blackbrook Collieries.[2] Later they claimed that at the Blackbrook Colliery two men had only earned 34s. in a fortnight, at the Royal Colliery three men had received just under 48s. for a fortnight's work, and at Rushy Park Colliery six men had between them only earned £6 13s. 0d. in the same length of time. The proprietors issued a rebuttal of these claims[3] in which they quoted pay sheets to show that each of these men (presumably singled out by the union as good examples of underpaid employees) was in fact earning about 4s. a day clear, or about 20s. a week. This would agree with the evidence of an underlooker in another part of the coalfield that the miner himself earned 20s. to 25s. a week,[4] his assistants receiving 4s. to 15s.[5] It accords, too, with evidence from Parr itself in 1842 that if a miner had members of his own family to help him, he might possibly make up to 40s. a week, not having to pay the usual 12s or 13s. for such assistance.[6]

This was at a time when trade was depressed. In 1844, an increase of 9d. a work (equivalent, it was said, to about 7s. per fortnightly reckoning)[7] was given to the men because trade was picking up again and the price of coal had been advanced. At the end of the next year " One of the Coal Trade," who claimed to have had much sympathy with the colliers two years previously in their struggle to obtain this increase, was able to write :

" . . . the amount of coal is only half as much as what is required and not half as much as what they might produce by working eight hours regularly per day. Instead of this, they can idle away entire days or they will work two or three hours a day while the masters must employ as many weekly hands and as much machinery as if a whole week's work was done."[8]

[1] P.R.O., H.O. 53/13. Deposition of Thomas Hartleigh.

[2] Bromilow Papers.

[3] St. H. Ref. Lib., Placard entitled *Public Facts*, Ansdell Papers.

[4] Ch. Emp. Comm., Kennedy, *op. cit.*, 204.

[5] *Ibid.*, 180.

[6] *Illustrated Itinerary*, 100.

[7] *Manchester Guardian* 10 Jan., 1844.

[8] *Lpool. Merc.* 21 Nov., 1845.

This was a highly partisan letter ; but it must have been based on good evidence. It was, indeed, a repetition of a grumble which had already been heard forty years earlier during a similar period of prosperity.

" . . . the labouring collier finds his services sought after, and instead of soliciting employment, that employment courting him, becomes saucy. His earnings permit him to idle half the week in an ale-house, which is to him enjoyment ; and by this debauched state of the working colliers, double the number of hands are required to what used to be, for the same quantum of work . . ."[1]

Comment in this vein makes it reasonably certain that when trade was booming, the miner was able to earn a sufficient amount to buy himself some additional leisure.

To summarise : colliers' earnings appear to have averaged 20s. to 25s. for a full week's work during the period 1820-45. During periods of depression they may have been lower and in times of prosperity they were almost certainly higher ; often family earnings must have added to the fortnightly reckoning very considerably. With members of the family helping as drawers, a collier could probably make as much as a skilled craftsman and even if he had to hire his own labour, he was still in the same wage group as a coarse yarn spinner.[2] It is impossible to resist the conclusion that the collier ought to be classed among the higher-paid workers. He usually had a little to spare when essentials—often very bare necessities in his case[3]—had been paid for. And sometimes, we suspect, he had more than a little to spare. Whether the collier was adequately compensated for the dangers and difficulties of his job at this time, will continue to raise conflicting opinions : that he was better off financially than many of his fellow workers in other occupations, there can be little doubt.

It was natural that men whose life was hard and dangerous should in their leisure time appear somewhat reckless and rough to those who knew nothing of conditions below ground. When Samuel Bishop referred to colliery folk as " rough and ignorant " he was thinking of them when their work was over. They were

---

[1] *Remarks on the Salt Trade* (Liverpool, 1804), 11.

[2] An iron moulder, for instance, was earning 30/- a week in 1832 and 36/- in 1845-6 (Clapham, *op. cit.*, I, 550) and a skilled journeyman bricklayer was receiving 30/- to 40/- a week (*ibid.*, 165). A third-grade male spinner turning out coarse yarn made 21/- in 1836 but only 18/- in 1849 (*ibid.*, 550-1).

[3] A colliery underlooker near Stalybridge estimated in 1842 (Ch. Emp. Comm., Kennedy *op. cit.*, 204) that a miner needed to spend on himself in one year only 33/- on a suit, 30/- on two singlets and two shirts and 12/- or 13/- on clogs. He would pay 5/- a week for fuel and rent. At St. Helens, however, the married miner had free coal.

great drinkers, gamblers and fighters. The miner's love of drink was a dominant theme in union leaders' speeches in later years ;[1] dog-fighting and pigeon-flying were favourite pastimes ;[2] prize fights, still very popular in the district even when no longer lawful,[3] and foot-racing were two familiar events giving ample scope for gambling : at one foot race in 1845, for instance, nearly £1,000 was said to have changed hands.[4] Colliers were also very fond of fighting among themselves in the most brutal manner. Although there are occasional local references to these extremely crude and primitive combats, none of them provides such a telling description as the following interview about a fight elsewhere on the Lancashire coalfield :

" Have you any fights?—Yes ; the colliers are great fighters and wrestlers. On Christmas Day I saw twelve pitch battles [sic] with colliers.

Were they stand up fights?—No ; it is all up and down fighting here. They fought quite naked, excepting their clogs. When one has the other down on the ground, he first endeavours to choke him by squeezing his throat, then he kicks him on the head with his clogs. Sometimes they are very severely injured ; that man you saw today with a piece out of his shoulder is a great fighter."[5]

It is hardly surprising that during the strikes and disturbances the local magistrates and others feared for their safety.

The miners formed the central core of what contemporaries were so fond of calling " the labouring population." So long as women and children continued to work in the pits, the mining community was insulated from the rest of the inhabitants of the district by their uncouth behaviour. Since they were sent down the mines so early, their children had hardly any opportunities of going to day school though in this respect the outlook was already brightening by 1840.[6] Colliers invariably married girls " out of the pit " so that they could help them in their coal-getting. The 1842 Coal Mines Act, however, led to great changes, particularly to a more frequent association between the mining

[1] William Pickard, one of the leaders, even asserted that union members threatened to dismiss him for preaching temperance and thrift (evidence to the S.C. on Coal, 1873, X, qq. 4209-10).

[2] Wigan Gazette 26 April, 1839 ; St. H. Stand., 31 Aug. 1872.

[3] Wigan Gazette 21 Oct., 1836 ; 21 June, 1839 ; St. H. N. 17 Oct., 1860, 27 April, 1861, 18 March, 1865, 8 April, 1865.

[4] Lpool. Merc. 16 May, 1845.

[5] Ch. Emp. Comm., Kennedy, op. cit., 185.   For a local colliers' fight, Wigan Gazette 22 Nov., 1839.

[6] Ch. Emp. Comm., Kennedy, op. cit., 149.   Cf. Illustrated Itinerary, 100.

community and the rest of the population. The Act also brought
its problems so far as St. Helens was concerned, for there were no
textile mills to absorb the female labour thus made available.
Many girls had to leave the district and seek employment elsewhere, a fact which was to affect the social structure of the town
considerably in later years.[1]

The unusual characteristics of the coalmining community
were the result of their occupation : those of the Irish were
due to their racial background. They came from a country desperately poor and plagued by over-population. After a visit to
Ireland in 1825, Sir Walter Scott noted in his *Journal* :

> " Their poverty is not exaggerated : it is on the extreme verge
> of human misery ; their cottages would scarce serve for pig-
> styes, even in Scotland, and their rags seem the very refuse of a
> rag-shop, and are disposed on their bodies with such ingenious
> variety of wretchedness that you would think nothing but some
> sort of perverted taste could have assembled so many shreds
> together."[2]

As he travelled through Ireland in search of orders, William
Pilkington experienced the same sights. He was everywhere confronted by swarms of ragged beggars : " misery in its worst
features—squalid filth and poverty, disease, deformity and every
thing which can distress and shock your feelings stands with
outstretched hands until your car again proceeds."[3]

When these poverty-stricken unfortunates visited England in
search of work, they were looked upon as outcasts of inferior race.
A few years before the Act of Union in 1800, two magistrates
from near Manchester wrote of " a very numerous and *foreign*
population (especially from Ireland), estranged, unconnected and
in general composed of persons who are in a species of exile."[4]
When this was written, the Irish were still " tied to the country "[5]
and usually came to England only as seasonal workers. It was not
until the 1820s that, drawn by higher wages or driven by famine,
they started to settle in Britain, and not until the 1840s that the
trickle of migrants became a torrent. The population of Ireland,
having grown from almost 5,500,000 in 1801 to over 8,000,000 in
1841, was reduced to 6,600,000 ten years later. In the later '40s,

---

[1] Below, p. 427.

[2] *Sir Walter Scott's Journal* (Nelson ed. n.d.) *sub* 20 Nov., 1825.

[3] Pilkington Brothers Ltd., William Pilkington to Richard Pilkington,
7 Nov., 1834.

[4] A. Aspinall, *The Early English Trade Unions* (1949), 1.

[5] *Arthur Young's Tour in Ireland*, ed. Hutton (1892), II, 57.

as a result of the famine, the great exodus was taking place at the rate of 250,000 a year.

The great majority came to Liverpool. In 1847 Irish refugees, " half naked and starving," were arriving in the Mersey at the rate of 700 per day[1] and even in the first years of the following decade the rate was 200 per day.[2] Most of them made the journey as deck cargo on the cattle steamers which, as we have noticed, had already established a regular service across the Irish Sea. On this crossing the wretched, vermin-ridden refugees fleeing from their homeland were treated worse than the cattle. Only after the animals and provisions had been loaded were the waiting human beings permitted to swarm on deck and stake their claim to a minute space—sometimes less than a square yard in extent—between the cattle pens. Here they stayed, huddled together, exposed to the rigours of storms and rough seas save for the protection, if they were lucky, of a tarpaulin and fortified only by the inevitable bottle of whisky, during a voyage of at least fourteen hours. Sometimes they reached Liverpool frozen to the deck, usually by that time awash with animal filth.[3] This terrible crossing was made not by thousands, nor by tens of thousands, but by hundreds of thousands. Most of them soon sailed from the Mersey to the United States. In 1847, for instance, 130,000 of the 250,000 Irish refugees embarked for America. Of the remaining 120,000 some stayed at Liverpool—many becoming beggars or thieves[4]—while others trudged wearily inland.

The sufferings of these miserable exiles often continued on this inland trek. A single example must suffice. Bridget Gallaghan, a widow forty years of age, landed at Liverpool on a day in April, 1850, with her cousin and four young children, the eldest of whom was fourteen. The little group set off at once on the road leading towards Yorkshire where they planned to stay with a relative. They stopped the first night at Knotty Ash, just outside Liverpool, and late on the second afternoon reached Bold, to the south of St. Helens. Here a local resident

" allowed them to make oatmeal porridge and also gave them some hot coffee. The poor woman and family left about five o'clock in the evening and crept with her children and cousin, under a hedge on the road. They remained there, although it rained heavily, until 5 o'clock the next morning ; the

[1] Letter to the Home Secretary from Edward Rushton, Stipendiary Magistrate of Liverpool, 1849 [266] XLVII.

[2] Report from the S.C. on Poor Removal, 1854 [396] XVII, appendix 8.

[3] Captain Denham's Report on Passenger Accommodation on Steamers between Ireland and Liverpool, May, 1848. 1849 [339] LI.

[4] Edward Rushton to the Home Secretary, 1849.

children began to cry, when a woman from the nearest house came to their assistance ; the poor woman was carried to a straw stack and laid down, her limbs being quite stiff, and she died a few minutes afterwards."[1]

This particular journey was reported in the papers because an inquest was held. Thousands of other Irish, hardier than Bridget Gallaghan, underwent the same bitter privation on their way inland but managed to survive until they eventually found somewhere to settle.

Those who took the more northerly branch of the turnpike at Prescot, instead of the southerly one leading through Bold, came to St. Helens, only twelve miles' tramp from Liverpool. Some of them stopped and found work in the town. The registers of St. Mary's, Lowe House, St. Helens, reveal that the settlement of Irish was taking place on an appreciable scale in the early 1830s and became more marked after 1837.[2] By 1841 there were more than 1,000 of them in the town. They lived in three distinct districts and were very rarely to be found elsewhere. More than 600 dwelt in Greenbank, more than 350 in the Smithy Brow-Parr Street neighbourhood and about 60 at Gerard's Bridge.[3]

Here they congregated, shunned by the rest of the population, and in these Irish quarters they were able to continue their own national feuds. On one occasion a man from Connaught savagely attacked one of his fellow countrymen from Leinster with a potato fork exclaiming: " I'm a Connaught man . . . I'll knock your brains out," or words to that effect. He did—and was subsequently sentenced to death for murder.[4] Here, too, they perpetuated the primitive habits and ways of life to which they had been accustomed in their rural homeland. So late as 1865 there were pigstyes in Greenbank ;[5] twenty years earlier, the pig had very likely lived indoors for, as Engels observed at the time :

" The Irishman loves his pig as the Arab his horse . . . he eats and sleeps with it, his children play with it, ride upon it, roll in the dirt with it, as any one may see a thousand times repeated in all the great towns of England. The filth and comfortlessness that prevail in the houses themselves it is impossible to describe."[6]

---

[1] *Lpool. Merc.* 16 April, 1850.

[2] The number of births to parents with recognisably Irish names, never more than 5 in any year before 1830, rose to 6 in that year, and then to 7 (1831), 11 (1832), 16 (1833), 24 (1834), 24 (1835), 23 (1836), 53 (1837), 68 (1838), 59 (1839), 68 (1840).

[3] P.R.O., H.O. 107/516 and /517.

[4] *Wigan Gazette* 6 Dec., 1839, 10 April, 1840.

[5] *St. H. N.*, 10 May, 1865. Letter from John G. Ackary.

[6] F. Engels, *The Condition of the Working Class in England in 1844* (1892), 92. See also P. Gaskell, *The Manufacturing Population of England* (1833), 137.

During the 1840s the size of these Little Irelands grew as more and more weary and verminous travellers arrived to join their fellow-countrymen, bringing with them famine-fever, dysentery and smallpox.

There were bitter feelings towards these Connors and Murphys and Duffys, partly on religious grounds and partly because the local inhabitants feared a new labour force which was often willing to accept wages lower than the English. Religious feelings certainly ran high. In 1838, for instance, the Protestants of the town made a show of their faith by celebrating the Battle of the Boyne and walking in a provocative procession towards Greenbank. Stones were thrown and a fight ensued during which two beershops were gutted and the windows and furniture of some of the cottages there seriously damaged.[1] Two years earlier two Roscommon men, who had just arrived in England and had secured employment on a farm in Sutton, were attacked by a railway labourer who set about one of them with a stick with fatal results. The survivor claimed that he had never seen their assailant before, and the attack appears to have been prompted entirely by anti-Irish prejudice, for the railway labourer was heard to call out after he had broken the helpless wretch's skull : " I'll have no Irish in this country."[2] As in the case of Bridget Gallaghan, this incident was reported because an inquest had been held ; if the beating-up of Irish was a common or even an occasional occurrence, it is not surprising that the newcomers kept within the security of their own quarters of the town.

The colliers, in particular, frequently picked quarrels with the Irish when they met face to face in public houses[3] and after the Fenian outrages later in the century the mining community of Parr, " armed with that formidable implement of their craft, the pick," descended upon the Irish colony at Smithy Brow one dark winter's night, causing the Irish inhabitants of that quarter to rally in self-defence brandishing pots and pans and various other blunt instruments.[4] Even in 1868 the Irish were still looked upon as intruders, to be kept in their place.

They usually made good unskilled labourers[5] and found

[1] *Wigan Gazette* 13 July, 1838.

[2] *Wigan Gazette* 21 Oct., 1836.

[3] *St. H. N.* 1 Feb., 1868.

[4] *Ibid.*

[5] For the Irish lack of skill, see G. Talbot Griffith, *Population Problems of the Age of Malthus* (Cambridge, 1926), 75-9. W. D. Boase in his Report on Vagrancy (1847-8 [987] LIII, 17) made the point that immigrants *via* Liverpool usually came from distant parts of Ireland " walking from Mayo to Drogheda and from Roscommon and Sligo to Dublin to take ship, which none but the able-bodied could do." There were therefore among the Irish entering Lancashire numbers of " lusty young men, willing to work."

employment in building and other industries which required heavy digging, hauling or carrying, " jobs which Englishmen disliked because the work was dirty, disreputable or otherwise undesirable."[1] St. Helens possessed one industry offering many such jobs : alkali making. About 80 per cent. of the employees at the Leblanc soda works were labourers[2] and everyone worked in a most unhealthy atmosphere. The escaping gases caused the men's teeth to decay and burnt their clothes " and when by any chance they inhale a more than usual quantity of gas, vomiting and fainting are brought on and they are obliged to be carried out of the Works for air."[3] In the bleaching powder department, work was particularly unpleasant, the men having to wear muzzles and goggles. Hours were generally long for all employees who usually worked a day shift one week and a night shift the next.[4]

It so happened that Muspratt entered the alkali trade on Merseyside at precisely the time when the first sizeable force of his fellow countrymen were being driven out of Ireland by the famine of 1822.[5] He appears to have given some of them a footing in the Leblanc trade from the outset, and, indeed, may have brought workmen with him from Dublin ; the Irish had never to face the same hostility from the English in this industry as, for instance, happened in textiles.[6] Although large numbers were never employed at the chemical works,[7] the industry as a whole did provide openings for many of the immigrant Irish and they in turn deserve recognition for their contribution to the development of the soda trade on Merseyside.

The Irish, a hardy people and accustomed to lower living standards than those prevailing in England, survived the ordeal of being uprooted from their native country and painfully transplanted to the heart of a growing industrial community. Here tasks distasteful to those who had never known such hunger and suffering were willingly accepted by men whose standards were based upon the meagrest pittance. By their habits and way

---

[1] A. Redford, *Labour Migration in England, 1800-1850* (Manchester, 1926), 133.

[2] D. W. F. Hardie, *A History of the Chemical Industry in Widnes* (I.C.I. General Chemicals Division, 1950), 119.

[3] L.R.O., Cross Papers. Gerard *v.* Crosfield, 1846. Brief for the Plaintiff, fo. 11.

[4] L.R.O., Cross Papers. Gerard *v.* Gamble. Evidence of James Haggarty.

[5] Redford, *op. cit.*, 120.

[6] Griffith, *op. cit.*, 85.

[7] E.g. in 1838 Muspratt was only employing 120 men at his Liverpool factory where 12 tons of salt were being decomposed per day. *Lpool. Merc.* 13 April, 1838. Evidence of John Ryan, foreman at the works.

of life the Irish created a grave social problem ; but by accepting
the thankless and unattractive jobs, and particularly by sustaining
one of the main local industries, they played an essential part in
the growth of the town.

The glassmakers of St. Helens were drawn from factories
elsewhere in Britain as well as from abroad. They formed a
mobile force, constantly on the move between the glasshouses of
Scotland, the north-east, Lancashire, the Midlands, London
and Bristol, whenever the termination of their contracts permitted them to go off in search of higher wages.[1] This mobility
of labour did not apply so much to the plate glass branch of the
industry, however, since manufacture was for many years confined
to Ravenhead and, even so late as the 1840s, was limited to only
five other concerns, two of which were in the St. Helens area.
In the crown and sheet branches of the trade, too, there were
some signs that the masters were trying to bring about greater
stability by means of longer contracts and by consultation among
themselves to prevent workmen from trying to play off one house
against another. At the same time, the custom of restricting the
trade to sons of existing glassmakers was being broken down.

The skilled craftsmen in the industry were able to command
a high wage. At the St. Helens Crown Glassworks it was usual for
sets of four blowers and four gatherers to be paid a fixed amount
for producing 1,200 tables (or flat circles of glass) a week and at
a higher rate for all additional tables, " plus " as it was called.
Before wages were increased in the middle of 1845 the basic
rates ranged from 27s. 6d. for the first 1,200 tables and 30s. for
1,200 tables of " plus," paid to the most skilled in a set, to 15s.
and 21s. respectively, paid to the least skilled. After the pay
increase of mid-1845, there was a general advance in basic rates
of 4s. for all except the lowest paid. In practice, a poor average
for a set was 1,600 tables and to make more than 2,400 tables
a week was quite common.[2] Assuming an output of 1,600
tables, the highest-paid men in each set were earning 37s. 6d.
per week and the lowest-paid 22s. before the increases of 1845.
In the sheet glass department, the blower's earnings were somewhat higher but his assistants' income was the same as that of
assistants in the crown houses. The sheet glass blower earned
53s. 8d. for a week's work of 425 sheets of prescribed size and

[1] This section is based upon contracts and correspondence still preserved
at Pilkington Brothers Ltd.,

[2] Henry Deacon, " The Manufacture of Blown Window Glass," *The
Builder* 5 April, 1851.

weight, with proportionately more for larger and thicker sheets, and he had a guaranteed minimum wage of 21s. The sheet glassmakers brought over from the continent when skilled labour became very scarce after the great expansion in trade in 1845, were offered appreciably more than this. Charles Singré, for instance, a sheet glass blower of Choisy-le-Roi near Paris, signed a contract in January, 1846, to work for two years at St. Helens at a weekly wage of £6 10s. 0d. with house and fuel free. He was to receive £240 of this in advance as a loan, to be stopped out of his wages at the rate of £3 a week, and his expenses were to be paid not only to St. Helens but also back again to France at the termination of the agreement.

The skilled men in the other two branches of the industry, bottlemaking and flint glassmaking, appear to have earned between 30s. and 40s. a week. The bottlemakers' basic rate, prior to a 3s. increase in 1845, ranged from 21s. to 15s. according to skill, but it was usual to blow twice as many bottles as the 63 dozen for which this rate was paid.[1] The flint glassmakers seem to have earned less. Figures before 1859 are lacking but in that year the basic rate ranged from 22s. to 12s., and the actual wage was about 50 per cent. more.[2]

In the glass factories at that time there was always a host of people who worked for the skilled men and their immediate assistants and it is important to distinguish between those who were directly engaged in the operation of glassmaking and the juvenile and unskilled labour engaged in fetching and carrying or in performing routine tasks. A list of wages at Pilkington's for a week in 1849 shows that the highest payment in the crown house was 57s. 9d. ; 17 received 30s. to 40s. and 24 received 20s. to 30s., while 74 were paid less than £1, the lowest amount—that of a juvenile—being 4s. In the sheet houses, the glassmakers were more highly paid but even here there were 122 workmen who received less than £1. Several hundred women and children, employed in the grinding, smoothing and polishing of plate glass or in the polishing of sheet glass, or as globe frosters at the flint glass factories, all received considerably less than the men, their earnings usually being between 5s. and 7s. per week. In cases where some of the younger girls helped other members of the family, they received no wages but were given " a trifle . . . to spend."[3]

These lower-paid workers were in the factories for 11½ to 12 hours per day[4] but the hours of the glassmakers themselves

[1] *The Lancashire Bottle Trade* (St. Helens, 1905), 4-5 ; Ch. Emp. Comm., 2nd Rep. 1843 [431] XIV, 55, and 4th, Rep. 1865 [8357] XX, 194.

[2] Ch. Emp. Comm., 4th Rep., 1865 [8357] XX, 199.

[3] *Ibid.*

[4] Ch. Emp. Comm., 2nd Rep., 1843 [431] XIV, B42.

depended on the processes then in use in the various branches
of the trade. In the manufacture of flint glass, the contents of the
large pots, each holding 18 cwts., took 30 to 40 hours to fuse.
This was done during the week-end in order to be ready for
working at 1 a.m. on Monday morning. The men were divided
into two groups, each group doing a six-hour shift night and day
until the pots were exhausted. This was usually on the following
Friday. Then they had two days free while the pots were being
re-charged for them to start again at 1 a.m. on the Monday.[1]
In crown, sheet and plate glassmaking, the men also worked
night and day but each shift was of longer duration, about twelve
hours at a time. At the plate glassworks, there was a night turn
and a day turn but, even so late as 1865, it was not possible to
prepare the pots for any prearranged time. This meant that, as a
Ravenhead witness testified, "though they start evenly at the
beginnings of the week, one set for the day and another for the
night, they get jumbled up by the end."[2] The crown and sheet
men were able to empty their pots in twelve hours or so and it
took 30 hours before they were re-charged again. As with plate
glass manufacture, it was impossible to guarantee when the metal
would be ready to work, and the juniors were used as call boys.
A twelve-year-old blockminder, named Gaskell, has left a
description of his duties :—

" We are about ten hours on and twenty-four off, that is the
journey ; but we boys always get called about three hours
before we start with the men, for we have to sweep up and get
ready for them before they come ; we could do it all in an hour
if we liked but we like to play in that time ; we are called at all
times, night and day ; the ' teazer ' or furnace man goes round
and calls every boy in the ' house ' when the furnace in that
house has heated the metal in the pots enough to start working
in about three hours. He comes to the door at home and
knocks and calls ' Gaskell ' and then, if it's night, my father
looks out of the window and the teazer says, ' No. — called ';
that is the number of the house ; so I get out of bed and go
off."[3]

In bottlemaking it took 8 or 12 hours for the set, or hole, of men
to use up all the metal and about 18 hours to re-charge the pots
again. This caused a further variation in working hours.

But, despite these unusual shifts and the heavy and exacting
nature of the work at the furnaces, the glass industry paid its
skilled men highly and treated them well. As a class, the glassmakers are said to have been " a very decent set of fellows " but
somewhat given to drinking.[4] The heat in the glasshouses and the

[1] Apsley Pellatt, *Curiosities of Glass Making* (1849), 48-50.

[2] Ch. Emp. Comm., 4th Rep., 1865 [8357] XX, 273.

[3] *Ibid.*, 276.

[4] Ch. Emp. Comm., 2nd Rep. 1843 [431] XLV, b55.

constant blowing gave them an enormous thirst and, at a time when water, tea and soft drinks were not so common as they are to-day, vast quantities of beer were consumed, beer money sometimes featuring in the glassmakers' contracts.[1]

The town of St. Helens was growing up in the midst of a district covered with a multitude of domestic workshops.[2] Although the concentration of those workshops where watch parts were made became greater in the direction of Prescot and the nailers' smithies became more numerous towards Billinge, these metal workers were to be found in some strength in the four townships and therefore merit some attention at this point.

The domestic workers at St. Helens were really a feature of an age that was passing. But their particular trades had not as yet been invaded by power-driven machinery and, as demand was constantly on the increase, they were enjoying a golden age of prosperity. Watchmakers were sometimes earning so much as £3 per week.[3] Of their hours of work, little is known ; it is impossible to discover how each man worked in his own home. Those who were employed by masters in workshops at Prescot sweated in the summer (for windows, necessary to provide adequate daylight for precision work, turned the workshops into hothouses) and strained their eyes in the winter working by candlelight after dark. This drudgery continued from six in the morning until eight at night.[4] It seems likely, however, that the craftsmen in their own homes, often assisted by members of their family, would have had an easier time.

The Lancashire nailers also continued to enjoy a producers' market. They were a rough set of men, " swarthy and dirty in appearance . . . ill-educated, drunken and profligate,"[5] great supporters of " Saint Monday and Saint Tuesday," two play days early in the week. This meant that they had to work overtime immediately before reckoning day, sometimes raising such a din

---

[1] For such a contract at the Eccleston Crown Glass Co., *Lpool. Merc.* 21 May, 1847. Excessive drinking at the Eccleston works on New Year's Eve, 1828—an interesting sidelight on Scottish influences in the factory—led to a fight and the killing of one of the workmen. *Lpool. Merc.* 16 Jan., 27 March, 1829 ; Cross Papers, DDCS 27/2.

[2] In 1851 the Prescot registration district included 710 watchmakers and 799 nailers.

[3] Ch. Emp. Comm., 3rd Rep., 1864 [3414] XXII, 202.

[4] *Ibid.*, 178.

[5] Ch. Emp. Comm., 2nd Rep., 1843 [431] XLV, B40.

V

in their smithies late at night that the whole neighbourhood was kept awake by the clatter.[1] One of the nail-masters alleged that many of them were dishonest as workmen :

> " Colliers are said to be bad, but nothing can beat nailers for dishonesty. . . . Sometimes they will exchange good iron . . . for bad and keep the difference. Sometimes they will make away with iron and never give any account of it,"

an occurrence of such regularity that special forms were printed, threatening the nailer with legal action if he did not appear either with the rod iron or the finished nails.[2] Unfortunately no nail-master's records have survived for this period to throw any light on the organisation of the trade. We must, therefore, be content with a glimpse of the local nailers which does not present them in a very favourable light.

The miners, Irish, glassmakers and domestic workers formed the four most distinct groups in the town. Others could be added : the iron and brass founders, for instance, or the growing shop-keeper class. But they do not stand out in quite the same relief as the groups that have just been considered.

The differences between these four groups emphasise the heterogeneous character of the local population. Their work and background, their customs and peculiarities, were all very diverse. The Irish and the glassmakers, for instance, were people who arrived in the town with outlooks very different both from each other and from those of the older inhabitants. There was a world of difference between the well-paid and highly-skilled Scottish glassmaker, brought up with an almost fanatical respect for cleanliness and thrift, and the poor and unskilled, though extremely vigorous and rather reckless, Irish refugee. The colliers, in their turn, although apparently Lancashire men for the most part,[3] were not only at daggers drawn with the Irish but were themselves looked down upon by the other local residents.

Since the different groups had so little in common, it would be a grave mistake to attempt to lump them all together and generalise indiscriminately about their standards of living and

---

[1] *Ibid.,* b45.

[2] *Ibid.,* b46. A comparison with the Midland nail trade is helpful ; *q.v.* W. H. B. Court, *The Rise of the Midland Industries* (Oxford, 1938), 191 *seq.*

[3] There is evidence of miners being brought from Wales and Stafford-shire in an attempt to break the 1831 and 1844 strikes, but the Parr poor law papers in the eighteenth century suggest that most of the labour force for the collieries was recruited locally.

conditions of work. Each group requires to be considered on its own. At this stage, only two very broad conclusions may be drawn: first, that at a time when piece-work was almost universal, many of the local workmen were well-paid and, second, that the tradition of family employment was still very strong. Although there was a cleavage between the skilled and semi-skilled on the one hand, and the general labourers on the other, the line of demarcation was often blurred. Many of the lower-paid fetchers and carriers, for instance, were the wives or children of men who could command a high wage. Nevertheless, there were families which consisted almost wholly of labourers ; of these it is probable that a very high percentage were Irish. For them, even a labourer's pay, brought in by several members of the family, was an improvement on the standards to which they had been accustomed.

Before we can carry our investigations into conditions in the town in the 1840s any farther, it is necessary first to consider how the problems raised by urban growth were being met—how streets were being paved and drained and water supplied—and then to investigate the poor law records to see what light they shed on the subject.

CHAPTER XX

THE GROWTH OF THE TOWN 1830-1845 AND THE BEGINNINGS OF LOCAL GOVERNMENT

ALTHOUGH the census returns give the population of the four townships of Eccleston, Parr, Sutton and Windle at ten-yearly intervals from 1801, no separate count was made for St. Helens itself until 1845. The town then numbered just under 11,800 people[1] and it was estimated to have grown by 3,000 or 4,000 between 1831 and 1841.[2] If, as seems likely, natural increase and immigration added a further 2,000 between 1841 and 1845, it doubled in size during the fifteen years now under consideration.

The need to accommodate the new population made house building the town's most essential industry. It provided a sure form of investment and appealed not only to wealthy industrialists like Peter Greenall and Joseph Greenough—rapidly making himself the leading property owner in Parr[3]—but also, through the agency of building societies, to those other local inhabitants who shared to a less extent in the general rise in prosperity. Peter Greenall, who had been the leading spirit in the first St. Helens Building Society of 1824,[4] became treasurer of its successor, formed in March, 1836. A year later, the 259 members held in all 743 shares, each worth £6. By the time it was wound up, in 1843, £34,535 had been invested.[5] This represented a considerable reinvestment of local profits, drawn from people in many walks of life.

Some of the wills of St. Helens men who died in the 1830s and 1840s provide us with a few details about these new property owners. James Shepherd, for instance, a grocer, possessed two houses and shops and five cottages, " newly erected," in Tontine Street when he died in August, 1833. He left instructions for his shares in the first St. Helens Building Society to be continued and for the building or purchase of one or more dwellinghouses.[6]

[1] L.R.O., Cross Papers, Population and number of houses, 1845.

[2] House of Lords Record Office. Evidence of Isaac Sharp to the S.C. on the St. H. Imp. Bill, 1845.

[3] St. H. Ref. Lib., Parr Poor Law Rate Books, 1840-7.

[4] Above, p. 170.

[5] Articles of agreement in package relating to Lee Watson, St. H. Town Hall, United Alkali Co. Ltd. deeds. Rules, annual reports and minute books at the St. Helens Brewery.

[6] Will proved at Chester, 9 Nov., 1833.

William Burrows, who described himself as an engineer of Parr, left a personal estate of less than £100. But he owned four houses in Greenbank and Tontine Street, one of them recently built.[1] William Hibbert, a chemist and druggist, had already established himself as a considerable property owner in Gerard's Bridge, Duke Street and Greenbank by the time of his death in 1847.[2] He was an original committee member of the St. Helens House and Cottage Owners' Society, formed in 1834 " for opposing any obnoxious Act of Parliament, unjust Rates, removal of Evil disposed and refractory Tenants or other encroachments on the Owners of House Property."[3] The lesser landlords were already sufficiently numerous to band together in an attempt to defend their savings and make sure of an adequate return on their capital.

It was possibly some of the cottage property put up by the members of this society that a visiting traveller observed was " chiefly of two storeys . . . as plain as a combination of lime and bricks can well be."[4] According to the medical officer for the St. Helens district of the Prescot Union, who had much experience of the insides as well as the outsides of these cottages, they were " generally small ; numbers of them being . . . only composed of two rooms, one below and the other over."[5] Most of these monotonous rows of red brick dwellings were erected at Greenbank, Gerard's Bridge and Smithy Brow, all of them districts where building had been begun before 1830. There was little attempt to break new ground. In 1845 Westfield was still able to live up to its name, though the builder had already started to encroach. During the 1830s an addition was made to the number of isolated hamlets which lay outside the town ; a small conglomeration of cottages came into existence at Sutton Oak to house the employees at the new factories there and at the railway company's locomotive and repair shed nearby.

The building up of Church Street, Market Street, Tontine Street and Bridge Street had taken place round a large field. This remained undeveloped until 1833 when its owners, the Society of Friends, laid out a square in the centre and sold the surrounding land as building sites. These plots fetched record prices from speculators eager to erect public houses, offices and shops

[1] Will proved at Chester, 11 Jan., 1834.

[2] Will proved at Chester, 24 July, 1847.

[3] Rules among the Ansdell Papers at St. H. Ref. Lib.

[4] *Chambers Edinburgh Journal* 11 April, 1846.

[5] Evidence of John Blundell to the S.C. on the St. H. Imp. Bill, 1845. See also Blundell's evidence published in the Report on Sanitary Condition of the Labouring Population of Great Britain, 1842, 1843 [509] XII.

around what was intended to be the town centre.[1] The New
Market Place, as the square was called, became the town's one
and only exhibit to which visitors could be taken. Its opening
caused William Pilkington to put his tongue in his cheek and write
home to his brother :

" I suppose . . . the New Market place will exceed or surpass
all that we have seen either in London or Paris."[2]

When the plots of building land were sold, a promise was made
that the square would be " left open and unbuilt upon."[3] By 1843,
however, the market people who met every Saturday at the
junction of Market Street and Church Street had become so
numerous that they, their stalls and their many milling customers
caused serious congestion along part of the main Liverpool to
Ashton turnpike road. The Society of Friends were prevailed upon
to permit the market to be removed to the new square and the
Inspector of Roads informed the stallholders in May, 1843, that,
unless they took advantage of this offer and ceased to obstruct the
main thoroughfare, they would be fined. No charge was made
for the use of the square and the market people appear to have
acquiesced in the change without protest. But the owners of
property were most annoyed, and their annoyance turned into
indignation when in the winter of 1843-4 the Society of Friends,
in an effort to shelter the shivering market people from a keen
south-westerly wind, put up two wooden sheds along the length of
the square and charged the stallholders toll for their use. The
property owners contended that this amounted to building on the
square and was a breach of the conditions under which they had
bought their building plots. This may have been so ; but by
taking this action the Society of Friends had, in fact, provided
the town with a new trading centre.[4]

As the rows of cottages became more numerous and the little
town showed more noticeable signs of bustle and activity, there
was a demand for improved transport facilities to neighbouring
towns, for supplies of water and gas, and for an adequate system
of drainage. These public services were provided in the first
instance by private venture.

[1] St. H. Town Hall, package 209. Memorandum on the St. H. Market,
1848.

[2] William Pilkington to Richard Pilkington, 15 Sept., 1834.

[3] St. H. Town Hall, package 209. Memorandum on the St. H. Market.
1848.

[4] *Ibid.*, minutes of St. H. I. C., 3 Dec., 1845 ; Ansdell Papers, placard
announcing the opening of the New Market Place.

Towards the end of the 1820s the Bolton-Liverpool coaches, which passed along the turnpike road through St. Helens, became incapable of carrying the growing number of people who wished to travel between St. Helens and Liverpool. Accordingly, in 1827, several of the local residents joined together and raised £90 to buy a small coach. They called it *The Regulator* and hired it out at £15 a year to a man named Lawton, who contracted to maintain a regular service between St. Helens and Liverpool. In 1833 *The Regulator* was sold to Lawton's successor for £10. During these seven years its proprietors received an annual dividend of 8s. upon each of their £2 shares. With the final dividend of 11s. 5d., paid after the coach's sale, this amounted to a total profit of 19s. 5d., or a return of almost 50 per cent. on their original outlay.[1]

Such a profitable venture was well worth repeating. When the railway was opened and it was found that there was no provision for the transport of passengers to and from the Liverpool-Manchester line at St. Helens Junction, several local residents again came forward and proposed to buy a carriage " to be propelled by horse power," agreeing to pay the railway company a quarter of the takings.[2] This method of conveyance from the town station (situated close to the present Peasley Cross Bridge) to St. Helens Junction may have satisfied the promoters but it aroused some indignation from one of the passengers, Sir George Head, who roundly condemned it as being " as disagreeable and as slow as can well be imagined."[3]

With both these ventures Peter Greenall was connected. He was a subscriber to *The Regulator* and actually hired it for his own use for five weeks before Lawton started the regular service to Liverpool. He may have been a promoter of the slow coach on the railway ; as chairman of the line, he would certainly have had a say in the matter. Other public services also had his support. When, for instance, a small Gas Light Company was floated in the spring of 1832, with a capital of £6,000 it was the distinctive signature of Peter Greenall that appeared on all the share certificates,[4] and, no doubt, he was interested in the adoption four years later of the Lighting and Watching Act which permitted elected inspectors to illuminate the streets of St. Helens with gas.[5]

[1] St. H. Ref. Lib., Ansdell Papers. Accounts of subscribers, 1827-33.

[2] St. H. and R.G. Mins., 29 Aug., 12 Sept., 1832.

[3] Sir George Head, *A Home Tour Through the Manufacturing Districts of England in the Summer of 1835* (1836), 85.

[4] L.R.O., Cross Papers, DDCS 37/4 ; 2 and 3 Wm. IV cap. XII ; *Lpool. Merc.* 10 Feb., 1832. The first plant occupied part of the present gasworks site.

[5] *Lpool. Merc.*, 10 Feb., 1836.

He was even more intimately concerned with supplying water to the town. The St. Helens Brewery had long enjoyed its own supply which was, apparently, piped from ponds fed by the Eccleston brook where it passed through Greenall land to the west of the town.[1] In 1824 Peter Greenall laid a system of pipes to cover the four main streets and Moorflat, and supplied the residents of this central area at a rent of upwards of 10s. 6d. a year.[2] As the population increased, however, the requirements of the inhabitants and the needs of the Brewery outstripped the capacity of the Greenalls' ponds. They therefore came to an agreement with Samuel Taylor of Eccleston Hall, whose estate lay on higher ground to the west of the town and was better situated for providing an unfailing supply of unpolluted water. Taylor was to receive £100 a year tax free—an interesting local sidelight upon a heated national issue—and the Greenalls were to be paid £150 a year, with a similar exemption from the responsibility of paying 7d. in the £1 to the Treasury. An Act of Parliament[3] was obtained permitting the formation of a limited company with a share capital of £4,000, to be spent partly on linking the Eccleston reservoirs[4] with the Greenalls' supply system in the town, and partly on laying additional mains. The promoters of the Bill, in addition to Taylor and the brothers Thomas, Peter and Gilbert Greenall, included Bateman and Fairbairn, the distinguished Manchester engineers.[5] By the middle of 1844 the necessary pipes had been laid and, during the first year of its operation the St. Helens Waterworks Company was able to satisfy all its consumers, despite an unusually severe drought.[6]

Even the town hall was a private venture, though in this case the promoters were driven to making a rather unprofitable investment out of a desire to restrict the spread of crime.

Until the middle of the 1830s the hand of the law lay very lightly upon the local inhabitants. Each township had a constable,

[1] II Geo. IV. cap. L, sec. 59 ; St. H. Town Hall, package 209, statement for the opinion of Counsel, 24 Dec., 1858. During extensions to the Brewery in 1896, some of the early pipes were dug up. They consisted of trunks of oak trees, 12 ins. long, through which a hole 6 ins. in diameter had been burned, and were surrounded by clay (St. H. N., 18 Jan., 1896). The first wooden water pipes in Liverpool are said to have been laid in 1799 (G. H. Morton, The Geology of the Country Around Lpool, 2nd ed., 1891, 172) and iron pipes came to replace wooden ones between 1810 and 1820 (William Garnett, A Little Book on Water Supply, Cambridge, 1922, 97).

[2] Rent Books, St. Helens Brewery.

[3] 6 & 7 Vict. cap. XXIII.

[4] One reservoir was already in existence and one had to be built. St. H. Town Hall, package 209, statement for Counsel's opinion. We are grateful to the late Mr. H. E. Hewitt for information concerning local water courses.

[5] Conveyance, 28 Oct., 1844, at the office of Maxwell Wood, Brewis and Co., St. Helens.

[6] L.R.O., Cross Papers. Brief on behalf of the landowners of Sutton, 1845.

and the town possessed a small and dilapidated lock-up at the Raven Inn and the inevitable stocks which stood at the end of Market Street.[1] The capture of law-breakers was very largely a matter of local publicity, the offer of rewards and a reliance on each person's sense of justice. In 1825, for instance, when a thief broke into the Independent Chapel and stole several books, the trustees took the law into their own hands. They went off to Liverpool in search of the robber, failed to detect him, and therefore distributed handbills throughout the neighbourhood offering five guineas reward on the conviction of the offender. A few days afterwards a Liverpool bookseller wrote to say that some books had been left at his shop which seemed to fit the description circulated. This was found to be the case and the thief was caught when he visited the shop a second time.[2] Such a casual police system appears to have worked well enough in a community so small that every person knew everyone else ; but when new faces began to appear in large numbers, it was no longer possible to pick out the stranger or to rely to the same extent upon local goodwill. In the heterogeneous population of the new towns, the sense of communal responsibility was not so strong as it had been in the rural districts. Consequently, it was necessary to copy the example of the large urban communities and form police forces to hunt out wrongdoers.

With this aim in view, a public meeting was held at St. Helens at the end of 1837. The meeting decided to rebuild the town's bridewell, to attempt to improve the policing arrangements and to request that the petty sessions, then held in Prescot where most of the legal business of the district was still transacted, should be held by adjournment once a month at St. Helens. This was necessary because, as the meeting pointed out, " from the trouble attendant upon prosecuting at such a distance in times past, many offenders must have been allowed to escape punishment."[3] The request was granted and the justices met for the first time at St. Helens in February, 1838.[4]

The magistrates were not satisfied, however, with the court-room accommodation afforded them at the Raven Inn, and the local residents were therefore obliged to erect a special building for the purpose or lose the advantage of a local session of the

---

[1] Interview with Abraham Hartley, *St. H. Lantern* 3 Jan., 1888. In 1837 the lock-up was in such a filthy state that the constable refused to lodge a disobedient apprentice there for the night. Instead, the apprentice was chained to his bed, " a large and savage dog keeping guard." *Wigan Gazette* 14 April, 1837.

[2] This account has been reconstructed from the solicitor's bill at St. H. Cong. Church.

[3] *Wigan Gazette* 29 Dec., 1837.

[4] *Wigan Gazette* 9 Feb., 1838.

justices.[1] Another public meeting was held at the end of April at which it was decided to raise £3,000 in £10 shares and to build a town hall which would include a court-room, a bridewell and a house for the constable.[2] The building, designed "on the modern Italian style" with "a Corinthian portico," was erected on a plot of land situated on the west side of the New Market Place.[3] Although the exterior was hybrid and incongruous, the inside was strictly utilitarian. The court room, we learn, was "ventilated by means of scroll-work panels which can be closed or opened by wires and cranks worked in the magistrates' retiring room . . . and when the room is required for balls or public dinners, by a very ingenious contrivance the table forms, witness box, etc. can be easily deposited below."[4]

The town hall became the centre and focus of social life for the next thirty years. The proprietors hired the rooms out for public meetings, church bazaars, local dances and visiting performances. Many musical concerts took place there, particularly after the installation of an organ in 1851. The Mechanics Institute made it their home and the first public library was shelved around the walls of one of its rooms. It was a town hall in the fullest sense of the term.

While it was being built, a new church was also in course of construction, intended to serve the growing population of Greenbank. St. Thomas's, as the church came to be called, was the result of the generosity of Peter Greenall. The town hall and St. Thomas's were both completed about the same time and it is symptomatic of Greenall's dominating influence in the St. Helens of his day that on 8 October, 1839, the guests who were entertained by Mrs. Greenall to luncheon at the opening of the town hall, of which her husband was the treasurer, later adjourned to attend the service of consecration at the church which he had built and endowed.[5]

The town hall, which had been erected primarily as a means of tightening up the policing arrangements of the neighbourhood and of checking the rise in crime, was completed just in time to meet the local needs of the Lancashire county police force which came into being a few months later. The decision to establish such a force was taken at the close of a year of agitation and excitement.

---

[1] Evidence of Isaac Sharp to the S.C. on the St. H. Imp. Bill, 1845.

[2] *Wigan Gazette* 11 May, 1838 ; L.R.O., Cross Papers DDCS 37/6, rough draft of deed appointing new trustees of the Town Hall Company.

[3] *Wigan Gazette* 11 Oct., 1839. The architects were A. and J. Williams of Tarleton Street, Liverpool.

[4] *Ibid.*

[5] *Wigan Gazette* 11 Oct., 1839. See also the issues of 28 July, 1837 and 29 June, 1838.

In the spring of 1839 the Assistant Poor Law Commissioner reported from Manchester that the Chartist Convention which began to meet at the beginning of February had increased popular excitement in Lancashire "to a ten fold degree." Operatives in the Leigh district were said to be dividing the land among themselves and calculating their share of the spoils, preparations were being made to light beacon fires, and the sales of the *Northern Star* in Lancashire were so heavy that a special van had to be chartered to carry the papers over from Leeds.[1] Nobody knew the strength the movement would reach and ordinary folk in Lancashire feared widespread disorder and rioting. A woman wrote from Bury that, " The Country is in such an agitation that not a man under the canopy of heaven can tell what will be the result of it."[2] From Hulme a mother and father wrote to their son : " You little know what we suffer at this time, work scarce, wages low and provisions high and the whole Country up in arms for rebellion ; we have need to pray to the Lord that things may turn out better than what is at present expected."[3] The Chartist Convention dissolved in discord, but the war of nerves was having its effect. With the depression deepening and winter setting in, the Lancashire magistrates at their Annual General Session of the Peace in Preston determined—as an interim emergency measure only[4]— to adopt the Rural Police Act which had just been placed on the Statute Book. Although the agitation was confined chiefly to the textile districts, the country west of Wigan being " entirely free from Taint,"[5] the magistrates of West Derby Hundred, in Quarter Session on 31 October, 1839, agreed with the resolution passed at Preston.[6] On 6 November the magistrates from all over the county met once more at Preston and, dismayed by the first news of the Newport Rising but probably not yet aware from later reports what a fiasco it had been, not only supported the establishment of the police force without any opposition, but even carried an amendment whereby the total strength was increased from 310 constables, as originally proposed, to 500.[7] On 18 December John Woodford of Preston, Captain and Adjutant of the Third Regiment of the Duke of Lancaster's Own Militia and a Captain on half pay, late of the Rifle Brigade,

[1] P.R.O., H.O. 73/55.   Mott to the Poor Law Commissioners, 27 March, 1839.

[2] P.R.O., H.O. 40/37.   Alice Scott (Bury) to her son in Lancaster Castle 7 March, 1839.

[3] *Ibid.*, Samuel and Anne Bowker to their son in Lancaster, 30 April, 1839.

[4] L.R.O., QEC 1/1.   Minutes of Constabulary Committee.

[5] P.R.O., H.O. 40/37, Letter from James Bancks, Wigan, 11 May, 1839.

[6] Minutes of the Constabulary Committee.

[7] *Ibid.* ; *Wigan Gazette* 15 Nov., 1839.

was appointed Chief Constable. Before the end of the month he was down in London studying Metropolitan Police methods and organization, and on his return to Lancashire swiftly set about creating an efficient county force based on the example of the Peelers.[1] The detachment at St. Helens, created in the spring of 1840, was commanded by Superintendent Storey, who had previously been constable of Hardshaw.[2] Already by May, 1840 the new police were making their presence felt in the neighbourhood " in bringing to justice the many idle and disorderly characters by whom the peace and order of the respectable inhabitants have been so much and so long disturbed."[3] The first five years were a period of extreme trial for Storey and his handful of constables ; a gang of ruffians, known as the Long Company, robbed travellers in the neighbourhood and are believed to have been connected with the murder of an elderly farmer at Denton's Green on 5 December, 1841. A period of distress and unemployment culminated in the colliers' strike of 1844, which, despite reinforcements from other districts, proved too much for the police to handle.[4] Nevertheless, the small force stationed in the town made a very determined attempt to maintain law and order in the face of an overwhelming majority of strikers, and a few months after the troubles had subsided, Samuel Taylor, one of the local justices, openly admitted that " if the constabulary disbanded, he did not believe that a single magistrate in the hundred of West Derby—at least, he could speak for himself— would sit on the magisterial bench."[5] The county police force was already building up at St. Helens a reputation for efficiency, the surest deterrent to the would-be lawbreaker. Storey was later described as " a terror to the thieves and vagrants for miles around."[6]

When the Lancashire Constabulary tendered the account for its additional services during the strike, the local ratepayers had a shock. The usual police charge of £25 a month rose to £73 in February, 1844, £209 in March and £138 in April, all of which had to be defrayed by the St. Helens district and was not chargeable to the county as a whole.[7] At the same time, the local inhabitants were obliged to share part of the burden of two new police stations proposed to be built at Woolton and Wavertree.

[1] Minutes of the Constabulary Committee, 18, 27 Dec., 1839.

[2] *Wigan Gazette*, 26 April, 6 Dec., 1839 ; *St. H. Intelligencer* 24 Feb., 1857.

[3] *Wigan Gazette* 1 May, 1840.

[4] *Lpool. Merc.* 1 March, 1844.

[5] *Lpool. Merc.* 17 Jan., 1845.

[6] *St. H. Intelligencer* 24 Feb., 1857.

[7] L.R.O., QEC 2/1. County Constabulary Accounts.

This led to a meeting of protest being held at St. Helens in December, 1844, at which it was urged that the St. Helens district should be severed completely from Prescot. A resolution was also unanimously carried against the excessive police rate for the year.[1] Although a more moderate tone prevailed when the objections of St. Helens were formally presented to the justices at a special session at Prescot a few weeks later, the demand for independence was clear enough.[2] It came at a time when plans were afoot to introduce into Parliament an improvement bill for the town, a clause of which proposed to bestow upon the new body powers to employ its own police force.[3] To a certain extent the St. Helens Improvement Bill profited from this local dissatisfaction. But it had a very positive side and to understand this more clearly we must turn again to the activities of Peter Greenall.

Peter Greenall had contested one of the parliamentary seats for the Borough of Wigan without success in 1837. But in 1841 when Peel and the Tories were swept to power, he was returned with a narrow majority.[4] He reached Westminster at a time when urban improvement, which only a few years earlier had aroused " hardly a glimmer of intelligent public interest,"[5] was beginning to attract considerable notice, thanks to the restless activity of Edwin Chadwick. Chadwick's *Sanitary Condition of the Labouring Population,* published in 1842, showed the extent of overcrowding and bad drainage in the built-up areas throughout the country, and led in the following year to the appointment of a Royal Commission to investigate the whole problem of urban sanitation in closer detail. The first instalment of its findings, issued in June, 1844, confirmed Chadwick's earlier report and was full of facts and figures which made excellent propaganda in the hands of the sanitary reformers.

Nowhere was this propaganda more keenly felt than among Members of Parliament and Peter Greenall seems to have been an early convert. A few months after the Royal Commission had issued its first report, he decided that the time had arrived to establish an Improvement Commission for St. Helens. In October, 1844, he conferred with Edward Johnson, a local solicitor, about drafting the necessary Bill, and gathered round him a group of younger men, foremost among whom were Arthur Sinclair, Secretary of the St. Helens and Runcorn Gap Railway,

[1] *Lpool. Merc.* 20 Dec., 1844.

[2] *Lpool. Merc.* 10, 17 Jan., 1845.

[3] Clause 234 of the original Bill.

[4] Duncombe Pink and Alfred B. Beavan, *The Parliamentary Representation of Lancashire* (1889), 241.

[5] Sir John Simon, *English Sanitary Institutions* (1890), 178.

and David Gamble, both still in their very early twenties.[1] The local movement for sanitary improvement was led by a benevolent despot and staunchly supported by a few youthful lieutenants.

It would be a mistake to conclude from the petition for an Improvement Bill that St. Helens was already as insanitary as some of the larger towns upon which the Royal Commission had reported. The supporters of the Bill claimed not that the measure was overdue but rather that they wanted to take action in time while the town was still growing. In general, the houses were spread out over a considerable area, chiefly along the sides of the main roads, and Dr. W. H. Duncan, the champion of public health at Liverpool and soon to be the City's first medical officer, gave his word that St. Helens was not at that time suffering from overcrowding.[2] But the districts which were claimed to be filthy, unpaved and undrained were those which were growing most rapidly : Greenbank and Smithy Brow—the Irish quarters, in fact. At Greenbank only one street was paved and sewered ; in wet weather the others became quagmires and in the heat of summer they were filled with the stench which arose from putrescent filth in " a great number of open cesspools."[3] Some houses were without privies and even when these had been provided, they were " within a few paces "[4] of doors and windows. When the privies were cleaned out once in three or six months, the contents were brought to the front of the houses where they sometimes lay a day or longer before being collected.[5] It was at Greenbank, not surprisingly, that most of the fever cases occurred.[6]

But of the central area of the town the supporters of the Bill had relatively little to say. It is true that they claimed that the old streets were paved only with large round stones which presented a very uneven surface, and that, despite the main sewer in Church Street, cellars were flooded in wet weather.[7] But there *was* a main sewer, 18 inches by 20 inches, made of stone and rubble, and it connected with four other drains running down from Church

---

[1] Sinclair and Gamble, for instance, tried to inspect the Sutton ratebooks at the beginning of November, 1844, in order to secure evidence for the proposed Bill. (Brief against the Bill on behalf of Sutton, Cross Papers). The committee for the Bill was reported to include Messrs. Bishop, Marsh, Haddock, Sinclair, Wadsworth, Daglish, Sharp, Bromilow and Fincham. *Lpool. Merc.* 8 Nov., 1844.

[2] House of Lords Record Office. Evidence to the S.C. on the St. H. Imp. Bill, 1845.

[3] *Ibid.*

[4] *Ibid.*

[5] *Ibid.* Evidence of Isaac Sharp.

[6] *Ibid.*, Evidence of John Blundell.

[7] *Ibid.*, Evidence of Richard Pankey.

Street to the brook.[1] This network, despite its inadequacy in
heavy rain, was sufficient to drain the central area under ordinary
conditions. The centre of the town was also lit by gas lamps—
some forty-six of them[2]—and, as we have seen, the houses were
supplied with water. In the struggle for the Bill the supporters
concentrated their attention on the areas which were unpaved,
undrained, and without water or gas,[3] while the opponents
stressed the measures which had already been taken to cope
with the increased population in Church Street, Market Street,
Tontine Street, Bridge Street, Moorflat and the New Market
Place.

But here Greenall and his friends had a very good reply. This
central area had been paved and drained because it came under
one local authority, the highway board of the hamlet of Hardshaw.[4]
Greenbank, however, was in Eccleston township, one side of
Smithy Brow was in Windle township and the other side in Parr,
and the area south of the Windle and Eccleston Brook was in
Sutton. Thus St. Helens as a whole came under five different local
authorities. Even if each of the four townships, as well as
Hardshaw, had decided to put its own part of the town in order,
the result would still have been chaotic. One of the primary
objectives of the reformers, therefore, was to create one local
authority with powers over the whole of the St. Helens drainage
area. They proposed, as the limits of the Act, Gerard's Bridge, the
Lingholme (then Four Lane Ends) and Boundary Road (then Gin
Lane), Thatto Heath, Peasley Cross, Ashcroft's Bridge and
Merton Bank. This included the built-up area in the four townships and the communities living at Gerard's Bridge, Ravenhead
and Thatto Heath but not those farther afield at Sutton Oak,
Parr Stocks and Ashton's Green.

Within this boundary it was proposed that certain minimum
standards of housing should be observed. No house was to be
built without one ground floor room measuring 108 square feet
and no rooms were to be lower than 7 ft. 6 ins. in height.[5] If any
house was certified filthy by a J.P., it was to be cleaned within
four days. No streets were to be made less than 30 feet wide, if

---

[1] *Ibid.* Evidence of George Harris.   Placard issued by William Eckersley,
1 July, 1845 (Ansdell Papers).   See above, p. 171.

[2] *Ibid.* Evidence of Isaac Sharp.

[3] Isaac Sharp stated in evidence that part of Eccleston township used
to be lit by gas but in 1843 " there were some dissatisfied people in the
township . . . the lower orders became clamorous and they assembled in
great force." The supply was, therefore, withdrawn.

[4] The Orderly Book of the Highways of the Hamlet of Hardshaw from
1839 may be seen in the St. H. Ref. Lib.

[5] Clause 141.

they were carriageways, or 20 feet if they were not, and the Commissioners were to have powers to remove buildings in order to improve the lines of the streets.[1] Clauses were also included in the Bill permitting the new body to establish its own police force,[2] to buy out the gas, water and town hall companies and to purchase the market place.[3]

But the original Bill, though bold in conception, took no account of the various vested interests which were already firmly entrenched in the town. The opposition made its appearance in force on 4 November, 1844, when a public meeting was held to enlist the necessary support for the Bill, Peter Greenall taking the chair. We learn that " a warm discussion " took place and further consideration of the matter had to be postponed for a week.[4] On the second occasion, with Peter Greenall again in the chair, there was a large majority—said to have been at least ten to one— against the Bill.[5] The property owners of St. Helens were afraid of the additional rates they might have to pay, those ratepayers of Sutton who were to be brought into the boundary had similar fears, and those who were to be left outside wondered from where their income was to come when the richest part of their township was swallowed up in St. Helens.[6] The men of property gave an overwhelming refusal to support the measure.

After the meeting on the 11 November it was believed that the project had been stifled. But Greenall held a trump card which he proceeded to play. He was a Member of Parliament and had already gained some experience of carrying his own ideas to the Statute Book when, in 1843, he had shepherded the St. Helens Waterworks Bill through the Commons.[7] Despite the strong feeling at St. Helens against the formation of the Improvement Commission, Greenall took the parliamentary initiative on his own ; many local inhabitants were surprised to learn that the Bill had been introduced into the Commons.[8] The measure was committed on 4 April, 1845, and Greenall saw to it that he was present as a member of the committee to exert his influence. He also took care that those who gave evidence were well chosen and

[1] Clauses 127, 138, 150.

[2] Clause 234.

[3] Clause 82 and 165.

[4] *Lpool. Merc.* 8 Nov., 1844 ; L.R.O., Cross Papers, Brief against the Bill on behalf of Sutton.

[5] *Ibid. ; Lpool. Merc.* 15 Nov., 1844.

[6] St. H. Ref. Lib., Ansdell Papers. Petition from the owners and occupiers of land in Sutton and St. Helens.

[7] *C.J.*, **98**, 99, 13 March, 1843.

[8] St. H. Ref. Lib., Ansdell Papers. Petition from Sutton.

primed. Isaac Sharp, the mainstay of the Greenall case, had a fluent tongue and spoke with effect of the horrors of Greenbank, though, when pinned down to specific streets, he had to confess : ' the place is occupied by the Labouring Classes and the Low Irish. I have no business that calls me there." John Blundell, the doctor, testified to the extent of disease in the Greenbank district, John Daglish, a land surveyor, confined himself to an imposing array of figures, and George Harris, the builder, spoke solely about drains and floods. Richard Pankey also gave evidence : he was an innkeeper—of a Greenall house.

The supporters and opponents of the measure developed their arguments in the ways which have already been indicated, but it is particularly significant that the opposition tried to launch a personal attack on Greenall and a great effort was made to suggest that he had promoted the Bill for his own personal profit. It was alleged that the gas and town hall companies were a liability the proprietors wished to be rid of[1] and that the owners of land in Greenbank wanted to see the roads paved at public expense to save their own pockets. Isaac Sharp, for instance, was quietly, logically and determinedly led to the point :

" Can you tell me the names of any of the owners of . . . land which is situate within Eccleston ?

—The land in Eccleston is in a great part leased off to a vast number of Individuals perhaps 100.

Leased off for what ?
—To a vast number of individuals to build upon.

Who is the lessor ?
—Mr. Mills I should say is the principal one and Messrs. Greenall and Bros. a great portion of it.[2]

Tell me the names of the Messrs. Greenall.
—Thomas Greenall, Peter Greenall and Gilbert Greenall, I think.

Peter Greenall the Member of Parliament ?
—Yes.

Sitting on this Committee ?
—Yes."[3]

This personal attack did not harm the measure, however. Two of the more radical clauses in the Bill—control of the police and

---

[1] L.R.O., Cross Papers. Brief against the Bill on behalf of Sutton. The gas company certainly did not pay high dividends : 5 per cent in 1833, 1835, 1836 and 1837 and only 2½ per cent in 1838 and 1843. St. H. Ref. Lib., Ansdell Papers, appendix to evidence of the St. H. Gas Bill, 1870.

[2] Above, p. 170.

[3] Evidence of Isaac Sharp to the S.C. on the St. H. Imp. Bill, 1845.

W

purchase of the gas undertaking—were struck out in the Commons
but it reached the Lords without vital alteration. But at this stage
the owners of land and property in Sutton, including the
proprietors of the St. Helens Crown Glassworks and the British
Plate Glassworks, made a very strong attack, and succeeded in
securing their exclusion from the area proposed to be covered by
the Improvement Commission.[1] This was a very weighty concession, made only to save the rest of the Bill. It meant that almost
all the township of Sutton, the southerly part of the drainage area
containing some of the most important industrial property, lay
outside the jurisdiction of the Commissioners ; but having
sustained this damaging, though not fatal, reverse at the hands of
a combination of industrialists and landowners, Peter Greenall
and his friends obtained their Act on 21 July, 1845, despite the
continued opposition in the town throughout the proceedings.[2]
A Tory Member of Parliament had triumphed over the ultra-
conservative elements of the St. Helens House and Cottage
Owners Society. The Improvement Commission was far from
being a tower of strength, but its creation did mark the beginning
of effective local government in the town.

[1] Evidence of Arthur Sinclair to the S.C. on the St. H. Imp. Bill, 1869.

[2] 8 & 9 Vict. cap. CLXXVI ; *Lpool. Merc.* 6 June, 1845 ; placards
issued by " A Rate Payer " and William Eckersley among the Ansdell
Papers.

CHAPTER XXI

THE NEW POOR LAW

BY 1830 the Old Poor Law had fallen into disrepute, particularly in the southern agricultural counties. There especially it had degenerated into the indiscriminate giving of assistance and often into the unfortunate policy of subsidizing labourers' wages from the rates. In the north, where township administration was more efficient and where the Speenhamland system of wage subsidy had not been introduced, the situation was by no means so bad, though even there the coming of the factory system was raising problems for the overseers.

Reform, essential in the south and desirable in the north, was provided by the Poor Law Amendment Act of 1834. This sought to return to the first principles laid down by the Elizabethan labour code : to tend the sick, to set the shiftless to work under conditions less attractive than those prevailing outside the poorhouse, and to deny doles of any kind to those who applied for outdoor relief.

But although the principles were old, the organisation was new. The maze of tiny poor law districts, some 15,000 in all, was rationalized into about 600 unions, each with its own large union workhouse capable of immuring several hundred inmates. Ratepayers, each possessing up to twelve votes according to the extent of their property, elected Guardians to administer the Poor Law within their own union. These elected representatives, however, were only able to make local decisions within the framework prescribed by a series of directives from the Commission in London and any such local decisions were subject to the Commission's confirmation. It is hardly surprising, therefore, that when the new *régime* started to effect administrative economies and to enforce the principles of less eligibility, it was the " three bashaws of Somerset House " and the " bastilles " that were signalled out particularly for attack.

Although the New Poor Law was greeted with widespread passive, and, in some cases, active resistance when it was introduced into the industrial north, its impact was not so keenly felt in the northern towns as in the country districts elsewhere. Alfred Power, the Assistant Poor Law Commissioner for Lancashire and the West Riding of Yorkshire, explained why this was the case :

" The high rate of wages and a superior spirit of independence have preserved the mass from all contact with pauperism during the ordinary circumstances of trade. Even in times of considerable depression, although not prepared to struggle with such an event of habits of prudence and forethought, the mass of the laboring population may be said to receive but little assistance from the poors rates in proportion at least to the vast amount of resources which are suddenly found withdrawn."[1]

Power went on to confirm that, on the whole, the local township administration under the Old Poor Law was well conducted in the industrial north :

" In my present district (more especially in Lancashire) the proportion of well-governed Townships is probably far greater than would be found in other parts of England previously to the formation of Unions."

In a part of the country so relatively free from lavish out-payments and local abuses, the Poor Law Commission's approach was based upon regional expediency rather than upon national principle. Local outpayments were not forbidden and the population continued to witness the use of some of the old workhouses while they were getting accustomed to the inevitability of a local " bastille."

The need to establish registration districts and to appoint civil registrars under the provisions of the Marriage Act of 1836 was seized upon by the Poor Law Commission as an opportunity to form unions in Lancashire.[2] " The proper area for an Union in England," wrote the Commission's secretary, " is considered to be the district in which the population resort to the same chief Market Town ; practically the Public business must be considered as an incident of the private business of the community."[3] With this is mind, the old town of Prescot at the head of the parish was selected as the administrative headquarters for a union, bounded by the Mersey on the south and Rianford on the north, and extending as far to the west as Speke and Woolton. The four townships of Windle, Parr, Sutton and Eccleston, all lay within its limits.

The first meeting of the Prescot Guardians took place on 2 February, 1837, at Prescot Town Hall. Thomas Kidd of Widnes was unanimously elected chairman and John Heyes was

[1] P.R.O., H.O. 73/53. Reply of Alfred Power, dated 21 Oct., 1837 to Chadwick's circular letter of 17 Aug.

[2] The Poor Law Commissioners wrote to Lord John Russell on 6 May, 1837 (H.O. 73/52) that they had originally planned to form the registration districts as a temporary measure but had later changed their minds and made them permanent.

[3] P.R.O., H.O. 73/52. Chadwick to Lord John Russell, 20 Jan., 1837.

appointed clerk to the Board.[1] At meetings on 9 February and 8 March Parr, Sutton, Windle and that part of Eccleston situated to the south of the Prescot-St. Helens turnpike road were formed into the St. Helens Registration District, with William Brunskill as Registrar.[2] The spring and summer of 1837 were taken up with resolving various administrative problems connected with the change-over to the new system and it was not until 19 October that the Prescot Guardians assumed full responsibility for the poor. It had previously been decided that, of the six workhouses which the union had inherited at Prescot, Bold, Sutton, Windle, Halewood and Much Woolton, those at Sutton, Windle and Much Woolton were best suited to the needs of the Guardians. Windle was to be used as a workhouse, Sutton as an asylum for old people and Much Woolton as a workhouse for children.[3] The appointment of relieving officers in November,[4] and of governors for the workhouse and the two poorhouses at the end of the following months[5] marked the real beginning of the new *régime* in the district.

A show of opposition was not long delayed. At the end of January, 1838, a large and well-attended meeting was held at St. Helens to protest against the New Poor Law and to launch a petition for the repeal of the Act of 1834. Feeling appears to have run high at this meeting. Mr. Arrowsmith, one of the Guardians who attempted to put in a word in favour of the union, was shouted down, but the critical remarks of the Rev. James Furnival,[6] incumbent of St. Mary's, met with loud applause. He attacked the " rigour and cruelty " of the new Poor Law compared with the " leniency, clemency and mercy " of the old, and had no difficulty in playing on local pride when he asked whether the growing town of St. Helens should be controlled by

---

[1] Minutes of the Prescot Guardians (Lancashire Record Office, PUP 1/1) hereafter referred to as Guard Mins. There were present from the four townships : John Johnson and Charles Neish (Eccleston), William Grundy (Parr), Robert Robinson and Richard Fildes (Sutton), and Peter Greenall, Thomas Arrowsmith and Richard Pilkington (Windle). Michael Hughes, Charles Orrell and Samuel Taylor also attended in their capacity as magistrates.

[2] Guard Mins., 9 Feb., 8 March, 1837.

[3] *Ibid.*, 8 March, 23 March, 1837 ; 11 Jan., 1838.

[4] *Ibid.*, 9 Nov., 1837.

[5] *Ibid.*, 28 Dec., 1837.

[6] The Rev. James Furnival came to St. Helens in 1836 from a curacy at Davenham, Cheshire. He became involved in the construction of a new and expensive parsonage which led to differences with the chapel trustees and to his resignation in 1841 (Mins. of trustees, 4 July, 1838, 22 April, 1841 ; *Wigan Gazette*, 9 Dec., 1836 ; art. by James Brockbank in biog. newscuttings at St. H. Ref. Lib.).

a Board of Guardians residing at Prescot.[1] Although the petition of protest is said to have been signed by 15,000,[2] the opposition appears to have been part of a more general anti-Poor Law movement rather than an outcry against the changes that were taking place locally. The people of St. Helens may have sympathised with those who were taking active measures to boycott the New Poor Law elsewhere, but there are no signs that the 15,000 signatories to the petition attempted to hinder the development of the new order in the four townships. On the contrary, Peter Greenall, who was chairman at the protest meeting, consented in the following year to be elected as a Guardian and the Rev. James Furnival, having at first refused to become chaplain, was later prevailed upon to consent when an honorarium of £50 a year was offered.[3]

The Guardians were very concerned about the susceptibilities of the opposition and, indeed, they themselves, far from being whole-hearted supporters of Benthamite ideas, disarmed their critics by making it clear that they were also partly, at least, on the side of their opponents. Thomas Kidd, Chairman of the Prescot Guardians, even went so far as to confess publicly :

" I have always condemned the principle and many of the provisions of the Act ; such as the separation of families and other clauses of a more delicate description and shall be happy to see it repealed altogether; though at the same time persuaded some good to the public may arise from a lenient administration of the law, which I contend is in the powers of the Commissioners to allow . . . The public will also find that the poor of the Prescot Union, by the same remission, are not to be immured in one common prison workhouse but divided, as well as circumstances will permit, into three separate houses, to accommodate each description of poor according to their relative situation and wants."[4]

As none of the Guardians chose to contradict this statement in the press or at subsequent meetings of the Board, we must assume that Kidd had the support of his fellow Guardians in making it. Three years later, in 1841, the Board carried a resolution " that

---

[1] *Wigan Gazette* 2 Feb., 1838.

[2] *Wigan Gazette* 9 Feb., 1838.

[3] Guard. Mins., 7 Feb., 4 April, 1839 ; 2, 16 Jan., 1840. Despite his willingness to stand as Guardian, Greenall still insisted that he was opposed in principle to the new Poor Law, believing that " the system is not fitted for the manufacturing and largely populated districts." (*Wigan Gazette* 18 June, 1841).

[4] *Wigan Gazette*, 16 Feb., 1838.

the New Poor Law might not be insisted upon in the Prescot
Union and that the Orders of the Poor Law Commissioners
relating to the Union might be rescinded."[1]

But, despite all these genuine protestations of sweet reasonable-
ness on the part of the Guardians, they were only agents of the
Commission. The constant flow of instructions and regulations
from Somerset House, and the Assistant Commissioner on his
regular visits from Manchester, repeatedly emphasised the need
for economy. Everything was advertised for purchase by tender:
food and fuel, coconut matting and coffins, clothes and clogs.
Local tradesmen, and occasionally manufacturers from far afield,
like Francis Barnett of Bristol who supplied " improved iron
Bedsteads,"[2] competed keenly to put in the lowest tender and we
are left to imagine the quality of the goods they supplied. As the
months passed, the diets became more and more spartan. In 1844,
for instance, it was ordered

> " that when Sweet Milk Porridge shall be made for the
> Paupers, it shall consist of one quart of Milk and five Quarts of
> Water ... Adult Paupers have Sweet Milk Porridge twice a
> week."[3]

When at one meeting a Guardian raised the question of increasing
the diet for those women who did the workhouse washing,

> " it was resolved unanimously that on Washing Days the
> Washerwomen be allowed Tea for their Breakfast and Bread
> and Butter for Lunch at ten o'clock in the forenoon."[4]

But perhaps the surest signs of the times were two orders made
in November, 1842. From then on Christmas dinner of roast
beef and plum pudding was to be discontinued and no pauper
was to be permitted any allowance of tobacco or snuff at any
time.[5] Ten years later and a few days before Christmas, the
Chairman of the Board was able to convey to the Governor and
Matron of the Workhouse the approbation of the Guardians
" especially in the reduction which has been effected in the cost
of Inmaintenance from 2/11 to 1/10¾ *per Head per week* without
affecting the comfort of the Inmates."[6]

The occupiers of the Windle Workhouse, the male paupers,
were soon set to work. In May, 1838, the Guardians from the
four townships were formed into a committee to decide what

[1] Guard. Mins., 25 Feb., 1841.
[2] *Ibid.*, 8 March, 1838.
[3] *Ibid.*, 13 June, 1844.
[4] *Ibid.*, 23 May, 1844.
[5] *Ibid.*, 24 Nov. 1842.
[6] *Ibid.*, 23 Dec., 1852. The italics are our own.

work should be provided and in July the committee was authorised
" to provide a quantity of old ropes for the able bodied Paupers
to pick into oakum."[1] In August it was resolved

> " that no Pauper be permitted to go out of the Sutton or
> Windle Workhouses without an order from the Visiting Com-
> mittee except to a place of Worship on the Sabbath day."[2]

A few years later, when it was discovered that only one pauper
had been to church, " the others having gone rambling about the
Country," it was ordered that

> " such of the Inmates as shall in future neglect to attend a
> place of worship when let out of the Workhouse for that
> purpose shall be deprived of their Sunday's Dinner."[3]

Having carefully watched local reaction to the gradual
introduction of the new system into the district, the Commissioners
awaited their opportunity to press upon the Guardians that large,
gaunt and terrifying symbol of the new order, the union workhouse. In February, 1839, Alfred Power admitted that he was
waiting for " a more favourable state of public opinion on the
subject " and reported that at Prescot " the project of a New
Union Workhouse will probably be brought forward before
long."[4] The next month a motion for the erection of a central
workhouse to cost less than £4,000 was carried at a meeting of
the Prescot Guardians by eleven votes to seven, though among
the seven were those of Grundy, Arrowsmith and Tomlinson, the
only representatives from the four townships present on that
occasion.[5] No further action was taken, however, until 1841
when Charles Mott, who had succeeded Power as Assistant
Commissioner for Lancashire and the West Riding of Yorkshire,
drew attention on one of his visits to Prescot to " the present
very inefficient workhouse accommodation " in the union and
persuaded five of the Guardians to inspect some recently-built
union workhouses at Chorlton-on-Medlock and elsewhere.[6] The
Guardians were apparently impressed by what they saw. On
their return they advised that an immediate start should be made
upon their own building. Accordingly, at the end of the year a
piece of land was acquired fronting upon the Prescot-Warrington
turnpike road as it passed through Whiston township ;[7] in June,

[1] *Ibid.*, 17 May, 5 July, 1838.

[2] *Ibid.*, 16 Aug., 1838.

[3] *Ibid.*, 25 Aug., 1842.

[4] P.R.O., H.O. 73/55. Report from Power, Feb., 1839.

[5] Guard. Mins., 28 March, 1839.

[6] *Ibid.*, 1 July, 1841.

[7] *Ibid.*, 19 Aug., 11 Nov., 1841.

1842, the tender for building went to Robert Morris of Liverpool[1] and just over a year later the Guardians were able to hold their first meeting in the Board Room of the new Union Workhouse.[2]

The operation of the New Poor Law in the district conforms very closely to the traditional workhouse story as told by Dickens. Yet there were never more than 100 inmates from the four townships of Windle, Parr, Sutton and Eccleston at any one time, apart from the period of depression at the beginning of the 'forties when the number reached 130. The figure for the mid-1840s was usually between 60 and 80 but it was sometimes less, on one occasion sinking to 32. Out-relief in the St. Helens district, on the other hand, varied from £20 to £40 per week with quarterly payments (presumably for rent) amounting to about £200. Even allowing an expenditure of 3s. per head per week on paupers in the workhouse and assuming that there were 100 such inmates from the four townships, the total payments on in-maintenance would only amount to £15, considerably less than what was being allowed to the needy in their homes. Accurate comparison is difficult, however, because the minutes of the Guardians give particulars of outpayments weekly and of inmates quarterly, and do not state the number of recipients of out-relief, only the total amount paid. There are, however, full returns, relating to the union as a whole and not particularly to St. Helens, for a week in February, 1846, and for another week in February, 1847. In the former, there were 99 inmates altogether, and 489 families, comprising 968 people, receiving out-relief amounting to £55 13s. 0d. In the latter week, there were 146 inmates, and 552 families (949 people in all) receiving out-relief totalling £69 3s. 0d.[3] In St. Helens itself the number in receipt of out-relief and in-maintenance was probably well below 600 in a population of more than 12,000.

From these totals, it would appear that the actual operation of the New Poor Law in the Prescot Union was not so harsh as the conditions prevailing in the workhouse would at first suggest. Of course, much depends upon the type of person who found himself an inmate. If he was a confirmed wastrel or idler, hardship, though not cruelty, may have been justifiable. But if he was a person who was down on his luck and unable to work—an unemployed handloom weaver, for example[4]—that would have been quite a different matter.

[1] *Ibid.*, 9 June, 1842.
[2] *Ibid.*, 7 Sept. 1843.
[3] Returns to an Address dated 30 May, 1848, 1847-8 [642] LIII.
[4] Of 8 weavers named in the St. H. Civil Death Registers between 1837 and 1843, 7 died in the poorhouse. This would refer to the Sutton poorhouse, then being used for the aged.

During the few years when trade was bad, the modest sums spent on out-relief could do little to alleviate the extreme hardship caused by widespread unemployment and part-time working. In the St. Helens district, weekly out-payments continued to fluctuate between £20 and £30 even during the severe depression of 1841-3. At the same time, however, there seems to be every justification for emphasising—as did the Assistant Commissioner[1]—the abundance of employment during good years rather than the undoubted misery during bad, for this was a period of unprecedented industrial growth. In general, St. Helens in these formative years presents a picture of prosperity rather than of poverty, of bustling activity rather than of idleness.

[1] Above, p. 306.

CHAPTER XXII

ST. HELENS IN THE 'FORTIES

THE reporter who described St. Helens both as a village and as a town in 1820 would have had no such doubts had he paid another visit twenty years later.

" The first view of St. Helens, as of most other manufacturing towns," wrote a correspondent in 1846, " is not very pre-possessing. It lies on a piece of level ground surrounded by a few gentle eminences, and seldom on any week-day is it without its overhanging cloud of smoke. Through this the visitor sees irregular masses of brick houses, two or three churches with square towers, tall chimnies vomiting smoke, and conical glass-houses, giving out occasional bright flashes of flame. The clank of hammers ringing against iron is heard from many a forge and foundry and a strange compound of smells proceed from a chemical work which rears its head close by the railway station and in the suburbs of the town. The streets have apparently been laid out without any plan, as chance or interest might direct. . . . In many of the streets only one side has been built up and there are therefore various vacant spaces of ground which, in rainy weather, contain pools of water and prove anything but conducive to health. Like many other manufacturing places, St. Helens seems to have been built in a hurry, the attention of the inhabitants being so absorbed in advancing manufactures that they would care little about the kind of houses they should provide for themselves."[1]

As the town expanded, fields became built-up areas, cart tracks became roads, green became black.

Yet, despite ugly urbanisation, much remained that was pleasantly rural. Although the low-lying tongue of land created by the Sankey Brook and its tributaries was being gradually covered with factories, shops and houses, there were still many open spaces and the inhabitants had only to walk a short distance to the " gentle eminences " surrounding the town to escape from the smoke and grime and enjoy the fresh air of the countryside. For the occupiers of the crowded and often insanitary cottage property in Greenbank, for instance, a stroll over nearby Comb-shop Brow was a pleasant country walk.[2] A recreation field down

---

[1] *Chambers Edinburgh Journal* No. 119 (new. ser.), 11 April, 1846.

[2] See, e.g., evidence given at the time of the Buckley murder (*Lpool. Merc.* 2 Dec., 1842).

in the town itself, as advocated by Samuel Taylor in 1847,[1] would, no doubt, have benefited the inhabitants, particularly the children, but it is open to doubt whether a public park had yet become a necessity with open country so close at hand. Nobody took up Taylor's offer of fifty guineas towards the purchase of a field suitable for use as a park and thirty years elapsed before the matter was broached again.

The countryside not only surrounded the townspeople : it was also in their blood. Some of them had been born and bred in St. Helens when it was only a village in the heart of a mining district. Others had grown up in isolated farmsteads or small hamlets or rude Irish cabins and had migrated to the town either in search of better wages or as refugees from starvation. For the most part, they came because they believed that the town offered them a higher standard of living than that to which they were accustomed. They brought with them a frankness and a spontaneity which has always typified country folk, and introduced a breath of fresh air that went far to counteract the discomfort and monotony of their urban surroundings. Their lack of discipline and their reluctance to be subjected to regulation, which raised serious problems for employers,[2] exercised a profoundly beneficial effect upon the social life of the new town. Their attitude of mind went far to make life worth living despite the deaths, fevers and discomforts which resulted from insanitary or overcrowded conditions.

They brought with them their country pastimes. Pigeon-flying, prize-fighting and foot-racing continued unabated and the inhabitants still thronged the various taverns in the town[3] as they had crowded into their favourite country inns. They showed a great zest for life and did not allow any opportunity for enjoyment to pass by—not even a public hanging.[4] Processions and feasting were particularly popular. When Queen Victoria came to the throne, for instance, the whole town participated *en masse* in a united demonstration of loyalty. A great procession, including Sunday School children, workmen from the various factories, members of friendly societies, tradespeople, magistrates, clergy and gentlemen—several thousands in all—headed by two

[1] *Lpool. Merc.* 25 June, 1847.

[2] See, e.g., the remarks of Andrew Ure in his *Philosophy of Manufactures* (3rd ed., 1861), 15.

[3] According to Pigot's *Directory*, there were 29 public houses and 46 beer shops in and around St. Helens in 1834. In 1855 the number had increased to 56 and 106 respectively (Mannex's *Directory*, 1855). In 1834 the St. Helens beersellers were powerful enough to defeat an attempt to change opening time from 6 a.m. to 8 a.m. (*Lpool. Merc.* 10 Oct., 5 Dec., 1834).

[4] See, e.g., the hanging of Clitheroe, a local man, who himself had been a frequenter of hangings at Kirkdale Gaol (*St. H. N.*, 20, 23 April, 1864).

trumpeters and interspersed by four bands, toured the town boundaries where the proclamation of the new queen was solemnly read out. Having thus shown their allegiance to the throne, everyone adjourned to parties and festivities which were prolonged deep into the night.[1] Demonstrations like this were not confined to rare state occasions : the Oddfellows, as has been seen, were very fond of them.

Three times every year there were particular opportunities for merrymaking : at the St. Helens Fair, held in the New Market Place in April and September, and during Newton Race Week, held in June. The two-day Fair originated in 1780, at the same time as the weekly market for the sale of cattle and horses, cloth, haberdashery, brassware and toys.[2] The sale of cattle and horses ceased about the end of the eighteenth century, however, and, as more local shops came to be built and the weekly market developed, the biannual fair became an occasion for amusement rather than for buying and selling. By the 1840s it was noted for its swing boats, merry-go-rounds, side shows, and stalls selling gingerbread and other kinds of food and drink. The Fair provided much excitement—and not a few opportunities for excess. The same was true of the week when the Newton Races were held, a period, as a contemporary described it, " much like Whitsun Week in Manchester when no one thinks of working if he can help it."[3] The incumbent of St. Mary's cautioned his congregation against the temptations of Newton Race Week[4] and Sunday School outings were organised on Race Friday in an attempt to

[1] *Wigan Gazette* 14 July, 1837. For a similar celebration at the accession of George IV, see *Lpool. Merc.* 3 March, 1820.

[2] *Gore's Gen. Ad.*, 10 March, 1780, carried the following notice :

"To the Public. Notice is hereby given that a FAIR will be holden in the Town of St. Hellen . . . on Friday and Saturday in Easter Week next, and continue annually for the Sale of Horned Cattle on Friday and for the sale of Horses, Woollen and Linen Cloth, Braziery, Toys, and all manner of Haberdashery Wares upon the Saturday—and also another FAIR will be holden upon the Friday and Saturday following the 5th November next, and continue annually, for the sale of the articles above-mentioned."

The sale of cattle appears to have ceased before the end of the eighteenth century, for, when the cattle fair was revived in 1840, mention was made of 45 years having passed since cattle had been sold at the Fair (*Wigan Gazette*, 20 Nov., 1840). According to Pigot's *New Commercial Directory* (1828), the Fair was held on the Monday and Tuesday after Easter and the Friday and Saturday after 8 Sept. During the following years, however, the days appear to have been altered to Saturday and Monday in each case.

[3] *St. H. Weekly News*, 22 June, 1861.

[4] Letter from Thomas Pigot, *Lpool. Merc.*, 13 Feb., 1835.

keep the children otherwise occupied.[1] In addition to these unofficial holidays, it is possible that the annual " works trips," noticed for the first time in the press in 1850,[2] may have become an institution a little before that time.

One of these trips was organised by Pilkington's Recreation Section which had started life in 1847 as a club organising games of cricket, a sport popular in the neighbourhood and already played by the St. Helens Cricket Club, formed in 1843.[3] The game of bowls also excited keen interest ; bowling matches were being held at Denton's Green so long ago as 1665 and continue to be held to this day.[4] A Bowling Green Inn, in Parr, was sold in 1778 and bowling matches were taking place about that time at the green belonging to the King's Head, next to St. Helen's chapel.[5] By the 1840s the Bird i' th' Hand at the end of Dunriding Lane (then Jack's Lane) was also the scene of many well-attended games from Easter onwards throughout the summer.[6]

When the cricket and bowling seasons came to an end and the nights began to draw in, the townspeople passed the evenings in the alehouses or at one or other of the churches which organised programmes of week-night activities. There were occasional visiting attractions, a circus, perhaps,[7] or a company of travelling players like those who erected their wooden " Thespian Temple " in the New Market Place and stayed so long as they received sufficient support.[8] A responsive audience does not seem to have been lacking, for in 1847 a permanent theatre was opened.[9] In the depths of winter, the hard frost and snow saw many people skating on the ice at Carr Mill dam and at other local ponds and lakes. Although we lack descriptions of these winter sports, this is probably because everyone took them for granted. Some of the happiest and most persistent traditions of this period relate to its hard winters. A leading article in an early issue of the *St.*

---

[1] See, e.g., *Lpool. Merc.* 11 June, 1847.

[2] In that year 400 workmen from the Ravenhead Plate Glassworks went to the Menai Straits and 150 from Pilkingtons visited Halton Castle (*Lpool. Merc.* 23 Jan., 1850).

[3] *Lpool. Merc.*, 16 Aug., 1844. The club used a ground behind the Raven Inn until 1858 when the land was required for the new railway station (*St. H. Intelligencer* 31 Jan., 10 July, 1858). The Cricket Club's annual ball is first mentioned in the *Manchester Courier* of 29 March, 1845.

[4] The Diary of Roger Lowe (ed. William L. Sachse, 1938) *sub.* 8 Aug., 1665 ; L.R.O., DDGe 658.

[5] *Gore's Gen. Ad.* 24 April, 1778 ; P.R.O., P.L. 7/86/175, 182.

[6] *Lpool. Merc.* 25 April, 1848.

[7] *Lpool. Merc.* 28 Feb., 1845.

[8] *Wigan Gazette* 19 Oct., 1838 ; James Brockbank, *History of the Drama in St. Helens* (St. H., 1901).

[9] *Ibid.*

Helens Intelligencer, in 1856, held that " the deficiency of occasions for merrymaking is not very great among us."[1] There is every indication that, had the journal been in existence ten or fifteen years earlier, it would have expressed the same opinion.

But there was another side to the picture. Against the boisterous fun and often reckless games must be set the strangeness of factory work, the drawbacks of having to live in an increasingly congested community and the discomfort of occupying a few rooms in a row of hastily-built cottages. Yet insanitary conditions were only starting to attract the attention of reformers in those parts of the town where property had been recently built. There were epidemics and fevers, but these were the result of medical ignorance rather than of sanitary negligence. Nobody at that time was in a position to cope with infectious and contagious diseases : they raged in country districts as well as in the towns. In 1819, for instance, when St. Helens was still little more than a village, a disease described as typhus but possibly typhoid was said to be " very prevalent " in the neighbourhood[2] and in the rural community of Ashton-in-Makerfield, a few miles away, a township committee had to be set up to deal with this same outbreak.[3] In the St. Helens of the 1840s the infant mortality rate—a sure guide to sanitary conditions—was only a little higher than the average for the nation as a whole. Throughout England and Wales there were 153 deaths under one year of age per 1,000 births :[4] in St. Helens the rate was 156 per 1,000.[5] Similarly, about one-third of the children born in the town died before reaching the age of five, as occured else where throughout the country. The high mortality rate was the penalty for failing to discover how diseases came to be spread. It is true that attention had been drawn to the close connection between health and living

---

[1] *St. H. Intelligencer* 12 April, 1856.

[2] L.R.O., DDPi 5/9-13. Eleanor Pilkington to Richard Pilkington, 6 April, 1819.

[3] Warrington Pub. Lib., Sibson Papers.

[4] *Matters of Life and Death* (H.M.S.O., 1948), 8.

[5] The Civil Death Registers show that in the St. Helens Registration District in 1840-9 there were 8,523 deaths. Of these, 1,326 were under one year of age. William Farr cast some doubt on the completeness of these early returns and estimated that throughout the country during the 1840s more than 38,000 births per year went unrecorded (*q.v.* T. H. Marshall, " The Population Problem During the Industrial Revolution," *Ec. Jour. Ec. Hist. Ser.* No. 4, Jan., 1929, 439). If this estimate is correct, the figures of births should be used with great caution. It may well be, however, that most of the unrecorded births occurred in places where there was most opposition to the new Poor Law. This was not the case at St. Helens and the local figures may, therefore, be more reliable than Farr's estimate suggests. See appendix 3.

conditions long before Chadwick's surveys gave much wider publicity to the subject.[1] But, even so, his conclusion that " the annual loss of life from filth and bad ventilation is greater than the loss from death or wounds in many wars in which the country has been engaged in modern times,"[2] did not make a deep impression upon the public as a whole, whose rudimentary knowledge of the subject was limited to an intuitive connection between foul smells and illness ; nor upon a medical profession which had only just distinguished typhus from typhoid[3] and had not yet proved the close correlation between the spread of cholera and contaminated water supplies.[4] Had Chadwick been able to cite the results of the later research of Pasteur and Lister, his task would have been far easier.[5]

The industries responsible for calling the insanitary new towns into existence went far to make amends by producing more abundantly and cheaply the materials required to promote cleanliness and to effect the necessary improvements in sanitation. Cheaper cotton, for instance, meant less typhus for, unlike woollens, cotton goods were boiled and boiling destroyed the body louse which carried the disease.[6] Local industries made their particular contribution. Cheaper alkali reduced the price of soap and a more abundant supply of window glass made possible the era of light and airy rooms, though the Victorians did not take easily to the idea of open windows. It was, however, the potteries of the neighbourhood which made the most direct and striking contribution to the improvement of public health.

When Edwin Chadwick and the other champions of sanitary reform were dogmatically urging the essential, if unspectacular, advantages bestowed by the non-porous drainpipe, their universal panacea had never before been produced on a commercial scale. Chadwick had been impressed by the experiments of John Roe,

---

[1] B. Keith-Lucas, " Some Influences Affecting the Development of Sanitary Legislation in England," *Ec. Hist. Rev.*, 2nd. ser., VI No. 3 (April, 1954), 290-6.

[2] Quoted by Sir John Simon in his *English Sanitary Institutions* (1890), 192.

[3] M. C. Buer, *Health, Wealth and Population in the Early Days of the Industrial Revolution* (1926), 193.

[4] *Ibid.*, 230.

[5] The germ theory of disease was being advanced by Pasteur at the end of the 1850s and Lister, who first used carbolic acid in 1866, acknowledged his debts to Pasteur's work (*q.v.* R. J. Dubos, *Louis Pasteur, Free Lance of Science*, 1951, particularly caps. 9-11 ; Hector Charles Cameron, *Joseph Lister, the Friend of Man*, 1948).

[6] Buer, *op. cit.*, 196.

engineer to one of the London Commissions of Sewers.[1] Roe had been able to obtain samples for these experiments from some of the potteries in Lambeth ; but to obtain bulk supplies was quite another matter. Although ordinary earthenware tubes were being used for agricultural purposes, no manufacturers had found it worth their while to concentrate upon making non-porous pipes with watertight joints until the extensive publicity of the sanitary reformers opened up a prospect of profit from this branch of pottery.

One of the first men to try his hand was Henry Doulton of Lambeth who in 1846 broke away from the family firm of Doulton and Watts and set up on his own at a small factory nearby. He later recalled :

> " There was a hard fight with the public outside, whilst inside we suffered from lack of suitable machinery. At first we had either to throw the pipes on the wheel, or turn them on drums . . . but within a year machinery was employed."

Assisted by technical advice from eminent engineers and aided financially by his father and brothers, he was soon able to embark upon large-scale production. Once Henry Doulton and Co. found themselves able to manufacture in bulk in London, they looked around for a suitable pottery from which they could supply the needs of the large towns and cities of the north. The coarse clays of St. Helens were admirably suited for their purposes and before 1850 Henry Doulton's elder brother, John, took charge of the Greenbank Pottery.[2]

There is always a time-lag between the growth of abuses and the taking of remedial action. In the case of sanitary reform, this was caused partly by a lack of knowledge about germs and delays in applying the technical results of scientific research, and partly by the apathy of a public only roused to action when widespread and devastating epidemics, such as those of the Asiatic Cholera, swept the land. The 'forties lay in the midst of this unhappy interval, when certain sections of the population underwent unusual trials. This time-lag between the growth of an abuse and its reform applied not only to those who lived in unhealthy

---

[1] This and the following paragraph are based upon S. E. Finer, *The Life and Times of Sir Edwin Chadwick* (1952) and " The Story of Doulton's," published in that company's magazine *Doulton News*, nos. 5-14 (1947-50), particularly the instalment in No. 8 on " The Dawn of Modern Sanitation."

[2] The exact date of Doulton's arrival at St. Helens is not clear. The carefully written *Doulton News* article states 1847 but the local rate books give the occupier of the Greenbank Pottery in that year as a Mr. Poulson and the proprietors as the executors of Thomas Harley (*q.v.* above, p. 129). This is confirmed by *Slater's Royal National Commercial Directory* of 1848. It is tempting to assume that Poulson was a mistaken reading for Doulton, but this was not the case, for Mr. Poulson was occupying the pottery in 1845 according to the rate book of that year.

X

surroundings but also to those who worked in industries where safety regulations were overdue. At St. Helens coalmining, which became more dangerous as the workings were extended, provides the best example. These widespread and persistent afflictions should not, however, be confused with the more acute, though temporary, distress which fell upon the town in the early 1840s. It is necessary to distinguish between times of thriving trade and years of depression.

In the fast-expanding local economy of the 1830s and 1840s, jobs were being created with extraordinary rapidity. New firms were springing up on all sides at an unprecedented rate. The demand for labour was so great, indeed, that there was a man-power shortage : workpeople had to be attracted to the town by offers of higher wages. This was particularly true of skilled craftsmen of whom the glassmakers formed the largest section.

A significant sign of the times was the presence of young men in positions of managerial responsibility. David Gamble had virtual control of the Gerard's Bridge Chemical works in his early twenties. Arthur Sinclair became secretary of the St. Helens Railway before he was twenty-one. Andrew George Kurtz succeeded to his father's business when he had just reached his majority and his manager, John Hutchinson, later the pioneer manufacturing chemist at Widnes, had been a fellow student with him in Paris. Henry Baxter, son of a local yeoman farmer, entered the Sutton Copper Works at sixteen and was manager by the age of twenty-five.[1] Admittedly, some of these young men were merely following in their father's footsteps ; but this was not true of all of them by any means. And for every one of such an age at the top of the ladder, several occupied the rungs immediately below. There was no shortage of remunerative careers open to talent at a time of such rapid industrial expansion.

There were periods, however, when this expansion was suddenly halted due to nation-wide depressions in trade. The years 1841-3 witnessed one of the most severe of all these slumps. The Sutton Plate Glassworks and two of the alkali companies, those of Darcy and Dearden and of the Cloughs, all failed and the men employed there were thrown out of work. The Union Plate Glassworks were temporarily closed with the same result. Elsewhere part-time working and reduced wages were general. In the autumn of 1843, when trade was starting to pick up again, a newspaper correspondent reviewed the havoc wrought at St. Helens during the slump :

" During the last two years, the trade of this town has suffered dreadfully in the general depression, many hundreds of persons —we have heard the number stated as high as 1,200 or 1,500—

[1] Below, p. 348.

having been thrown out of employment by the stoppage of
several large works, not only inflicting much misery upon the
workpeople, but seriously injuring the shopkeepers and house-
owners of the town, a large amount of property having been all
at once vacated by the unemployed tenants. Within the last
month or two, however, we are glad to say, there are evident
indications of a revival in several branches of trade . . ."[1]

The withdrawal of wages on such a scale occasioned great hardship
and set many of the unemployed on the tramp for work. In such
difficult times the vast resources of the friendly societies, and
particularly the contacts offered in other towns by the larger
Orders, must have been a great boon. Despite these alleviating
circumstances, however, 1841-3 were undoubtedly years of
extreme privation and it seems probable that the celebrated story,
recounted by Engels, of the poor, helpless wretch, found " in a
miserable damp cellar " at St. Helens mending the stockings of
his wife who was out working, was a product of this period.[2]
But the story is told at third hand and written up in a highly
emotional style. It was a case of special pleading and in no way
typical of life in the town, even during the slump. St. Helens was
a place where women often assisted men at their work but could
rarely replace them ; the very nature of the jobs made that
impossible. Indeed, there was a drift from the town to the textile
areas where more suitable employment was available for women.[3]
Again, the suggestion that the local inhabitants lived in cellars, is
to say the least, most misleading. A sanitary reformer, in evidence
before the committee on the St. Helens Improvement Bill in 1845,
mentioned some " dark, damp cellars," not fit for habitation, at
Gerard's Bridge. Yet only sixteen cellars are mentioned in the
rate books of that year, and John Daglish, a land surveyor, told
the committee of 1845 that they were not inhabited.

In 1847-8 there was another, though much less severe, recession
in trade. Its limited extent is indicated by the small reduction in
the coal traffic carried on the St. Helens Canal and Railway : only
50,000 tons in the period June 1847-8 below the previous year's
total. Income from the carriage of passengers and merchandise
even continued to increase slightly during the period.[4] In some
respects more dislocation was caused during this minor depression
by the arrival of hordes of starving Irish fleeing from the famine
than by the mild setback in trade.

[1] *Manchester Courier*, 30 Sept., 1843.

[2] F. Engels, *The Condition of the Working Class in England in* 1844 (1892)
45-6.

[3] Below, p. 427.

[4] *Railway Record*, 5 Aug., 1848.

The sufferings of these poverty-stricken, vermin-ridden refugees was shared to some extent by all those living and working near them who were obliged to bear with their unconventional habits and, on occasions, to contract their diseases. Although the Irish settled in particular districts, these Little Irelands did not consist exclusively of Irish people and the introduction of men and women with totally different outlooks and habits, accustomed to a lower standard of living, inevitably tended to exercise a depressing influence upon their neighbours.

The lot of the Irish settler may serve as a warning against any too materialistic interpretation of the 1840s solely in terms of sanitation or standards of living. The Irishman had been accustomed to eking out a precarious existence on the verge of starvation and under the most primitive conditions. He was, therefore, satisfied with the most elementary necessities of life ; indeed, he clung to them for in the past they had sufficed to make him happy. It may be contended that happiness for him, when he came over to England, consisted in maintaining as many of his old customs as he could. To deny him his pig, filthy though it may have been, or his glass of whisky, even though it often led him to trouble, would certainly have caused him pain, not pleasure. Similarly with the other elements in the population, the need for regulation was not readily appreciated, for everyone was accustomed to greater freedom of action. For a true understanding of the 'forties, it is essential to bear firmly in mind the conditions prevailing earlier, to concentrate upon 1800 rather than upon 1900. His sports and recreations—brutal and coarse though some of them were—and some of his less refined habits probably meant more to the townsman of the 1840s than the laying of drains.

So far as St. Helens was concerned, although the 1840s saw much hardship and inconvenience, the inevitable accompaniment of any vigorous transition, they were no more remarkable as a period of shortage and suffering than the 1820s or 1830s had been or any other ten-yearly period which included intervals when trade—or the harvest—was bad. The small number of inmates in the Prescot Union Workhouse, it is true, was kept on short rations and the Irish refugees certainly endured great privation until they settled down. To refer to the 'forties indiscriminately as " hungry," however, is quite misleading. The suggestion that the essentials of life could not be afforded is completely at variance with the ascertainable local evidence. Nor was there any thirst for knowledge and culture in the town. Two attempts to form a Mechanics Institute had failed and a third met with a very scant measure of success.[1] A library, when it was

---

[1] Below, p. 386.

formed, attracted few borrowers. Though the progressive reformers might preach self-help and self-government, they found few ardent followers. The vast majority of men and women appear to have been quite content to concern themselves with their family, their friends and the doings of their immediate neighbourhood. Then, as always, births, marriages and deaths, sickness and health, work, sport and scandal seem to have formed the chief topics of interest. It is, perhaps, fair comment upon the validity of the " Hungry Forties " so far as St. Helens is concerned, to notice that the phrase did not come into common usage until the beginning of the present century when it was employed by the free-traders for propaganda purposes.[1]

Clearly, St. Helens had several advantages over its neighbours. It was quite unlike the textile centres, usually quoted as the classical examples of urban growth. It developed later than these mill towns and was still comparatively small by the middle of the nineteenth century. In consequence, it was not so overcrowded and was less troubled by insanitary conditions. Nor did it have to carry the burden of a horde of domestic weavers who stubbornly clung to their looms in the face of overwhelming competition. On the contrary, instead of being obliged to support a section of the population floundering in abject poverty, St. Helens derived considerable benefit from possessing a high percentage of well-paid workpeople. All these facts contribute to make the picture which we have been painting rather brighter than the classical examples. The complete absence of Chartism,[2] is obviously not without significance.

But there were other new towns which, like St. Helens, grew up later than the textile districts ; they, too, do not conform to the standard pattern. And further enquiry may show that some of the relieving features—such as the thriving friendly societies and the numerous leisure activities—which helped to make life more endurable and enjoyable at St. Helens were to be found throughout all the industrial districts of the country. Indeed, our evidence causes us to wonder whether writers about urban conditions at this time, who have drawn mainly on sources which relate to the larger towns and looked at their information through twentieth-century eyes, may not have reached conclusions which are gloomier than the facts merit. They have presented only part of the picture. There is another side to it which ought not to be ignored.

[1] W. H. Chaloner, " The ' Hungry Forties ' : The Origin of a Legend," *History To-day*, July, 1951, 78.

[2] This statement is based on a study of the Liverpool, Manchester and Wigan papers of the period. See also above, p. 297.

After the enactment of the St. Helens Improvement Bill, some of the inhabitants of the town, in recognition of the part played by Peter Greenall, subscribed to have his portrait painted. But before the artist had had time to complete the canvas, his sitter was dead. Peter Greenall had a stroke on 18 September, 1845, and passed away before medical help could reach him. The loss of the man who at the age of forty-nine might have been expected to continue to guide the fortunes of St. Helens for another twenty years or more, was a sad blow. The whole town went into mourning, " feeling as if they had lost a near and valued friend."[1] On the day of his funeral,

" Churchman and Dissenter, rich and poor, Conservative and Liberal, as if by common consent, *without the slightest arrangement*, suspended all business, that they might pay tribute of their deep feelings of sorrow over the tomb of their late respected townsman ; every shop was fully closed and continued so during the day. So early as eight in the morning strangers were seen wending their way to the town from Wigan and the other towns and villages surrounding, all clad in the usual habiliments of mourning as if coming to pay their homage of respect to some dear and departed relative. At ten o'clock all the county constabulary of the district were drawn up to pay their last token of respect to their late resident magistrate. By this time the streets near the church were liberally crammed and at half past ten there could not have been fewer than 6,000 persons waiting as spectators."[2]

This year, 1845, ended the formative period in the town's development. The amalgamation of the Canal and Railway changed considerably its economic prospects by re-establishing a transport monopoly ; the removal of the excise duty stimulated the local glass industry ; and the setting up of an Improvement Commission marked the beginning of modern local government. Peter Greenall passed away with the age with which he had been so vitally and successfully associated, an age owing so much to his influential direction. His sudden and untimely removal left the town to face the middle years of the century much the poorer for his loss.

---

[1] *Lpool. Merc.* 19 Sept., 1845. For obituary notices, see also *Manchester Guardian* and *Manchester Courier* 20 Sept., 1845 and the *Annual Register* 1845, 296-7.

[2] *Lpool. Merc.* 26 Sept., 1845. The italicised words are in the original report.

PART THREE

THE MIDDLE YEARS
1845-1870

CHAPTER XXIII

THE TRANSPORT MONOPOLY

1845-1872

AT the time of the amalgamation of the St. Helens Canal and Railway in 1845, the latter was in dire need of repair and certain fundamental improvements in the line were also required. The stationary engine and inclined planes were a serious and costly handicap to the expansion of the all-important coal traffic ; the two docks at Widnes, intended as outlets into the Mersey free from the effects of " neaping," could only be entered by fully-laden boats for two hours at each high tide and were totally inaccessible for about eighty days in the year.[1] Moreover, the collieries in the Blackbrook district, mining the profitable Rushy Park and Little Delf coals, then in great demand, were not served at all by the Railway. The need for removing the inclines, building new docks farther down the river and extending the line to the north of St. Helens became even more pressing during the Railway Mania of 1845-46. The Grand Junction company at the close of 1845 proposed to construct a line over the Mersey at Runcorn to connect with the Liverpool and Manchester at Huyton and to continue north-eastwards towards the coalfield at St. Helens.[2]

The St. Helens Canal and Railway countered this threat by embarking upon an ambitious scheme of development of their own. Early in July 1845 the directors called in John Meadows Rendel, an eminent civil engineer whose plans for the proposed docks at Birkenhead had brought him before the public eye. He was instructed to carry out a survey of south-west Lancashire with a view to extending the St. Helens Railway through Black-brook to the Wigan coalfield in one direction and to the pro-posed bridge at Runcorn in the other, " so as to give a direct Railway communication from the St. Helens and Wigan Coal Fields to the Cheshire Salt Works." He was also " to make such improvements on the inclined planes on the Railway as shall enable them to work the line with greater economy and dispatch " and to improve the approach from the Mersey to the Widnes

[1] Evidence of Samuel Stock to the S.C. (Lords) on the St. H. C. and R. Bill, 1847 ; evidence of Samuel Palin to the S.C. on the St. H. C. and R. Bill, 1846.

[2] St. H. and R. G. Mins., 8 Dec., 1845.

Docks.[1] Rendel reported in September that it would not be possible to avoid neaping at Widnes and strongly urged the construction of a completely new dock at Garston where coal could be loaded directly into seagoing vessels by means of staithes ; this would avoid the breakage of coals in transhipment.[2] The Railway's extension from Widnes to Garston, $7\frac{1}{2}$ miles, would not be costly, for the land was flat and of poor quality and there was " no ornamental property on the route."[3] This recommendation, coming from the foremost dock engineer of his day, was unanimously accepted and within a month the necessary land was obtained at Garston.[4]

A decision was not reached so quickly about the future of the inclined planes, however, nor about the proposed line to Wigan. Rendel in his first report favoured a railway link between the Parr branch and the Wigan coalfield,[5] but more mature consideration apparently caused him to drop the idea, for it was never mentioned again. He certainly opposed any attempt to level down the inclined planes and put forward instead what became known as the Sankey Valley Scheme : the abandonment of the original route and the laying of a completely new line along the banks of the Sankey Canal, now the property of the Company.[6] This proposal had the advantage that coal could be carried on a down-gradient from any of the collieries at St. Helens or at Blackbrook. It would also be easy to lay a short branch from Sankey Bridges into Warrington to link up with the proposed Birkenhead, Lancashire and Cheshire Junction Railway of which Rendel was also the engineer. Once again the proprietors accepted Rendel's advice and appointed a sub-committee to investigate the matter in closer detail. This sub-committee reported early in December, agreeing with Rendel's original re-routing and adding a branch to Rainford, another from Eccleston Lane Ends past Gillar's Green Colliery to Gerard's Bridge, and a connection with the Grand Junction Railway at Winwick Quay.[7]

The proprietors, obviously by now firmly in the grip of the Railway Mania, sought parliamentary sanction for these

[1] St. H. and R. G. Mins., 22 July, 1845.

[2] *Ibid.*, 5 Sept., 1845 ; 14 Feb., 1846.

[3] *Ibid.*, 14 Feb., 1846.

[4] *Ibid.*, 5 Sept., 1845. For Rendel, see *D.N.B.* and obits. *Proc. Inst. C.E.*, XVI (1857), 133-42 ; *Proc. Roy. Soc. Lond.*, VIII (1857), 279-283 His report on the proposed Mersey Bridge is published in Parl. Papers, 1846 [379] XXVIII.

[5] St. H. and R. G. Mins., 5 Sept., 1845.

[6] St. H. and R. G. Mins., 10 Oct., 1845.

[7] *Ibid.*, 8 Dec., 1845.

radical additions to their line which amounted, in fact, to the construction of a completely new railway and dock at a cost of £330,000.[1] In evidence to the Parliamentary committee in the Commons, the Company based its case on the assertion that the Bill was " essentially a protective measure to St. Helens " for, as Rendel pointed out :

> " We found last year that in all directions the trade of the St. Helens Canal was invaded ; that the salt district which consumes a large portion of the trade carried on the St. Helens Canal, was about to be accommodated with Coals from Wales . . . It was very clear that unless we could give the salt works railway accommodation at once and permanently that that invasion of our property would take place."[2]

Although informal negotiations between the directors of the St. Helens Canal and Railway and officials of the Grand Junction Company had taken place in London on 13 March, 1846, no agreement had been reached and the Grand Junction therefore opposed the Bill with all its might.[3] Bowing before the storm, the St. Helens Company dropped their proposals to build branches to Eccleston and Rainford.[4] But even after throwing overboard these two non-essentials, the favourable petitions from the colliery owners and lessees at St. Helens and from the merchants, manufacturers and inhabitants of Warrington were no match for the combined opposition of the Grand Junction Company, interested landowners and others;[5] in the end Parliament only sanctioned the Garston extension.[6] The comprehensive plans of the St. Helens Company were severely curtailed ; but so were those of the Grand Junction. The bridge over the Mersey did not materialise and the threatened invasion from the south was postponed.

In the light of this reverse Rendel had second thoughts about his Sankey Valley scheme and came to the conclusion that it would, after all, be possible to reduce the inclined planes on the existing line to about 1 in 100 so that locomotives could haul their loads along the whole length of the existing track and the stationary engine could be scrapped. A Bill was introduced to extend the Railway to Blackbrook in the north and from Widnes, along the banks of the Sankey Canal and into Warrington to the east. Despite

---

[1] Evidence of Rendel to the S.C. on the St. H. C. and R. Bill, 1846.

[2] *Ibid.*

[3] St. H. and R. G. Mins., 1 Aug., 1846.

[4] *Ibid.*, 15 May, 1846.

[5] *C. J.*, **101**, 233, 477, 580, 674, 753, 2 March, 3, 28 April, 11, 22 May, 1846.

[6] 9 and 10 Vict. cap. CLXXXIII.

the opposition of the London and North Western Railway (the product of the amalgamation of the Grand Junction and several other lines, including the Liverpool and Manchester, in July, 1846), the Bill passed into law on 22 July, 1847.[1]

The Acts of 1846 and 1847 authorised an expenditure of £400,000 (£100,000 more than the existing share capital of the Company[2]) in order to transform a very inferior and inefficient mineral line, possessing only 9 second-hand tank engines and 20 trucks[3] and manned by a total staff of 112,[4] into a self-compact network linking the entire St. Helens coalfield with Warrington and Widnes, and (*via* Garston) with the Irish and other coastal and foreign markets. As an earnest of this sweeping change and a foretaste of the future, holders of Railway stock at last received a dividend—1½ per cent.—a month after the passing of the 1847 Bill.[5]

An immediate start was made on the reconstruction of the inclined planes[6] and land was acquired close to Raven Street, opposite the Raven Inn, for a new station and offices.[7] The line to this station was certified as fit for traffic by a Government inspector in December, 1849.[8]

The station and the purchase of a Patent Steam Carriage early in 1850[9] were indications of the Company's keenness to increase its passenger traffic now that the time taken to cover the distance between St. Helens and Widnes had been reduced by the removal of the inclined planes. Passengers had previously travelled on the Railway despite, rather than with the assistance of, the Company, for the proprietors had been preoccupied with the goods traffic and regarded the conveyance of passengers as very secondary and incidental. A horse-drawn passenger carriage had been placed on the line between St. Helens and the junction with the Liverpool and Manchester Railway by several St. Helens residents as a private speculation,[10] and Thomas Kidd, the ironfounder—a director of the Railway—had offered to

---

[1] 10 & 11 Vict., cap. CCLXXI. For petitions concerning the Bill, *C. J.*, **102**, 176, 213, 295, 468, 1, 8 March, 29 March, 3 May, 1847.

[2] 9 and 10 Vict. cap. CLXXXIII, sec. 3 ; 10 and 11 Vict. cap. CCLXXI. sec. 26.

[3] Gauge Commissioners' Report, 1846 [684] XVI. The local coal proprietors owned 400 waggons.

[4] Return 1847 [579] LXIII.

[5] *Railway Record*, 21 Aug., 1847.

[6] St. H. and R. G. Mins., 21, 24 July, 1847.

[7] *Ibid.*, 28 Feb., 1848 ; 19 March, 1849. The building that housed the offices is still standing.

[8] *Ibid.*, 19 Dec., 1849.

[9] *Ibid.*, 15 April, 20 May, 1850.

[10] Above, p. 293.

provide similar facilities between St. Helens and Widnes Dock.[1] In 1834 the Liverpool-Manchester Railway had been approached to run through carriages to St. Helens[2] and they probably did this soon afterwards. They were certainly running their carriages into St. Helens in the early 1840s when the St. Helens and Runcorn Gap Railway was able to issue a time-table showing that there were four trains a day for Manchester, with connections for Warrington (presumably from Newton Junction), Wigan and Preston (from Parkside) and Bolton (from Kenyon), and five trains a day for Liverpool.[3] As the population of the town increased and more people passed through St. Helens on their way to Southport,[4] much larger numbers came to be carried between St. Helens and the Liverpool-Manchester line, the 100,000 mark being exceeded between June 1845 and June 1846.[5] But even at this time the St. Helens Railway took no interest in the growing and lucrative passenger traffic, almost entirely in the hands of the Liverpool and Manchester.[6] Occasionally an unwary visitor would attempt to make the journey down the line to Widnes Dock. One such traveller gave vent to his indignation in a contribution to the *Manchester Courier* in 1840 :

" The writer of this paragraph booked himself by the quarter to six o'clock train from St. Helens to Runcorn Gap and received a ticket from the book-keeper at the former place. At ten minutes to six the train—one coach—started, and in a few minutes arrived at the foot of the incline which carries the railway across the Liverpool to Manchester line. Here Runcorn passengers alight and a walk to the stationary engine followed. There the Parr engine, with a train of coal wagons, was waiting. After some ten minutes delay, the writer was told to mount the tender of the engine his carriage being there to take him in the end [*sic*] of the journey. Another short ride brought him to the top of the second incline, on reaching which he was told to dismount from the coal-box and walk on to Runcorn, some two miles distance. After a walk and a wait he was picked up by the Runcorn engine, and on that finally arrived

[1] St. H. and R. G. Mins., 13 March, 1833.

[2] *Ibid.*, 8 Sept., 1834.

[3] The time-table, dated 14 Oct., 1842, is to be seen at the St. H. Ref. Lib.

[4] According to the 1842 time-table, " Edward Fidler's Patent Safety Coaches leave St. Helens Station for Southport every Day (Sundays excepted) on the arrival of the two o'clock train from Manchester."

[5] Return of Passengers, 30 June, 1845 to 30 June, 1846, 1847 [706] LXIII.   Cf. 26,290 passengers in 1838 (Second Report from the S.C. on the State of Communications by Railways, 1839 [517] X. Appendix, p. 398).

[6] Gauge Commissioners' Report, 1846 [684] XVI.

at the station at Runcorn Gap at twenty-five minutes past
seven, having travelled the whole line of the Runcorn Gap
and Saint Helens railway, some seven miles, in the amazing
short space of one hour and forty minutes, which is about
five minutes longer than would take a tolerable pedestrian
to walk over the same distance."[1]

He was lucky. Sir George Head, who had made the same journey
a few years before by carriage, had to dismount at one place
and was kept waiting for an hour and a quarter, the journey
of seven miles taking him nearly three hours.[2] After the reconstruction of the line, the same journey took twenty-five minutes.[3]

The original line having been vastly improved and a new station
built at St. Helens, the company turned to the various extensions ;
these were made by John Smith, a local railway contractor of
note.[4] The Blackbrook branch was being laid in the middle of
1850[5] and a connection to the Haydock Collieries was commenced early in the following year.[6] Meanwhile, as a result of
pressure from the St. Helens coal-owners, a start was made in 1850
on the line to Garston and work began on the dock there.[7] The
stretch of single track between Widnes and Garston was opened
on 1 July, 1852[8] and the line along the Canal bank to Sankey
Bridges and into Warrington was opened on the following
1 February[9], though the joint station with the Warrington and
Stockport Railway was not completed until the following year.[10]
The official opening of the Garston Dock on 21 June, 1853,

---

[1] *Manchester Courier*, 2 May, 1840. We are grateful to Mr. S. H. P.
Higgins for this reference.

[2] Sir George Head, *A Home Tour through the Manufacturing Districts of
England in the Summer of 1835* (1836), 88-91.

[3] Time-table of 1853 at St. H. Ref. Lib.

[4] John Smith, who had previously reported on the state of the line in
1840, became a director in 1849 and was in charge of all extensions after
that date. In June, 1851 he became superintendent of the locomotive
department. He owned land in the vicinity of St. Helens Junction and
was a prominent benefactor of the Roman Catholic Church, being largely
responsible for the building of St. Anne's Monastery, opened in October,
1853 (obit. *St. H. N.*, 13 June, 1863 ; Directory 1844 ; St. H. & R. G. Mins.)

[5] St. H. and R. G. Mins., 27 June, 1850. For criticisms of this branch,
see *Lpool. Merc.*, 13 and 16 March, 1849. It was originally a single line
and was doubled shortly before 1864.

[6] St. H. and R. G. Mins., 7 March, 1851.

[7] *Ibid.*, 16 April, 1849 ; 29 Aug.; 18 Nov., 1850.

[8] *Railway Times*, 7 Aug., 1852 ; report of Capt Wynne on the Widnes
and Garston extension in Report of the Privy Council Committee on
Railways, 1852 [1533], XLVIII, appendix, p. 32. There was a double line
from St. Helens to Widnes.

[9] *Railway Times*, 19 Feb., 1853.

[10] St. H. and R. G. Mins., 20 Feb., 1854.

crowned six years of intensive railway building and the event was marked by a speech by the Mayor of Liverpool in which he emphasised that they were celebrating that day " the energy and the enterprise of St. Helens."[1] The Dock was indeed an impressive achievement. It embraced an area of water more than six acres in extent, and was entered from the Mersey through two gates, each fifty feet wide. The coal drops thirty feet high, manufactured at the St. Helens Foundry, could load 250 tons of coal aboard a vessel in the space of two and a half hours, a rate never before equalled anywhere on Merseyside.[2]

While the Garston Dock was nearing completion, the St. Helens Canal and Railway was obliged to ward off a second attempt to break its monopoly of traffic to and from St. Helens. This came from the East Lancashire Railway, whose directors proposed to build a line into the town from Ormskirk. To this possible threat to its independence the St. Helens Canal and Railway responded with plans to build their line northwards to meet that of the East Lancashire at Rainford, thereby both staking a claim to an interest in whatever profits might accrue from the traffic and preventing the East Lancashire from exercising any influence in St. Helens itself. It was decided at the same time to revive the idea of a branch to Eccleston, though from Ravenhead not from Gerard's Bridge, and Parliamentary sanction was sought and obtained for both these extensions in the session of 1853.[3] Neither of them was built immediately ; the Rainford line was not opened until 1 February, 1858[4] and a trial engine did not travel over the newly-laid track to Gillar's Green Colliery in Eccleston until March, 1859.[5] An additional £100,000 had been authorized in 1857 for constructing these extensions, thus raising the capital of the Company to about £1,000,000.[6] This also enabled the Company to purchase an extensive area of land lying between Hall Lane (later Hall Street) and the Canal for a new station and goods yard.[7]

All these improvements and extensions brought more traffic. No longer were shareholders only too eager to dispose of their unremunerative holdings. Even before the opening of

[1] Lpool. Merc., 24 June, 1853.

[2] Lpool. Merc., 24 June, 1853 ; Railway Times, 6 Aug., 1853. William Laird in The Export Coal Trade of Liverpool (Lpool, 1850) used the projected Garston Dock as a stick with which to beat the Liverpool Dock Trust for failing to provide similar facilities.

[3] 16 & 17 Vict. cap. CXXXIV.

[4] Railway Times, 13 Feb., 1858. A trial trip on this line was reported in the St. H. Intelligencer, 31 Oct., 1857.

[5] St. H. Intelligencer, 5 March, 1859.

[6] 20 & 21 Vict., cap. XVI.

[7] St. H. and R. G. Mins., 8 April, 1857. The station was built on part of the site of the present Shaw Street Station.

the Garston and Warrington branches, Gilbert Greenall, M.P., who succeeded his brother, Peter Greenall, as chairman of the Company, remarked that shares were unobtainable, and in the year ending June 1859 revenue reached £100,000, 40 per cent. of which was paid out in dividends.[1]

The flourishing state of the Company was due in no small measure to the appointment as engineer in 1854 of a young Scot of twenty-five named James Cross.[2] Cross showed in the everyday working of the line the same ability and resource that Arthur Sinclair was revealing as commercial head of the concern. Together they formed a most efficient and valuable partnership and in later years Sinclair, the businessman, did not conceal the debt the Company owed to its engineer.[3] Under Cross's direction, repair and maintenance reached such proportions that the original locomotive sheds at Sutton Oak became inadequate[4] and in 1857-8 new engineering shops had to be built on the St. Helens line just south of the Liverpool-Manchester Railway.[5]

But the growing prosperity of the Company was obtained in a way that made certain its early disappearance as a separate entity. It had been hoped that the loading facilities at Garston Dock, by attracting sea-going vessels, would enable St. Helens coal to rival that of the Wigan coalfield in the export trade from the Mersey. If this hope had been realised, the revenue of the St. Helens Canal and Railway would have been derived very largely from purely local traffic on its own network, and the goods transferred to and from other lines would not have been of great consequence. Unfortunately, however, the Garston Dock proved a disappointment[6] because the approach to it from the river was, according to a St. Helens coal proprietor, so " bad and dangerous " that there was considerable difficulty in inducing sea captains to take their vessels into it.[7] Moreover, the traditional Mersey and Weaver coal traffic continued to be carried on the Canal, for it was less injurious to the coal to load the flats at quays close to the collieries and sail them direct to their destination, than to load the coal into railway trucks, and transfer it into flats at Garston.[8]

[1] *St. H. Intelligencer*, 5 March, 6 Aug., 1859.

[2] For Cross, see below, p. 366 and obits. *Proc. Inst. M.E.*, 1894 ; *Proc. Inst. C. E.*, 1894-5.

[3] *St. H. N.*, 13 Aug., 1864.

[4] For the location of these sheds, see the 1848 O.S.

[5] St. H. and R. G. Mins., 23 Sept., 1857 ; 25 Aug., 1858.

[6] See, e.g., the chairman's remarks reported in the *Railway Times*, 9 Aug., 1856 and in the *St. H. Intelligencer*, 7 Feb., 1857.

[7] Evidence of David Bromilow to the S.C. on the St. H. C. and R. Transfer Bill, 1864.

[8] *Ibid.*, Evidence of Samuel Stock.

The Garston Dock having failed to gain a prominent place for St. Helens coal in the Liverpool export trade, the income from passengers and goods exchanged with the London and North Western (at St. Helens Junction), the Warrington and Stockport (at Warrington) and the Lancashire and Yorkshire (at Rainford Junction) formed a proportionately larger item in the annual profit and loss account than would otherwise have been the case. The St. Helens Canal and Railway's fortunes inevitably became bound up with those of its three neighbours. Each presented a potential threat. That from the Lancashire and Yorkshire, dating only from 1858, was very remote. So was that from the Warrington and Stockport. Indeed, in the latter case, the danger came from its weakness rather than its strength. The Warrington and Stockport was an unprofitable line and in 1859 the St. Helens Canal and Railway was drawn into leasing it along with the powerful London and North Western.[1] After this the London and North Western's net closed rapidly and the St. Helens Canal and Railway soon found itself completely enmeshed. In the same Parliamentary session that the Warrington and Stockport Leasing Bill was passed, the London and North Western was empowered to link Edge Hill by rail with Garston.[2] The following year, 1860, they took a twenty-one years lease of the Warrington-Garston section of the St. Helens Railway for £12,000 per annum.[3] In 1861, they were permitted to build a line from Aston (on the railway between Crewe and Warrington) to Ditton (on the St. Helens Railway) which was to cross the Mersey by bridge at Runcorn.[4] The threat of 1845 had finally materialised.

Amalgamation with the London and North Western was now only a matter of time, agreement on a satisfactory transfer price, and arrangements to safeguard the interests of the traders at St. Helens and Widnes.[5] A settlement of all these issues was reached and, by the St. Helens Canal and Railway Transfer Act,[6] the Railway which had started as a mineral line with a capital of £120,000, had acquired the Sankey Canal by amalgamation, had greatly widened its influence throughout south-west Lancashire by enlarging its one ramshackle line into a small but prosperous railway network catering for passengers and goods alike, and had eventually raised more than one million pounds in share capital,[7]

[1] 22 & 23 Vict. cap. CXXXVIII.

[2] 22 & 23 Vict. cap. II.

[3] 23 & 24 Vict. cap. LXXIX.

[4] 24 & 25 Vict. cap. CXXVIII.

[5] Below, p. 351.

[6] 27 & 28 Vict. cap. CCXCVI.

[7] According to Schedule II of the Transfer Act, the share capital stood at £1,059,200 and there were also mortgages of £319,700 and £33,300.

finally lost its independence and was absorbed into the London and North Western system on 1 August, 1864.[1]

The new owners made a gesture to compensate the local population for the removal of control to Euston and the displacement of Arthur Sinclair, James Cross, John Wolfenden—stationmaster at St. Helens since 1837[2]—and other well-known members of the staff. They promised an immediate expenditure of £100,000 on improvements, including a bridge from Cotham Street[3] to Parr Street to be completed within twelve months.[4]   A new line to Wigan was opened in 1870.[5] It was built primarily in an attempt to link the Wigan coalfield with the St. Helens-Garston line so that Wigan, as well as St. Helens, coal could be exported from Garston where a second dock was opened in 1875.[6] In 1880 a by-pass was laid *via* Blackbrook so that this coal traffic did not have to pass through St. Helens.[7] Meanwhile, the new owners started in 1868 and completed in December, 1871, a branch from St. Helens to join the Liverpool-Manchester line at Huyton, thereby providing a more direct route to Liverpool.[8] Apart from the ill-starred line into the town from Glazebrook Junction, not opened until twenty years later,[9] this completed the local railway system.

There remains to be mentioned only the new station—still in use. When it was opened in July, 1871, it was claimed to have

[1] *St. H. N.*, 3 Aug., 1864.

[2] Obit., *St. H. N.*, 7 Aug., 1880.   He was succeeded as stationmaster by David Moss who held that position for more than twenty years.   In an amusing interview, printed in the *St. H. Lantern*, 6 Sept., 1888, Moss recalled the time when " station-masters never had the least idea where the train was, or how it was running, or when it would turn up " and illustrated his point with the recollection of seeing the stationmaster at Earlestown climb the ladder of one of the signals to look for a train, long overdue. See also obit., *St. H. N.*, 10 Aug., 1895.

[3] Later re-named Corporation Street.

[4] *St. H. Standard*, 16 July, 1864.

[5] George P. Neele, *Railway Reminiscences* (1904), 175.

[6] Evidence of George Findlay, Chairman of the L. and N.W.R., to the S.C. on the St. H. and Wigan Junc. Rly. Bill, 1885.

[7] *Ibid.*

[8] *St. H. Standard*, 8 May, 1869 ; *St. H. N.*, 23 Dec., 1871.

[9] This railway was originally planned to break the L. and N.W.R.'s monopoly and was intended to run through St. Helens to Liverpool. Although work began in Feb., 1888, the line (a single track from St. Helens to Ashton and a double track from there to Glazebrook Junction where it joined the C.L.C.) was not opened until 1 July, 1895. The promoters were John Leith, an alkali maker, (Sir) Joseph Beecham, the pill manufacturer, and other local men. Ev. to S.C., 1885 ; *St. H. N.*, 17, 30 Jan., 18, 25 April, 25 July, 1885 ; *Prescot Reporter*, 6 March, 1886 ; *St. H. N.*, 15 Oct., 1887 ; 4 Feb., 1888 ; *St. H. Lantern*, 22 March, 19 July, 2 Aug., 1888 ; *St. H. N.*, 17 Aug., 1895.

and continued to outstrip them all under the direction of Robert Daglish, junr., whose father, also named Robert, was probably the " person of respectability " who had gone into partnership with Lee Watson in 1820.[1] In some ways the careers of the two Daglishes (b. 1777 and 1809) recall those of their more famous contemporaries, George and Robert Stephenson.[2] Possibly the elder Daglish, like the Stephensons, came from the north-east ; family tradition has it that this was so. He is said to have come to Wigan in 1804 as manager of the important Haigh Foundry and Brock Mill Forge, the property of Lord Balcarres.[3] There he superintended the construction of colliery engines and pumping equipment which came to be well known for their reliability. He later became manager of the Orrell Colliery, situated between Wigan and St. Helens, and in 1812 built a Blenkinsop rack locomotive to haul coals from the pithead down to the banks of the Leeds and Liverpool Canal, possibly the first locomotive to be made in Lancashire.[4] He soon became an authority on coal-mines and railways. His advice was sought by many a colliery proprietor in the Lancashire and North Wales coalfields and he was also consulted by British and American railway promoters, including those of that little-known but important early line from Bolton to Leigh.[5] In the mid-1830s he won a prize offered by the London and Birmingham Railway for an improved form of rail and chair and his design was universally adopted throughout the country. His merits as an engineer were recognised in 1830 in his election as member of the Institution of Civil Engineers.

Robert Daglish, junior, started to work at the St. Helens Foundry in 1830 after completing his apprenticeship with Hick and Rothwell of Bolton. In 1834 he married Harriet Speakman and thereby became brother-in-law of Lee Watson, then managing partner of the firm. Seven years later the younger Daglish was given a six years' contract for the supply of locomotive power on the St. Helens Railway.[6] After the death of Lee Watson in 1843,[7]

[1] Above, p. 129.

[2] This paragraph is based upon the obit. to Robert Daglish, senior, *Proc. Inst. C. E.* (1866-7).

[3] Speech of an employee at Haigh, whose father started work there in 1792 (*Wigan Examiner* 2 May, 1856).   For these works, see Dr. Alan Birch's " The Haigh Ironworks : A Nobleman's Enterprise During the Industrial Revolution," *Bull. John Rylands Lib.*, March, 1953.

[4] Daglish made the claim in a letter to the press in 1856, partly repro-duced in J. H. M. Banks, " Records of Mining in Winstanley and Orrell, near Wigan," *Trans. L. and C. Antiq. Soc.*, LIV (1939), 58-9.   The locomotive was made at the Haigh Foundry (*Wigan Examiner* 2 May, 1856).

[5] Lois Basnett, " The History of the Bolton and Leigh Railway," *L. and C. Antiq. Soc.*, LXII (1950-1), 165, 169, 171-2.

[6] St. H. and R. G. Mins., 2, 16 Aug., 1841, 14 Aug., 1843.   The contract was extended to 1849 (*ibid.*, 4 Oct., 1847).

[7] He d. 23 July, 1843, aged 50 (Vault in Old Graveyard, St. Helens ; will proved at Chester, 16 Jan., 1844).

2A

he became managing partner, the concern being known as Rober Daglish Junior and Company.

Under Daglish's direction, the St. Helens Foundry assumed more than local importance. It served not only the industries of the neighbourhood—specialising particularly in the manufactur of horizontal, self-acting, high-pressure winding engines for collieries[1]—but also supplied many orders elsewhere. In the late 1840s Daglish fulfilled contracts for bridges on the Lancashire and Yorkshire Railway and in 1856 his firm constructed the Barrack Bridge over the Liffey in Dublin.[2] The St. Helens Foundry also made many of the pumping engines installed at waterworks so far away as Bristol and Newark. The Foundry already covering an acre of land when Daglish took control of it doubled in size between 1850 and 1865 and by the time of his death in 1883 covered close upon five acres.[3]

The ropery belonging to James William Glover may perhaps be mentioned at this juncture for it provided many of the hempen (and later wire) ropes which were attached to the collier winding engines of Daglish and the other engineering firms Glover, who came of the brewing family who had owned the King's Head Inn,[4] served his apprenticeship at a Wigan ropery and returned to St. Helens where he set up business on the Moorflat in 1818.[5] He later removed to Greenbank where James Bromilow entered into partnership with him for a time.[6] With the exception of a solitary and short-lived interloper,[7] this was the sole rope-walk in the district.

Only one other industry, that of brewing, increased in size during this period. As the population of the town and neighbourhood

[1] George H. Daglish, " On Direct-Acting Winding Engines for Mines," *Proc. Inst. M. E.* (1875), 219.

[2] Obit., Robert Daglish, junior, *Proc. Inst. C. E.*, **74**, 1883. Daglish' name is prominently displayed on the ironwork of the Barrack Bridge.

[3] *Ibid.*, St. H. I. C. Rate Books. George Heaton Daglish (1893-1913) nephew of Robt. Daglish, junior, was responsible for designing much that was made at the St. H. Foundry and became a partner in 1869 and a member of the Inst. C. E. in 1876. Thomas Windus, who joined the firm in 1843, was for many years the general manager (*St. H. Lantern* 7 April, 1893).

[4] Above, p. 55n.

[5] Obit., *St. H. Weekly News* 12 April, 1862 ; advt. *St. H. Weekly News* 9 Aug., 1862.

[6] Bromilow Papers. Letter from James Bromilow to his father, 7 Feb. 1832 ; ref. to fire at Bromilow and Glover's, *Wigan Gazette* 1 Sept., 1837

[7] This ropery was situated at Parr Mount and was advertised for auction in the *St. H. N.* 14 Jan., 1871.

ST. HELENS FOUNDRY ABOUT 1860

[Photo : R. K. Robertson]

grew, so did the demand for beer. Greenalls rebuilt their brewery in 1856-7 and added considerably to its capacity.[1] Some ten years later they purchased the Denton's Green Brewery from Charles Speakman and Co. and pulled it down.[2] After that they had a virtual monopoly of brewing in the district, the three tiny brewhouses that survived at Thatto Heath,[3] Peckers Hill[4] and Langtree Street[5] being of little consequence. In 1880 the St. Helens and Wilderspool Breweries were incorporated as Greenall Whitley and Company Ltd.[6]

The local potteries do not appear to have made any very marked progress in these middle years. Some proprietors failed : others succeeded. On balance we are left with the impression that if the total amount of business increased, it could not have been to any great extent. The Gerard's Bridge Potteries, conducted by William, Thomas and John Lightfoot, three sons of Richard Lightfoot the founder of the concern, were in difficulties for some time before they were actually closed in the 'seventies ;[7] and Benjamin Blake, an experienced potter from Chesterfield, ran into trouble with a mortgage at the Ravenhead Pottery.[8] On the other hand, a second pottery was opened at Sutton Heath[9] and Swaine's original Sutton Heath Pottery across the road was leased to Thomas and Francis Grace who already owned a similar business at Marshall's Cross.[10] At the Greenbank Pottery, Doultons

---

[1] St. H. Town Hall. Statement for the opinion of Counsel, 24 Dec., 1858 (package 109) ; *St. H. Intelligencer* 31 Oct., 1857.

[2] For sale of plant, *St. H. N.* 3 May, 1865 ; by Oct., 1866, the brewery was said to have been pulled down (*The Incorporation of St. H.*, St. H. 1869, Donnelly Inquiry, 31).

[3] *St. H. N.*, 28 May, 1895.

[4] *St. H. N.* 19 Sept., 3 Oct., 1896. For obits. of two members of the Wilcock family, the proprietors, *St. H. N.* 30 Jan., 1877, 13 Jan., 1895.

[5] *St. H. N.* 6 Oct., 1883.

[6] The first directors were Sir Gilbert Greenall, Peter Whitley, T. J. Downs, Joseph Robinson and R. I. Wynne Jones. Joseph Robinson was the son of Samuel Robinson, who came from Wilderspool in 1835 to manage the St. H. Brewery and was in charge there for 31 years (obits. *St. H. N.*, *St. H. Standard* 16 Sept., 1871).

[7] *St. H. N.* 14 Sept., 1867 ; *St. H. Standard* 27 Feb., 1869 ; *Directory* 1871 ; *St. H. Standard* 12 Dec., 1874, 3 July, 1875 ; *St. H. N.* 2 Feb., 1878. Of the 3 brothers, William d. 1862, Thomas 1874 and John 1894 ; for obit. of John Lightfoot, *St. H. N.*, 28 July, 1894. Most of the site of these potteries was acquired by J. C. Gamble and Son.

[8] *St. H. N.* 4 May, 1878 ; *Directory* 1884 ; information from Mr. Blake's son.

[9] According to the *Directory* of 1876, this pottery belonged to Yates and Co.; Mr. T. Davies, the present proprietor, has informed us that his grandfather was Yates's manager before taking a lease of the property.

[10] L.R.O., Cross Papers. Lease of 23 Aug., 1872. Obit. James Grace, *St. H. N.* 17 Dec., 1887.

were doing a brisk trade in drainpipes and all kinds of stoneware,[1] while at Lea Green, Roughdales Fire Clay Company Limited were also advertising sanitary pipes as well as bricks and tiles.[2]

If brewing was on the increase and pottery-making more or less stationary, the domestic metal trades, having enjoyed a period of considerable prosperity, were by 1870 floundering and faced with certain extinction. Improved nailmaking machinery introduced about 1864 which enabled four nails to be cut from a strip of iron in a single operation,[3] gradually drove the wrought iron nail off the market. At St. Helens itself William Swire was soon to be manufacturing cut nails at a factory in Haydock Street[4] and John Anderton, the leading maker of wrought iron nails in the town, took the wise precaution of adding the duties of house and estate agent to his thirty-year-old nailmaking business.[5]

Protective tariffs in the United States, also dating from the early 1860s, reduced the demand for locally-produced hand-made nails just at the time that improved slitting machinery was about to come into use. These protective duties did great harm to the domestic watchmaking industry of the district as well. A 30 per cent. tariff was imposed upon watches entering the United States and a considerable encouragement thereby given to American producers.[6] The output of American-made watches grew eightfold between 1862 and 1872, in which year three times as many watches were being made in the United States as in Great Britain.[7] Meanwhile the Swiss were developing their watch industry and many of their products were competing with the British on the home market ; imports of watches from Switzerland rose from 42,000 in 1853 to 90,000 in 1855 and 160,000 in the early 1860s.[8]

When times started to become hard in the early 1860s, some of the masters took to paying part of their men's wages in kind, a practice previously " only done in a few instances here and

[1] Advt. *St. H. N.* 8 Nov., 1873.

[2] *St. H. N.*, 25 Dec., 1869. The plant and machinery at Lea Green were advertised for sale in the *St. H. N.* 17 Oct., 1885. The company is still in business at Marshall's Cross.

[3] G. C. Allen, *Industrial Development of Birmingham and the Black Country* (1929), 183.

[4] *St. H. N.* 2 March, 1878. When Swire died five years later, the machinery was put up for sale (*St. H. N.* 9 June, 1883).

[5] *Directory*, 1853 ; *St. H. N.* 28 Jan., 1882 ; 3 Jan., 1885.

[6] Evidence of John Wycherley to the S.C. to Inquire into the Truck System, 1871 [C. 327] XXXVI, q. 33,525.

[7] T. P. Hewitt, *English Watchmaking Under Free Trade* (Liverpool, 1903), 4.

[8] Speech to the British Horological Institute quoted in the *Prescot Reporter* 11 Jan., 1862.

there."[1] This caused great misgiving and some of the men complained to a commission which was investigating alleged violations of the Truck Act. Two of the commissions' members came to Prescot at the end of 1870 and heard evidence from various people engaged in the industry in and around Prescot and St. Helens. This sheds much light on domestic watchmaking in south-west Lancashire during its declining years.

The local craftsmen—" a few hundreds " at Prescot and " about ninety " at St. Helens[2]—still cut and shaped almost all the watch parts made in England, their only competitors being some of the Coventry men who were interested " a little in one class of works and movements."[3] Coventry was more a centre for the assembling of finished watches, as were London, Birmingham, Liverpool and " a few outstanding places in the country."[4] The masters employed some men as piece workers and others on a time basis. John Wycherley of Prescot, for instance, had nearly fifty men working for him and of these, twenty were time workers.[5] The men, who owned their own workshops attached to their homes, chose their own masters. They sometimes worked for more than one at the same time[6] and at least two of the witnesses were kept busy with orders from Coventry.[7] This free choice of employer was to the domestic workman's advantage when his handiwork was in great demand but when trade deteriorated during the 1860s, the choice became severely restricted and the men considered themselves lucky to find anyone who would give them work, even if they had to accept part of their payment in kind.

Complaints were lodged against three of the employers at St. Helens.[8] It was alleged that Peter Burrows, who also owned a provision shop, paid in meat[9] or butter;[10] that Peter Mercer, who had no shop, made his workmen take watches at £5 for which they

---

[1] Evidence of Thomas Prescott to the S.C. to Inquire into the Truck System, 1871 [C.327] XXXVI, q. 34,250.

[2] *Ibid.*, Luke Healey, qq. 32,881-2.

[3] *Ibid.*, John Wycherley, q. 33,526.

[4] *Ibid.*, John Wycherley, q. 33,532.

[5] *Ibid.*, Wycherley, qq. 33,551-2.

[6] *Ibid.*, Chesworth, q. 32,153.

[7] *Ibid.*, Healey, q. 32,899 ; Travis, q. 32,871.

[8] Two others were mentioned, Thelwall and Chadwick, but these always paid in cash. (*ibid.*, Travis, qq. 32,774-5 and qq. 32,830-2). Ralph Foster was another employer (*ibid.*, Lucas, q. 33,410).

[9] *Ibid.*, Chesworth q. 32,225.

[10] *Ibid.*, Healey, q. 32,914. It had to be rendered down to remove the dirt.

could only get £2 10s. at the pawnbroker's[1]; and that Mrs. Watkinson had just opened a little store where the men were expected to make their purchases.[2]   Mercer, in his defence, was quite frank : he had to pay in watches or be undersold at Coventry (where he took the movements)[3] by those who paid in provisions.   Mrs. Watkinson was more cautious.   When the members of the commission sought to discover whether her newly-opened store was used generally by the public or particularly by her workmen, she hedged—but without success :

" Does the provision shop face the street ?
—No, not exactly.
Does it face the back yard ?
—Yes, but there is an entry "[4]

Peter Burrows did not appear at all to defend himself ; he sent along a doctor's certificate that he was " suffering from nervous excitement... rendered worse by any public appearance or examination."[5]

While some employers were attempting to reduce their costs at the expense of their men's wages, others were already trying to face the flood of foreign watch production by an efficiency drive in their own workshops and among their own domestic workers. In the early 1860s about half the men employed at Prescot worked in shops provided by their employers and not at their own homes.[6]   We do not know to what extent the domestic system was breaking down in St. Helens as well ; of the employers mentioned in the 1870 enquiry, only Mrs. Watkinson had her own workshop, employing twenty to thirty men who paid sixpence per week for the use of the machinery provided.[7]   At the same time, Wycherley in Prescot was attempting to standardise the type of movements and to introduce equipment for the manufacture of eight standard sizes.[8]   But, despite the master's workshop and such attempts at standardisation, Prescot and St. Helens watch-movement makers went out of business one by one ; the trade disintegrated and in

---

[1] *Ibid.*, Travis, q. 32,784 and q. 32,799.   825 watches had been pawned in St. Helens (by watchmakers and others) in the previous six months. (*Ibid.*, Berry, q. 33,867).

[2] *Ibid.*, Renshall, q. 33,097.

[3] *Ibid.*, Mercer, q. 34,113.

[4] *Ibid.*, Jane Watkinson, qq. 33,590-1.

[5] *Ibid.*, Burrows, q. 34,082.

[6] Third Report of the Ch. Emp. Comm., 1864.   Evidence of Johnson (Prescot), 202.

[7] Evidence before the S.C. Appointed to Inquire into the Truck System. Jane Watkinson, q. 33,613.

[8] David Glasgow, *Watch and Clock Making* (1891), 36.

1885 the " confined and decayed little factories " were reported to be " almost deserted."[1] The once flourishing domestic industry was virtually extinct. The end came a few years later when a courageous band of survivors joined together to launch the Lancashire Watch Company Limited and opened a large factory in Prescot.[2]

Competition from abroad, particularly from new concerns in the United States, which overwhelmed the domestic nail- and watch-makers and drove them out of business, was soon to strike hard at the plate glass and chemical industries of St. Helens, which also counted on customers across the Atlantic for much of their trade. But before moving on to consider the dislocation of these two basic industries, it is necessary to turn to the growth of the town itself during the prosperous middle years of the century before these black storm clouds blew into sight.

[1] *Prescot Reporter*, 12 Sept., 1885.

[2] For the origins of the Prescot Watch Factory, opened in January, 1890, see *The Lancashire Watch Company Limited : Its Rise and Progress* (Prescot, 1893). The first watch made completely at the new factory, was produced three years later (*St. H. N.* 14 Jan., 1893). The Society for Promoting Industrial Villages was interested in this venture, *q.v.* William Ashworth, *The Genesis of Modern British Town Planning* (1954), 138.

Chapter XXV

URBAN GROWTH

1845-1870

THE tap of bricklayers' hammers and the scrape of their trowels were sounds very familiar to the inhabitants of St. Helens a hundred years ago. The population of the town itself, having probably doubled between 1830 and 1845, certainly doubled again between 1845 and 1870, increasing from some 12,000 to about 25,000. This was the number actually living within the boundary of the Improvement Commission ; another 20,000 people were by 1870 living outside the boundary but within the limits of the four townships of Eccleston (excluding part in the Prescot registration district), Parr, Sutton and Windle.[1] Accommodation for these many additional families was provided in rows of brick cottages, repetitive, dull and uninteresting, though if within the town boundary built to certain minimum specifications laid down by the Improvement Commission.[2] These monotonous new streets radiated outwards from the original nucleus of buildings. In the late 'forties the builders were hard at work between Liverpool Road and Westfield Street fitting as many houses to the acre as they could, and the same was happening in Parr to the south of the St. Helens-Ashton turnpike.[3] During the 'fifties they were running up cottages near the newly-opened factories at Pocket Nook and starting to obliterate Westfield, extending their operations as far as Duke Street in the north and Boundary Road in the west. In the 'sixties they developed the southern slope of Cowley Hill, laid open by the cutting of North

---

[1] For the population within the boundaries of the Improvement Commission in 1845, see above, p. 290. At the census of 1851 it was 14,866, in 1861, 18,396 and in 1869, according to the Borough Treasurer giving evidence on the Improvement Bill of that year (q. 275), it was " about 25,000." The population of the St. Helens sub-district (the four townships with Eccleston in Prescot excluded) was 25,020 in 1851, 37,961 in 1861 and 45,280 in 1871.

[2] Above, p. 301. The Improvement Act of 1855, which laid down that houses not more than two storeys high were to be of 9 in. brickwork, brought forth a protest from the builders " on the ground that it increased the cost of Building " but their protests fell on unresponsive ears (St. H.I.C. Mins., 7 May, 1856).

[3] This summary is based upon the appearance of new streets in the St. H.I.C. Rate Books.

Road a few years earlier,[1] and eventually linked up with other builders who were striking south and west from Gerard's Bridge. At the same time shops and offices, as well as private houses, were being built in Cotham Street, Claughton Street, Hardshaw Street and George Street, thereby extending the heart of the town northwards. Outside the Improvement Commission's boundary, housing schemes were being pressed forward with equal vigour. The scattered hamlets in Parr were growing quickly and tending to merge ; more accommodation was required for the workpeople at the factories of Sutton Oak ; houses were springing up in some numbers just outside the boundary to the south of the town ; Alma Place and Alma Street, close to Kurtz's works, bear the distinctive marks of the mid-1850s.

All this building activity meant that the labour of bricksetters and masons, joiners and plasterers, painters and plumbers, was in great demand. It is not surprising, therefore, that the Society of Operative House Carpenters and Joiners (formed in 1830),[2] the Operative Painters' and Plumbers' Association (formed in 1857)[3] and the Bricklayers' and Plasterers' Society were the most active trade unions in the town at this period, constantly demanding higher pay and shorter hours, usually with success.[4] The leading builder at St. Helens in the earlier part of the century was James Latham[5] and, after his death in 1841, the firm of Harris and

---

[1] In 1856 John Blundell and David Gamble, owners of the Great Cowley Hill Estate, negotiated with Samuel Cross's trustees with a view to constructing what came to be called North Road. The trustees agreed to permit a deviation of the proposed road through their estate until property at the end of Duke Street could be purchased. John Knowles, the owner, refused to sell and it was not until 1880 that the two houses, the cause of the deviation, were pulled down (St. H. Cong. Ch., package 14, mins. of meeting 14 Aug., 1856 ; diary of Newton Lacey in the possession of Mrs. Campbell of Rhos-on-Sea, who kindly placed it at our disposal).

[2] Above, p. 262. There was also a local branch of the Friendly Society of Operative Stonemasons, whose membership grew from 5 in 1859 to 44 in 1868 (11th Report of the R.C. on Trade Unions, 1899, appendix, pp. 305,313).

[3] *St. H.N.* 3 Sept., 1864.

[4] They were involved in a strike lasting twelve months in 1859-60 for an increase in pay from 2/8 to 3/- per day, which was conceded to the men in May, 1860. This was part of a wider movement and delegates came from London to assist in raising strike funds (*St. H. Intelligencer* 28 May, 15 Oct., 1859; *Prescot Reporter* 5 May, 1860; evidence of T. Winters to the S.C. on Masters and Operatives, 1860 [307] XXII, *q.* 272 *et seq.*). For other refs. to union activities in the building industry at St. H., see *Wigan Times* 19 June, 1853; *St. H.N.* 16, 23, 30 Jan., 22 April 6, 18 May, 6 July, 3, 10 Sept., 1864; 22 Aug., 1865; 1, 8 May, 1869; 4 May, 1872; 10 May, 1873; 5 May, 1877.

[5] His will was proved at Chester, 5 Oct., 1841. A ledger of 1840-1, now in the possession of Mr. Thomas, Mill Lane, Sutton, St. Helens, probably refers to Latham's business.

Sherratt (later George Harris and Son)[1] rose to take his place.
They put up not only cottage property but many larger buildings
as well : factories, public buildings, churches—particularly
Wesleyan churches, a speciality of theirs—and spacious private
houses to create the new residential districts of Cowley Hill and
St. Ann's.[2] Harris's foreman, William Barton, branched out on
his own and built much of the cottage property in Westfield ; it
was claimed at the time of his death in 1878 that he had built about
a quarter of the houses in the town.[3]

So long as the population continued to grow at a rapid rate,
property continued to be a wise form of investment, particularly
if it was well situated, within easy reach of a mine or factory, or
close to the centre of the town. A house in Bridge Street, for
instance, which was sold for £55 in the middle of the 1840s and
re-sold for £95 in 1848, fetched no less than £350 at a public
auction in 1851.[4] Even if property only occasionally appreciated
to this extent, that would be sufficient to attract the investor.
As has been noticed, building capital had previously been provided
chiefly by coal proprietors and manufacturers and, latterly, by
a host of smaller men through building societies. The middle
years of the century saw the rise of the permanent building
society, which did not terminate upon the completion of a
particular housing scheme as had previously been the case. In
1855, for instance, the St. Helens Permanent Building Society,
launched three years before,[5] claimed to be the " most profitable
bank for saving " and substantiated this claim by offering the
realisation of a £30 share in seven or eight years in return for an
annual deposit of £3—a profit of about 30 per cent.[6] The St.
Helens and Rainford Building Society, established three years
later, " promoted by men of great practical knowledge (many of
whom have been connected with building societies for 20 years
past)," promised a profit of " more than three times the rate of

---

[1] George Harris (1810-75) was the grandson of the Joseph Harris
who came to St. H. to manage the copper works (above, p. 83). He was
in partnership with Richard Sherratt until 1 Jan., 1857 (*St. H. Intelligencer*
10 Jan., 1857). His son, George, particularly concerned with the architec-
tural side, became a partner in 1873. (Obits. *St. H. Standard* 25 Sept.,
2 Oct., 1875; *Prescot Reporter* 17 April, 1886. Sale of West Park House,
St. H.N. 30 Oct., 1886).

[2] For a list of buildings erected by the firm, *Prescot Reporter* 17 April,
1886.

[3] *St. H.N.* 3 Aug., 1878; 5 June, 1880. For John Middlehurst, another
prominent local builder, below, p. 402n.

[4] *Wigan Times* 13 June, 1851.

[5] In 1865 it was stated to have been established 13 years. (*St. H. Standard*
14 July, 1865).

[6] *St. H. Intelligencer* 3 Feb., 1855.

interest to be obtained in the Savings Bank."[1]   A year later 1,062 £60 shares had been taken up.[2]

This was a golden age for the shopkeeper as well as for the builder. The market for consumer goods was expanding with extraordinary rapidity ; retailers flocked into the town from other parts of Lancashire and from farther afield in the hope of supplying some of the new customers who were daily making their appearance. James Hatton, for instance, came to St. Helens from Warrington in 1854, and, after serving for a few years with a butcher in Church Street, branched out on his own (as he later recalled) with only 8s. 6d. in his pocket.[3]   John Cotton, who was born in Congleton, had three years' medical training behind him when in the early 'fifties he went as assistant to a Prescot doctor. He soon saw an opening for a chemist and druggist at St. Helens, found a vacant shop and removed to the town in 1854.[4]   George William Griffin, a native of Dudley, took up the new trade of photography, first at Liverpool, then at Southport, and finally in St. Helens, where he later added the sale of furniture to his business.[5] Henry Ratcliffe Lacey, who arrived from his home town of Wotton-under-Edge in Gloucestershire in 1858 to join his brother, Newton Lacey, as a teacher, later set up shop as a hosier.[6] A niece of the Laceys married Jesse Boydell ; he came from Lowton, and after serving his time with a Wigan tailor opened a shop of his own in Hardshaw Street, St. Helens in 1864.   Ten years later he removed to Church Street and when his brother, Joshua, joined him in 1878, opened a second shop there.   In 1883 Boydell Brothers started business in Market Street, Manchester and in 1886 in Ranelagh Street, Liverpool.[7]   These few examples of bustling activity need to be multiplied many times to catch the sense of opportunity prevailing among the hopeful retail traders, each seeking to attract the custom of newcomers at the expense

---

[1] *St. H. Intelligencer* 22 May, 1858.

[2] *St. H. Intelligencer* 28 May, 1859. There was also a Ravenhead Building Society about this time (*St. H. Weekly News* 29 Dec., 1860) and a few years later a St. Helens and Widnes Co-operative Building Society (*St. H. Standard* 2 Dec., 1865). The St. Helens and Sutton Victoria Building Society was established in April, 1868, and the Sutton, Bold and District Permanent Building Society in January, 1878. (*St. H. Standard* 2 Jan., 1869; *St. H. N.* 5 Jan., 1878).

[3] *St. H. Lantern* 11 Oct., 1889.

[4] *Ibid.*

[5] Obit., *St. H.N.* 17 Oct., 1896.

[6] H. R. Lacey was a very active supporter of the Mechanics Institute and, particularly, of its library.   When the Corporation took control, he became chairman of the Library Committee, an office he held for many years (Obit. biog., newscuttings at St. H. Ref. Lib.).

[7] *St. H.N.* 6 June, 1874, 15 Nov., 1879; *St. H. Lantern* 11 Oct., 1889.

of his equally hopeful and persistent rivals. The advertisement columns of the earliest newspapers accurately reflect this bitter struggle to become firmly established so as to grow with the market. They contain notices from those who have just arrived and announcements from those who have moved on to larger and better-situated premises—and from the assignees of those who have failed. Everyone was on the move, either up or out.

By far the most successful of all the salesmen who reached St. Helens in the 1850s was a man whose name later became a household word not only in St. Helens but throughout the whole country. Thomas Beecham was born in Oxfordshire in 1820 and at the age of eight was sent out to work as a shepherd's boy for 1s. 6d. a week. In 1840, to quote his own words, " a slight wave of opportunity presented itself and I launched my tiny barque on the ever-shifting sea of commercial uncertainty."[1] He is believed to have taken the knowledge of various herbal remedies from his native Oxfordshire to Wigan where in 1847 he was granted a medicine licence.[2] While at Wigan, he sold " Beecham's Celebrated Herbal Pills " at 1s. 6d. a box, together with other patent medicines including " a never-failing remedy for Deafness, providing the Drum of the Ear is not broken."[3] At the end of 1858 or early in 1859,[4] Dr. Beecham (as he called himself at this period) removed to St. Helens. At first, he sold his pills on the St. Helens market and advertised them for sale by post from his residence at 13 Milk Street at 6d. a box, " one box sent post free for 8 stamps to any address."[5] His famous slogan is supposed to have been coined by a Mrs. Ellen Butler of St. Helens, a spontaneous and unprompted appreciation of Beecham's pills,[6] but, if that were so, it must have been very soon indeed after his arrival in the town, for " worth a guinea a box " headed his first advertisement in the *St. Helens Intelligencer* on 6 August, 1859. His postal business appears to have grown quite rapidly ; it may well have been transferred from Wigan, as is indicated by a testimonial from Golborne which he printed in 1859.[7] A year later a complimentary letter was published from an appreciative

---

[1] *St. H.N.* 31 May, 1890, quoting a letter from Beecham in *Tit Bits*.

[2] A photograph of this licence is printed as part of an article appearing in *The Chemist and Druggist* 10 Oct., 1942.

[3] Beechams Pills Ltd. Undated poster issued from his residence ' No. 7 New Square, near the Savings Bank, Standishgate, Wigan '.

[4] A poster advertising the auction of the stock-in-trade of a grocer and druggist's business at 120 Wallgate on 8 and 9 Nov., 1858, is preserved at Beechams Pills Ltd. This, presumably, referred to Beecham himself but there is no mention of him on the document.

[5] *St. H. Intelligencer* 6 Aug., 1859; *St. H. Weekly News* 14 Sept., 1861.

[6] James Brockbank, *History of St. Helens* (St. H. 1896), 42.

[7] *St. H. Intelligencer* 6 Aug., 1859.

customer who wrote from Pendlebury,[1] in 1863 from satisfied correspondents at Leyland, Croston, and Cambridge,[2] and in 1865 from Bath and Barnsley.[3] In that year he had wholesale agents in Liverpool, Manchester and London and in the following year at Leeds, York and Wolverhampton as well.[4]

So the business grew. In 1863 he removed from Milk Street to 32 Westfield Street and shortly afterwards took the premises next door as a workshop[5] where his son (later Sir) Joseph Beecham joined him.[6] The real expansion came in the 1880s when the firm embarked on a great advertising campaign, one of the first in the country on such a scale. In 1884 £22,000 were spent on advertising and in 1889 this sum had been increased to £95,000.[7] The campaign was a great success. The output of the firm in the following year, 1890, totalled 9,000,000 pills per day,[8] a result which was obtained at a remarkably low labour cost. In 1884, nineteen men were employed and in 1889, eighty-eight.[9] By the latter date new premises had been built in Westfield Street at a cost of over £30,000.[10] They were opened towards the end of 1887.[11] As Beecham himself wrote on that occasion, as he surveyed the success of his business during the previous years : " There is no doubt that advertising—properly and judiciously done—pays."[12]

If a list were to be drawn up of successful traders at St. Helens

[1] *St. H. Weekly News* 22 Sept., 1860.

[2] *St. H.N.* 4 Feb., 1863.

[3] *St. H. Standard* 7 July, 1865.

[4] *St. H. Standard* 10 March, 1866.

[5] *St. H.N.* 10 Oct., 1863. The address is subsequently given as 29 West-field Street (*St. H. Standard* 7 April, 1866; St. H.I.C. Rate Books). This change of address may have been due to a further removal or to a re-numbering of the street. In 1866 he was also owner and occupier of 27 Westfield Street (St. H.I.C. Rate Books).

[6] He was b. at Wigan on 8 June, 1848, and first mentioned in the local directories in 1876 as ' assistant chemist ' at the works. He was given a half share in the concern in 1889 and obtained complete control in 1895. He became a Councillor in 1889 and was Mayor in 1899-1900 and 1911-12. He was a very keen cyclist and musician. Knighted 1911 and created a baronet 1915 (obits. *St. H.N.* and *St. H.R.* 3 Oct., 1916; deeds at Beechams Pills Ltd.).

[7] *St. H.N.* 10 Jan., 1885; *St. H. Lantern* 1 Aug., 1890.

[8] *St. H. Lantern* 1 Aug., 1890.

[9] Wages books at Beechams Pills Ltd.

[10] *St. H.N.* 2 Aug., 1890.

[11] *Prescot Reporter* 12 Nov., 1887. The works manager, Walter Andrews, was then said to have ' grown up with the business '. Charles Rowed, a cycling companion of Joseph Beecham, at that time secretary, succeeded Andrews soon afterwards.

[12] Quoted in the *Prescot Reporter* 12 Nov., 1887.

with Thomas Beecham, the retailer turned wholesaler, at the head, we should expect to find the first fitful attempts to launch a co-operative store somewhere near the foot. The co-operative movement was essentially a product of east Lancashire and drew its support in the early days chiefly from the textile towns. When in May, 1851, for instance, more than eighty delegates from Lancashire, Yorkshire and Cheshire met at Bury, south-west Lancashire was unrepresented,[1] and it was not until the following month that we hear of " a few friends " joining together to start a co-operative store at Liverpool.[2] Later in the year, when Ludlow made a tour of co-operative societies in Lancashire and travelled from Liverpool to Golborne, he remarked upon " a large and flourishing store at Haddeck [Haydock] "[3] but did not mention another co-operative venture at Worsley Brow in Sutton. This had been launched in the previous year, 1850.

The intention of the Sutton Co-operative Friendly Society was (to quote the rules) " to give the Inhabitants of Sutton and its vicinity, the opportunity of purchasing from the Society's stores the common necessaries, such as provisions, or any other commodities that may be required, which shall be the best quality and sold at the lowest remunerating price."[4] Any member could hold up to twelve 5/- shares, dividend was to be paid once a year, and 2s. 6d. credit was allowed per share. All members were expected to shop at the store and, if they did not do so, were " subject to an examination by the Committee, so as to ascertain the cause." The committee was democratically elected at six-monthly meetings. Of the three original trustees, one was a railway porter, one a Chelsea Pensioner and one a farmer. By the end of 1850 it was reported that between 800 and 900 shares were taken up " and the shop . . . set to work in good earnest." This, it was said, caused the other grocers in the neighbourhood to reduce the price of their butter, cheese and bacon by 2d., and their sugar by $\frac{1}{2}$d., per lb.[5] We know nothing of the store's history between 1850 and 1870 but its appeal does not seem to have been very extensive ; at the end of the latter year, although the shares had been advanced to £1 each and the total capital stood at £324, there were only 44 members.[6] Possibly some of its business was lost when the Sutton Glassworks Co-operative Society opened a shop nearby in 1859 and when the Sutton Rolling Mills Co-operative

[1] *Christian Socialist* 3 May, 1851.

[2] *Christian Socialist* 21 June, 1851.

[3] *Christian Socialist* 11 Oct., 1851.

[4] No. 2079 Lancs. at the Registry of Friendly Societies, London.

[5] *Wigan Times* 22 Nov., 1850.

[6] Return 1871 [190] LXII.

Society was started in 1861 ; by 1865 they had 54 and 83 members respectively.[1]

Meanwhile two stores had been opened at St. Helens itself. The Sutton Alkali Works Co-operative Society originated in a meeting called at Kurtz's chemical works in mid-1860. Owen Duffy, the works manager, supported the men's proposal and A. G. Kurtz, the proprietor, contributed £50 besides building suitable premises which he leased to the society at a moderate rent. This gave the venture a flying start and at the first annual meeting Owen Duffy, who had become treasurer and president, reported that the 133 members would receive $7\frac{1}{2}$ per cent. on their shares and all customers would be paid 1s. 3d. in the £1 dividend on their purchases.[2] The membership soon reached 200.[3] In the following year, 1862, the St. Helens Equitable Co-operative Society was started in Liverpool Road. It survived the scandal caused when its manager was accused of bigamy[4] but the total membership did not exceed 50 at the end of the 1860s.[5] Two later societies, the St. Helens Co-operative Watch Movement Makers' Society (registered in July, 1867, and dissolved in 1869) and the Sutton Co-operative Industrial Society (registered in May, 1868, and dissolved the following year) can hardly have had time to prove of much benefit to their members.[6]

As in the case of the pioneer society at Toad Lane, Rochdale,[7] these early attempts at co-operation seem to have been the product of slack trade. A reduction in earnings appears to have caused the more thoughtful and thrifty workpeople to band together (often, as at Kurtz's, with their masters' blessing[8]) to make their reduced earnings go farther. The only periods of depression at St. Helens between 1850 and 1870 which were severe enough to be referred to in the newspapers were in 1850[9] and between 1858 and 1862.[10] They coincide with the formation of co-operative societies in the district. Conversely, the unparalleled boom of 1870-3 when wages were exceptionally high,[11] destroyed most of these rather

[1] Return 1866 [355] XXXIX.

[2] *St. H. Weekly News* 8 June, 12, 19 Oct., 1861.

[3] *St. H.N.* 12 April, 1864.

[4] *St. H.N.* 14 Jan., 1863.

[5] Returns 1867 [492] XXXIX; 1871 [190] LXII.

[6] Return 1872 [418] LIV.

[7] G. D. H. Cole, *A Century of Co-operation* (n.d.), 62.

[8] James Shanks and Samuel Bishop, were also warm supporters (*St. H. Standard* 9 Dec., 1865; *Co-operative News* 30 Dec., 1871).

[9] *Lpool. Merc.* 30 April, 1850.

[10] Below, p. 412.

[11] Below, p. 433.

feeble efforts at co-operation. In those four years the local pioneer of 1850, the Sutton Alkali Works society of 1860, and the Sutton Glassworks society, all went out of business,[1] leaving the store in Liverpool Road and the Sutton Rolling Mills societies to keep the flag flying for a few more years before they, too, succumbed.[2] Even if the management of these early ventures was rather lax, as was alleged to be the case with the Sutton Alkali Works society,[3] this by itself hardly explains why they were accorded such lukewarm support. Their failure is all the more remarkable in the light of the immediate and overwhelming success which attended the present St. Helens Industrial Co-operative Society Ltd., which was able to boast well over 2,000 members within five years of its formation at the close of 1883, and nearly 7,000 by the close of the century.[4]

While these earlier co-operators were struggling to introduce a measure of public control into what had previously been the preserve of the private trader, individual enterprise continued to provide public services, sometimes from purely philanthropic motives (for instance, the fountain erected by Charles Bishop in the old market place, Church Street, for the benefit of travellers[5]) and sometimes in the hope of covering the initial cost and making a profit. As has been seen, the first passenger service by road to Liverpool and by rail to St. Helens Junction was such a private speculation and the town was supplied with water and gas by private companies. A. G. Kurtz maintained this tradition when in 1861 he built the first public baths in the town next to his factory.[6] The charge of 4d. for first class, and 3d. for second class bathers[7] can hardly have met the heavy running costs,[8] particularly

---

[1] Return 1872 [418] LIV; *St. H.N.* 30 March, 13 April, 5 Oct., 7 Dec., 1872.

[2] They had certainly closed by 1882, when a correspondent in the *St. H. N.* 7 Jan., deplored the fact that there was no co-operative store in the town. According to the *Directory* of 1881, the Sutton Rolling Mills society was still in being but had an address at Parr Stocks. It was formally wound up under an order of June, 1883 and debts were still being collected two years later (*St. H. N.* 11 April, 1885).

[3] *St. H. N.* 5 Oct., 1872.

[4] Below, appendix, 2.

[5] St. H. I. C. Mins., 3 June, 5 Aug., 1857.

[6] *St. H. N.* 8 June, 1861. A scheme to launch a St. Helens Baths and Washhouses Co. Ltd. in 1858, with capital of £5,000 (*St. H. Intelligencer* 21 Aug., 1858) did not reach fruition. A. G. Kurtz was to have been one of the directors ; perhaps it was the failure of this venture that caused him to take action on his own.

[7] *St. H. N.* 8 June, 1861.

[8] Mining subsidence caused the baths to be completely reconstructed in 1864-5, a costly operation. *St. H. N.* 12 Sept., 1863, 21 May, 1864, 10 May, 1865.

as very few people chose to use the baths. " The public do not appreciate the baths ...," it was reported in 1865, " [Bathing] has always been the luxury of rich and educated men and will be. Working men ... seldom bathe and women scarcely ever."[1]

Perhaps the best example of a privately-sponsored public service was the local press. Before the 'fifties, local news had to be called out by a town crier[2] or spread by public placards or by brief paragraphs in the Liverpool, Wigan and Manchester papers which circulated in the district. Owing to the high cost of these papers—about 5d. each even after the newspaper duty was reduced to 1d. in 1836—the local inhabitants clubbed together and read them communally in newsrooms at the local inns ; the Eagle and Child, for instance, had well over a hundred such subscribers in 1840.[3] Many of the early placards were printed by Isaac Sharp. The son of the local Independent minister, he had served his apprenticeship with a printer in Wigan and with Longmans in London. He returned to St. Helens in 1821 to take over a printing, bookselling and stationery business at the corner of the Old Market Place, previously owned by Henry Lyon.[4] Sharp, however, was no journalist and it was left to a later arrival, William Foreman, to edit and print the earliest local paper. He is first encountered as a purveyor of straight news without comment : he ran off score cards at a cricket match in the summer of 1853.[5] On the following 3 December, encouraged, no doubt, by the removal of the advertisement duty in that year, he issued the first number of a paper entitled *What's Wanted : Containing St. Helens Intelligence*, four pages of advertisement and news (the former predominating) for the price of 2d. In it he announced that the *St. Helens Intelligencer*, as the paper was to be called, would appear on or about the first of each month " until we find ourselves wanted oftener."[6] The repeal of the

---

[1] *St. H. Standard* 18 Aug., 1865. According to the *St. H. N.* 25 April, 1868, fewer than 500 people per week attended the baths even in the heat of summer.

[2] The St. H. I. C. resolved on 7 Feb., 1849 " That the Town Bell be delivered to Thomas Houghton to be used by him as Town Crier on condition that he return it when called on to do so by the Commissioners ". The bell is still to be seen at the St. H. Museum, Victoria Park. A label attached to it states that it was in use until *c.* 1890.

[3] *Wigan Gazette* 7 Feb., 1840.

[4] Obit. Isaac Sharp, *St. H. N.* 18 March, 1865. For a circular printed by Lyon, see Sibson Papers at Warrington Ref. Lib.

[5] *Wigan Times* 13 May, 1853.

[6] Issues 1 and 14 (the latter dated 3 Feb., 1855) are in the St. H. Ref. Lib. Samuel Bishop is said to have backed Foreman financially and Canon Carr, the Vicar, was intimately associated with its affairs (*St. H. N.* 11 Jan., 1896). Until the issue of 22 Oct., 1859, only the local news was printed at St. H., the rest of the paper being printed in London.

newspaper stamp duty in 1855[1] as well as a growing demand for
local news led to the first issue of a weekly *St. Helens Intelligencer*
on 29 December of that year.

One of the most regular contributors was a determined young
man named Bernard Augustine Dromgoole.[2] Born in Warrington
of Irish parents in 1819, he worked for a time at Grace's Marshall's
Cross Pottery (where he married his employer's daughter), and
then opened a pawnbroker's shop in Liverpool Road, St.
Helens in 1853. Dromgoole had a distinct flair for journalism
combined with a deep social conscience which caused him to make
frequent use of his talent. He contributed to the second number
of the *Intelligencer*[3] and later claimed that by 1860 he had " penned
many hundred pages of manuscript besides spending scores of
hours . . . reading and correcting proofs."[4] But Dromgoole was
an ex-Chartist, a Liberal and a Radical : the *Intelligencer* was
Conservative. When the Tories won a sweeping victory in South
Lancashire at the general election of 1859, the electors of the
newly-formed St. Helens Polling District voting strongly in the
Conservative cause, he was among the small band of Liberals
who met together to consider the possibility of launching a Liberal
paper. The would-be promoters did not come to a working
agreement, however, so Dromgoole, " foreseeing that a paper
managed by a number of persons whether as a committee or as
shareholders would only create confusion and unpleasantness and
quickly end in failure,"[5] decided to launch the new Liberal organ
on his own and at his own expense.[6] This was a step requiring very
considerable courage, for he was not a printer nor had he access
to a printing press. Nevertheless, on 22 September, 1860, the
first edition of *The St. Helens Weekly News*, printed outside the
town, made its appearance on the stalls and in the shops. It was
produced by a staff of one, Dromgoole being his own reporter as
well as editor and business manager. But he could write well and
the courage which had revealed itself when he embarked upon the
paper did not desert him when he sat down to write the editorials.
Even the Improvement Commissioners were roundly denounced
in an early number as " a public nuisance and a reproach ; a
nuisance indeed that is daily becoming more offensive and

[1] A. Aspinall, *Politics and the Press* (1949), 383.

[2] For details of Dromgoole's life, see obit., *St. H. N.* 8 Jan., 1909.

[3] *St. H. N.* 11 Jan., 1896. This appears to refer to the monthly paper

[4] *St. H. Weekly News* 27 July, 1861.

[5] *St. H. N.* 27 Sept., 1862.

[6] He claimed two years after the launching of the paper that his losses
had been " considerable up to within a recent period ", amounting " on a
moderate calculation to near £500, more than £280 being cash out of
pocket ". Help had been promised but in fact only £5 : 5 : 0 had been
received from one well-wisher. *Ibid.*

mischievous and one that ought to be abated "[1]—words made quite intelligible to the local inhabitants by the all-pervading noxious vapours. These attacks lost him much revenue and made him several bitter enemies ; but they also gained a large number of readers. In 1862 he was able to buy a rotary printing machine and introduce a mid-week edition. He also changed the title to *Dromgoole's St. Helens Newspaper and Advertiser*.[2] " It was hard work," he later confessed, " and when we got the rotary machine and had to turn it by hand, it was harder still. But we went on mangling away."[3] The *Newspaper*, which sold 4,000 copies during the last week of 1863,[4] soon drove the *Intelligencer* out of business. The rights of the latter were bought by Dromgoole who was then able to claim that his paper dated from 1853.[5] This left the Conservatives without a newspaper so in 1865—another election year—they made good the loss of the *Intelligencer* by launching the *St. Helens Standard*, the managing editor being first E. H. Johnson and then Frederick Hodgson.[6] The *Standard* just contrived to hold its own against the local thunderer but in 1877, when Culshaw, Brown and Culshaw, proprietors of the *Prescot Reporter*, announced their intention of removing the head office of that paper to St. Helens, Hodgson " felt that the time had come when he could favourably retire from the field of newspaper labour and leave the work in more willing hands."[7] The combined paper continued to be known as the *Prescot Reporter and St. Helens Central Advertiser* until the edition of 8 June, 1888, when it appeared for the first time as the *St. Helens Reporter*.[8]

[1] *St. H. N.* 20 April, 1861.

[2] *St. H. N.* 29 March, 27 Sept., and 15 Nov., 1862.

[3] *St. H. N.* 11 Jan., 1896.

[4] *St. H. N.* 27 Feb., 1864.

[5] For conflicting views on the date on which the *Intelligencer* ceased publication, see the *St. H. N.* 3 Jan., 24 Oct., 1863 and 19 Jan., 1867 ; and the *St. H. Standard* 7 July, 1865. The files at the St. H. Ref. Lib. do not continue beyond 1859 and the B.M. Newspaper Lib. has no copies at all.

[6] For Hodgson, see obit., *Prescot Reporter* 24 Sept., 1887.

[7] *St. H. Standard* 24 Nov., 1877. The first number of the *Prescot Reporter* was published by John Culshaw, postmaster of Prescot, on 12 Nov., 1859. From the very first edition it contained some St. Helens news.

[8] The following newspapers were also published locally before 1900 :
The St. H. Leader (monthly). Journal of the St. H. Y.M.C.A., containing much local news. 1 Sept., 1877—2 Sept., 1878.
The St. H. Examiner (estd. 1878). Copies from 24 May, 1879, at the B. M. Newspaper Lib. None available locally.
St. H. Chronicle ceased pubn. Feb., 1894 after 5 years, having lost more than £2,000 (*St. H. N.* 10 Feb., 1894). No copies at St. H. Ref. Lib. or the B. M. Newspaper Lib.
St. H. Lantern, 6 Jan., 1887—12 May, 1893. Monthly, 1887, fortnightly 1888 and weekly in and after 1889. Ed. Henry Lindon Riley (q.v. below, p. 469).

The sale of several thousand copies of these local newspapers every week is a good indication that in all probability the majority of the town's adult population could read.[1] A further indication came only a few weeks after the first copy of the *Intelligencer* was published, when a move was made to form a public library. The Mechanics Institute, when it was established in 1852, had toyed with the idea of a library for its own members, but in the end the committee had decided to be content with a newsroom in part of the Town Hall.[2] Towards the end of 1853, however, the matter was broached again and a meeting was convened in January, 1854. It was addressed by Lord Stanley, who had spoken at a similar meeting in Prescot early in the previous month.[3] Robert Daglish pointed out that it would be very unwise to confine the library to members of the Mechanics Institute for that body might fail. He therefore proposed to give £100, instead of the £50 he had originally intended, if it were decided to make the library public and vest it in the St. Helens Improvement Commission. Gilbert Greenall, M.P., the Pilkingtons and the Bromilows warmly supported Daglish's suggestion and each gave £100. In all, more than £600 was forthcoming. A committee was formed consisting of members of the Mechanics Institute, the St. Helens Improvement Commission and other interested persons, and rules (based upon those in force at the Manchester Public Library) were drawn up.[4] The books were shelved in a room in the Town Hall and could be borrowed by anyone who lived in any of the four townships for 1d. a week, members of the Mechanics Institute paying at the reduced rate of 2s. a year.[5] By 1857 the library possessed almost 2,500 volumes and these were taken out at the rate of 600 a month[6]—a disappointing total when there were between 20,000 and 30,000 potential borrowers. Support for the Mechanics Institute was even more disappointing. After losing strength steadily throughout the 1860s,[7] the Institute was said to be

[1] According to Robert K. Webb, "Working Class Readers in Early Victorian England," *Eng. Hist. Rev.*, LXV., July, 1950, the commonest figure for literacy in the 1840s was between ⅔ and ¾ of the working classes, "perhaps nearer the former."

[2] This paragraph, unless otherwise stated, is based upon the recollections of Robert Kirkman, an eye-witness of the events he described (*St. H.N.* 13 May, 1893).

[3] *Lpool. Merc.* 9 Dec., 1853.

[4] St. H. Ref. Lib., Mins. of the St. H. Pub. Lib., 1853-70, 9 June, 1854.

[5] *Ibid.*, 20 Jan., 30 Oct., 1854.

[6] *St. H. Intelligencer* 13 June, 1857.

[7] St. H. Ref. Lib., Mins. of the Mechanics Institute, 1861-73, 31 May, 1866, 23 Feb., 1869.

" between life and death " in 1870.[1]   It died[2]; and its offspring was left helpless until the Corporation later took charge and revived it in a new form.   In August, 1877, a Public Free Library containing 5,000 volumes was opened in the new Town Hall.

That a high proportion of the local inhabitants was able to read, reflects considerable credit upon the schools of the town, by this time sufficiently numerous to provide a basic grounding in the three Rs for almost the whole child population.   " Drunken and dissolute fathers and mothers . . . are the only ones except poor widows who do not now get their children some education, at all events in St. Helens," a local employer commented in 1865.[3] " A young person who cannot read and write," added another, " goes with a positive disadvantage in the labour market."[4] Of course, this schooling was in most cases rudimentary in the extreme by modern standards.   Accommodation was cramped, classes were very large,[5] attendance was frequently irregular and brief, and the teachers were themselves sometimes unable to spell.[6]   But, armed with a cane—or in one case with a pick shaft[7]—they drove what little they knew into the heads of their pupils.   It was a strict, harsh and painful *régime* but it achieved its limited aim.   The boys and girls were taught to read and write (usually in a bold, copper-plate hand).   And they were taught to obey.

Although the noxious vapours drove away the boarding academies, a few private day schools survived to give a more advanced form of education—usually of a commercial nature— to the sons and daughters of those who could afford to pay the fees.   The responsibility for elementary education, however, continued to rest, with the exception of a few factory schools,[8] almost wholly upon the churches.

Most of the churches in the neighbourhood made great efforts

[1] *St. H. Standard* 10 Sept., 1870.

[2] On 7 Nov., 1870 the name was changed to the St. H. Atheneum, rooms acquired in Hardshaw Street and billiard and bagatelle tables installed. These had to be sold in 1873 (Minutes; *St. H.N.* 29 Nov., 1873).

[3] Evidence of Samuel Bishop to the Ch. Emp. Comm., 4th Rep., 1865 [8357] XX, 271.

[4] *Ibid.*   Evidence of Crossley and Sivewright, 273.

[5] E.g. the headmaster of Holy Trinity Boys' School thought that a class of 50 for P.T. was " not large " (Log book, kept at the school, 29 April, 1885).

[6] *St. H. Intelligencer* 5 July, 1856.

[7] William Stubbs, master at Moorflat School from 1857 (John Kerr in *Cullet*, staff magazine of Pilkington Brothers Ltd.).

[8] There were factory schools attached to the Ravenhead Plate Glassworks and the St. Helens Crown Glassworks.   The British and Foreign Copper Co. also supported an infants' school in 1850.

to open schools. The case of the parish of Sutton provides a good example of how important the Anglicans believed their schools to be. Sutton was formed into a separate parish in 1848 and on 4 June in the following year the church of St. Nicholas was consecrated.[1]   Six months later, the Rev. Henry Edward Francis Vallancey, a Fellow of King's College, Cambridge, who had been presented to the living,[2] wrote to the Principal and Fellows of Brasenose College, Oxford, the owners of a small estate in his parish :

> " On taking possession of my living, I found everything had to be created in the parish. My attention was first of all directed to the almost total want of schools . . . In the present circumstances of the educational question, it did not appear to me advisable to build, unless prepared to build without extraneous assistance, which I was unable to do. A further survey of my parish having convinced me of the extreme necessity of schools, I am determined to avail myself of the only spot suited for the purpose, the old Township poorhouse of which I have agreed to take a lease for 21 years with the usual conditions. The whole of this rent of £30 per annum I am perfectly willing to take upon myself if I can raise enough in my parish to meet the annual expenses of the schools. This I was perfectly confident about but now I am not so confident as I was, in consequence of not having been met by the principal landowner as liberally as I had every right to expect and I am therefore forced to turn to the non-resident proprietors for assistance. I have obtained an excellent schoolmaster and mistress . . ."[3]

The school was opened in February 1850[4] and a year later the Vicar declared that he had " every reason to be satisfied with the state of the Schools . . . especially the boys' School."[5] The printed report for 1850, which he enclosed, showed that 95 boys and 74 girls were receiving education in the converted poorhouse and 130 infants were being taught at a kindergarten on the premises of the British and Foreign Copper Company, supported by the proprietors, Newton Keates and Company. The total cost of two teachers (a man and his wife), equipment and fuel for the first year was about £120. In June, 1856, the Vicar wrote again to say that the schools were permanently established but he wanted to put them on a firmer footing :

---

[1] Supplement to the *London Gazette* 15 Aug., 1848, issued 17 Aug. ; *Lpool Merc.* 8 June, 1849.

[2] For Vallancey, who remained Vicar of Sutton until he d. in 1888, see obit., *St. H. N.* 22 Sept., 1888.

[3] Brasenose College, Oxford, package 46.   Letter dated 13 Dec., 1849.

[4] *Ibid.*   Letter dated 6 Feb., 1850.

[5] *Ibid.*   Letter dated 17 March, 1851.

" My present Schools are contiguous to my Church but far removed from the mass of my population. The great mass of my people reside around the works and many have to come more than a mile every day and some nearly two miles. Down where the majority reside, there is a population of full 2,500 and, as much building is going on there, there can be no doubt that the population there will increase still more ; in fact, it had increased largely since I came here. The only day schools down there are those belonging to a Roman Catholic Monastery —this building was projected before I came and has been built since [St. Anne's Monastery, opened October, 1853]. A suitable plot of ground has been given, valued at £200. The schools must necessarily be large and with requisite residences will cost about £1,500. Towards this I am entitled to receive one half from the government and therefore I must raise £800. The Company that has given the land [The British and Foreign Copper Co.] will likewise largely help with building materials, which become valuable by saving the expense of brickwork. From the Glass works I expect to receive £300 and possibly glass for the windows. Mrs. Hughes of Sherdley Park gives £100."[1]

The forthright language which had to be used by the Vicar to obtain this £100 from Mrs. Hughes is worthy of notice. He wrote to her on 28 March, 1856 :

" You will pardon me, I trust, for what I am going to say for I must speak out very plainly. You are beyond question my wealthiest Parishioner and what is the amount I receive from you as your annual subscription for the support of our Schools? Merely five pounds! . . . If I obtain the land from you, I shall not look for any further assistance from you for the building fund: if you are still indisposed to give it, I must tell you that I conceive I have every right to look to you for a subscription of £100: less than this I do not expect from you . . ."[2]

Only the Vicar could address the leading local landowners in this dictatorial way. Only the church could exert such strong pressure to finance new schools by voluntary gifts.

The most valuable of these gifts were bequests of land, particularly those given during the early stages of industrialization before land values had risen greatly or the underlying coals had been removed. John Allanson, for instance, entrusted his small estate in Parr to the Independent Chapel in 1792. About one-third of the income from it was to be spent on Bibles, psalm and

[1] *Ibid.* 19 June, 1856.

[2] Sherdley Estate Office. Letter dated 28 March, 1856. The Vicar's schemes did not materialise so early as he hoped. The foundation stone of the Sutton National Schools was not laid until August, 1863, and the schools, built on land given by Newton Keates and Co., were not opened until the following February. They cost £1,300, only £50 being received from the Committee of Education (*St. H. N.* 19 Aug., 1863, 27 Feb., 1864).

hymn books " and in the purchase of other Divine Books for . . .
the raising and supporting a Library for the use of the Congregation attending Divine Service in the Dissenting Chapel."[1] In 1830
the coal measures under the estate started to be mined and the
annual income rose suddenly from £24 to £224 for each of the
following thirty years.[2] A sizeable library was built up and the
interest from this income not only helped to pay off the debt on the
new chapel but also made possible the erection of a Sunday
School building in 1837.[3]

The Sarah Cowley Charity is an even better local example
of a humble bequest appreciating in value. This small estate
yielded £10 a year immediately after Sarah Cowley's death
in 1716.[4] At the beginning of the nineteenth century, as has been
noticed,[5] coalmining increased the value of the property considerably. In 1856 and 1858 the St. Helens Canal and Railway
Company, at that time requiring land for their new Rainford
branch and for a goods yard, leased the greater part of the estate
at an annual rent of £666.[6] The trustees, who were still receiving
a considerable income from the exploitation of the coal measures
in addition to this new windfall,[7] at once planned to extend the
scope and size of the Cowley Schools. According to their *Scheme
for the Regulation of Sarah Cowley's Charity*, filed in Chancery
on 29 June, 1860,[8] there were in future to be three departments : for boys aged 6-17, for girls aged 6-16 and for infants
of 2-7 years. The boys and girls were to be taught reading,
writing, arithmetic, general English literature and composition,
history, geography and book-keeping, the boys the " elements
of the Latin language "[9] and mathematics and the girls needle-
work. No pupil was to pay more than 3d. a week and the trustees
were empowered to reduce or abolish this head money in needy
cases. In 1861 the necessary new building was erected to house

[1] Will of John Allanson proved at Chester, 21 May, 1792.

[2] St. H. Cong. Ch., package 10. Petition to Lord Lyndhurst, 1833 ;
letter from Benjamin Biram to Isaac Sharp, 18 Dec., 1860.

[3] The new schoolroom, with accommodation for 500 children, cost
£600. An infants' room was added shortly before 1856 (*Lpool. Merc.*
7 March, 1856). This was replaced by the present, three-storey building
in 1872 (*St. H. N.* 9 Sept., 1871 ; papers in package 18 at St. H. Cong. Ch.).

[4] St. H. Ref. Lib. MS. Account Book of the Management of Sarah
Cowley's Estate.

[5] Above, p. 176.

[6] Charity Commissioners' Report, 1905 [313] C, 37.

[7] St. H. Town Hall. Cowley Trust papers.

[8] *Ibid.*

[9] Some idea of the meaning of " elements " may be grasped from the
headmaster's diary—e.g., " Solus in mea sede in ecclesia " (Diary of Newton
Lacey, *sub.* 1 Aug., 1886).

the boys' department and the older school (in the revealing words
of the Charity Commissioners' Report) was "abandoned to
the use of the girls and infants."[1] At the end of the year 1861
when the annual examinations were held, there were 285 boys,
114 girls and 159 infants benefiting from the more advanced
form of education which was to be had at these, the largest schools
in the town.[2] The high standard reached was due in no small
measure to the personality of the headmaster, Newton Lacey,
who directed the teaching there from 1846 until his retirement
in 1875.[3] During these twenty-nine years he calculated (with
a meticulous accuracy typical of him) that 6,208 scholars had
passed through his hands.[4] He had become so much a part
of the place during this long period that it came to be known
popularly as Lacey's School.

The Cowley School, managed by a joint committee of Independents and Anglicans (the former predominating slightly)
was non-sectarian. It was a British school where religious instruction was limited to Bible teaching and exposition without
any particular denominational bias or doctrinal teaching.
Moorflat, on the other hand, was a National school under
Anglican management and had developed out of the seventeenth
century foundation at the old St. Helen's Chapel.[5] It, too,
reaped the harvest of timely endowments which increased in
value as the town grew, and was able to offer to " respectable
tradesmen's sons " not only " the elementary parts of an English
education " but also " Euclid, Algebra, Mechanics, Book-
keeping by double entry, Mensuration, Drawing, Painting,
Chemistry and Music (use of harmonium) " for from 6s. to 12s.
per quarter.[6] Moorflat, attended by 250 scholars in the late '50s
and early '60s, was about the size of the new boys' department
of Cowley School.[7]

While Moorflat was providing a higher grade of education,
other National Schools were being built to teach the " elementary
parts." These elementary schools arose from the new Anglican
churches which were being built to serve the rapidly-growing
population, as in the case of St. Nicholas's, Sutton. There

---

[1] Charity Commissioners' Report, 1905 [313] C, 37 ; St. H. N. 21 Dec.,
1861.

[2] St. H. N. 21 Dec., 1861.

[3] For Newton Lacey, see obit., St. H. N. 21 May, 1896, and his diary,
1871-92.

[4] Diary of Newton Lacey, 24 July, 1875.

[5] Above, p. 175.

[6] St. H. Intelligencer 7 Feb., 1857.

[7] For attendance figures, Wigan Times 22 July, 1853 ; St. H. Intelligencer 20 Dec., 1856 ; St. H. N. 5 Dec., 1863.

were schools attached to St. Thomas's from its opening, for instance, and these were extended in 1843.[1] At a meeting held in March of the following year, the early commencement of National Schools in Parr (where a chapel-of-ease had been consecrated in the previous month[2]) was announced.[3] In 1857 a second chapel-of-ease, Holy Trinity in Parr, was opened and a day school erected[4] and in 1858 the Vicar of St. Helens claimed that £5,000 had been spent on educational building in the previous five years.[5]

The Roman Catholic population was ill-served with schools until the close of the 1840s when local Catholics took energetic measures to make good the deficiency. In 1849 when the full effect of the Irish immigration into the district was being felt and the number of Catholic schoolchildren in and about St. Helens was stated to be 1,500, the schoolroom attached to St. Mary's, Lowe House, could only accommodate 100. But in that year new premises were opened for 1,100 children.[6] This was followed by new schools at St. Anne's Monastery in Sutton (1853),[7] at St. Joseph's in Parr (1857)[8] and those at Holy Cross,[9] Sacred Heart and Gerard's Bridge were built soon afterwards.[10] The Catholics appear to have made provision for the higher education of girls earlier than of boys ; on 3 May, 1858, the Sisters of Notre Dame of Namur began to provide " every essential for a polite education " for young ladies at 10, Hardshaw Street.[11]

The Methodists, who already conducted day schools outside the town at Nutgrove and Sutton, opened premises at Waterloo Street in January, 1855, where 150 boys and girls and 150 children

---

[1] *Lpool. Merc.*, 8 Sept., 1843.   A separate school for orphans, supported by Mrs. Greenall, stood nearby.

[2] *Lpool Merc.* 23 Feb., 1844.   The church was burnt down in Jan., 1864 and a new church consecrated in Dec., 1865 (*St. H. N.* 20 Jan. 1864 ; 2 Jan., 1866).

[3] *Lpool Merc.* 15 March, 1844.

[4] *St. H. Intelligencer* 24 Feb., 1857.

[5] *St. H. Intelligencer* 6 March, 1858.

[6] *Lpool Merc.* 25 Sept., 1849 ; 23 Aug., 1850.

[7] Catholic Churches' Guide, 1899.

[8] *St. H. Intelligencer* 22 March, 1856, 28 Nov., 1857.

[9] When Joseph McGarigle d. in 1889, he was said to have been headmaster at Holy Cross for 31 years—i.e., since 1858.   (obit. *St. H. N.* 7 Sept., 1889).   Holy Cross Church itself, however, was only opened in 1862 (*St. H. N.* 3 May, 1862 ; 25 Nov., 1863).

[10] *St. H. N.* 21 Nov., 1900.   Prior to the opening of Sacred Heart Church in 1878, the schools were known as Victoria Schools.

[11] *St. H. Intelligencer* 17 April, 1858.

could be accommodated.[1] The Independents did not hold with sectarian, day school education but, as we have seen, were closely associated with the Cowley Schools. Some of their members were also to be found among the leading supporters of the Ragged School in Arthur Street opened in 1861.[2]

In the aggregate, the results of this church-dominated day school building was impressive. By 1870 there were more than 8,000 scholars on the registers[3] and public elementary education costing only a few pence per week was almost universal. The town was not obliged to establish a school board and, when a school attendance committee was set up to assist teachers in checking truancy, the *St. Helens Leader* commented, with some justification :

> " We may be able to congratulate ourselves upon the attainment of most of the objects of School Boards without their usual accompaniment—large expenditure."[4]

By this time more children attended day schools than Sunday schools,[5] a remarkable transition since the earlier years of the century. As the day schools came to assume more responsibility for the standards of literacy in the town, the Sunday schools, freed from this duty, were able to concentrate to a greater extent upon religious instruction.

These middle years marked the heyday of the voluntary principle and of private initiative. These were the golden years of opportunity little troubled by disturbances of trade, when local speculators, having acquired experience and capital in minor ventures, could embark to advantage on bolder schemes. Their cumulative success was magnetic : other speculators were drawn into the district from outside with equal hope of success

[1] *Lpool Merc.* 13 June, 1854. For Nutgrove School, see the will of Jonas Nuttall, proved at Chester, 12 July, 1838, and for the school at Sutton, established 1845, see Cook, *MS. Hist. of St. H.*, 45.

[2] Obit. W. W. Pilkington, *St. H. N.* 20 March, 1914 ; obit. J. F. Allen, *St. H. N.* 30 Aug., 1912 ; obit. the Rev. W. A. Mocatta, *St. H. Standard* 30 Dec., 1876 ; *St. H. Standard* 1 Sept., 1865 ; Charity Commissioners' Report 1905 [313] C, 60-1.

[3] *St. H. N.* 18, 25 March, 1 April, 7 Oct., 1871.

[4] *St. H. Leader* 1 Nov., 1877.

[5] Of 7,413 on the registers of local Sunday schools in 1869, 2,402 were Anglicans, 1,496 Wesleyans, 998 Independents, 996 Catholics, 438 Primitive Methodists, 120 United Free Methodists, 120 Presbyterians, 180 Baptists, 75 Christian Brethren, 540 Ragged School and 48 Town Mission (*St. H. Standard* 5 June, 1869).

and they, in turn, gave added strength to the town's growth. On the fringes of all this private effort for motives of profit were established many of the public services. As the townsmen saw all these new buildings—works, houses, shops, schools and churches—going up around them on every hand and at such a rapid rate, it is hardly surprising that they came to the conclusion that progress and individual effort were synonymous. This was the age of continuous economic growth and modest requirement, an age when individual effort could be exerted with greatest effect. The time was yet to come when economic growth was arrested by foreign competition and when public requirements became more exacting and expensive ; then it was no longer possible to rely to the same extent upon voluntary contribution and piecemeal organisation.

The changes in the character of local government, particularly the grouping of the poor law authorities and the formation of new bodies for sanitary purposes, were already pointing the way to the future. It is the development of local government at St. Helens, the growth of the organisation that was eventually to take control of much that had been started by private venture, that must concern us next.

Chapter XXVI

THE IMPROVEMENT COMMISSION

THE St. Helens Improvement Commission came into being under remarkably inauspicious circumstances. The exclusion of that part of Sutton immediately to the south of the town prevented the new sanitary authority from exercising control over the whole of the natural drainage area and robbed it of income from the rich industrial property in the rapidly-developing Ravenhead district. Moreover, membership of and electoral votes for the Commission were subject to strict property qualifications. Only those local residents who were assessed for the poor rate at more than £20, or received an income from rent exceeding £50, or possessed personal estate worth more than £1,000, could stand as Commissioners ; and only those rated under the Act at more than £4 were given the power of election.[1] This placed responsibility for the working of the new sanitary authority squarely upon the shoulders of the leading property owners, the very men who had opposed the Bill with such vehemence and were quite out of sympathy with the spirit of the measure. Clearly, all the ingenuity and influence of the chief architect of the new local authority was needed to secure its success. But Peter Greenall died less than a month after the Commissioners held their first meeting.

Although Greenall's able lieutenants did their best to support the venture which they had helped to promote (Samuel Bishop, Arthur Sinclair and David Gamble were successively chairmen of the Commission between 1845 and 1862), and although Edward Johnson, the local solicitor who had been Greenall's chief legal assistant in securing the Act, was appointed clerk to the Commissioners—a position which he held until his death in January, 1866—the disabilities under which the new body laboured soon

---

[1] 8 and 9 Vict. cap. CLXXVI, sec. 2, 16. Commissioners had to be resident within the Commission's boundary or within two miles of it. The first Commissioners, named in sec. 1 of the Act., were : John Ansdell, Samuel Bishop, David Bromilow, Robert Daglish, Frederick Fincham, David Gamble, Peter Greenall, John Haddock, William Hibbert, William Johnson, John Marsh, jr., Isaac Sharp, Edward Webster, George Webster and Thomas Walmesley. According to the St. H. I. C. Mins., Fincham and Haddock, property owners in Sutton, declined to serve, and James Shanks and John Blundell were co-opted in their stead. H. G. Bromilow became a Commissioner in the room of his brother and, when Peter Greenall died, his brother-in-law, Richard Pilkington, was appointed to take his place but never attended any meetings. Nor did Walmesley. One-third of the Commission of 15 retired on 1 Jan. each year but could be re-elected.

damped their initial enthusiasm.   The property within the
Commission's boundary was only valued at £17,000 in 1845
and the rates permitted by the Act brought in less than £1,500
in the first year.[1] In consequence the indigent Improvement
Commission, tolerated but not liked by those responsible for its
working, achieved the minimum amount of routine paving and
draining necessary to justify its existence, but progressed by slow,
awkward, leaden-footed steps, moving only when compelled to
do so, spurred on by inescapable necessity and irate ratepayers.
It soon became an object of ridicule rather than of respect.

The fate of one of the Commission's earliest resolutions,
authorising negotiation with the Society of Friends for the
purchase of the New Market Place and the market sheds, was an
augury of what was to be expected in the future. Bargaining
dragged on and on, final agreement not being reached for five
years. The building of the market hall, once the New Market
Place had been acquired, was quick by comparison. The tender
for £2,030, put in jointly by Harris and Sherratt, and Robinson
and Cook, was accepted in October 1850 and the market hall,
with accommodation for 118 stalls, was opened in September
of the following year.[2]

The inadequacy of the town's water supply confronted the
Commissioners with their first important challenge. As the
numbers of domestic and industrial consumers increased, the
reservoirs on Samuel Taylor's estate, capable of supplying only
130,000 to 150,000 gallons per day, were unable to satisfy the
additional demand and in hot weather, when the dams were almost
dry, the water which reached the town was often far from crystal
clear. The only action taken by the Commissioners in response
to the " frequent complaints . . . of the filthy, noxious, unhealthy
condition of the water supplied to the town "[3] was to remonstrate
with the existing Waterworks Company, despite the fact that they
were themselves fully empowered by the Act of 1845 to take
control.[4] But as the population increased the water shortage became rapidly more acute and it was evident that each summer
would bring louder cries of indignant protest from the hot and
thirsty townspeople. Unlike Peter Greenall, who led public
opinion, the reluctant Commissioners delayed until they were overwhelmed by it.

[1] 8 and 9 Vict. cap. CLXXVI, sec. 267-9; St. H. I. C. Rate Books. The
Act permitted the Commission to levy a 10d. rate for paving and highway
development, a 4d. rate for sewering and a 7d. rate for lighting and general
purposes.

[2] St. H. I. C. Mins., 1 May, 31 July, 16 Oct., 1850 ;   *Wigan Times* 19
Sept., 1851.

[3] St. H. I. C. Mins., 5 June, 1850.

[4] 8 and 9 Vict. cap. CLXXVI, sec. 82.

In October, 1850, it was eventually decided to apply to Parliament for another Improvement Act " for general purposes and especially for powers to enable the Commissioners to take Water from the Liverpool Water Works (Rivington Scheme) and to lay pipes for the supply of the Town."[1] This course was approved by a meeting of ratepayers at the end of December,[2] the Waterworks Company's property was taken on a 5,000 year lease in March 1851 at an annual rent of £300[3], and the second St. Helens Improvement Bill passed into law a few months later.[4]

The Commissioners expected to be able to end the water shortage by tapping the Rivington-Liverpool pipeline as it passed through St. Helens and they had already appointed Thomas Hawksley, the eminent water engineer and promoter of the Rivington Pike Scheme,[5] as their expert adviser by February, 1851.[6] But the laying of the Rivington main progressed very slowly ; it did not supply water to Liverpool until 1857, ten years after the scheme had been authorised.[7] The Commissioners could not afford to delay and they therefore asked Hawksley to investigate other sources of water. This was a wise decision, particularly in the light of Liverpool Corporation's subsequent decision to lay the Rivington pipeline farther to the north of St. Helens than had been previously intended.[8] Hawksley, having taken into account that the town was built over coal

---

[1] St. H. I. C. Mins., 4 Sept., 1850. The St. H. Waterworks Co. also applied to Parliament in the 1851 session " to raise more Money, to receive Water from the Liverpool Corporation Waterworks and to sell their Undertaking to the St. H. Improvement Commissioners " but this Bill was later abandoned. (*C.J.*, **106**, 12, 13, 18 Feb., 1851).

[2] W. Ranger, *Report to the President of the General Board of Health on a Preliminary Inquiry into the Sewerage, Drainage and Supply of Water and the Sanitary Condition of the Inhabitants of the Town of St. Helens in the County Palatine of Lancaster* (1855), 44-5 (hereafter referred to as *Ranger Report*).

[3] St. H. I. C. Mins., 5 March, 1851. This was equivalent to $7\frac{1}{2}$ per cent on each of the 160, £25 shares. Water rents in 1850 totalled about £1,000 and expenditure in that year amounted to £592. Previous dividends had averaged 14/6 per share (a little under 3 per cent) and £636 had been laid out in improvements since the Company's formation (St. H. I. C. Mins., 20 Nov., 1850, 5 Feb., 1851).

[4] 14 & 15 Vict. cap. CXXXII. This Act also raised the number of Commissioners from 15 to 18 and incorporated the Commissioners Clauses Act, the Town Improvement Clauses Act, the Town Police Clauses Act, the Markets and Fairs Clauses Act and the Waterworks Clauses Act., all passed in 1847.

[5] For Hawksley, see the *D.N.B.*

[6] St. H. I. C. Mins., 5 Feb., 1851.

[7] 9 & 10 Vict. cap. CXXVII ; William Fergusson Irvine, *A Short History of the Township of Rivington* (Edinburgh, 1904), 150.

[8] Below, p. 401.

measures which were constantly being pumped dry for mining purposes, and that any water from the vicinity of the alkali works was liable to be polluted,[1] recommended the sinking of a shaft in the red sandstone where it outcropped at Eccleston Hill to the west of the town. Here the height of the pumping station would give a pressure of about 150 ft. The new source, he estimated, would yield an additional 550,000 gallons per day, much more than was required at that time for domestic purposes. This would allow the 130,000 to 150,000 gallons per day, then being obtained from the existing reservoirs at a pressure of only 60 ft., to be used in the local factories.[2]

The Commission accepted these recommendations and work began on the Hawksley Scheme at the end of 1852. The sinking of the shafts and the erection of pumping machinery, however, took longer than was expected : operations continued during 1853 and 1854.[3] While this search for a new source of water was going on, the water shortage in the town became more acute each year, particularly in the broiling summer of 1853 when there was " considerable alarm," lest the supply should prove inadeqate for the town's basic needs.[4] Moreover, delays added to the cost of the new " high pressure " water supply (as it came to be called) ; the total expenditure eventually amounted to £19,000, £7,000 more than the Improvement Commission was permitted to raise by mortgage on the security of the rates. In order to legalise this overspending the Commissioners were obliged to apply to Parliament for yet another Improvement Act ; this enabled them to increase their borrowing powers from £12,000 to £30,000.

Meanwhile a second crisis was rapidly coming to a head. By 1851 the Commissioners had laid sewers in the main streets of the town but in their campaign against cesspools they had created another and equally harmful nuisance. In laying the new sewers, the surveyor had followed the previous practice of running each pipe or brick culvert[5] down into a central brook which wound its way through the town. As more sewers discharged into this brook, its sluggish waters became the more polluted and foul smelling, particularly in the heat of summer. By 1851 the surveyor reported to the Commissioners that from Westfield Street to the St. Helens Foundry it was

[1] Evidence of Hawksley to the S.C. on the St. H. Improvement Bill, 1855.

[2] Hawksley to St. H. I. C., 3 June, 1852 in *Ranger Report*, 42-3.

[3] *Ranger Report*, 20-1.

[4] St. H. Town Hall, package 209. Statement for the opinion of Counsel, 29 July, 1861.

[5] In 1855, more than two-thirds of the sewers of the town were still made of brick (*Ranger Report*, 24).

" exceedingly offensive and dangerous to public health."[1] This open main sewer, which received the outfall from all the smaller drains, was obviously in need of immediate attention if the town was not to be plagued with a huge cesspool much larger in extent than those which the local sewers had removed. But no action was taken and the pollution became far worse as more street sewers were connected. By 1854 a local resident was able to describe the brook as " an open ditch running among the dwellings for at least *a mile* and exposing in its course an evaporating surface of filth but a few yards less than an acre in extent".[2]

Once again the Commissioners acted only when compelled to do so by public opinion. On this occasion it was the outbreak of cholera in 1854, the second in five years,[3] that re-kindled an interest in sanitary reform. Although the disease took its heaviest toll among those who lived outside the town in the hamlets of Parr Flat and Parr Stocks,[4] there were some deaths in St. Helens itself and Robert Daglish, junior, was prompted to complain to the Poor Law Guardians of

" the neglect of the Improvement Commissioners to apply any remedy to the causes of disease for some time in operation and (in his judgment) in a great measure the cause of the alarming prevalence of Fever at St. Helens at the present time."[5]

The Guardians, anxious to keep to a minimum any additional charge on the poor rate, wrote to the St. Helens Improvement Commission urging the immediate removal of the nuisances and also sought the assistance of the General Board of Health. But the only advice that the General Board had to offer was that " it would be best that local authorities should co-operate."[6] After three months' futile correspondence with the St. Helens Improvement Commission, the Guardians came to the conclusion that it was high time that " this correspondence, productive of little or no good to the public, should cease."[7]

[1] St. H. Ref. Lib., Mins. of the St. H. I. C. Sewering and Highway Purposes Committee, 24 Sept., 1851.

[2] J. Barnes Barrow, quoted in *Ranger Report*, 51-2.

[3] The previous epidemic, in 1849, lasted from June until November, Peasley Cross, Parr Street, Parr Stocks and Merton Bank suffering the most severely. There were over 100 deaths. W. Farr, *Report on the Mortality of Cholera in England* (1852), 278.

[4] According to the Rev. A. A. Nunn, incumbent of St. Peter's, Parr, the outbreak resulted in 48 deaths in that parish (*St. H. Intelligencer* 7 Nov., 1857).

[5] Guard. Mins., 26 Oct., 1854.

[6] *Ibid.*, 1 March, 1855.

[7] *Ibid.*, 1 Feb., 1855.

The Guardians' prodding, however, seems to have caused the Commissioners, already obliged to obtain a new Improvement Act to legalise their overspending at the waterworks, to seek at the same time additional powers " for the more effectual suppression of nuisances and improving the sanitary condition " of the town, and, particularly, " a main arterial sewer."[1] They had at last been driven to take action or, more precisely, to state publicly that they intended to take some (unspecified) action at some (unspecified) future date. This was their answer to criticism when, in April 1855, a meeting of ratepayers was called to protest against the insanitary condition of the town,[2] and it was their reply to a General Board of Health Inspector when, in October 1855, he carried out an enquiry at St. Helens in response to a petition signed by 460 indignant ratepayers.[3]

Although the Inspector could not recommend the application of the Public Health Act to St. Helens because the Commissioners had secured their own local Act so recently,[4] his sweeping criticism of the existing local government was a bitter indictment of ten years of slow and reluctant progress:

" He should certainly have imagined that there had been no Acts of Parliament in existence for the cleansing of the town . . . Certainly the provisions of their own Act of Parliament and the bye-laws elaborately and properly set forth for the guidance of their working officer, should have reminded the Commissioners that something more was required, namely to give effect to them."[5]

But when the Inspector returned to London and wrote his report he toned down his criticisms considerably. He pointed out that rather more than half the houses and more than three-quarters of the streets had been sewered, and nearly $6\frac{1}{4}$ miles of roadway had also been slagged and paved,[6] Set against this record of achievement, the long list of delapidated privies, the roads still to be adopted and the absence of an arterial sewer (" a work too long delayed "),[7] did not seem such severe strictures upon the Commissioners' sloth. But to many of the townspeople, expecting an outright denunciation of the Commissioners and all their works, the report came as an unpleasant surprise. The *St. Helens*

[1] St. H. I. C. Mins., 2 Nov., 1854.

[2] *Lpool. Merc.* 10 April, 1855.

[3] *Ranger Report*, 5.

[4] 18 & 19 Vict. cap. LXXIV. This Act also divided the town into three wards ; Eccleston ; Windle ; and Hardshaw and Parr.

[5] *Lpool. Merc.* 21 Aug., 1855.

[6] *Ranger Report*, 24, 55, 62.

[7] *Ibid.*, 34. See also 59-61.

Intelligencer remarked: " As a whole, it falls much short of what we were led to expect."[1]

Nevertheless, the greater frankness of the Inspector while he was in St. Helens conducting his inquiry was sufficient to spur the Commission to a belated show of action at last. During the inquiry it had been emphasised that the brook nuisance was very much aggravated both by the large deposits of alkali waste which had been allowed to grow up " under the eyes and under the noses of the Commissioners,"[2] and by the acid, poured away from the chemical works in such quantities that Liverpool Corporation decided to divert their iron water main to skirt the town lest it should be destroyed by corrosion.[3] A few days after the Inspector's visit, a sub-committee was set up to consider the best means of abating the nuisance from the alkali waste[4] and shortly afterwards a Nuisance Removal Committee was established and an Inspector of Nuisances appointed.[5] By June, 1856, an agreement had been reached with Sutton township for paving the bed of the brook between Westfield Street and the St. Helens Foundry[6] but it was not until the middle of the following year that contractors were sought for this *cloaca maxima*.[7] They laid a pitched invert in the bed of the brook at a cost of £274—very much less than the £4,016 which the main sewer, much mentioned at the time of the Inspector's visit, would have cost.[8]

This unhealthy economy might have aroused fiercer opposition had not public attention been temporarily diverted away from the Commissioners' meetings to the proceedings of the Burial Board. This was established in May, 1856,[9] to select a suitable piece of ground, lay it out, and conduct it as a cemetery to take the place of the existing graveyards of the various individual churches as they became occupied.[10] The new combined cemetery at Denton's Green covering twenty Cheshire acres was opened

[1] *St. H. Intelligencer* 2 Feb., 1856.

[2] *Lpool. Merc.* 21 Aug., 1855.

[3] Evidence of Hawksley to the S.C. (Lords) on the St. H. Gas Bill, 1870, qq. 422-3.

[4] *Lpool. Merc.* 28 Aug., 1855.

[5] St. H. I. C. Mins., 4 Oct., 1855 ; 5 March, 1856.

[6] St. H. I. C. Mins., 4 June, 1856.

[7] *St. H. Intelligencer* 20 June, 1857.

[8] Report of the Rivers Pollution Commission 1870 [C. 109] XL, 15 ; *Ranger Report*, 52.

[9] *St. H. Intelligencer* 17 May, 1856. It was set up under the terms of the Burial Boards Act of 1855 (18 & 19 Vict. cap. CXXVIII).

[10] For the condition of the various graveyards, see *Ranger Report*, 62.

in the spring of 1858.[1] Its hillside position, sufficiently far removed from the smoke and smell of the town to be pleasantly rural and yet sufficiently close at hand to be easily accessible, was ideal, and it had the additional advantage of including within its walls the ruins of the fifteenth-century Windleshaw Chantry and the old Roman Catholic burial ground nearby. The Burial Board could hardly have achieved a more successful result; but its proceedings were marred by much petty sectarian bickering and this for a time aroused more popular attention than the cemetery itself.[2]

When the excitement over the Burial Board had died down, the public attack on the Improvement Commission was resumed. It was reinforced by B. A. Dromgoole, who was himself a Commissioner at the time he launched the *St. Helens Weekly News* in 1860 and therefore knew his target well. He singled out particular members for criticism of the most violent and personal nature. One man was called (by name) a " nondescript Methodist preacher of morality and encourager of vice . . . who may with great propriety be henceforth styled ' The Devil's Chaplain',"[3] and when another member was voted to the Chair of the Commission Dromgoole asked: " Has not his career at the Local Board of Commissioners been marked by the most wishy-washy drivel—the most milksop twaddle? "[4] Incompetent officials were hounded[5] and scorn poured upon the inefficient fire brigade, which on one occasion took fifty minutes to travel a few yards[6] and on another failed to arrive until all danger was over because

---

[1] *St. H. Intelligencer* 3 April, 22 May, 1858.   The Burial Board, authorised by the Treasury to raise £10,000, had spent £6,000 of this in purchasing the land from Sir Robert Tolver Gerard (L.R.O., DDGe 1457-61). The cemetery was laid out and the chapels built by John Middlehurst, a well-known local builder, responsible for many of the Catholic churches and schools of the town.   Born at a farm in Hard Lane, where his father was proprietor of the quarry, he later occupied various farms himself and was for some years tenant of Hardshaw Hall, where he worked the colliery on the estate.   He died at Birchley Hall (obit. *St. H. N.* 11 April, 1896 ; evidence of Moubert to the S.C. on Noxious Vapours, 1862, qq. 99-100).

[2] See, e.g., *St. H. Intelligencer* 17 April, 1, 15, 29 May, 7 Aug., 1858 ; 22, 29 Jan., 9 July, 1859.

[3] *St. H. Weekly News* 26 April, 1862.

[4] *St. H. N.* 10 Sept., 1864.

[5] E.g. the attack on the Collector of Rates, *St. H. Weekly News* 21 Sept., 2 Nov., 1861.

[6] *St. H. N.* 7 March, 1863.   The St. H. I. C. inherited " fire engines and water carts belonging to the Town " (Mins., 1 April, 1846).   A fire brigade committee was set up as a sub-committee of the St. H. I. C. in 1858 and in the following year a " fire engine shed " was in course of erection. In May the committee was authorized to engage and retain men to form the Brigade at a cost not exceeding £30 a year " (St. H. I. C. Mins., 19 May, 24 Aug., 1858 ; 11 May, 1859).

the wheel fell off the engine.[1] At the local elections he did not hesitate to make the most sweeping charges. In 1863, for instance, he wrote :

" Purity in elections is not one of the virtues for which St. Helens is famous; on the contrary, the town—but more especially the Hardshaw and Parr Ward—has become notorious for its drunkenness, its rowdyism and its total disregard of all decency, fair play and honesty in its elections. To such an extent is this system carried, that honest, respectable and intelligent men stand but a poor chance of being returned, whilst any dolt who will give away beer by gallons—give a *posse* of publicans a *carte blanche* and provide cabs and omnibuses to convey such ' fine and independent electors ' as had already been made half drunk, to the polling places—is pretty certain of being returned at the head of the poll. Not only is bribery by drink carried on to a great extent, but personation and false representation are practised to a degree unknown in any other town and a great disgrace to this . . . The system has been carried to such a height in this town that were it not for a few persons now and then at these recurring elections, bestirring themselves to secure the return of a few intelligent and independent men to the Board, the government of the town would soon be solely in the hands of the incapable and beery faction, who are returned by the ignorant, the duped and the drunken —who are a disgrace to the electoral body and whose representations at that Board are but too true a reflection of themselves . . ."[2]

One may wonder how Dromgoole escaped having to face innumerable actions for libel.[3] But that his paper was an important, stirring influence in local affairs, there can be little doubt.

For all their venom, the editorials written by Dromgoole were essentially realistic. He realised that although the polluted brook was a disgrace and the action of hydrochloric acid upon the calcium sulphide from the alkali works caused the most repulsive of smells, the town was not particularly unhealthy by mid-

---

[1] *St. H. N.* 29 April, 1863.

[2] *St. H. N.* 3 Sept., 1864.

[3] Dromgoole settled out of court libel actions, brought against him by the Rev. W. A. Mocatta in 1856 and by Dr. McNicoll in 1872, and a third action, brought by Thomas Thomson, a local tailor, in 1874 was decided in Dromgoole's favour. Hodgson, of the *St. H. Standard*, who was not nearly so outspoken, was fined £50 in 1871 for libelling L. W. Evans. Even Dromgoole, however, had to make amends in 1894 to the tune of £200 for calling Mr. Rose, a local confectioner, " the last Rose of summer " and much else in the same vein (*St. H. N.* 2, 16 Sept., 7 Oct., 1865 ; 2 Jan., 1866 ; 8 April, 1871 ; 27 July, 17 Aug., 1872 ; 28 March, 1874 ; 8 Dec., 1894).

nineteenth-century standards.[1] When the Earl of Derby brought the destructive effects of the noxious vapours to public notice in May 1862, the *St. Helens Weekly News* did not declare itself wholeheartedly in favour of immediate Parliamentary action but commented :

" Noxious as are the vapours, St. Helens cannot be said to be unhealthy. The large amount of high-priced labour which these works provide, would cause the inhabitants to rise as one man to resist by every legitimate means any attempt on the part of the legislature to pass any bill which would have the effect of crippling so important a branch of the trade of this district."[2]

Here lay the crux of the problem : although the Commissioners were certainly lax in much that they did and preferred to proceed at a casual jog-trot while everyone around them was galloping, they were quite unable to cope with the chief impediment to sanitary development, the by-products of the Leblanc process. The Nuisance Inspector went round seeking out the petty offender but was powerless to prevent the mass generation of noxious vapours and offending smells, for they were an integral part of the prosperity of the town. As James Haddock, the local coal proprietor, pertinently expressed it, St. Helens " seems to be a place in which they are licensed to make smells."[3] Until it became technically possible to put the by-products of the Leblanc process to profitable use, the noxious vapours continued to hang over the town. Sanitary improvement at St. Helens was due in great measure not to Parliamentary legislation nor to the St. Helens Improvement Commission but to Walter Weldon and those who followed in his footsteps.[4] David Gamble's chief motive, in encouraging Weldon, was, no doubt, to reduce the cost of making bleaching powder. But Gamble, one of Greenall's young lieutenants of 1845, was a keen supporter of sanitary improvement and had been chairman of the Improvement Commission from 1856-62. Public motives may, to some extent, have reinforced his desire for private advantage when he decided to back Weldon's research in 1866.

By the middle of the 'sixties, the town had outgrown its official limits and the Improvement Commission's boundary was already an anachronism ; there were almost as many people living within the immediate vicinity of St. Helens as in St. Helens

[1] See below, p. 416.

[2] *St. H. Weekly News* 17 May, 1862.

[3] Evidence of James Haddock to the S.C. on the St. H. Imp. Bill, 1869, q. 181.

[4] Above, pp. 354-5.

itself.[1] Sutton, with a rateable value of nearly £50,000—almost as great as that of St. Helens—established a Local Board in 1864[2] and Parr, a much poorer district, with a rateable value of only £13,600,[3] followed suit in the next year.[4] Both of these new authorities confined their activity to maintaining the roads and clearing the ashpits and privies.[5] Sutton, however, was soon faced, as St. Helens had been, with the considerable expense of supplying the township with water, for the local wells were insufficient and often polluted. When in October, 1866 two cases of cholera broke out in a house in Peasley Cross, a medical man reported that " most of the [well] water in the district was unfit to drink."[6] This particular outbreak of disease forced Sutton's hand ; it was obliged either to reach an agreement with the St. Helens Improvement Commission[7] or embark on a costly waterworks scheme of its own. The possibility of St. Helens and Sutton competing between themselves for water in the same bed of red sandstone appalled even the sturdiest advocates of local independence. They were driven to the conclusion that if they embarked upon an unpredictable and costly scheme of their own, the rates might be heavier than if they were to throw in their lot with St. Helens. The water crisis won many followers to the cause of those who had for some time been agitating for the incorporation of St. Helens and for the extension of the town boundary.

The leading advocate of incorporation was B. A. Dromgoole, who seems to have been greatly influenced in the matter by the invigorating effect of such a step upon local government in his native Warrington.[8] " New blood was introduced," he wrote, " and with it new spirit . . . men of wealth and position, who had hitherto stood aloof and would not accept a seat at the Commissioners' Board, sought a seat in the Council Chamber."[9] Incorporation became his panacea for all the shortcomings in

[1] Above, p. 374.

[2] St. H. Town Hall. Mins. of Sutton Local Board ; *St. H. N.* 19 Dec., 1863. The Local Board was formed by adopting the Local Government Act, 1858.

[3] *Incorporation of St. Helens* (Donnelly Inquiry), 9.

[4] *St. H. N.* 29 April, 1865.

[5] Rivers Pollution Comm., 1870 [C. 109] XL, 8, 66.

[6] Guard., Mins., 25 Oct., 1866.

[7] The Commission was permitted to supply water to any point in the four townships but had no powers to compel householders on the route of their mains to take their water if they lived outside the boundary (*Incorporation of St. Helens*, Donnelly Inquiry, 15).

[8] For the incorporation of Warrington in 1847, see George A. Carter's article in *Warrington Hundred* (Warrington, 1947), 57-9.

[9] *St. H. N.* 4 Feb., 1865.

the public life of the town. A letter signed " Mentor " appearing in the *St. Helens Intelligencer* so early as February 1855, urging the advantages of borough status, may possibly have come from his pen.[1] He was certainly campaigning hard for incorporation from 1862 onwards and when two years later a committee was formed to further this end, Dromgoole became its secretary.[2] The attempted adoption of the Local Government Act in Windle in the same year, 1864, called forth a strong leading article on the need for a more comprehensive form of local authority[3] and these events in Windle also caused the Improvement Commissioners to lend an ear to Dromgoole's opinions. They considered the advisability of petitioning for a municipal charter and ordered their clerk to find out how Warrington had become incorporated and how Southport was at that time seeking incorporation. A week later, however, the matter was adjourned *sine die*.[4] Undaunted by this rebuff, the incorporation committee pressed on hotly with its campaign. They very soon achieved some success. At the request of 89 ratepayers, the chairman of the Improvement Commission called a town meeting on 7 February, 1865, and this meeting passed a resolution in favour of incorporation. A petition was signed and sent to the Privy Council Office.[5]

The incorporation party now awaited developments. But no reply from London was received. Accordingly, in April 1866— more than a year later—a further meeting was held to enable the faithful to demonstrate once more in favour of a charter.[6] A month later, however, news was received that gained the incorporation party many new supporters. It was learned that St. Helens had not been included among six towns to be enfranchised by the Re-distribution of Seats Bill just introduced into Parliament.[7] This came as an unpleasant shock to those who had been led to believe that St. Helens had a strong claim to separate representation in the House of Commons instead of

[1] *St. Helens Intelligencer* 3 Feb., 1855.

[2] *St. H. Weekly News* 22 March, 1862 ; *Incorporation of St. Helens*, 3.

[3] *St. H. N.* 12 Nov., 1864. Windle's attempt to form a Local Board was refused by the Home Office on the ground that there were fewer than 3,000 inhabitants in the district concerned. (*St. H. N.* 9 Nov., 31 Dec., 1864).

[4] St. H. I. C. Mins., 16, 23 Nov., 1864.

[5] *St. H. N.* 28 Jan., 11 Feb., 1865 ; *Incorporation of St. Helens*, 6.

[6] *St. H. Standard*, 14 April, 1866.

[7] The Bill had its first reading on 7 May. It was proposed that one Member be given to each of the six unrepresented municipal boroughs with populations over 18,000 : Burnley, Stalybridge, Gravesend, Hartlepool, Middlesborough and Dewsbury (*Parliamentary Debates*, 3rd ser., CLXXXIII, col. 496.).

merely forming part of the South Lancashire division.[1] The Improvement Commission detailed three of its number to wait upon Mr. Gladstone " to urge upon him the claim of St. Helens to be included in the list of New Boroughs "[2] but Mr. Gladstone had no time to see them.[3] At a public meeting, Arthur Sinclair voiced the town's sense of injustice : 106 of the 186 boroughs returning M.P.s had populations smaller than the 23,000 or so who resided within the limits of the St. Helens Improvement Act and " even Burnley, the most populous of the proposed new boroughs had only a population of 28,700 while St. Helens and its districts with a population of 41,000 had been altogether ignored."[4] But Burnley was already a municipal borough and, though St. Helens might in fact be the focal centre of a district of 41,000 inhabitants, officially it ranked as a growing sanitary district which, at the last census of 1861, numbered only 18,396.

The Redistribution Bill was, however, defeated.[5] But it had taught the town a lesson and brought home the importance of borough status. There was a great revival of interest in incorporation and the petitions and protests sent up to London in connection with the 1866 Bill appear to have been responsible for causing the Privy Council Office to take action at last. At the end of October, 1866, Captain Donnelly was sent to St. Helens to conduct an inquiry into the whole matter.

This investigation revealed that there was a very large measure of support for incorporation not only in St. Helens itself but also in the surrounding rural districts which had previously fought against any encroachment by the town. This change of front may be attributed partly to developments beyond the Commissioners' boundary (emphasised by the critical water supply position) and partly to a more diplomatic handling of likely opponents. The possibility of extending the boundary in Windle was made easier by the fact that the legal adviser of those who sought incorporation was also Sir Robert Gerard's solicitor,[6] and the plans for fixing limits to take in the new St. Ann's

---

[1] That St. Helens should have its own M.P., had been an opinion expressed by the Mayor of Liverpool on the occasion of the opening of Garston Dock in 1853, and by speakers at the elections of 1859 and 1865 (*Lpool. Merc.*, 24 June, 1853 ; *St. H. Intelligencer*, 30 April, 1859 ; *St. H. N.*, 15 July, 1865).

[2] St. H. I. C. Mins., 23 May, 1866.

[3] *Ibid.*, 6 June, 1866.

[4] *St. H. N.*, 26 May, 1866.

[5] When the Conservatives' Reform Bill was introduced in the following year, St. Helens was among the new towns to be given representation, but it was soon dropped from the Bill (*Parliamentary Debates*, 3rd ser., CLXXXVI, col. 24 ; *St. H. N.*, 6 July, 1867).

[6] Evidence of E. P. Cearns to the S.C. on the St. H. Imp. Bill, 1869.

district of Eccleston were made in close consultation with
Samuel Taylor, the chief landowner concerned.[1] Leading
members of the Sutton and Parr Local Boards spoke in favour
of the Charter provided the entire township was included in each
case and not merely the built-up areas.[2] When Captain Donnelly
returned to London the prospects of early incorporation seemed
reasonably good. But the promoters had counted without Lord
Salisbury, a considerable landowner in Sutton, who turned out
to be most hostile and caused Captain Donnelly to hold a second
inquiry at St. Helens in March 1867 to hear the grounds of his
opposition.

As another summer approached, the need for an improved
water supply in Sutton became more urgent and an additional
supply was also required by this time at St. Helens itself,
particularly for industrial users.[3] Meanwhile, a private concern,
named the Rainhill and Sutton Waterworks Company and launched
towards the end of 1866, was proposing to sink two wells at
Rainhill to a greater depth than those at Eccleston Hill,[4] thereby
depriving St. Helens of first call on its chief source. From this
pumping station the new company planned to supply Rainhill
and Sutton and those districts of Eccleston and Parr outside
the town limits of St. Helens.[5] The Improvement Commission
attempted to persuade their potential rivals to drop their Bill
in Parliament, while at the same time making its own plans
to deepen the wells at Eccleston Hill should that be required.[6]
The Commission also tried to reach agreement with Sutton
Local Board but talks broke down at the beginning of April
1867[7] and, at the end of May, Sutton decided to apply for powers
to borrow £40,000, " for the purpose of establishing Water
Works in the District."[8] At this juncture the private company
threw in its lot with Sutton and later sold to the Sutton Local
Board the land that it had acquired for a pumping station site.[9]

[1] *St. H. N.*, 20 Oct., 1866.

[2] *Incorporation of St. Helens.* Donnelly Inquiry, 19-22.

[3] The works were supplied with " low pressure " water from the reservoirs, the " high pressure " water going to domestic users, who paid a higher
rate. As more works were opened, the " low pressure " supply became
lower than ever.

[4] St. H. I. C. Mins., 23 Nov., 1866 ; St. H. Town Hall, package 209,
statement for the opinion of Counsel, 10 Oct., 1867.

[5] *C.J.*, 7 Feb., 1867.

[6] St. H. I. C. Mins., 7 Dec., 1856.

[7] *Ibid.*, 11 March, 3 April, 1867 ; Mins. of Sutton Local Board, 27 March,
4 April, 1867.

[8] Mins. of Sutton Local Board, 29 May, 1867. Only £30,000 was eventually sanctioned (*ibid.*, 12 Aug., 1867).

[9] *Ibid.*, 19 Sept., 1867.

On 25 September, 1867, Sutton decided to approach Bateman, the Manchester engineer, to enquire if he would become their expert adviser.[1] Two days later the St. Helens Improvement Commission, led by William (Roby) Pilkington,[2] re-opened negotiations and on 16 October a settlement was reached whereby the Commissioners assumed responsibility for the expenditure that Sutton had already incurred and promised to supply Sutton with water on the same terms as they supplied consumers in St. Helens.[3]

These commitments made it certain that the St. Helens Waterworks would have to be considerably extended and that, in turn, meant that the Commissioners would have to seek a further Improvement Act, for they had already raised £24,000 of the £30,000 permitted by the Act of 1855.[4] The knowledge that the town was to be saddled with this additional debt revived the dying embers of opposition to the charter of incorporation and a protest meeting was planned for 3 February, 1868. But it was never held ; on the previous day the news arrived that Her Majesty the Queen had been pleased to grant St. Helens a municipal charter.[5]

The Corporation was soon in being. The roll of burgesses was completed by March[6] and the eighteen councillors (three from each of the six wards into which the borough was divided) were elected by universal household suffrage in May.[7] The chief honours were evenly divided between the two most prominent local families ; William Pilkington was Returning Officer and

---

[1] *Ibid.*, 25 Sept., 1867.

[2] *Ibid.*, 27 Sept., 1867. William (Roby) Pilkington, who had consented to stand for Eccleston at the election earlier in Sept. in order to strengthen the town's claim to incorporation, was unanimously voted to the chair of the St. H. I. C. and it was he, John Fidler and Robert McNicoll who formed the delegation to the Sutton Local Board which settled the difference between the two bodies so speedily.

[3] *Ibid.*, 16 Oct., 1867.

[4] Evidence of E. P. Cearns to the S.C. on the St. H. Imp. Bill, 1869 ; St. H. I. C. Mins., 24 Oct., 1867. At that time St. Helens had ideas of building waterworks in Burtonwood.

[5] *Incorporation of St. Helens*, 8-9. For a printed copy of the charter, see L.R.O., DDCS 37/9.

[6] *St. H. N.* 21 March, 1868.

[7] *St. H. N.* 16 May, 1868. Those elected to the first Council were :
Windle : David Gamble, Henry Johnson, William Webster.
Eccleston : James Bayley, Robert McNicoll, John Fisher.
Hardshaw : (previously Hardshaw and Parr) Joseph Cook, Edward Johnson, Llewellyn William Evans.
Parr : Joseph Greenough, Robert Reeves, John Wolfenden.
East Sutton : James Cross, W. J. Blinkhorn, E. P. Twyford.
West Sutton : William Roberts, jun., James Radley, Hadden W. Todd.

David Gamble became the first Mayor. The Council chose one
of their number from each ward as aldermen and six other
councillors were elected in their stead.[1] On 28 July the Commissioners sealed the formal deed transferring all their powers
to the St. Helens Corporation.[2]

The champions of incorporation would have had every
reason to be satisfied with the successful outcome of their campaign had it not soon become evident that they—and, so it seems,
everyone else in the town—had unwittingly exaggerated the
powers that a municipal charter conferred. As the Mayor later
confessed :

" We hoped on obtaining the charter of incorporation that we
should be able to do away with the governing bodies of the
adjoining districts without an Act of Parliament, but we
were advised afterwards that it was not possible."[3]

The formal deed of the Commissioners gave the Corporation
the same authority over the town within the limits described
in the Act of 1855 that the Commissioners had enjoyed : but
it did not convey the powers over Sutton and Parr then held
by the two Local Boards, nor did it permit the Corporation
to impose rules and regulations in the newly-incorporated parts
of Windle and Eccleston which had previously lain outside the
1855 boundary.[4] The borough was obliged to enlarge the scope
of its impending Improvement Bill to extend its geographical
limits as well as to increase its borrowing powers. The Corporation also took the opportunity to include in the Bill clauses
giving authority to erect a new town hall,[5] to establish libraries
and to purchase land for parks. It was also compelled by the
London and North Western Railway Company, the owners of
the Canal, to insert a clause whereby St. Helens undertook to

[1] The aldermen were : Webster, McNicoll, Evans, Greenough, Cross and
Radley ; and the new councillors : James Harrison, Charles A. Hard-
wick, John Cotton, William Hibbert, Henry Baxter and William Pilkington,
junr.

[2] St. H. I. C. Mins.

[3] Evidence of David Gamble to the S.C. on the St. H. Imp. Bill, 1869,
q. 418.

[4] St. H. Town Hall, package 209.   Statement for the opinion of Counsel,
1 June, 1868.

[5] The Town Hall, purchased by the Corporation from the private company
in Sept., 1870 for £2,150, was seriously damaged by fire in May of the
following year and, when repaired, was again damaged in July, 1873 (*St. H.
N.*, 13 May, 1871 ; 5 July, 1873).   The plans for the new town hall, the
present building, were submitted in Nov., 1872 and the foundation stone
laid a year later, the opening ceremony taking place in June, 1876 (*St. H. N.*,
30 Nov., 1872, 8 Nov., 1873, 10 June, 1876.

take immediate action to improve the condition of the Sankey Brook.[1]

The Charter of 1868 replaced a rather shabby and strictly utilitarian body, which commanded very little public confidence, by a form of urban government to which centuries of tradition had lent dignity and prestige. The Improvement Act of 1869 bestowed the powers necessary to maintain that prestige in the eyes of those who lived within the new limits. These boundaries were extensive, encircling more than 5,558 acres—ten times the area within the old limits and twice the area governed by Liverpool Corporation at that time[2]—and including a population of 45,000. The yield from the rates was twice the amount that the Improvement Commission had been in a position to collect immediately prior to incorporation, the total rateable value of the borough being £139,000.[3] In addition to this, the waterworks brought in almost £7,000 per year and the market more than £700.[4] The new boundary included the whole of the natural drainage area and made possible the construction of a trunk sewer to replace the open brook. Local government had now the opportunity to take on a new lease of life.

[1] 32 & 33 Vict. cap. XXX. The Bill received the Royal Assent on 12 July, 1869.

[2] Evidence of Joseph Johnson to the S.C. on the St. H. Imp. Bill, 1869, q. 428 ; *St. H. Standard*, 16 March, 1867.

[3] Evidence of Joseph Johnson, qq. 372-4, 429.

[4] Evidence of Sinclair, qq. 164-70. Of this, £1,536 went to assist the rates.

CHAPTER XXVII

TOWN LIFE,

1845-1870

AS the town continued to grow, the separate groups formerly distinct elements of the local population tended to merge into one. The colliers mixed more with those who worked in other industries, though the Irish for long remained anathema to them ; the immigrant Catholics intermarried with the local Catholic population, though here again deep-seated prejudices had to be broken down ; the glassmakers became an integral part of the town as their occupation became less nomadic. Gradually, the different sections of the community came to ignore, if not to forget, their own individual backgrounds and developed a new outlook dictated by conditions then prevailing in the town rather than by prejudices inherited from the past. As new generations grew up, this broader outlook became generally accepted.

The twenty years after 1850 formed an ideal period for the beginnings of such an adjustment of views. Unlike the periods before and after it, 1850 to 1870 were years of almost continuous prosperity uninterrupted by serious depressions or industrial disputes. It is true that trade was slack during 1858-62. At St. Helens in the winter of 1860-61 soup kitchens had to be provided for the needy[1] ; in the following autumn it was reported in the local paper that " trade is bad here and people have but little money to spare " ;[2] and during that winter, from August 1861 until April 1862, the three plate glass factories were only working for four days each week.[3] But this recession was, in fact, relatively mild compared with the very severe interruptions of trade on previous occasions. The short time at the three plate glassworks, for instance, is to be compared with the complete failure of one of these factories and the temporary closing of another during the paralysing slump of the early '40s.[4] Moreover, the state of affairs in St. Helens was very much brighter than that in the textile towns, rendered idle by the Cotton Famine, the product of the American Civil War. " It is some consolation," wrote the *St. Helens Weekly News* on 19 April, 1862, " amid the general distress

[1] *St. H. Weekly News* 19 Jan., 1861.

[2] *St. H. Weekly News* 28 Sept., 1861.

[3] *St. H. Weekly News* 19 April, 1862.

[4] Above, p. 320.

arising from the scarcity of employment throughout the cotton
districts of this county and the consequent depression of trade,
that St. Helens has felt comparatively little privation . . . "   A
year later, when a local fund was launched to aid the unemployed
in the cotton towns, £2,800 was raised, half of it in small
contributions from working men.[1]

Economic prosperity, reflected by an increase in real wages,
was accompanied by comparative industrial peace, broken only
during the period of recession by a few rather half-hearted
strikes, wholly lacking in the bitterness shown during the disputes
of previous years.   The coalminers' union, for instance, concentrated on encouraging its members to take individual
grievances to court ; on at least two occasions W. P. Roberts,
known as " the miners' Attorney General," appeared for the
prosecution at the petty sessions in the town.[2]   There is no evidence
of the union's having supported any general stoppages in the St.
Helens area before 1860, when the miners struck in opposition
to a wage reduction. The strike on that occasion lasted for three
weeks.[3]   In 1862 a new union was formed which professed the
most moderate aims.   It was directed from Wigan by William
Pickard, himself a holder of shares in the Wigan Coal and Iron
Company worth £365.[4]   In the following year this union joined
with the newly-established Miners' National Provident Society
and Pickard became the Vice-President.[5]   As its title suggests, the
union provided friendly society facilities[6] and at its meetings
speakers urged upon members the advantages of education and
the dangers of drink, rather than the need for better wages and
shorter hours.[7]

[1] *St. H. N.*, 21 Feb., 1863.

[2] *St. H. Intelligencer*, 17 May, 1856 ;   *St. H. N.*, 18 Oct., 1862.   He also
took part in labour troubles at the St. H. Crown Glassworks in 1845 (Cross
Papers).

[3] *Prescot Reporter* 18, 25 Feb., 3, 10 March, 1860.   An isolated strike
at Laffak Colliery was reported in the *Lpool. Merc.*, 19, 30 April, 21 May,
1850 and one at Broad Oak Colliery in the *St. H. Intelligencer*, 18, 25 Sept.,
30 Oct., 1858.

[4] Evidence of William Pickard to the S.C. on Coal, 1873, 144, 147, and
to the R.C. on Trades Unions (8th Rep.). q., 15,794.

[5] R. Page Arnot, *The Miners : A History of the Miners Federation of
Great Britain, 1889-1910* (1949), 45.   The membership of the union reached
2,600 at St. Helens in Jan., 1864—more than half the total—but dropped
to a quarter of this by 1868 (*St. H. N.*, 6 Jan., 1864 ; evidence of James
Haddock to the R.C. on Trades Unions (6th Rep., 1868), q. 12,053).   The
agents at St. Helens were Henry Davidson (to 1866) and then Edward
Rymer.

[6] For details see evidence of Pickard to the R.C. on Trades Unions
(8th Rep.), q. 15,766 *et seq.*

[7] *St. H. N.* 6 Jan., 28 May, 1864 ;   4 Jan., 8 April, 1865 ; *St. H. Standard*,
6 Jan., 1866.

The same spirit of cautious moderation characterised the activities of the other trade unions in the town during these middle years, the building workers' aggressive attitude being quite exceptional.[1] The bottlemakers went on strike in 1858 against a proposed reduction of 4s. in their weekly pay, then averaging 36s., but after twelve weeks their masters went more than half way to meet them ; the cut was reduced to 1s. and even this was restored within six months.[2] In the following year, 1859, the local flint glassmakers staged a strike in sympathy with members of their union who had stopped work at Stourbridge. The stoppage at St. Helens was conducted with great courtesy and was notable for a dinner at which the strikers drank their employers' health.[3] At a time when increased production and expanding markets led to a rising standard of living, a spirit of co-operation sweetened even the occasional strike.

While the friendly society aspect of trade unionism appears to have assumed greater importance, the lower-paid labourers, who with the exception of some of those who worked at the alkali factories[4] had no trade union of their own, continued to secure much the same benefits from joining one or other of the numerous friendly societies which continued to flourish in the town. In the middle of the 'sixties, for instance, the Oddfellows of the Manchester Unity had 1,395 members in the St. Helens district and the Ancient Order of Shepherds reported a membership of more than 1,500.[5] Memberships of this size make it certain that the labouring classes were well represented and this conclusion is confirmed by the records of one of the Oddfellows' lodges : several members sign with a mark only and Irish names are very much in evidence.[6]

Such prosperity and providence were a boon to the Poor

[1] Above, p. 375.

[2] *St. H. Intelligencer* 27 Feb. 1858 ; *The Lancashire Glass Bottle Trade* (St. Helens, 1905), 4.

[3] *St. H. Intelligencer* 15 Jan., 1859.

[4] For an early chemical workers' society, see above, 261. Three sets of rules relating to the Chemical Workers' Burial, Accident and Provident Benefit Society, printed in St. Helens in 1866, were enrolled at the Registry of Friendly Societies. All met in Parr. Two closed within a year " for want of support of the lodge." There is no information as to when the third was wound up. These lodges seem to have been part of a wider organisation, for one of the trustees came from Appleton-in-Widnes and another from Farnworth near Bolton. Possibly the collapse of the union in 1867 was connected with the verdict given in the case of the Bradford Boilermakers' Society (*q.v.* S. & B. Webb, *History of Trade Unionism*, 2nd ed. 1920, 261).

[5] *St. H. N.* 18 May, 14 Dec., 1864.

[6] The records of the Perseverance Lodge, March, 1857—March, 1885, including a minute book, an account book and a weekly contribution book, are in the possession of Mr. J. Ashton, secretary of the Sacred Heart Guild, who kindly permitted us to consult them.

Law Guardians. Throughout these years there were usually only between 60 and 80 inmates at the Union workhouse from the whole of the four townships, though this figure rose to 109 in March, 1862.[1] Out-relief payments over the same area grew in proportion to its population : £40-£50 per week in the 1850s, £50-£60 in the earlier, and £70-£80 in the later 1860s. On several occasions the Poor Law Inspector observed that the proportion of pauperism in the Prescot Union was considerably below the average throughout the region under his supervision.[2] In such conditions, the Guardians could well afford to relax the extreme harshness of the *régime* at the workhouse. By 1856 the inmates were again being fed on roast beef and plum pudding at Christmas[3] and in later years they had a Christmas party complete with Christmas tree from which gifts were distributed ; these included tobacco and snuff, indulgences most rigidly forbidden in earlier years.[4]

Although there is little evidence of abject poverty or acute distress at St. Helens, there continued to be much discomfort—inevitable in any rapidly-growing hive of industry, where so many people were pushing and jostling their neighbours in an attempt to elbow themselves into a position of greater economic security. There was, for instance, a considerable housing shortage, particularly on the outskirts of the town, where several new factories were growing up. " The trouble that the men have to get cottages near those outlying parts," observed Arthur Sinclair in 1869, " is terrible. They have to go two miles off for lodgings constantly until they have got cottages gradually built up."[5] The housing shortage did not, however, drive the population into cellars. Only 24 cellars within the town boundary were rated in 1855, 17 in 1860 and 16 in 1869.[6] Overcrowding in existing houses, however, was not unusual. By a clause in the St. Helens Improvement Act of 1845, lodging houses were to be registered and kept under supervision. Although the actual number of dwellings so registered is not known, the frequent references to the appearances of unregistered lodging house keepers at the local court, indicate quite clearly that overcrowding was one of the town's main problems. In 1854, for instance, the owner of unregistered premises in Traverse Street, close to the rapidly-developing industrial site at Pocket Nook, admitted that his

[1] Guard. Mins. 20 March, 1862.

[2] *Ibid.*, 8 July, 1852, 12 Oct., 1854, 4 Oct., 1856.

[3] *St. H. Intelligencer* 27 Dec., 1856.

[4] *St. H. N.*, 20 Jan., 1854.

[5] Evidence of Arthur Sinclair to the S.C. on the St. Helens Improvement Bill, 1869, q. 317. As a partner in the locomotive works near St. Helens Junction, Sinclair was speaking from personal experience.

[6] St. H. I. C. Rate Books ; 1st Rep. of the Rivers Pollution Comm. 1870 [C. 109] XL, 33.

house contained 28 people.[1] At the petty sessions two years later, no fewer than 15 people were fined for lodging house offences in the same day.[2] Even in some of the houses that were registered, there were between four and six occupants per room.[3]

Another cause of discomfort was the compound of smells that filled the air on so many occasions. The stench from the brook—" an open sepulchre full of pestiferous odours," a local doctor called it[4]—was a perennial cause of complaint, and the ashpit privies, 6,000 of them within the borough limits in 1869, had become an abomination. Water closets were quite a novelty; only 250 houses had them at that date.[5] In addition to such cloacal smells then common to all towns, St. Helens had its own particular brand caused by the effluvia from the decomposed alkali waste. " Good heavens !" exclaimed a visitor from Manchester on breathing St. Helens air for the first time, " I have heard that St. Helens is a dirty place, but how can they exist in such a stench? "[6] In fact, the local inhabitants became acclimatised without any great difficulty. Hydrochloric acid gas was certainly harmful and many employees at the alkali works suffered from pulmonary troubles.[7] But this gas was well diluted by the time it spread over the town and after 1863 when 95 per cent. condensation was compulsory, the " noxious vapours," consisting chiefly of sulphuretted hydrogen, were not particularly harmful. As the town's first medical officer of health put it, the gases

" do not kill anybody ; they act as a depressant, keeping people somewhat below par in health, not making them ill of themselves, but combining with other things which may be going . . . to give the patient a worse chance of recovery . . ."[8]

There is little evidence of additional leisure during these middle years of the century. The timetable at some of the local factories— at the glassworks, for instance—was dictated by the methods of

[1] *Lpool. Merc.* 16 June, 1854.

[2] *St. H. Intelligencer* 12 April, 1856.

[3] *St. H. N.* 15 May, 1869.

[4] *St. H. Standard* 15 Sept., 1866.

[5] Report of the Rivers Pollution Commission, 1870 [37] XL, 24, 45.

[6] *St. H. Intelligencer* 16 April, 1859.

[7] Below, p. 459.

[8] Evidence of Robert McNicoll to the R.C. on Noxious Vapours, 1878, q. 1647.

production and could not be altered until new inventions permitted its revision. But elsewhere, and particularly in most labouring jobs, the employees were not tied by particular processes. Robert Daglish introduced a 5½-day week at the St. Helens Foundry in April, 1857, though it is not known how long this continued ;[1] a rival engineering firm was still working on Saturday afternoons eight years later.[2] It was not until the introduction to the town of the nine-hour movement in 1871— adopted at " nearly all the large establishments " by the following year[3]—that a shorter working week became general.

Various attempts to curtail the hours of shop assistants, who usually worked until 8 o'clock on most weeknights and might be serving until midnight on Saturdays (pay day for most people), also met with a very limited response. An early closing movement was reported in 1856 but it collapsed in the following year[4] and the idea was not revived until 1865 with the founding of the St. Helens Early Closing Association.[5] But this new body achieved no more success than its predecessor and the hard-worked shop assistants had to wait until 1884 before they obtained their Thursday half-holiday.[6]

Until the half-holiday was introduced, there was no possibility of the rise of the sports club in its modern guise. Forms of recreation changed little and the old attractions continued to draw the crowds. The biannual fair went on, to the accompaniment of violent attacks by the local shopkeepers who hated to see so much money evading their own tills and falling into the pockets of visiting salesmen. Dromgoole dubbed it a " half yearly remnant of a barbarous age."[7] Newton Race Week also continued to draw supporters from St. Helens and attempts were made to start a similar race meeting nearer home, at Denton's Green, at a later date in the year; but these met with a very poor reception.[8] Prize fights were still held whenever the police relaxed

---

[1] *St. H. Intelligencer* 4 April, 1857.

[2] *St. H. Standard* 25 Nov., 1865.

[3] *St. H. N.* 18 Nov., 1871 ; 24 Feb., 1872.

[4] *St. H. Intelligencer* 12 Jan., 1856 ; 21 Nov., 1857.

[5] *St. H. Standard* 28 Oct., 1865.   The St. Helens Chamber of Trade's formation was reported in the *St. H. N.*, 18 Nov., 1871.

[6] *St. H. N.* 5 Jan., 1884.

[7] *St. H. N.* 13 Sept., 1862.   The fair ceased to be held in the New Market Place in 1863 and was moved to a site near the Salisbury Hotel. When this site was taken by Messrs. Holman Michell in 1882, the fair was moved to land near the Town Hall (*St. H. N.*, 15 April, 1863 ; 22 April, 1882).

[8] *Lpool. Merc.* 6 Aug., 1850 ; *Wigan Times* 24 Oct., 1851 ; *St. H. Standard* 27 Oct., 1866.

their vigilance and pigeon-flying and foot-racing still retained their popularity. One enterprising promoter of foot-racing opened a pleasure ground in Parr " for the accommodation of Pedestrians and other Athletic Sportsmen and Pleasure Seekers," offering as first prize a quarter barrel of Greenall's ale and 10s. in money.[1]

The railway extensions, particularly the Rainford Junction branch of 1858 which connected with the line to Ormskirk and Southport, made it easier to get away to the seaside or into the country during the summer. Many local people went on works' trips, annual events from the early '50s. At St. Helens itself the same summer sports of bowls and cricket continued to be popular and there were also innovations : open air dancing at Thatto Heath Gardens, for instance, and floral and horticultural shows.[2] In the winter the theatre, housed in a new building in Milk Street from 1862,[3] had its own regular supporters and concerts, recitals and lectures were held at the town hall. Politics, too, created much enthusiasm. We do not know to what extent non-voters interested themselves in elections to the Improvement Commission, but from 1859 when St. Helens became the centre of a polling district in the south-west Lancashire division,[4] Parliamentary elections certainly aroused a considerable stir. In 1868, when the new Reform Act had swelled the number of local voters from about 800 to 2,200,[5] Mr. Gladstone, a candidate for the division, chose to open and close his election campaign in the town.[6]

Many townsmen devoted their spare time to soldiering with the Volunteers. Such a national defence force had existed during the Napoleonic Wars ; when the French armies crossed the Alps into Italy early in 1859, it was decided to revive it. At St. Helens, £500 was soon subscribed by the leading industrialists of the neighbourhood, who also took a prominent part in raising the necessary companies among their own workmen.[7] By February, 1860, the men were " in a very efficient state of drill . . . anxiously waiting for their uniform and muskets."[8] William Pilkington,

[1] *St. H. N.* 3 Aug., 1864.

[2] *Lpool. Merc.* 3, Sept., 1850 ; *Wigan Times*, 13 Aug. 1851 ; *St. H. Intelligencer* 6 Sept., 1856.

[3] *St. H. N.* 29 March 1862 ; James Brockbank, *A History of the Drama in St. H.* (St. H. 1901).

[4] Local voters previously polled at the Legh Arms, Newton.

[5] W. W. Bean, *The Parliamentary Representation of the Six Northern Counties of England* (Hull, 1890), 191-4.

[6] *St. H. N.* 8 Aug., 21 Nov., 1868. See appendix 1.

[7] *St. H. Intelligencer*, 3, 10, 31 Dec., 1859 ; art. on " St. Helens and the Volunteer Movement " by an old 1860 member, from *St. H. N.* of 1926, in St. H. Ref. Lib.

[8] *Prescot Reporter*, 18 Feb., 1860.

who had taken the initiative locally in forming the Volunteers was too old to take an active part in their drilling. Command, therefore, passed to David Gamble, 23 years his junior, who had taken a great interest in the movement from the outset. Gamble was gazetted lieutenant-colonel in July, 1860, and in the following year he built headquarters for the St. Helens battalion in Mill Street.[1] The Volunteers outlasted the emergency ; many joined their ranks and spent much of their leisure drilling at the Volunteer Hall.

The growing number of public houses and beer shops, however, continued to make the greatest claim on the inhabitants' leisure. In the four townships there was one such establishment for every 150 people ; if children are subtracted from the total, this amounted to one for every 80.[2] Week after week a procession of defendants appeared at the local court charged with being drunk and disorderly. In the 1860s there were between 500 and 700 cases a year, rising to 911 in 1869, 970 in 1872 and 1,783 in 1878.[3] When the public houses eventually closed their doors for the night, their inebriated patrons often staggered out and rolled forth, only to collapse in the street where they were either taken into custody by the police or allowed to stay and sleep off their drunken stupor. Within eighteen months there were two cases of men who fell, helpless, in the middle of a railway line. These cases were reported only because one of them was run over and killed and the other miraculously saved by the life guard on the locomotive.[4] Railway lines did not occupy a great proportion of the land in the town, so, presumably, very many more " drunks " came to rest in less dangerous places but passed unnoticed because no accident occurred. The editor of the *St. Helens Intelligencer* was not exaggerating when he deemed drink to be " the monster evil of society."[5] As the Vicar of St. Mary's later remarked, " It seemed . . . as if Englishmen were intended to live by suction."[6]

Hand in hand with excessive drinking went lawlessness and immorality. There were some ugly fights and stabbings. At one of these which took place just after closing time, a glassmaker

[1] *Prescot Reporter* 11 May, 1861 ; *St. H. N.*, 16 Nov., 1861.

[2] *St. H. N.*, 9 Sept., 1865 ; *St. H. Standard* 24 Aug., 1872. In 1860 there were 160 public houses and beer shops within the boundary of the St. H. I. C. (Rate Books).

[3] The following figures are taken from annual returns, published in the local press : year ending Aug., 1863, 619 ; 1865, 537 ; 1866, 710 ; 1868, 596 ; 1869, 911 ; 1872, 970 ; 1874, 1,344 ; 1875, 1,559 ; 1878, 1,783 ; 1879, 1,078.

[4] *St. H. Intelligencer* 30 Jan., 1858 ; 18 June, 1859.

[5] *St. H. Intelligencer* 29 Dec., 1855.

[6] *St. H. N.* 10 March, 1883.

was knifed to death.[1] The small police force, consisting of a
superintendent, 5 sergeants and 27 men,[2] had to be constantly on
the alert. They were kept fully occupied.

Many of the public houses did not confine their activities to
providing liquid refreshment. As the manager of a local glass
works testified :

> " St. Helens is not a very moral place ; there are dancing
> saloons all over the town ; nearly every public house has one ;
> young fellows take their girls there and make them half tipsy
> and then there follows what might be expected."[3]

Some of these public houses developed into common brothels.
In 1862 it was alleged that

> " notorious brothels . . . are now infesting the town in almost
> every street, every one of which has grown up within the last
> six or seven years ; . . . previous to that time there was scarcely
> a common prostitute to be seen in the streets and now many
> of the thoroughfares are infested with them. As to publicly
> and openly-avowed brothels, such a thing was unknown."[4]

It was against this seamy side of life in the town that the
churches set their face. They realised that by attacking drunkenness they could strike at the root cause of delinquency and
eradicate much of the grosser forms of lawlessness and immorality.
But before investigating how the churches of the town took
their stand on this vital issue, it is necessary first of all to take
stock of the extent of their support at this time.

Between 1851 and 1871, church building more than kept pace
with the growth of population. In 1851 the Anglicans in their
two churches within the boundary of the Improvement Commission, St. Mary's and St. Thomas's, could seat 2,500, almost
200 more than the 2,332 that the Roman Catholics, Independents
and Wesleyans could accommodate. In 1871, however, the Free
Churches and the Catholics had seats for 7,300, while the Anglican
total, augmented by Holy Trinity, Parr Mount,[5] had only risen

---

[1] *St. H. Intelligencer* 2 Oct., 18 Dec., 1858.

[2] *St. H. Intelligencer* 25 June, 1859. Ten years later there were 29
constables. (*St. H. Standard* 1 May, 1869.)

[3] 4th Report of the Ch. Emp. Comm., 1865 [8357] XX, 271.

[4] *St. H. N.* 16 Aug., 1862. The first mention of the committal of " a
notorious prostitute " from St. Helens to Kirkdale gaol is to be found
in the *Lpool. Merc.* 21 March, 1845. Thereafter references are frequent.

[5] Consecrated as a chapel of ease in 1857 (*St. H. Intelligencer* 24 Feb.,
1857).

to 3,681.[1] This change was brought about by the opening of places of worship by the United Methodists, Primitive Methodists, Presbyterians and other sects, as well as by increased support for the older chapels.[2] In this period the town's population

[1] Census of Religious Worship, 1851 ; *St. H. N.* 1 Feb., 1873.

[2] The Methodist Church in Park Road of 1861 (*q.v. St. H. Weekly News* 16 March, 20 July, 1861) and the Wesleyan Chapel in Cotham Street (Corporation Street) of 1869 (*q.v. St. H. Standard,* 5 June, 1869) increased the Wesleyans' sittings from 450 in 1851 (at the old chapel in Tontine Street) to 1,880 in 1871. The Roman Catholics who had 1,000 sittings in 1851, had 2,400 in 1871 owing chiefly to the extension of St. Mary's, Lowe House in 1857 and the opening of Holy Cross in 1862. (*St. H. Intelligencer,* 26 Dec., 1857 ; *St. H. N.* 3 May, 1862). Extensions at the Independent Chapel, completed in 1869, increased the capacity from 800 to 1,000. (*St. H. Standard* 20 Feb., 1869). The new chapels provided in all 2,020 sittings. They were : (1) the Presbyterian Church (1868) (The Presbyterians had previously worshipped since 1863 in the Quaker's Chapel, *q.v. St. H. N.* 2 May, 1863 ; 3 Sept., 1864 ; 21 Dec., 1867 ; 15 Aug., 1868) ; (2) the United Methodist Free Church, Ormskirk Street (1861, extended 1870). An offshoot of the Reform Methodists of Arthur Street, they had previously met in a large room at Moorflat from Sept., 1859 (*St. H. Intelligencer* 24 Sept., 1859 ; *St. H. N.* 29 June, 1861 ; *St. H. Standard* 16 July, 17 Sept., 1870) ; (3) the Primitive Methodists (*c.* 1850, rebuilt 1876. (They had previously worshipped at Mount Street, Greenbank *q.v. Directory* 1848 ; *St. H. N.* and *St. H. Standard* 4 Sept., 1875) ; (4) Reform Wesley Chapel Arthur Street (1854) (*Lpool. Merc.* 8 Aug., 1854) ; (5) Other sects, e.g. the Christian Brethren who started to worship in a room in Arthur Street in 1859 (*St. H. Intelligencer,* 24 Sept., 1859) and the Latter Day Saints (Mormons) who met at the Old Workhouse and later in the Raven Buildings (*Wigan Times* 10 July, 1851 ; *St. H. Intelligencer* 1 Aug., 1857, 25 Sept., and 6 Nov., 1858 ; 28 Jan., 1863). There were no Quakers living in the town in the middle of the century and they therefore permitted other religious bodies to use their buildings on occasion. The seating capacity of this old chapel would appear to be the difference between the sum of the totals given above (7,300) plus the Anglican total (3,681) and the grand total of 11,099, that is, 118.

This list does not include the churches outside the boundary of the St. H. I. C. These were :

(i) Baptist, Park Road, 1869. The Baptists had previously worshipped at Hoole Bank House, home of James Shanks, who left £600 towards this chapel (*St. H. N.,* 17 Nov., 1866 ; *St. H. Standard,* 2 Oct. 1869).

(ii) Primitive Methodist, Park Road, 1862. The congregation had worshipped at a cottage in Coalpit Lane since 1859 (*St. H. Weekly News* 14 June, 1862).

(iii) Methodist, Sutton Road, 1871 (*St. H. N.,* 19 Nov., 1870). There was an earlier Methodist chapel in Sutton, opened in 1845 (Cook, *MS. Hist. of St. Helens,* 45).

(iv) Congregational, Peasley Cross, 1865 (*St. H. N.,* 5 Oct., 1864).

(v) Anglican, Christ Church, Eccleston, 1838 (*Wigan Gazette* 12 Oct., 1838). St. Peter's, Parr, 1844 (rebuilt 1865 after fire) (above, p. 392). St. Nicholas, Sutton, 1849 (above, p. 388). St. John the Evangelist, Ravenhead, 1869 (*St. H. N.* 28 Dec., 1869).

(vi) Roman Catholic. St. Anne's Monastery, 1853. St. Mary's, Blackbrook (formerly a private chapel of the Orrells). Catholics at Peasley Cross worshipped in a temporary church from 1862, St. Joseph's being opened in 1878 (*St. H. N.* 7 Sept., 1878).

had grown from nearly 15,000 to 26,000, while the number of sittings in its churches had risen from 4,832 to 11,099.

But even in 1871 it would have been impossible to accommodate more than two-thirds of the local adult population, even had all these sittings been free—and it is known that most of them were privately rented.[1] It was estimated from figures taken at the 1851 census that throughout the country less than half the population went to church, the fraction being even smaller in the new industrial towns. This would appear to have been true for St. Helens. On the Sunday in March, 1851, when the religious census was taken, there were only 25,289 attendances out of a total population in the Prescot division of 56,174, and this figure certainly included many who went to church more than once on that day. In the following twenty years, the proportion of churchgoers to non-churchgoers may have increased (the larger number of sittings suggests that it did) but the increase, if any there were, could not have been very appreciable. About half the population went to church and the other half did not.

The non-churchgoers were not a vocal section of the community and, in consequence, there is less to be learnt about this great cleavage than about the divisions among the churches themselves which were frequently advertised. The Anglicans, in particular, were most hostile to the Catholics who were very strong in the area. In 1839 the curate of St. Mary's preached a series of sermons on " The Errors of the Church of Rome " and the same topic was the subject of a similar course of lectures delivered by the incumbent eleven years later at the time of the outcry against " Papal Aggression."[2] Samuel Bishop, the glass manufacturer, who attended St. Mary's, became well-known for his fiery Protestantism. In 1862 he was responsible for bringing to the town an Irish Protestant who tried to hold an open-air campaign ; but the only two attempts to stage meetings were frustrated by an indignant crowd, said to be several thousands strong.[3] Whatever opinions the Roman Catholics may have entertained privately, they did not voice them in public and they appear to have borne these attacks with remarkable dignity and calm. Indeed, some of them are reported to have attended the sermons at St. Mary's, taking books with them in order to check any quotations which might be made.[4] After 1854 when Father Thomas Ullathorne[5]

[1] In 1851 only 8,367 sittings out of 24,094 in the Prescot census district were free.

[2] *Wigan Gazette*, 31 May, 13 Sept., 4, 11 Oct., 14 Nov., 13 Dec., 1839 ; *Wigan Times* 22, 29 Nov., 1850.

[3] *St. H. N.* 14, 28 June, 1862.

[4] *Wigan Gazette* 11 Oct., 1839.

[5] Obit., *St. H. N.* 20 April, 1900 ; Reginald Riley, *History of Lowe House* (St. Helens, 1940).

became Superior at St. Mary's, Lowe House, official moderation was assured. Father Ullathorne was a man of saintly disposition, widely respected by Catholic and Protestant alike. The religious life of St. Helens owed much to the wise counsel which he gave during his thirty-two years as head of the Jesuit Order in the town.

The Anglicans were also placed at an advantage by having no break in their leadership during these middle years. The Rev. Edward Carr[1] was presented to the perpetual curacy of St. Mary's in 1846 and remained as incumbent (after 1852, when St. Helens was created a separate parish, as vicar) until his death in 1886. He was a man of a very different stamp from Father Ullathorne. Always on the look-out for an argument (he was an Irishman and, moreover, took a degree at Trinity College, Dublin, in law), he seemed to attract trouble. Almost as soon as he arrived in the town, he became involved in a most unfortunate dispute with the daughter church of St. Thomas's over surplice fees and the issue had to be fought out in court.[2] Ten years afterwards he aroused discontent among Nonconformists and Catholics alike by his undiplomatic handling of the arrangements for the new cemetery and, disputatious to the end, he later made an unsuccessful attempt to defend the legality of private pews against the very strong advice of the churchwardens.[3]

There were many other examples of this kind of internal squabbling and inter-denominational rivalry. The incumbent of Holy Trinity, Parr, for instance, felt it his duty to attempt to break up meetings of the Latter Day Saints[4] and the non-resident property-owning Society of Friends came in for a considerable amount of criticism on all sides because (as the local Methodist historian put it, politely cloaking his words in scripture) they " reaped [the town's] carnal things, though they sowed in it spiritual things sparingly."[5] It was, indeed, only towards the non-churchgoing half of the community that the different religious bodies showed any signs of a unity of purpose. This revealed

---

[1] Edward Carr had been vicar of St. John's, Guernsey, for nine years before coming to St. Helens. When Liverpool was formed into a separate diocese in 1880, he was created an honorary canon. He married three times (obit. *Prescot Reporter* 26 June, 1886 ; funeral, *ibid.*, 3 July, 1886).

[2] *Law Journal Reports* 1850, n.s. **19**, pt. 2, 249-258 ; correspondence among the papers of the St. H. Parish Church trustees.

[3] *Case, Counsel's Opinion and Statement as to the Seats in the Parish Church of St. Helens* (St. Helens, 1884). The Vicar replied in *Facts and Fallacies Respecting the Parish Church of St. Helens* (St. Helens, 1884). A speaker complained in 1884 that, although the church could hold 1,800, only 500 usually attended (*St. H. N.*, 19 April, 1884). See also *My Pew !* by A Late Warden (St. H., 1885) and newscuttings at the St. H. Ref. Lib.

[4] *St. H. Intelligencer* 25 Sept., 1858.

[5] Cook, *MS. History of St. Helens*, 109.

itself first in the co-operation between Anglicans and Non-
Nonconformists in combing the neighbourhood for new scholars
for their Sunday Schools. The field of combined operations was
gradually extended as the churches came to take a firmer stand
against drunkenness and all it led to. The campaigns to argue
into conformity those who held other beliefs gradually gave place
to resolute, if often independent, action against a common
menace.

The religious census of 1851 made it quite clear that the
" alarming number of non-attendants " at church consisted, in
fact, of " the labouring myriads ":

> " They fill, perhaps, in youth, our National, British and Sunday
> Schools and there receive the elements of a religious education ;
> but no sooner do they mingle in the active world of labour
> than ... they soon become as utter strangers to religious
> ordinances as people of a heathen country."[1]

" The workers," remarked a French observer, " stand on their
doorsteps or collect in groups until the time when service is over
and the public houses open."[2] Resolute attempts were made to
end this state of affairs. The Methodists were making some
headway locally among these " myriads " and, largely as a result
of their efforts, the leading spirits in the coalminers' newly-formed
union were even able to include in their speeches religious passages
which sound surprising and even out of place to the modern ear.
At an open air meeting at St. Helens, William Pickard concluded
a speech by expressing the hope that " when they had done with
thraldom, bickering and backbiting, they would all meet in
Heaven " and his words were greeted with cheers.[3] At another
meeting six hundred miners stood to hear a converted collier
exhort them to follow his example.[4] Nor were the Methodists
the only people making an attempt to carry their religion to those
who did not attend church. The Rev. W. A. Mocatta of St.
Thomas's gave at least one course of open air addresses at
Greenbank[5] and the Rev. J. A. Macfadyen, minister of the
Independent Chapel—later to earn a great reputation in Manchester[6]—conducted a series of services for working men at the
theatre on Sunday afternoons during the winter of 1862-3.[7] But

---

[1] Report on Religious Worship (1853), cli.

[2] L. Faucher, *Etudes sur l'Angleterre* (1845) I, 351-2 quoted in Elie Halevy,
A History of the English People, 1841-52 (The Age of Peel and Cobden)
(1947), 343.

[3] *St. H. N.* 28 May, 1864.

[4] *St. H. Standard* 6 Jan., 1866.

[5] *St. H. N.* 13 Aug., 1864.

[6] For Macfadyen, see A. Mackennal, *J. A. Macfadyen, D.D., Memoir
and Sermons* (1905).

[7] *St. H. N.* 18 March, 1863.

these evangelical campaigns were only partially successful. The
" myriads " remained. The incidence of drunkenness and
immorality increased, apparently unchecked, as the town grew.

Perhaps the substitution of tea and oranges for warm ale and
buns at the Independent Sunday School's annual treat in 1827[1]
may be said to indicate the beginnings of the temperance movement at St. Helens. In 1838 the Independents held what they
called a temperance festival[2] and the Temperance Reading Room
in Brook Street, mentioned a few years later, was probably located
in their Sunday School.[3] Although the protests against excessive
drinking—though not against drinking itself—grew with the years,
it was not until 1867 that two Catholic priests, an Anglican clergyman and the Independent minister appeared on the same platform
at a temperance meeting. And, even at that late date, they only
went so far as to urge the closing of public houses on Sundays.[4]
It took the rapid rise in convictions during the 1870s to produce
positive action. In December, 1873, the Catholic Association for
the Suppression of Drunkenness was formed, with its alternative
pledges of temperance or total abstinence,[5] followed, in 1878, by
the establishment of a local branch of the Congregational Temperance Society of England and Wales.[6] In the next year, 1879,
Cardinal Manning addressed a temperance rally in the town[7] and
in 1882 a campaign by the Blue Ribbon Movement is said to have
caused 6,000 people to sign the pledge at St. Helens within
sixteen days.[8] Meanwhile several leading townsmen, headed by
James Radley the mayor at the time, launched the St. Helens Café
and Recreation Company, " to provide places of public resort,
refreshment and recreation . . . apart from the sale and use of
intoxicating liquors."[9] It was soon operating three cafés in the
town. Two of them did good business and the company paid a
regular tax-free dividend of 10 per cent. This caused Dromgoole
to dub the directors " 10 per cent. philanthropists."[10]

By the 1870s, therefore, the religious bodies and their

---

[1] Recalled by the Rev. John Edmonds at the Sunday School's 50th anniversary (*Lpool. Merc.*, 7 March, 1856).

[2] *Wigan Gazette* 8 June, 1838.

[3] *Lpool. Merc.* 15 Dec., 1843.

[4] *St. H. N.* 11 May, 1867.

[5] *St. H. N.* 13 Dec., 1873.

[6] *St. H. N.*, 23 Feb. 1878.

[7] *St. H. N.*, 6 Sept. 1879.

[8] *St. H. N.* 11, 18, Nov., 1882.

[9] *St. H. N.* 30 Sept., 1876. William Windle Pilkington, Richard Pilkington, H. S. Hall, Joseph Cook, R. A. Gaskell, James McBryde, H. A.
Binney, Christopher Sharples and A. J. Speeden were the other directors.

[10] *St. H. N.* 9 March, 1889.

individual members had taken their stand. For many, this meant accepting a rigid total abstinence ; for a few it became an all-absorbing mania. No doubt much of the strictness and prudery which characterised the " respectable " part of the population, particularly in the case of those who inherited puritan principles, came down from the past. But one is led to wonder how much of it was a Victorian creation, part of the campaign against what Victorians saw as the evil all around. When fighting drunkenness, one is driven to be a total abstainer. When trying to combat influences revealing themselves in frivolity and recklessness, one must maintain a straight face and be the soul of circumspection. To some extent the churchgoer fitted the part before he was obliged to play it, but circumstances appear to have caused him to don an even more characteristic costume and to speak sterner lines than would otherwise have been necessary.

The middle years, then, while witnessing the gradual removal of some of the divisions in the community, also saw the deepening of the main cleavage between one half of the population and the other. This period of industrial peace and increasing prosperity allowed the divergent groups in the population to grow up together in greater harmony ; but the deep division between the " respectable " people and the rest of the population became more marked. Here, indeed, if anywhere, were the two nations. It was not simply a division between rich and poor, though the well-to-do and the middle classes, not yet disturbed in their religious beliefs by the twin attacks of utilitarianism and scientific discovery, were still found almost to a man on the side of the " respectable " church-goers, and the poverty-stricken were usually beyond the pale of respectability. Yet many of the " labouring myriads," not rich by any means, were careful and thrifty and spent their modest and hard-earned wages on basic necessities rather than on luxuries and pleasures, on the home and the family rather than in the public house and on the racecourse, on saving rather than on spending. These prudent men and women were to be seen in their hundreds sitting in their places at church or chapel Sunday after Sunday. Many of them, by husbanding their slender resources and by gaining a reputation for painstaking effort and constant reliability, made their way in the world. Others lived to see their children reach positions which carried them into what was generally called—for want of a better name—the middle class.

For the deserving, there was certainly no lack of openings : the great swirling tide of economic growth did not permit anything or anybody to remain at rest. Of the opportunities at St. Helens, what has been said in an earlier chapter[1] is equally true of these middle years of the last century. A new feature, however, is the growing tendency for people to emigrate from the district in an effort to make a better living elsewhere.

Women, in particular, could find little employment at St. Helens in the great factories. Apart from jobs as smoothers at the glassworks[2] and pit brow lasses at the collieries,[3] the three local industries of coal, glass and chemicals had nothing to offer them. Women therefore left for the textile towns, particularly after the mid-1840s when they were no longer permitted to go down the mines, and female immigrants also tended to make for the textile areas. The population returns illustrate this movement of female labour. Taking the country as a whole during the past century, there has been an excess of women over men.[4] In 1801 this was true of the local population : there were 3,799 women in the four townships and 3,774 men. By 1821, however, the balance was already starting to tip ; there were only 5,270 women and 5,333 men. By 1851 there were 500 fewer women than men in a population of 45,000 ; by 1861, 1,041 fewer in a total of 38,000 and by 1871, 1,250 fewer in a total of 45,000.

A number of St. Helens people took advantage of their proximity to Liverpool, the port in the United Kingdom from which most emigrants sailed,[5] to seek their fortunes abroad. Thomas Melling of Moss Bank, for instance, who served his apprenticeship at the locomotive sheds of the St. Helens Railway, became an engine driver on the line between Rouen and Paris and later went to Egypt, where he drove the Viceroy's train.[6] William and Peter Barton, who had been converted to Mormonism, went to settle in Utah.[7] Others went to Australia where gold was the particular attraction. Thomas Grundy, who emigrated there in 1850 related in his first letter home seven years later—he promised to write oftener in future—how he had been unsuccessful at the

---

[1] Above, p. 320.

[2] See, e.g., *St. H. Intelligencer* 1, 8, 15 Nov., 1856.

[3] The Act of 1842 only forbade the employment of women underground. The pit brow lasses continued to be a familiar sight in the district throughout the period, despite various efforts to end their employment (see, e.g., *St. H. N.*, 17 April, 1886). There were 1,600 of them at work in West Lancashire in the early 1890s (evidence of George Caldwell to the R.C. on Labour, Gp.A., I (1892), q. 5936).

[4] Report of R.C. on Population (Cmd. 7695 of 1949), 97.

[5] Thomas Baines, *Liverpool in* 1859 (1859), 22.

[6] *St. H. N.* 2 Nov., 1867. At first all the engine drivers on the Rouen—Paris railway were Englishmen (*q.v.* W. O. Henderson, *Britain and Industrial Europe, 1750-1870* (Liverpool, 1954), 70.

[7] *St H. Intelligencer* 25 Sept., 1858 ; diary of Newton Lacey, 3 Sept., 1874.

diggings but had earned enough by carting provisions for the more fortunate prospectors to enable him to remove to Otago, New Zealand, where he had bought a farm for £115.[1] Grundy was followed to Australia in 1856 by Robert Whyte, Pilkingtons' mining agent,[2] and in 1857 by T. Graham, an employee of the London and Manchester Plate Glass Company.[3]

In 1864 a strong and athletic young engineer, not yet twenty years of age, Richard John Seddon by name, also took the emigrants' boat from Liverpool. He was born in 1845 at the Eccleston Free Grammar School[4] on the side of the turnpike road half way up Eccleston Hill, where his father, Thomas Seddon a native of Bickerstaffe, was for many years schoolmaster. In 1861, however, Thomas Seddon gave up this appointment and, in February 1862, became Relieving Officer for St. Helens. His tenure of this office was brief, for it was discovered that he had not kept the books correctly and this led to his resignation in January 1863.[5] This family misfortune may well have some bearing upon Richard Seddon's leaving the St. Helens Foundry, where he had been apprenticed in 1859, and taking a job at the Vauxhall Foundry in Liverpool in September, 1863.[6] But, as he himself later recalled, " a restlessness to get away to see new broad lands " seized him and in the next year he took ship from Liverpool bound for Australia. Like Grundy and so many other optimists, he headed straight for the diggings but—also like so many of the others—his luck was out and he was obliged to find employment in the railway workshops at Williamstown. Late in the next year, 1865, he joined in the gold rush on the west coast of New Zealand, but, once again, he had no notable success as a prospector. He opened a store and established himself as one of the leading figures in the rough community that sprang up at the goldfield. He was elected miners' representative on various local government bodies and in 1879 became their choice for the lower house of the New Zealand Parliament. He quickly distinguished

---

[1] St. H. Intelligencer, 16 Jan., 1858.

[2] St. H. Intelligencer 12 July, 1856.

[3] St. H. Intelligencer 3 July, 1858.

[4] The Eccleston Free Grammar School, a late sixteenth century foundation, was closed at the end of the eighteenth century. It was reopened in 1827 as the result of the discovery of certain legal documents. There is information concerning the school in the Cross Papers, DDCS 14/120 and in the Report of the Schools Inquiry Commission, 1867-8 [3966] XXVIII, part XVI, 248.

[5] Guard. Mins., 20 Feb., 1862 ; 20 Jan., 1863. He later became a grocer in St. Helens.

[6] Speech by Seddon on his return to St. H. in 1897 (St. H. R., 11 June, 1897). This account is based on this and other speeches and reports made on the occasion of his visits to St. Helens in 1897 and 1902 (see also St. H. R., 4 June, 1897 ; St. H. N., 20, 27 June, 11 July, 1902).

himself as a parliamentarian and in 1893 became Prime Minister, holding the office until his death in 1906. He never forgot his friends at St. Helens and corresponded regularly with his old foreman at the St. Helens Foundry, W. Melling.[1] On his two official visits to England in 1897, for Queen Victoria's jubilee, and in 1902, for King Edward's coronation, he came to his native town and was given a tumultuous welcome, on the second occasion being presented with the freedom of the Borough.[2]

Richard Seddon provides St. Helens with its greatest success story.

[1] *St. H. R.* 11 April, 1895.   He also sent Christmas greetings every year to H. R. Lacey.

[2] For an outline of Seddon's life, see James Drummond, *The Life and Work of Richard John Seddon* (1907), which includes a photograph of his birthplace and of him as a 16-year-old apprentice. For obit., see news-cuttings at St. H. Ref. Lib. and *Letters and Telegrams of Condolence* (Wellington, 1906). The *D.N.B.*, supplement, 1901-11, contains an article for which information was privately supplied.

PART FOUR

INDUSTRIAL GROWTH AND THE RISE
OF RESPECTABILITY
1870-1900

CHAPTER XXVIII

INDUSTRIAL DEVELOPMENT,

1870-1900

THE period 1873-96 is usually known as the Great Depression. It was marked by more severe fluctuations in economic activity than had occurred during the previous quarter of a century and by an intensification of industrial competition. Foreign countries, particularly Germany and the United States, were now beginning to produce for themselves goods formerly imported from Britain, and manufacturers came to depend increasingly upon British markets. Despite these changes in the pattern of trade, however, productivity continued to rise, though not so fast as previously. Prices became more competitive and renewed emphasis was placed upon plant efficiency ; new technical processes were introduced and widely applied.

The Great Depression was preceded by a short period of great prosperity, in which the coal industry had more than its fair share. The outstanding feature of the boom was an acute coal shortage which caused prices to soar to unprecedented heights. Slack from the Ravenhead Colliery, which had been delivered to the nearby St. Helens Copper Company for 3s. 6d. a ton at the end of 1870,[1] fetched 5s. at the pithead twelve months later and coal 8s.[2] The price continued to rise spectacularly until the spring of 1873 when slack was being quoted at the pithead at 16s. and coal at 20s.[3] Although prices dropped a little during the summer, slack was still being sold for 12s. and coal for 18s. in September, 1873, and for 11s. and 17s. respectively in the following December.[4]

The high price of coal enticed speculators into the industry on a scale unknown at St. Helens for more than fifty years ; some extreme optimists even chanced their luck after the boom was over, possibly in the hope of its recurrence. Benjamin Bradshaw Glover opened the Phoenix Colliery at Ravenhead[5] and W. J. Menzies of the Greenbank Alkali Works took over

[1] Pilkington Brothers Ltd., Mins of the Ravenhead Colliery, 9 Nov., 1870.

[2] *Ibid.*, 14 Dec., 1871.

[3] *Ibid.*, 6 March, 1873.

[4] *Ibid.*, 11 Sept., 18 Dec., 1873.

[5] *Ibid.*, 18 July, 15 Aug., 1872.

the Greengate Colliery not far away.[1] John Cross, a working collier who had risen to be Menzies' right-hand man in this venture, later branched out on his own by re-opening some of the old workings of the Royal Colliery at Thatto Heath.[2] To the north of the town, G. A. Bates was selling coal at the City Colliery, Windle,[3] and to the east, sinkers were being sought for the Redgate Colliery in Parr, the property of George Molyneux.[4] But only one of these new speculations was able to survive long enough to become firmly established. The two that sounded the most inspiring—the City and the Royal—were the first to go, in 1876 and 1878 respectively.[5] The Greengate Colliery, together with its neighbouring Brick and Tile Works, was put up for auction in 1882[6] and the Redgate Colliery was sold in the following year.[7] Only the Phoenix Colliery continued as a going concern and in this case, B. B. Glover, its chief proprietor, had outstanding advantages in his favour. He had been articled in 1856, at the age of seventeen, to a Wigan mining engineer and between 1861-4 had gained valuable managerial experience with Richard Evans and Company at Haydock. Then he joined a firm of mining surveyors at St. Helens and in the following year, 1865, was appointed mining engineer to William John Legh.[8] He probably also possessed some other, non-technical, advantages, for he came of the old-established family who owned the King's Head Estate, his father being J. W. Glover, the ropemaker. The Glovers had parted with the surface land of their estate in the 1820s but had reserved the mineral rights.[9]

[1] W. Walmesley & Co. were advertising coal from the Greengate Colliery from the beginning of 1869 and the tone of the advertisements suggests that they had only just gone into business. Menzies was offering coal from the colliery in October, 1872 (*St. H. Standard* 2 Jan., 20 Feb., 1869 ; Ravenhead Colliery Mins., 10 Oct., 1872).

[2] *St. H. N.* 26 June, 12 Oct., 1875.   In the *St. H. N.* of 15 July, 1876 Cross advertised that he was " Proprietor of best Glass House, Pot and Crucible Clay, Manufacturer of Glass House Furnace Bricks, Blast Furnace Bricks and Lumps, Tiles and Fire Bricks of every description." Many of his bricks were used to build the houses of Eccleston Park. We are grateful to Mr. Cross of 30 Fir Street, Thatto Heath, for information concerning his father.

[3] *St. H. N.* 17 Jan., 1871.

[4] *St. H. N.*, 20 March, 1877.

[5] *St. H. N.* 5 Feb., 1876 ; 26 March, 14 Dec., 1878.

[6] *St. H. N.* 1 April, 1882.

[7] *St. H. N.* 4 Aug., 1883.

[8] Memoir in the *St. H. Lantern* 11 Oct., 1889.   Between 1879 and 1889 B. B. Glover was also general manager for Richard Evans & Co., and in charge of the Greenbank Ropery.

[9] *Lpool. Merc.* 26 April, 1822 ; Pilkington Brothers Ltd., package 11. Lease dated 21 July, 1826. According to Pilkington Brothers' Board Mins., 19 March, 1863, the Glovers were still in possession of the mineral rights at that date.

While these events were taking place in the immediate vicinity of St. Helens, Richard Evans and Company of Haydock were rapidly invading the coal measures of Parr. In 1863 they had opened the Havannah Colliery in that township[1] and immediately prior to 1870 they sank three additional pits there.[2] The failure in 1869 of the Sankey Coal Company Ltd., formed only seven years before to take over the Sankey Brook and Ashton's Green Collieries,[3] left the Haydock firm dominant in that part of the coalfield and they extended their operations even more after purchasing several estates in the townships of Parr and Sutton.[4] By 1889, when Richard Evans's became a limited company, the concern had grown into a great undertaking, operating pits over more than ten square miles (those in Parr being the most westerly) and owning estates and property worth more than £700,000.[5] Six years later, this one company was raising 2,000,000 tons of coal annually.[6]

Nearer to St. Helens and to the south of the town, the old Ravenhead Colliery merged with Pilkingtons' St. Helens Colliery in 1876, the new concern being known as the St. Helens Collieries Company Ltd.[7] Farther to the south, where the coal measures were only met at a greater depth, Bold Colliery was opened in the mid-1870s.[8] Ten years later, Bromilow Foster and Company, who had taken over Ashton's Green Colliery in 1883, sank a shaft there to a depth of 554 yards in order to work the Little Delf mine.[9]

Now that the district no longer suffered from the disability of penalising transport charges, the prosperity of the early 1870s induced local manufacturers and, to a smaller extent, outsiders, to

[1] St. H. Chronicle 7 June, 1889.

[2] Mining Journal 18 June, 1870 (Supplement).

[3] St. H. Town Hall, United Alkali Co. Ltd., Deeds (Baxter's Works) ; L.R.O., Cross Papers, DDCS 30/41, 43, 44, 47 ; Brasenose College, Oxford, correspondence in packages 46 and 372.

[4] When purchasing Barton's Bank Estate from Brasenose College, Oxford, the representatives of Joseph Evans (the chief proprietor after the death of his father in 1864 and his brother, Josiah, in 1873) stated that Evans had recently acquired " several estates adjoining, both in Parr and Sutton " (Brasenose College, Oxford, package 46, letter from Amos Hanson dated 25 Feb., 1874).

[5] St. H. N. 16 Nov., 1889.

[6] St. H. N. 9 March, 1895.

[7] Pilkington Brothers Ltd., printed notice of extraordinary meeting held 27 April, 1876. The shareholders in the Ravenhead Colliery received £10,950 in 5 per cent debentures and three £50 shares for each share they already held.

[8] St. H. N. 18 April, 1874 ; 21 June, 1879 ; 22 May, 1886 ; 27 June, 1896.

[9] Prescot Reporter 5 June, 1886.

embark fresh capital in glass and chemicals as well as in coal.
Pilkingtons decided to take up the manufacture of cast plate glass
and in 1874 acquired a site for this purpose at Cowley Hill.[1]
The new factory went into production in August, 1876.[2] About
the same time, Henry Baxter, the copper smelter, and Cannington
Shaw and Company, the bottle makers, both branched out into
alkali manufacture, the former near his smeltery in Parr, the latter
at the Sutton Lodge Chemical Works.[3] It was not surprising that
Baxter should embark upon the manufacture of soda, an industry
allied to copper smelting, and Cannington Shaw and Company, no
doubt, derived considerable advantage from possessing their own
source of alkali. But it is difficult to suggest a reason for George
Harris, the builder, being drawn into alkali making, save that of
pure speculation. He was not successful. The small Merton Bank
Alkali Works which he had just erected were mortgaged for
£700 in June, 1872.[4] His affairs took a turn for the worse, possibly
on account of this venture into alkali making, possibly on account
of his heavy building commitments elsewhere, and he died in
Liverpool in 1875 under most unfortunate circumstances.[5] The
following year all his property was put up for auction and the
Merton Bank Alkali Works passed into the hands of Thomas
Walker, described as a manufacturing chemist of St. Helens.[6]
Another new alkali concern had an even shorter life than Harris's.
This was the St. Helens and Liverpool Alkali Company Ltd.,
which took over the iron foundry in Boundary Road belonging to
James Varley, who became one of the shareholders. The company
failed in November, 1873, only seventeen months after the original
conveyance of land had been signed.[7] These Boundary Road
Chemical Works were acquired a few months later by William
Lockwood of Rainhill and John Leith, Lockwood being the
financier and Leith the practical chemist.[8]

The only successful newcomer of this period was a Scot from
Campbeltown named Duncan McKechnie. He had gained

[1] Pilkington Brothers Ltd. Deeds, package 51.

[2] Papers at Pilkington Brothers Ltd.

[3] *Directory*, 1876.

[4] St. H. Town Hall. United Alkali Co. Ltd. Deeds, Walker's Works.

[5] *St. H. Standard* 25 Sept., 2 Oct., 1875.

[6] *St. H. N.*, 26 Aug., 1876 ; United Alkali Co. Ltd. Deeds, Walkers' Works.

[7] British Electricity Authority, Clarke's Gardens, Lpool. Conveyance dated 2 June, 1872. According to information supplied by I.C.I. (General Chemicals Division) Ltd., the original shareholders were : Joseph Busby (350), John Busby (300), James Varley (300), William Cannon (200), S. T. Thompson (100), Exors. Thomas Grandage Edwards (300), Exors. Isaac Scott (300), Henry Baxter (20). The shares were each worth 5/-.

[8] Deed dated 23 March, 1874 ; *Chem. Trade Jour.* 31 March, 1888.

considerable experience in operating Henderson's wet copper process for extracting metals from low-grade ores, at Runcorn, first at Johnson's soapery and then at the Old Quay works, where he was a partner. But there were differences within the partnership and McKechnie, backed by Mason and Barry, two men with interests in pyrites mines, launched out at St. Helens in 1871.[1]

All these ventures, the product of the boom, soon had to struggle for their existence when exposed to the rigours of competition and less favourable trading conditions. And the bleakest prospect of all was soon to face the Leblanc alkali trade which had attracted much support during the years of prosperity.

The depression of the late 'seventies, already severe at St. Helens towards the close of 1878, reached its nadir during the following year.[2] The industrial casualties of the district were confined to the chemical trade and it was the older and apparently well-established firms that went out of business. J. K. Leathers, who had conducted the wet copper process at his Bridgewater Smelting Works for a quarter of a century, failed in July, 1878.[3] Six months later John Marsh and Company went bankrupt and their Parr Alkali Works, more than forty years old, were put up for auction.[4] Most surprising of all, Crosfield Brothers and Company ran up a debt of more than £20,000[5] and were obliged to sell their extensive factory, part of which had formed Muspratt and Gamble's original works, the first in the town.

While these two alkali companies were being mortally weakened—so it was alleged—by inefficient management,[6] a greater threat to the Leblanc manufacturers was looming up in the form of a new method of making soda, which was eventually to be the chief cause of the closing of every chemical factory in the town.

Brunner-Mond's Solvay ammonia-soda process, in operation at Winnington Hall near Northwich from the mid-'seventies, was

[1] Obit. *St. H. N.* and *St. H. R.* 12 Dec., 1913 ; D. W. F. Hardie, *A History of the Chemical Industry in Widnes* (I.C.I. Ltd., General Chemicals Division, 1950), 78-9. The site of McKechnie's first works was near where Todd Brothers Ltd. now stands. The works were later moved to the foot of Peasley Cross Lane.

[2] For local comments on the depression, see *St. H. N.* 30 Nov., 14, 21 Dec., 1878 ; 11, 25 Jan., 1 March, 29 Nov. 1879.

[3] Above, p. 346.

[4] *St. H. N.* 4 Jan., 1879 ; 23 Feb., 1884.   Marsh's Ravenhead Chemical Works were advertised to be sold in the *St. H. N.* 10 Nov., 1883.

[5] St. H. Town Hall.   United Alkali Co. Ltd. Deeds, Globe Works.

[6] The allegation was made in the case of Crosfields', by Sir Frederick Norman and in the case of Marsh's by Messrs. Huyton and Weatherilt, two old alkali works employees.

not looked upon in its early days as a substitute for the existing means of alkali production. Although soda could be manufactured more cheaply by the new process, there were no chlorine by-products to furnish an additional profit. The prevailing opinion—held, among others, by Ludwig Mond himself—was that ammonia-soda production would grow so long as the Leblanc makers continued to increase their sales of chlorine products, but when the market for chlorine products was satisfied, then ammonia-soda output would also have reached its limit. Moreover, supplies of ammonia from the gas and coking industries were by no means unlimited and, in any case, the price of this essential raw material would rise as the demand grew.[1]

Before the close of the 1870s, therefore, the Leblanc soda makers were far from downcast as they surveyed the industrial scene. From all appearances they had every reason for self-assurance. Costs were falling as more efficient labour-saving machinery and furnaces were installed.[2] During the 'seventies the selling price of soda fell only a little and the market was not appreciably affected by Brunner Mond's production, which had only reached 10,000 tons by 1878.[3] At the same time the Leblanc makers were reaping benefits from the developments of the previous decade and, in particular, from the Weldon process. The cost of making bleaching powder had been reduced from about £9 to £2 a ton,[4] while the selling price had only fallen from about £10 to £5. Here, indeed, was a great source of profit in which the manufacturer of ammonia-soda could have no share.

But self-assurance soon turned to alarm as the enormous possibilities of the rival process came to be realised. Between 1878 and 1882 ammonia-soda production jumped from 10,000 tons to 52,000 tons, one seventh of the total output of soda from all the Leblanc works. The threatened shortage of ammonia did not materialise : on the contrary, there was an extraordinary increase in supplies from the coke ovens and the price of ammonia actually fell despite the greater demand for it.[5] Taken by itself,

[1] Hardie, *op. cit.*, 137-8.

[2] Between 1872 and 1882, coal consumption was reduced from 336 tons to 216 tons per 100 tons of total products. Wages were reduced by 44 per cent in the same period (Walter Weldon, " The Present Condition of the Soda Industry," *Jour. Soc. Chem. Ind.*, 29 Jan., 1883, 9).

[3] *Ibid.*, 3.

[4] E. K. Muspratt stated in 1869 that when bleaching powder was sold at £14 to £18 a ton, there was a profit of £5 to £8 a ton (evidence to the Rivers Pollution Commission, 1870, II, q. 2030). Deacon stated in a private letter on 29 July, 1871 (now in the possession of I.C.I. (General Chemical Division) Ltd.,) that bleaching powder could be made by his process for £1/11/4 a ton and Weldon in a propaganda document claimed it could be made for about £2 by his magnesite process. These figures indicate the range of costs at the time.

[5] Hardie, *op. cit.*, 138

the rapid rise in ammonia-soda production in Britain was serious enough. But, in addition, other works had been built abroad which were also able to compete with Leblanc soda in the world markets. In 1882 Solvay's original works in Belgium were making 8,000 tons of soda. The plant at Dombasle in France (opened in 1876) produced 57,000 tons and one in Baden, started in 1880, 44,000 tons. Most significant of all, 1,000 tons of ammonia-soda were manufactured in that year in the United States.[1]

Merseyside had grown up on the American trade. Thomas Baines could still write in the middle of the nineteenth century that " This great trade with the new world . . . is the chief support of the commerce of Liverpool."[2] He added that Liverpool was the main port of shipment for 40,000 tons of soda ash, sent abroad annually from Britain.[3] In 1857 Liverpool's own export trade in soda amounted to nearly 33,600 tons.[4] Much of this alkali, like other exports from Liverpool, was sent to the United States which never developed a Leblanc industry of its own.[5] Local evidence confirms that the trade in chemicals with America was very important. In 1865 trade with the United States had grown so extensive that the manufacturers of the town requested the U.S. Consul at Liverpool to open a Consular Agency at St. Helens so that they would no longer be troubled with taking their invoices into Liverpool for verification. In his message to Washington forwarding this request, the Consul described St. Helens as " a town . . . engaged almost entirely in manufacturing and doing a large business with the United States."[6] The request was granted and John Hammill became the

[1] Weldon, *op. cit.*, 2.

[2] Thomas Baines, *History of the Town and Commerce of Liverpool* (1852), 809.

[3] *Ibid.*, 767.

[4] Thomas Baines, *Liverpool in 1859* (1859), 20.

[5] An article which appeared in the *Chem. Trade Jour.*, 28 Jan., 1899, entitled " The Caustic Soda Trade in the States " refers to occasional factories but Walter Weldon in his survey of soda production in 1882 does not credit the United States with any soda made by the Leblanc process. The *Chem. Trade Jour.* article mentions a small works at South Wilmington near Boston, managed first by a man named Wolf who had been foreman at the Greenbank Works, St. Helens and later by one Bradley, who had also been foreman at works in St. Helens. Victor S. Clarke in his *History of Manufactures in the United States, 1860-1914* (Washington 1928), 524, asserts that the " first successful " soda works there were opened at Bay City, Michigan about 1880.

[6] Thomas H. Dudley to Secretary of State Seward, 1 Sept., 1865 (Despatches, Liverpool, volume 32, fo. 527 at the State Department, Washington). We are grateful to Mrs. Julia B. Carroll of the National Archives, Washington for making a search of documents upon which this section is based and to the Rev. P. F. Atherton for visiting the National Archives on our behalf.

first United States Consular Agent at St. Helens in October, 1865.[1] His appointment is eloquent testimony to the large and expanding trade flowing from St. Helens across the Atlantic and this is confirmed by the records relating to the Agency, still preserved among the National Archives in Washington from the year 1873.[2] All the traffic, of course, did not consist of chemical products. Glass, as we shall presently see, formed an important part of the shipments. But there can be no doubt that much of the profits of local Leblanc alkali makers was earned on the other side of the Atlantic. And it is significant that when St. Helens ceased to be a centre of the alkali trade during the first World War, the consular agency was closed.[3]

So with ammonia-soda production rapidly on the increase at home and threatening to invade a most profitable and long-established market abroad, the Leblanc makers were obliged to sell their alkali at more competitive prices and to look to by-products for their profits. By 1883, however, so many Leblanc factories were making bleaching powder that the supply had exceeded demand and the price had slumped to £3 7s. 6d. a ton,[4] enough to yield a small profit, it is true, but insufficient to maintain the whole Leblanc edifice. Addressing the Society of the Chemical Industry, Weldon suggested how the Leblanc makers could reduce their soda costs still further so as to save an additional £1 a ton which, he estimated, was the difference between the cost of production in the two processes.[5] But the manufacturers took a shorter cut to solve their difficulties : they joined together in an association to maintain bleach prices.

The idea of trade agreements among the Leblanc makers was not new. They had joined together in 1862 to form a common front at the time of the Alkali Works Regulation Bill and there were even earlier agreements in the industry.[6] In 1867 some manufacturing chemists, including David Gamble, had joined together to form the Tharsis Copper and Sulphur Company to ensure their sulphur supplies.[7] Now, in 1883, they formed

[1] On the death of John Hammill in 1870, his son, also named John, succeeded him.

[2] This volume entitled *Record of Fees* covers the period 1 April, 1873 to 31 December, 1892.

[3] The last Agent was Ernest Phillips, appointed in 1908. The Agency was closed on 10 June, 1916.

[4] *Chem. Trade Jour.* 13 Oct., 1888.

[5] Weldon, *op. cit.*, 8.   [6] Above, p. 253.

[7] This company established works at Widnes where 48 per cent. sulphur and 2½ per cent. copper were abstracted from low-grade ores from its own mines in Spain. The ore was first sent to the alkali works, where all but 5 per cent of the sulphur was removed, and then sent to Widnes, or other works belonging to the company elsewhere in the country, for the remaining sulphur and copper to be extracted (*The Ironmonger* 3, 10 Sept., 1887 ; Hardie, *op. cit.*, 82).

the Lancashire Bleaching Powder Manufacturers' Association and each company, having been allocated an "accepted make," was obliged to keep below that limit. It was the same method that had already been employed with success, as has been seen, in the salt and glass industries. For the alkali manufacturers the result of this regulation of output was most satisfactory : the selling price of bleaching powder rose from £3 7s. 6d. to £7 a ton.[1]

But the very success of such limitation of output attracted the interloper who hoped for large sales by slightly underselling the Association. The St. Helens firm of Lockwood and Leith tried to recoup their losses in this way. Their history is of interest, for it shows how very possible it was for the Leblanc process to be barren and profitless at this time. Between 1874, their first year of production, and 1886, Lockwood and Leith made a profit in only two years : in 1881 of £166 and in 1884 of £269. In other years they ran their works at losses ranging from £120 in 1883 to £2,631 in 1880 and totalling £10,502 in all. The firm was able to withstand such heavy losses because Lockwood continued to supply capital until he had invested £5,000 and he prevailed upon his brother-in-law, William Lees Evans, to embark more than that amount. In 1887, having lost £10,000, it was decided to make a bold bid for solvency by entering the bleaching powder trade on a large scale and underselling the Association. The derelict Parr Alkali Works were purchased for £10,000, and £7,000 were spent in restoring them to a working condition. But all to no avail. The bleach ring thwarted them by buying up all their production and re-selling it at the fixed price. In 1887 Lockwood and Leith registered a loss of £5,341 and in March of the following year they appeared in the Liverpool Bankruptcy Court.[2] Three months later it was announced that the Bleaching Powder Manufacturers' Association had acquired the property and was about to dismantle it.[3] This was done with speedy and ruthless efficiency.[4]

By maintaining the selling price of the Leblanc industry's one great asset at a level which yielded a profit of about 200 per

[1] *Chem. Trade Jour.* 13 Oct., 1888.

[2] This account is based on the public inquiry into the firm's affairs, reported in the *Chem. Trade Jour.* 31 March, 1888. This report gave W. L. Evans's share in the firm as £3,000 but the deeds (now held by the British Electricity Authority, Clarke's Gardens, Liverpool) show that he had, in fact, lent £5,000 by the 1 Sept., 1877 and he lent a further £1,500 after that. A list of the industrial creditors is printed in the same *Journal* on 12 May, 1888.

[3] *Chem. Trade Jour.* 28 June, 1888.

[4] For the auction of the Boundary Road Chemical Works, see the *St. H. N.* 29 Sept., 1888 and for that of the Parr Alkali Works, the *St. H. N.* 15 June, 1889

cent. after transport costs had been met, the Lancashire Bleaching
Powder Manufacturers' Association gave the industry a breathing
space. But few of its members can have looked upon it as anything but a stop-gap solution of their dilemma. They had before
them the examples of past associations in the salt industry which
gave good results so long as they lasted, but revealed a tendency
to break up after a time owing to internal stresses and strains.
A period of free competition thereupon ensued until the prices fell
so low that the manufacturers were once again obliged to combine in their common interest. This appears to have occurred
in the Leblanc trade in the course of the year 1889. The agreements lapsed and the price of bleaching powder fell to £5 a ton.[1]
A closer alliance was clearly required which would not be subject
to interruptions of this kind.

Once again, the salt industry showed the way. In November,
1888, saltmakers claiming to produce among them more than
90 per cent. of the salt output of the United Kingdom, joined
together to form the Salt Union Ltd., a company in which all the
smaller concerns became shareholders, thereby losing their individual identity. The Salt Union was a huge undertaking with
a nominal capital of £4,000,000. It got off to a flying start and
was able to declare a dividend of 10 per cent. on the first fourteen
months' working, having raised salt prices to 70 per cent. above
their previous level.[2]   This apparently most conclusive proof
of the soundness of the new company coming at the beginning
of 1890 when the Leblanc makers were casting about for a more
permanent form of organisation, seems to have had a profound
influence upon their deliberations. The United Alkali Company
Ltd., when it came into being in November, 1890, was even
larger than its prototype. It had a share capital of £5,000,000
and controlled forty-eight factories in England, Scotland and
Ireland.[3]

The whole of the chemical industry in St. Helens was involved
in the new concern. More than £1,150,000 were paid out to the
chemical manufacturers of the town as compensation for their
works.[4] In most cases almost the whole of this amount took the
form of ordinary, preference and debenture shares in the new
company, evidence that the local manufacturers were not
seizing the opportunity to cut their losses and bolt from what

[1] *Chem. Trade Jour.* 4 Jan., 1890.

[2] Clapham, *An Economic History of Modern Britain* (Cambridge, 1936),
III, 215.   For the Salt Union Ltd., see Calvert, *Salt in Cheshire* (1915),
549-596.   The successful results of the first fourteen months' working
were not repeated.

[3] Hardie, *op. cit.*, 146.

[4] These details are taken from the deeds of the various works, now at
the St. H. Town Hall.

they thought to be a dying industry.[1] In all, 85 per cent. of the share capital in the United Alkali Co. Ltd. was held by those within the chemical trade.[2]

Although each manufacturer naturally sought the highest rate of compensation for his property and, no doubt, some succeeded in driving better bargains than others, the selling-out prices of the local works may be taken as an indication of their size and importance. Heading the list came the two works of J. C. Gamble and Son at Gerard's Bridge and Hardshaw Brook for which £320,000 were paid.[3] The pioneer factory at the New Double Locks, re-started in 1880 by the Globe Alkali Co. Ltd.,[4] came next with £191,490 and was followed closely by the Greenbank works (£181,000)[5] and Kurtz's (£172,050). Baxter's fetched £138,940— a remarkable achievement in less than twenty years—and McBryde's £90,200. The Pocket Nook factory which had once belonged to Balmain and had passed to the St. Helens Chemical Co. Ltd. and then in 1877 to Chadwick and Sons, Manchester paper makers, was acquired for £39,000 and Walker's nearby brought only £12,000. McKechnie's works passed into the hands of the new company in the course of 1891.[6]

This great merger of 1890 was, without doubt, the most important single event in the industrial history of St. Helens during the nineteenth century. The transfer of more than £1,000,000 worth of property, most of it for shares in the new company, meant that the allegiance of the former proprietors of local factories was now owed not to the chemical industry in St. Helens but to the Leblanc industry as a whole throughout the country. They had everything to gain from the rationalisation of the industry in the low-cost areas. From the beginning the view appears to have been taken by the Widnes-dominated board of directors[7] that the works at St. Helens gave less satisfactory

---

[1] For Baxter's works, £92,000 were paid in cash. McBryde's and Chadwicks only received one-third of their payment in cash and Gambles received no cash at all.

[2] Hardie, *op. cit.*, 146.

[3] J. C. Gamble & Son. at the time of the transfer presented 15 of their workmen with £2,900 in shares in the new company (*Chem. Trade Jour.* 7 Nov. 1891).

[4] St. H. Town Hall. United Alkali Co. Ltd. Deeds.

[5] The deeds in this case are at Pilkington Brothers Ltd. The Greenbank Co. was allowed to retain its sulphate of copper plant, but Menzies promised not to make any chlorine products except as a shareholder of the United Alkali Co. Ltd.

[6] *Chem. Trade Jour.* 2 April, 1892. Duncan McKechnie's sons started a factory at Widnes in 1891 (Hardie, *op. cit.*, 79).

[7] 10 of the first 23 Directors were associated with Widnes. John Brock was the chairman (Hardie, *op. cit.*, 148-9).

results than those at Widnes. The new order did not favour the older town.

As the 1890s progressed, the deepening crisis in the soda trade strengthened the hands of those who kept on urging the most ruthless rationalisation. Trade at home was slack, particularly in 1893, and sales on the other side of the Atlantic fell at a greater rate after the McKinley Tariff came into force in the United States in 1890 and encouraged the expansion of the American chemical industry. In 1897 the Dingley Tariff, considerably higher than its predecessor of 1890, reduced soda ash exports from England to the United States from 125,000 to 29,000 tons and caustic soda shipments from 33,000 to 11,000 tons.[1] As a result of this falling-off in demand both at home and abroad, some plants at St. Helens were completely closed for long periods and operations were frequently interrupted on instructions from headquarters in Liverpool. The *St. Helens Newspaper* had ample justification for asserting that the formation of the United Alkali Company had been " a bad thing for the town."[2]

While the chemical industry at St. Helens was being weakened by the competition from ammonia-soda, a third method of decomposing salt was discovered. This was the electrolytic process, which produced not only caustic soda but also bleaching powder, the Leblanc manufacturers' last hope. The Castner-Kellner Alkali Company, formed to exploit the new invention, started to build a factory at Weston Point near Runcorn in February, 1896,[3] and the plant was partially at work early in 1897.[4] Two years after this the General Electrolytic Alkali Company was floated to commercialise another electrolytic process employing a diaphragm instead of a mercury cell, the invention of James Hargreaves and Thomas Bird who had carried out their researches at Farnworth, near Widnes. This firm went into production at Middlewich in 1901.[5] Yet a third type of cell, the Holland-Richardson, had been patented[6] and the Electro-Chemical Company Ltd. was formed with a share capital of £200,000 to work it commercially. This company's choice of St. Helens for its

[1] *Chem. Trade Jour.* 25 March, 1899.

[2] *St. H. N.* 8 Feb., 1896.

[3] *Chem. Trade Jour.* 15 Feb., 1896.

[4] *Ibid.*, 3 April, 1897.

[5] *Ibid.*, 23 Dec., 1899 ; Hardie, *op. cit.*, 197. For an extremely informative and lucid account of the various electrolytic processes and the attitude of the United Alkali Co. Ltd. to them, see Hardie, *op. cit.*, chap. 11.

[6] British Patents 2297/1890 and 5525/1893. For a brief description of the cell, see 31st Ann. Rep. of the Alkali Inspector (for 1894), 12. It was operating at a pilot plant in Snodland, Kent, in 1892.

operations extended to the chemical industry of the town hope of a last-minute reprieve from otherwise certain extinction.

The Electro-Chemical Company's prospectus, issued early in 1894, did not divulge where it was intended to work the new process, but among the " eminent experts " who testified to the " unequivocal success " of the Holland-Richardson cell was John Leith, " the well-known Lancashire Alkali Manufacturer and Chemical Engineer."[1] He was, indeed, well-known. Possibly his powers of persuasion, well-developed during his term as managing partner of the Boundary Road and Parr Alkali Works, were in some measure responsible for the company's choice of site (the old Parr copper works) and of manager (Leith himself).[2] The chairman of the company (Col. T. J. Holland, Bombay Army, Retd.) reported to the shareholders in November, 1895, that

" We have proved and are daily practically demonstrating to the sceptical chemical world and to the expectant electrical profession, that purer and better bleach and caustic soda can be made by our simple electrical process than by any of the older processes"

and added that a licence had been granted at a cost of £6,000 for the use of their cell in Russia.[3] According to the Alkali Inspector, however, these works " were hardly in complete operation at the close of the year [1895]".[4] This, as the chairman of the company confessed later, was due to "the inefficiency of the first machinery supplied," an ominous admission. Nevertheless, by the end of 1897 the company had " excellent engines and dynamos," and was producing 70 tons of 70 per cent. caustic soda, 130 tons of 37-38 per cent. bleach and 5-6 tons of " exceptionally pure " chlorate of potash per week. Moreover, it had sold licences for the cell's use in Japan, France and Belgium, as well as in Russia, for £43,000 in all.[5]

But, despite these hopeful trumpetings, the Electro-Chemical Company, though it had the advantage of an early start, was unable to stay the course once its chief competitors had appeared. The Holland-Richardson cell was not so efficient and reliable as either Castner's or the Hargreaves-Bird cell and this reflected itself in relative production costs. By 1901 the St. Helens firm, remodelled in the previous year,[6] was attempting to sell out

---

[1] *Chem. Trade Jour.* 24 Feb., 1894.

[2] *St. H. N.* 8 Feb., 1896.

[3] *Chem. Trade Jour.* 23 Nov., 1895.

[4] 32nd Ann. Rep. (for 1895), 11.

[5] *Chem. Trade Jour.*, 27 Nov., 1897.

[6] *Ibid.*, 3 March, 1900.

and negotiations with possible foreign buyers were reported.[1] They came to nothing and the Electro-Chemical Company (1900) Ltd. was obliged to go into liquidation in 1904.[2] The hopes of a reprieve for the chemical industry at St. Helens were finally dashed. The United Alkali Co. Ltd. was left unchallenged in the district and during the first three decades of the present century the great Leblanc works at St. Helens were closed one by one. The chemical industry passed away, leaving behind many derelict acres of ugly alkali waste as a reminder of its former presence.

By then the copper industry had already left the area. In this case, competition came almost entirely from abroad. The Royal Commission investigating noxious vapours had reported in 1878 that :

> " the copper trade, so far from being in so flourishing a condition as to enable it to bear a large additional outlay, is unfortunately depressed and declining . . . The trade appears to have in large part been transferred to Chile which formerly supplied Swansea with copper ore."[3]

As more copper was smelted where it was mined, there was a decline in British smelting. Moreover, when Henderson's wet copper process came into more general use, the alkali maker took his supplies of sulphur from this new source rather than from the ' dry ' copper smelter. The British smelters, therefore, were obliged first to reduce their output and then to close down altogether. Newton Keates and Company at Sutton Oak, for instance, employed about a hundred men until the beginning of the 1890s, when the number was cut to sixty. In December 1895 the works were closed.[4] Baxter's Copper Works in Parr, as has been seen, were already closed by 1894 when the site was sold to the Electro-Chemical Company. By 1900 the only smelting works remaining at St. Helens were the smaller establishments employing the " wet " process.

In the 1890s it seemed as if the economic forces which had combined to bring about the growth of the town were now joining to bring about its downfall. Certainly the disappearance of " dry " copper smelting and the impending departure of the alkali trade were equivalent to the loss of one of the chief supports upon which the industrial life of the town rested. But the loss in

[1] *Ibid.*, 9 March, 1901.

[2] St. H. Town Hall. United Alkali Co. Ltd., Deeds, Baxter's Works. During the First World War a Gibbs diaphragm cell was set up at the Hardshaw Brook Works of the U. A. Co. Ltd. and this was operated until 1926 (information from Dr. D. W. F. Hardie).

[3] Report, 18.

[4] *St. H. N.* 7 Dec., 1895.

this case took place gradually and it was possible for the other main industry—glass manufacture—to bear the extra weight and prevent a more serious economic collapse.

Technical development, so disastrous to the local chemical industry, proved a great boon to the glassworks of the town. In particular, the introduction of Siemens' tank furnaces for the manufacture of window glass at Pilkingtons in 1874,[1] almost twenty years before such furnaces were used by their rivals, Chances, enabled the St. Helens firm to seize supremacy in that branch of the industry. As Mr. Walter Lucas Chance later confessed :

" it was the adoption of the tank system for making sheet glass by their St. Helens competitors . . . that finally deprived them of the predominant position which they had hitherto held."[2]

The local bottle manufacturers also adopted tank furnaces and, as will be seen presently, new machinery greatly influenced the development of the bottleworks and plate glass factories at St. Helens.

The glass industry had, however, to withstand foreign competition on a scale far larger than anything the manufacturing chemists knew. Its intensity may be seen from the following table of glass imports from Britain's chief competitor, Belgium.

AVERAGE ANNUAL IMPORTS OF PLATE AND WINDOW GLASS
FROM BELGIUM TO THE UNITED KINGDOM (£1,000s)[3]

			Plate		Window
1875-79	......	......	124	......	424
1880-84	......	......	132	......	358
1885-89	......	......	159	......	343
1890-94	......	......	275	......	333
1895-99	......	......	392	......	408

The trebling of the value of Belgian imports of plate glass occurred at the same period that the Americans, previously dependent on Europe for this product, started to make plate glass themselves. Already in 1883 a skilled glassmaker from Ravenhead, who had been enticed over to America in the hope of earning higher wages, was writing home about the newly-built factory near Pittsburgh

[1] Information from Pilkington Brothers Ltd.

[2] J. F. Chance, *A History of the Firm of Chance Brothers & Company* (privately printed, 1919), 279.

[3] Report of the Tariff Commission, Vol. VI (1907), tables 8 and 10.

where he had found employment. It was, he said, the fourth to
be started in that neighbourhood.[1] Ten years later the United
States possessed eight such works.[2]

The deluge of Belgian plate glass and the loss of American
customers affected St. Helens particularly for, as has been
noticed,[3] two-thirds of all the plate glass in the country was made
at its three plate glassworks in the 1860s and since that date the
opening of Pilkingtons' large factory at Cowley Hill made the
fraction even greater. The effect of this competition at home and
across the Atlantic may be illustrated by the history of the London
and Manchester Plate Glass Company during this period. This
was a large concern, employing 1,500 men at its Sutton Oak
factory and 1,200 at Ravenhead.[4]

Once the boom of the early 'seventies was over, there was a
constant and unchecked fall in prices ; in 1887 they stood 45
per cent. lower than they had been in 1876. In 1887 an association
was formed among the manufacturers which succeeded in raising
prices by about 26 per cent. by 1891 but this meant that they
were still 35 per cent. below their 1876 level. At this juncture
foreign competition was intensified. New works were opened
in Belgium, France and Germany. Britain was flooded with
foreign glass and it was no longer possible for English manufacturers to maintain prices on account of the extent of this
foreign interloping. They fell by 40 per cent. between 1891 and
1893 and stood at 60 per cent. below the 1876 level in June, 1893.
At the same time the McKinley Tariff of 1890 caused a reduction
in shipments of plate glass to the United States and the export
trade from St. Helens to America was described as " enormously
worse than at any period for a large number of years past."
To add to these perplexities, the coal strike of 1893 caused serious
interruptions at the works.

Confronted by these misfortunes, the London and Manchester
Company started to introduce more modern machinery for
grinding, smoothing and polishing their glass, but this programme
of re-equipment came to an abrupt end. In the two years following August 1891, there had been a loss of nearly £83,000 and when
the deficit grew by £60,000 in the following year, the chairman
thought it was high time to inform shareholders that the company was at the end of its tether. Faced with the prospect of
closing the works or increasing the share capital to continue
their re-equipment, it was decided to cease production. The

[1] *St. H. N.* 14 April, 21 July, 25 Aug., 1883.

[2] Clark, *op. cit.*, 796.

[3] Above, p. 363.

[4] *St. H. Lantern* 15 March, 1889. The following account is based upon
information given at meetings of the company in 1894. We are grateful
to Mr. Crouch, of Eyton Villa, Leach Lane, St. H., for newscuttings.

Sutton works were closed and the lease of Ravenhead surrendered. The latter was re-opened in 1895 by its owners, the British Plate Glass Company ;[1] the former was eventually purchased by a new company for about £150,000 and re-opened at the end of 1896. But it did not prosper. Plate glass was cast there for the last time in 1903.[2]

With one notable exception, the fate of the London and Manchester Plate Glass Company was suffered by the other plate glass concerns in the country. At St. Helens, the Union Plate Glass Company Ltd., at Pocket Nook, was in difficulties so early as 1889 when the directors sought to reduce the share capital " in consequence of losses through the depression in trade."[3] By the middle 1890s, despite re-equipment,[4] it was tottering to its fall. Glass ceased to be cast there before the end of the century.[5]

The only plate glass manufacturers to survive this widespread annihilation were Pilkington Brothers, from 1894 a limited company with share capital of £800,000.[6] They managed to maintain production only because they were not wholly dependent upon plate glass and were able to keep alive by the profits they made from other branches, particularly from window glass. But the drain was very serious indeed and could not be endured indefinitely. Fortunately for Pilkingtons and for St. Helens, the Belgian glass industry was irreparably weakened by a strike which broke out in August, 1900, and lasted until May, 1901.[7] This paved the way for the formation, in 1904, of an international syndicate of plate glass manufacturers which controlled output and prices.[8] The acquisition of the Ravenhead works in 1901 and the Sutton Oak works in 1905[9] considerably strengthened Pilkingtons' bargaining position when they came to meet the foreign manufacturers and thus helped to secure more favourable output quotas. Possession of these two factories also meant that, by the

[1] St. H. N. 27 June, 1896 ; *Now Thus, Now Thus* (Pilkington Brothers Ltd.), 58.

[2] St. H. N. 27 June, 4, 11 July, 1896 ; 29 May, 12, 26 June, 1903.

[3] St. H. N. 10 Aug., 1889.   The firm had become a limited company in 1864.

[4] St H. N., 26 Dec., 1891 ; 6 Feb., 15 Oct., 1892.

[5] According to Hudson A. Binney, manager at Sutton Oak, in a statement published in the St. H. N. 27 Nov., 1903, the Union Plate Glassworks were closed five years before.

[6] *Chem. Trade Jour.* 14 July, 1894.

[7] *The Times* 22 May, 1901 ; information kindly supplied by Mr. A. Cecil Pilkington.

[8] Annual Series of Diplomatic and Consular Trade Reports, 1905 [Cd. 2682] XXX.

[9] St. H. N. 15 Feb., 1901 ; 1 Sept., 1905 ; 21 Sept., 1906.   The Sutton Oak Works were used for warehousing purposes only.

beginning of the present century, Pilkington Brothers Ltd. of St. Helens had become not only the chief manufacturers of window glass in Britain but also the sole producer of cast plate glass.

The town's pre-eminence as a glassmaking centre was further emphasised by the rapid development of local bottlemaking. This branch of the industry started to expand rapidly about 1870 and in the following thirty years the three firms at St. Helens made great progress. By 1889 Cannington, Shaw and Company were employing 870 people at their Sherdley Glass Works, Nuttall and Co. at Ravenhead, 450, and Lyon Brothers of the Peasley Glass Works about 200.[1] Lyon Brothers became a limited company in 1886 with a share capital of £60,000[2] They attempted to reduce wages in the following year by introducing foreign workmen whom they brought over specially from Sweden. The arrival of the Swedes was the signal for a strike of the local bottle-makers and within a fortnight the foreign contingent was on its way home again, its repatriation having been financed by the bottlemakers' union.[3] Lyon Brothers Ltd. showed a loss of £200 on this year's working and the deficit grew to £2,600 in 1888.[4] In October, 1890, the Lyons finally admitted defeat and went out of business, their Peasley Glass works being purchased by Cannington, Shaw and Company.[5] In 1892, when Cannington, Shaws acquired limited liability with a share capital of £250,000[6] they were employing 1,188 men and women.[7] It was described later in the same year as the largest works of its kind in the world.[8]

Although bottlemaking machinery had already by the end of the 'eighties reached the stage when it could be used commercially, the Lancashire bottlemakers resolutely refused to countenance its introduction into their district. When in 1897 Cannington, Shaw and Co. finally decided to install machinery at Sherdley, the union at first forbade its members to work in the factory. But it was a little late in the day for such demonstrations. Negotiations followed, and three months afterwards the union agreed to the introduction of bottlemaking machines " so long as they are not injurious to us as workmen."[9] This new machinery

---

[1] *St. H. Lantern* 15, 22 March, 1889.

[2] *St. H. N.* 23 Jan., 1886.

[3] *The Lancashire Glass Bottle Trade*, 123-131 ; *St. H. Lantern* 3 Feb., 1887.

[4] *St. H. Lantern* 31 Oct., 1890.

[5] *The Lancashire Glass Bottle Trade*, 8.

[6] *Chem. Trade Jour.* 13 Feb., 1892.

[7] Royal Commission on Labour. Answers to Schedules of Questions. Group C., 1892 [C.6795—IX] XXXVI, 418.

[8] *Chem. Trade Jour.* 12 March, 1892.

[9] *The Lancashire Glass Bottle Trade*, 133-4.

caused the proprietor of a local engineering firm to enter the bottle industry. John Forster, who had served his apprenticeship at Robinson and Cook's and had been in business on his own account as iron founder and engineer first at Grove Street and then in Atlas Street, obtained the British rights for a semi-automatic bottlemaking machine. The bottle manufacturers, however, were very reluctant to use it, so Forster, rather than admit defeat, erected one in part of his works. The venture proved a great success, so much so, in fact, that he was later able to take over the vacant Union Plate Glassworks nearby for bottlemaking purposes.[1]

The St. Helens Flint Glassworks of S. and C. Bishop and Co., the only surviving flint glassworks in the town, appears to have continued more or less untroubled by the momentous happenings of these critical years. In 1892, 155 workpeople were employed there,[2] approximately the same number as thirty years before. For its failure to expand, the firm blamed restrictive practices on the part of the men :

" Large quantities of glass are imported from abroad which would be made in this country if we could get men to make it. One apprentice should be allowed to every two journeymen to meet the requirements of the trade. It is useless to spend money on technical education as long as the trades unions are allowed to prevent a reasonable number of boys from learning a trade in which there is ample scope for them."[3]

The occupation returns which form part of the decennial censuses provide a helpful summary of the main industrial trends at St. Helens towards the close of the nineteenth century.

Coalmining, the basis upon which all other industrial life in the neighbourhood depended, continued to grow in importance. In 1881, some 3,000 people living within the borough limits were employed in the industry. By 1901 this number had doubled, a rate of growth quicker than that of the population as a whole. The numbers at the local glassworks also grew during the same twenty years, from 3,764 to 6,255, and more than a quarter of

[1] *St. H. N.* 5 July, 1884 ; 28 April, 1894 ; 20 July, 1895 ; 22 Aug., 1896. Obit., *St. H. N.* 3 Jan., 1928. John Forster was keenly interested in politics and was elected to the Town Council in 1884. He played a great part in rallying the Liberal Party in the neighbourhood and in 1895 was chosen as their candidate for Parliament but was not returned.

[2] Royal Commission on Labour. Answers to Schedules of Questions. Group C., 1892 [C6795-IX] XXXVI, 417.

[3] *Ibid.*, 700.

these in 1901 were concerned with bottlemaking. By contrast, the chemical industry, which employed 1,132 in 1881 and reached a peak of 1,748 ten years later, slumped back again to 1,077 in 1901. The strength of metal workers, the core of which consisted of engineers and iron founders, increased from about 900 in 1881 to about 1,300 at the turn of the century, by which time domestic nailmaking and watchmaking were virtually extinct. More than 600 people still made a living in industries depending on the rich local clays. Many were engaged in making bricks and drainpipes ; the firm of Doulton and Co., for instance, continued to thrive at St. Helens, despite a change of site.[1] Not all those working in clay were concerned with bricks and sanitary ware, however. Away to the south of the town in the rural parts of Sutton, removed from the smoke and din, the potter could still be found sitting quietly at his wheel, as his predecessors in the craft had been doing in the same district time out of mind.

By the beginning of the present century, therefore, competition and new techniques were responsible for consolidating at St. Helens the industry that could benefit most from the raw materials available in the immediate vicinity ; the town had become the foremost glassmaking centre in the country, relying on the local coal and sand and, in the case of the bottlemaking branch, on the local clays as well. The copper industry, on the other hand, which depended on foreign ores, collapsed when those ores came to be smelted abroad, and the chemical industry, also dependent on raw materials from outside the St. Helens area, suffered a mortal blow in 1890 and was obviously doomed. Seen in perspective, the copper and chemical industries were unnatural growths, important to the local economy in their day, but subject to transport costs from which the glass industry was relatively free. The first important industrial arrival at St. Helens, glassmaking, survived the longest.

[1] As the result of a Chancery order of 10 April, 1891, Doulton and Co. agreed to sell their Greenbank Pottery to the neighbouring Greenbank Alkali Co. within five years for £9,000. The pottery was removed to Boundary Road, where Doultons already possessed a clay-hole. Pipemaking was started there in 1896 and bricks were made from surface clay until 1906 (Pilkington Brothers Ltd., United Alkali Co. Ltd. Deeds, Greenbank Works ; Memoir of A. E. Marshall at Doulton & Co. Ltd., Lambeth).

CHAPTER XXIX

SOCIAL CONDITIONS
1870-1900

IN Victorian St. Helens, as in other towns, there was always plenty of business for the undertaker and even more for any-one who sold cradles. An elderly inhabitant who died in 1866 had seen 23 of his grandchildren and 13 of his great grand-children die during his lifetime ; but these represented only a quarter of the total born and he still had 61 grandchildren and 37 great-grandchildren to tease him in his old age.[1] This particular family was mentioned in the local press at the time as being one of extraordinary size but there is no doubt that many others were not much smaller. The birth-rate at St. Helens was particularly high ; in the census year of 1871 it stood at 47.52 per 1,000 and it never fell below 40 until 1885, when a slight downward trend set in. By 1900 it had fallen to 37.3 These totals were far above the average for the country as a whole and considerably higher than those for either Liverpool or London where, in the early 1870s, the birth-rate stood at about 38 and 35 respectively.[2]

William Farr, the Victorian demograper, after many years of patient study, reached the conclusion that in the industrial towns

" the excess of births is due to the men getting good wages and bringing women there and marrying ; and there being a great excess of people at the child-bearing age, you consequently have a great excess of births ; and the population, increasing fast, attracts young men to the works."[3]

This would explain the high fertility rate at St. Helens ; but it does not suggest why it should have been higher than in other towns where the same conditions prevailed. The fact that St. Helens was a younger town than many of the others is certainly of relevance. Immigration continued on a considerable scale and most of the new arrivals were young people, in the prime of life. Reinforcements of Irish, for instance, were constantly arriving ; an editorial on the census of 1881 in one of the local newspapers commented on the " pretty constant inflow of stalwart young

---

[1] St. H. Standard 20 Jan., 1866.

[2] These and the following population figures are taken from the reports of the local Medical Officer of Health.

[3] Evidence of William Farr to the R.C. on Noxious Vapours, 1878, [2159] XLIV, q. 6865.

men from Ireland."[1] Perhaps one should also consider the possibility of a connexion between the preponderance of men in the local population[2] and the high birth-rate.

Whatever may have been the reason, or combination of reasons, for the high birth rate, the cause of the large number of deaths was left in no doubt, for the sanitary condition of the town was still most unsatisfactory.[3] This high mortality rate acted as a considerable brake upon the natural increase of the population ; during the years immediately after 1870 it usually stood at about 21 or 22 per 1,000 and was occasionally driven up by outbreaks of fever or disease, as in 1874 when it reached 30 during an outbreak of scarlet fever. There was, however, a tendency for the death-rate, like the birth-rate, to fall, and by the last years of the century it had dropped below 20.

In the early 1870s there were just over 2,000 births per year and 1,000 deaths ; and in the late 1890s about 3,000 and 1,600 respectively. Throughout the period there was a natural increase of about 35,750,[4] and a gain by migration of about 3,280. This occurred between 1871-81 and 1891-1901 but not in the intervening decade when there was a net loss by migration of 112.[5] In all, the population, which stood at 45,000 in 1871, gained 39,030, making the total 84,310 at the census of 1901.

The population thus increased by about the same number in these thirty years as it had done in the previous seventy. This meant that the builders were busier than ever, and the building force passed the thousand mark. The date stones on many of the houses show how the urban area was gradually enlarged during these later years of the century. The town limits were steadily advanced towards Windle City in the north, Denton's Green in the north-west, St. Ann's and Toll Bar[6] in the west, Robins Lane and St. Helens Junction in the south, and Blackbrook in the east.

---

[1] St. H. N. 30 April, 1881.

[2] Above, p. 427.

[3] Below, p. 466.

[4] The exact figure for 1873-80 was 8,665. There are no Medical Officer's reports for the years 1871 and 1872, so 8,665 has been taken as 80 per cent of the total for the decade.

[5] The population grew from 45,280 to 57,403 between 1871 and 1881, an increase of 12,123. The estimated natural increase during this decade was 10,831, giving a gain by migration of 1,292. The corresponding figures for 1881-91 were 11,225, 11,337 and —112 and for 1891-1901, 15,682, 13,582 and 2,100.

[6] Tolls continued to be levied by the Turnpike Trust until 1870 when the newly-formed Corporation assumed responsibility for the upkeep of the road to Prescot. St. H. N. 3, 31 July, 18 Sept., 1869 ; St. H. Standard 29 Jan., 1870 ; St. H. N., 13 May, 23 Dec., 1871.

Those residents who went to live in the new houses farther from the town centre—and often farther from their place of work—created a demand for a regular transport service and this, in turn, added to the attractiveness of what may perhaps by now be called the suburbs. The St. Helens and District Tramways Company Ltd., formed in 1879, started to run an hourly horse-tram service to Prescot in November, 1881, and lines were laid to Denton's Green, Peasley Cross and Haydock by the following spring.[1] Steam cars were introduced in 1889[2] but it was not until the coming of the electric tram ten years later that the company had a means of conveyance capable of forming the basis of a profitable transport undertaking.

By the later years of the century the town had grown to the point where generalisation becomes difficult. The complexities are such that the historian is aware of entering the province of the social scientist and wishes for the writings of a Booth or a Rowntree to draw upon. In the absence of any such contemporary analysis, he must be content to pick out two dominant themes. The first consists of the various social repercussions of the changing pattern of trade. The second deals with the craving for respectability and attempts to follow up some of the ideas on this outstanding feature of Victorian life mentioned in a previous chapter. These were two sharply-contrasted themes and they might be expected to produce a jarring discord when put together : a period of economic disturbance, including years of considerable depression and intensified competition, was hardly the most fitting time to indulge in sedate convention or polite ceremonial. But, as we shall see, the two themes, in fact, harmonised quite well.

The interruptions in trade caused hundreds of men to be thrown out of work for weeks on end ; unemployment in Britain was higher in the slump of 1878-79 than at any other time during the half century before 1914.[3] At St. Helens a central distress committee was formed to distribute soup and bread to 530 needy families and, in an effort to provide work, the Corporation took on additional hands for labouring jobs at 12s. a week.[4] Ten years later, when the town was in the grip of another widespread depression, the unemployed staged a protest meeting and some 500 workless attended it.[5] At the end of 1894 when the plate glassworks were closed and first one and then

[1] *St. H. N.* 2 Aug., 6 Sept., 1879 ; 5, 19 Nov., 1881 ; 6 May, 1882.

[2] *St. H. Lantern*, 2 Aug., 1889.

[3] W. W. Rostow, *British Economy of the Nineteenth Century* (Oxford, 1948), 181.

[4] *St. H. N.* 30 Nov., 14, 21 Dec., 1878 ; 11 Jan., 1 March, 1879.

[5] *St. H. N.* 17 March, 1888.

another of the alkali factories were idle for brief spells, the *St. Helens Newspaper* observed : " destitution is developing in our midst at a rapid rate."[1] Another distress fund was launched and the £1,350 raised helped to feed 400 familes during the hard winter months.[2] Trade picked up a little during 1895 and many glassmakers found work again in the following year when the Sutton Oak works resumed casting. The decision to hold a special service of thanksgiving is an indication of the importance attached to that event.[3]

Distress on this scale had been unknown since the severe slump of the early 'forties. It foreshadowed the future rather than reflected the past. But the Great Depression is in some ways a misnomer. Mechanisation, increased competition and cheaper foodstuffs from abroad brought down prices ; industrial production was greater *per capita* and real wages continued to rise.[4] This growth of real wages was an alleviating circumstance, though it could hardly offset the effects of short-time working to any great extent. The very successful co-operative venture, launched at the close of 1883, also had the effect of making the weekly earnings go farther. By the end of 1887, 2,000 townspeople had joined and, by 1892, 3,000. In 1899 almost half the population shopped either at the large central store in Baldwin Street, recently opened, or at one or other of the ten branches. More than £23,000 was in that year divided among the members.[5]

Greater numbers of workmen were protected by trade unions during this period than had been the case during earlier depressions. The Lancashire Miners' Federation, which came into being in 1881, pressed its wage claims with vigour and, with the Miners' Federation of Great Britain, formed in 1889, the men at last had a national body to safeguard their interests.[6] Miners' wages were advanced 40 per cent. between 1888 and 1890[7] and when the price of coal fell, the union resolutely opposed any wage reduction. This stand led to a lockout between July and October 1893 but the Miners' Federation withstood the owners' pressure and the existing rates were continued until the following year, when a board of conciliation in London, presided over by Lord Rosebery, agreed upon a 10 per cent. cut. This represented

[1] 15 Sept., 1894.

[2] *St. H. N.* 16 Feb., 23 March, 1895.

[3] *St. H. N.* 5 Dec., 1896.

[4] Rostow, *op. cit.*, 26.

[5] See appendix, 2

[6] R. Page Arnot, *The Miners: A History of the Miners' Federation of Great Britain, 1889-1910* (1949), 102.

[7] Sutton Heath Miners' Lodge. Price List Aug., 1917 ; Page Arnot, *op. cit.*, 116.

a considerable triumph for the miners, for the price of coal
had fallen by more than 20 per cent.[1] Much of their success
was due to the wise leadership and counsel of Samuel Woods,
a native of St. Helens, who was the first president of the
Lancashire Miners' Federation and vice-president of the Miners'
Federation of Great Britain from its formation until his death
in 1909.[2]

While the miners, long accustomed to trade unionism, were at
last achieving a working unity, the unorganised labourers at the
glass and chemical works of the town were starting to combine,
encouraged, no doubt, by the success of the New Unionism
elsewhere and the outcome of the Dock Strike. The United
Plate Glass Workers' Society, formed at the beginning of 1889,
claimed to have 800 members by June of that year,[3] though this
early promise was not sustained.[4] In the late autumn of 1889
P. J. King, an Irishman who had come to St. Helens as the
Liberals' registration agent, started to organise the alkali workers,
in the ranks of whom were so many of his fellow countrymen.[5]
In September, 1890, he stated that his Chemical and Copper
Workers' Union had 5,000 members[6] and in 1892 most of the
alkali workers in Lancashire were said to have joined.[7] Although
this union, like the plate glassmakers', lost many of its initial
members, it did bring about considerable improvements in the
chemical worker's lot. King's first annual report, issued in 1891,
included an impressive list of wage increases at the various

---

[1] Page Arnot, *op. cit.*, 209-11, chapter 8. *St. H. N.* 5 Aug., 18 Nov., 1893.

[2] Samuel Woods was born in Sutton on 10 March, 1846. He went to
help his father at the Pimbo Lane Colliery, Upholland, so it was later
said, at the age of seven, and at nine returned to school. He was a collier
at Laffak until 1875 and, while there, came under the influence of Frederick
Greening, master at the colliery school. Greening was a Baptist and in
June, 1863 Woods was himself baptised and eventually became a local
preacher. He became a check-weigher in 1875, an agent in 1881 and, so
that he might understand the problems of management the better, took
his manager's certificate in 1886. He was later a Member of Parliament.
St. H. Lantern 26 Oct., 1888 ; ev. of Woods to the R.C. on Explosions
from Dust in Coal Mines. First Rep. 1891, qq. 5182, 5194, 5263 ; Page
Arnot, *op. cit.*, 204.

[3] *St. H. N.* 22 June, 1889.

[4] According to a return to the R.C. on Labour, 1893 [7062-1] XXXIX,
97, there were only 112 members on 31 Dec., 1891.

[5] For King, see *St. H. N.* 23 Nov., 1889, 12 April, 1890 ; *St. H.
Lantern* 12 Sept., 1890 ; *St. H. Reporter* 25 May, 1894 ; *St. H. N.*
15 Sept., 1894 ; ev. of Patrick Healey, his successor as president of the
union, to the R.C. on Labour, 1893, qq., 22,313-8, 22,366.

[6] *Chem. Trade Jour.* 20 Sept., 1890.

[7] *Ibid.*, 26 March, 1892.

factories.[1] He was then pressing for eight-hour shifts and this aim was achieved a few years later.[2]

There was much room for improvement. Shortly after the union was formed, an employee at one of the local chemical works, in a letter to Mr. Gladstone complaining of the long hours, explained that they worked from 7 in the morning to 5 at night on the day shift and from 5 at night to 7 the next morning on night turn. They started the latter with a continuous shift of 24 hours from 8 o'clock on Sunday morning to 8 o'clock the next day and ended it with two spells from 5 p.m. on Friday until 6 a.m. on Saturday and again from 1 p.m. on Saturday until 8 o'clock the following morning : 112 hours' work in a week. The following week, when they were on the day shift, they worked 56 hours. The men who fired the pots had an even more laborious life. " For these men," wrote Mr. Gladstone's correspondent, " there is no New Year's Day, no Christmas Day, no Good Friday. These works ignore all such days. It is *one eternal round of drudgery*." In twelve years, the writer had not spent one of these holidays with his family.[3]

When this letter was published, critics were quick to point out that only the men who were responsible for maintaining continuous processes worked such long hours. Most of the labourers were employed from 6 in the morning until 5 at night from Monday to Friday and from 6 to 1 on Saturday.[4] They had no answer, however, to the facts concerning the almost unbearable lot of the skeleton staff who had to be on duty night and day. Nor was the unhealthiness of the work discussed in this correspondence. Details of this were revealed later by two official committees and by a journalist who " had to climb over the wall at the back " in order to get his story.[5]

The bleaching powder department was said to be " undoubtedly by far the most trying of all to those employed in chemical works."[6] Here men had to enter the Weldon chambers, which had been filled with chlorine for four days, and shovel out the powder while it was still intermixed with gas. They wore goggles over their eyes, and muzzles over their nose and

[1] *Ibid.*, 6 June, 1891.

[2] *St. H. N.* 25 July, 1896.

[3] The letter was published in the *Chem. Trade Jour.* 30 Nov., 1889.

[4] *Chem. Trade Jour.* 7 Dec., 1889.

[5] Report on the Conditions of Labour in Chemical Works, 1893 [C.7235] XVII. Mins. of ev. before group C. of the R.C. on Labour (vol. III), 1893. Robert H. Sherard, " The White Slaves of England," *Pearson's Magazine*, III, No. 4, 1896.

[6] Report on the Conditions in Chem. Works, 2.

mouth and smeared any exposed parts of their body with tallow as a protection. Sometimes, despite these precautions, they were overcome by gas and had to be revived by a dose of whisky. Some took to whisky as a regular antidote ; one of them claimed that he needed a glass three or four times a day and usually took another before he went to bed at night in order to sleep off the gas.[1] Admittedly, the pay was extremely good, 35s. to 50s. per week, and the hours short, less than six or seven per day ;[2] but this was small compensation for quickly-ruined health. Nor was the caustic department much less dangerous : a man at one factory lost an eye as a result of being splashed and his father died after falling up to the elbow into a caustic pot.[3] As a local doctor observed : " It would not be wise to pass a chemical yard man at the ordinary rate for life insurance."[4]

There appear to be good reasons for suggesting that these appalling conditions were to some extent the results of the industry's bitter struggle during the previous twenty years. In order to fight the ammonia-soda process many economies had to be made, and the bleaching powder department at each factory—where conditions were worst of all—was greatly extended as a result of the introduction of the Weldon process.[5] Although the chemical industry in the town was always renowned for its extremely unpleasant and laborious jobs, it would be unwise to assume too readily that because conditions were bad in 1890 they must necessarily have been worse forty or fifty years earlier. In this particular industry the reverse would seem to have been true.

By 1890 these new unions, together with others of longer standing, were co-operating together for political ends. Two attempts had been made earlier in the century to form a Trades Council. Of the first, all that is known is that it was in being in 1867.[6] The second was formed in 1885 but was disrupted by internal tension between the skilled and the unskilled unions.[7] The third attempt, however, was successful.

This arose out of a meeting called in September, 1890, by

[1] Ev. of John Carey to the R.C. on Labour, qq. 22,519, 22, 523-4.

[2] *Ibid.*, qq. 22,502, 22,551.

[3] Ev. of Robert Hankinson. Report on the Conditions in Chem. Works qq. 138, 175-82.

[4] Quoted by Sherard, 49.

[5] The chambers used in the Deacon process of bleaching powder manufacture were less unhealthy but there were none at St. Helens. Ev. of John Beetle in Report on the Conditions in Chem. Works, q. 107.

[6] *St. H. N.*, 16 March, 1867.

[7] *St. H. N.*, 19 Sept. 1885 ; 27 Sept., 1890.

Thomas Glover, the miners' agent,[1] and attended by representatives of seventeen unions.[2] In all, twenty-four trades eventually joined and Thomas Glover became the first secretary.[3] At the local elections a month later Robert Hunter, the bottle-makers' leader, gave notice of the new political influence that had just been created by defeating William Windle Pilkington in the North Eccleston Ward.[4] Although the Trades Council had its teething troubles and the old schism between the skilled and unskilled unions recurred,[5] its formation foreshadowed the sweeping changes of later years. At the close of 1902 the Labour Representation Committee was approached by the Trades Council and the local Socialist Society about a suitable candidate for the next parliamentary election. The miners pressed Glover's claim, while many of the other representatives preferred another candidate. Glover was adopted by a vote of more than two to one on 29 August, 1903,[6] and he was returned as the first Labour

[1] Thomas Glover was born at Prescot, 1852. His father, a collier, removed to Blackbrook 18 months later. He himself went down the pit at the age of ten and experienced " every stage of a miner's life, short of being manager " until 1884 when he succeeded John Cross as miners' agent for the district. Although a Radical Liberal, he was already, in 1888, in favour of sending independent Labour Members to Parliament, and thought that " a real Conservative working-man ought to be put in a museum as a curiosity." Interview in *St. H. Lantern*, 26 Oct., 1888.

[2] *St. H. N.*, 11 Oct., 1890. These were : J. Bradbury, St. Helens United Plate Glass Workers' Society. Robert Hunter, Glass Bottle Makers' Trade Protection Association. Henry Johnson and Joseph Shewell, Glass Bottle Makers' Society. T. Seddon, Flint Glass Makers' Society. Joseph Chisnall and Thomas Farrell, General Union of House Carpenters. G. Wilkinson and William Battersby, Miners' Federation. William Croft, J. Kirkham and James Taylor, Amalgamated Society of Carpenters and Joiners. Fred Eden, James Cross and Joseph Goulding, Engine Winders' Society. Thomas Clitheroe and John Jones, Coopers' Society. John Davies, Robert Dancer and Thomas Fishwick, Stonemason's Society. John Murkett and John Fowles, Amalgamated Society of Railway Servants. Robert Logan and W. Jackson, Plasterers' Society. Edward Skelland, Painters' Society. James Chadwick, Chemical Workers' Union. George Abbott, Operative Bricklayers' Society. R. Billington, Life Insurance Agents' Society. James Winstanley, Journeyman Cloggers' Society. *St. H.. N.* 27 Sept., 1890.

[3] *St. H. N.* 11 Oct., 1890.   [4] *St. H. N.* 25 Oct., 8 Nov., 1890.

[5] *St. H. N.* 27 Jan., 1894.

[6] Minutes of the Joint Committee of the St. Helens Trades Council and the St. Helens Socialist Society to consider the advisability of adopting a direct and independent Labour candidate for the Parliamentary Borough of St. Helens. The Secretary of the committee was J. H. Standring who in 1910 left St. Helens to become the Lancashire Divisional Organiser of the I.L.P., an office he held until 1918. He was afterwards divisional organiser and agent at Bermondsey and at Rushcliffe and then North Western Area Organiser of the Labour Party until his death in 1928. The Minutes of the Joint Committee of 1903, together with other material relating to the early Labour movement at St. Helens are in the possession of Mrs. Standring, to whom we are indebted for lending them to us.

M.P. for the town at the election of 1906. The Town Council, too, soon had a Labour majority.

The growth of real wages and the spread of trade union activity both helped to maintain a steady rate of social progress despite the disturbances of trade. And, as the town expanded, stabilising forces grew more powerful. The inhabitants had ceased to be a diverse collection of country folk playing their part in the creation of a town : for every newcomer between 1870 and 1900, ten people were born and bred in the town itself and many more had qualified as townspeople by many years' residence. They possessed an urban outlook. The spontaneity and exuberance of the countryman were fading away into the past. In their place came discipline, order and, above all, organisation. The factory hooter was heard at St. Helens for the first time in January, 1869.[1]

This new urban outlook came to pervade the inhabitants' leisure as well as their working hours. As the half holiday became general, there was more time for sport. But it was sport of a different kind from the rough games to which earlier generations had been accustomed. There were no prize fights, secretly organised when the police were not looking. The collier no longer went in for " up and down " fisticuffs in his clogs. Instead, there arose the sports club which promoted games that were played according to rules.

The local press started to report football matches in the early 1880s and in 1888 the town, which already possessed its " Saints " and " Recs," was described as " a hotbed of Rugbyism."[2] Cricket, too, was well organised by this time and each club issued an imposing fixture list at the beginning of the season. The ramblers had their own club by the early 1870s[3] and the runners formed themselves into the St. Helens Harriers ten years later.[4] But the most characteristic clubs of all, truly symbolic of the age, were those which catered for the enthusiasts of that new-fangled creation—the bicycle.

Cycles were first manufactured in quantity during the 1870s[5] and by 1878 it was reported that " the choice of bicycle has now become quite a serious matter ; there is such a multitude of different makes."[6] The St. Helens Cycling Club was formed in

---

[1] *St. H. N.* 6, 13, 20 Feb., 1869.

[2] *St. H. Lantern* 16 Feb., 18 March, 1888. The St. Helens Recreation Football Club was started in 1879. Art. by H. Logan, *Cullet*, Jan., 1929.

[3] *St. H. Standard* 13 June, 1874.

[4] *St. H. N.* 24 April, 1886.

[5] Clapham, *Economic History of Modern Britain*, II, 96-7

[6] *St. H. Leader*. 1 July, 1878.

May, 1876 by (Sir) Joseph Beecham and W. J. Ashton.[1] Although the members, wheelists or wheelmen as they were called, must all have been fairly well-to-do—the early bone-shakers cost about £20 each—their activities attracted a large popular following. The route of the annual championship race along the turnpike from Warrington to Prescot and from there back to St. Helens became so thronged with eager spectators that regular traffic was held up.[2] The cyclists' feats of endurance over long distances also excited widespread attention. A local wheelist, described as the Sub-Captain of the St. Helens Club, set off from Land's End at midnight on 12 August, 1888, on his Rudge's Number One Tricycle in an attempt to break the record for a ride to John o' Groats. He reached Edinburgh in 106 hours having had only $2\frac{1}{2}$ hours' sleep on the journey. This was a distance of 704 miles, and he estimated that he had ridden a further 100 miles by taking the wrong turnings.[3]

These more refined methods of revealing one's prowess were in keeping with the times. They reflect the changes that were taking place in social habits and illustrate the prevailing trend towards a more settled and routine life. As such, they were an integral part of the rise of respectability. In this process there was often a strong element of expediency. The churches' campaign against drunkenness, for instance, was an attempt to stamp out what had recently become a serious public menace. This same element of expediency may also be seen in the sphere of education.

Although the town continued to be relatively well served with elementary schools, there was a shortage of schools capable of providing courses of a more advanced nature. As more complex processes came into general use at local factories, employers began to clamour for the provision of technical education. At the same time middle class parents wanted a school other than the existing privately-run commercial academies to which they could send their children. To meet this need, the trustees of Cowley's Charity in 1874 put forward a scheme whereby the income from the trust would be devoted to a boys' and girls' Middle School. The existing Cowley Schools were to continue to provide elementary education but were to be financed by the Government grants that were then available. The Middle School was to be for boys and girls between 8 and 17 whose parents could pay yearly tuition fees of £4 to £8 with an extra charge of not more than £3 for those boys who used the laboratory. The headmaster was to be a university man and of the governors, six

[1] *St. H. N.*, 17 June, 1876 ; *St. H. Lantern* 16 Feb., 1878. A second club, the Excelsior was formed two years later. *St. H. N.* 20 March, 1880.

[2] *St. H. Lantern* 8 March, 1888.

[3] *St. H. Lantern* 20 Sept., 1888.

were to be elected by the Town Council and six co-opted.[1] These proposals were approved but there was a long delay before the necessary building fund could be raised. Even when building had been started, operations had to be suspended for lack of funds and it was not until October, 1882, that the schools in Cowley Hill Lane were opened.[2]

Meanwhile the Science and Art Department had already begun to hold evening classes in the town[3] and a Literary and Scientific Association had been formed for adults.[4] But these new creations did not suffice to provide all the necessary technical knowledge which the employers demanded. They were conducted on too small a scale. There were, for instance, fewer than 130 boys at the Middle School nine years after its opening.[5] The early '90s, however, witnessed great strides. The Act of 1889 which permitted the Council to levy a penny rate for technical education, and the income from " whisky money " which was granted for the same purpose in the following year, led to the formation of a Technical Education Committee which took charge in 1892 of the classes previously run by the Science and Art Department.[6] In the following year there were 23 evening classes and the Committee was hard pressed for accommodation ; even the court room had to be used on one occasion.[7] It was at this critical juncture that David Gamble offered to build a technical school " for the purpose of assisting our people to make themselves equal or superior to those countries where technical education has been an institution for a great number of years."[8] This most generous, though not entirely disinterested, gesture was accepted at once and the Gamble Institute, which cost its

[1] St. H. Town Hall. Papers of the Cowley Trustees. Endowed Schools Commission. Scheme for the Management of the Charitable Foundation of Sarah Cowley at St. Helens in the County of Lancaster.

[2] *St. H. N.* 9, 14 Oct., 1882. Of the total cost of £15,000, £5,000 was raised from the accumulated funds of the Trust, £1,600 from the sale of Consols., £3,200 from the Governors and £3,000 from the general public. £2,500 was raised by a loan. The first headmaster was E. J. Simpson, M.A. (Cantab.) and the first headmistress, Kate Jurgenson, L.L.A. (St. Andrews). L.L.A. stood for Ladies Licentiate in Arts, a qualification granted to women from 1877 until they came to be admitted to full membership of St. Andrews University. (Information from Dr. D. W. F. Hardie on the authority of two L.L.As. Cf. R.G.Cant., *University of St. Andrews* (1946), 120).

[3] *St. H. N.* 5 Oct., 1878.

[4] *St. H. N.* 31 Jan., 1880.

[5] St. H. Town Hall. Papers of the Cowley Trustees. Return of the R.C. on Secondary Education.

[6] *St. H. N.* 6 Oct., 1894.

[7] *Ibid.*

[8] *Ibid.*

donor £25,000, was opened on 5 November, 1896.[1] It became
the home of the Public Library as well as of technical education
in the town.

There were still such opportunities for private benefactors to
provide public services. The local hospitals furnish another
example of this. Peter Greenall broached the need for an infirmary in the early 1840s and the matter was repeatedly raised
subsequently without any action being taken.[2] When in October,
1872, John Fenwick Allen, the copper smelter, visited A. G.
Kurtz to solicit a donation for the Ragged School, Kurtz urged
him to find a suitable building for a hospital and promised to
provide the money to equip it.[3] Fenwick Allen decided upon
part of a house near Peasley Cross, which he leased from Michael
Hughes for £20 a year. Although a portion of the building was
still occupied, the part which was acquired for the hospital had
been untenanted for some time and was in a very dilapidated
condition : the windows were out, slates were missing from
the roof and the plaster was crumbling off the walls. Michael
Hughes repaired and painted the outside and an expenditure of
£462 put the interior to rights again. Three rooms were furnished
and nine beds installed. Mrs. Martha Walker, a Quaker lady of
wide experience and determined character, who had served in an
American hospital camp during the Civil War and was in Paris
during the Commune, was chosen as the first matron, and three
little orphan girls were obtained from the Whiston workhouse
to help her. Such were the humble origins of the Cottage
Hospital, opened in January, 1873.[4]

There is no indication that, even at this late stage, the hospital
was looked upon as an essential institution. The management
committee was lax in its attendance and the matron, content with
nothing but the best, soon ran up a debt of more than £1,000.
Kurtz again intervened : he purchased the whole house and
three acres of land surrounding it and presented them to the
town. Mrs. Walker, who refused to economise, was obliged
to resign in October, 1875. A penny-a-week fund was launched,
the debt was paid off and the new institution at last began
to prosper. By 1882 the weekly pennies added up to almost
£500 over a year. Shortly afterwards the number of beds was
increased to 36 and in 1894 it was further increased to 50. Four

[1] *St. H. N.* 7 Nov., 1896.

[2] *St. H. Intelligencer* 15 Aug., 1857 ; *St. H. Weekly News* 8, 15 June,
1861 ; *St. H. Standard* 14 July, 16, 23 Sept., 1865 ; 6 Jan., 1866 ; 26 March,
1870.

[3] The following account is based upon articles by J. Fenwick Allen in the
St. H. Lantern, 10 Nov., 1887 and the *St. H. N.* 1904 or 1905, the latter
to be found under " St. Helens—Hospitals " at the St. H. Ref. Lib.

[4] *St. H. N.* 11 Jan., 1873.   Each patient paid 1/- per day.

years later the handsome bequest of £27,000 by Miss Ann Jane
Garton, the daughter of a local doctor,[1] provided the hospital
with an additional income of more than £700 a year. This en-
encouraged the management committee to embark upon further
extensions which were completed in 1904.

Meanwhile a second hospital had been opened in Hardshaw
Hall by a Roman Catholic order, the Poor Servants of the Mother
of God, who had been nursing from 1882 at a house in George
Street.[2] The Providence Hospital, as it was called, was opened
on 15 September, 1884, by Cardinal Manning.[3] It also benefited
in due course from Miss Garton's generosity.

Despite these notable examples, the field of benevolence and
private initiative was being curtailed as the scope of local government was extended. The isolation hospital, unlike the general
hospitals, was a municipal responsibility from the outset.[4] The
privately-owned St. Helens Gas Light Company was acquired
by the Corporation in 1878 after it had supplied the town with
gas for almost fifty years and, towards the end of the century,
the Corporation took the initiative in providing an electricity
supply.[5] It also leased the baths from Kurtz and in 1890 built
larger ones in Boundary Road.[6] So far as water supply was concerned, the battle with the private company had already been
fought ; the Corporation gradually increased its sources of
supply as more consumers were connected to the rapidly-growing
network of pipes. Pumping stations were opened at Whiston
in 1872, Collins Green Colliery in 1878, Knowsley in 1886 and
Kirkby in 1891.[7]

In 1873 Robert McNicoll, a doctor who had been in practice
at St. Helens since 1848, was appointed the town's first Medical
Officer of Health. It was a good choice, for Dr. McNicoll had
considerable experience of the workings of local government
as well as a sound medical knowledge, the fruits of a three-year
training at Dublin, Liverpool Royal Infirmary and St. Thomas's

[1] For her father, William Garton, F.R.C.S., who died 3 March, 1847,
see the vault in the Old Graveyard, St. Helens and Letters of Admin. at
the L.R.O.

[2] *St. H. N.* 18 Feb., 4 March, 1882.

[3] *St. H. N.* 20 Sept., 1884.

[4] *St. H. N.* 21 Aug., 4 Nov., 1880 ; 17 March, 1894.

[5] *St. H. Leader* 1 Feb., 1878 ; *St. H. N.* 24 Nov., 1883. The first power
station, at the gasworks, supplied electricity to private consumers at 6d.
per unit. *St. H. R.*, 4 Dec., 1896. A small generating plant had previously
supplied the Town Hall and Gamble Institute.

[6] *St. H. N.* 13 April, 1878, 2 Aug., 1890.

[7] *St. H. N.* 26 Aug., 1871, 25 May, 1872, 1 June, 1878, 12 June, 1886,
23 May, 1891.

Hospital in London. He had been a member of the Improvement Commission from 1859 and its chairman in 1864-65. When the town was incorporated, he became one of the first aldermen.[1] As Medical Officer, he exercised great vigilance and in his annual reports was forever pleading for the improvement of the town's grossly inadequate sanitary arrangements. But his advice was rarely heeded. In particular, the vital trunk sewer to replace the open brook, which had been projected and promised at the time of Ranger's visit in 1855, was not even started until 1889, and then the Council was only stirred to action by a widespread outbreak of typhoid in the course of which six guests contracted the disease at a mayoral banquet in the town and two of them died.[2] The trunk sewer was constructed in two stages ; to Ashcroft's Bridge and then to the Old Double Locks. It was not until 1895 that this long-delayed but very important piece of sewerage was within sight of completion.[3] No wonder the death rate was so slow in falling !

By the end of the century the town did, however, possess a few open spaces where the inhabitants could escape from the bricks and mortar during their leisure time. The Corporation had to buy all but one of these parks and recreation grounds. The one exception was Taylor Park, presented to the town by Samuel Taylor in 1893.[4] Of the others, Thatto Heath was bought from the Crown in 1884 for £600,[5] and Cowley House and its surrounding 31 acres were bought from the trustees of John Ansdell for £11,000. The latter estate was opened to the public in June, 1886, and named Victoria Park in the following year as part of the Jubilee celebrations. The house later accommodated the St. Helens Museum.[6] The smaller Queen's and

[1] For McNicoll, see interview in *St. H. Lantern* 5 July, 1888 and obit. *St. H. N.* 3 Nov., 1894.

[2] *St. H. N.* 8 Dec., 1888, 8 June, 1889.

[3] *St. H. N.* 25 Feb., 1895.

[4] *St. H. N.* 20 May, 1893. Samuel Taylor removed to Westmorland c. 1850 and leased Eccleston Hall to William Pilkington. He returned to Eccleston a few years before his death in 1881. His son having predeceased him, the estate passed to his grandson who lived near Newby Bridge in north Lancashire. The rest of the Eccleston estate, apart from what became Taylor Park, was sold to the Greenall family. *Prescot Reporter* 9 April, 1881 ; *V. C. H. Lancs.*, III, 365 ; *St. H. N.* 25 Feb., 1893.

[5] Return of the Charity Commissioners for the County Borough of St. Helens, 1905, 66 ; *St. H. N.*, 5 April, 1884 ; 7 Feb., 1885.

[6] *St. H. N.* 19 June, 1886 ; *Lpool. Weekly Post* 27 March, 1886. Ansdell was a local solicitor with various business interests. He acquired part of the Cowley Hill Estate after the death in 1847 of John Speakman—he himself had married the widow of John's brother, Richard Speakman—and built Cowley House in 1849-50. *Lpool. Merc.* 22 Feb., 1850 ; obits. *St. H. N.* and *Prescot Reporter* 7 Nov., 1885.

Parr Recreation Grounds were purchased in 1899 and 1900 respectively.[1]

To their contemporaries all these amenities and improvements were but the visible fruits of progress, the legitimate return for their successful labours. To anyone like David Gamble, whose life spanned the growth of the town, it could hardly have seemed otherwise. He had watched the place grow from an outsized village to a large and flourishing borough. He had guided the fortunes of his business from very modest and faltering beginnings until it had become a large and prosperous concern and had seen other factories grow up all around. He had every reason to have pride in his generation which had accomplished so much, and faith in progress which seemed inevitable.

The creation of the town within the space of little more than half a century, it was felt, redounded to the credit of all its inhabitants. This was made clear from the attitude taken before the town's incorporation : St. Helens, it was contended, deserved a municipal charter because it had earned the privilege. Other symbols of urban success were accepted later as matters of right : the Borough Bench in 1882,[2] separate Parliamentary representation in 1884[3] and County Borough status in 1889.

As with the town, so with its leading inhabitants ; they too, deserved recognition : a seat on the Council, a place on the Bench, or the Mayoral Chain were their perquisites. Some even had hopes of a seat in Parliament : when the Borough was enfranchised, David Gamble, Arthur Sinclair and John Forster each in turn tried to secure election.[4] The publication of the Gamble, Haddock and Pilkington pedigrees was in keeping with the spirit of the times. So, too, was the raising of public subscriptions to have portraits of some of the leading townsmen painted. Gamble's cost nine hundred guineas.[5]

---

[1] Report of the Charity Commissioners, 1905 [313], C, 68.

[2] *St. H. N.* 29 April 1882. The new Borough Bench consisted of the nine existing J.P.s: David Gamble, J. C. Gamble, H. S. Hall, William Windle Pilkington, Richard Pilkington, William (Roby) Pilkington, Thomas Pilkington, Dr. Twyford and William Blinkhorn, together with nine additional magistrates : Joseph Cook, J. Harrison, James McBryde, James Radley, A. Walmesley, Dr. R. A. Gaskell, Arthur Sinclair, Henry Baxter and C. J. Bishop. The town had previously possessed a court for the collection of small debts ; the Court of Requests was established in 1841 (*C.J.* 96, 12 Feb., 24 May, 21 June, 1841) and this was replaced by a County Court in March, 1847 (*Lpool. Merc.* 12 March, 1847). The County Court was housed at the corner of East Street and Market Street from April, 1866 (*St. H. Standard* 14 April, 1866).

[3] *St. H. N.* 6 Dec., 1884. The first M.P. for the town was elected in Nov., 1885. For a summary of the political history in the nineteenth century, see Appendix I.

[4] Appendix I.

[5] *St. H. N.* 7 Sept., 1889.

When these patriarchal civic leaders had occasion to speak about their road to success, they were able to cite a long and impressive record of achievement, the result of painstaking effort and true economy. Their story could be repeated on a smaller scale by many of those who moved in humbler walks of life. Whatever his occupation might be, the man who " got on " and bettered his position in the world looked upon the respect of his fellows as his due.

In these years when attitudes were changing, opinion hardened against many of the institutions which had been willingly tolerated and, indeed, welcomed in former years. The murmurs of criticism against the biannual fair and its accompanying carefree lack of restraint grew into an active campaign with the result that it was forbidden to be held after April, 1882.[1] As the temperance and teetotal movements gathered way, the public house was frowned upon, if not condemned, by many. Even the theatre aroused sharply divided opinions.[2]

In their place many more seemly pursuits and occupations were encouraged, such as the organised sports which have already been mentioned. The churches took the lead by providing a wider range of week-night activities. Concerts were held ; the " Messiah " was performed at St. Helens for the first time in January, 1874, for instance, with local choirs and principals and instrumentalists from Manchester ; although a critic tartly commented that " it seemed as if sweetness were sacrificed to volume,"[3] the oratorio became an annual event in the town. There were also opportunities to hear more professional performances, such as those given by the D'Oyly Carte Opera Company on its regular visits from the middle of the '80s onwards.

Debating was very much in vogue at this time and a St. Helens Parliamentary Debating Society was formed. Those who participated were able to make a study of the various styles employed by visiting politicians such as John Burns, David Lloyd George and John Morley, all of whom spoke at St. Helens within the space of a month in 1890.[4] Those who preferred the academic lecture were also catered for. A fairly close liaison had already grown up with University College Liverpool by the end of the '80s and members of the staff were often heard in the

---

[1] St. H. Ref. Lib. Newscutting *sub.*, April, 1882.

[2] Sir Thomas Beecham, *A Mingled Chime* (1944), 16. The Theatre Royal in Corporation Street, opened in 1890, was gutted by fire nine years later. The present theatre was opened in 1901. James Brockbank, *A History of the Drama in St. Helens* (St. H., 1901).

[3] *St. H. N.* 24 Jan., 1874.

[4] *St. H. N.* 6 Sept., 4 Oct., 1890.

town. Professor Oliver Lodge was among those who paid several visits.[1]

Not that the town was short of talent of its own. The legal profession produced more than its quota. H. Linden Riley sparkled wherever he appeared, especially in the pages of the *St. Helens Lantern* which he edited before he went to the Liverpool Bar. One of his predecessors there, Thomas Swift, had also been a solicitor at St. Helens, and his son, Rigby Swift, born at St. Helens in 1874, followed in his father's footsteps. He was even more successful, entered politics, became M.P. for St. Helens in 1910 and was created a judge in 1920.[2]

The most colourful character of all, however, made his first big public appearance in the town right at the end of the century. (Sir) Thomas Beecham, the grandson of the founder of the pill firm, was born at St. Helens in 1879 and grew up, as he tells us, in a house overflowing with musical boxes.[3] He was put to study the piano at an early age by his father (Sir) Joseph Beecham, his first teacher being Oswald Barton, organist at St. Mary's, Lowe House.[4] When in his seventh year the family moved out to Huyton, his piano teacher from St Helens continued to give him lessons.[5] He became as enthusiastic a musician as his father and his keenness grew during his schooling at Rossall and his brief college life at Oxford. In 1899 St. Helens was the scene of his *début* as a conductor. He formed an orchestra in the town consisting of local talent with a leaven of professional players, and (as he himself has put it) " burst upon my fellow townsmen with a series of classical concerts. At once I realised that here was the medium which I had vainly sought in the piano or any other solo instrument."[6] It so happened that his father, Mayor in that year, had arranged for the Hallé Orchestra to give a concert in the town. At the last minute Hans Richter, their celebrated conductor, was unable to appear and Beecham suggested to his father that he could conduct in his stead. His father—and the orchestra—eventually agreed: as Sir Thomas later reflected, his father probably saw advertising possibilities in the move.[7] So the people of St. Helens were able to witness one of their own townsmen, though not yet twenty years of age, conducting what many thought to be the finest British orchestra of the day.

[1] *St. H. Lantern* 16 Feb., 18 March, 1888 ; 30 March, 1889.

[2] For Rigby Swift and references to his father and H. Linden Riley, see E. S. Fay, *The Life of Mr. Justice Swift* (1939).

[3] Beecham, *op. cit.*, 12.

[4] B.B.C. broadcast by Sir Thomas Beecham together with additional information, published in the *St. H. R.* 13 March, 1953.

[5] Beecham, *op. cit.*, 13-4.

[6] *Ibid.*, 34.

[7] *Ibid.*, 35.

It is an interesting paradox that this rather drab and certainly inartistic industrial town happened to be the place where the man who was destined to become the country's foremost orchestral conductor first decided what his medium of musical expression was to be. In its turn, this pioneer Beecham concert serves to emphasise the new spirit in the town ; such a concert could not have been held fifty, or even thirty, years earlier.

The people of St. Helens made the most of the period immediately after the main rough-and-tumble of unorganised urban growth was over, to settle down and engage in more genteel pursuits. They were able to do so because of their firm faith in the inevitability of progress along existing lines. Industrialisation had brought about a general improvement in living standards. A handful had made fortunes ; a small number were occupying well-paid positions ; the vast majority enjoyed a higher standard of living than their predecessors had done. Why should the march of progress not continue along this well-tried road ?

This optimistic outlook was already, however, giving way to doubts. The dislocation of the town's industries was a very clear sign of an age that was passing. The increased scale of the public services, the curbing of unplanned individualism and the new political winds that were already starting to blow strongly, were further indications of change. Progress there was indeed to be. But it was not continuous nor was it along the lines mapped out by the leaders of the nineteenth century.

APPENDIX I

POLITICS AT ST. HELENS

1832-1900

ST. HELENS did not become a Parliamentary Borough until 1884. For the greater part of the century, therefore, we are concerned merely with an aspect of the Lancashire county elections and with the growth of the local electorate.

This was a slow and not particularly lively process. There was not even a polling station in the town prior to 1859 and the electors had to journey into Newton in order to declare their votes. The Legh Arms in that town was the centre of political activity for the neighbourhood at election time, though there is evidence that, in Peter Greenall's day, there was a considerable amount of priming of the local freeholders beforehand. A correspondent complained to the Liberal *Liverpool Mercury* in 1835 that

" On the day of nomination of the candidates for South Lancashire, a quantity of beef, mutton, etc. was purchased and distributed among the proprietors of freehold tenements in St. Helens and the immediate neighbourhood (of which, by the by, there is no scarcity) and sent with Mr. ——s respects and should be glad if Mr. —— would vote for his friends Egerton and Wilbraham ; to others a cask of ale was sent with the kind assurance that should they want it refilled, the request would be complied with. With some, good beef and wholesome malt liquor (being home-brewed) had not the desired effect ; but this was easily obviated by presenting the obsequious spouse with seventeen or eighteen yards of silk. Their manoeuvres did not terminate here ; in order to swell out their list of *free* and *independent* voters, the living were dragged to the hustings to speak the sentiments of the dead and the healthy to personate the sick."[1]

There were, however, very few occasions for such engaging and profitable diversions to take place. An appeal was made to the electorate of South Lancashire in 1833, 1835 and 1837. But between 1837 and 1859 the two seats were not contested at any

[1] *Lpool. Merc.* 6 Feb., 1835.

general election and there was only one by-election. This occurred in 1844 ; a large meeting was staged at the Town Hall on behalf of the Free Trade candidate and this was addressed by Cobden.[1] If the leading townspeople held strong views upon the events of the day, they had few enough opportunities to air them.

With the opening of a separate polling station at St. Helens in 1859 there was a sensible quickening in the interest taken in the election even though there were still only 500 voters on the local lists. Both sides formed their own committee to sponsor meetings at which their candidates were to speak. Most of the leading industrialists of the neighbourhod, though by no means all of them, were ranged, as would be expected, in the Liberal camp. James Shanks was chairman of their local committee which included David Gamble, A. G. Kurtz, William Blinkhorn, Francis Dixon, John Merson, L. W. Evans, A. R. Arrott, and James Radley. In addition, Richard and William Pilkington, Arthur Sinclair and James McBryde were closely associated with the Liberal cause. The Conservative leaders included fewer industrialists, though Robert Daglish, junior, Samuel Bishop and the Bromilows were staunch supporters. But the Tories were able to exert much influence on account of their landed property : the Gerard, Hughes, Taylor and Greenall families were all ranged on the Conservative side. And their party also controlled the only local paper. The Tories had won at the elections in South Lancashire in 1835, 1837 and 1844 (though a Liberal filled one of the seats by arrangement after 1846) and the St. Helens electorate voted in the ratio of two to one for Egerton and Legh, the Conservative candidates, in 1859.[2]

The heat generated by the 1859 election may be said to have aroused local interest in politics at last. Dromgoole, who had been the Vice-President of the Liberals' district committee, launched his *St. Helens Newspaper* in 1860 (above, p. 384) and started at once to attack the brewing interests (i.e., the Greenalls) and the prevalence of " corruption." When in August, 1861, another election was held—this time to fill a third seat which had just been bestowed upon South Lancashire—the Liberals put up a

[1] *Lpool. Merc.* 24 May, 1844. Josias Christopher Gamble also spoke. The Free Traders had organised a meeting at St. Helens in the previous November. It was presided over by Joseph Crosfield of Warrington, and F. Fincham of the Ravenhead Plate Glassworks was also present. For details of the South Lancashire elections, see D. Pink and A. B. Beavan, *The Parliamentary Representation of Lancashire, 1258-1885* (1889) and W. W. Bean, *The Parliamentary Representation of the Six Northern Counties of England* (Hull, 1890).

[2] *St. H. Intelligencer* 23, 30 April, 7 May, 1859. In the St. Helens Polling District, 318 votes were cast for Egerton, 306 for Legh, 168 for Cheetham and 168 for Heywood.

stronger fight. But they were again defeated. At St. Helens
the margin was very small : 254 to 245.[1] But this near-success
did not represent a permanent trend in local opinion. At the
general election of 1865, which attracted greater attention on
account of the candidature of W. E. Gladstone—at last (as he
put it) " unmuzzled "—the balance tipped more markedly against
the Liberals in the St. Helens polling district than in the constituency as a whole. The Tories again secured a two to one
majority. Even Gladstone, who was elected as third on the list,
owed his success to votes from the other districts ; at St. Helens
he fared little better than his fellow Liberals.[2] " The sorry figure
the Liberal candidates cut in the St. Helens polling district," commented the friendly *St. Helens Newspaper*, " is a reflection on
the Liberal party . . . Yet it is but fair to say that if the votes
of the town were separated from those of the rural district polling
here, there would be sufficient evidence to prove that even St.
Helens is on the side of Liberal principles."[3]

The passing of the second Reform Bill in 1867 injected new
life into both parties. The electorate at St. Helens was doubled
in size : in the 1868 election there were 2,206 voters on the
local register. The Conservatives appear to have been the first
to indulge in any party organisation in the town. Just before the
1868 election we learn of the existence of a St. Helens Working
Men's Conservative Association which was, no doubt, intended
to appeal to the newly-enfranchised section of the local electorate.[4]
It may have played a decisive rôle, for the voting at St. Helens
was very close. Gladstone, who opened his campaign in the town,
polled 818 votes, 10 and 20 fewer than his two Conservative
opponents. (The South Lancashire district had been replaced
by the geographically smaller South-West Lancashire constituency in 1867 with two Members.) On this occasion the local
poll was representative of the constituency as a whole, and,
although his party was successful in gaining office, the Liberal
leader was obliged to sit in Parliament for Greenwich. In a
gloomy letter from Knowsley, Derby was able to report one

---

[1] These are the figures for the four townships of Eccleston, Parr, Sutton
and Windle, given (with names) in the *St. H. N.* 31 Aug., 1861. For the
electoral district as a whole the Conservative candidate, Turner, polled
445 votes and Cheetham, his Liberal opponent, 306. (Bean, *op. cit.*, 191).

[2] The figures for the St. Helens Polling District were : Egerton 477,
Turner 460, Legh 459, Gladstone 248, Thompson 222, Heywood 214.
Those for the constituency as a whole were 9,171, 8,806, 8,476, 8,786,
7,703 and 7,654 respectively. (Bean, *op. cit.*, 191 ; *St. H. Standard* 28 July,
1865.)

[3] *St. H. N.* 22 July, 1865.

[4] *St. H. N.* 25 July, 1868.

bright spot in the election : " My county at least has done its duty."[1]

With the increase in the size of the electorate, it was more difficult for pressure to be brought to bear upon individual voters. When there were only a few hundred with the vote, it was possible to coerce those who were not freeholders and persuade those who were : it was alleged in 1844, for instance, that Mrs. Hughes of Sherdley Hall had sent a circular to all her tenants instructing them to vote Tory.[2] But when the electorate was counted in thousands, dictation by either method was another matter. It is true that in 1868 coercion was alleged among employees at the glass and copper works at Sutton Oak[3] but there is evidence that the chief glass firm in the town expressly repudiated any such political dictation. William Pilkington and William Windle Pilkington issued the following notice to their employees on 24 November, 1868 :

" The undersigned hereby give notice that all voters employed by the Firm of Messrs. Pilkington Brothers whether at the Glass Works or Colliery are perfectly at liberty to vote for any candidate they think proper neither shall any person be authorised to use our names in any way to influence their votes."[4]

With the passing of the Ballot Act in 1872, the freedom of the vote was assured, though a comment in the *St. Helens Newspaper* fifteen years later suggests that local voters were rather suspicious of the ballot at first. " Voting by ballot," it wrote on 5 November 1887, " is becoming with every recurring election better understood and now a man can go and give his vote without letting either one party or the other know the bent of his mind."

The age of " influence " being over, both parties developed their own local organisations in order to strengthen the force of their popular appeal. Although the two Conservative Members were returned unopposed at the election of 1874, the local Liberals made preparations for a future contest by forming a Liberal Association and opening a club in Hardshaw Street.[5] The Conservatives followed suit the next year (1875) and established

---

[1] Derby to Disraeli, 22 November, 1868 q. in G. E. Buckle, *The Life of Benjamin Disraeli* (1920) V, 92. At the St. Helens Polling District, which from this time onwards apparently included only voters in the four townships, there voted for Cross 834, for Turner 824, for Gladstone 818 and for Grenfell 764 (Bean, *op. cit.*, 192).

[2] *Lpool. Merc.* 28 May, 1844.

[3] *St. H. N.* 5 Dec., 1868.

[4] Notice found in the purse of W. W. Pilkington after his death, now preserved at Pilkington Brothers Ltd.

[5] *St. H. N.* 5 May, 1874 ; *St. H. Standard* 4 July, 1874.

their headquarters in Hall Street.[1]   But the people of St. Helens
had to wait until 1880, twelve years after the previous contested
election, before they again had the opportunity to express their
political views. The Conservatives retained the seats.[2]

As a result of the redistribution of 1884, St. Helens became
a Parliamentary Borough, thus obtaining the right to elect its
own Member. The Conservatives at once set about angling for the
new voters and established a registration association for the town
in March, 1885.[3]   The Liberals took heart once more, particularly as they were able to prevail upon their leader, David
Gamble, to stand in their interest. The Conservatives looked to
William (Roby) Pilkington to meet this challenge but he was
unwilling to stand. They approached other prominent Conservatives in the district but without success.[4]   In the end the
choice fell upon William Pilkington's son-in-law Henry Seton-
Karr, the son of a member of the Indian Civil Service, who
had been educated at Harrow and Oxford. He had been called
to the Bar in 1879 but had not had a very successful career as a
lawyer, as he readily admitted, and, as he was also prepared to
admit, his chief interest lay in a cattle ranch in Wyoming and the
hunting of wild animals.

" I had not previously paid much attention to political
questions [he later confessed] having been so much occupied
in travel and sport—when not working in my profession in
London—but the legal training I had, enabled me to readily
gather up the threads of political controversy."[5]

From all accounts, he was an able man and a proficient candidate. He said nothing out of turn. And he had the greatest of
good fortune. A few days before polling began, Parnell issued
his famous manifesto urging all Irish voters to support the
Conservative candidates in the interest of Home Rule. The
strong Irish faction at St. Helens obeyed, and Gamble was
defeated by 57, the figures being Seton-Karr 3,750, Gamble

---

[1] *St. H. Standard* 23 Jan., 9 Oct., 1875.

[2] There voted for Cross 11,420, for Blackburne 10,905, for Rathbone
9,666 and for Molyneux 9,207. More than 900 Liberal votes were said
to have been cast at St. Helens but no detailed figures for the St. Helens
Polling District are available. (*St. H. N.* 10 April, 1880.)

[3] *Prescot Reporter,* 7 March, 1885.

[4] *St. H. N.,* 14 Feb., 1885. According to H. Linden Riley, writing in
the *St. H. Lantern* 2 Aug., 1888, the Conservatives invited the Hon. William
Gerard, Michael Hughes, Henry Baxter and Thomas Baxter to stand but
they all refused.

[5] Interview published in the *St. H. Lantern* 2 Aug., 1888. He was
knighted in 1902. After his defeat at St. Helens in 1906, he stood for
Berwickshire in 1910 but was again defeated. He was drowned when
the *Empress of Ireland* went down in the mouth of the river St. Lawrence
in 1914. (Obits. *St. H. N., St. H. R.* 5 June, 1914).

3,693.[1] The Liberals never came nearer to winning St. Helens
than on this first occasion, for after 1885 the split in the party
on Home Rule was very evident in a town where religious and
Irish feelings still ran high.   Gamble, true to his Northern
Ireland forbears, became a Liberal Unionist.[2]

This vital division in the Liberal ranks was made worse by
squabbles and a lack of effective party organisation in the town.
When, in 1886, Seton-Karr defeated Arthur Sinclair, another
local candidate and a popular figure, by 217 votes, the position
was aptly summed up by B. A. Dromgoole :

> " In St. Helens dissent ruins the Liberal cause. Whatever
> pluck there may be in individuals and groups, there is no
> training ; the Liberal rank and file are like the militia, called
> up once a year or seldomer when everybody is out of harness ;
> all are officers or think themselves fit to command ; there is
> no captain and consequently no submission, no recognised
> and trusted leader for the ranks to look up to and follow
> implicitly . . . Success as a party is impossible under such
> conditions."[3]

Prior to 1900, though the Liberals were never far behind at the
polls, they never succeeded in summoning up that extra ounce
of strength to achieve victory. In 1892, W. R. Kennedy, Q.C.,
failed by a narrow margin and in 1895 Alderman John Forster,
a local man, lost by 609.[4] In 1900 C. A. V. Conybeare sustained
a more decisive defeat, Seton-Karr's majority rising to 1,898.
This was the foundation year of the Labour Representation
Committee and the local trade unions had already been politically
articulate for ten years. When Labour ran its own candidate,
Thomas Glover, in 1906, he polled over 6,000 votes—1,400 more
than the man who had successfully held the Liberals at bay for
21 years.

[1] *St. H. N.* 28 Nov., 1885.

[2] *St. H. N.* 7 June, 1890.

[3] *St. H. N.*, 10 July, 1886.

[4] *St. H. N.* 13 July, 1895.

APPENDIX II

THE RAPID GROWTH OF CO-OPERATION AFTER 1884

THE success of the St. Helens Industrial Co-operative Society Ltd., formed at the close of 1883, was quick and overwhelming. Its remarkable record of development, recounted in the minute books, quarterly reports and annual returns (preserved at the Society's head office), is in sharp contrast to the feeble attempts at co-operation which had taken place in earlier years at St. Helens. Previously it had been hard to find any members : now the major problem was how to accommodate them all.

Towards the end of 1883 a number of workmen at Cannington and Shaw's Bottle Works waited upon Thomas Killey, who was also employed there, with a view to launching yet another co-operative venture to fill the void left by the collapse of the previous societies.[1] A preliminary meeting was held at the Blue Ribbon Club House in Bridge Street on 17 November, 1883, at which it was decided to embark on a store as soon as 150 members had joined the society. Thomas Killey was voted to the chair and James Appleton became the secretary. At later meetings, held in the St. Thomas's Schools, a committee was appointed,[2] a set of rules adopted, the Co-operative Wholesale Society in Manchester approached for a price list, and a scrutiny made of the best premises in which to open a store. Number 17 Market Square was eventually decided upon and on 1 March, 1884, members were informed that the store would be opened within a fortnight.

At the conclusion of the first quarter's trading, which had been confined to the sale of groceries most of which were purchased from the C.W.S. in Manchester, the committee was able to report a net profit of £50 on sales totalling £646 and was able to pay the 164 members a dividend of 1s. 6d. in the £1, and non-members 9d. This was a modest but very satisfactory start.

[1] Statement by T. Killey at the laying of the foundation stone of the new central stores, reported in the *St. H. N.* 12 Oct., 1896. He did not specify the works at which he was employed but Miss B. Killey informs us that it was Cannington and Shaw's. This is confirmed by the obit. in the *St. H. N.* 1 Oct., 1926.

[2] The first committee consisted of : T. Killey, President ; R. Baddeley, Vice-President ; W. Barwise, Treasurer ; James Appleton, Secretary ; Peter Anders, Geo. F. Armytage, Jno. Binns, Jno. Gorse and J. T. Hopgood. The auditors were Thomas Cross and Robert Hunter.

The new store caught the public's fancy. Mr. Winterbottom, the manager, and his young assistant, were soon very busy indeed. In the second quarter ending 9 September, £916 worth of groceries were sold and the membership had risen to 218. Later the same month the society started to deal in coal and at the next quarterly meeting receipts totalled £1,228, the 269 members receiving a dividend of 1s. 9d.

The little shop in the Market Square soon became quite inadequate to meet the growing scale of business and other premises, in Lowe Street, had to be leased at the end of the year.[1] The tide of success was rising and the management committee was resolved to make the most of it. Arrangements were made with Mr. Coop, a local tailor, for him to serve members at rates upon which dividend was payable by the society and these agreements were extended until they included 31 private shopkeepers who supplied baby linen, boots and shoes, butchers' meat, clogs, clothing, dresses, drapery, furniture and ironmongery, earthenware, jewellery, hats, photographs and picture frames. In April, 1885, plans were afoot for a bakery and in October the first of a series of branches was opened at Higher Parr Street. In the following March it was reported that deliveries to Thatto Heath and Sutton were so heavy that auxiliary stores were required in those districts to relieve the strain on the Lowe Street shop. The former was opened in the spring and the latter in the autumn of 1886. In May, 1887, another shop was taken in Lowe Street in which a butchery department was opened, the first step in the process of extending the scope of the business to include those commodities which had been temporarily allocated by arrangement to the private retailer. By December, 1887, the membership was close on 2,000 and the sales in the last quarter exceeded £12,000. Dividends, which had been paid at the rate of 2s. 2d. in the £1 from September, 1885, were raised to 2s. 4d. at the end of 1888 and 2s. 6d. at the end of 1889.

Success bred further custom and the rapid rate of development was sustained. The membership exceeded 3,000 in 1892 and 6,000 in 1898. More new branches were authorised : Peter Street and Thatto Heath (1888), Peasley Cross (1892), Haydock (1893), Denton's Green and Newtown (1897) and Derbyshire Hill (1898). In October, 1896, the foundation stone of the new central stores, which were to cost the society £20,000, was laid on the site of the old Moorflat School.[2] In the last year of the nineteenth century, sales totalled £165,000 and £23,171 were divided among the 6,833 members. If we assume five persons to a family, this meant

[1] These premises were leased from Thomas Beecham, having been previously occupied by Pemberton the builder.

[2] *St. H. N.* 12 Oct., 1896. New Schools to replace Moorflat were opened at Wolseley Road at the beginning of 1895. (*St. H. N.* 5 Jan., 1895).

that almost half the population of the town was using the co-
operative stores : an impressive achievement in fifteen years
from an initial outlay of less than £200.

No doubt much of this spectacular success may be attributed
to the disturbed economic conditions at the close of the century,
circumstances which, as we have suggested, were conductive to
the rise of such money-saving societies. But much depended upon
the vigour and resource shown by the management committee,
upon the presence or absence of what Dromgoole had called
" palaverish schemers." The committee of 1883 consisted of
most able men. It is significant that two of them, Killey and
Hopgood, though in relatively humble circumstances at the time
the society was formed, were later to become directors of
Cannington Shaw and Co. Ltd. The committee as a whole
showed both diligence and ingenuity. Any faults were swiftly
remedied and any laxity sternly reprimanded. On 3 November
1884, the secretary recorded :

" The Chairman was authorised to see John Price, the assistant,
and caution him against mistakes and promise him an advance
in his wages in one month if he showed amendment and greater
readiness to assist the manager in the correct dispatching of
goods."

Again, on 12 May, 1887 :

" It having come to the knowledge of the Committee that
Mr. Higginbottom disgraced himself on two occasions of late,
it was resolved that he be asked to sign the Pledge."

The affairs of the store were scrutinised to the minutest detail.
On 17 October, 1885, it was

" Resolved that the shopmen shall be provided with tea Friday
and Saturday and that the necessary crockery be got for the
purpose . . ."

But on the following 2 December,

" It was found that expenses were going up and owing to the
increased staff in the shop, it was resolved that the teas provided
for shopmen be dispensed with for the present."

Every effort was made to buy in the cheapest market—which was
not always the C.W.S. On 28 July, 1884, the manager was empowered to go to Liverpool to enquire into the prices there.
When a sale took place at St. Helens, he was permitted to attend
and to " purchase whatever he thought useful for the stores "
(20 January, 1886). On 7 July, 1887, he " was instructed to make
inquiries regarding Warrington market with a view to attending
same for cheese and potatoes."

Such efficiency, resource and adaptability commanded confidence. The steady rise in sales and (distributed) profits encouraged others to join. Success, given such able surveillance,
was assured.

2H

APPENDIX III

BIRTHS AND DEATHS IN THE ST. HELENS REGISTRATION DISTRICT 1837-49.

Year	Births	Deaths Under One	Deaths Under Five	Deaths Total All ages	Infant Mortality Rate (Deaths under one per 1000 births)	Typhus	Cholera	Smallpox	Scarlet Fever	Measles	Phthisis	Pneumonia	Croup	Consumption	Child Birth	Typhoid	Hydro-cephalus	Whooping Cough
July-Dec 1837	259	45	77	163	175	5	1	5	—	—	—	—	2	1	2	—	4	—
Year 1838	760	95	181	403	125	15	2	*60*	—	—	—	—	11	1	5	—	12	3
1839	782	151	278	471	193	31	2	12	36	3	1	1	14	32	6	—	19	4
1840	865	129	340	598	147	15	2	21	37	*92*	23	11	29	41	6	—	12	14
1841	858	107	232	471	125	5	2	2	28	—	50	41	37	10	5	—	23	12
1842	765	134	241	463	175	14	2	—	4	2	86	80	16	—	2	—	26	27
1843	791	127	215	401	161	10	1	—	3	29	73	52	15	1	3	—	20	2
1844	793	115	163	340	145	8	1	—	6	—	62	41	5	1	1	—	20	7
1845	772	99	209	429	127	7	—	*64*	1	7	56	51	13	2	—	—	15	11
1846	868	156	345	634	157	8	6	9	*96*	3	46	46	8	16	4	—	36	8
1847	909	169	341	677	186	27	4	12	*57*	11	49	45	21	13	1	11	24	1
1848	941	147	254	491	156	11	1	—	18	5	37	34	10	16	4	—	18	2

CHIEF CAUSES OF DEATH (Epidemics printed in italics)

APPENDIX IV

NOTE ON BANKING AND CREDIT AFTER 1830[1]

IT is clear from the deeds which we have been able to consult that the chief local source of credit in the nineteenth century was Parr's Bank at Warrington. They advanced £20,000 to the Pilkington Brothers on the security of the St. Helens Crown Glassworks and were particularly active in financing the alkali trade : Darcy and Dierden's was mortgaged to them, so was Balmain's and so was Crosfield's. When Parr's became a joint-stock bank in 1865, eight of the provisional committee of 29 were St. Helens men (John Ansdell, David Bromilow, Alfred Crosfield, David Gamble, A. G. Kurtz, William Pilkington, junior, Arthur Sinclair and Samuel Stock). A month or two later, David Gamble was chosen to be one of the directors. Parr's loomed so large in the local economy that without access to papers relating to the Old Bank at Warrington (now part of the Westminster Bank) it would be pointless to attempt any consideration of banking operations in the district.

Parr's opened a branch in East Street, St. Helens, during the 1840s, the first mention of it being in the *Directory* of 1848. In 1838 the Phoenix Bank of Liverpool (established 1837) had a St. Helens office in the New Market Place. Although this bank was still in existence in 1841, it appears to have collapsed soon afterwards and it seems very probable that its failure added to the difficulties of the local inhabitants during the depression. After the departure of this short-lived rival, Parr's had no other local competition until 1868 when the Manchester and Salford Bank opened a branch in the town.

[1] Based upon United Alkali Co. Ltd. deeds ; Pilkington Bros. Ltd. deeds ; Cross Papers DDCS 43/22 ; *St. H. N.* 29 April, 3 June, 1865, 23 Feb., 1867 ; Pigot's *Directory of Manchester and Salford*, 1838, 1841 ; note upon the deed of settlement of the Phoenix Bank at the Picton Ref. Lib., Liverpool ; advertisement of Jonathan Wrigley, dated 12 October, 1838, among the Ansdell Papers at the St. H. Ref. Lib.)

INDEX

Abbott, George 460n
Abram, 38, 41.
Ackary, John G., 281n.
Accidents at chemical works, 459.
Accidents in coalmines, 200, 272, 273, 341.
Adams, John, 6n.
Adamson, Henry, 134.
Affleck, Philip, 57, 83, 84, 112, 113n.
Africa trade, 12n, 49, 50, 51, 76, 128, 129, 170n, 181n.
Agriculture, 3, 63, 132n, 155.
Ale, see Beer, Breweries Greenall's St. Helens Brewery.
Alexandra, Princess of Wales, 340.
Alexandra Colliery, 340.
Alkali Association, 253, 440-1.
Alkali trade, see Chemical Industry.
Alkali waste, 352-5, 401, 416.
Alkali Works Regulation Act, 350, 440.
Allanson, John, 389.
Allen, John Fenwick, 227n, 236, 464.
Allerton, manor of, 203, 205.
Alton, Staffs., 76.
Amalgamated Society of Carpenters and Joiners, 460n.
Amalgamated Society of Railway Servants, 460n.
America, United States of, 233, 280, 356, 367, 439, 439n, 447-8, 464.
American Consular Agency at St. Helens, 439-40.
American continent, trade with, 60, 124, 240-2, 370, 439-40, 444, 448.
American War of Independence, dire effects of, 49-54.
Amlwch, see Anglesey.
Ammonia-soda, see Solvay ammonia-soda process.
Anders, Peter, 477n.
Anderton, John, 370.
Anderton, 58n.
Andrews, Walter, 379n.
Anglesey, copper mining in, 76-82, 88, 89, 240-2.
Anglesey, supply of beer to, 100.
Ansdell, John, 203n, 395n, 466, 466n, 481.
Appleton, James, 477, 477n.
Appleton, William, senr., 71.
Appleton, William, junr., 71.
Appleton, 38, 414n.
Apprenticeship, 136, 138, 142-4.
Armytage, George F., 477n.

Arnott, Alexander Robertson, 345, 472.
Arrowsmith, Thomas, 307, 307n, 310.
Arrowsmith's estate, 55n.
Ashcroft's Bridge, 301, 466.
Ashes Colliery, 33-4.
Ashton, Anna, 51.
Ashton, John, 15-17, 20-2, 41, 51, 185n.
Ashton, J., 414n.
Ashton, Nicholas, senr., 16, 16n, 143.
Ashton, Nicholas, junr., 41, 49n, 51, 60, 72, 101, 132, 150-1, 184, 185n, 195, 200.
Ashton, N. C. E., 16n.
Ashton, William, 68.
Ashton, W. J., 462.
Ashton's estate, 56.
Ashton-in-Makerfield, 7, 15n, 16, 41, 62, 69, 76, 87, 91, 123, 126, 197, 265, 317, 336n.
Ashton-under-Lyne, 264.
Ashton's Green, 69, 301.
Ashton's Green Colliery, 69, 190, 200, 435.
Aspinall, Professor, A., 159.
Aspinall's estate, 57.
Associations of Manufacturers, 52, 95, 103, 246-255, 350-1, 440-4, 448-9.
Astley, Edward, 68.
Aston, 335.
Atherton, the Rev. P. F., 439n.
Atherton, —., 89.
Australia, emigration to, 427-8.
Australia, trade with, 243, 358.

Baddeley, R., 477n.
Bailey, F. A., 129n.
Baines, Thomas, 439.
Baldwin, Frances, 142.
Balmain, William Henry, 244, 344-5, 481.
Balmain and Parnell, 244, 344-5, 351.
Banks, see Chester and N. Wales, Manchester and Salford, Parr's, Phoenix.
Banner and Doke, 171n.
Baptist Church, see Churches.
Barges, canal, see Flats.
Barilla, 117, 223-5.
Barker, Thomas, 186n.
Barnes, John, gentleman, 42.
Barnes, John, solicitor, 203, 203n, 207.

483

Streets at St. Helens—*continued.*
  Duke Street, 200*n*, 291, 374, 375*n*.
  Dunriding Lane, 316.
  East Street, 467*n*, 481.
  Eccleston Street, 118.
  George Street, 375.
  Gin Lane, *see* Boundary Road.
  Grove Street, 358-9, 451.
  Hall Street, 333, 475.
  Hard Lane, 402*n*.
  Hardshaw Street, 375, 377, 387*n*, 392, 474.
  Haydock Street, 370.
  High Street, 344.
  Higher Parr Street, 478.
  Jack's Lane, *see* Dunriding Lane.
  Langtree Street, 369.
  Liverpool Road, 374, 381, 384.
  Liverpool Street, 365.
  Lowe Street, 478.
  Market Place, 291-2, 296, 315, 316, 396, 477, 478, 481.
  Market Street, 169, 171, 172, 174*n*, 291, 292, 295, 301, 365*n*, 467*n*.
  Milk Street, 378, 418.
  Mill Street, 419.
  Mount Street, 421*n*.
  North Road, 374-5, 375*n*.
  Ormskirk Street, 421*n*.
  Park Road, 421*n*.
  Parr Street, 281, 336, 399*n*.
  Peasley Cross Lane, 437*n*.
  Prescot Road, 197.
  Raven Street, 330.
  Robins Lane, 454.
  St. Mary's Street, 365.
  Smithy Brow, 281, 282, 291, 300, 301.
  Sutton Road, 421*n*.
  Tontine Street, 120, 169, 174, 290, 291, 301, 421*n*.
  Traverse Street, 415.
  Water Street, 364.
  Waterloo Street, 365, 392.
  Watson Street, 365, 366*n*.
  Welsh Row, 82, 87.
  West's Row, 170.
  West's New Row, 170.
  Westfield Street (Church Street, Westfield), 291, 374, 379, 398, 401.
  Wolseley Road, 478*n*.
Strikes, 159-63, 263-8, 298, 375*n*, 413-4, 448, 449, 450.
Stubbs, William, 387*n*.
Stubs, Peter, 59*n*, 171*n*.
Subsidence, colliery, 63.
Sullivan, Admiral Sir Charles, 362.

Sullivan, Sir Edward, 361-2.
Sulphur, 243, 352, 440, 440*n*.
Sulphur recovery, 353-4.
Sulphuretted hydrogen, 352-5, 416.
Sulphuric acid, 81, 224*n*, 225, 225*n*, 233, 243, 244, 346.
Sunday Schools, *see* Schools.
Sutton, Thomas, 101.
Sutton, township of, 3, 7, 9, 20*n*, 27, 32, 33, 42, 54, 55*n*, 66, 68, 89, 108, 109, 131, 131*n*, 150-3, 156, 158, 162, 165, 170, 176, 177, 178, 301, 302, 303, 306, 307, 360*n*, 374, 380-1, 388-9, 395, 405, 408, 410, 435, 452, 478.
Sutton Alkali Works Co-operative Society, 381, 382.
Sutton Colliery (Peasley Cross), 190, 198, 200.
Sutton Co-operative Friendly Society, 380.
Sutton Co-operative Industrial Society, 381.
Sutton Cottage, 128.
Sutton Glassworks Co-operative Society, 380-2.
Sutton Grange, 360*n*.
Sutton Hall, 185.
Sutton Heath, 7, 129*n*, 369.
Sutton Lodge, 89, 150-1, 153.
Sutton National Schools, *see* Schools.
Sutton Oak, 291, 301, 334, 375.
  See also glassworks, Newton Lyon & Co., Newton Keates & Co.
Sutton Rolling Mills Co-operative Society, 380-1, 382, 382*n*.
Sutton, Bold & District Permanent Building Society, 377*n*.
Swaine, —., 369.
Swansea, 75, 76, 80, 88, 89, 166, 240, 240*n*, 242.
Swift, Rigby, 469.
Swift, Thomas, 469.
Swire, William, 370.

Tarbuck family, 64.
Tarbuck, Alexander, 28, 29, 67, 68.
Tarbuck, Barton, 53, 68.
Tarbuck, F. R., 366*n*.
Tarbuck, James, 110.
Tarbuck, John, 31.
Tarbuck, John of Ormskirk, 124.
Tarbuck, Robert, 31.
Tarbuck's estate, 55*n*.
Tarbuck, township of, 38, 65*n*.
Taylor, Alice, 136.
Taylor, A. J., 266*n*.
Taylor, James, 460*n*.
Taylor, Michael, 136, 140.

CHARLESWORTH'S
Chiropodial Orthopædics